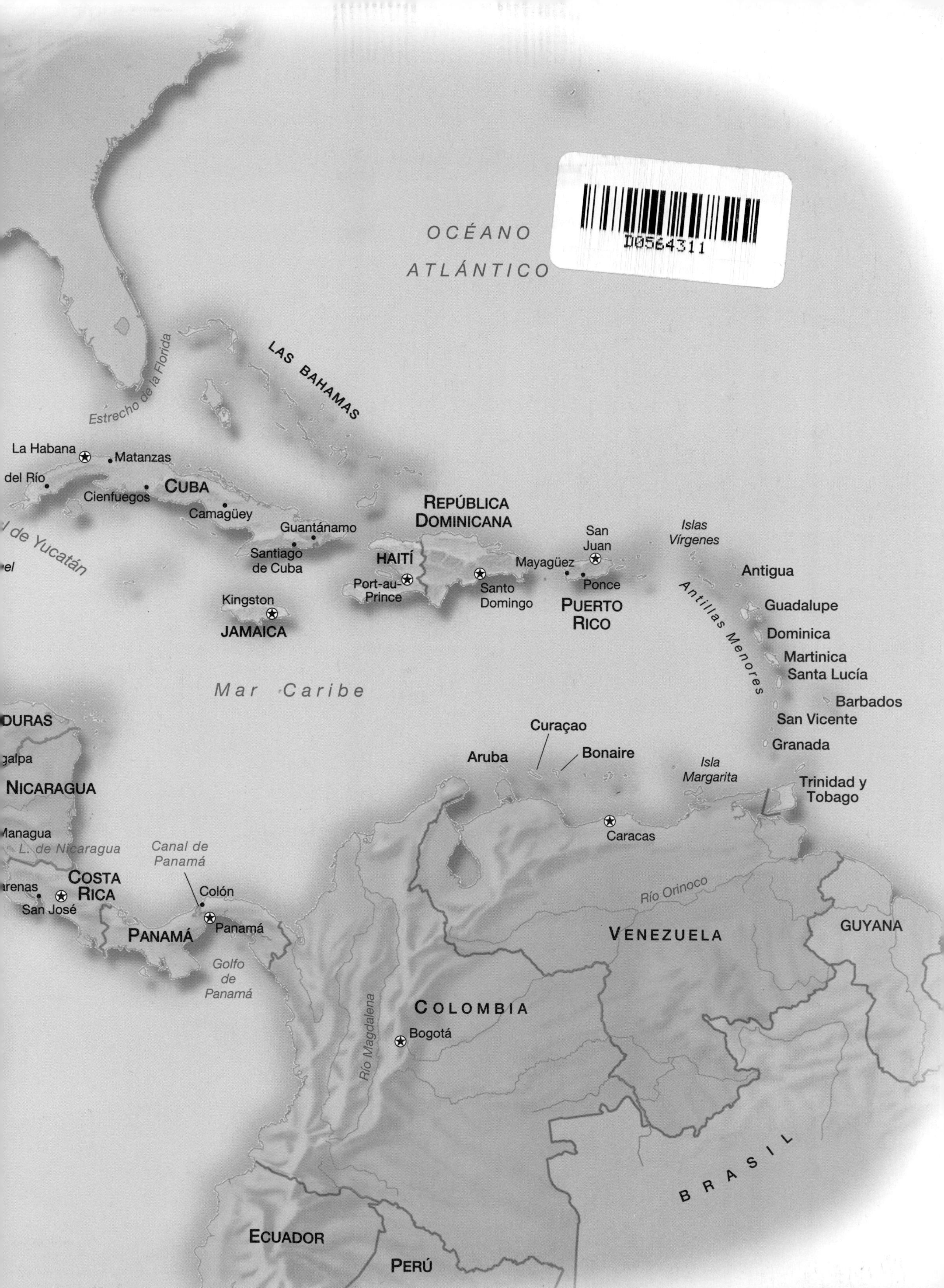

OCÉANO
ATLÁNTICO
D0564311
LAS BAHAMAS
Estrecho de la Florida
La Habana
Matanzas
del Río
CUBA
Cienfuegos
Camagüey
Guantánamo
Santiago de Cuba
de Yucatán
REPÚBLICA DOMINICANA
HAITÍ
Port-au-Prince
Santo Domingo
San Juan
Mayagüez
Ponce
PUERTO RICO
Islas Vírgenes
Antigua
Antillas Menores
Guadalupe
Dominica
Martinica
Santa Lucía
Barbados
San Vicente
Granada
Kingston
JAMAICA
Mar Caribe
DURAS
Curaçao
Aruba
Bonaire
Isla Margarita
Trinidad y Tobago
NICARAGUA
Managua
L. de Nicaragua
Canal de Panamá
COSTA RICA
San José
Colón
Panamá
PANAMÁ
Golfo de Panamá
Caracas
Río Orinoco
VENEZUELA
GUYANA
Río Magdalena
COLOMBIA
Bogotá
BRASIL
ECUADOR
PERÚ

Brief Edition

¡Arriba! Comunicación y cultura

Fifth Edition

Eduardo Zayas-Bazán
Emeritus, East Tennessee State University

Susan M. Bacon
University of Cincinnati

Holly J. Nibert
Western Michigan University

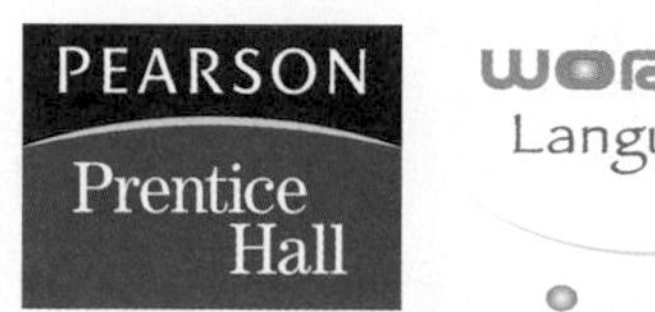

Upper Saddle River, New Jersey 07458

Publisher: *Phil Miller*
Editorial Supervisor/Assistant Development Editor: *Debbie King*
Director of Marketing: *Kristine Suárez*
Director of Editorial Development: *Julia Caballero*
Development Editor: *Janet García-Levitas*
Development Editor for Assessment: *Melissa Marolla Brown*
Production Supervision: *Nancy Stevenson*
Composition/Full-Service Project Management: *Natalie Hansen and Sandra Reinhard, Black Dot Group*
Assistant Director of Production: *Mary Rottino*
Supplements Editor: *Meriel Martínez Moctezuma*
Senior Media Editor: *Samantha Alducin*
Prepress and Manufacturing Buyer: *Brian Mackey*
Prepress and Manufacturing Manager: *Nick Sklitsis*
Interior Design: *Black Dot Group*
Cover Design: *Lisa Delgado, Delgado & Company*
Art Manager: *Maria Piper*
Illustrator: *Andrew Lange*
Director, Image Resource Center: *Melinda Reo*
Manager, Rights & Permissions IRC: *Zina Arabia*
Manager, Visual Research: *Beth Brenzel*
Image Permissions Coordinator: *Joanne Dippel*
Photo Researcher: *Elaine Soares*
Marketing Coordinator: *William J. Bliss*
Cover Image: *Getty Images/Laura Ronchi Collection*

This book was set in 10/12 Meridian Roman by Black Dot Group and was printed and bound by Von Hoffmann. The cover was printed by Phoenix Color Corp.

Printed in the United States of America
10 9 8 7 6 5 4 3 2 1

Student Edition: 0-13-513636-9 / 978-0-13-513636-2
Brief Student Edition: 0-13-513635-0 / 978-0-13-513635-5

Pearson Education LTD., *London*
Pearson Education Australia PTY, Limited, *Sydney*
Pearson Education Singapore, Pte. Ltd.
Pearson Education North Asia Ltd., *Hong Kong*
Pearson Education Canada, Ltd., *Toronto*
Pearson Educación de Mexico, S.A. de C.V.
Pearson Education—Japan, *Tokyo*
Pearson Education Malaysia, Pte. Ltd.
Pearson Education, *Upper Saddle River*, New Jersey

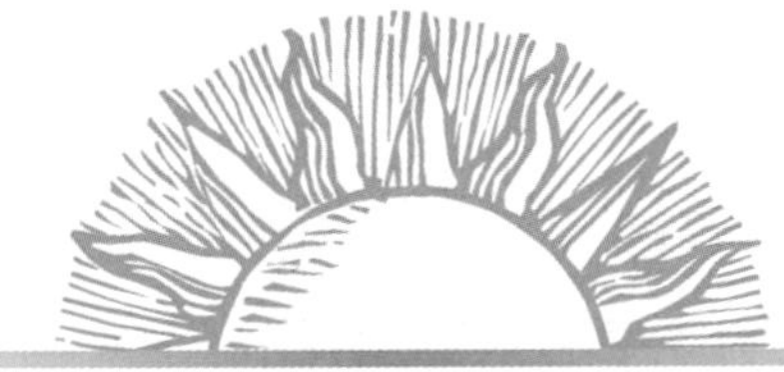

Dedicado a Mabel J. Cameron (1914–2004)

Y a Manuel Eduardo Zayas-Bazán Recio (1912–1991)

"Y aunque la vida murió, nos dejó harto consuelo su memoria"

—**JORGE MANRIQUE**

Brief Contents

Scope and Sequence

	COMMUNICATIVE OBJECTIVES	VOCABULARY
1 **Hola, ¿qué tal?** 2	Meeting and greeting others Spelling your name Performing simple math problems Talking about the calendar and dates Describing your classroom Responding to classroom instructions Talking about yourself and others Identifying colors and talking about your favorite color	Saludos y despedidas En la clase **LETRAS Y SONIDOS:** Spanish vowels
2 **¿De dónde eres?** 38	Describing yourself, other people, and things Asking and responding to simple questions Asking for and telling time Talking about what you like to do (*me gusta/te gusta*) Talking about what you have and what you have to do	Adjetivos descriptivos y adjetivos de nacionalidad ¿De dónde eres? ¿Qué haces? ¿Qué te gusta hacer? **LETRAS Y SONIDOS:** More on vowels in Spanish
3 **¿Qué estudias?** 74	Exchanging information about classes Talking about things that belong to you Talking about how you and others feel Describing yourself and others Asking for and giving simple directions	Las materias académicas y la vida estudiantil Los edificios de la universidad **LETRAS Y SONIDOS:** Syllabification in Spanish
4 **¿Cómo es tu familia?** 114	Talking about your family Expressing desires and preferences Planning activities Extending invitations Making spatial references Discussing things you know	Miembros de la familia El ocio **LETRAS Y SONIDOS:** Word stress and written accent marks in Spanish
5 **¿Cómo pasas el día?** 154	Describing your daily routine and habits Expressing needs related to personal care Expressing emotional states Comparing objects and people Talking about what you do around the house Discussing people or things using superlatives Describing what is happening at the moment	Las actividades diarias Los quehaceres domésticos **LETRAS Y SONIDOS:** The consonants "h, ch" in Spanish

STRUCTURES	CULTURE	READING AND WRITING
The Spanish alphabet The numbers 0–100 The days of the week, the months, and the seasons Nouns and articles Adjective form, position, and agreement Subject pronouns and the present tense of *ser* (to be)	**COMPARACIONES:** El mundo hispano **OBSERVACIONES:** *¡Pura vida!*, Episodio 1 **PANORAMAS:** El mundo hispano **RITMOS:** "Salsa en Nueva York", Típica Novel (Cuba, Nueva York)	**PÁGINAS:** "Versos sencillos, XXXIX", José Martí **TALLER:** Una carta de presentación
Telling time Formation of yes/no questions and negation Interrogative words The present tense of regular *-ar* verbs The present tense of regular *-er* and *-ir* verbs The present tense of *tener*	**COMPARACIONES:** Nombres, apellidos y apodos **OBSERVACIONES:** *¡Pura vida!*, Episodio 2 **PANORAMAS:** España: Tierra de Don Quijote **RITMOS:** "Cuéntame alegrías", Tachú (España)	**PÁGINAS:** "*E-milios*" por correo tradicional **TALLER:** Una entrevista y un sumario
The numbers 101–3,000,000 Possessive adjectives Other expressions with *tener* The present tense of *ir* (to go) and *hacer* (to do; to make) The present tense of *estar* (to be) Summary of uses of *ser* and *estar*	**COMPARACIONES:** Las universidades hispánicas **OBSERVACIONES:** *¡Pura vida!*, Episodio 3 **PANORAMAS:** ¡México lindo! **RITMOS:** "La Bamba", Mariachi Vargas de Tecalitlán (México)	**PÁGINAS:** El Museo de Antropología de México **TALLER:** Una carta personal
The present tense of stem-changing verbs: *e→ie*, *e→i*, *o→ue* Direct objects, the personal *a*, and direct object pronouns The present tense of *poner*, *salir*, and *traer* Demonstrative adjectives and pronouns *Saber* and *conocer*	**COMPARACIONES:** La familia hispana **OBSERVACIONES:** *¡Pura vida!*, Episodio 4 **PANORAMAS:** La América Central I: Guatemala, El Salvador, Honduras **RITMOS:** "Marimba con punta", Los Profesionales (Honduras)	**PÁGINAS:** "Querida Dolores" **TALLER:** Una invitación
Reflexive constructions: pronouns and verbs Comparisons of equality and inequality The superlative The present progressive	**COMPARACIONES:** El ecoturismo en Costa Rica **OBSERVACIONES:** *¡Pura vida!*, Episodio 5 **PANORAMAS:** La América Central II: Costa Rica, Nicaragua, Panamá **RITMOS:** "Ligia Elena", Rubén Blades (Panamá)	**PÁGINAS:** Playa Cacao **TALLER:** Vendo casa

Scope and Sequence

	COMMUNICATIVE OBJECTIVES	VOCABULARY
6 ¡Buen provecho! 188	Discussing food, eating preferences, and ordering meals Talking about things and expressing to whom or for whom Expressing likes and dislikes	Las comidas y las bebidas
	Discussing cooking and recipes Talking about events in the past	En la cocina **LETRAS Y SONIDOS:** The sequences "s, z, ce, ci" in Spanish
7 ¡A divertirnos! 222	Talking about activities you like to do in your free time Making plans to do something Talking about indefinite people and things, and people and things that do not exist	El tiempo libre
	Talking about different sports Reporting past events and activities Taking shortcuts in conversation	Los deportes **LETRAS Y SONIDOS:** The sequences "ca, co, cu, que, qui, k" in Spanish
8 ¿En qué puedo servirle? 256	Shopping at a department store Talking about what used to happen and what you used to do in the past Describing a scene in the past	Las compras y la ropa
	Reading and responding to advertisements Describing a product Contrasting what happened in the past with something else that was going on Making general statements about what people do	Tiendas y artículos personales **LETRAS Y SONIDOS:** The sequences "j, ge, gi, x" in Spanish
9 Vamos de viaje 292	Requesting travel-related information Making travel arrangements	En el aeropuerto
	Describing travel experiences Trying to influence another person Giving advice	Los viajes **LETRAS Y SONIDOS:** The letter "g" in sequences other than "ge, gi" in Spanish

STRUCTURES	CULTURE	READING AND WRITING
The verbs *decir* and *dar* Indirect objects and indirect object pronouns *Gustar* and similar verbs The preterit of regular verbs Verbs with irregular forms in the preterit (I)	**COMPARACIONES:** La compra de la comida y la cocina chilena **OBSERVACIONES:** *¡Pura vida!,* Episodio 6 **PANORAMAS:** Chile: un país de contrastes **RITMOS:** "Tren al sur", Los Prisioneros (Chile)	**PÁGINAS:** "El Santiago" (Reseña periodística) **TALLER:** Una reseña de un restaurante
Irregular verbs in the preterit (II) Indefinite and negative expressions Irregular verbs in the preterit (III) Double object pronouns	**COMPARACIONES:** La vida social de los hispanos **OBSERVACIONES:** *¡Pura vida!,* Episodio 7 **PANORAMAS:** Las islas hispánicas del Caribe: Cuba, la República Dominicana y Puerto Rico **RITMOS:** "El pregonero", Tito Nieves (Puerto Rico)	**PÁGINAS:** "Sensemayá", Nicolás Guillén **TALLER:** Una entrada en tu diario
The imperfect tense of regular and irregular verbs Ordinal numbers Preterit versus imperfect Impersonal and passive *se*	**COMPARACIONES:** De compras **OBSERVACIONES:** *¡Pura vida!,* Episodio 8 **PANORAMAS:** El reino inca: el Perú y el Ecuador **RITMOS:** "Junto a ti", Yawar (Perú)	**PÁGINAS:** "Los rivales y el juez", Ciro Alegría **TALLER:** Una fábula
Por or *para* Adverbs ending in *-mente* The Spanish subjunctive: An introduction The subjunctive to express volition	**COMPARACIONES:** El turismo en los países hispanos **OBSERVACIONES:** *¡Pura vida!,* Episodio 9 **PANORAMAS:** Los países caribeños de Sudamérica: Venezuela y Colombia **RITMOS:** "Tu ausencia", Los Tupamaros (Colombia)	**PÁGINAS:** Un folleto turístico **TALLER:** Un folleto turístico

Scope and Sequence

	COMMUNICATIVE OBJECTIVES	VOCABULARY
10 ¡Tu salud es lo primero! 328	Talking about your health and explaining what part of your body hurts Inviting others to do something Making suggestions indirectly	Las partes del cuerpo humano
	Talking about how to stay fit Expressing emotions Giving your opinion about something	Los alimentos **LETRAS Y SONIDOS:** The consonants "r, rr" in Spanish
11 ¿Para qué profesión te preparas? 362	Describing professions and occupations using work-related terms Talking about the advantages of different professions Persuading others and expressing your opinion	Los oficios y las profesiones
	Reading the want ads Writing a brief business letter Interviewing for a job Giving and following instructions and commands	La búsqueda de empleo **LETRAS Y SONIDOS:** The consonants "b, v" in Spanish
12 El futuro es tuyo 396	Discussing technology Talking about what will happen and what has happened	La computadora y otros aparatos electrónicos
	Talking about the environment Talking about what could happen Giving and following instructions and commands	El medio ambiente **LETRAS Y SONIDOS:** The consonants "t, d" in Spanish

STRUCTURES	CULTURE	READING AND WRITING
Nosotros commands Indirect commands The subjunctive to express feelings and emotions The subjunctive to express doubt and denial	**COMPARACIONES:** El ejercicio y la dieta **OBSERVACIONES:** *¡Pura vida!,* Episodio 10 **PANORAMAS:** Los países sin mar: Bolivia y el Paraguay **RITMOS:** "Sol de primavera", Inkuyo (Bolivia)	**PÁGINAS:** "El ñandutí" (Leyenda paraguaya) **TALLER:** Un artículo sobre la salud
The subjunctive with impersonal expressions Formal commands The subjunctive and the indicative with adverbial conjunctions	**COMPARACIONES:** Los empleos y las relaciones personales **OBSERVACIONES:** *¡Pura vida!,* Episodio 11 **PANORAMAS:** El virreinato de la Plata: la Argentina y el Uruguay **RITMOS:** "Todo cambia", Mercedes Sosa (Argentina)	**PÁGINAS:** "No hay que complicar la felicidad", Marco Denevi **TALLER:** Un *currículum vitae* y una carta de presentación para solicitar trabajo
The past participle and the present perfect indicative The present perfect subjunctive The future and the future of probability The conditional and conditional of probability *Tú* commands	**COMPARACIONES:** La tecnología y el idioma **OBSERVACIONES:** *¡Pura vida!,* Episodio 12 **PANORAMAS:** Los hispanos en los Estados Unidos **RITMOS:** "Caminando", Millo Torres y El Tercer Planeta (Puerto Rico)	**PÁGINAS:** *La casa en Mango Street* (fragmento), Sandra Cisneros **TALLER:** Un relato personal

PREFACE

¡Arriba! continues to rise! We were very pleased by the enthusiastic response to the changes we made in the fourth edition of ***¡Arriba!,*** and our aim has been to make the fifth edition an even more complete and flexible program for first-year Spanish courses, one that instructors with varying teaching styles can adopt with confidence. With help from an unprecedented number of reviewers, we have made many important refinements in the student text. But we have also extensively revised the other components of the ***¡Arriba!*** program, with the goal of creating a completely integrated whole that will allow students to have a successful and rewarding learning experience.

Since it was first published in 1993, ***¡Arriba! Comunicación y cultura*** has been used successfully by thousands of instructors and hundreds of thousands of students throughout North America. Originally conceived to address the need for an elementary Spanish text that went beyond grammar drills to develop cultural insight and communication skills, it has come to be known as a highly flexible program—one that can be used effectively in a wide range of academic settings by instructors who teach the course in different ways. Adopters have consistently praised ***¡Arriba!*** for its clarity and for providing materials that are both motivating and easy to use in the classroom. We believe that they will find those qualities reflected in the fifth edition as well.

Organization and Pedagogy

Like its predecessors, the fifth edition of ***¡Arriba!*** consists of fifteen thematically organized chapters. The first twelve chapters present essential communicative functions and structures, along with basic cultural information about the countries that make up the Hispanic world. The last three chapters present more advanced structures together with thematically focused, cultural material. (A brief version of the text, consisting of the first twelve chapters only, is also available.)

All chapters have the same basic organizational structure, with content presented in three major sections. The language material that forms the core of each chapter is divided into two distinct instructional units, ***Primera parte*** and ***Segunda parte.*** The third, entitled ***Nuestro mundo,*** is a synthesizing section that presents cultural information along with activities designed to develop students' reading and writing skills. A two-page spread at the beginning of each chapter serves as an advanced organizer and presents the chapter's communicative objectives.

The ***Primera*** and ***Segunda partes*** are largely parallel in their organizational structure. They include the following sections:

- ***¡Así lo decimos!*** presents new vocabulary related to the chapter theme. This section begins with ***¡Así es la vida!,*** lively conversations and readings that set the stage for the communicative functions and culture to be presented more formally later in the chapter. Drawings (many of them new to this edition) are used extensively to provide visual context for vocabulary learning and practice. Words are listed in practical, functional groups to facilitate student retention. This section also offers a wide variety of practice activities, ranging from more guided to more open-ended activities, among them an audio activity that builds on the language sample introduced in ***¡Así es la vida!***

- ***¡Así lo hacemos!*** presents grammar structures related to the chapter's communicative objectives. We have tried to make the explanations as clear and concise as we could, with short, bulleted points followed immediately by examples. Wherever possible we have supplemented the words with helpful and (we hope) entertaining illustrations. **Study Tips** boxes assist students with structures that non-native speakers of Spanish often find difficult, and additional structures are elaborated further in the ***Expansión*** boxes, also located in this section. A wide variety of practice activities is provided for each grammatical topic, moving from form-focused to meaning-focused to more open-ended communicative activities.
- The ***¿Cuánto sabes tú?*** boxes at the end of each part serve as a form of self-assessment. They are designed to remind students of the communicative objectives for the chapter and assist them in determining how well they have mastered the material.
- ***Letras y sonidos*** boxes (new to this edition) offer a brief presentation of an important pronunciation topic. The purpose of these boxes is to help students improve their listening and speaking skills.
- ***Comparaciones*** (in the ***Primera parte*** only) presents information regarding the Spanish-speaking world as a whole, then asks students to compare what they have learned with aspects of their own culture. The ***En tu experiencia*** questions invite students to reflect on their experiences within their own culture, while the ***En tu opinión*** activities encourage them to discuss topics further in small groups.
- ***Observaciones*** (in the ***Segunda parte*** only) offers a comprehensive and engaging set of activities based on the corresponding episode of a new video filmed specifically to accompany the fifth edition of ***¡Arriba!*** This sitcom-like video, entitled ***¡Pura vida!,*** features the interactions of five young adults who have all found their way to a residence in Costa Rica. The pre-viewing, viewing, and post-viewing activities in the text are designed to help students follow the story that unfolds in each episode.

The ***Nuestro mundo*** section of each chapter includes the following elements:

- ***Panoramas*** is a visually and textually panoramic presentation of the Hispanic country or region that is the focus of the chapter. The material is supported by activities that encourage students to discuss the regions and topics, do additional research on the web, and make comparisons between the targeted country's culture and their own.
- ***Ritmos*** is designed to help students understand and appreciate the musical culture of the targeted country or region. The text offers pre-listening, listening, and post-listening activities to accompany the musical selections. The selections themselves are available to instructors on an accompanying audio ***Ritmos de nuestro mundo*** CD.
- ***Páginas*** focuses on the development of reading skills. The readings include excerpts from magazine and newspaper articles, a fable, poems, short stories, plays, and novel excerpts. All are authentic texts written by contemporary Hispanic writers from various parts of the Spanish-speaking world, including the United States. All of the readings are accompanied by pre- and post-reading activities.
- ***Taller*** provides guided writing activities that incorporate the vocabulary, structures, and themes covered elsewhere in the chapter. Writing assignments are varied, ranging from personal and business letters to fables. Each assignment is presented in a process-oriented manner, encouraging

students to follow a carefully planned series of steps that includes both self-monitoring and peer editing.

Each chapter concludes with a comprehensive, clearly organized list of all active vocabulary words introduced in the chapter. This section (which is new to this edition) also includes grammatical references for quicker access to information.

New to This Edition

Drawing on the success of previous editions, the fifth edition of ***¡Arriba!*** has been carefully crafted to introduce another generation of students to Spanish language and culture. Like its predecessors, the new edition has been designed as an eclectic and flexible text that is clear, easy to use, and motivating to students. But while the goals remain the same, many refinements and additions have been made as a result of extensive feedback from over 150 reviewers. The comprehensive array of supplemental materials has also been carefully reviewed and revised, and several new items have been added to the program. Specific changes include the following:

- **A new, more visual layout** in the *¡Así lo decimos!* sections has been designed to aid and motivate vocabulary learning. Small drawings are used to convey the meaning of many individual vocabulary words, lessening dependence on English translations. Larger, more complex drawings are also provided so that students can visualize the context in which new vocabulary words could be used. Audio recordings of all the vocabulary items in this section are available online and on an accompanying set of CDs.
- At the end of each chapter, a **new summary** listing all the active vocabulary words introduced in the chapter facilitates review and serves as a quick reference.
- **A new pronunciation section** in each chapter, titled ***Letras y sonidos,*** helps students with pronunciation of new words as well as those introduced in previous chapters. In early chapters these sections focus on aspects of pronunciation that may affect the speaker's ability to communicate meaning. Later chapters deal with topics that contribute to the perception of a non-native accent in Spanish. Each ***Letras y sonidos*** section includes exercises that the instructor may elect to use with students for more focused practice.
- **Four new songs** in the ***Ritmos*** sections allow students to experience engaging and motivating music from around the Hispanic world. The new songs include *Salsa en Nueva York, La Bamba, Junto a ti,* and *Que viva el son montuno.*
- **Four new readings** in the ***Páginas*** sections reflect current events and create balance in the text between cultural and literary readings. The new readings include "*E-milios* por correo tradicional," "El Museo de Antropología de México," "El Santiago" (Reseña periodística), and "Un folleto turístico."
- **A completely new video**, carefully scripted to reinforce the sequence of topics in the fifth edition of ***¡Arriba!,*** is the focus of the revised ***Observaciones*** sections in the second part of each chapter. This sitcom-like video, entitled ***¡Pura vida!,*** features the interactions of five young adults who have all found their way to a residence in Costa Rica. The pre-viewing, viewing, and post-viewing activities in the text are designed to help students follow the story that unfolds in each episode.

- **Many new annotations** in the **Annotated Instructor's Edition** provide a wealth of additional suggestions that will help instructors get the most out of each chapter's contents. The new annotations were added to provide more support to instructors, to facilitate different teaching styles, and to provide clear direction for lesson planning. These annotations enhance activities in the text by offering ideas for pre-activity warm-ups and tips on implementation, as well as suggestions for wrap-up and expansion. The new annotations likewise include additional activities made available for extra practice or as alternatives to activities in the text. Finally, various notes are included that suggest ways an instructor can deepen student understanding of certain structures in the target language.
- The sequencing of grammar topics has been revised to achieve a better balance between chapters and across semesters. Specific changes include the following:
    - In Chapter 2, *-ar* verbs and *-er*/*-ir* verbs are now presented as two separate topics, giving students the opportunity to practice *-ar* verbs before moving on to *-er*/*-ir* verbs.
    - Coverage of the present progressive has been moved from Chapter 3 to Chapter 5 to better balance the grammatical load and discourage misuse of the progressive form in Spanish.
    - The treatment of pronouns has been reorganized and spread over a larger number of chapters in order to allow students to learn each set of pronouns and their functions in a clearer, more efficient manner. "Indirect object pronouns, *decir* and *dar*" and "*Gustar* and similar verbs" have moved from Chapter 5 to Chapter 6; "Double object pronouns" from Chapter 6 to Chapter 7; and "Impersonal and passive *se*" from Chapter 7 to Chapter 8.
    - Coverage of superlatives has moved from Chapter 6 to Chapter 5 to maintain a balance of grammar topics in light of changes to the pronoun sequence.
- The student text now includes icons with cross-references to supplemental material available in the accompanying **Student Activities Manual** and in the ***¡Arriba!*** audio and video programs. For more information, see "A Guide to ***¡Arriba!*** Icons," pages xxii–xxiii.

Program Components

Student Resources

AUDIO CDS TO ACCOMPANY THE TEXT

The recordings on this CD set correspond to the listening activities in the textbook as well as the ***¡Así es la vida!*** dialogues, the ***¡Así lo decimos!*** vocabulary words, and the new ***Letras y sonidos*** pronunciation section.

STUDENT ACTIVITIES MANUAL

The ***¡Arriba!*** **Student Activities Manual** includes "workbook" activities as well as audio- and video-based activities for each chapter of the text. The activities are integrated and organized to mirror the corresponding textbook chapter. Each chapter of the manual includes a ***Letras y sonidos*** section, two ***¿Cuánto sabes tú?*** sections, comprehensive activities on the ***Observaciones*** video segments, and an extended ***Nuestro mundo*** section. The contents of this manual are also available in online formats.

- **ANSWER KEY TO ACCOMPANY THE STUDENT ACTIVITIES MANUAL**
  The **Answer Key** contains answers to all activities in the **Student Activities Manual.**

- **AUDIO CDS TO ACCOMPANY THE STUDENT ACTIVITIES MANUAL**
  The recordings on this CD set correspond to the listening activities in the *¡Arriba!* **Student Activities Manual.**

ADDITIONAL PRACTICE ACTIVITIES
This ***¡Arriba!*** supplement provides additional activities that can be used in class or assigned for out-of-class work. Integrating highly motivational activities such as games, crossword puzzles, fill-in-the-blank activities, and paired activities, it is a rich resource for a variety of teaching situations.

QUICK GUIDE TO SPANISH GRAMMAR
This brief supplement (with laminated pages to ensure durability) provides students with a handy reference source on the key points of Spanish grammar. It is available at a special discount in value packs with the ***¡Arriba!*** student text.

¡PURA VIDA! **VIDEO**
¡Pura vida! is an original story-line video filmed specifically to accompany the fifth edition of ***¡Arriba!*** Over the course of its fifteen episodes, students follow the interactions of five principal characters who find themselves living together in a youth hostel in San José, Costa Rica. Students are able to see the vocabulary and grammar structures presented in the textbook in use in realistic situations while gaining a deeper understanding of Hispanic culture. The sitcom-like format allows instructors to show or assign segments for some chapters without being obligated to do so for others. Pre-viewing, viewing, and post-viewing activities are found in the ***Observaciones*** sections of the textbook and the **Student Activities Manual.** The video is available for student purchase on DVD, but is also available within **MySpanishLab.** In addition, the video is available to instructors on DVD and VHS cassette.

Meet the Cast!

Here are the main characters of ***¡Pura vida!*** whom you will get to know when you watch the video:

Doña María

Felipe

Hermés

Silvia

Patricio

Marcela

VISTAS CULTURALES **VIDEO**

The new, Telly™ award-winning ***Vistas culturales*** video provides students with a rich and dynamic way to expand, enhance, and contextualize the cultural materials they study in the ***Panoramas*** section of the textbook. The eighteen ten-minute vignettes include footage from every Spanish-speaking country. Each of the accompanying narrations, which employ vocabulary and grammar designed for first-year language learners, was written by a native of the featured country or region. The video is available for student purchase on DVD, but is also available within **MySpanishLab.** In addition, the video is available to instructors on DVD and VHS cassette.

- *VISTAS CULTURALES* **VIDEO GUIDE**
  The video guide includes useful vocabulary and pre-, during-, and post-viewing activities designed to guide students as they view each country segment.

ENTREVISTAS **VIDEO**

The new ***Entrevistas*** video consists of guided but authentic interviews with native Spanish speakers on topics related to each chapter's theme. Participants employ target grammatical structures and vocabulary while providing broader cultural perspectives on chapter themes. The video is available for student purchase on DVD, but is also available within **MySpanishLab.** In addition, the video is available to instructors on DVD and VHS cassette.

Instructor Resources

ANNOTATED INSTRUCTOR'S EDITION (AIE)

The ***¡Arriba!* AIE** now has a new format, with slightly larger pages, to allow inclusion of a great deal of helpful new material. Icons are placed at appropriate points throughout each chapter to indicate related resources available in other components of the *¡Arriba!* program (see chart on pages xxii–xxiii for the icon key). The number of marginal instructor annotations has been greatly increased. The annotations fall into several categories:

- **Pre-activity Preparation:** Suggestions for instructor preparation, such as what the instructor might need to bring to the classroom, beyond the text, to carry out an activity.
- **Warm-up:** Suggestions for activating students' prior knowledge or helping set up an activity before carrying it out.
- **Implementation:** Ideas for implementing an activity that go beyond the direction lines.
- **Expansion:** Ideas for lengthening or adding to an activity, e.g., by asking additional questions or by applying the information to students' lives.
- **Wrap-up:** Suggestions for concluding an activity effectively, e.g., by drawing a conclusion based on the students' responses or by sampling or reviewing student responses.
- **Additional Activity:** Independent activities separate but related to those in the student text that offer instructors further options for classroom practice with students.
- **Note:** Additional information on how a structure functions or how a word is used, beyond what is provided in the student text.
- **Audioscript:** The written script of what is heard on the accompanying audio program.
- **Lyrics to *Ritmos* songs:** Full lyrics of all of the songs on the ***Ritmos de nuestro mundo*** CD.

INSTRUCTOR'S RESOURCE MANUAL (IRM)
The ***¡Arriba!*** **IRM** is a comprehensive resource that instructors can use for a variety of purposes. Contents include:

An introduction that discusses the philosophy behind the ***¡Arriba!*** program, a guide to using the text's features, and a guide to other program components.

Pointers for new instructors, including lesson planning, classroom management, warm-ups, error correction, first day of class, quizzes/tests, and other teaching resources.

An explanation of the North American educational system, written (in Spanish) for instructors who may be unfamiliar with it.

Sample syllabi showing how the ***¡Arriba!*** program can be used in different educational settings and at different paces.

Detailed lesson plans for selected chapters.

The audioscript for the **Student Activities Manual** audio program.

The videoscripts for all three ***¡Arriba!*** videos (***¡Pura vida!, Vistas culturales,*** and ***Entrevistas***), as well as suggested activities for the ***Entrevistas*** video. (Activities for ***¡Pura vida!*** and ***Vistas culturales*** are available in other components of the program.)

IN-CLASS COMMUNICATIVE PROJECTS
This unique supplement (new to this edition of ***¡Arriba!***) consists of highly interactive classroom activities coordinated with the text's communicative objectives. It includes student handouts as well as tips for instructors. These activities offer instructors additional opportunities to motivate students while enhancing their communication skills.

MUSIC CD: *RITMOS DE NUESTRO MUNDO*
This music CD contains recordings of all songs featured in the ***Ritmos*** sections of ***¡Arriba!*** The songs have been carefully selected to represent a variety of musical genres and styles and to reflect the culture of the country or region featured in the corresponding chapter of the text.

TRANSPARENCIES
The ***¡Arriba!*** transparency set consists of all the maps from the textbook as well as the drawings found in the ***¡Así lo decimos!*** sections. It also includes some drawings not found in the student text.

POWERPOINT PRESENTATIONS
This new set of **PowerPoint Presentations** includes all of the visual material in the ***¡Arriba!*** transparencies set, together with dynamic presentations on each grammar point covered in the text.

IMAGE RESOURCE CD
Digital versions of all illustrations in the ***¡Arriba!*** student textbook are provided on this CD. Instructors can use the images to create their own handouts, transparencies, PowerPoint slides, and test questions.

TESTING PROGRAM
The ***¡Arriba!*** **Testing Program** has been completely revised and greatly enhanced for this edition. In addition to two finished, ready-to-use tests for each chapter, it contains over 500 testing modules from which instructors can draw to create customized tests. The finished tests and modules have been carefully edited to ensure close coordination with the textbook and **Student Activities Manual.** The content area, assessment goal, and response type are identified for each module. Available within **MySpanishLab** is a user-friendly test-generating program known as **MyTest** that allows instructors to select, arrange, and customize testing modules to meet the needs of their courses. Once created, tests can be printed on paper or administered online.

- **TESTING PROGRAM AUDIO ON CD**
  This CD contains the recordings to accompany the listening activities in the *¡Arriba!* **Testing Program.**

Online Resources

MYSPANISHLAB™
MySpanishLab™ is a new, nationally hosted online learning system created specifically for students in college-level language courses. It brings together—in one convenient, easily navigable site—a wide array of language-learning tools and resources, including an interactive version of the ***¡Arriba!*** **Student Activities Manual,** an electronic version of the ***¡Arriba!*** student text, and all materials from the ***¡Arriba!*** audio and video programs. Readiness checks, chapter tests, and tutorials personalize instruction to meet the unique needs of individual students. Instructors can use the system to make assignments, set grading parameters, listen to student-created audio recordings, and provide feedback on student work. Instructor access is provided at no charge. Students can purchase access codes online or at their local bookstore.

QUIA™ STUDENT ACTIVITIES MANUAL
An interactive version of the ***¡Arriba!*** **Student Activities Manual,** including the related audio and video materials, is available in the highly regarded **Quia™** platform. Instructors' access is provided at no charge. Students can purchase access codes online or at their bookstore.

COMPANION WEBSITE™
The open-access **Companion Website™** features access to the ***¡Arriba!*** audio program, web resources such as cultural activities and links, practice activities, and comprehensive chapter review materials.

ACKNOWLEDGMENTS

The fifth edition of *¡Arriba!* is the result of careful planning between ourselves and our publisher and ongoing collaboration with students and you—our colleagues—who have been using the first, second, third, and fourth editions. We look forward to continuing this dialogue and sincerely appreciate your input. We owe special thanks to the many members of the Spanish-teaching community whose comments and suggestions helped shape the pages of every chapter. We gratefully acknowledge and thank in particular our reviewers for this fifth edition:

Riyad Abifaker, *University of North Carolina at Charlotte*
Claudia Acosta, *College of the Canyons*
Ana Almonte, *Hudson Valley Community College*
Raysa Amador, *Adelphi University*
Carol Amman, *Alfred State College*
Yuly Asención, *Northern Arizona University*
J. Stewart Bankhead, *University of North Carolina at Charlotte*
Gabriel Barreneche, *Rollins College*
Hilario Barrero, *Borough of Manhattan Community College, CUNY*
Anne Becher, *University of Colorado at Boulder*
Camile Bethea, *Wofford College*
Paola Bianco-Sobejano, *Wilkes University*
Brian Boisvert, *University of Massachusetts at Amherst*
Amanda Boomershine, *University of North Carolina at Wilmington*
Judy Brandon, *Clovis Community College*
Darren Broome, *Gordon College*
Laura Brown, *University of North Carolina at Charlotte*
Suzanne M. Buck, *Albuquerque Technical Vocation Institute*
Valerie Budig-Markin, *Humboldt State University*
Julia Bussade, *University of Mississippi*
Wendy Caldwell, *Francis Marion University*
Gina Carrion, *Angelo State University*
Horacio Castillo-Pérez, *University of North Carolina at Charlotte*
Laura Chamberlain, *Coastal Carolina Community College*
Deb Cohen, *Slippery Rock University*
Francesca Colecchia, *Duquesne University*
Elizabeth Contreras, *University of Mississippi*
Mary Cook, *Coastal Carolina Community College*
Angelina Craig-Flórez, *Columbia University*
Cathy Davis, *Rockland Community College*
John F. Day, *St. Norbert College*
Fidel de León, *El Paso Community College*
Jesus de León, *El Paso Community College*
María de los Santos Onofre-Madrid, *Angelo State University*
Douglas Deane, *Albuquerque Technical Vocation Institute*
Mark Del Mastro, *The Citadel*
Nancy Di Bella, *University of Southern Florida*
Christopher DiCapua, *Community College of Philadelphia*
Debra Dickerson, *University of Tennessee at Chattanooga*
Lisa Dillon, *Oakland Community College*
Conxita Domenech, *Front Range Community College*

Patrick Duffy, *La Salle University*
Lucia Dzikowski, *Seminole Community College*
Gilta Engman, *Nova Southeastern University*
Héctor M. Enríquez, *University of Texas at El Paso*
Norma Espinosa-Parker, *Compton Community College*
Enric Figueras, *Boise State University*
Patricia Figueroa, *Pima Community College*
Tanya Flores, *Boise State University*
Roberto Fuertes-Manjón, *Midwestern State University*
Guadalupe C. Gámez, *University of Texas at El Paso*
Ricardo García, *San Jacinto College South*
José M. García-Paine, *Front Range Community College at Boulder*
Linda Gianoulis, *Northwestern College*
Zoila Gil, *University of North Carolina at Charlotte*
Nathan Glockle, *Dakota County Technical College*
Concepción Godev, *University of North Carolina at Charlotte*
Gail Grosso, *Albuquerque Technical Vocation Institute*
Karen Guffey, *Gordon College*
Hannelore Hahn, *College of Saint Elizabeth*
Eric Henager, *Rhodes College*
Lorenza Hernández, *Clovis Community College*
Amarilis Hidalgo de Jesús, *Bloomsburg University of Pennsylvania*
Anneliese Horst Foerster, *Queens University of Charlotte*
Diana Huey, *Clovis Community College*
Silvia Huntsman, *Sam Houston State University*
Margarita Jacome, *Denison University*
J. Eduardo Jaramillo-Zuluaga, *Denison University*
Alexis Jardine, *Reading Area Community College*
Shannie Jessup, *Surry Community College*
Valerie Y. Job, *South Plains College*
David Knutson, *Xavier University*
J. Grady Lacy, *Surry Community College*
Nilsa Lasso-von Lang, *Moravian College*
Luis E. Latoja, *Columbus State Community College*
Jacquelyn Linnes, *North Central University*
Iraida H. López, *Ramapo College*
Nuria López-Ortega, *University of Cincinnati*
Thedore Maier, *Danville Community College*
Martha Manier, *Humboldt State University*
Laura Manzo, *Modesto Junior College*
Delmarie Martínez, *Nova Southeastern University*
Angelica McMillan, *Front Range Community College*
Neal A. Messer, *Virginia Military Institute*
Brenda Miller, *Northeast Iowa Community College*
Charles H. Molano, *Lehigh Carbon Community College*
Alexis Moore, *Albuquerque Technical Vocation Institute*
Carlos Murrell, *North Carolina Central University*
Lisa Nalbone, *University of Central Florida*
Mary Newcomer McKinney, *Texas Christian University*
Trista Nicosia, *Cape Fear Community College*
Lola Norris, *Texas A&M International University*
Cristina Ortiz, *University of Wisconsin at Green Bay*
Jayne Ortiz, *University of North Carolina at Charlotte*
Luisa Ossa, *La Salle University*
Sue Otto, *University of Iowa*
Eliezer Oyola, *Evangel University*
Milta Oyola, *Evangel University*

Mirta Pimentel, *Moravian College*
Alcibíades Policarpo, *Sam Houston State University*
Harriet Poole, *Lake City Community College*
Comfort Pratt, *Texas Tech University*
Nicole Price, *Denison University*
Mónica Prieto, *Florida International University*
Anne M. Prucha, *University of Central Florida*
Kay E. Raymond, *Sam Houston State University*
Kathleen Regan, *University of Portland*
Alejandra Rengifo, *Central Michigan University*
Ray Rentería, *Sam Houston State University*
Danielle L. Richardson, *Randolph Community College*
Sheila Rivera, *University of Central Florida*
Ignacio Rodeño, *Xavier University*
Joaquín J. Rodríguez-Barberá, *Sam Houston State University*
Nilsa Rodríguez-Jaca, *The Culinary Institute of America*
Caroline Rueda, *University of Cincinnati*
Ivan Ruiz-Ayala, *Georgia College & State University*
Maritza Salgueiro-Carlisle, *Bakersfield College*
Ruth Sánchez Imizcoz, *The University of the South*
Loreto Sánchez-Serrano, *Johns Hopkins University*
Carmen Schlig, *Georgia State University*
Rosalba E. Scott, *University of North Carolina at Charlotte*
Gilberto Serrano, *Columbus State Community College*
Paul Sexton, *Tarrant County Northwest*
Albert Shank, *Scottsdale Community College*
Michele Shaul, *Queens University of Charlotte*
Margaret L. Snyder, *Moravian College*
Mary Stevens, *SUNY New Paltz*
Rosa María Stoops, *University of Montevallo*
Charles Swadley, *Oklahoma Baptist University*
Katheryn A. Thompson, *University of Tennessee at Chattanooga*
John Verbick, *University of Oklahoma*
Gayle Vierma, *University of Southern California*
Valerie Watts, *Asheville Buncombe Technical College*
Norman Weinstein, *Boise State University*
Kathleen M. Wheatley, *University of Wisconsin at Milwaukee*
Peter T. Whelan, *Francis Marion University*
Norma Williamson, *Sam Houston State University*
Joseph Wilson, *Catawba College*
Timothy D. Wilson, *University of Alaska, Fairbanks*
Tanya S. Wilder, *Washington State Community College*
Melinda J. Wise, *University of Cincinnati*
Bridget E. Yaden, *Pacific Lutheran University*
Erica Yozell, *Moravian College*
Irina Zager, *Davenport University*
Elizabeth Zahnd, *Francis Marion University*
Mikela Zhezha-Thaumanavar, *Western Michigan University*
Nancy Zimmerman, *Kutztown University*
U. Theresa Zmurkewycz, *Saint Joseph's University*

We owe many thanks to Pepe Fernández, a longtime contributor and friend, and to Enric Figueras and Lisa Nalbone for the **Student Activities Manual.** Special thanks are due to Héctor Torres, for his knowledgeable advice about music and for his tenacity in obtaining permissions for the ***Ritmos de nuestro mundo*** CD, and to Anne Prucha, for creating the ***Ritmos*** activities in the text. Thank you also to Pamela Ranallo for the development of the web site to accompany the new edition. Special thanks are also due to Catherine Hebert and Daphne Villatoro for all of their careful work on the testing program, to William R. Cisco for authoring the innovative **PowerPoint Presentations,** to Mary Stevens and José M. García-Paine for their contributions to the **Instructor's Resource Manual,** to Evelyn F. Brod and Teresa Roig-Torres for their work on the **Additional Practice Activities,** to Chris DiCapua for his contribution to the **Companion Website,** and to Comfort Pratt for her many helpful suggestions and for authoring the **In-class Communicative Projects.**

We wish to express our gratitude and appreciation to the many people at Prentice Hall who contributed their ideas, tireless efforts, and publishing experience to the fifth edition of ***¡Arriba!*** We are especially indebted to Janet García-Levitas, our Development Editor, for all of her hard work, suggestions, attention to detail, and dedication to the text; and to Julia Caballero, Director of Editiorial Development, for helping to shape the fifth edition in every detail and for supervising every aspect of the ***¡Arriba!*** program.

We would like to sincerely thank Phil Miller, Publisher, for his support and commitment to the success of the text. Many thanks are also due to Mary Rottino, Assistant Director of Production; Nancy Stevenson, Senior Production Editor; our Photo Researcher, Elaine Soares; Andrew Lange, for clever illustrations; and Siren Design for the creative reproductions of the realia.

Thanks are due to Samantha Alducin, Senior Media Editor, for her excellent work on the ***¡Pura vida!*** video and other media components. We would also like to thank Melissa Marolla Brown, Development Editor for Assessment, for the diligent coordination between the text, **Student Activities Manual,** and **Testing Program;** and Meriel Martínez Moctezuma, Supplements Editor, for her efficient and meticulous work in managing the preparation of the other supplements; Bob Hemmer, Samantha Alducin, Andrea Michael, and Dan Cooper for their hard work on **MySpanishLab™,** Debbie King, Assistant Development Editor, for her impressive work and efficiency in her work on the glossary, obtaining permissions and reviews, and in attending to many administrative details; Kristine Suárez, Director of Marketing, and Bill Bliss, Marketing Coordinator, for their creativity and efforts in coordinating marketing and promotion for the new edition.

We thank our partners at Black Dot Group for their careful and professional editing services, design, and project management, and Natalie Hansen, Editorial Project Manager, in particular.

Finally, our love and deepest appreciation to our families: Lourdes, Cindy, Eddy, and Lindsey, Elena, Ed, Lauren, and Will; Wayne, Alexis, Sandro, and Ignacio, Camille, Chris, Eleanor, and Theresa; and Pete, Valayda and Jesse, Roger and Britt, Dave, Nancy, Wesley, and Megan, Leisa and David, and Tammy.

EDUARDO ZAYAS-BAZÁN
SUSAN M. BACON
HOLLY J. NIBERT

A GUIDE TO ¡ARRIBA! ICONS

Activity Types

	Pair Activity	This icon indicates that the activity is designed to be done by students working in pairs.
	Group Activity	This icon indicates that the activity is designed to be done by students working in small groups or as a whole class.
A B	Information Gap Activity	This icon indicates that the activity is designed to be done in pairs, with each student having access to information that the other student does not see. The information needed by Student A is included in the chapter; Student B's information is found in **Appendix 1,** pp. A1–A15.
WWW	Web Activity	This icon indicates that the activity involves use of the World Wide Web. Helpful links can be found on the accompanying ***¡Arriba!*** web site.

Supplemental Student Resources

	Student Activities Manual	This icon indicates that there are practice activities available in the ***¡Arriba!*** **Student Activities Manual.** The activities may be found either in the printed version of the manual or in the interactive versions available through ***MySpanishLab*** and **Quia.** Activity numbers are indicated in the text for ease of reference.
	Text Audio Program	This icon indicates that recorded material is available in the ***¡Arriba!*** text audio program. The recordings may be found either on the accompaning set of CDs or on the ***¡Arriba!*** web site. The CD and track numbers are indicated in the text for ease of reference.
	¡Pura vida! Video	This icon indicates that a video recording is available in the ***¡Pura vida!*** video that accompanies the ***¡Arriba!*** text. The video is available on the ***MySpanishLab*** and **Quia.** web sites and in DVD and VHS formats.
	Vistas culturales Video	This icon indicates that a video recording is available in the ***Vistas culturales*** video that accompanies the ***¡Arriba!*** text. The video is available on the ***MySpanishLab*** web site and in DVD and VHS formats.

Instructor Resources

	Instructor's Resource Manual	This icon indicates that there are additional resources available in the ***¡Arriba!* Instructor's Resource Manual.** These resources include lesson plans as well as video scripts to accompany the ***¡Pura vida!*** episodes.
	Additional Practice Activities	This icon indicates that practice activities are available in the ***¡Arriba!* Additional Practice Activities** supplement.
	Transparency	This icon indicates that there is a relevant transparency available. Some transparencies replicate the images included in the student text, while others are additional images drawn from other sources.
	PowerPoint Presentation	This icon indicates that there is a PowerPoint grammar presentation or image available to supplement your lessons. A "G" in the icon reference indicates that there is a grammar presentation available on PowerPoint. A "T" in the icon indicates that the image is available on transparency as well as on PowerPoint.
	Ritmos de nuestro mundo CD	This icon indicates the track number for the songs presented in the ***Ritmos*** section of *¡Arriba!*
	In-class Communicative Projects	This icon, presented with all ***¿Cuánto sabes tú?*** boxes, indicates that there are communicative projects available. Students can use these to put each of the communicative objectives into practice, within context, in class.
	Testing Program	This icon refers to the ready-made tests, to tests A and B, and to the modules available in that chapter if you prefer to create your own test.

1 Hola, ¿qué tal?

PRIMERA PARTE

¡Así lo decimos! Vocabulario	Saludos y despedidas
¡Así lo hacemos! Estructuras	The Spanish alphabet
	The numbers 0–100
	The days of the week, the months, and the seasons
Comparaciones	El mundo hispano

- Meeting and greeting others
- Spelling your name
- Performing simple math problems
- Talking about the calendar and dates

SEGUNDA PARTE

¡Así lo decimos! Vocabulario	En la clase
¡Así lo hacemos! Estructuras	Nouns and articles
	Adjective form, position, and agreement
	Subject pronouns and the present tense of **ser** (*to be*)
Observaciones	¡Pura vida! Episodio 1

- Describing your classroom
- Responding to classroom instructions
- Talking about yourself and others
- Identifying colors and talking about your favorite color

NUESTRO MUNDO

Panoramas	El mundo hispano
Ritmos	"Salsa en Nueva York" (Típica Novel, Cuba/Nueva York)
Páginas	Versos sencillos, "XXXIX" (José Martí, Cuba)
Taller	Una carta de presentación

El descubrimiento de América por Cristóbal Colón. Salvador Dalí, 1958.

Source: Salvador Dali (1904–1989), "The Discovery of America by Christopher Columbus, 1958–1959, oil on canvas, 410.2 x 310 cm. Salvador Dali Museum, St. Petersburg, Florida, USA. The Bridgeman Art Library International Ltd. © 2004 Salvador Dali, Gala-Sal

El mundo hispano

«Si vives alegre, rico eres.»*

Source: Diego Rivera, "Mexico from the Conquest to 1930." Mural. (Detail) Location: National Palace, Mexico City, Mexico. Photo: Leslye Borden/Photoedit. © Banco de Mexico Diego Rivera & Frida Kanlo Museums Trust. Av. Cinco de Mayo, No. 2, Col. Centro, Del. Cuau

Historia de México desde la conquista hasta el futuro. Diego Rivera, 1930.

***Refrán:** If your life is happy, you are rich.

PRIMERA PARTE

¡Así lo decimos![1] Vocabulario

CD 1, Track 1

1-1 to 1-3

¡Así es la vida![2] Saludos y despedidas

En el pasillo (*hallway*) de la universidad

Jorge: Hola, Roberto. ¿Qué tal? ¿Cómo estás?
Roberto: Muy bien, Jorge, ¿y tú?
Jorge: Eh... más o menos...

En la puerta (*door*) de la clase

Profesor López: Hola, buenas tardes. ¿Cómo se llama usted?
María Luisa: Me llamo María Luisa Gómez.
Profesor López: Mucho gusto. Soy el profesor López.
María Luisa: Encantada.

[1]That's how we say it!
[2]That's life!

Saludos y despedidas

1-4 to 1-8

el estudiante

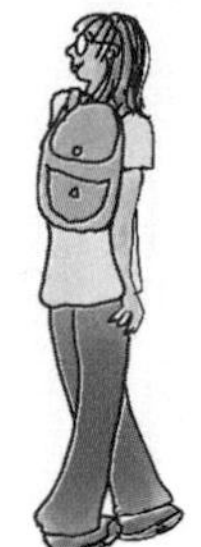
la estudiante

el profesor

la profesora

Saludos	*Greetings*
Buenos días.	*Good morning.*
Buenas tardes.	*Good afternoon.*
Buenas noches.	*Good evening.*
¿Cómo está usted?	*How are you? (formal)*
¿Cómo estás?	*How are you? (informal)*
Hola.	*Hello; Hi.*
¿Qué pasa?	*What's happening? What's up? (informal)*
¿Qué tal?	*What's up? (informal)*

Respuestas	*Responses*
De nada.	*You're welcome.*
¿De verdad?	*Really?*
Encantado/a.	*Delighted; pleased to meet you.*
Gracias.	*Thank you.*
Igualmente.	*Likewise.*
Mucho gusto.	*Nice to meet you.*
(Muy) Bien.	*(Very) Well.*
(Muy) Mal.	*(Very) Bad.*
Más o menos.	*So, so.*

Sustantivos	*Nouns*
la clase	*class*
la universidad	*university*

Despedidas	*Farewells*
Adiós.	*Good-bye.*
Hasta luego.	*See you later.*
Hasta mañana.	*See you tomorrow.*
Hasta pronto.	*See you soon.*

Presentaciones	*Introductions*
¿Cómo se llama usted?	*What's your name? (formal)*
¿Cómo te llamas?	*What's your name? (informal)*
Me llamo...	*My name is...*
Mi nombre es...	*My name is...*
Soy...	*I am...*

Títulos	*Titles*
el señor (Sr.)	*Mr.*
la señorita (Srta.)	*Miss*
la señora (Sra.)	*Mrs.; Ms.*

Otras palabras y expresiones	*Other words and expressions*
con	*with*
mi/mis	*my*
o	*or*
tu/tus	*your (informal)*
y	*and*

Aplicación

1-1 ¿Qué tal? If you heard the statements or questions on the left, how would you respond? Choose from the list of options on the right.

Modelo: Adiós.
Hasta luego.

1. _____ Hola, ¿qué tal?	a. Me llamo Pedro Guillén.
2. _____ Gracias.	b. Muy bien, ¿y tú?
3. _____ ¿Cómo se llama usted?	c. Buenas tardes, profesora.
4. _____ Mucho gusto.	d. Hasta mañana.
5. _____ ¿Cómo estás?	e. ¿De verdad?
6. _____ Buenas tardes, Tomás.	f. De nada.
7. _____ Adiós.	g. Igualmente.
8. _____ Estoy muy mal.	h. Estoy muy mal.

CD 1, Track 3

1-2 ¿Quiénes son? (*Who are they?*) Listen to the short conversations on your **¡Arriba!** audio program or as read by your instructor. Write the number of each conversation next to the corresponding situation below.

_____ two friends saying good-bye
_____ a teacher and student introducing themselves
_____ a young person greeting an older person
_____ two friends greeting each other
_____ two students introducing themselves

1-3 ¡Hola! The following people are meeting for the first time. What would they say to each other?

Modelo:

el profesor Solar, Ester Muñoz

Profesor Solar: *Buenas tardes. Soy el profesor Solar.*
Ester: *Buenas tardes, profesor Solar. Soy Ester Muñoz.*
Profesor Solar: *Mucho gusto.*
Ester: *Igualmente.*

1. 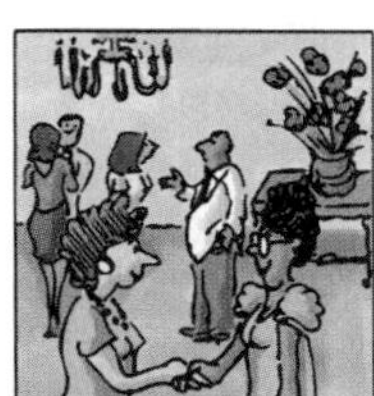
la Sra. Aldo, la Sra. García

2. 
Patricia, Marcos

3. 

Eduardo, Manuel

María, ¿cómo estás?

1-4 Saludos. How do you greet people you're meeting for the first time? How do you greet relatives? Friends? Does the age of the person you are greeting make a difference? When do people embrace, hug, or kiss each other on the cheek in the U.S. and Canada? Read about greetings in Latin America and Spain and think about how you would react to them and why.

> Many Spanish speakers use nonverbal signs when interacting with each other. These signs will vary, depending on the social situation and on the relationship between the speakers. In general, people who meet each other for the first time shake hands (*dar la mano*) both when greeting and when saying good-bye to each other. Relatives and friends, however, are usually more physically expressive. Men who know each other well often greet each other with an *abrazo*, or hug, and pats on the back. Women tend to greet each other and their male friends with one (Latin America) or two (Spain) light kisses on the cheeks.

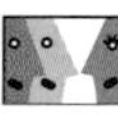
1-5 Presentaciones. Introduce yourself to five of your classmates. Shake hands or kiss lightly on the cheek as you ask them their names and how they are doing. Then say good-bye.

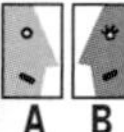
A B

1-6A ¿Cómo está usted? (*When you see the **A/B** icon, one of you will assume the **A** role given in the text; the other, the **B** role in Appendix 1 for **B Activities.***) Assume the role of instructor—Sr./Sra. Pérez. Your partner is your student. Greet each other and ask how things are. Use the following information about yourself and the day. Student B, please see **Appendix 1,** page A1.

- It's morning. You greet the student.
- You feel great today. Ask a student his/her name.
- Respond to the student.

CD 1, Track 4

1-9 to 1-13

LETRAS Y SONIDOS

Spanish vowels

The vowels of Spanish are short and stable. Their pronunciation is fairly predictable based on spelling, where each of the five *letters a, e, i, o, u* corresponds to one vowel *sound.* In English, these same five letters correspond to many different vowel sounds, which tend to be long and glided. For example, the letter *a* creates five different vowel sounds in the following words: f*a*ther, c*a*t, *a*pproach, bl*a*me, *a*we.

What vowel sound corresponds to each of the letters *a, e, i, o, u* in Spanish?

1. The letter *a* is pronounced like the *a* in f*a*ther, but is shorter.
   más pasa nada mañana encantada
2. The letter *e* is pronounced like the *e* in th*e*y, but is shorter with no final glide.
   es tres mesa deporte interesante
3. The letter *i* is pronounced like the *i* in mach*i*ne, but is shorter.[1]
   mi niño libro tímido inteligente
4. The letter *o* is pronounced like the *o* in al*o*ne, but is shorter with no final glide.
   o hola color exótico nosotros
5. The letter *u* is pronounced like the *u* in fl*u*te, but is shorter.
   tú azul lunes gusto música

[1]Be careful to avoid the *i* sound in s*i*t in the following words, since this sound does not exist in Spanish: *inteligente, interesante, introvertido, impaciente, tímido, simpático, misterioso.*

¡Así lo hacemos![1] Estructuras

CD 1, Track 5

1-14 to 1-17

1. The Spanish alphabet

The Spanish alphabet contains twenty-seven letters, including one that does not appear in the English alphabet: **ñ.**[2]

Letra (*Letter*)	Nombre (*Name*)	Ejemplos (*Examples*)
a	a	Ana
b	be (grande)	Bárbara
c	ce	Carlos; Cecilia
d	de	Dios; Pedro
e	e	Ernesto
f	efe	Fernando
g	ge	gato; Germán
h	hache	Hernán; hola
i	i	Inés
j	jota	José
k	ka	kilómetro
l	ele	Luis
m	eme	María
n	ene	Nora; nachos
ñ	eñe	niño
o	o	Óscar
p	pe	Pepe
q	cu	Quique; química
r	ere	Laura
s	ese	Sara
t	te	Tomás
u	u	usted; Úrsula
v	be (corta) or uve	Venus; vamos
w	doble be (or uve doble)	Washington
x	equis	excelente; México
y	y griega	Yolanda; soy
z	zeta	Zorro

- The letters **b** and **v** are pronounced exactly alike, as a **b.**
- The letters **k** and **w** are not common, and appear only in words borrowed from other languages, such as **karate** and **whiskey.**
- At the beginning of a word, **r** is always pronounced as a trilled **rr,** for example, **Ramón**, **Rosa**, **reloj.**

[1]That's how we do it!

[2]Until mid-1994 the Spanish alphabet had three additional letters: *ch, ll,* and *rr.*

- Depending on its position, the letter **y** can be a semivowel as in the English words *boy* and *toy*: **Paraguay, voy.** It can also be a consonant as in the English words *yard* and *yesterday*: **yo, maya.**
- The letter **c** is pronounced like **s** before **e** or **i: cero, cita.** It sounds like the English **k** before **a, o,** or **u: casa, Colombia, Cuba.**
- The letter **z** is pronounced like the English **s: gazpacho, zona, lápiz.**
- In most of Spain, **c** before **e** and **i,** and **z** are pronounced like the English **th,** as in **zorro** or **Celia.**
- The letter **g** is pronounced like the Spanish **j** (or hard English **h**) before **e** or **i: Germán, gitano.** The combinations **ga, go, gu, gue,** or **gui** are pronounced like the English **g** in **gate: gato, Gómez, Gutiérrez, guerra, guía.**
- The letter **h** is always silent: **hotel, hospital.**
- When a letter carries an accent, say **con acento** after saying the name of the letter: **eme - a - ere - i con acento - a** (**María**).

Aplicación

1-7 ¿Qué vocal falta? What vowels are missing from the following names of famous people?

Modelo: S_____nt_____n_____
Santana

1. J_____nn_____fer L_____p_____z (actriz y cantante)
2. C_____mer_____n D_____ _____z (actriz)
3. R_____b_____rt_____ Cl_____m_____nt_____ (beisbolista)
4. Ósc_____r d_____ l_____ H_____y_____ (boxeador)
5. P_____bl_____ P_____c_____ss_____ (pintor)

1-8 ¿Qué letra falta? What consonants are missing from these countries' names in the Spanish-speaking world?

Modelo: Mé_____i_____o
x (equis), c

1. Ar_____enti_____a
2. Bo_____i_____ia
3. _____erú
4. E_____ua_____or
5. Ve_____e_____ue_____a
6. El Sa_____ _____ado_____
7. Re_____ública Do_____ini_____ana
8. Co_____ _____a _____ica
9. Para_____ua_____
10. Espa_____a

1-9 ¿Quién soy yo? (*Who am I?*) Take turns dictating your full name to each other. Then check to see if your spelling is correct.

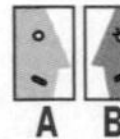
A B

1-10A Otra vez, por favor (*please*). Take turns spelling out your words to each other. Be sure to say what category they are in. If you need to hear the spelling again, ask your partner to repeat by saying, **Otra vez, por favor.** Student B, please see **Appendix 1,** page A1.

MODELO: cosa (*thing*) (enchilada)
e - ene - ce - hache - i - ele - a - de - a

YOU SPELL...	YOU WRITE...	
1. persona famosa (Andy García)	1. persona famosa:	________
2. ciudad (Lima)	2. ciudad (*city*):	________
3. cosa (banana)	3. cosa:	________
4. ciudad (Taos)	4. ciudad:	________

1-18 to 1-20

2. The numbers 0–100

0–9	**10–19**	**20–29**	**30–39**
cero	diez	veinte	treinta
uno	once	veintiuno	treinta y uno
dos	doce	veintidós	treinta y dos
tres	trece	veintitrés	treinta y tres
cuatro	catorce	veinticuatro	treinta y cuatro
cinco	quince	veinticinco	treinta y cinco
seis	dieciséis	veintiséis	treinta y seis
siete	diecisiete	veintisiete	treinta y siete
ocho	dieciocho	veintiocho	treinta y ocho
nueve	diecinueve	veintinueve	treinta y nueve

40–49	cuarenta, cuarenta y uno, cuarenta y dos, cuarenta y tres...
50–59	cincuenta, cincuenta y uno, cincuenta y dos, cincuenta y tres...
60–69	sesenta, sesenta y uno, sesenta y dos, sesenta y tres...
70–79	setenta, setenta y uno, setenta y dos, setenta y tres...
80–89	ochenta, ochenta y uno, ochenta y dos, ochenta y tres...
90–99	noventa, noventa y uno, noventa y dos, noventa y tres...
100–109	cien, ciento uno, ciento dos, ciento tres...

- **Uno** becomes **un** before a masculine singular noun and **una** before a feminine singular noun.

un libro	*one book*	**una mesa**	*one table*
un profesor	*one professor (male)*	**una profesora**	*one professor (female)*

- In compound numbers, **-uno** becomes **-ún** before a masculine noun and **-una** before a feminine noun.

veintiún libros	*twenty-one books*
veintiuna profesoras	*twenty-one female professors*

- The numbers **dieciséis** through **diecinueve** (16–19) and **veintiuno** through **veintinueve** (21–29) are generally written as one word. The condensed spelling is not used after 30.

- **Cien** is used when it precedes a noun or when counting the number 100 in sequence.

  cien estudiantes — *one hundred students*

  noventa y ocho, noventa y nueve, cien

- **Ciento** is used in compound numbers from 101 and 199.

ciento uno	**ciento cuarenta y cinco**
ciento diez	**ciento noventa y nueve**

Aplicación

1-11 ¿Qué número falta? Complete the following sequences with the logical number in Spanish.

MODELO: uno, *tres*, cinco, *siete*, nueve

1. dos, ________, seis, ocho, ________, doce, ________
2. ________, ________, cinco, siete, ________, once
3. uno, cinco, ________, ________, diecisiete
4. cinco, diez, ________, veinte, veinticinco, ________, ________
5. treinta, cuarenta, ________, ________, setenta, ________, ________
6. ________, veintidós, ________, cuarenta y cuatro, ________, ________, setenta y siete, ________
7. veintiuno, veintitrés, ________, veintisiete, veintinueve
8. noventa y cinco, setenta y dos, ________, veintiséis, ________

¿Cuál es tu número favorito?

1-12 Te toca a ti (*It's your turn*). Challenge a classmate with an original sequence of numbers. See the previous activity for models.

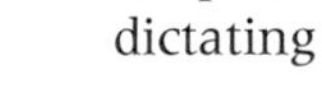

1-13 ¿Cuál (*What*) es tu número de teléfono? Write your telephone numbers, including the area code, and take turns dictating them to each other.

MODELO: E1: *¿Cuál es tu número de teléfono?*
E2: (513) 556 2240: *cinco, trece, cinco, cincuenta y seis, veintidós, cuarenta*

1-14 ¿Qué hacer en Madrid? On what page of the tourist guide can you find information about what to do in Madrid?

En Madrid

La **Semana Santa** en Madrid ofrece un buen número de procesiones.

El 30 se corre la famosa **Mapoma** (Maratón Popular de Madrid).

El 23 se celebra el **Día del Libro**. Se ofrece una gran variedad de libros por todo el centro de la ciudad.

Atención: Noten que los museos tienen horas especiales durante la Semana Santa.

Bienvenida a los participantes del Congreso de Inmunología Humana que tiene lugar en el Hotel Principado.

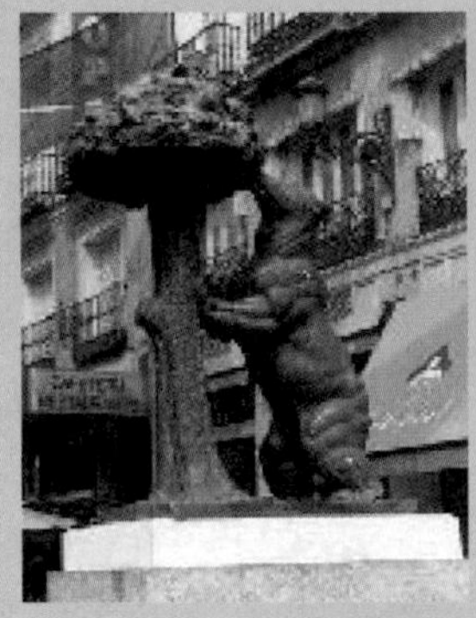

El teléfono turístico: 902 202 202.

La línea turística proporciona amplia información sobre hoteles, restaurantes, camping, hostales, etc., las mejores ofertas para viajar, dónde y cómo reservar.

010 Teléfono del consumidor.

Toda la información cultural y de servicios del Ayuntamiento de Madrid.

MARZO - 2008

EDITA Patronato Municipal de Turismo Mayor, 69, 28013
Madrid. Tel. 91 588 29 00
El p.m.t. no se responsabiliza de los cambios de última hora.

Modelo: __20__ música
en la página veinte

1. ____ puntos de interés
2. ____ datos útiles
3. ____ congresos
4. ____ niños
5. ____ conciertos
6. ____ ballet
7. ____ paseo del arte
8. ____ deportes
9. ____ fiestas
10. ____ ópera

3. The days of the week, the months, and the seasons

1-21 to 1-27

Los días de la semana

- The days of the week in Spanish are not capitalized and are all masculine.
- Calendars begin the week with Monday, not Sunday.
- The definite article is not used after **es** when telling what day of the week it is.

  Hoy **es jueves.** — *Today is Thursday.*
- On Monday ..., on Tuesday ..., etc., is expressed by using the definite article, **el** or **los.**

  El examen es **el lunes.** — *The exam is on Monday.*
- Days that end in **-s** have the same form in the singular and the plural.

  el lunes — **los lunes**
- In the plural, the days of the week express the idea of doing something regularly.

  La clase de filosofía es **los lunes, los miércoles** y **los viernes.** — *Philosophy class is on Mondays, Wednesdays, and Fridays.*
  Los sábados voy al gimnasio. — *I go to the gym on Saturdays.*

septiembre 2008

lunes	martes	miércoles	jueves	viernes	sábado	domingo
1	2	3	(4)	5	6	7
8	9	10	11	12	13	14
15	16	17	18	19	20	21
22	23	24	25	26	27	28
29	30					

¿Qué día es hoy? Es jueves, 4 de septiembre.

Los meses del año

- Months are not capitalized in Spanish.

  Mi cumpleaños es en **noviembre.** — *My birthday is in November.*
  Hay veintiocho días en **febrero.** — *There are twenty-eight days in February.*

enero

L	M	M	J	V	S	D
						1
2	3	4	5	6	7	8
9	10	11	12	13	14	15
16	17	18	19	20	21	22
23	24	25	26	27	28	29
30	31					

febrero

L	M	M	J	V	S	D
		1	2	3	4	5
6	7	8	9	10	11	12
13	14	15	16	17	18	19
20	21	22	23	24	25	26
27	28					

marzo

L	M	M	J	V	S	D
		1	2	3	4	5
6	7	8	9	10	11	12
13	14	15	16	17	18	19
20	21	22	23	24	25	26
27	28	29	30	31		

abril

L	M	M	J	V	S	D
					1	2
3	4	5	6	7	8	9
(10)	11	12	13	14	15	16
17	18	19	20	21	22	23
24	25	26	27	28	29	30

mayo

L	M	M	J	V	S	D
(1)	2	3	4	(5)	6	7
8	9	(10)	11	12	13	14
15	16	17	18	19	20	21
22	23	24	25	26	27	28
29	30	31				

junio

L	M	M	J	V	S	D
			1	2	3	4
5	6	7	8	9	10	11
12	13	14	15	16	17	18
19	20	21	22	23	24	25
26	27	28	29	30		

julio

L	M	M	J	V	S	D
					1	2
3	4	5	6	7	8	9
10	11	12	13	14	15	16
17	18	19	20	21	22	23
24	25	26	27	28	29	30
31						

agosto

L	M	M	J	V	S	D
	1	2	3	4	5	6
7	8	9	10	11	12	13
14	15	16	17	18	19	20
21	22	23	24	25	26	27
28	29	30	31			

septiembre

L	M	M	J	V	S	D
				1	2	3
4	5	6	7	8	9	10
11	12	13	14	15	(16)	17
18	19	20	21	22	23	24
25	26	27	28	29	30	

octubre

L	M	M	J	V	S	D
						1
2	3	4	5	6	7	8
9	10	11	(12)	13	14	15
16	17	18	19	20	21	22
23	24	25	26	27	28	29
30	31					

noviembre

L	M	M	J	V	S	D
		1	2	3	4	5
6	7	8	9	10	11	12
13	14	15	16	17	18	19
20	21	22	23	24	25	26
27	28	29	30			

diciembre

L	M	M	J	V	S	D
				1	2	3
4	5	6	7	8	9	10
(11)	12	13	14	15	16	17
18	19	20	21	22	23	24
25	26	27	28	29	30	31

Las estaciones del año

- The definite article is normally used with seasons. Seasons are not capitalized.

  ¿Cómo es **la primavera** aquí? *What is spring like here?*

el invierno

la primavera

el verano

el otoño

Aplicación

1-15 Fechas importantes en los Estados Unidos y el Canadá. Write out the date of the following celebrations.

Modelo:

el diecisiete de marzo

1. 

2. 

3. 

4. 

1-16 Fiestas importantes en el mundo hispano. Refer to the calendar on page 13 and match the dates with the probable event.

Modelo: El día de la Independencia de México es en el otoño.
El 16 de septiembre es el día de la Independencia de México.

1. _____ La batalla de Puebla se celebra en la primavera.
2. _____ El día de la Raza (o el día de Colón) es en el otoño.
3. _____ La fiesta de la Virgen de Guadalupe es en el invierno.
4. _____ El día festivo (*holiday*) para los trabajadores es en la primavera.
5. _____ En México, el día de las madres también es en la primavera.
6. _____ En Pamplona, España, se celebran los sanfermines[1] por nueve días en el verano.

a. el 12 de diciembre
b. del 6 al 14 de julio
c. el 5 de mayo
d. el 10 de mayo
e. el 12 de octubre
f. el primero de mayo

Ernest Hemingway escribió sobre las fiestas de San Fermín.

[1]"Los sanfermines" is a masculine plural noun referring to the festivities that honor Saint Fermin (*San Fermín*).

1-17 Trivia. Take turns asking each other questions.

MODELO: E1: ¿Qué mes tiene veintiocho días?
E2: *febrero*

1. los días de la semana en que no hay clases
2. los meses de la primavera
3. un mes con treinta y un días
4. un día malo (*bad*)

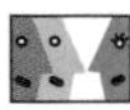

1-18 ¿Cuándo es tu cumpleaños? Take turns reporting your birthdays. Have one person fill in the information on a twelve-month graph, like the one below, for the class.

1. ¿Cuál (*Which*) es el mes más (*most*) común?
2. ¿Cuál es el mes menos (*least*) común?

	Número de estudiantes
enero	
febrero	
marzo	
abril	
mayo	
junio	
julio	
agosto	
septiembre	
octubre	
noviembre	
diciembre	

¿Cuánto sabes tú? *How much do you know? Can you...*

1-28 to 1-31

- ☐ introduce yourself to your teacher? to a classmate? to a person at a party?
- ☐ greet and say good-bye to friends from class? use the Hispanic ways of greeting?
- ☐ spell your name in Spanish? write down a classmate's name when it is dictated?
- ☐ dictate your phone number and take down a phone number dictated to you?
- ☐ talk about the calendar and dates: say when your birthday is? ask when a friend's birthday is? say which days you have class? say which months you're in school? give today's date?

El mundo hispano

1-19 En tu experiencia. How many countries can you name whose official language is English? Can you think of differences in accents or in expressions that people use in regions of the United States and other English-speaking countries? As you read about the Spanish-speaking world, think about how geography influences language and culture.

There are over 425 million Spanish speakers in the world today. Spanish is the official language of Spain, Mexico, much of Central and South America, and much of the Caribbean. Spanish is spoken in some Asian countries, such as the Philippines, and by a portion of the population in Equatorial Guinea and Morocco in Africa. The United States has over 42 million people who are of Hispanic heritage, which is 14.5% of its population, and some 1.8 million Hispanic-owned businesses. The United States is considered the fourth largest Spanish-speaking country in the world. Today, only Mexico, Spain, and Colombia have more Spanish speakers than the United States and by the year 2050, one in every four United States citizens will be Hispanic.

The enormous diversity among Spanish speakers results in differences in pronunciation and vocabulary, similar to differences in expressions and accents in English. Different neighbors and ethnic groups influenced the words and accents of each country. Below are some examples.

1-20 En tu opinión. Take turns telling each other in which country you are, based on what you need.

MODELO: E1: *Necesito un coche.*
E2: *Estás en España.*

	España	**Colombia**	**México**	**Argentina**
car	coche	carro	carro	auto
apartment	piso	apartamento	departamento	departamento
bus	autobús	bus	camión	ómnibus
sandwich	bocadillo	sándwich	sándwich; torta	sándwich; bocadillo

SEGUNDA PARTE

¡Así lo decimos! Vocabulario

CD 1, Track 6

1-32 to 1-33

¡Así es la vida! En la clase

Profesora García: Buenos días, abran el libro en la página cincuenta, por favor, y escriban el número seis.

Paulina: Ay, necesito un lápiz.

Miguel: Pues, no tengo papel.

Ramón: Y yo no tengo libro.

Profesora García: ¡Pero qué barbaridad! (*What nonsense!*) ¡Qué estudiantes!

En la clase

CD 1, Track 7

1-34 to 1-39

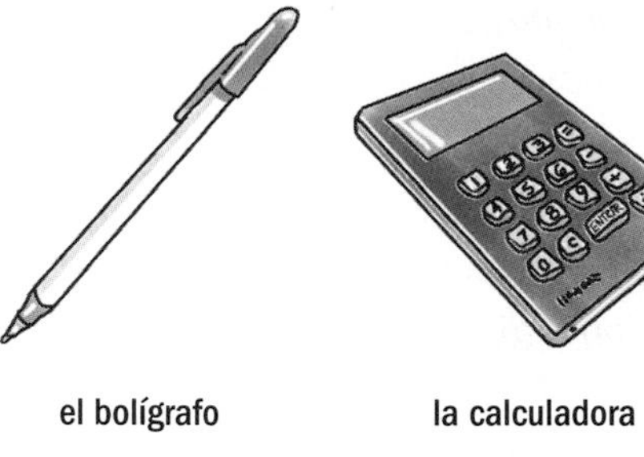
el bolígrafo

la calculadora

el cuaderno

el diccionario

el libro

el mapa

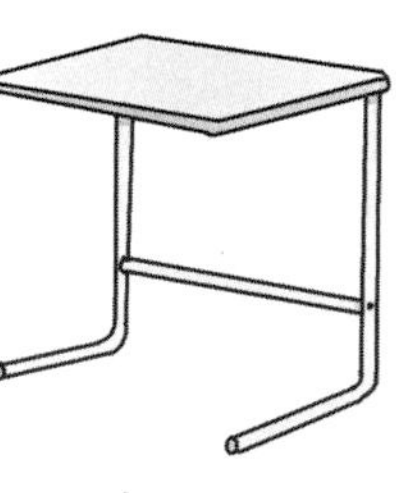
la mesa

la mochila

la pizarra

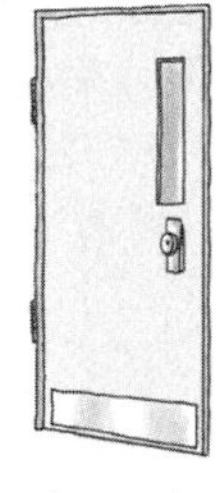
la puerta

el reloj

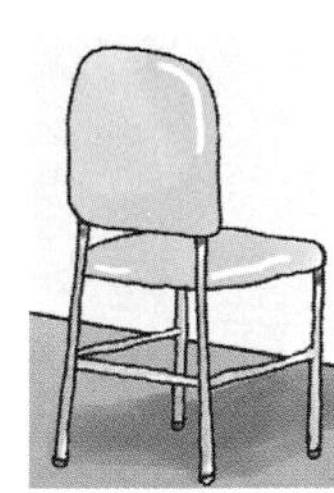
la silla

Colores	*Colors*
amarillo/a	
anaranjado/a	
azul	
blanco/a	
gris	
morado/a	
negro/a	
rojo/a	
rosado/a	
verde	
moreno	Brown

Más objetos en la clase	*More objects in the classroom*
el lápiz	*pencil*
el papel	*paper*

Verbos	*Verbs*
necesitar	*to need*
ser	*to be*
tener (ie)	*to have*

Adjetivos	*Adjectives*
aburrido/a	*boring*
barato/a	*cheap; inexpensive*
bueno/a	*good*
caro/a	*expensive*
extrovertido/a	*outgoing*
fascinante	*fascinating*
grande	*big*
inteligente	*intelligent*
interesante	*interesting*
malo/a	*bad*
pequeño/a	*small*
simpático/a	*nice*
tímido/a	*shy; timid*
trabajador/a	*hard-working*

Adverbios	*Adverbs*
aquí	*here*

Expresiones para la clase[1]	*Expressions for class*
Abre (Abran) el libro.	*Open your book(s).*
Cierra (Cierren) el libro.	*Close the book.*
Contesta (Contesten) en español.	*Answer in Spanish.*
Escribe (Escriban) en la pizarra.	*Write on the board.*
Escucha (Escuchen).	*Listen.*
Estudia (Estudien).	*Study.*
Lee (Lean) el diálogo.	*Read the dialogue.*
Repite (Repitan).	*Repeat.*
Ve (Vayan) a la pizarra.	*Go to the board.*

[1]These commands are for one student. Commands for the whole class are given in parentheses.

EXPANSIÓN — More on structure and usage

To ask and reply to basic questions in Spanish, use the following questions and answers:

PREGUNTAS	***QUESTIONS***
¿Cómo es/son?	*What is/are (it/they) like?*
¿Cuántos(as)?	*How many?*
¿De qué color es...?	*What color is...?*
¿Necesitas...?	*Do you need...?*
¿Qué hay en...?	*What is/are there in...?*
¿Qué es esto?	*What's this?*
¿Tienes...?	*Do you have...?*
RESPUESTAS	***ANSWERS***
Es.../Son...	*It is... / They are...*
Hay un/a (unos/as)...	*There is a (are some)...*
Necesito...	*I need...*
Tengo...	*I have...*

Aplicación

1-21 ¿Qué hay en la clase? Take inventory of your classroom. Indicate how many of each item there are.

Modelo: __20__ estudiantes
Hay veinte estudiantes.

_____ pizarra(s)
_____ bolígrafo(s)
_____ mesa(s)
_____ mapa(s)
_____ cuaderno(s)
_____ silla(s)
_____ reloj(es)
_____ libro(s)

1-22 Ellos, ellas y los colores. This reading comes from *Vanidades,* a popular magazine throughout Latin America. The article is based on a survey of men and women and their color preferences. Skim the reading. Don't try to understand every word. Read for general meaning to answer the questions below.

Ellos, ellas y los colores.

En un hospital de París se desarrolló un estudio en el que se les pidió a pacientes adultos, hombres y mujeres, que pintaran acuarelas con sus colores favoritos. En los resultados se observó que el 85% de los hombres prefirió usar los tonos verdes y los azules, mientras que la mayoría de las mujeres escogió los rojos y los amarillos, mostrando así —una vez más— las marcadas diferencias que en cuanto a preferencias de colores existen entre los dos sexos.

Vanidades, 34 (20), p. 16.

1. Where did the study take place?
2. Who were the subjects interviewed?
3. What percentage of men is referred to?
4. What colors are mentioned?
5. Now compare your class with the subjects in the article by responding **Sí** or **No** to these statements:

"Los hombres del estudio son como (*like*) los chicos (*guys*) de la clase".
"Las mujeres del estudio son como (*like*) las chicas (*girls*) de la clase".

CD 1, Track 8

1-23 ¿Qué haces cuando...? (*What do you do when...?*) Listen to a Spanish teacher make various requests in the classroom and write the number of each request by your corresponding reaction.

_____ I answer in Spanish.	_____ I close the book.
_____ I open my book.	_____ I listen to the music.
_____ I read the dialogue.	_____ I repeat the month.
_____ I write the sentence.	_____ I go to the board.

A B

1-24A Necesito... Below is a list of items you need. Tell a classmate what you need and ask if he/she has them. Mark the items your classmate has. When you finish, compare your lists. Student B, please see **Appendix 1,** page A1.

MODELO: E1: *Necesito ochenta bolígrafos. ¿Tienes ochenta?*
E2: *Sí, tengo bolígrafos.*
E1: *Necesito treinta y tres libros. ¿Tienes treinta y tres libros?*
E2: *Sólo* (only) *veintidós.*

Necesito...

_____ 1 puerta	_____ 14 cuadernos	_____ 11 mesas
_____ 10 sillas	_____ 80 bolígrafos	_____ 20 diccionarios
_____ 100 papeles	_____ 17 lápices	_____ 75 pizarras
_____ 16 mochilas	_____ 95 mapas	_____ 33 libros

1-25 Veo algo... (*I see something...*) Describe an object to see if your classmate can guess what it is. Use colors and adjectives from **¡Así lo decimos!**

MODELO: E1: *Veo algo verde y grande.*
E2: *¿Es la pizarra?*

1-26 De compras (*Shopping*). You are responsible for buying supplies for an academic department. Figure out how many of the following items you need to order. (Be sure to show your calculation.)

Hay nueve profesores y dos secretarias. Cada (*each*) profesor necesita una mesa. Tres profesores necesitan un cuaderno y diez bolígrafos cada uno. Tres profesores necesitan ocho lápices y una silla cada uno. Dos profesores necesitan veinticinco cuadernos y una pizarra cada uno. Un profesor necesita cuatro diccionarios, un reloj y dos cuadernos. Cada secretaria necesita quince bolígrafos, una computadora, veinte lápices, quince relojes y una mochila.

MODELO: *9 mesas (9 × 1 = 9)*

1. cuadernos ___________	5. mochilas ___________
2. computadoras ___________	6. bolígrafos ___________
3. lápices ___________	7. diccionarios ___________
4. pizarras ___________	8. relojes ___________

¡Así lo hacemos! Estructuras

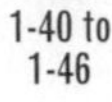

1-40 to 1-46

4. Nouns and articles

Words that identify persons, places, or objects are called nouns. Spanish nouns—even those denoting nonliving things—are either masculine or feminine in gender. Note how the definite article (*the*) must agree with the noun.

Masculine		Feminine	
Singular	**Plural**	**Singular**	**Plural**
el hombre	los hombres	la mujer	las mujeres
el muchacho	los muchachos	la muchacha	las muchachas
el libro	los libros	la mesa	las mesas
el profesor	los profesores	la profesora	las profesoras
el lápiz	los lápices	la clase	las clases
el mapa	los mapas	la universidad	las universidades

There are many clues that will help you identify the gender of a noun.

- Most nouns ending in **-o** or those denoting male persons are masculine: **el libro, el hombre.** Most nouns ending in **-a** or those denoting female persons are feminine: **la mesa, la mujer.** Some common exceptions are: **el día** (*day*) and **el mapa,** which are masculine.
- Many person nouns have corresponding masculine **-o** and feminine **-a** forms.

  el amigo/la amiga **el niño/la niña** (*boy / girl*)
- Most masculine nouns ending in a consonant simply add **-a** to form the feminine.

  el profesor/la profesora **el francés/la francesa**
- Certain person nouns use the same form for masculine and feminine, but the article used will show the gender.

  el estudiante/la estudiante (*male / female student*)
- If it is provided, the article will tell you what the gender of the noun is.

  la clase **el lápiz**
- Most nouns ending in **-ad** and **-ión** are feminine.

  la universidad **la nación**
- Most nouns ending in **-ema** are masculine.

  el problema **el poema**

- Use the definite article with titles when talking about someone, but not when addressing the person directly.

  El profesor Gómez habla español. — *Professor Gómez speaks Spanish.*
  ¡Buenos días, profesor Gómez! — *Good morning, Professor Gómez!*

- Nouns that end in a vowel form the plural by adding **-s.**

  mesa → mesas

- Nouns that end in a consonant add **-es.**

  mujer → mujeres **universidad → universidades**

- Nouns that end in a **-z** change the **z** to **c** in the plural.

  lápiz → lápices

- When the last syllable of a word that ends in a consonant has an accent mark, the accent is no longer needed in the plural.

  lección → lecciones

	Masculine		Feminine	
Singular	**un** bolígrafo	*a pen*	**una** silla	*a chair*
Plural	**unos** bolígrafos	*some pens*	**unas** sillas	*some chairs*

- Indefinite articles (*a, an, some*) also agree with the noun they modify. **Un** and **una** are equivalent to *a* or *an*. **Unos** and **unas** are equivalent to *some* (or *a few*).
- In Spanish, the indefinite article is omitted when telling someone's profession, unless you qualify the person (good, bad, hard-working, etc.).

  Lorena es profesora de matemáticas. — *Lorena is a mathematics professor.*
  Lorena es **una** profesora buena. — *Lorena is a good professor.*

Aplicación

1-27 ¿Masculino o femenino? Say which of the following words are masculine (M) or feminine (F). Then provide the article.

MODELO: _____ libro
M: el libro

1. _____ universidad
2. _____ mesa
3. _____ muchacho
4. _____ mujer
5. _____ problema
6. _____ lápiz
7. _____ silla
8. _____ poema

1-28 ¿Qué necesita? Say what the following people or places need. Use the indefinite article.

MODELO: ¿Qué necesita un profesor de informática (*computer science*)?
Necesita una computadora…

bolígrafos	cuaderno	mapas	papeles	lápices
diccionario	mesa	reloj	sillas	computadora
calculadora	estudiantes	microscopio	puerta	libros

¿Qué necesita…

1. un profesor de historia?
2. un científico?
3. una profesora de biología?
4. un matemático?
5. una profesora de ingeniería?
6. un/a estudiante?

1-29 Más de uno. Give the plural form of each of these nouns.

Modelo: el libro
los libros

1. la profesora	3. la lección	5. el reloj	7. el mapa
2. el lápiz	4. la puerta	6. el día	8. la mujer

1-30 En la clase de María Luisa. Complete the paragraph about María Luisa's class by using the correct form of the definite or indefinite article in each blank.

En (1) ___________ clase de español, hay (2) ___________ mapa, (3) ___________ pizarra, (4) ___________ mesa y (5) ___________ sillas. (6) ___________ estudiantes son (*are*) muy inteligentes. (7) ___________ profesora es (8) ___________ señora López. Todos (9) ___________ días (*every day*), estudiamos (*we study*) (10) ___________ lección y hablamos (*we speak*) mucho.

5. Adjective form, position, and agreement

1-47 to 1-53

- Descriptive adjectives, such as those denoting size, color, and shape, describe and give additional information about objects and people.

un libro **fascinante**	*a fascinating book*
una clase **grande**	*a big class*
un cuaderno **rosado**	*a pink notebook*

- Descriptive adjectives agree in gender and number with the noun they modify, and they generally follow the noun. Note that adjectives of nationality are not capitalized in Spanish.

el profesor **colombiano**	*the Colombian professor*
la señora **mexicana**	*the Mexican lady*
los estudiantes **españoles**	*the Spanish students*

- Adjectives whose masculine form ends in **-o** have a feminine form that ends in **-a.**

el profesor **argentino**	*the Argentine professor (male)*
la profesora **argentina**	*the Argentine professor (female)*

- Adjectives ending in a consonant or **-e** have the same masculine and feminine forms.

un coche **azul**	*a blue car*
una silla **azul**	*a blue chair*
un libro **grande**	*a big book*
una clase **grande**	*a big class*

- For adjectives of nationality that end in a consonant, and adjectives that end in **-dor,** add **-a** to form the feminine. If the masculine has an accented final syllable, the accent is dropped in the feminine and the plural forms.

el profesor **español**	*the Spanish professor*
la estudiante **española**	*the Spanish student*
un libro **francés**	*a French book*
una mujer **francesa**	*a French woman*
un señor **trabajador**	*a hard-working man*
una profesora **trabajadora**	*a hard-working professor*

Aplicación

1-31 Parejas. Match the following objects with the colors. Pay close attention to the gender and number of the nouns.

1. las mesas	_____ amarillos
2. el bolígrafo	_____ blanca
3. los relojes	_____ rojas
4. la silla	_____ negro

1-32 ¿De qué color? Look at the following items in your classroom and state what color they are.

MODELO: la pizarra
La pizarra es negra.

1. el mapa	5. las sillas
2. el lápiz	6. la puerta
3. el libro	7. los papeles
4. los cuadernos	8. la mochila

1-33 ¿Cómo es? ¿Cómo son? Combine nouns and adjectives to make logical sentences in Spanish. Remember that articles, nouns, and adjectives agree in gender and number.

MODELO: los estudiantes
Los estudiantes son buenos.

el libro de español		fascinante
los profesores		interesante
las sillas		simpático
la clase		inteligente
los estudiantes		bueno/malo
la pizarra	es/son	norteamericano/español, etcétera
el libro de inglés		rojo/anaranjado/amarillo/negro, etcétera
el bolígrafo		barato/caro
la universidad		grande/pequeño
los cuadernos		trabajador

1-34 ¿Cómo es? Describe your Spanish professor and one or more students in the class. Use at least two descriptive words for each person.

MODELO: *Cristina es inteligente y trabajadora.*

1. El profesor (La profesora) es...
2. (Nombre de un/a estudiante) es...

1-35 Palifruta. Answer the following questions based on the ad.

1. ¿De qué color es el palifruta de limón?
2. ¿De qué color es el palifruta de grosella?
3. ¿Son buenos o malos los palifrutas? ¿Por qué?

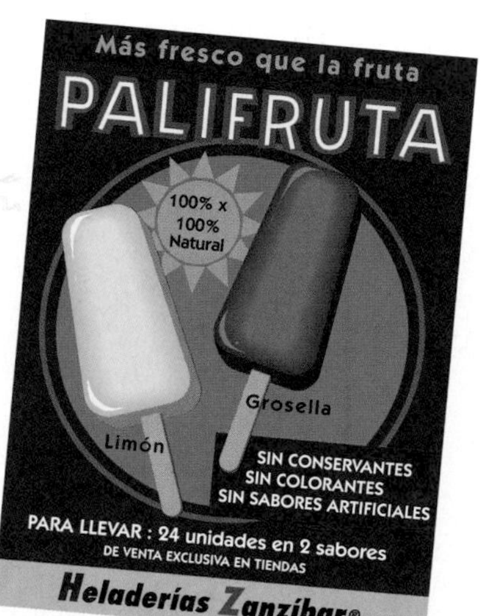

6. Subject pronouns and the present tense of *ser* (to be)

1-54 to 1-60

In Spanish, subject pronouns refer to people (*I, you, he,* etc.).[1]

Subject pronouns

Singular		Plural	
yo	I	**nosotros/nosotras**	we
tú	you *(inf.)*	**vosotros/vosotras**	you *(inf. Spain)*
usted (Ud.)	you *(for.)*	**ustedes (Uds.)**	you *(for.)*
él	he	**ellos/ellas**	they
ella	she		

Just like the verb *to be* in English, the verb **ser** in Spanish has irregular forms. You have already used several of them. Here are all of the forms of the present indicative, along with the subject pronouns.

ser (*to be*)

Singular			Plural		
yo	**soy**	*I am*	nosotros/as	**somos**	*we are*
tú	**eres**	*you are (inf.)*	vosotros/as	**sois**	*you are (inf.)*
él, ella, Ud.	**es**	*he/she is, you are (for.)*	ellos/as, Uds.	**son**	*they are, you are (for.)*

- Because the verb form indicates the subject of a sentence, subject pronouns are usually omitted unless they are needed for clarification or emphasis.

¿Eres de Puerto Rico?	*Are you from Puerto Rico?*
Sí, soy de Puerto Rico.	*Yes, I'm from Puerto Rico.*
Yo no, pero **ellos** sí son de Puerto Rico.	*I'm not, but they're from Puerto Rico.*

- There are four ways to express *you*: **tú, usted, vosotros/as,** and **ustedes. Tú** and **usted** are the singular forms. **Tú** is used in informal situations, that is, to address friends, family members, and pets. **Usted** denotes formality or respect and is used to address someone with whom you are not well acquainted or a person in a position of authority (e.g., a supervisor, teacher, or older person).[2]
- **Vosotros/as** and **ustedes** are the plural counterparts of **tú** and **usted,** but in most of Latin America, **ustedes** is used for both the familiar and formal plural *you*. **Vosotros/as** is used in Spain to address more than one person in a familiar context (e.g., a group of friends or children).[3]

---

[1]Subject pronouns are not generally used for inanimate objects or animals (except when referring to pets).

[2]In the families of some Hispanic countries, children use ***usted*** and ***ustedes*** to address their parents as a sign of respect.

[3]*¡Arriba!* uses ***ustedes*** as the plural of ***tú*** except where cultural context would require otherwise.

- The pronouns **usted** and **ustedes** are commonly abbreviated as **Ud.** and **Uds.** or **Vd.** and **Vds.**
- The verb **ser** is used to express origin, occupation, or inherent qualities.

¿De dónde **eres**?	*Where are you from?*
Soy de Toronto.	*I am from Toronto.*
Mi madre **es** profesora.	*My mother is a professor.*
Ustedes **son** muy pacientes.	*You are very patient.*

Aplicación

1-36 Dos artistas importantes. Read the description of the two artists below and underline the uses of **ser**. Then answer the questions that follow.

Salvador Dalí y Diego Rivera son dos de los artistas más famosos del mundo. Sus pinturas son admiradas por expertos y por estudiantes de arte. Los dos son del siglo xx, pero sus experiencias y sus estilos son muy diferentes. Salvador Dalí es español. Es de Figueras, un pueblo cerca de Barcelona. Dalí es famoso no sólo por su arte surrealista, sino también por su apariencia extravagante. *El descubrimiento de América por Cristóbal Colón* conmemora el famoso viaje de Colón en 1492. La muerte de Dalí es en 1989 a la edad de 84 años.

Diego Rivera es mexicano. Es de Guanajuato, una ciudad colonial al norte de la Ciudad de México. La fecha de su nacimiento es 1886 y la fecha de su muerte es 1957. Rivera es famoso por sus murales que describen la historia de México, especialmente la conquista de México por los españoles. *Historia de México desde la conquista hasta el futuro* es un mural muy grande. Su estilo es realista.

Now answer in Spanish.

1. What do Rivera and Dalí have in common?
2. What else do they have in common?
3. How do they differ?

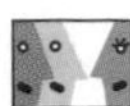

1-37 Una encuesta. Take a survey of class members to find out what they consider to be the ideal qualities of the following people, places, and things. Respond with your own opinions as well.

MODELO: E1: ¿Cómo es la clase ideal?
E2: *La clase ideal es pequeña.*
E3: *La clase ideal es interesante.*

1. ¿Cómo es el/la profesor/a ideal?
2. ¿Cómo es el/la amigo/a ideal?
3. ¿Cómo es el libro ideal?
4. ¿Cómo es la universidad ideal?

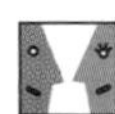

1-38 Yo soy... Introduce and describe yourself to a classmate, then ask what he/she is like. Follow the model.

MODELO: Me llamo... Soy..., y... (adjectives).
¿Cómo eres tú?

¿Cuánto sabes tú? *How much do you know? Can you...*

1-61 to 1-64

- ☐ identify the objects in your classroom using the correct definite or indefinite article?
- ☐ follow your teacher's instructions in Spanish?
- ☐ describe yourself using several adjectives?
- ☐ describe items using colors and other adjectives?

Observaciones

Episode 1

1-65 to 1-68

¡Pura vida! Episodio 1

¡Pura vida! is an on-going *serie* that takes place in Costa Rica.

Antes de ver el video

1-39 ¿Cómo es Costa Rica? Costa Rica is known for its natural beauty and national efforts to maintain the varied ecosystem. It is a tropical country with several climatic zones and four mountain ranges with seven active volcanoes. Earth tremors and small quakes shake the country from time to time. Read about San José, its capital, and answer the questions that follow in English.

San José, la capital de Costa Rica, está situada (*located*) en el valle central del país (*country*) a una elevación de 3.795 pies de altura, con los volcanes Poás, Irazú y Barba al norte y la Sierra de Talamanca al sur. La ciudad tiene una población de 350.000 habitantes; la temperatura promedio (*average*) oscila entre los 19 y 22 grados centígrados.

En el centro de San José los turistas pueden ver (*see*) el Teatro Nacional, con su arquitectura barroca y neoclásica. Es el edificio *(building)* más notable de la ciudad. Otros lugares (*places*) de interés son el Museo de Oro Precolombino, el Museo de Jade, el Museo Nacional y el Centro Costarricense de Ciencias y Cultura. El suburbio de Escazú tiene excelentes restaurantes y una animada (*lively*) vida nocturna.

San José está situada entre dos volcanes.

1. Where is the capital of Costa Rica located?
2. What volcanoes are to the north of San José?
3. What is San José's average temperature?
4. What is the most remarkable building in the capital?
5. Where can you find excellent restaurants and lively nightlife?

A ver el video

1-40 Los personajes. Watch the first episode of *¡Pura vida!* and watch for the ways in which the characters greet each other. Take note of what seems to cause cultural confusion. Then, identify the characters using the brief descriptions below.

La casa de doña María

Hermés

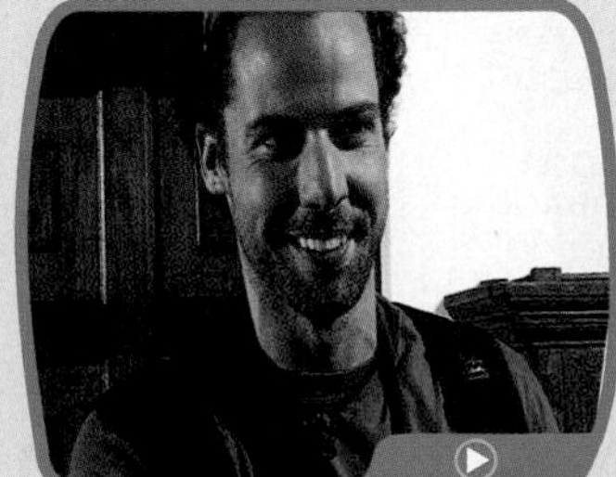
Felipe

1. _____ Es fotógrafo.
2. _____ Tiene una camioneta (*van*).
3. _____ Compra (*buys*) fruta.
4. _____ Va al trabajo *(work)*.

Después de ver el video

WWW

1-41 La ciudad de San José. Connect with your **¡Arriba!** website to see photographs of the city of San José and write three adjectives to describe it.

Modelo: La ciudad es…

NUESTRO MUNDO

Panoramas

Vistas culturales

1-69

El mundo hispano

You will soon see that our world (*nuestro mundo*) is full of diversity and surprises. Throughout **¡Arriba!** we hope to emphasize that the Hispanic world is one of many cultures with the Spanish language tying it together across five continents. As you make these discoveries, we hope that you remember and appreciate the diversity. To begin, what do you already know about the Spanish-speaking world? Supply as much of the following information as you can.

1-42 ¿Ya sabes? (*Do you already know?*) How many of the following can you name?

1. the names of some Spanish-speaking countries
2. a coffee-producing country
3. states in the United States where Spanish is an important language
4. a petroleum-producing country

On the next two pages, you will find the answers to some of these questions, as well as other information about the Spanish-speaking world. Use the images and your guessing skills to understand the text, then test your comprehension with the activities that follow.

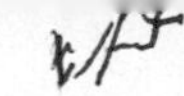

La topografía, el clima y la economía de Sudamérica varían de región en región. La majestuosa cordillera de los Andes, donde hace mucho frío (*it's very cold*) y donde hay poca vegetación, contrasta con la rica y calurosa (*warm*) zona del Amazonas.

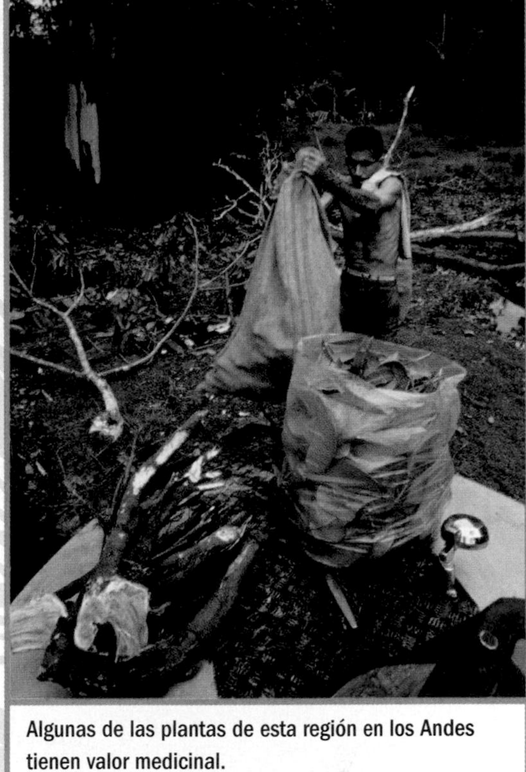

Algunas de las plantas de esta región en los Andes tienen valor medicinal.

Muchas capitales sudamericanas son metrópolis grandes y modernas con sus rascacielos (*skyscrapers*), su comercio, su gente (*people*) y su contaminación (*pollution*).

Santa Fe de Bogotá, la capital de Colombia, incluye un nombre con origen indígena (Bogotá) y español (Santa Fe).

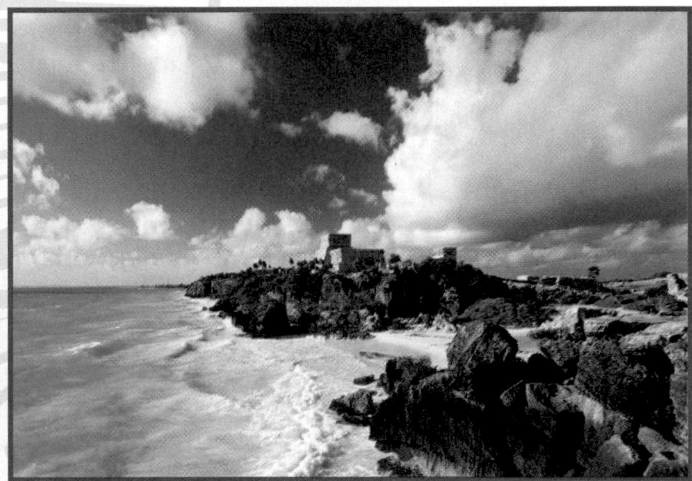

Los yacimientos arqueológicos, como el de Tulum, México, son testigos (*witnesses*) de las civilizaciones precolombinas.

La presencia de los hispanos en los EE.UU. (*U.S.*) se nota en muchas partes, especialmente en las grandes ciudades y en el sur del país. Este desfile en febrero es parte de la celebración del Carnaval de la Calle Ocho de Miami, donde muchas personas son de origen hispano.

1-43 ¿Cierto o falso? Identify whether the following statements are true or false. Correct any false statement.

MODELO: _____ Bogotá es la capital de Chile.
__*F*__ *Bogotá es la capital de Colombia.*

1. _____ Hay muchos hispanos en Miami.
2. _____ Los Andes están en Norteamérica.
3. _____ Tulum está en la costa de Guatemala.
4. _____ El Carnaval en Miami es en el otoño.
5. _____ Algunas plantas de los Andes tienen valor medicinal.
6. _____ La capital de Colombia es pequeña.

1-44 Conexiones. Connect with your **¡Arriba!** web site to find out the following information about the Spanish-speaking world.

1. a Central American country where English is the official language
2. where Patagonia is
3. three very long rivers
4. three important mountain ranges in the Hispanic world
5. what and where Titicaca is
6. a city in the United States with a large Spanish-speaking population

1-45 ¡Vamos! Work with another student to choose three Spanish-speaking countries you are going to visit. Once you choose the countries, connect to the Internet and print information about them. Be prepared to justify why you chose the three countries.

MODELO: *Vamos a Chile, a Bolivia y a la Argentina.*

Ritmos

1-70

"Salsa en Nueva York" (Típica Novel, Cuba/Nueva York)

This song, by the Cuban group Típica Novel, very simply tells of the joys of *salsa* music and its influence on the city of New York. Metaphorically speaking, the lyrics of the song represent the far-reaching influence of Hispanic music on the peoples and cultures of the world where it has flourished.

"Salsa en Nueva York"
Llegó la salsa a Nueva York, cuna del ritmo y del sabor
de Puerto Rico, Cuba y demás se unen así salsa y sabor.
(se repite)

Oye, lleva mi ritmo, salsa y sabor. (se repite)
Hace tiempo, que hacía falta que la Novel le traiga salsa.
(se repite)
Oye, lleva mi ritmo, salsa y sabor. (se repite)

Antes de escuchar (*Pre-listening*)

1-46 Estilos musicales. "Salsa en Nueva York" is typical of the cheerful, catchy, and very danceable rhythms of *salsa* music. Are you or your classmates familiar with *salsa*? Have you ever heard *salsa* music? What ideas or thoughts do you associate with it? What ideas or thoughts do you associate with Hispanic or Latin music in general? What musical styles are typical of your country or the region you are from? Which are your favorites and why?

1-47 La música hispana. Before listening to "Salsa en Nueva York," write down as many styles of Hispanic or Latin music as you can, working in pairs. Then share your list with your classmate and discuss any artists whom you know and whether or not you like their music.

A escuchar (*Listening*)

1-48 Los instrumentos. As you listen to the song indicate with an "X" which instruments you hear. The names of the instruments are written in Spanish. They are all cognates, words that are identical or similar in both Spanish and English.

_____ el piano
_____ la trompeta
_____ el violín
_____ la flauta
_____ el banjo
_____ el acordeón
_____ la guitarra
_____ el clarinete

Después de escuchar (*Post-listening*)

1-49 Descripciones. Imagine that you are a true *aficionado*, or fan, of *salsa* music. Indicate in the spaces below with an "X" which statements you would most likely believe to be true of "Salsa en Nueva York." Each statement uses a cognate.

_____ Es interesante.	_____ Es terrible.
_____ Es mala.	_____ Es emocionante.
_____ Es fascinante.	_____ Es romántica.
_____ Es misteriosa.	_____ Es exótica.
_____ Es aburrida.	_____ Es buena.

Páginas

1-71

Versos sencillos, "XXXIX" (José Martí, Cuba)

The readings in **Páginas** come from the Spanish-speaking world and were written for native Spanish speakers. Remember that you do not have to comprehend every word in order to understand the passage and glean essential information. The related activities will help you develop reading comprehension strategies.

José Martí (1853–95) was an artist, intellectual, and patriot. Besides being known for his struggle to gain Cuba's independence from Spain, he is famous for his poetry, some of which has been popularized through song (*Guantanamera*). This selection comes from a series of short poems entitled *Versos sencillos* and discusses how the poet treats both his friends and his enemies.

Antes de leer (*Pre-reading*)

1-50 Los cognados. Spanish and English share many cognates, words or expressions that are identical or similar in two languages—for example, *profesor*/professor and *universidad*/university. When you read Spanish, cognates will help you understand the selection. Skim the poem and list the cognates you see. Then for each cognate, guess the meaning of the phrase in which it appears.

A leer (*Reading*)

1-51 El poema. Read the following poem.

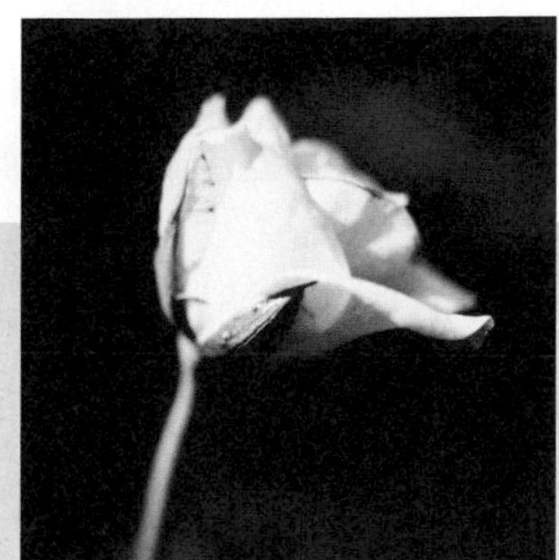

"XXXIX"

Cultivo una rosa blanca,
En julio como en enero,
Para el amigo sincero
Que me da (*gives*) su mano (*hand*) franca.
Y para el cruel que me arranca (*yanks out*)
El corazón (*heart*) con que vivo,
Cardo (*thistle*) ni ortiga (*nettle; a prickly plant*) cultivo:
Cultivo una rosa blanca.

Después de leer (*Post-reading*)

1-52 ¿Comprendiste? (*Did you understand?*) Which of the following seem to describe the poet from what he writes?

1. Es blanco.
2. Es optimista.
3. Tiene amigos.
4. Tiene enemigos.
5. Es generoso.
6. Su mes favorito es julio.

1-53 Los símbolos. We often use colors as symbols for other things. Work with a classmate to match these colors with what you believe they could symbolize. What else do they symbolize for you?

1. _____ el rojo
2. _____ el amarillo
3. _____ el blanco
4. _____ el verde
5. _____ el negro

a. la pureza (*purity*), la paz (*peace*)
b. el misterio
c. la juventud (*youth*)
d. la pasión
e. la cobardía (*cowardice*)

Taller

1-72 to 1-74

1-54 Una carta de presentación. When you write a letter of introduction, you want to tell something about your physical and personal characteristics and something about your life. In this first introduction, think of information you would share with a potential roommate. Follow the steps below to write five sentences in Spanish to include with a housing application.

> Santa Clara, CA
> 25 de septiembre de 2007
>
> ¡Hola!
>
> Me llamo Susanita. Soy extrovertida y simpática. Tengo clases muy interesantes y fascinantes. Mi profesora de español es la señora Carro. Es muy inteligente y trabajadora. Mi cumpleaños es el 10 de abril. Mi color favorito es el amarillo. . .
>
> ¡Hasta pronto!
>
> *Susanita*

Antes de escribir (*Pre-writing*)

- Write a list of adjectives that you identify with yourself.
- Write a list of adjectives to describe your classes and your professors.

A escribir (*Writing*)

- Introduce yourself.
- Using adjectives from your list, describe what you are like. Use the connector **y** (*and*) to connect thoughts.
- Describe your classes and your professors.
- Say what your favorite color is (**Mi color favorito es el...**).
- Add any other personal detail about yourself (your birthday, favorite day of the week, etc.).

Después de escribir (*Post-writing*)

- **Revisar (*Review*)**
  - ☐ Go back to make sure all of your adjectives agree with the nouns they modify.
  - ☐ Check your use of the verb **ser.**
- **Intercambiar (*Exchange*)**

  Exchange your description with a classmate's. Then make suggestions and corrections and add a comment about the description.
- **Entregar (*Turn in*)**

  Rewrite your letter, incorporating your classmate's suggestions. Then turn in the letter to your instructor.

Vocabulario

Primera parte

Saludos	*Greetings*
Buenos días.	*Good morning.*
Buenas noches.	*Good evening.*
Buenas tardes.	*Good afternoon.*
¿Cómo está usted?	*How are you? (for.)*
¿Cómo estás?	*How are you? (inf.)*
Hola.	*Hello; Hi.*
¿Qué pasa?	*What's happening? What's up? (inf.)*
¿Qué tal?	*What's up? (inf.)*

Presentaciones	*Introductions*
¿Cómo se llama usted?	*What's your name? (for.)*
¿Cómo te llamas?	*What's your name? (inf.)*
Me llamo...	*My name is...*
Mi nombre es...	*My name is...*
Soy...	*I am...*

Respuestas	*Responses*
De nada.	*You're welcome.*
¿De verdad?	*Really?*
Encantado/a.	*Delighted; pleased to meet you.*
Gracias.	*Thank you.*
Igualmente.	*Likewise.*
(Muy) Bien.	*(Very) Well.*
(Muy) Mal.	*(Very) Bad.*
Más o menos.	*So-so.*
Mucho gusto.	*Pleased to meet you.*

Despedidas	*Farewells*
Adiós.	*Good-bye.*
Hasta luego.	*See you later.*
Hasta mañana.	*See you tomorrow.*
Hasta pronto.	*See you soon.*

Títulos	*Titles*
el señor (Sr.)	*Mr.*
la señora (Sra.)	*Mrs.; Ms.*
la señorita (Srta.)	*Miss*

Otras palabras y expresiones	*Other words and expressions*
con	*with*
mi/mis	*my*
o	*or*
tu/tus	*your (inf.)*
y	*and*

Sustantivos	*Nouns*
la clase	*class*
el/la estudiante	*student*
el/la profesor/a	*professor*
la universidad	*university*

Segunda parte

En la clase	*In the classroom*
el bolígrafo	*pen*
la calculadora	*calculator*
el cuaderno	*notebook*
el diccionario	*dictionary*
el lápiz	*pencil*
el libro	*book*
el mapa	*map*
la mesa	*table*
la mochila	*backpack*
el papel	*paper*
la pizarra	*blackboard*
la puerta	*door*
el reloj	*clock; watch*
la silla	*chair*

Adjetivos	*Adjectives*
aburrido/a	*boring*
barato/a	*cheap; inexpensive*
bueno/a	*good*
caro/a	*expensive*
extrovertido/a	*outgoing*
fascinante	*fascinating*
grande	*big*
inteligente	*intelligent*
interesante	*interesting*
malo/a	*bad*
pequeño/a	*small*
simpático/a	*nice*
tímido/a	*shy; timid*
trabajador/a	*hard-working*

Los colores	*Colors*
amarillo/a	*yellow*
anaranjado/a	*orange*
azul	*blue*
blanco/a	*white*
gris	*grey*
morado/a	*purple*
negro/a	*black*
rojo/a	*red*
rosado/a	*pink*
verde	*green*

Adverbios	*Adverbs*
aquí	*here*

Verbos	*Verbs*
necesitar	*to need*
ser	*to be*
tener (ie)	*to have*

Expresiones para la clase	*Expressions for class*
Abre (Abran) el libro.	*Open your book(s).*
Cierra (Cierren) el libro.	*Close the book.*
Contesta (Contesten) en español.	*Answer in Spanish.*
Escribe (Escriban) en la pizarra.	*Write on the board.*
Escucha (Escuchen).	*Listen.*
Estudia (Estudien).	*Study.*
Lee (Lean) el diálogo.	*Read the dialogue.*
Repite (Repitan).	*Repeat.*
Ve (Vayan) a la pizarra.	*Go to the board.*

Numbers 0–100	*See page 10.*
The days of the week	*See page 13.*
The months and the seasons	*See page 13–14.*
Subject pronouns	*See page 26.*

2 ¿De dónde eres?

PRIMERA PARTE

¡Así lo decimos! Vocabulario	Adjetivos descriptivos y adjetivos de nacionalidad
¡Así lo hacemos! Estructuras	Telling time
	Formation of yes/no questions and negation
	Interrogative words
Comparaciones	Nombres, apellidos y apodos

- **Describing yourself, other people, and things**
- **Asking and responding to simple questions**
- **Asking for and telling time**

SEGUNDA PARTE

¡Así lo decimos! Vocabulario	¿De dónde eres? ¿Qué haces? ¿Qué te gusta hacer?
¡Así lo hacemos! Estructuras	The present tense of regular **-ar** verbs
	The present tense of regular **-er** and **-ir** verbs
	The present tense of **tener**
Observaciones	¡Pura vida! Episodio 2

- **Talking about what you like to do (*me gusta/te gusta*)**
- **Talking about what you have and what you have to do**

NUESTRO MUNDO

Panoramas	España: Tierra de Don Quijote
Ritmos	"Cuéntame alegrías" (Tachú, España)
Páginas	"*E-milios*" por correo tradicional
Taller	Una entrevista y un sumario

Pablo Picasso, pintor prolífico, nació en Málaga. Esta obra es una de sus más famosas.

España: Tierra de Don Quijote

«Buenas acciones valen más que buenas razones.»*

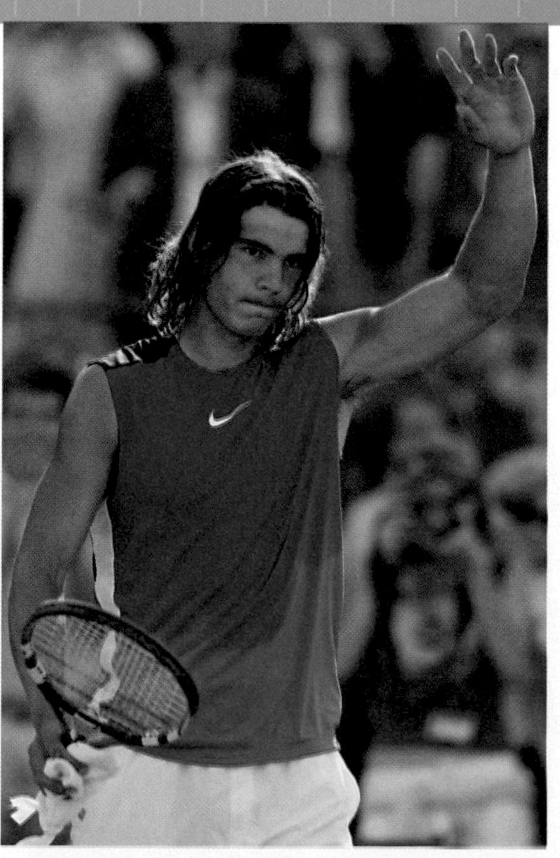

Rafael Nadal, de Manacor, Mallorca, España, ganó más de 12 torneos de tenis internacionales en 2005.

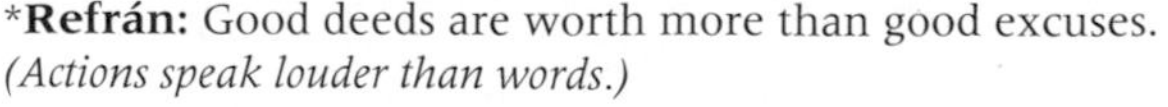
*__Refrán:__ Good deeds are worth more than good excuses. *(Actions speak louder than words.)*

¡Así lo decimos! Vocabulario

CD 1, Track 9

2-1 to 2-2

¡Así es la vida! ¿Quiénes somos?

La *Casa del Café* es un lugar muy popular en la Calle Mayor de Madrid. Hoy hay muchas personas.

En una mesa están José e Isabel. José Ortiz Pérez es el estudiante moreno. Estudia en la Universidad de Salamanca, pero es de Algeciras, un puerto en el mar Mediterráneo. La muchacha rubia, amiga de José, se llama Isabel Rojas Lagos. Es de Sevilla. Es muy inteligente y muy trabajadora. También es muy simpática. En otra mesa hay dos muchachas, Marta y María. Marta es dominicana y su amiga, María, es mexicana.

Paco, el muchacho rubio, y su amigo Daniel compran café. Paco es colombiano. Es alto y delgado. Daniel es de Madrid, la capital de España.

¡Cuántas personas interesantes hay en la *Casa del Café*!

Adjetivos descriptivos y adjetivos de nacionalidad

CD 1, Track 10

2-3 to 2-7

(la chica) **rubia**

(el chico) **moreno**

(el chico) **joven**

(la mujer) **vieja**

(el hombre) **pobre**

(la mujer) **rica**

(el muchacho) **alto**

(el muchacho) **bajo**

(la perra) **flaca**

(el perro) **gordo**

(el suéter) **nuevo**

(el suéter) **viejo**

Más adjetivos descriptivos	*More descriptive adjectives*
bonito/a	*pretty; cute*
feo/a	*ugly*
grande	*big*
guapo/a	*good-looking*
pequeño/a	*small*
perezoso/a	*lazy*

Algunos adjetivos de nacionalidad[1]	*Some adjectives of nationality*
PAÍS	NACIONALIDAD
la Argentina	**argentino/a**
el Canadá	**canadiense**
Chile	**chileno/a**
Colombia	**colombiano/a**
Cuba	**cubano/a**
la República Dominicana	**dominicano/a**
el Ecuador	**ecuatoriano/a**
España	**español/a**
los Estados Unidos	**norteamericano/a (estadounidense)**
México	**mexicano/a**
Panamá	**panameño/a**
el Perú	**peruano/a**
Puerto Rico	**puertorriqueño/a**
El Salvador	**salvadoreño/a**
Venezuela	**venezolano/a**

Los lugares	*Places*
la capital	*capital city*
la ciudad	*city*
el país	*country*

Las personas	*People*
el/la amigo/a	*friend*
el/la muchacho/a	*boy/girl*
los padres	*parents*

Adverbios	*Adverbs*
ahora (mismo)	*(right) now*
también	*also*
tarde	*late*
temprano	*early*

Conjunciones	*Conjunctions*
pero	*but*
porque	*because*

[1]Adjectives of nationality are not capitalized in Spanish.

Aplicación

CD 1, Track 11

2-1 ¿Quién eres tú? Listen to José and the others on your **¡Arriba!** audio program or as read by your instructor. Based on the information in **¡Así es la vida!**, write the number of each monologue next to the corresponding name.

_____Isabel _____María _____Paco _____Daniel _____José

2-2 Asociaciones. What do you associate with the following people and places? Choose terms in the two right columns that you associate with the people and places in the left column.

MODELO: Madrid—*ciudad, grande*

México	**dominicano/a**	**moreno/a**
Barcelona	**bonito/a**	**norteamericano/a**
Salma Hayek	**capital**	**país**
Bolivia	**ciudad**	**pequeño/a**
Buenos Aires	**colombiano/a**	**peruano/a**
Alex Rodríguez	**delgado/a**	**grande**
Penélope Cruz	**español/a**	**puertorriqueño/a**
Lima	**joven**	**rico/a**
Los Ángeles	**mexicano/a**	**rubio/a**
Madrid	**ecuatoriano/a**	**viejo/a**

2-3 En una fiesta en Salamanca. Complete the conversation between Juan and Marisol with words and expressions from the word bank below.

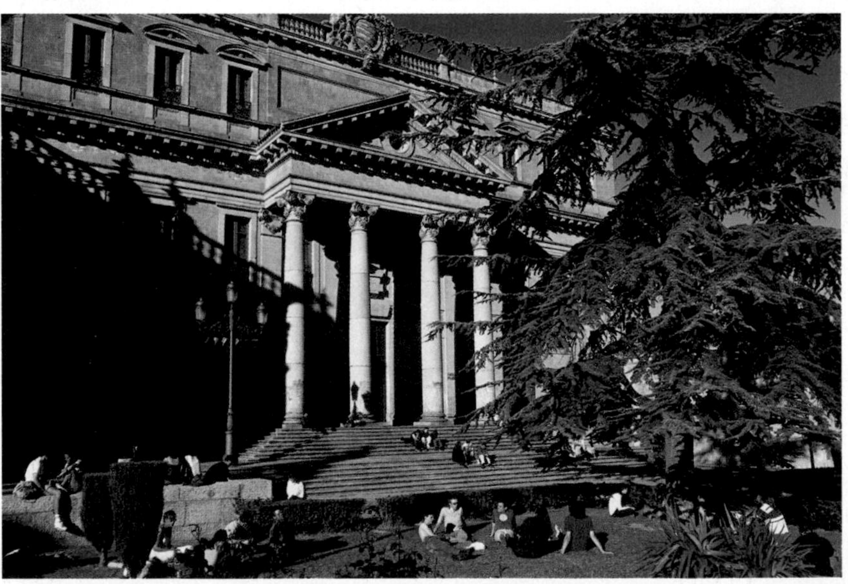

La Universidad de Salamanca, fundada en 1218, es la más antigua de España.

amiga	aquí	capital	cómo
dominicano	eres	española	me llamo

Juan: ¡Hola! Soy Juan Luis Ruiz. ¿(1) ________ te llamas?
Marisol: (2) ________ Marisol. ¿De dónde (3) ________, Juan?
Juan: Soy (4) ________.

Marisol: ¡Ah! Mi (5) ________ Ana es de Punta Cana, en la costa de la República Dominicana.

Juan: Yo soy de Santo Domingo, la (6) ________. ¿Y tú, Marisol? ¿De dónde eres?

Marisol: Ay, yo soy (7) ________. Soy de (8) ________, de Salamanca.

2-4 ¿Cómo son? Take turns describing these people, places, and things to see if you agree with each other. When you agree, say: **Sí, es cierto.** When you disagree, offer your own opinion. Choose from the adjectives in the three columns, making sure that they agree with the nouns they modify.

MODELO: la universidad
E1: *La universidad es pequeña.*
E2: *Sí, es cierto. (No, es grande.)*

alto/a	grande	pequeño/a
bajo/a	guapo/a	pobre
bonito/a	joven	puertorriqueño/a
delgado/a	mexicano/a	rico/a
español/a	moreno/a	rubio/a
feo/a	norteamericano/a	simpático/a
gordito/a	nuevo/a	trabajador/a
gordo/a	panameño/a	viejo/a

1. la ciudad de...
2. el/la profesor/a
3. Benicio del Toro
4. la clase
5. un estudiante de la clase
6. una estudiante de la clase
7. Antonio Banderas
8. España

2-5 ¿Cuál es su (*his/her*) nacionalidad? Give the name of the country where the following people are from and their nationality.

MODELO: Felipe de Borbón / España
E1: *¿De dónde es Felipe de Borbón?*
E2: *Es de España. Es español.*

1. Juanes / Colombia
2. Juan Carlos de Borbón y Pedro Almodóvar / España
3. Celia Cruz / Cuba
4. Rubén Blades / Panamá
5. Salma Hayek / México
6. Pedro Martínez / La República Dominicana
7. Yo...
8. Nosotros...

2-6 Yo soy... Take turns introducing yourselves, saying where you are from and what you are like.

Modelo: *Hola, soy _____. Soy de_____ . Soy_____ y_____. No soy_____.*

¡Así lo hacemos! Estructuras

2-8 to 2-11

1. Telling time

¿Qué hora es?

- The verb **ser** is used to express the time of day in Spanish. Use **Es la** with **una** (singular for one hour). With all other hours use **Son las.**

Es la una.	*It's one o'clock.*
Son las dos de la tarde.	*It's two o'clock in the afternoon.*

- To express minutes *past* or *after* an hour, use **y.**

  Son las tres **y** veinte. — *It's twenty past three. (It's three twenty.)*

- To express minutes *before* an hour (*to* or *till*) use **menos.**[1]

  Son las siete **menos** diez. — *It's ten to (till) seven.*

- The terms **cuarto** and **media** are equivalent to the English expressions *quarter* (fifteen minutes) and *half* (thirty minutes). The numbers **quince** and **treinta** are interchangeable with **cuarto** and **media.**

  Son las cinco menos **cuarto (quince).** — *It's a quarter to five. (It's four forty-five.)*

  Son las cuatro y **media (treinta).** — *It's half past four. (It's four thirty.)*

- For *noon* and *midnight* use **(el) mediodía** and **(la) medianoche.**

  Es **mediodía.** — *It's noon (midday).*

  Es **medianoche.** — *It's midnight.*

---

[1]This is how time is traditionally told. It is now common to use **y** for :01 to :59. 3:40 = **Son las tres y cuarenta.**

- To ask at what time an event takes place, use **¿A qué hora...?** To answer, use **a la/las** + *time*.

¿**A qué hora** es la clase?	*(At) What time is the class?*
Es **a las** ocho y media.	*It is at half past eight.*

- The expressions **de la mañana, de la tarde,** or **de la noche** are used when telling specific times. **En punto** means *on the dot* or *sharp*.

La fiesta es a las ocho **de la noche.**	*The party is at eight o'clock in the evening.*
El partido de fútbol es a las nueve **en punto.**	*The soccer game is at nine sharp.*

- The expressions **por la mañana, por la tarde,** and **por la noche** are used as a general reference to *in the morning, in the afternoon,* and *in the evening.*

No tengo clases **por la mañana.**	*I don't have classes in the morning.*

- In many Spanish-speaking countries, the 24-hour clock is used for schedules and official timekeeping. The zero hour is equivalent to midnight, and 12:00 is noon. 13:00–24:00 are the P.M. hours. To convert from the 24-hour clock, substract twelve hours from hours 13:00 and above.

  21:00 (or 21,00) = **las nueve de la noche**
  16:30 (or 16,30) = **las cuatro y media de la tarde**[1]

STUDY TIPS

Learning to tell time in Spanish

1. To become proficient in telling time in Spanish, you'll need to make sure you have learned Spanish numbers well. Practice counting by fives to thirty: **cinco, diez, quince, veinte, veinticinco, treinta.**
2. Think about and say aloud times that are important to you: **Tengo clases a las nueve, a las diez..., Hay una fiesta a las...,** etc.
3. Every time you look at your watch, say the time in Spanish.

Aplicación

2-7 Rafael y sus actividades. Refer back to page 39 to see a photo of Rafael Nadal, the famous Spanish tennis player. Write an **X** next to the activities you think he normally does.

_____ Se levanta (*gets up*) al mediodía.
_____ Practica tenis por tres horas.
_____ Lee (*reads*) poemas.
_____ Juega (*plays*) al tenis con su instructor.
_____ Se acuesta (*goes to bed*) a las once y media de la noche.
_____ A las once de la mañana está en el gimnasio.
_____ A las dos de la tarde está en casa.

[1]The punctuation used in giving the time varies from country to country. You might see periods or commas as well as the colon used in English.

2-8 La vida diaria de Rafael Nadal. Read about Rafael Nadal's daily schedule, then answer the questions that follow in Spanish.

> Rafael Nadal, el famoso tenista español, tiene un día muy activo. A las siete de la mañana, está en la cancha de tenis. Practica con su instructor hasta (*until*) las diez de la mañana. A las once y media de la mañana, está en casa con su familia. A la una y cuarto de la tarde, está en la universidad. A las cinco de la tarde, está en un restaurante. A las nueve de la noche, está otra vez en casa con su familia. Ahora, son las once y media de la noche y Rafael ve (*watches*) la televisión. Mañana es otro día.

1. ¿A qué hora está en la universidad?
2. ¿Dónde está a las cinco?
3. ¿A qué hora está en casa con su familia?
4. ¿Qué hora es ahora?
5. Y tú, ¿dónde estás a las siete y media de la mañana?

2-9 ¿Qué hora es? Look at the clocks and say whether the following statements are **cierto** or **falso.** Correct any false statements.

MODELO:

Son las dos y cuarto de la tarde.
Falso, son las dos y media de la tarde.

Son las dos y cuarto de la noche.

Son las siete menos quince de la mañana.

Son las ocho menos veinte de la noche.

Son las cuatro menos cuarto de la mañana.

Son las doce menos diez de la noche.

Es medianoche.

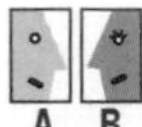

2-10A ¿A qué hora? Complete your calendar by asking your partner when the events with times missing take place. Student B, please see **Appendix 1,** page A2.

Modelo: la fiesta (20:30)
E1: *¿A qué hora es la fiesta?*
E2: *Es a las ocho y media de la noche.*

Hora	Actividad
10:15	la clase
	la conferencia (*lecture*)
12:05	la reunión
	el examen
16:30	el partido de fútbol
	el programa "Amigos" en la televisión
20:30	la fiesta

2. Formation of yes/no questions and negation

2-12 to 2-16

La formación de preguntas *sí/no*

- A yes/no question has rising intonation. There are three ways to form yes/no questions, depending on the intent of the speaker. Note that an inverted question mark (¿) is used at the beginning of a question, and a standard question mark (?) closes one.
- To request new information, invert the order of the subject (S) and verb (V) found in a declarative sentence.

  Declarative (S + V):
  Miguel es de Barcelona. *Miguel is from Barcelona.*

  Request for new information (V + S):

  ¿Es Miguel de Barcelona? *Is Miguel from Barcelona?*
- To express disbelief about information already given, maintain the declarative order (S + V) but with rising intonation (called an *echo question*).

  Disbelief (S + V):

  ¿Miguel es de Barcelona? *Miguel is from Barcelona?*
- To confirm information already given or supposed, simply add to the end of a statement a tag word or phrase with rising intonation (such as *¿no?, ¿verdad?, ¿no es cierto?*).

  Confirmation (S + V):

  Miguel es de Barcelona, ¿verdad? *Miguel is from Barcelona, right?*

Negación

- To make a sentence negative, simply place **no** before the verb.

Tú **no** eres de Portugal.	*You're not from Portugal.*
Nosotros **no** somos de España.	*We're not from Spain.*

- When answering a question in the negative, the word **no** followed by a comma also precedes the verb phrase.

¿Son Elena y Ramón de Segovia?	*Are Elena and Ramón from Segovia?*
No, no son de Segovia.	*No, they're not from Segovia.*

Aplicación

2-11 ¿Verdad? Ask each other questions based upon the following statements by inverting the subject and the verb or using a tag question. Respond to your partner's questions in a truthful manner.

MODELO: Cervantes es autor.
E1: *¿Es autor Cervantes? (Cervantes es autor, ¿verdad?)*
E2: *Sí, Cervantes es autor.*

1. Penélope Cruz es baja y fea.
2. Pedro Almodóvar es director de cine.
3. Pablo Picasso es pintor.
4. Antonio Gaudí es de Barcelona.
5. Santiago Calatrava es perezoso.
6. Edgar Rentería es jugador de béisbol.
7. Antonio Banderas y Melanie Griffith son poetas.
8. El SEAT es un automóvil norteamericano.

2-12 ¿Es verdad? Take turns asking and answering yes/no questions. Comment on the truthfulness of each other's responses.

MODELO: E1: *¿Eres norteamericano/a?*
E2: *No, no soy norteamericano/a.*
E1: *¿De verdad?*
E2: *Sí, de verdad. Soy de Francia.*

1. ¿Eres canadiense?
2. ¿Son profesores tus padres?
3. Tus amigos son trabajadores, ¿no?
4. ¿Eres de San Francisco?
5. Tu familia es rica, ¿verdad?
6. ¿...?

3. Interrogative words

2-17 to 2-22

- Interrogative words are often used at the beginning of a sentence to form questions. The most frequently used are:

¿Cómo...?	*How...? What...?*
¿**Cómo** eres?	*What are you like?*
¿Cuál(es)...?	*Which (one/ones)...?*
¿**Cuál** es tu libro?	*Which one is your book?*
¿Cuándo...?	*When...?*
¿**Cuándo** es tu clase de español?	*When is your Spanish class?*
¿Cuánto/a(s)?	*How much (many)...?*
¿**Cuántos** estudiantes hay?	*How many students are there?*
¿Dónde...?	*Where...?*
¿**Dónde** hay una pizarra?	*Where is there a blackboard?*
¿De dónde...?	*From where...?*
¿**De dónde** es Paz Vega?	*Where is Paz Vega from?*
¿Adónde...?	*(To) Where...?*
¿**Adónde** vas?	*Where are you going?*
¿Por qué...?	*Why...?*
¿**Por qué** no hay clase hoy?	*Why is there no class today?*
¿Qué...?	*What...?*
¿**Qué** estudias?	*What are you studying?*
¿Quién(es)...?	*Who...?*
¿**Quién** es el profesor Suárez?	*Who is Professor Suárez?*
¿De quién(es)...?	*Whose...?*
¿**De quién** es el bolígrafo azul?	*Whose is the blue pen?*

- When you ask a question using an interrogative word, your intonation will fall.

¿Cómo se llama el profesor?

Aplicación

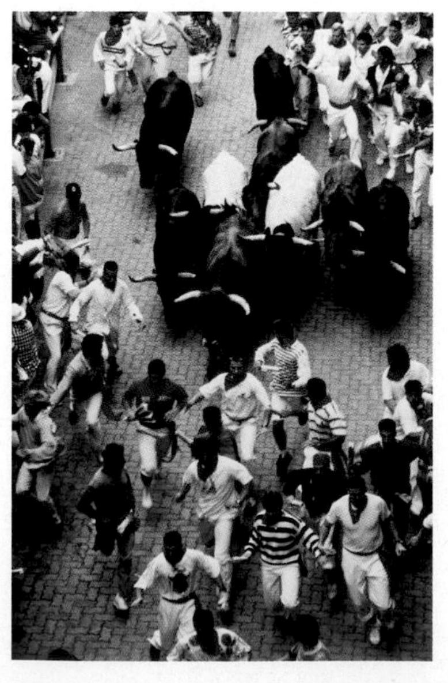

2-13 Los sanfermines. Read the description of one of Spain's most popular festivals and match the questions that follow with their responses.

La fiesta de San Fermín en España es muy famosa. Siempre es en Pamplona, en el norte de España. El primer día es el 6 de julio y el último día es el 14 de julio. Durante nueve días sueltan (*turn loose*) los toros (*bulls*) que corren (*run*) por las calles. Los jóvenes corren delante (*in front*) de los toros. Es muy peligroso (*dangerous*), pero también muy emocionante. El novelista norteamericano Ernest Hemingway, famoso por *The Sun Also Rises*, describió (*described*) muy bien la fiesta de los sanfermines.

1. _____ ¿Dónde es la fiesta?
2. _____ ¿Cuándo es el primer día de la fiesta?
3. _____ ¿Cuál es el último día de la fiesta?
4. _____ ¿Quiénes corren por las calles?
5. _____ ¿Cómo es la fiesta?
6. _____ ¿Quién es el autor norteamericano que se asocia con esta fiesta?

a. Ernest Hemingway
b. es emocionante
c. el 6 de julio
d. en Pamplona, España
e. los toros y los jóvenes
f. el 14 de julio

2-14 Rafael (Rafa) Nadal. Read the following description about Rafael Nadal, and then answer the questions below.

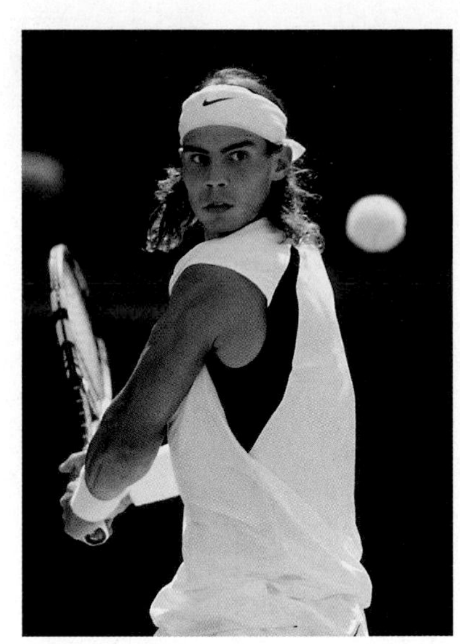

Rafael Nadal Perera es uno de los tenistas más famosos del mundo. Nace (*he is born*) en la isla de Mallorca, España el 3 de junio de 1986. En 2002, a los quince años, gana en Mallorca el primer torneo importante. Hoy es considerado el tenista número dos del mundo y es el primer tenista, desde (*since*) Boris Becker, en alcanzar (*reach*) esa posición antes de (*before*) los veinte años. En 2005 gana más de doce torneos, incluyendo los *ATP Master Series* de Monte Carlo, Roma, Montreal y Madrid. Sus fanáticos (*fans*) están convencidos de que Rafa pronto será (*he will be*) el tenista número uno del mundo.

1. ¿De dónde es Rafael Nadal?
2. ¿Cuándo nace?
3. ¿Qué gana a los quince años?
4. ¿Cuántos torneos gana en 2005?
5. ¿De qué están convencidos sus fanáticos?

EXPANSIÓN More on structure and usage

¿Qué...? versus ¿Cuál(es)...?

The interrogatives **qué** and **cuál** may cause some confusion for English speakers learning Spanish because each may be translated as *what* or *which* in different contexts. Generally, **qué** is used to request a definition and/or explanation and is translated as *what.*

¿**Qué** tienes?	*What do you have?*
¿**Qué** es esto?	*What is this?*

When followed by a noun, **¿qué?** means *which?*

¿**Qué** clase necesita?	*Which class does he/she need?*
¿**Qué** clase tienes ahora?	*Which (What) class do you have now?*

Cuál also means *which* but is generally not followed by a noun. In some cases, it can be translated as *what,* but it always implies a choice indicating *which one(s).* Use the plural **cuáles** when that choice includes more than one person or thing.

¿**Cuál** de las clases necesita?	*Which (of the) classes does he/she need?*
¿**Cuál** prefieres?	*Which (one) do you prefer?*
¿**Cuáles** son tus amigos?	*Which (of those people) are your friends?*
¿**Cuál** es la fecha de hoy?	*What is today's date?*
¿**Cuáles** son las capitales de los dos países más grandes de Latinoamérica?	*Which are the capitals of the two biggest countries in Latin America?*

2-15 ¿Qué? o ¿Cuál? Complete the questions with **qué** or **cuál(es)** depending on the context. Then answer the questions.

MODELO: ¿ Cuál es la fecha de hoy?
Es el 2 de octubre.

1. ¿_____ hora es?
2. ¿_____ es tu clase favorita?
3. ¿_____ es tu cuaderno?
4. ¿_____ día es hoy?
5. ¿A _____ hora es la clase de español?
6. ¿_____ es la fecha de tu cumpleaños?

 **2-16 ¿Quiénes son? ¿Cómo son?** Ask each other at least four original questions about the people depicted on the I.D. cards.

Modelo: E1: *¿Dónde estudia Luisa?*
E2: *Estudia en la Universidad Nacional.*

 **2-17 Una entrevista.** Interview each other to complete the biographical information requested on the card below.

Modelo: Nombre:
E1: *¿Cómo te llamas?*
E2: *Me llamo Ramón.*

Nacionalidad:
E1: *¿De dónde eres?*
E2: …

Nombre: ______________________________

Nacionalidad: __________________________

Domicilio: _____________________________

Descripción física: ______________________

Clase favorita: _________________________

Nombres de amigos/as: ___________________

2-18 Profesor/a... Ask your teacher any question and then react with **¿De verdad?, ¿Es cierto?,** or **¡No!**

Modelo: ESTUDIANTE: *Profesor/a, ¿de dónde es usted?*
PROFESOR/A: *Soy de Bolivia.*
ESTUDIANTE: *¿De verdad?*

¿Cuánto sabes tú? *Can you…*

2-23 to 2-26

- ☐ describe yourself and others using the verb **ser** and descriptive adjectives, including nationality?
- ☐ tell time and say at what time events happen?
- ☐ find out information from others by asking questions using inversion and interrogative words?

Comparaciones

Nombres, apellidos y apodos (*nicknames*)

2-19 En tu experiencia. How does a name reflect a person's heritage? When do women in the United States and Canada keep their maiden name after marriage? Are there instances when married women use both their maiden and their married names? Do you have a nickname? Who uses it, and under what circumstances? Do you prefer to be called by your nickname? This reading explains the naming patterns used in the Spanish-speaking world. As you read it, think about what your complete name is.

People with Hispanic backgrounds generally use both their paternal surname (**el apellido paterno**) and maternal surname (**el apellido materno**). For example: **María Fernández Ulloa** takes her first surname, Fernández, from her father and her second, Ulloa, from her mother. Many Hispanic women keep their paternal surname when they marry. They may attach their husband's paternal surname using the preposition **de.** For example, if María Fernández Ulloa marries Carlos Alvarado Gómez, her married name could be María Fernández de Alvarado. Many would refer to her as **la señora de Alvarado,** and to the couple as **los Alvarado,** although María would be known as **María Fernández,** as well. There are some advantages to these naming practices, including less confusion if a woman gets divorced since she keeps her paternal surname as well as knows that her children will keep the family name alive. Nonetheless, these traditional naming conventions are also changing as attitudes toward gender equality evolve, and some women choose to make no alterations to their name when they marry. What remains relevant is that a family name can be very important for a person, his/her identification, and family pride.

The use of a nickname (**apodo**) in place of a person's first name is also very common in Hispanic countries. A person's nickname is often a diminutive form of his/her given first name, formed using the suffix **-ito** for men or **-ita** for women. For example, **Clara** becomes **Clarita.** As in English, there are also conventional nicknames like those listed below.

Male		Female	
Alejandro	Alex, Alejo	Ana	Anita
Antonio	Tony, Toño	Carmen	Menchu
Enrique	Quique, Quiqui[1]	Concepción	Concha
Francisco	Paco, Pancho[1]	Dolores	Lola
Guillermo	Memo, Guille	Graciela	Chela
José	Pepe, Chepe, Cheo	Guadalupe	Lupe
Ignacio	Nacho	María Isabel	Maribel, Mabel
Luis	Lucho	María Luisa	Marilú
Manuel	Manolo	Mercedes	Mencha, Meche, Merche
Ramón	Mongo	Rosario	Charo, Chayo
Roberto	Beto	Teresa	Tere

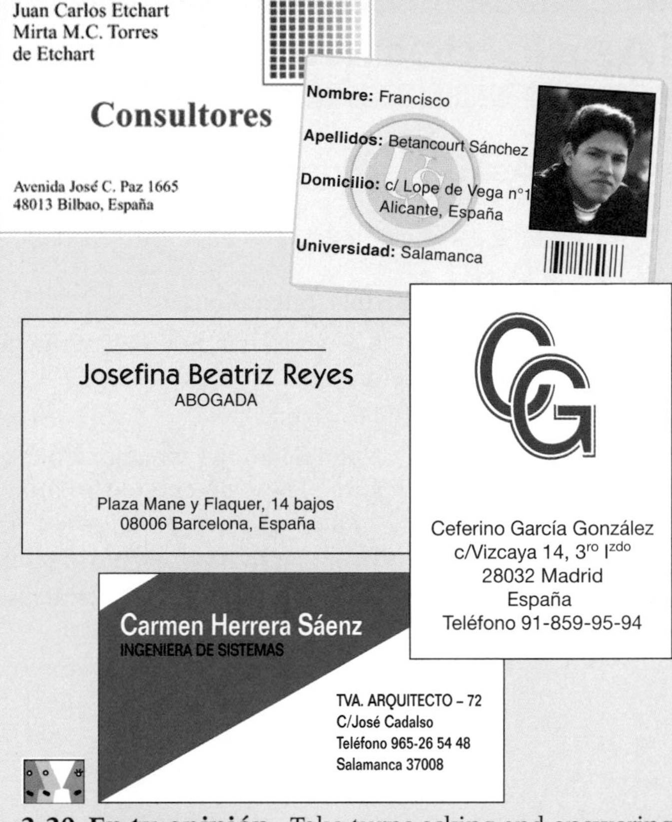

2-20 En tu opinión. Take turns asking and answering the following questions.

1. ¿Cuál es el apellido paterno de Carmen? ¿Y el apellido paterno de Ceferino?
2. ¿Cuál es el apellido materno de Carmen?
3. ¿Cuál es la nacionalidad de Josefina? ¿Y la nacionalidad de Francisco?
4. ¿Dónde estudia (*study*) Francisco Betancourt? ¿Cuál es su (*his*) apodo?
5. ¿Cuál es tu apellido materno? ¿Y tu apellido paterno?
6. ¿Cuál es tu apodo?

[1]Not all nicknames are used in every country. For example, ***Quique*** is used in Spain, ***Quiqui*** in Cuba. ***Paco*** is used in Spain, ***Pancho*** in Mexico. Some nicknames like ***Chema*** combine the first and second names, ***José María.***

SEGUNDA PARTE

¡Así lo decimos! Vocabulario

CD 1, Track 12

2-27 to 2-28

¡Así es la vida! ¿Qué haces?

En la Facultad de Idiomas en la Universidad Complutense de Madrid…

Secretaria: Hola, buenas tardes.

Celia: Buenas tardes. Soy Celia Cifuentes Bernal. Hablo español, francés,… y…

Secretaria: Muy bien, ¿y?

Celia: Estudio idiomas y mañana hay examen de alemán a las dos de la tarde. Los exámenes de mi profesora no son fáciles. Yo leo mucho y todavía no comprendo bien la materia. Necesito ayuda.

Secretaria: Ya entiendo. Debes hablar con Rogelio. Rogelio estudia portugués y alemán. Es muy inteligente. Rogelio, ¿ayudas a esta muchacha con un examen de alemán?

Rogelio: Pues, no ahora. Estudio y tomo café con varios amigos los lunes, miércoles y viernes por la noche después de practicar tenis y esta noche asisto a un concierto de música jazz. ¿Mañana?

¿De dónde eres? ¿Qué haces? ¿Qué te gusta hacer?

CD 1, Track 13

2-29 to 2-33

(el) alemán - Alemania

(el) chino - China

(el) coreano - Corea

(el) español - España, México

(el) francés - Francia, el Canadá

(el) inglés - Inglaterra, los Estados Unidos, el Canadá

(el) italiano - Italia

(el) japonés - el Japón

(el) portugués - Portugal, el Brasil

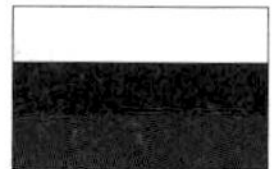
(el) ruso - Rusia

Sustantivos	*Nouns*
el idioma/la lengua	*language*

¿Qué haces?	*What do you do?*
abrir	*to open*
asistir (a)	*to attend*
aprender	*to learn*
ayudar	*to help*
bailar	*to dance*
beber	*to drink*
buscar	*to look for*
caminar	*to walk*
comer	*to eat*
comprar	*to buy*
comprender	*to understand*
conversar	*to converse*
creer	*to believe*
decidir	*to decide*
enseñar	*to teach*
escribir	*to write*
escuchar	*to listen*
estudiar	*to study*
hablar	*to speak*
leer	*to read*
llegar	*to arrive*
mirar	*to look at*
nadar	*to swim*
practicar	*to practice; to play (a sport)*
preparar	*to prepare*
recibir	*to receive*
regresar	*to return*
tomar	*to drink; to take*
trabajar	*to work*
viajar	*to travel*
vender	*to sell*
ver	*to see*
vivir	*to live*

Algunos deportes[1]	*Some sports*
(el) baloncesto/el básquetbol	*basketball*
(el) béisbol	*baseball*
(el) fútbol	*soccer*
(el) fútbol americano	*football*
(la) natación	*swimming*
(el) tenis	*tennis*

Adjetivos	*Adjectives*
difícil	*difficult*
fácil	*easy*

Otras palabras y expresiones	*Other words and expressions*
¿Qué te gusta hacer?	*What do you* (inf.) *like to do?*
Me gusta[2] (+ infinitive)	*I like* (+ infinitive)
Te gusta (+ infinitive)	*You* (inf.) *like* (+ infinitive)

[1]You will learn more about sports in **Capítulo 7.**

[2]You will learn more about **Gustar** and similar verbs in **Capítulo 5.**

Aplicación

2-21 ¿Quién es? Refer to **¡Así es la vida!** on page 54 and identify the speaker of each statement below.

C: Celia **R**: Rogelio

1. _____ Practico tenis.
2. _____ Me gusta la música.
3. _____ Tengo un examen mañana.
4. _____ Estudio con mis amigos.
5. _____ Leo mucho para mi clase.

CD 1, Track 14 **2-22 ¿Qué pasa?** Listen to your **¡Arriba!** audio program or your instructor to hear a description of what is happening. Match each drawing with the corresponding statement you hear.

_____

_____

_____

_____

_____

_____

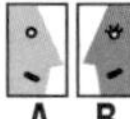

A B **2-23A ¿Dónde estoy?** Take turns identifying the country where you speak the language. Student B, please see **Appendix 1,** page A2.

MODELO: E1: Hablo italiano.
E2: Estás en Italia.

HABLO...	**TU COMPAÑERO/A ESTÁ EN...**
1. inglés	Alemania
2. coreano	el Japón
3. ruso	China
4. portugués	España

2-24 ¿Qué te gusta? Tell a classmate the names of three activities that you like and three that you don't like. Do you have any interests in common?

MODELO: *Me gusta practicar fútbol, pero no me gusta leer novelas.*

CD 1, Track 15

2-34 to 2-35

LETRAS Y SONIDOS

More on vowels in Spanish

While the letters *i, u* correspond to vowel sounds in Spanish (*li-bro, lu-nes*), these letters also may correspond to *glides*, which are brief, weak sounds that combine with a vowel to form a single syllable. The letter *y* also produces a glide in some words. It is important to distinguish a glide from a vowel in speech, since meaning can be affected: *reí* ("I laughed"), where the letter *i* is a vowel and there are two syllables (i.e., *re-í*), versus *rey* ("king"), where the letter *y* is a glide and there is only one syllable. A glide can precede or follow a vowel, and in some words, it does both. The following examples all contain glides, shown underlined. Be sure not to pronounce these glides as a separate syllable.

a-diós	*sie-te*	*vein-te*	*soy*	*hay*
nue-vo	*gua-po*	*Eu-ro-pa*	*es-tu-diáis*	*U-ru-guay*

The letters *i, u,* when next to other vowels, are not always glides in Spanish, however. When they indeed are vowels and not glides, a written accent mark is used to indicate that they constitute a separate syllable.

dí-a *rí-o* *pa-ís* *Ra-úl*

In English, the sounds *e* in *they* and *o* in *alone* always carry a final glide. Be careful not to insert a glide with these vowels automatically in Spanish, since the meaning may be changed: *pe-na* ("pity") versus *pei-na* ("he/she combs").

¡Así lo hacemos! Estructuras

2-36 to 2-40

4. The present tense of regular *-ar* verbs

Spanish verbs are classified into three groups according to their infinitive ending **(-ar, -er,** or **-ir).** Each of the three groups uses different endings to produce verb forms (conjugations) in the various tenses.

- The present tense endings of **-ar** verbs are as follows.

hablar (*to speak*)		
yo	habl + o	→ habl**o**
tú	habl + as	→ habl**as**
él, ella, Ud.	habl + a	→ habl**a**
nosotros/as	habl + amos	→ habl**amos**
vosotros/as	habl + áis	→ habl**áis**
ellos/as, Uds.	habl + an	→ habl**an**

- The following verbs are regular **-ar** verbs that are conjugated like **hablar.**

ayudar	*to help*	**llegar**	*to arrive*
bailar	*to dance*	**mirar**	*to look at*
buscar	*to look for*	**nadar**	*to swim*
caminar	*to walk*	**necesitar**	*to need*
comprar	*to buy*	**preparar**	*to prepare*
conversar	*to converse*	**regresar**	*to return*
enseñar	*to teach*	**tomar**	*to take; to drink*
escuchar	*to listen*	**trabajar**	*to work*
estudiar	*to study*	**viajar**	*to travel*

The Spanish present indicative tense has several equivalents in English. In addition to the simple present, it can express on going actions and even the future tense. Note the following examples.

Estudio ingeniería. { *I study engineering.* / *I am studying engineering.* }

Practicamos golf mañana. *We will practice golf tomorrow.*

STUDY TIPS

Learning regular verb conjugations

1. The first step in learning regular verb conjugations is being able to recognize the infinitive stem: the part of the verb before the ending.

INFINITIVE	**STEM**	
hablar	habl~~ar~~	→ habl
estudiar	estudi~~ar~~	→ estudi
trabajar	trabaj~~ar~~	→ trabaj

2. Practice conjugating several **-ar** verbs in writing first. Identify the stem, then write the various verb forms by adding the present tense endings listed above. Once you have done this, say the forms you have written out loud several times.
3. Next you will need to practice **-ar** verb conjugations orally. Create two sets of index cards. In one, write down the subject pronouns listed above (one per card). On the other set, write some of the regular **-ar** verbs you have learned. Select one card from each set and conjugate the verb with the selected pronoun.
4. Think about how each verb action relates to your own experience by putting verbs into a meaningful context. For example, think about what you and each of your friends study:

   Estudio matemáticas. **Juan estudia ingeniería.**

Aplicación

2-25 ¿Qué te gusta hacer? Choose from the activities below to say what you like and do not like to do.

Modelo: *Me gusta jugar al fútbol.*
No me gusta nadar.

(No) Me gusta...

bailar con mis amigos
conversar con mi familia
viajar en avión
caminar por el parque
comprar chocolate
ganar dinero
preparar comida mexicana
practicar golf
llegar temprano a clase
escuchar música
tomar café
trabajar por la noche

2-26 Preguntas y respuestas. With a classmate, take turns matching the following questions with logical responses.

1. _____ ¿Qué compras en la librería?
2. _____ ¿Quién enseña literatura española?
3. _____ ¿Qué necesitas para la clase de matemáticas?
4. _____ ¿Con quiénes estudias?
5. _____ ¿Qué instrumento musical practicas?
6. _____ ¿Quién prepara la comida en tu casa?
7. _____ ¿Dónde trabajas?
8. _____ ¿Cuándo y dónde escuchas música?

a. con mis amigos de la residencia
b. una calculadora
c. mi padre (*father*)
d. la profesora Rodríguez
e. libros y lápices
f. por la noche en mi dormitorio
g. en una oficina
h. el trombón

2-27 ¿Qué hacen? Match each drawing with an activity listed below, then create a sentence based on the information you have.

MODELO:

Eugenia

practicar tenis
Eugenia practica tenis.

1. _____ bailar en una fiesta
2. _____ mirar la televisión
3. _____ estudiar en la biblioteca
4. _____ preparar una pizza
5. _____ hablar por teléfono
6. _____ caminar por la tarde
7. _____ conversar durante el almuerzo (*lunch*)
8. _____ nadar mucho
9. _____ escuchar música
10. _____ trabajar en el laboratorio

a.

Jacinto

b.

Arturo / Abuela

c.

Jorge / Carlos / Leo

d.

Leonor

e.

Lucy / Memo

f.

Sonia

g. 

Ramona

h. 

Pedro

i. 

Katia / Giselle

j. 

Víctor / Catalina

 **2-28 ¿Y tú?** Take turns asking each other questions about your routine at the university.

Modelo: ¿Dónde / estudiar?
E1: *¿Dónde estudias?*
E2: *Estudio en la residencia.*

1. ¿Cuándo / trabajar?
2. ¿Con quién / hablar por teléfono?
3. ¿Con quiénes / conversar en clase?
4. ¿Por qué / estudiar español?
5. ¿Cuándo / comprar los libros?

5. The present tense of regular *-er* and *-ir* verbs

2-41 to 2-45

- You have just learned the present tense forms of regular **-ar** verbs. The following chart includes the forms for regular **-er** and **-ir** verbs.

	comer (*to eat*)	vivir (*to live*)
yo	com**o**	viv**o**
tú	com**es**	viv**es**
él, ella, Ud.	com**e**	viv**e**
nosotros/as	com**emos**	viv**imos**
vosotros/as	com**éis**	viv**ís**
ellos/as, Uds.	com**en**	viv**en**

- The present tense endings of **-er** and **-ir** verbs are identical except for the **nosotros** and **vosotros** forms.
- The following verbs are regular **-er** and **-ir** verbs.

-ER		-IR	
aprender (a) (+ infinitive)	*to learn (to do something)*	**abrir**	*to open*
beber	*to drink*	**asistir (a)**	*to attend*
comer	*to eat*	**decidir**	*to decide*
creer	*to believe*	**escribir**	*to write*
leer	*to read*	**recibir**	*to receive*
vender	*to sell*	**vivir**	*to live*

- **Ver** (*to see, to look at*) is an **-er** verb with an irregular **yo** form. Also note that the **vosotros/as** form has no accent because it is only one syllable.

ver (*to see, to look at*)			
yo	**veo**	nosotros/as	**vemos**
tú	**ves**	vosotros/as	**veis**
el, ella, Ud.	**ve**	ellos/as, Uds.	**ven**

Aplicación

2-29 Me gusta/No me gusta. Complete the following sentences stating which activities you like to do and which you do not like to do.

Modelo: Me gusta ver *fútbol en la televisión*.
No me gusta asistir a *los partidos de fútbol*.

1. (No) Me gusta ver ____________.
2. (No) Me gusta beber ____________.
3. (No) Me gusta vivir ____________.
4. (No) Me gusta asistir a ____________.
5. (No) Me gusta comer ____________.

2-30 Una semana típica. Fill in the blanks to complete the following paragraph about a typical week for Celia at the university. Use the correct form of a logical verb from the word bank.

asistir (a)	escuchar	practicar	ver	mirar
bailar	estudiar	tomar	comer	trabajar

(1) Yo ____________ ingeniería en la Universidad Complutense de Madrid. (2) ____________ a mis clases por la mañana donde (3) ____________ a mis amigos. Mi amigo Antonio y yo (4) ____________ en la cafetería de la universidad. (5) Yo ____________ los lunes y miércoles. Antonio (6) ____________ los miércoles y jueves. Los sábados Antonio y su amigo Luis (7) ____________ tenis por la mañana. (8) Yo ____________ un poco de televisión o (9) ____________ música. Por la noche, Antonio y yo (10) ____________ en la discoteca Kapital con amigos.

2-31 Maribel y la doctora Recio. Use the following information to write short news articles.

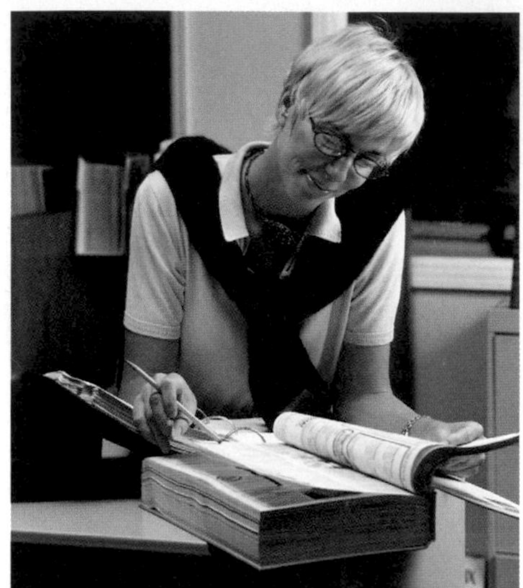

La doctora Recio:
profesora, historia
elegante, alta
Universidad del País Vasco
Bilbao
inglés y alemán
bailar, música clásica

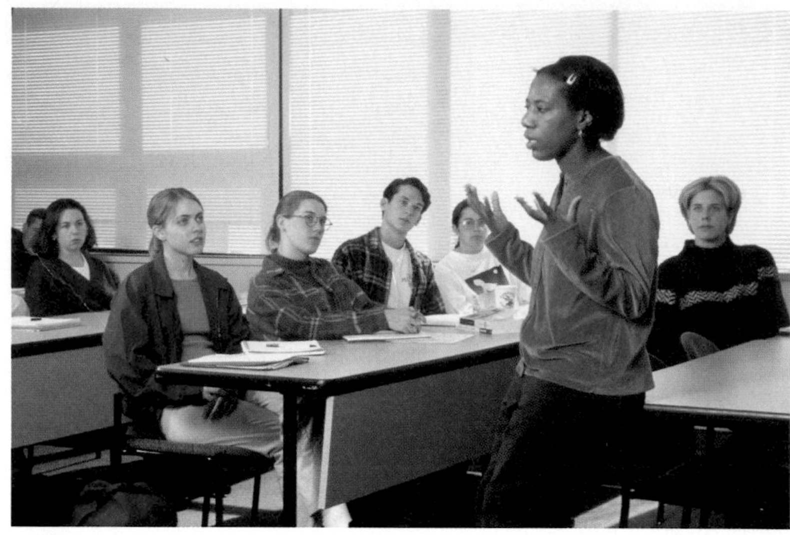

Maribel:
estudiante, inteligente
simpática, ciencias políticas
Universidad Complutense de Madrid
España
francés y japonés
fútbol y natación

2-32 ¿Qué hacen? Take turns using the verbs listed below to describe the scene in the photograph: include what is there, who the people are, what they are like, and what they are doing.

MODELO: (haber) *Hay siete estudiantes.*

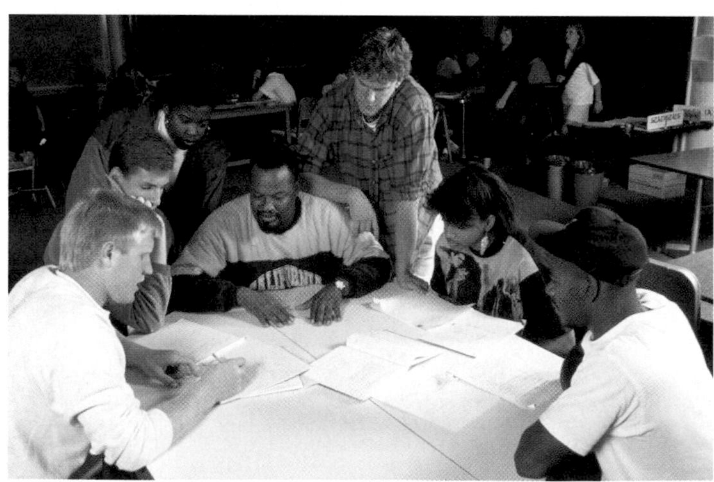

abrir	escribir	hablar	ser
asistir (a)	escuchar	leer	ver
comprender	estudiar	mirar	vivir

2-33 Pablo Picasso. Read the description of Pablo Picasso to a classmate and ask three questions that he/she can respond to with either **sí** or **no.**

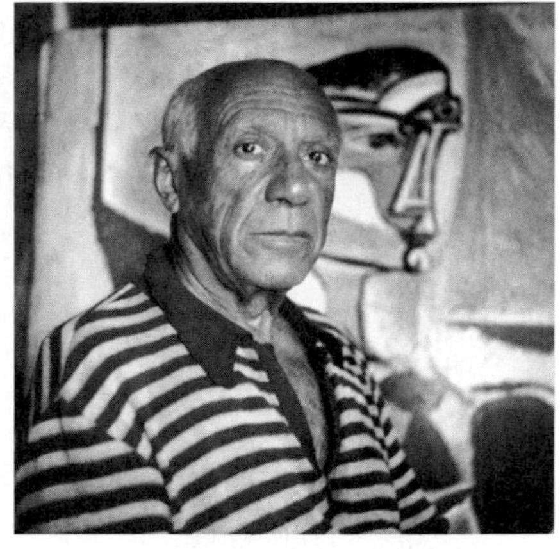

Pablo Picasso es uno de los artistas más importantes del siglo XX. Es de Málaga, España, pero vive gran parte de su vida en Francia. Su padre (*father*) es profesor de arte. Su nombre original es Pablo Ruiz, pero usa su apellido materno, Picasso. Estudia en Barcelona y en Madrid. Después vive en París. Es famoso por sus períodos "azul" y "rosa" y también por el estilo que se llama "cubismo". Una de sus obras más impresionantes es *Guernica*, un cuadro que representa los horrores de la Guerra Civil española y que Picasso pinta en 1937. El cuadro ahora está en el Museo Reina Sofía de Madrid.

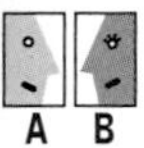

2-34A Entrevistas. Ask each other questions to obtain information. Be prepared to report back to the class. Student B, please see **Appendix 1,** page A2.

MODELO: E1: *¿A qué hora llegas a clase?*
E2: *Llego a las dos.*

1. ¿Cuándo estudias, por la tarde o por la noche?
2. ¿Qué idiomas hablas bien?
3. ¿Lees el periódico (*newspaper*)?
4. ¿Siempre asistes a clase?
5. ¿Qué deportes practicas?

2-35 ¿Y tú? Write a short paragraph in which you discuss your activities using verbs that end in **-ar, -er,** and **-ir.** Connect your thoughts by using the expressions **pero, y,** and **también.**

MODELO: *Estudio dos idiomas: inglés y español. También estudio ciencias y administración de empresas. Trabajo en la cafetería. Me gusta escribir poesía y asistir a conciertos de música rock.*

2-46 to 2-50

6. The present tense of *tener* (to have)

- The Spanish verb **tener** is irregular. As in English, **tener** is used to show possession.

Tengo tres clases y un laboratorio.	*I have three classes and a laboratory.*
¿**Tienes** un bolígrafo?	*Do you have a pen?*

tener (*to have*)			
yo	**tengo**	nosotros/as	**tenemos**
tú	**tienes**	vosotros/as	**tenéis**
él, ella, Ud.	**tiene**	ellos/as, Uds.	**tienen**

- **Tener** is used in many idiomatic expressions, including **tener que** + *infinitive* (to have to [do something]).

Mañana **tengo que** asistir a clase.	*Tomorrow I have to attend class.*
¿**Tienes que** leer una biografía de Picasso?	*Do you have to read a biography about Picasso?*

Aplicación

2-36 Mi tarea. Check off the activities you need to do today.

Tengo que...

☐ asistir a clase.
☐ llegar temprano a clase.
☐ estudiar la lección.
☐ comprar comida.
☐ escribir una composición.
☐ hablar con el/la profesor/a.
☐ bailar en la discoteca.
☐ escuchar música
☐ ayudar a mi amiga.

2-37 ¿Qué tienes que hacer? Discuss what you do and do not have to do tomorrow.

MODELO: E1: *¿Qué tienes que hacer mañana?*
E2: *Mañana tengo que practicar tenis y tengo que hablar con el profesor. No tengo que estudiar. ¿Y tú?*

2-38 ¿Qué tienen en común? Write eight sentences in Spanish, saying what various people have in common. Use verbs that end in **-ar** as well as **ser** and **tener.**

MODELO: *Christina Aguilera y Gloria Estefan son bonitas. Tienen muchos amigos. Cantan bien.*

Christina Aguilera
Jude Law
Paz Vega
yo
Bill Gates
Venus Williams
el príncipe Felipe de España
Gloria Estefan
Enrique Iglesias
Pedro Almodóvar
tú
Rafael Nadal
Shakira
Barack Obama
Eva Longoria
Jessica Simpson
Tiger Woods
Benjamín Bratt

A B

2-39A ¿Tienes? Take turns asking each other if you have the items on your list. If your partner has the item you want, you make a pair. The first person who has five pairs of items wins. Student B, please see **Appendix 1,** page A2.

MODELO: ☐ un libro de historia
E1: *¿Tienes un libro de historia?*
E2: *Sí, tengo. (No, no tengo.)*

☐ un libro de español
☐ una pintura de Picasso
☐ un examen fácil
☐ una mesa roja
☐ un lápiz azul
☐ una mochila negra
☐ una novela de Hemingway
☐ un reloj grande
☐ un buen amigo
☐ un/a profesor/a inteligente
☐ un libro nuevo
☐ un cuaderno viejo

¿Cuánto sabes tú? *Can you...*

2-51 to 2-54

☐ describe your activities: what you do, what you like to do, when, where, and with whom?
☐ identify the language spoken in several different countries?
☐ say what you and others have?
☐ say what you and others have to do?

Observaciones

Episode 2

¡Pura vida! Episodio 2

2-55 to 2-59

In this episode you'll learn more about each character as he/she shares his/her opinions of each other.

Antes de ver el video

2-40 Silvia es española. Read the following information about Spain and match the questions that follow with the appropriate answers.

España es el tercer país más grande de Europa, después de Rusia y Francia. Por su diversidad y su mezcla *(mixture)* de gentes y tradiciones, España es un país muy diferente al resto de Europa. Los grupos que han influido *(have influenced)* en la historia de este país son: los íberos, los celtas, los griegos, los romanos, los godos, los árabes y los judíos.

Ahora, España está dividida en diecisiete comunidades autónomas. Aunque existen diferencias entre las comunidades, todos comparten *(share)* muchas tradiciones y costumbres, como el horario.

En España el horario es muy diferente al de los Estados Unidos y Canadá. Por ejemplo, se desayuna (*one eats breakfast*) entre las ocho y las diez de la mañana. El almuerzo (*lunch*), en los restaurantes, se sirve entre las 13:00 y las 15:30 horas. La cena (*dinner*) se sirve de las 20:30 a las 23:00 horas. En los bares y restaurantes se puede comer "tapas", los deliciosos aperitivos españoles, todo el día.

Se puede (*One can*) comer tapas a cualquier hora (*at any time*) en España.

1. _____ ¿Qué países europeos son más grandes que España?
2. _____ ¿Cuándo se sirve la cena en España?
3. _____ ¿Dónde se puede comer tapas en España?

a. de las 20:30 a las 23:00
b. Rusia y Francia
c. en muchos establecimientos epecialmente los bares y restaurantes

A ver el video

2-41 Los otros personajes. Watch the second episode of *¡Pura vida!* and listen to the characters describe each other. Then, write a description for Silivia, Patricio, and Marcela using the correct forms of logical adjectives from the following list.

alegre mexicano español moreno colombiano guapo cubano inteligente simpático

Silvia

Patricio

Marcela

Después de ver el video

2-42 ¿Cuál es tu opinión? Choose two of these countries and state why you would visit them.

MODELO: Visito __________ porque es __________ y __________.

México Argentina Costa Rica Colombia España Cuba

NUESTRO MUNDO

Panoramas

Vistas culturales

España: Tierra de Don Quijote

2-60 to 2-61

2-43 ¿Ya sabes...? How many of the following can you name?

1. la capital de España
2. un arquitecto español famoso
3. un producto importante de España
4. el nombre del otro país que ocupa la Península Ibérica
5. un director de cine español famoso

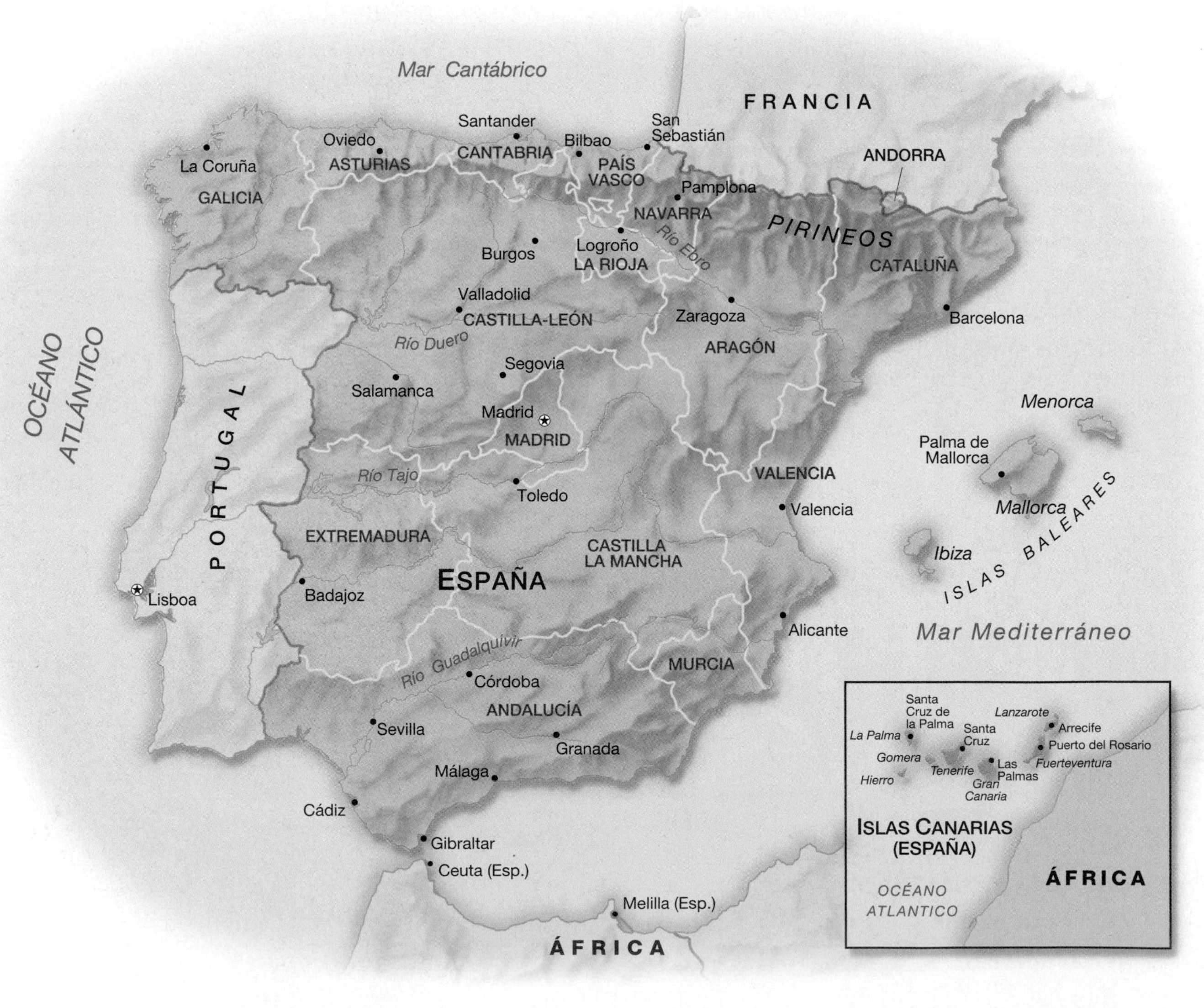

La fabricación de automóviles tiene lugar en el norte de España. El SEAT es un auto pequeño y económico muy popular.

El arquitecto Santiago Calatrava diseñó L'Hemisfèric (*Planetarium*) en Valencia.

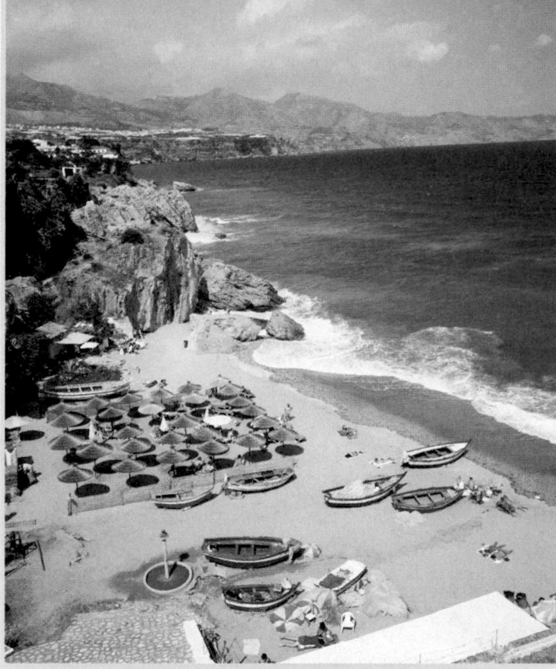

El clima agradable del sur de España, particularmente en la Costa del Sol, atrae a millones de turistas de todo el mundo.

En las largas y ricas costas de España, la pesca (*fishing*) es maravillosa. La gastronomía española es famosa por sus (*its*) excelentes platos.

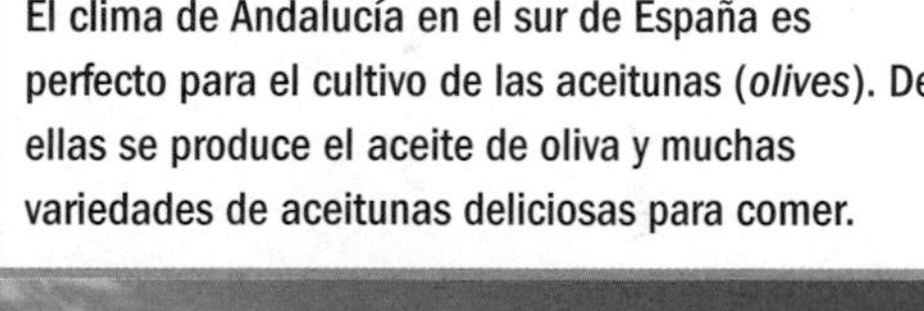

El clima de Andalucía en el sur de España es perfecto para el cultivo de las aceitunas (*olives*). De ellas se produce el aceite de oliva y muchas variedades de aceitunas deliciosas para comer.

Pedro Almodóvar es el director de cine español más prestigioso. Entre sus (*his*) notables películas se incluyen *Mujeres al borde de un ataque de nervios, Mala educación, Todo sobre mi madre,* y *Hable con ella.* Almodóvar recibió un Óscar por las dos últimas.

2-44 ¿Dónde? Identify a place on the map where you might find the following.

1. playas (*beaches*)
2. montañas
3. arquitectura interesante
4. el gobierno
5. buena gastronomía
6. arquitectura moderna
7. la producción de aceite de oliva
8. la fabricación de automóviles

2-45 Conexiones. Connect with your **¡Arriba!** web site to find out the following information about Spain.

1. dónde hay otros diseños de Santiago Calatrava
2. el nombre del rey (*king*) de España
3. la población
4. una de las lenguas, además del castellano, que se habla en España
5. el nombre de un/a tenista profesional famoso/a
6. una comida (*meal*) popular de España

2-46 Guía turística. Complete this description of Spain with the correct form of the appropriate adjectives from the list below. Refer to the reading and photos in **Nuestro mundo.**

Modelo: *España tiene playas* *<u>bonitas</u>*.

bonito	delicioso	económico	excelente
famoso	grande	hermoso	importante
largo	moderno	prestigioso	popular

España tiene una gastronomía ____________, un director de cine ____________, arquitectura ____________, fábricas ____________, aceitunas ____________, automóviles ____________ y una costa ____________.

Ritmos

2-62

"Cuéntame alegrías" (Tachú, España)

The guitar rhythms and singing style of "Cuéntame alegrías" are reminiscent of Spanish flamenco music, which originated in southern Spain and was greatly influenced by the gypsies in the middle of the nineteenth century.

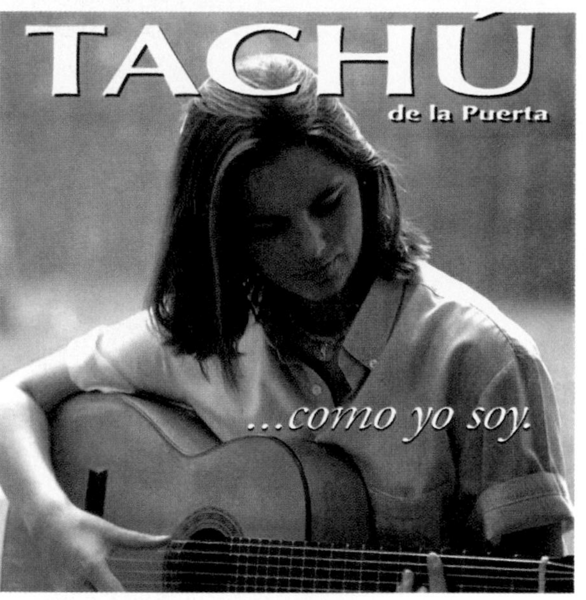

Antes de escuchar

2-47 La letra. Complete the table below with the correct definite and indefinite articles for the words found in the lyrics of "Cuéntame alegrías." Then, use a bilingual dictionary and the glossary at the back of the textbook to find out the meanings of the words.

PALABRA	ARTÍCULO DEFINIDO	ARTÍCULO INDEFINIDO
vida		
amor		
caricia		
sonrisa		
corazón		
alma[1]		
flor		
cielo		
cariño		

A escuchar

2-48 La canción. As you listen to the song, choose the word or phrase that best completes the following sentences.

1. El grupo que canta "Cuéntame alegrías" se llama...
   a. Amor b. Tachú c. Alegría
2. El grupo es de...
   a. España b. México c. La República Dominicana
3. En la canción canta...
   a. un hombre b. un niño c. una mujer
4. Uno de los ritmos de la canción tiene influencias de la música...
   a. clásica b. flamenca c. rock
5. Uno de los temas de la canción puede ser...
   a. el amor b. los estudios c. España

[1]Note: Singular feminine nouns that begin with a stressed "a" or "ha" require the masculine definite or indefinite article. For example, *el alma buena*, but *las almas buenas*; *el agua fría*, but *las aguas frías*.

Después de escuchar

2-49 Comprensión. Answer the following questions with a complete sentence in Spanish and then practice asking and answering the questions with a partner.

1. ¿Cuál es el título de la canción?
2. ¿Qué instrumentos oyes (*hear*) en la canción?
3. ¿Cómo es el ritmo de la canción?
4. ¿Te gusta la canción? ¿Por qué?

Páginas

2-63

"E-milios" por correo tradicional

Antes de leer

2-50 Pistas extratextuales. Look at the illustration and guess what the reading is about.

2-51 Busca los cognados. Underline the cognates in the text. Do they coincide with your guess about what the text is about?

A leer

"*E-milios*" por correo tradicional

Una noticia interesante: ¡en España los carteros *(mail carriers)* reparten *(deliver)* e-milios! Sí, el Departamento de Correos tiene una "oficina virtual" en la Red *(Internet)*, que está abierta las 24 horas del día durante todo el año, y así puedes mandar *(you can send)* "cartas" sin necesidad de sobres *(envelopes)* o de sellos *(stamps)*.

Sólo tienes que escribir el texto en computadora y entrar en www.correos.es/. Ellos después imprimen la carta y la envían a cualquier dirección postal del mundo. Los responsables aseguran que el servicio es más rápido porque la carta entra en el circuito de reparto *(delivery route)* antes, porque no es necesario sacarla del buzón *(mailbox)*, aunque también es más caro *(expensive)*. Mandar una carta electrónica a cualquier destino nacional cuesta *(costs)* 48 céntimos de euro. Una carta normal cuesta 28 céntimos. Pero además de tiempo, se ahorra *(you save)* el precio del sobre y del papel. Muchas personas han comentado que quizás *(perhaps)* la idea venga del "cibernético" príncipe Felipe de España.

Después de leer

2-52 Haz las preguntas. Complete the questions with the most appropriate interrogative word. Use the answers in Spanish to help you form the questions.

1. ¿_____ es el país que tiene un servicio electrónico de cartas?
2. ¿_____ cuesta una carta normal en comparación con una carta por e-*milio*?
3. ¿_____ horas al día está abierta esta oficina de correos?
4. ¿_____ no tienes que comprar?
5. ¿_____ es más rápido el servicio por *e-milio* que el servicio normal?
6. ¿_____ es posiblemente esta idea?

2-53 ¿Qué opinas tú? Respond to the following statements to express your opinions.

1. Me gusta usar el correo electrónico.
   a. Mucho. b. Un poco. c. No me gusta nada (*at all*).
2. Paso más de dos horas diarias en la Red (*Internet*).
   a. Siempre. b. De vez en cuando. c. Nunca.
3. Recibo cartas normales.
   a. A menudo (*Often*). b. De vez en cuando. c. Casi nunca.
4. Me gusta escribir cartas normales.
   a. Mucho. b. Un poco. c. No me gusta nada.
5. Soy una persona muy cibernética.
   a. Sí. b. Posiblemente. c. No.

WWW **2-54 Correos en la Red.** Connect with your **¡Arriba!** web site to find out the following information about sending mail from Spain.

1. the cost to send a letter (*carta*) or post card (*tarjeta postal*) to the U.S. _____
2. the cost to send a 2-page fax to the U.S. _____
3. the cost to send a 10-word (*palabra*) telegram to Canada _____
4. how long it takes to deliver an urgent money order (*giro postal*) _____

Taller

2-55 Una entrevista y un sumario.

2-64 to 2-66

Antes de escribir

- Write questions you'd like to ask a famous Spaniard if you could interview him/her, for example, el príncipe Felipe, Pedro Almodóvar, Antonio Banderas, Penélope Cruz, Felipe de Borbón, Picasso, Salvador Dalí, Rafael Nadal. You may log onto your **¡Arriba!** web site to see some famous people in the Spanish-speaking world. Use the following interrogatives:

  ¿Cómo? ¿Dónde? ¿Qué? ¿Cuándo?
  ¿Por qué? ¿Cuál(es)? ¿Quién(es)? ¿De dónde?

- Write at least one question using the verb **tener.**
- **Entrevista.** Interview a classmate who will role-play as a famous Spaniard, then write up the responses.

A escribir

- Summarize the information for an article in *¡Aló!*, a Spanish magazine that depicts the lives of the rich and the famous. Use connecting words such as **y, pero** (*but*), and **por eso** (*therefore*).
- Write at least six sentences about your famous person.

Después de escribir

- **Revisar.** Review your summary to assure the following:
  - ☐ agreement of nouns, articles, and adjectives
  - ☐ agreement of subjects and verbs
  - ☐ correct spelling, including accents
- **Intercambiar**
  Exchange your summary with a classmate's; make suggestions and corrections.
- **Entregar**
  Rewrite your summary, incorporating your classmate's suggestions. Then turn in the summary to your instructor.

Vocabulario

Primera parte

Adjetivos de nacionalidad	*Adjectives of nationality*
argentino/a	*Argentine*
canadiense	*Canadian*
chileno/a	*Chilean*
colombiano/a	*Colombian*
cubano/a	*Cuban*
dominicano/a	*Dominican*
ecuatoriano/a	*Ecuadorian*
español/a	*Spanish*
mexicano/a	*Mexican*
norteamericano/a (estadounidense)	*American (US)*
panameño/a	*Panamanian*
peruano/a	*Peruvian*
puertorriqueño/a	*Puerto Rican*
salvadoreño/a	*Salvadorian*
venezolano/a	*Venezuelan*

Adjetivos descriptivos	*Descriptive adjectives*
alto/a	*tall*
bajo/a	*short*
bonito/a	*pretty; cute*
delgado/a	*thin*
feo/a	*ugly*
flaco/a	*skinny*
gordo/a	*chubby*
grande	*big*
guapo/a	*good-looking*
joven	*young*
moreno/a	*brunette*
nuevo/a	*new*
pequeño/a	*small*
perezoso/a	*lazy*
pobre	*poor*
rico/a	*rich*
rubio/a	*blond*
viejo/a	*old*

Los lugares	*Places*
la capital	*capital city*
la ciudad	*city*
el país	*country*

Las personas	*People*
el/la amigo/a	*friend*
el/la muchacho/a	*boy/girl*
los padres	*parents*

Adverbios	*Adverbs*
ahora (mismo)	*(right) now*
también	*also*
tarde	*late*
temprano	*early*

Conjunciones	*Conjunctions*
pero	*but*
porque	*because*

Segunda parte

Verbos	*Verbs*
abrir	*to open*
asistir (a)	*to attend*
aprender (a)	*to learn*
ayudar	*to help*
bailar	*to dance*
beber	*to drink*
buscar	*to look for*
caminar	*to walk*
comer	*to eat*
comprar	*to buy*
comprender	*to understand*
conversar	*to converse*
creer	*to believe*
decidir	*to decide*
enseñar	*to teach*
escribir	*to write*
escuchar	*to listen*
estudiar	*to study*
hablar	*to speak*
leer	*to read*
llegar	*to arrive*
mirar	*to look at*
nadar	*to swim*
practicar	*to practice; to play (a sport)*
preparar	*to prepare*
recibir	*to receive*
regresar	*to return*
tomar	*to drink; to take*
trabajar	*to work*
viajar	*to travel*
vender	*to sell*
ver	*to see*
vivir	*to live*

Algunos deportes	*Some sports*
el baloncesto/ el básquetbol	*basketball*
el béisbol	*baseball*
el fútbol	*soccer*
el fútbol americano	*football*
la natación	*swimming*
el tenis	*tennis*

Adjetivos	*Adjectives*
difícil	*difficult*
fácil	*easy*

Los idiomas	*Languages*
el alemán	*German*
el chino	*Chinese*
el coreano	*Korean*
el español	*Spanish*
el francés	*French*
el inglés	*English*
el italiano	*Italian*
el japonés	*Japanese*
el portugués	*Portuguese*
el ruso	*Russian*

Otras palabras y expresiones	*Other words and expressions*
¿Qué te gusta hacer?	*What do you* (inf.) *like to do?*
Me gusta (+ infinitive)	*I like* (+ infinitive)
Te gusta (+ infinitive)	*You* (inf.) *like* (+ infinitive)

Telling time — *See page 44.*
Interrogative words — *See page 50.*

3 ¿Qué estudias?

Objetivos comunicativos

Primera parte

¡Así lo decimos! Vocabulario	Las materias académicas y la vida estudiantil
¡Así lo hacemos! Estructuras	The numbers 101–3,000,000
	Possessive adjectives
	Other expressions with **tener**
Comparaciones	Las universidades hispánicas

- Exchanging information about classes
- Talking about things that belong to you
- Talking about how you and others feel

Segunda parte

¡Así lo decimos! Vocabulario	Los edificios de la universidad
¡Así lo hacemos! Estructuras	The present tense of **ir** (*to go*) and **hacer** (*to do; to make*)
	The present tense of **estar** (*to be*)
	Summary of uses of **ser** and **estar**
Observaciones	¡Pura vida! Episodio 3

- Describing yourself and others
- Asking for and giving simple directions

Nuestro mundo

Panoramas	¡México lindo!
Ritmos	"La Bamba" (Mariachi Vargas de Tecalitlán, México)
Páginas	El Museo de Antropología de México
Taller	Una carta personal

Frida Kahlo empezó su carrera artística como terapia después de sufrir un horrible accidente. Aunque recibió poca atención durante su vida, hoy en día se le considera una de las mejores (*best*) pintoras del mundo hispano. Fue la esposa del gran muralista mexicano, Diego Rivera.

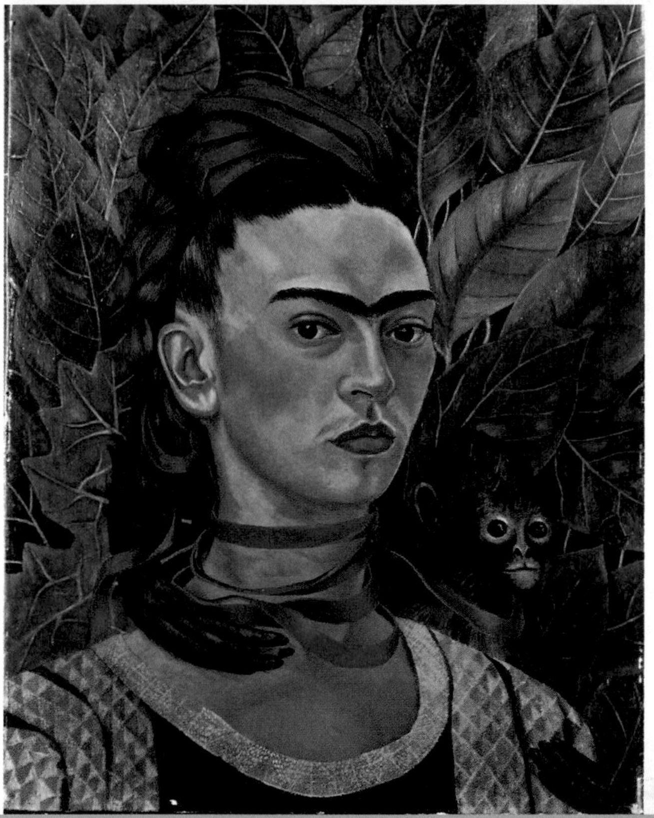

¡México lindo!

«La educación no es para enseñar qué pensar, sino a pensar.»*

Carlos Santana, el gran artista de música de rock, nació en Autlán de Navarro, México. En el año 2000, ganó cuatro Grammys.

***Refran:** "Education serves not to teach what to think, but rather to think."

PRIMERA PARTE

¡Así lo decimos! Vocabulario

CD 1, Track 16

3-1 to 3-2

¡Así es la vida! ¿Qué materias vas a tomar?

En el laboratorio de lenguas de la Universidad Autónoma de México…

Carmen: Pedro, mira el horario de clases de este semestre.

Pedro: Sí, ¿qué materias tienes tú?

Carmen: Mi horario es bastante complicado. Tengo cinco materias: español, química, historia, inglés y cálculo.

Pedro: ¡Estás loca! Yo tengo que tomar cuatro materias este semestre… ¡Y eso ya es mucho!

Carmen: ¿Tienes hambre? Yo sí. ¿Vamos a comer algo?

Pedro: Ahora no. No tenemos tiempo. Tenemos que asistir a la clase de biología.

Carmen: ¡Es verdad! ¿Qué hora es?

Pedro: Ya son las nueve. La clase es en cinco minutos.

Carmen: ¡Tienes razón! ¡Vamos! Y todavía tengo que comprar un libro para mi clase de química.

Las materias académicas y la vida estudiantil

CD 1, Track 17

3-3 to 3-7

Horario de clases
Semestre de otoño de 2007

Álgebra 101	12:00-1:00	lunes, miércoles y viernes
Antropología 252	9:00-10:00	lunes, miércoles y viernes
Cálculo 300	18:30-21:30	martes
Geología 120	9:30-11:00	martes y jueves
Literatura 310	11:00-12:00	lunes, miércoles y viernes
Música 111	9:30-11:00	martes y jueves
Psicología 101	18:30-21:30	jueves
Química 300	10:00-11:00	lunes, miércoles y viernes
Laboratorio	14:00-17:00	jueves
Sociología 160	8:00-9:00	lunes, martes, miércoles, jueves y viernes

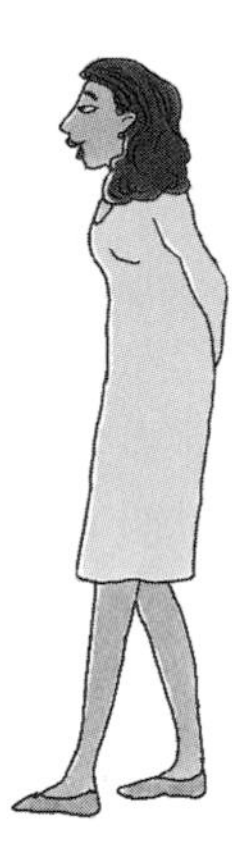

la chica

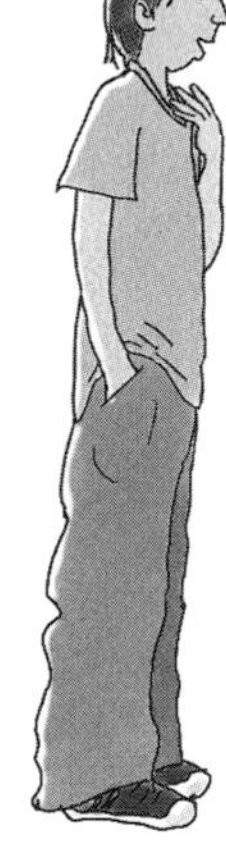

el chico

la computadora

Más materias académicas	***More academic subjects***
la administración de empresas	*business administration*
la arquitectura	*architecture*
el arte	*art*
la biología	*biology*
las ciencias políticas	*political science*
las ciencias sociales	*social science*
las comunicaciones	*communications*
la contabilidad	*accounting*
el derecho	*law*
el diseño	*design*
la educación física	*physical education*
la estadística	*statistics*
la filosofía	*philosophy*
las finanzas	*finance*
la física	*physics*
la geografía	*geography*
la historia	*history*
la informática/la computación	*computer science*
la ingeniería	*engineering*
la ingeniería eléctrica	*electrical engineering*
las matemáticas	*mathematics*
la medicina	*medicine*
la pedagogía	*teaching*
la veterinaria	*veterinary science*

Sustantivos	***Nouns***
el horario (de clases)	*(class) schedule*
el semestre	*semester*
el trimestre	*trimester*

Adjetivos	***Adjectives***
complicado/a	*complicated*
exigente	*challenging; demanding*

Adverbios	***Adverbs***
bastante	*quite; fairly*
después de	*after*
solamente	*only*

EXPANSIÓN More on structure and usage

Todo is used in many expressions in Spanish, with the equivalent *every* and *all* in English.

todo (pron.)	*everything, all*
todo/a (adj.)	*all (of)*
todo el día	*all day*
todo el mundo	*everyone, everybody*
todas las noches	*every night*
todos/as	*all*
todos los días	*every day*
Todos asisten a **todas** sus clases **todos** los días.	*Everyone attends all of their classes every day.*

Aplicación

3-1 Y tú, ¿qué estudias? Check off the subjects you have this term. Compare your list with another student.

Modelo: *Estudio…*
☑ biología, ☑ cálculo, ☑ español y ☑ química.

☐ administración de empresas
☐ alemán
☐ álgebra
☐ antropología
☐ árabe
☐ arte
☐ biología
☐ cálculo
☐ ciencias políticas
☐ ciencias sociales
☐ comunicaciones
☐ coreano
☐ chino
☐ derecho
☐ educación física
☐ español
☐ filosofía y letras
☐ física
☐ francés
☐ geografía
☐ geología
☐ historia
☐ informática
☐ ingeniería
☐ inglés
☐ japonés
☐ literatura
☐ matemáticas
☐ medicina
☐ música
☐ pedagogía
☐ portugués
☐ psicología
☐ química
☐ ruso
☐ sociología

3-2 Tengo. Match what you have and what you study, based on the item.

Modelo: un libro de Milton Friedman
Tengo un libro de Milton Friedman. Estudio economía.

TENGO:	**ESTUDIO:**
1. _____ una novela	a. español
2. _____ un mapa	b. biología
3. _____ un libro de los aztecas	c. geografía
4. _____ un piano	d. historia
5. _____ un microscopio	e. informática
6. _____ una computadora	f. literatura
7. _____ un diccionario bilingüe	g. matemáticas
8. _____ una calculadora	h. música

3-3 Campus Querétaro. *El Instituto Tecnológico de Estudios Superiores de Monterrey (El Tecnológico de Monterrey)*, popularly known as *El Tec*, has campuses all over Mexico, each with a particular academic strength. Here you have a brief description of the *Campus Querétaro*. Read the selection and then answer the questions that follow.

El Tec de Monterrey, Campus Querétaro, empezó a construirse el 14 de agosto de 1974.

Las clases comenzaron en agosto de 1975 con 344 alumnos: 174 en preparatoria y 170 en profesional. Hoy en día, cuenta con unos 3.000 estudiantes.

Las carreras profesionales que se ofrecieron en un principio fueron:

- Ingeniería en Agronomía
- Ingeniería de Sistemas Computacionales
- Licenciatura en Administración de Empresas

Actualmente (*Currently*) el Campus Querétaro tiene 17 carreras completas además de la preparatoria. Algunas de las carreras que se ofrecen son:

- Arquitectura
- Veterinaria
- Ingeniería Industrial y de Sistemas
- Ingeniería en Mecánica y Administración
- Ingeniería en Agronomía
- Licenciatura en Administración de Empresas
- Licenciatura en Ciencias de Comunicación
- Licenciatura en Contabilidad y Finanzas
- Licenciatura en Diseño Industrial

1. ¿Cuántos años tiene (*How old is*) el Campus Querétaro?
2. ¿Cuántos estudiantes había (*were there*) en el primer año?
3. Si te gusta el arte y el diseño (*design*), ¿qué carrera(s) estudias?
4. Si te gusta el comercio, ¿qué estudias?
5. Si te gustan los animales, ¿qué estudias?
6. En tu opinión, ¿cuál es la especialidad académica del Tec?

 **3-4 Materias.** Here is a schedule of classes for students in international business at *El Tec.* Ask each other what you are going to study and when each class meets.

MODELO: E1: ¿Qué vas a estudiar?
E2: *Administración de empresas.*
E1: ¿Cuándo?
E2: *Los lunes y los miércoles a las ocho y media.*

Curso	Días	Hora
Administración de empresas	lunes y miércoles	8:30–10:00
Análisis de información	lunes y miércoles	10:30–12:00
Contabilidad financiera I	viernes	16:00–19:00
Derecho privado	lunes y miércoles	8:30–10:00
Japonés II	martes y jueves	15:00–17:00
Derecho público	viernes	16:00–19:00
Matemáticas II	lunes y miércoles	10:30–12:00
Psicología avanzada	lunes y miércoles	8:30–10:00
Estadística administrativa	martes y jueves	15:00–17:00
Principios de microeconomía	martes y jueves	15:00–17:00
Recursos humanos	lunes y miércoles	8:30–10:00
Negocios internacionales	martes y jueves	15:00–17:00
Principios de macroeconomía	lunes y miércoles	8:30–10:00

CD 1, Track 18

3-5 El horario de Alberto y Carmen. Listen to Alberto and Carmen talk about their schedules on your **¡Arriba!** audio program or as read by your instructor. Then underline the statements that apply to each of them.

1. Estudia matemáticas. Alberto Carmen
2. Estudia química. Alberto Carmen
3. Tiene examen hoy. Alberto Carmen
4. Tiene que hablar con el profesor. Alberto Carmen
5. Trabaja esta noche. Alberto Carmen
6. Va a una fiesta esta noche. Alberto Carmen
7. Tiene una clase difícil. Alberto Carmen
8. Tiene un profesor exigente. Alberto Carmen

3-6 ¿Cuántas? In a group of three to four students, ask what each other is studying this semester and at what times the classes meet. Which class is the most common among you? What time is the most popular? Which class is the most difficult? Use these questions to guide you and complete the chart below.

1. ¿Qué estudias este semestre (trimestre)?
2. ¿A qué hora es la clase?
3. ¿Es difícil o fácil?

Nombre	Materia	Hora	Fácil	Difícil

¡Así lo hacemos! Estructuras

3-8 to 3-12

1. The numbers 101–3,000,000

101	ciento uno/a	800	ochocientos/as
200	doscientos/as	900	novecientos/as
300	trescientos/as	1.000	mil
400	cuatrocientos/as	4.000	cuatro mil
500	quinientos/as	100.000	cien mil
600	seiscientos/as	1.000.000	un millón (de)
700	setecientos/as	3.000.000	tres millones

- **Ciento** is used in compound numbers between 100 and 200.
  ciento diez, ciento treinta y cuatro, etcétera
- When 200–900 modify a noun, they agree in gender with it.
  cuatrocient**os** libros quinient**as** sillas doscient**as** universidades
- **Mil** is never used with **un** and is never used in the plural for counting.
  mil, dos mil, tres mil, etcétera

- The plural of **millón** is **millones,** and when followed by a noun, both take the preposition **de.**

  dos millones de dólares

- In Spain and in most of Latin America, thousands are marked by a period and decimals by a comma.

UNITED STATES/CANADA	SPAIN/LATIN AMERICA
$1,000	$1.000
$2.50	$2,50
$10,450.35	$10.450,35
2,341,500	2.341.500

Aplicación

3-7 ¿En qué año? Match the following dates with historical events. Then give another important event and its date.

Modelo: 1776
mil setecientos setenta y seis; la independencia de los Estados Unidos

1. _____ 1492	a. los Juegos Olímpicos en China
2. _____ 2008	b. la Guerra Civil española
3. _____ 2000	c. la Gran Depresión
4. _____ 1929	d. el nuevo milenio
5. _____ 1861	e. la conquista de México por Cortés
6. _____ 1936	f. la Guerra Civil norteamericana
7. _____ 1521	g. la llegada (*arrival*) de Cristóbal Colón a Santo Domingo
8. _____ ¿...?	h. ¿...?

3-8 ¿Qué número es? Write the numerals that are represented below.

Modelo: doscientos cuarenta y nueve
249

1. quinientos noventa y dos _____
2. diez mil setecientos once _____
3. un millón seiscientos treinta y tres mil doscientos nueve _____
4. novecientos mil ciento veintiuno _____
5. dos millones ochocientos mil ochocientos ochenta y ocho _____
6. ciento cuarenta y cinco _____

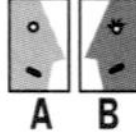

3-9A Inventario. Take turns dictating your inventory numbers to each other in Spanish. Which items do you have in common? **¡Ojo! (*Watch out!*)** Watch for agreement. Student B, see **Appendix 1,** page A3.

Modelo: 747 mesas
setecientas cuarenta y siete mesas

1. 200 diccionarios	5. 1.526 libros
2. 5.002 escritorios	6. 2.700.000 calculadoras
3. 816 pizarras	7. 111.000 sillas
4. 62 mapas	8. 672 computadoras

3-10 Una empresa nueva. Together you have a budget of *un millón de pesos* to equip an office. Decide which items you must have, but do not go over budget.

MODELO: E1: *Necesitamos comprar dos escritorios ejecutivos por veinte mil pesos.*
E2: *No, necesitamos comprar uno ejecutivo y uno pequeño por once mil pesos.*

PRESUPUESTO (*BUDGET*) $1.000.000 (Pesos)

escritorio ejecutivo	$10.000	escritorio pequeño	$1.000
carro económico	$120.000	carro lujoso	$320.000
silla de plástico	$250	sillón	$3.000
computadora	$15.000	papel, bolígrafos	$1.000
fotocopiadora	$10.000	estante (*bookshelf*)	$1.200
mesa pequeña	$800	mesa grande	$2.500
fax	$1.500	miscelánea	¿...?

3-13 to 3-17

2. Possessive adjectives

Subject pronoun	Singular	Plural	
yo	**mi**	**mis**	*my*
tú	**tu**	**tus**	*your* (inf.)
él, ella, Ud.	**su**	**sus**	*your* (form.), *his, her*
nosotros/as	**nuestro/a**	**nuestros/as**	*our*
vosotros/as	**vuestro/a**	**vuestros/as**	*your* (inf.)
ellos/as, Uds.	**su**	**sus**	*your* (form.), *their*

- Possessive adjectives agree in number with the nouns they modify. Note that **nuestro/a** and **vuestro/a** are the only possessive adjectives that show both gender and number agreement.

- In Spanish, possessive adjectives are always placed before the noun they modify.

Mis clases son grandes.	*My classes are big.*
Nuestros amigos llegan a las ocho.	*Our friends arrive at eight o'clock.*

- In Spanish, the construction **de** + *noun* can also be used to indicate possession. It is equivalent to the English *apostrophe s.*

El libro **de Raúl** es interesante.	*Raúl's book is interesting.*
La hermana **de Laura** estudia derecho.	*Laura's sister studies law.*

- When the preposition **de** is followed by the definite article **el,** it contracts to **del: de** + **el** = **del.**[1]

Los libros **del** profesor son difíciles.	*The professor's books are difficult.*
No es mi cuaderno, es **de él.**	*It's not my notebook, it's his.*

EXPANSIÓN More on structure and usage

Su and *sus*

The possessive adjectives **su** and **sus** can have different meanings (*your, his, her, their*). The context in which they are used indicates who the possessor is.

María lee **su** libro.	*María reads her book.*
Ramón y José hablan con **sus** amigos.	*Ramón and José speak with their friends.*

When the identity of the possessor is not clear, the construction **de** + *noun* or **de** + *prepositional pronoun* can be used for clarification.

¿**De quién** es el libro?	*Whose book is it?*
Es **su** libro. Es el libro **de Paco.**	*It's his book. It's Paco's book.*
¿Son **sus** amigas?	*Are they her friends?*
Sí, son las amigas **de ella.**	*Yes, they're her friends.*

With the exception of first and second person singular (**yo** and **tú**), prepositional and subject pronouns are the same: **de él, de usted, de nosotros/as, de ellos/as.** The prepositional pronouns for **yo** and **tú** are **mí** and **ti.** The preposition **con** has special forms with **yo** and **tú: conmigo** and **contigo.**

Aplicación

3-11 José Antonio. Read about a Mexican student named José Antonio. Underline all of the possessive adjectives.

Soy José Antonio O'Farrill, estudiante del Tec de Monterrey. Mi carrera es ingeniería eléctrica. Tengo clases por la mañana y trabajo por la tarde. Vivo en un apartamento cerca de la universidad, pero voy a mi casa los fines de semana. Mi familia vive en Guanajuato. Mis clases más difíciles son informática y estadística. El profesor de estadística tiene su doctorado de una universidad norteamericana. Este año voy a ser estudiante de intercambio *(foreign exchange student)* en el Canadá, donde voy a estudiar francés, también. Mi novia *(girlfriend)* es de Quebec.

[1]The preposition **de** does not contract with the subject pronoun **él.**

3-12 Habla José Antonio. Now complete the questions for José Antonio with logical possessive adjectives. Then respond to the questions as if you were José Antonio.

Modelo: ¿Cuál es <u>*tu*</u> número de teléfono?
<u>*Mi*</u> *número de teléfono es el 555-2550.*

1. ¿Cuál es _____ carrera en la universidad?
2. ¿Cuáles son _____ cursos más difíciles?
3. ¿Dónde vive _____ familia?
4. ¿De dónde tiene _____ doctorado _____ profesor de estadística?
5. ¿De dónde es _____ novia?

3-13 ¿Cómo es? Take turns telling each other what the following things and people are like.

Modelo: clase
E1: *¿Cómo es tu clase de inglés?*
E2: *Mi clase es buena. ¿Cómo es tu clase de matemáticas?*

1. amigos
2. apartamento
3. libros
4. universidad
5. profesor/a de...
6. familia
7. trabajo
8. horario

3-14 ¿Dónde? Take turns asking where each other's class takes place and what the professor is like. Use the following questions as a guide.

1. ¿Dónde es tu clase de...?
2. ¿Cómo es tu profesor/a de...?

3-18 to 3-20

3. Other expressions with *tener*

¡Maribel tiene miedo!

You have used **tener** to show possession and to say you *have to* (*do something*).

Tengo muchos amigos.	*I have many friends.*
Tienes que asistir a clase.	*You have to attend class.*

- There are other common expressions that use **tener** where English uses the verb *to be*. Note that many of these refer to things we might feel (hunger, thirst, cold, etc.).

¿**Tienes** hambre?	*Are you hungry?*
No, pero **tengo** frío.	*No, but I'm cold.*
Tenemos prisa.	*We're in a hurry.*

- Use the verb **tener** also to express age.

tener... años	*to be... years old*
¿Cuántos años **tienes**?	*How old are you?*

Aplicación

3-15 En el camerino (*dressing room*) de Carlos Santana. Read the conversation between Carlos Santana and his agent and underline all of the expressions with **tener.**

Agente: El concierto es en media hora. ¿Necesita algo?

Santana: Sí, tengo mucha sed. Pero si tomo agua, tengo frío.

Agente: ¿Por qué no toma café?

Santana: ¡Porque luego tengo calor! Y si tomo café descafeinado, tengo sueño durante el concierto.

Agente: Tengo una idea. Ud. debe tomar un poco de té ahora y comer algo para tener energía durante el concierto.

Santana: Tomo un poquito de té ahora, pero no como porque tengo prisa. Tengo que vestirme (*get dressed*).

Agente: Tiene razón. Vamos a comer después del concierto. ¡A las once de la noche vamos a tener mucha hambre!

3-16 ¿Qué tiene Santana? Answer the questions using an expression with **tener.**

1. ¿Qué tiene Santana?
2. ¿Qué no toma? ¿Por qué?
3. ¿Por qué tiene prisa?
4. ¿Quién tiene razón?
5. ¿Cuándo van a tener hambre?

3-17 ¿Y tú...? Match these statements to say when you feel the following. If none of the choices are appropriate, supply a new one.

1. _____ Tengo frío...	a. en el desierto.
2. _____ Tengo calor...	b. en el verano.
3. _____ Tengo hambre...	c. en un examen.
4. _____ Tengo sed...	d. a las dos de la mañana.
5. _____ Tengo prisa...	e. en el invierno.
6. _____ Tengo cuidado...	f. en una película (*movie*) de horror.
7. _____ Tengo sueño...	g. en un buen restaurante.
8. _____ Tengo miedo...	h. cuando tengo que llegar a tiempo (*on time*).

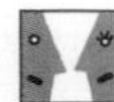

3-18 ¿Cuántos años tienen? You may be familiar with these famous Mexicans. Take turns saying how old they are, as if they were all still alive.

¿Cuántos años tiene Vicente Fox?

Modelo: Vicente Fox, ex-presidente de México (1942)
Tiene... años.

1. Frida Kahlo, pintora (1907)
2. Diego Rivera, muralista, esposo de Frida (1886)
3. Alfonso Cuarón, director de cine, *Y tu mamá también* (1961)
4. Carlos Santana, músico (1947)
5. Salma Hayek, actriz (1966)
6. Carlos Contreras, deportista de NASCAR (1970)
7. Laura Esquivel, novelista, *Como agua para chocolate* (1950)
8. Alejandro González Iñárritu, director de cine, *Amores perros* (1963)

3-21 to 3-24

¿Cuánto sabes tú? *Can you...*

- ☐ talk about your classes; say what you are studying; ask other students about their classes?
- ☐ talk about to whom things belong, using possessive adjectives? **(¿De quién es el libro? No es mi libro, es de Antonio.)**
- ☐ talk about how you feel using expressions with **tener**? **(Tengo hambre cuando...)**

Comparaciones

Las universidades hispánicas

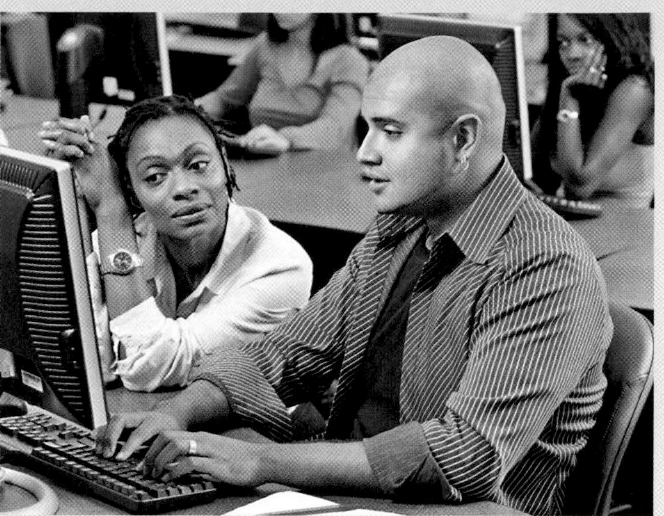

3-19 En tu experiencia. ¿Cuántos estudiantes hay en una clase típica en tu universidad? ¿En una clase de idiomas? ¿Cuántas clases hay por semana? ¿Es muy importante el examen final? ¿Participan mucho los estudiantes en tus clases?

Read this article to find out more about the system in many Hispanic universities.

Generalmente, las clases en las universidades hispánicas ocurren en un ambiente más formal que las clases en las universidades de los EE.UU. y del Canadá. En muchas universidades hispanas...

- las clases son mucho más grandes. Hay entre 50 y 200 estudiantes en cada clase.
- muchas de las clases son conferencias (*lectures*) dictadas por profesores y hay poco tiempo para intercambio entre profesores y estudiantes.
- muchos profesores no tienen horas de oficina.
- las clases son uno o dos días a la semana.
- la nota (*grade*) final es el resultado de un examen final.

Sin embargo (*nevertheless*), universidades como El Tec de Monterrey tienen instalaciones (*physical facilities*) muy modernas para los estudiantes y clases más pequeñas.

3-20 En tu opinión. Read the following statements and take turns expressing your opinion about them.

1. ¡Ni modo! No estoy de acuerdo. (*No way! I disagree.*)
2. No es probable.
3. No sé. (*I don't know.*)
4. Es posible.
5. Estoy completamente de acuerdo.

a. Las clases grandes son más aburridas.
   1 2 3 4 5
b. Los profesores buenos son informales.
   1 2 3 4 5
c. Me gusta tener varios exámenes en un semestre.
   1 2 3 4 5
d. Me gusta hablar en clase.
   1 2 3 4 5
e. Me gusta el sistema norteamericano.
   1 2 3 4 5

SEGUNDA PARTE

¡Así lo decimos! Vocabulario

CD 1, Track 19

3-25 to 3-26

¡Así es la vida! ¿Dónde está la librería?

El campus de la Universidad Autónoma de México es muy grande y tiene muchos edificios. Carmen y Pedro hablan después de clase.

Pedro: Carmen, ¿qué vas a hacer después del almuerzo (*lunch*)?

Carmen: Pues, debo ir a la librería para comprar un diccionario de inglés-español.

Pedro: ¿Dónde está la librería? Tengo que ir esta tarde.

Carmen: Mira el mapa. Está enfrente de la Facultad de Medicina. ¿Por qué no vamos juntos ahora?

Pedro: No, gracias, Carmen. Tengo que ir a la biblioteca, ¿sabes dónde está?

Carmen: Mira, está al lado de la librería.

Pedro: Es que necesito terminar de escribir una biografía sobre Frida Kahlo. Estoy nervioso, porque su vida es muy complicada y tiene muchas pinturas.

Carmen: Debes llamar a Marisa. Ella lee mucho y su especialidad es el arte mexicano.

Pedro: ¿Dónde vive Marisa?

Carmen: Cerca de aquí, con sus padres en Coyoacán, pero sólo asiste a clase los martes y jueves.

Pedro: Gracias. Y también tengo que ir al estadio, ¿sabes dónde está?...

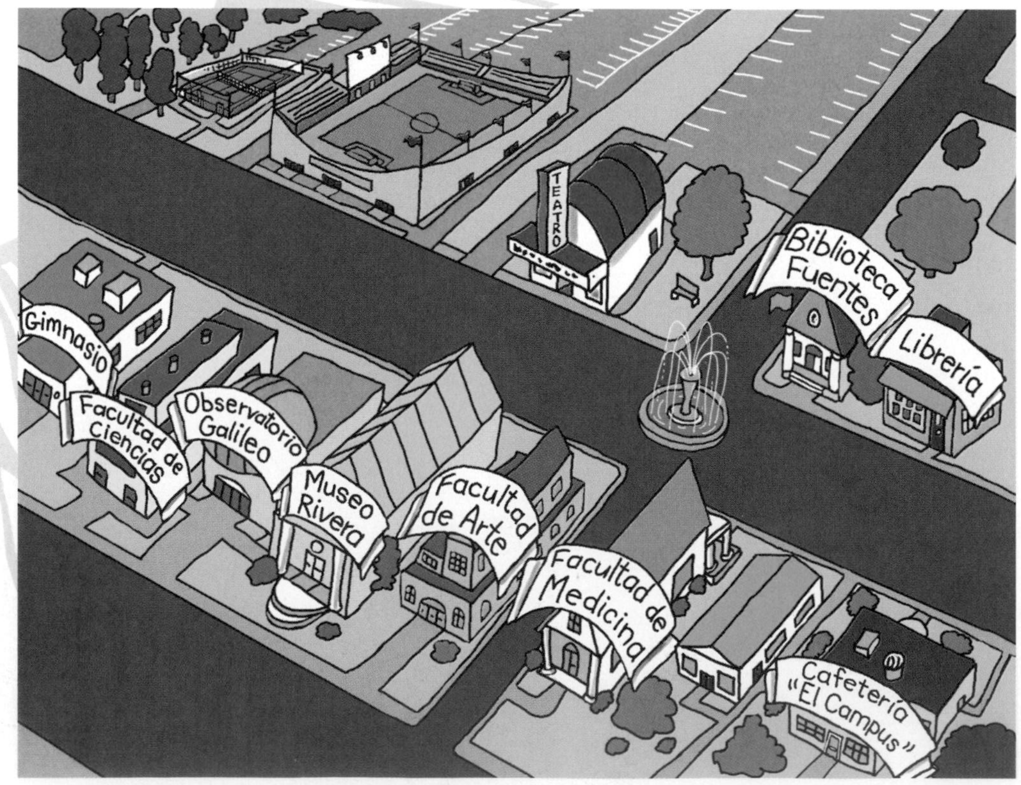

Los edificios de la universidad

la biblioteca

la cafetería

la cancha de tenis

el estadio

la Facultad de Arte

la Facultad de Ciencias

la Facultad de Medicina

el gimnasio

la librería

el museo

el observatorio

el teatro

Más edificios	*More buildings*
el auditorio	*auditorium*
el centro estudiantil	*student union*
la Facultad de Derecho	*School of Law*
la Facultad de Filosofía y Letras	*School of Humanities*
la Facultad de Ingeniería	*School of Engineering*
la Facultad de Matemáticas	*School of Mathematics*
el laboratorio de lenguas	*language laboratory*
la rectoría	*President's office*

Adverbios	*Adverbs*
siempre	*always*
sólo	*only*

Expresiones	*Expressions*
pues	*well*

¿Dónde está?	*Where is...?*
al lado (de)	*next to*
a la derecha de	*on the right*
a la izquierda de	*on the left*
cerca (de)	*nearby (close to)*
delante de	*in front of*
detrás de	*behind*
enfrente (de)	*facing; across from*
entre	*between*
lejos (de)	*far (from)*

Verbos	*Verbs*
estar	*to be*
hacer	*to do; to make*
ir	*to go*

CD 1, Track 21

3-31 to 3-32

LETRAS Y SONIDOS

Syllabification in Spanish

In Spanish, a syllable is a unit of timing for rhythm. Every syllable contains one vowel, which may be accompanied by glides and/or consonants.[1] Consonants combine with vowels to form syllables as follows.

1. Spanish prefers open syllables, or ones that end in a vowel. Thus, a single consonant (including *ch, ll, rr*) always attaches to the vowel that follows.
   se-ño-ri-ta *po-e-ma* *mu-cha-cho* *bo-ca-di-llo* *pi-za-rra*
2. Two consonants also attach to the vowel that follows, given that they consist of a strong consonant (*p, b, t, d, c, g, f*) followed by *r* or *l*.
   a-brir *pro-ble-ma* *no-so-tros* *pa-dre* *bo-lí-gra-fo*

   If they do not form this combination, two consonants are separated, creating a closed syllable.
   tar-de *de-por-te* *blan-co* *Car-los* *es-tu-dian-te*
3. In groups of three consonants, the last two attach to the vowel that follows, given that they consist of a strong consonant (*p, b, t, d, c, g, f*) followed by *r* or *l*.
   com-pli-ca-do *hom-bre* *es-cri-to-rio* *in-glés*

   If the last two consonants do not form this combination, only the last one attaches to the vowel that follows.
   pers-pec-ti-va *ins-ta-lar* *cons-tan-te* *sols-ti-cio*
4. In groups of four consonants, the last two always attach to the vowel that follows.
   ins-truc-tor *abs-trac-to*

[1]Syllables with glides are discussed in **Capítulo 2.**

Aplicación

3-21 ¿Dónde está...? Give the location of the following buildings using the map on page 90.

Modelo: _____ la cancha de tenis
Está cerca del estadio.

LUGARES

1. _____ el estadio
2. _____ el observatorio
3. _____ la cafetería
4. _____ la Facultad de Arte
5. _____ la Facultad de Ciencias
6. _____ la librería
7. _____ el museo
8. _____ la biblioteca

DIRECCIONES

a. Está al lado del gimnasio.
b. Está entre el observatorio y la Facultad de Arte.
c. Está al lado de la biblioteca.
d. Está al lado de la cancha de tenis.
e. Está a la izquierda del museo.
f. Está al lado de la Facultad de Medicina.
g. Está a la derecha de la Facultad de Medicina.
h. Está a la izquierda de la librería.

CD 1, Track 22

3-22 En la cola (*Standing in line*). Listen to your **¡Arriba!** audio program or to your instructor to hear a description of where the people are standing in line. Place the numeral in front of the name of each person.

_____ Marcela
_____ Mercedes
_____ Pepe
_____ Adrián
_____ Paula

3-23 ¿Dónde están? ¿Quiénes son? Where or who are the people in the following drawings?

Modelo:

El profesor Romero está en un laboratorio de...
la Facultad de Ciencias.

1. Lisa está en una clase de...

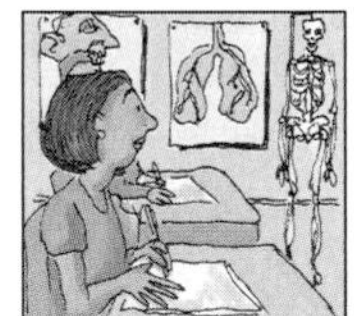

2. Arcadio está en...

3. Ana y Germán están en...

4. Catalina y Jacobo están en...

5. Gabriela Estrada es profesora de...

3-24 La Universidad Nacional Autónoma de México. Read about the most important university in Mexico. Indicate whether the statements are **cierto (C)** or **falso (F)** based on the following text.

La comunidad de la UNAM se compone de estudiantes, profesores, otro personal de apoyo (*support*) y egresados (*alumni*). En total, la población activa es más de 300.000 personas; 137.000 de ellas son estudiantes subgraduados. El recinto de la Universidad es enorme. Tiene aproximadamente 1.700.000 metros cuadrados con 997 edificios, y casi todos son edificios académicos.

La infraestructura de la Universidad también es importante. Hay 143 bibliotecas con más de 4.000.000 de libros; 19 librerías; 28 clínicas, dos jardines botánicos, dos observatorios, una supercomputadora, además de más de 15.000 computadoras personales. Tiene también gran riqueza cultural con muchos edificios históricos importantes, grandes murales, esculturas y pinturas. Además, tiene salones para concierto, teatros, acuarios y museos. Para los que practican deportes, hay dos estadios, siete piscinas y otras áreas para hacer 39 deportes diferentes. Finalmente, la UNAM tiene 24 comedores, 35 cafeterías y tres supermercados.

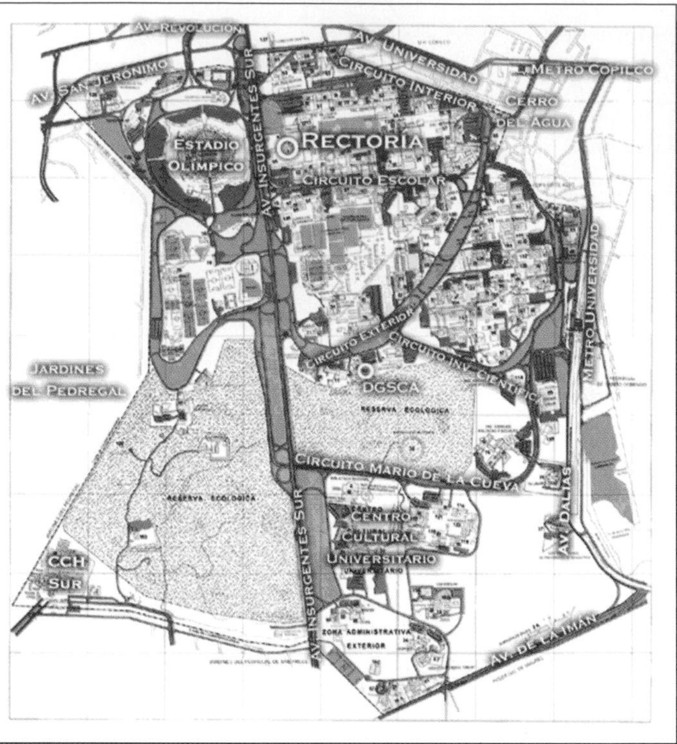

1. _____ La UNAM es una universidad importante de México.
2. _____ Muchos estudiantes mexicanos asisten a la UNAM.
3. _____ Si tienes hambre, no es posible comer en la universidad.
4. _____ Hay muchos eventos culturales: conciertos, obras de teatro, etc.
5. _____ Es difícil practicar deportes en la UNAM.
6. _____ La tecnología es bastante anticuada.
7. _____ Es difícil hacer investigación porque hay pocos libros en las bibliotecas.
8. _____ La UNAM es más grande que mi universidad.

 **3-25 Tu universidad.** Draw and label a map of your university in Spanish. Include at least five important buildings. Then tell a classmate where the buildings are located in relation to each other.

Modelo: *La biblioteca está cerca del estadio.*

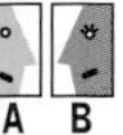
A B

3-26A Las materias, la hora, el lugar. Take turns asking and answering questions in order to complete the missing information on your class schedules. Student B, see **Appendix 1,** page A3.

MODELO: E1: *¿A qué hora es la clase de...?*
E2: *¿Qué clase es a la/s...?*
E1: *¿Dónde es la clase de...?*
E2: *¿Quién es el/la profesor/a de...?*

Hora	Clase	Lugar	Profesor/a
	cálculo		*María Gómez García*
	diseño	*Facultad de Arte*	*Ramón Sánchez Guillón*
10:00	*biología*		*Julia Gómez Salazar*
12:00			
	física		*Carlos Santos Pérez*

¡Así lo hacemos! Estructuras

3-33 to 3-41

4. The present tense of *ir* (to go) and *hacer* (to do; to make)

ir *(to go)*

Singular		Plural	
yo	**voy**	nosotros/as	**vamos**
tú	**vas**	vosotros/as	**vais**
él, ella, Ud.	**va**	ellos/as, Uds.	**van**

hacer *(to do; to make)*

Singular		Plural	
yo	**hago**	nosotros/as	**hacemos**
tú	**haces**	vosotros/as	**hacéis**
él, ella, Ud.	**hace**	ellos/as, Uds.	**hacen**

- The Spanish verbs **ir** and **hacer** are irregular. **Hacer** is irregular only in the first-person singular: **hago.**

  Hago la tarea por las noches. — *I do homework at night.*

- **Ir** is always followed by the preposition **a.** When the definite article **el** follows the preposition **a,** they contract to **al: a + el = al.**

  Luis y Ernesto **van al** centro estudiantil. — *Luis and Ernesto are going to the student union.*

- The construction **ir a** + *infinitive* is used in Spanish to express future action. It is equivalent to the English construction *to be going to + infinitive.*

  ¿Qué **vas a hacer** esta noche? — *What are you going to do tonight?*
  Voy a estudiar en la biblioteca. — *I'm going to study in the library.*

- When you are asked a question using **hacer,** you usually respond with another verb.

  Ricardo, ¿qué **haces** aquí? — *Ricardo, what are you doing here?*
  Busco un libro para mi clase. — *I'm looking for a book for my class.*

Aplicación

3-27 La familia de Santana. Read the following newspaper article about what Santana and his family are going to do. Underline all forms of the verb **ir.**

LAS NOTICIAS

Después de ganar los cuatro Grammys, Carlos Santana anuncia que va a dedicar su tiempo a su familia y a sus obras de caridad (*charity*). Su esposa Deborah (desde 1974) y sus tres hijos, Salvador, Stella y Angélica, van a vivir en su casa en Santa Ana, California. Santana y su esposa van a pasar mucho tiempo trabajando en su Fundación Milagro que ayuda a mejorar la educación, la salud y la vivienda (*housing*) de los niños pobres del mundo. Toda la familia va a trabajar también con Buster Brown, la empresa que fabrica zapatos (*shoes*) que llevan el nombre del artista. Buster Brown va a vender los zapatos "Carlos" en Macy's y otros almacenes importantes. Santana va a donar sus ganancias a la Fundación Milagro. Deborah también tiene mucho talento. Este año ella va a hacer su autobiografía.

3-28 Preguntas para Santana. Now write questions based on the previous article. You can begin the questions as indicated.

Modelo: *¿Quién va a escribir su autobiografía?*

1. ¿Dónde...?
2. ¿Cuándo...?
3. ¿Qué...?
4. ¿Quiénes...?
5. ¿Por qué...?
6. ¿Cómo...?

3-29 ¿Qué hacen? Guess what the following people are doing according to where they are and what they have.

Modelo: (el) sándwich
En la cafetería, la señora *hace los sándwiches*.

(los) ejercicios (la) lección (la) tarea (el) trabajo

1. En la biblioteca, yo ____________.
2. En clase, nosotros ____________.
3. En el gimnasio, tú ____________.
4. En la oficina, los secretarios ____________.

3-30 Planes para ver un concierto. Make plans to see a concert. Use the following questions to guide you.

Modelo: ¿Adónde van?
Vamos a Colombia a ver a Shakira.

1. ¿Con quiénes van?
2. ¿Adónde van?
3. ¿Por cuánto tiempo van?
4. ¿A qué hora van?
5. ¿Qué van a hacer?
6. ¿Qué no van a hacer?
7. ¿Qué van a comprar?
8. ¿Cuándo van a regresar?

5. The present tense of *estar* (to be)

3-42 to 3-46 The English verb *to be* has two equivalents in Spanish, **ser** and **estar.** You have already learned the verb **ser** in **Capítulo 1,** and you have used some forms of **estar** to say how you feel, to ask how someone else feels, and to say where things and places are. The chart shows the present tense forms of **estar.**

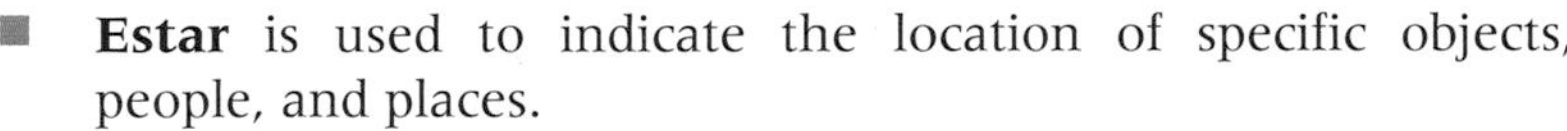

yo	**estoy**	nosotros/as	**estamos**
tú	**estás**	vosotros/as	**estáis**
él, ella, Ud.	**está**	ellos/as, Uds.	**están**

- **Estar** is used to indicate the location of specific objects, people, and places.

  Ana Rosa y Carmen **están** en la cafetería. — *Ana Rosa and Carmen are in the cafeteria.*
  La cafetería **está** en el centro estudiantil. — *The cafeteria is in the student union.*

- **Estar** is also used to express a condition or state, such as how someone is feeling.

  ¡Hola, Luis! ¿Cómo **estás**? — *Hi, Luis! How are you?*
  Hola, Sara. **Estoy** cansado. — *Hi, Sara. I'm tired.*
  Elena **está** enferma. — *Elena is sick.*

- Adjectives that describe physical, mental, and emotional conditions are used with **estar.**

aburrido/a	*bored*	**enfermo/a**	*sick*
cansado/a	*tired*	**enojado/a**	*angry*
casado/a (con)	*married (to)*	**ocupado/a**	*busy*
contento/a	*happy*	**preocupado/a**	*worried*
enamorado/a (de)	*in love (with)*	**triste**	*sad*

Carlos y Deborah Santana **están casados.** — *Carlos and Deborah Santana are married.*
El profesor Martínez **está divorciado.** — *Professor Martínez is divorced.*
Alicia **está enamorada** del novio de Úrsula. — *Alicia is in love with Úrsula's boyfriend.*

La casa de Frida Kahlo

Aplicación

3-31 Frida y Diego. Read the description of Frida Kahlo and Diego Rivera in 1950 and underline the uses of **estar.**

Frida y Diego están casados y viven en la Ciudad de México. Su casa está en la colonia (*neighborhood*) de Coyoacán, un barrio bonito que está cerca de la UNAM. La casa está pintada de azul, el color favorito de Frida. En este momento, Frida está en su estudio donde pinta uno de sus cuadros famosos, con colores muy vivos, frutas y animales. Diego no está, porque está en California. Frida está triste y enferma. Extraña (*she misses*) mucho a Diego.

3-32 ¿Cómo está Frida? Answer the following questions based on what you read in activity **3-31.**

1. ¿Dónde está la casa de Frida y Diego?
2. ¿De qué color está pintada la casa?
3. ¿Qué hace Frida ahora?
4. ¿Por qué no está con Diego?
5. ¿Cómo está Frida? ¿Por qué?

Source: Frida (Frieda) Kahlo, "Frieda and Diego Rivera," 1931, oil on canvas, 39 3/8 in. x 31 in. (100.01 cm x 78.74 cm). Ben Blackwell/San Francisco Museum of Art. © 2003 Banco de Mexico. Diego Rivera & Frida Kahlo Museums Trust. Estate of Frida Kahlo.

3-33 Una conversación telefónica. Complete the telephone conversation between Frida and her agent, Marcelo, with the correct forms of the verb **estar.**

Marcelo: ¿Bueno?
Frida: Marcelo, habla Frida. ¿Cómo (1) _____ (tú)?
Marcelo: Muy bien, ¿y tú?
Frida: Yo (2) _____ bastante bien, gracias. ¡Oye!, ¿dónde (3) _____ (tú) ahora?
Marcelo: (4) _____ en mi oficina.
Frida: ¿(5) _____ Diego y su asistente?
Marcelo: No, ellos (6) _____ en el Palacio del Gobierno.
Frida: Y ¿qué hacen allí? ¿(7) _____ ocupados con algo?
Marcelo: No, (8) _____ aburridos. Diego (9) _____ cansado de pintar.
Frida: Bueno, (10) _____ en mi estudio. Ahora voy al Palacio del Gobierno a buscar a Diego.
Marcelo: (11) _____ bien. Hablamos después. Hasta luego.

3-34 En la cafetería. Describe how these people in the drawing feel and why. Work together to write a conversation between two of the people and then write a description of another person in the drawing. Use **estar** with adjectives and expressions with **tener.**

Modelo: *Pedro está enfermo. Tiene mucho frío y necesita regresar a casa.*

enojado/a	enfermo/a	contento/a	ocupado/a
cansado/a	nervioso/a	enamorado/a	preocupado/a

3-35 ¿Cómo estás? Imagine that you are in the following situations. Say how you feel using the verb **estar** and the appropriate adjectives.

Modelo: en una fiesta
Estoy contento/a.

aburrido/a	contento/a	enojado/a	nervioso/a	enfermo/a
cansado/a	enamorado/a de	ocupado/a	triste	preocupado/a

1. a la medianoche
2. en clase
3. después de un examen
4. cuando hay mucho trabajo
5. en el hospital
6. con una persona especial
7. con una persona importante
8. en una ciudad grande
9. en el gimnasio
10. lejos de mi familia

3-36 Lo siento, no está aquí. Take turns inventing excuses for why a friend can't come to the telephone.

Modelo: E1: *Hola, ¿está Carlos?*
E2: *Lo siento, Carlos está ocupado ahora. Está con su padre.*

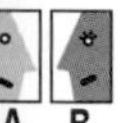

3-37A ¿Dónde estoy? Take turns acting out your situations while your partner tries to guess where you are. Student B, see **Appendix 1,** page A3.

Modelo: E1: (act out reading a book) *¿Dónde estoy?*
E2: *Estás en la biblioteca.*

1. (eating)
2. (listening to headphones)
3. (watching a ball game)
4. (walking)
5. ¿...?

6. Summary of uses of *ser* and *estar*

3-47 to 3-52

Ser is used

- with the preposition **de** to indicate origin, possession, and to tell what material something is made of.

Frida y Carlos **son** de México.	*Frida and Carlos are from Mexico.*
Las pinturas **son** de Diego.	*The paintings are Diego's.*
La mesa **es** de plástico.	*The table is (made of) plastic.*

- with adjectives to express characteristics of the subject, such as size, color, shape, religion, and nationality.

Tomás **es** alto y delgado.	*Tomás is tall and thin.*
Los jóvenes **son** católicos.	*The young men are Catholic.*
Somos mexicanos.	*We are Mexican.*

- with the subject of a sentence when followed by a noun or noun phrase that restates the subject.

Mi hermana **es** abogada.	*My sister is a lawyer.*
Leo y Ligia **son** mis padres.	*Leo and Ligia are my parents.*

- to express dates, days of the week, months, and seasons of the year.

Es primavera.	*It's spring.*
Es el 10 de octubre.	*It's October 10th.*

- to express time.

Son las cinco de la tarde.	*It's five o'clock in the afternoon.*
Es la una de la mañana.	*It's one in the morning.*

- with the preposition **para** to tell for whom or for what something is intended or to express a deadline.

¿**Para** quién **es** esa calculadora?	*For whom is that calculator?*
La composición **es para** el viernes.	*The composition is for (is due) Friday.*

- with impersonal expressions.

Es importante ir al laboratorio.	*It's important to go to the laboratory.*
Es fascinante estudiar la cultura hispana.	*It's fascinating to study Hispanic culture.*

- to indicate where and when events take place.

La fiesta **es** en mi casa.	*The party is at my house.*
El concierto **es** a las ocho.	*The concert is at eight.*

Estar is used

- to indicate the location of persons and objects.

La librería **está** cerca.	*The bookstore is nearby.*
Guadalajara **está** en México.	*Guadalajara is in Mexico.*

- with adjectives to describe the state or condition of the subject.

Las chicas **están** contentas.	*The girls are happy.*
Pedro **está** enfermo.	*Pedro is sick.*

- with descriptive adjectives (or adjectives normally used with **ser**) to indicate that something is exceptional or unusual. This structure is often used this way when complimenting someone, and in English is sometimes expressed with *look*.

Carlitos, tienes ocho años; ¡**estás** muy grande!	*Carlitos, you're eight years old; you are (look) so big!*
Señora Rubiales, usted **está** muy elegante esta noche.	*Mrs. Rubiales, you are (look) especially elegant tonight.*

EXPANSIÓN More on structure and usage

Changes in meaning with *ser* and *estar*

Some adjectives have different meanings depending on whether they are used with **ser** or **estar.**

ADJECTIVE	WITH *SER*	WITH *ESTAR*
aburrido/a	*to be boring*	*to be bored*
bonito/a	*to be pretty*	*to look pretty*
feo/a	*to be ugly*	*to look ugly*
guapo/a	*to be handsome*	*to look handsome*
listo/a	*to be clever*	*to be ready*
malo/a	*to be bad, evil*	*to be ill*
verde	*to be green (color)*	*to be green (not ripe)*
vivo/a	*to be smart, cunning*	*to be alive*

Remember: To locate an entity or event modified by an indefinite article, or a quantifier (such as **mucho, poco,** or a number), use **hay.**

Esta noche **hay** una fiesta en mi casa.	*There's a party at my house tonight.*
Hay más de 42.000.000 de hispanos en los EE. UU.	*There are more than 42,000,000 Hispanics in the U.S.*
Hay muchos jóvenes en la discoteca.	*There are many young people at the disco.*

Aplicación

3-38 La familia de la Mora. Read the description of the de la Mora family and underline all the uses of **ser** and **estar.**

La familia de la Mora es una familia mexicana que vive en Guadalajara. Guadalajara está cerca de la costa Pacífica de México. Guillermo, el papá, es muy trabajador. Olga Marta, la mamá, es de la Ciudad de México y es muy simpática. Ellos tienen tres hijos: Billy, Martita y Érica. Billy es muy responsable. Ahora está en Alemania donde estudia ingeniería. Martita es muy inteligente. Ahora está en la capital donde visita a sus abuelos. Érica es muy alta y delgada y además, es muy trabajadora, como su papá. Ella está en la biblioteca porque necesita hacer su tarea. Esta noche la familia está muy contenta porque va a tener una fiesta para el aniversario de Guillermo y Olga Marta. Es importante invitar a toda la familia y a todos los amigos.

La familia de la Mora

3-39 Preguntas para la familia de la Mora. Write questions that you could ask the de la Mora family.

Modelo: *¿Dónde está Guadalajara?*

1. ¿Cómo...?
2. ¿Por qué...?
3. ¿Cuándo...?
4. ¿Quién...?
5. ¿Dónde...?
6. ¿Qué...?

3-40 En mi casa esta noche. Complete Ana's description of her family and what is happening tonight using the correct forms of **ser** or **estar,** or the verb **hay.**

Mi familia (1) _____ grande, (2) _____ quince personas. Mi casa (3) _____ pequeña. (4) _____ en la calle *(street)* Florida que (5) _____ en el centro de la ciudad. Esta noche (6) _____ una fiesta en mi casa. La fiesta (7) _____ a las ocho de la noche. Mis tíos siempre llegan temprano y ahora (8) _____ en la sala con mi mamá. Mi tío Alfredo (9) _____ alto y guapo. (10) _____ dentista. Mi tía Julia (11) _____ baja y simpática. Ella (12) _____ psicóloga. Mis hermanos (13) _____ en el patio con mi papá, pero mi hermano, Rafa, no, porque (14) _____ enfermo. Rafa (15) _____ en cama *(bed)*. (16) _____ las ocho y quince de la noche y (17) _____ muchas personas en mi casa. Carlos (18) _____ el chico alto y guapo; Saúl (19) _____ el joven bajo y fuerte *(strong)*. (20) _____ argentinos, de Buenos Aires, la capital. ¡Bienvenidos, amigos! (21) _____ música, refrescos y comida. ¡Todo (22) _____ para nosotros!

3-41 Te toca a ti. Now write a short paragraph about someone you know. Include the following information.

¿Quién es?	¿Dónde está en este momento?
¿De dónde es?	¿Qué va a hacer ahora?
¿Cómo es?	¿Por qué?

3-42 Entrevístense. Write out six questions you can ask a classmate using **ser, estar,** or **hay.** Then take turns asking each other your questions.

MODELO: E1: *¿Cómo eres?*
E2: *Soy alto y guapo.*
E1: *¿De dónde eres?*
E2: *Soy de Ohio.*

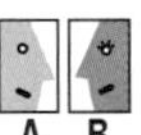

3-43A Dibujos (*Drawings*). Take turns describing a person using the following information while your classmate tries to draw the person described. Then compare your drawings with the descriptions. Student B, see **Appendix 1,** page A3.

MODELO: chica: dieciocho años, alta, bonita, triste, oficina
E1: *Es una chica. Tiene dieciocho años. Es alta y bonita. Está triste y está en la oficina.*
E2: *Es un hombre...*

1. hombre, viejo, bajo, enojado, librería
2. chico, siete años, pequeño, feo, miedo, clase
3. chica, veinticuatro años, gorda, tímida, nerviosa, rectoría

¿Cuánto sabes tú? *Can you...*

3-53 to 3-56

☐ talk about yourself using the verb **ser** to say where you are from, your profession, and what you are like, and the verb **estar** to say how you feel and where places are located?

☐ ask others about themselves?

☐ ask and answer questions about what you are doing (**¿Qué haces?**)?

☐ ask and answer questions about where you are going (**¿Adónde vas?**) and make plans (**¿Vamos a...?**)?

Observaciones

Episode 3

3-57 to 3-60

¡Pura vida! Episodio 3

In this episode you'll learn more about Patricio and his ambitions.

Antes de ver el video

3-44 Nuestra Tierra. Patricio and Silvia decide to meet at *Nuestra Tierra*, a restaurant in San José. Read the following review, then judge the statements that follow as **cierto** (true) or **falso** (false). Correct any false statements.

¡Qué lugar más divertido! Este restaurante ofrece "cocina local típica" y tiene una atmósfera atractiva para complementar la comida. A primera vista es un lugar rústico, sin embargo hay un señor que toca la guitarra y camareros que sirven la comida de una manera cordial. Como decoración hay cebollas (*onions*) que cuelgan del techo (*hang from the ceiling*), y cestas de legumbres (*vegetables*) frescas.

En este restaurante se puede comer bien y barato, y tomar la deliciosa cerveza *Imperial.* Sirven platos típicos costarricenses y es un gran lugar para empezar la noche. Está abierto (*open*) veinticuatro horas todos los días y está ubicado en la Calle 15 con la Avenida 2, de San José.

Nuestra Tierra

1. _____ *Nuestra Tierra* es un restaurante de comida francesa.
2. _____ Los camareros son impacientes.
3. _____ Es un lugar muy elegante.
4. _____ Se sirve la cerveza *Imperial.*
5. _____ Está cerrado (*closed*) los lunes.

A ver el video

3-45 Los otros personajes. Watch the third episode of *¡Pura vida!* where you will hear Silvia use the word *manzana* and Patricio will correct her using the word *cuadra*. Can you guess what the word means? Then, complete the following sentences by matching the phrases below.

Silvia

Patricio

Hermés

1. _____ Silvia está cerca de...	a. en una universidad norteamericana.
2. _____ El restaurante está...	b. bastante lejos.
3. _____ Patricio desea estudiar...	c. una beca *Fulbright.*
4. _____ Es necesario tomar un examen...	d. la Avenida Central.
5. _____ Patricio solicita...	e. colombiano.
6. _____ Uno de los requisitos para Patricio es ser...	f. de inglés.

Después de ver el video

WWW

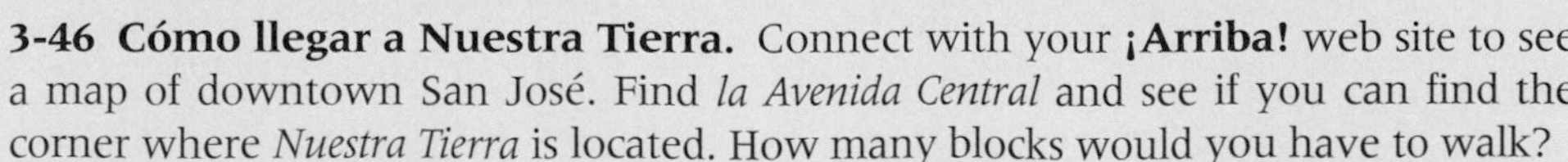

3-46 Cómo llegar a Nuestra Tierra. Connect with your **¡Arriba!** web site to see a map of downtown San José. Find *la Avenida Central* and see if you can find the corner where *Nuestra Tierra* is located. How many blocks would you have to walk?

NUESTRO MUNDO

Panoramas

¡México lindo!

Vistas culturales

3-47 ¿Ya sabes...? How many of the following can you name?

3-61 to 3-63

1. la capital de México
2. un producto de México
3. una antigua civilización
4. los colores de la bandera mexicana
5. una playa que atrae a muchos turistas

Las figuras de madera son hechas a mano por artesanos de Oaxaca. Representan animales y seres fantásticos.

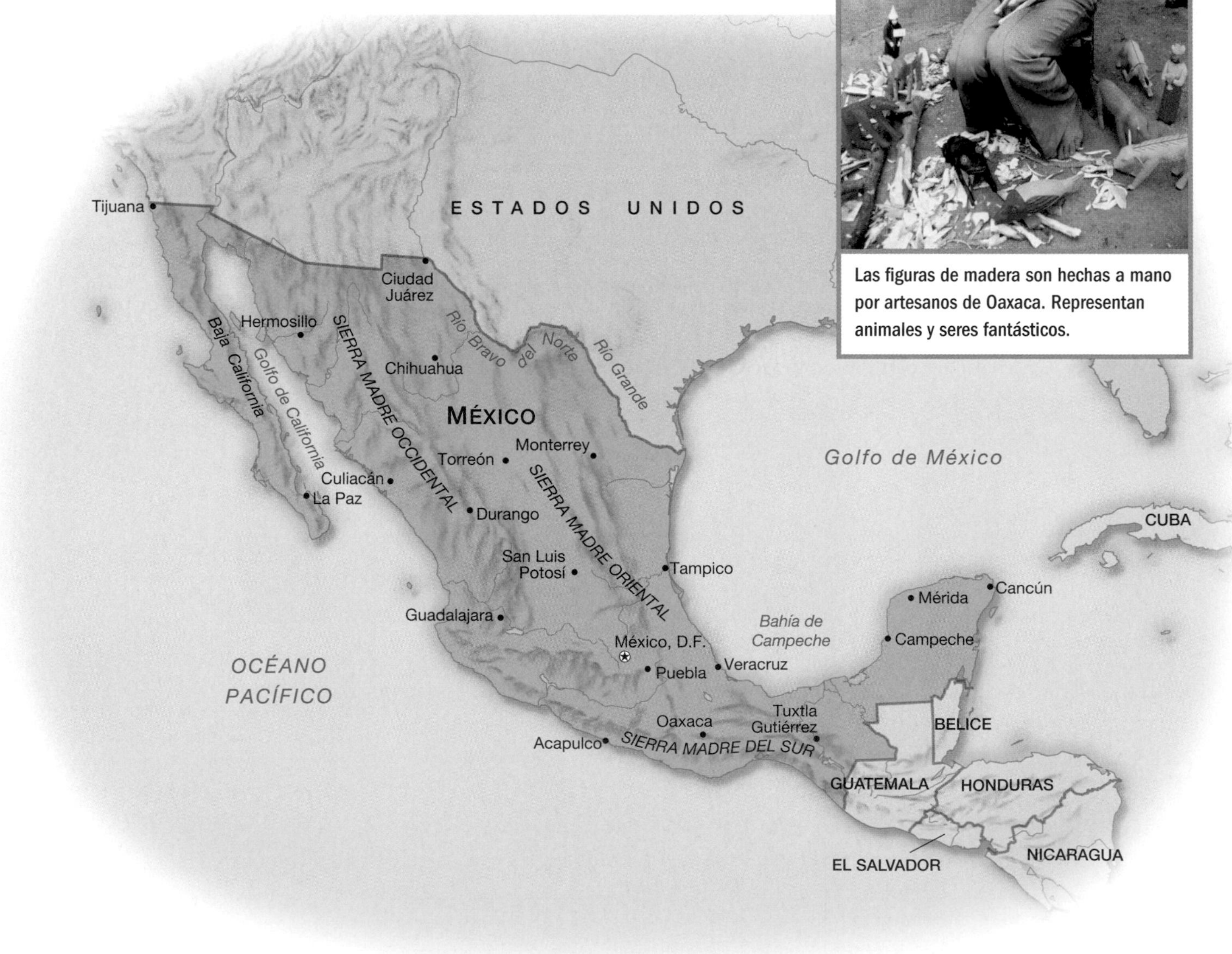

México es famoso por su artesanía. Si visitas la antigua ciudad colonial de Taxco, vas a ver su rica tradición de platería (*silver*).

La vida marina y el agua cristalina azul verdosa atrae a muchos turistas a la isla de Cozumel.

Para muchas personas, los mariachis con sus guitarras, bajos y trompetas representan la música folklórica mexicana. Aunque los mariachis tienen origen en el siglo XVII, todavía son populares en las fiestas y las bodas. Si vives en Guadalajara, parte de la celebración de tu cumpleaños probablemente va a ser una serenata con *Las mañanitas*, una canción popular mexicana.

Las maquiladoras situadas cerca de la frontera de los EE.UU. ensamblan los componentes de automóviles y aparatos electrónicos. Aunque las maquiladoras son tan importantes para la economía mexicana como para la norteamericana, los trabajadores mexicanos reciben sueldos (*wages*) muy inferiores a los sueldos de los norteamericanos.

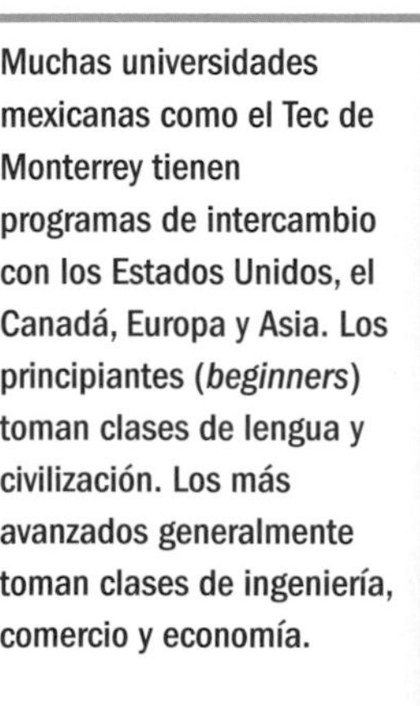

Muchas universidades mexicanas como el Tec de Monterrey tienen programas de intercambio con los Estados Unidos, el Canadá, Europa y Asia. Los principiantes (*beginners*) toman clases de lengua y civilización. Los más avanzados generalmente toman clases de ingeniería, comercio y economía.

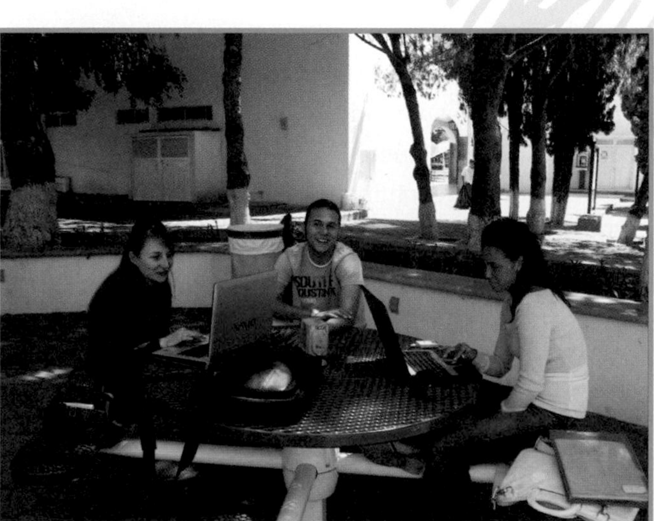

3-48 ¿Dónde? Identify a place on the map of Mexico where you might find the following.

1. playas
2. ruinas arqueológicas
3. música folklórica
4. la casa de Frida Kahlo y Diego Rivera
5. coral
6. figuras de madera (*wood*)

3-49 ¿Cómo es México? Complete each statement logically.

1. México es nuestro vecino del...
   a. norte. b. sur. c. este.
2. La isla de Cozumel es popular entre...
   a. los artistas. b. los turistas. c. los diplomáticos.
3. Los mariachis se originaron en...
   a. la ciudad de Guadalajara.
   b. la frontera con los Estados Unidos.
   c. la costa del Caribe.
4. Los mariachis cantan...
   a. jazz y rock. b. música folklórica. c. música espiritual.
5. Los trabajadores de las maquiladoras son...
   a. aztecas. b. estadounidenses. c. mexicanos.
6. Frida Kahlo...
   a. vive en la capital. b. es famosa por sus pinturas. c. es actriz.
7. En cada región de México hay...
   a. artesanía. b. maquiladoras. c. pirámides.
8. En muchas universidades mexicanas hay...
   a. programas de televisión.
   b. programas de música folklórica.
   c. estudiantes de intercambio.

WWW

3-50 Investigar. Connect with your **¡Arriba!** web site to see more images by Frida Kahlo and Diego Rivera. Choose one picture or mural that you like and write a brief description. Use these questions as a guide.

1. ¿Cómo se llama la pintura? ¿Quién es el artista?
2. ¿Hay personas? ¿Cuántas? ¿Cómo son?
3. ¿Hay objetos? ¿Qué son?
4. ¿Hay animales? ¿Cómo son?
5. ¿Qué colores predominan?
6. ¿Te gusta la pintura?

Ritmos

3-64

"La Bamba" (Mariachi Vargas de Tecalitlán, México)

This song, which was made popular in the United States by the Mexican American pop singer Ritchie Valens, is an example of *mariachi* music, which has its roots in the Mexican state of Jalisco and is influenced by Spanish, African, and native traditions. *Mariachi* music, which is played primarily by string instruments such as guitars and violins, can be characterized by enthusiastic and "catchy" rhythms and lyrics, whether the theme is one of sadness and heartbreak or one of a playful and lighthearted nature. Lyrics to traditional songs may also vary, as performers improvise; this is the case with the version of "La Bamba" by Mariachi Vargas de Tecalitlán.

Antes de escuchar

3-51 La letra. Work in pairs to find the meaning of one of the following lines of the lyrics to "La Bamba" and then share your findings with your classmates.

1. ... para cantar la bamba se necesita una poca de gracia...
2. ... yo no soy marinero, por ti seré...
3. ... cuando canto la bamba yo estoy contento...
4. ... yo no soy marinero, soy capitán...
5. ... que bonita es la bamba en la madrugada cuando todos la bailan...

3-52 A conversar. Use the following questions as a guide to discuss the song.

1. ¿Cuál es/son el/los tema/s de la canción?
2. ¿Qué opinión tienes de la letra (*lyrics*)?
3. ¿Qué palabras asocian tus compañeros y tú con la canción?

A escuchar

3-53 La canción. As you listen to "La Bamba" complete the following sentences with the correct form of **ser** or **estar** based on what you already know about the song and on what you hear and read in the lyrics.

1. "La Bamba" _____ una canción mariachi y _____ de origen mexicano.
2. Richie Valens _____ el artista que escribió (*wrote*) esta canción *pop*.
3. Cuando cantan, los narradores de "La Bamba" _____ muy felices y emocionados.
4. Dos instrumentos típicos en la música mariachi _____ la guitarra y el violín.

Después de escuchar

3-54 Expresiones. The Spanish word *arriba*, which is the title of this textbook and which can be found in *La Bamba*, means "up" or "upward." It is also an exclamation — *¡Arriba!* — and when used this way can mean "All right!" or "Let's go!" Look at the following Mexican exclamations and try to match them to their English meanings. Then, with a partner, practice saying them aloud with the correct Spanish pronunciation and intonation.

1. _____ ¡Ándale!	a. *What a surprise!*
2. _____ ¡Híjole!	b. *Disgusting!*
3. _____ ¡Está padrísimo!	c. *Let's go!*
4. _____ ¡Qué chido!	d. *Fantastic!*
5. _____ ¡Guácala!	e. *How nice!*

Páginas

3-65

El Museo de Antropología de México

Antes de leer

3-55 Una hipótesis. Use the text format, title, and other visual clues or background knowledge to get an idea of what the text is about. As you read, test your hypothesis to see if your initial guesses were correct. Sometimes, you will have to revise your hypothesis as you read.

3-56 Formular una hipótesis. Answer these questions before reading to formulate a hypothesis about its content.

1. ¿Dónde? 2. ¿Quiénes? 3. ¿Cuándo?

A leer

3-57 El museo. Read the following text to discover more about this world-famous museum.

El Museo Nacional de Antropología del Distrito Federal de México fue inaugurado en 1964 para albergar *(house)* lo más representativo de los avances de la época en la investigación antropológica sobre el mundo prehispánico y sus descendientes, los pueblos indígenas de México.

La Sala de los mayas en el museo contiene una importante colección de piezas *(pieces, items)* de las ancestrales comunidades mayas, que nos permiten apreciar diferentes etapas *(stages)* y escenarios de su historia y su visión del mundo. En la sala hay testimonios de la vida diaria *(daily)*, de sus costumbres y tradiciones en torno a *(pertaining to)* la guerra *(war)*, al comercio y a su pensamiento *(thought)* religioso con prácticas rituales.

Los mayas desarrollaron una brillante cultura, construyendo grandes centros cívico-ceremoniales con pirámides y bellas obras *(works)* de arte.

De martes a domingo de 9:00 a 19:00 hrs.
El lunes permanece cerrado.

ADMISIÓN:

$45.00 M.N., de martes a sábado

Exentos de pago de 9:00 a 17:00 hrs:

- Niños menores de 13 años
- Estudiantes y profesores con credencial vigente *(in force; in effect)*
- Adultos mayores de 60 años
- Jubilados *(retired persons)*, pensionados y discapacitados *(disabled)*
- Pasantes *(teachers)* e investigadores *(researchers)* que cuenten con el permiso del INAH (Instituto Nacional de Antropología e Historia)
- Todos los visitantes están exentos de pago los domingos de 9:00 a 17:00 hrs.

Source: Ceremonial procession—detail of musicians. From Mayan Fresco Series found at Bonampak. (East wall, room 1). Museo Nacional de Antropologia, Mexico City, D.F., Mexico. © SEF/Art Resource, NY.

Después de leer

3-58 ¿Comprendiste? Complete each statement logically.

1. El museo está en…
   a. Teotihuacán. b. México, D.F. c. Cancún.
2. La colección maya incluye…
   a. figuras de guerreros.
   b. pinturas de los años 1950.
   c. animales prehistóricos.
3. La colección refleja…
   a. la vida religiosa.
   b. las fiestas del pueblo.
   c. el uso de animales domésticos.
4. Si no quieres pagar, lo visitas el…
   a. sábado. b. domingo. c. lunes.
5. Los martes no paga(n)…
   a. nadie (*no one*). b. las mujeres. c. los adultos mayores de 60 años.

3-59 El Museo de Antropología. Connect with your **¡Arriba!** web site to visit this renowned museum in Mexico City. Look for the following information.

1. tres salas permanentes
2. una exposición temporal
3. una pieza interesante

3-60 En mi opinión. Compare your opinions with a classmate's by responding to the following statements.

Sí, seguramente… Sí, probablemente… No…

1. Voy a visitar México algún día.
2. Voy a visitar el Museo de Antropología.
3. Voy a visitar las pirámides.
4. Me gusta la arqueología.
5. Me gusta el arte.

Taller

3-66 to 3-67

3-61 Una carta personal.

Monterrey, 14 de octubre de 2007

Querida Raquel:

Hoy es 14 de octubre y estoy aquí en la biblioteca del Tec...

Un abrazo de...

Antes de escribir

- Respond to these questions before writing a letter to a friend or family member about your student experience.

¿Cuál es la fecha de hoy?

¿Dónde estás?

¿Te gusta la universidad?

¿Qué estudias este semestre (trimestre/año)?

¿A qué hora son tus clases?

¿Recibes buenas notas (*grades*)?

¿Cómo son los profesores?

¿Con quién asistes a tus clases?

¿Dónde comes?

¿Adónde vas por la noche?

¿Dónde haces tu tarea?

¿Qué vas a hacer mañana?

¿...?

A escribir

- Use the letter format above, beginning with the place, date, and a greeting.
- Incorporate your answers to the previous questions in the letter. Connect your ideas with words such as **y, pero,** and **porque.**
- Ask your addressee for a reply to your letter.
- Close the letter with a farewell: **Un abrazo de...**

Después de escribir

- **Revisar.** Review the following elements of your letter:
  - ☐ use of **ir, hacer,** and other **-er** and **-ir** verbs
  - ☐ use of **ser** and **estar**
  - ☐ agreement of subjects and verbs
  - ☐ agreement of nouns and adjectives
  - ☐ correct spelling, including accents
- **Intercambiar**
  Exchange your letter with a classmate's; make grammatical corrections and content suggestions. Then, respond to the letter.
- **Entregar**
  Rewrite your original letter, incorporating your classmate's suggestions. Then, turn in your revised letter and the response from your classmate to your instructor.

Vocabulario

Primera parte

Las materias	*(Academic) Subjects*
la administración de empresas	*business administration*
el álgebra	*algebra*
la antropología	*anthropology*
la arquitectura	*architecture*
el arte	*art*
la biología	*biology*
el cálculo	*calculus*
las ciencias políticas	*political science*
las ciencias sociales	*social science*
las comunicaciones	*communications*
la contabilidad	*accounting*
el derecho	*law*
el diseño	*design*
la educación física	*physical education*
la estadística	*statistics*
la filosofía	*philosophy*
las finanzas	*finance*
la física	*physics*
la geografía	*geography*
la geología	*geology*
la historia	*history*
la informática/ la computación	*computer science*
la ingeniería	*engineering*
la ingeniería eléctrica	*electrical engineering*
la literatura	*literature*
las matemáticas	*mathematics*
la medicina	*medicine*
la música	*music*
la pedagogía	*teaching*
la psicología	*psychology*
la química	*chemistry*
la sociología	*sociology*
la veterinaria	*veterinary science*

Sustantivos	*Nouns*
el chico/la chica	*boy/girl*
la computadora	*computer*
el horario (de clases)	*(class) schedule*
el semestre	*semester*
el trimestre	*trimester*

Adverbios	*Adverbs*
bastante	*quite; fairly*
después de	*after*
solamente	*only*

Adjetivos	*Adjectives*
complicado/a	*complicated*
exigente	*challenging; demanding*

Segunda parte

Los edificios de la universidad	*University buildings*
el auditorio	*auditorium*
la biblioteca	*library*
la cafetería	*cafeteria*
la cancha de tenis	*tennis court*
el centro estudiantil	*student union*
el estadio	*stadium*
la Facultad de Arte	*School of Art*
la Facultad de Ciencias	*School of Science*
la Facultad de Derecho	*School of Law*
la Facultad de Filosofía y Letras	*School of Humanities*
la Facultad de Ingeniería	*School of Engineering*
la Facultad de Matemáticas	*School of Mathematics*
la Facultad de Medicina	*School of Medicine*
el gimnasio	*gymnasium*
el laboratorio de lenguas	*language laboratory*
la librería	*bookstore*
el museo	*museum*
el observatorio	*observatory*
la rectoría	*President's office*
el teatro	*theatre*

¿Dónde está?	*Where is...?*
cerca (de)	*nearby (close to)*
delante (de)	*in front of*
detrás (de)	*behind*
a la derecha (de)	*to (on) the right (of)*
enfrente (de)	*facing; across from*
entre	*between*
a la izquierda (de)	*to (on) the left (of)*
al lado (de)	*next to*
lejos (de)	*far (from)*

Adverbios	*Adverbs*
siempre	*always*
sólo	*only*

Expresiones	*Expressions*
pues	*well*

Verbos	*Verbs*
estar	*to be*
hacer	*to do; to make*
ir	*to go*

Expressions with todo/a/os/as	*See page 78.*
Numbers 101–3,000,000	*See page 81.*
Possessive adjectives	*See page 83.*
Expressions with *tener*	*See page 85.*

4 ¿Cómo es tu familia?

PRIMERA PARTE

¡Así lo decimos! Vocabulario	Miembros de la familia	• Talking about your family
¡Así lo hacemos! Estructuras	The present tense of stem-changing verbs: **e → ie, e → i, o → ue**	• Expressing desires and preferences
	Direct objects, the personal **a,** and direct object pronouns	• Planning activities
	The present tense of **poner, salir,** and **traer**	
Comparaciones	La familia hispana	

SEGUNDA PARTE

¡Así lo decimos! Vocabulario	El ocio	• Extending invitations
¡Así lo hacemos! Estructuras	Demonstrative adjectives and pronouns	• Making spatial references
	Saber and **conocer**	• Discussing things you know
Observaciones	¡Pura vida! Episodio 4	

NUESTRO MUNDO

Panoramas	La América Central I: Guatemala, El Salvador, Honduras
Ritmos	"Marimba con punta" (Los Profesionales, Honduras)
Páginas	"Querida Dolores"
Taller	Una invitación

Rigoberta Menchú recibió el Premio Nobel por su lucha por los derechos humanos de los indígenas de Guatemala.

La América Central I: Guatemala, El Salvador, Honduras

«Al hombre mayor, dale honor.»*

*__Refrán:__ Respect your elders.

La civilización maya era (*was*) una de las más avanzadas de las Américas.

PRIMERA PARTE

¡Así lo decimos! Vocabulario

CD 1, Track 23

4-1 to 4-2

¡Así es la vida! Un correo electrónico

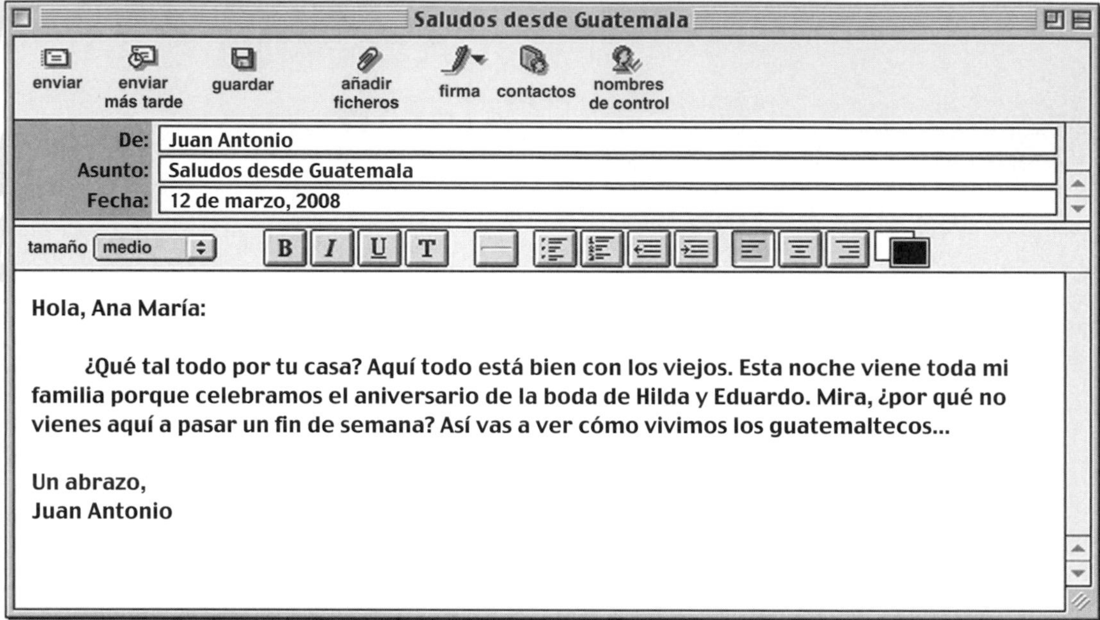

Saludos desde Guatemala

enviar | enviar más tarde | guardar | añadir ficheros | firma | contactos | nombres de control

De: Juan Antonio
Asunto: Saludos desde Guatemala
Fecha: 12 de marzo, 2008

tamaño medio

Hola, Ana María:

¿Qué tal todo por tu casa? Aquí todo está bien con los viejos. Esta noche viene toda mi familia porque celebramos el aniversario de la boda de Hilda y Eduardo. Mira, ¿por qué no vienes aquí a pasar un fin de semana? Así vas a ver cómo vivimos los guatemaltecos...

Un abrazo,
Juan Antonio

Miembros de la familia

CD 1, Track 24

4-3 to 4-6

la abuela

el abuelo

Eduardo, el esposo de Hilda

la hermana, Hilda

el hermano

Juan Antonio

la madre

el padre

la prima

la tía

el tío

Otros miembros de la familia	***Other family members***
el/la cuñado/a	*brother-in-law/sister-in-law*
el/la hermanastro/a	*stepbrother/stepsister*
el/la hijo/a	*son/daughter*
la madrastra	*stepmother*
el/la nieto/a	*grandson/granddaughter*
el/la novio/a	*boyfriend/girlfriend; groom/bride*
la nuera	*daughter-in-law*
el padrastro	*stepfather*
el/la sobrino/a	*nephew/niece*
el/la suegro/a	*father-in-law/mother-in-law*
el yerno	*son-in-law*

Verbos	***Verbs***
almorzar (ue)	*to have lunch*
costar (ue)	*to cost*
dormir (ue)	*to sleep*
empezar (ie)	*to begin*
encontrar (ue)	*to find*
entender (ie)	*to understand*
jugar a (ue)	*to play*
pasar	*to spend (time)*
pensar (ie)	*to think*
pedir (i)	*to ask for; to request*
perder (ie)	*to lose*
poder (ue)	*to be able; can*
poner	*to put; to place*
preferir (ie)	*to prefer*
querer (ie)	*to want; to love*
recordar (ue)	*to remember*
repetir (i)	*to repeat*
salir	*to leave; to go out*
servir (i)	*to serve*
soñar (ue) (con)	*to dream (about)*
traer	*to bring*
venir (ie)	*to come*
volver (ue)	*to return*

Adjetivos	***Adjectives***
casado/a	*married*
divorciado/a	*divorced*
mayor	*older*
menor	*younger*
soltero/a	*single; unmarried*
unido/a	*close; close-knit*

Aplicación

4-1 ¿Quién es mayor? Look at the drawing of Juan Antonio's family and decide who is older and who is younger.

MODELO: el padre de Hilda, o el esposo de ella
El padre es mayor. El esposo es menor.

1. la hermana de Juan Antonio, o su abuela
2. la madre de Juan Antonio, o su abuelo
3. el hermanito de Juan Antonio, o su cuñado
4. la prima de Juan Antonio, o su hermano
5. el tío de Juan Antonio, o la sobrina de su madre

Joaquín Beléndez Buenahora
Hilda Ferrero Bravo
y
José Luis Sosa Loret de Mola
María Elena Fernández de Sosa
tienen el honor de invitarle
al matrimonio de sus hijos
Hilda Teresa y
Eduardo Antonio
el viernes veintiséis de mayo
de dos mil siete
a las tres de la tarde
Misa Nupcial en
Iglesia San Jorge
Guatemala, Guatemala

4-2 La boda (*wedding*) de Hilda y Eduardo. Answer the following questions based on the wedding invitation.

1. ¿Quiénes son los novios?
2. ¿Cómo se llama el padre del novio?
3. ¿Cómo se llama la madre?
4. ¿Quiénes son los padres de la novia?
5. ¿Cuál es el nombre completo de Hilda antes de casarse (*getting married*)?[1]
6. ¿Cuál es el nombre completo de Hilda después de casarse?
7. ¿Dónde es la ceremonia?
8. ¿En qué fecha y a qué hora es la ceremonia?

[1]See **Comparaciones: Nombres, apellidos y apodos** in **Capítulo 2** for information on Hispanic last names.

CD 1, Track 25

4-3 Entre familia. Listen to Eduardo describe his family. As he talks, complete Eduardo's family tree, writing in the names of the three generations of family members that he discusses.

4-4 ¿Quién es quién? Take another look at the family tree you completed in **4-3** and give the relationships for each of these people.

Modelo: *Eduardo es el hijo de José Luis... (etc.)*

4-5 Tu árbol genealógico. Draw your family tree, or an imaginary one. Then tell your partner about the family based on the tree.

¡Así lo hacemos! Estructuras

4-7 to 4-15

1. The present tense of stem-changing verbs: *e → ie, e → i, o → ue*

You have already learned how to form regular **-ar, -er,** and **-ir** verbs and a few irregular verbs. This group of verbs, including **querer,** requires a change in the stem vowel[1] of the present indicative forms, except **nosotros/as** and **vosotros/as.**

querer (*to want; to love*)			
yo	qu**ie**ro	nosotros/as	queremos
tú	qu**ie**res	vosotros/as	queréis
él, ella, Ud.	qu**ie**re	ellos/as, Uds.	qu**ie**ren

El cambio e → ie

empezar	*to begin*
entender	*to understand*
pensar *(+ infinitive)*	*to think; to plan (to do something)*
perder	*to lose*
preferir	*to prefer*

Te **quiero,** mi amor.	*I love you, my love.*
Pensamos mucho en nuestro abuelo.	*We think about our grandfather a lot.*
Pienso ver una película esta noche.	*I plan to see a movie tonight.*
¿A qué hora **empieza** la función?	*At what time does the show start?*

[1]In these forms the stem contains the stressed syllable.

- Some common **e** → **ie** verbs, such as **tener** and **venir** (*to come*), have an additional irregularity in the first person singular.

	tener	venir
yo	**tengo**	**vengo**
tú	tienes	vienes
él, ella, Ud.	tiene	viene
nosotros/as	tenemos	venimos
vosotros/as	tenéis	venís
ellos/as, Uds.	tienen	vienen

Tengo que pasar por mi novia a las ocho.	*I have to stop by for my girlfriend at eight.*
Si Ester y Rubén **vienen** el viernes, yo **vengo** también.	*If Ester and Rubén come Friday, I'll come too.*

El cambio e → i

Another stem-changing pattern changes the stressed **e** of the stem to **i** in all forms except the first- and second-person informal plural.

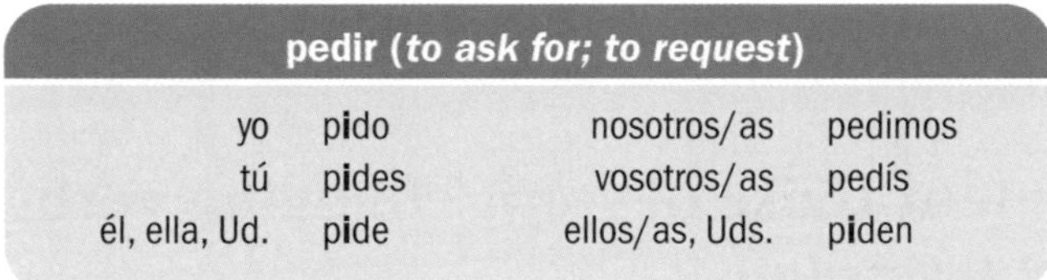

pedir (*to ask for; to request*)			
yo	p**i**do	nosotros/as	pedimos
tú	p**i**des	vosotros/as	pedís
él, ella, Ud.	p**i**de	ellos/as, Uds.	p**i**den

- All **e** → **i** stem-changing verbs have the **-ir** ending. The following are some other common **e** → **i** verbs.

repetir	*to repeat; to have a second helping*
servir	*to serve*

La instructora **repite** las oraciones sólo una vez.	*The instructor repeats the sentences only one time.*
¿**Servimos** la sopa primero?	*Do we serve the soup first?*

El cambio o → ue

volver (*to return; to come back*)			
yo	v**ue**lvo	nosotros/as	volvemos
tú	v**ue**lves	vosotros/as	volvéis
él, ella, Ud.	v**ue**lve	ellos/as, Uds.	v**ue**lven

- Another category of stem-changing verbs is one in which the stressed **o** changes to **ue.** As with **e** → **ie** and **e** → **i,** there is no stem change in the **nosotros/as** and **vosotros/as** forms.

- Other commonly used **o** → **ue** stem-changing verbs are:

almorzar	*to have lunch*
costar[1]	*to cost*
dormir	*to sleep*
encontrar	*to find*
jugar[2] **a**	*to play*
poder	*to be able; can*
recordar	*to remember*
soñar (con)	*to dream (about)*

Mañana **juego** al tenis con mi tía.	*Tomorrow I'm playing tennis with my aunt.*
Almorzamos con mis abuelos todos los domingos.	*We have lunch with my grandparents every Sunday.*
¿**Sueñas con** ser rico algún día?	*Do you dream about being rich one day?*
No **recuerdo** a mi tía muy bien.	*I don't remember my aunt very well.*

Aplicación

4-6 ¿Quién dice qué? At family functions people often seem to all be talking at once. Match the questions and statements on the left with logical rejoinders on the right.

1. _____ Oye, Pancho, ¿cuándo vuelves a casa esta noche?
2. _____ Sarita, ¿quieres agua *(water)* o un refresco *(soft drink)*?
3. _____ Tomás, ¿a qué hora vienes mañana?
4. _____ Abuelita, ¿puedes jugar con los niños?
5. _____ Papá, ¿vas a dormir todo el día?
6. _____ Toño, son las ocho y media. ¿Cuándo empieza la fiesta?
7. _____ Pedro, ¿quiénes juegan en la serie mundial?
8. _____ Tía, ¿quién sirve los refrescos?

a. Prefiero café, por favor.
b. Es que no duermo bien por la noche.
c. Vuelvo antes de la medianoche.
d. Empieza a las nueve y media.
e. Seguramente los Astros de Houston.
f. Yo sirvo el café; tu tío sirve la limonada.
g. Vengo a las cinco y media.
h. Ahora, no. Juego con ellos más tarde.

---

[1]**Costar** is conjugated only in the third person of singular and plural.

[2]**Jugar** follows the same pattern as **o** → **ue** verbs, but the change is **u** → **ue.**

4-7 Una entrevista con Rigoberta Menchú. Rigoberta Menchú received the Nobel Peace Prize in 1992 for her work with the indigenous peoples of Guatemala. Read the interview with her and underline all of the stem-changing verbs.

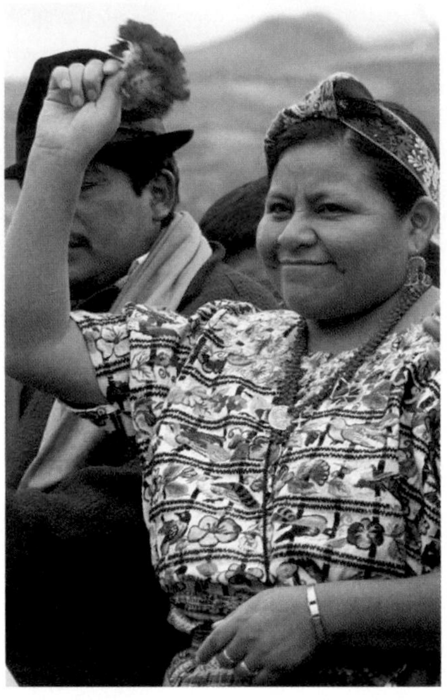

Reportera: Señora, usted es famosa por su trabajo con los indígenas de Guatemala. ¿Qué piensa hacer ahora?

Rigoberta: Pienso trabajar por los derechos humanos para todos los guatemaltecos.

Reportera: ¿Viene a Washington este año?

Rigoberta: No, pero sirvo en un comité de las Naciones Unidas. Por eso, pienso ir a Nueva York.

Reportera: ¿Recuerda bien la ceremonia de los Premios Nobel?

Rigoberta: Sí, recuerdo muy bien la ceremonia, pero no puedo recordar los nombres de toda la gente. Algún día voy a volver a Estocolmo para visitar los museos también.

Reportera: ¿Con qué sueña usted, señora?

Rigoberta: Sueño con la paz en el mundo.

4-8 ¿Comprendes? Answer the following questions based on the interview.

1. ¿Por qué es famosa Rigoberta Menchú?
2. ¿Qué piensa hacer este año?
3. ¿Por qué va a Nueva York?
4. ¿Qué no recuerda bien de su tiempo en Estocolmo?
5. ¿Por qué quiere volver a Estocolmo?
6. ¿Con qué sueña ahora?

4-9 Ana María y Juan Antonio hacen planes. Juan Antonio has invited his friend, Ana María, to visit him in Guatemala. Complete her explanation with a logical verb from the list. (In some cases you have a choice of more than one verb.)

cuestan	juego	piensa	pierdo	queremos
entiende	pensamos	prefiero	puede	quiere

Juan Antonio y yo (1) ___________ hacer planes para el viernes. Nosotros (2) ___________ ir al cine. Juan Antonio (3) ___________ ver una película (*movie*) de acción pero para mí no son interesantes. Yo (4) ___________ las películas francesas, pero Juan Antonio no (5) ___________ francés. Su madre (6) ___________ que debemos jugar al tenis. Juan Antonio (7) ___________ jugar al tenis, pero yo no (8) ___________ muy bien. A Juan Antonio le gusta jugar conmigo porque yo siempre (9) ___________. También hay un concierto el viernes, pero los boletos (*tickets*) (10) ___________ mucho. ¡Es mejor pasar el viernes en casa con la familia!

4-10 ¿Y tu familia? Use the following information to form at least six sentences in Spanish that describe your activities and those of your friends and family. Add other words as necessary.

Modelo: *Almuerzo con mis amigos en la cafetería.*

yo	**almorzar**	temprano (tarde)
tú	pedir	**cafetería**
mis padres	pensar	fútbol (tenis, béisbol…)
mi abuelo/a	dormir	casa (restaurante…)
tú y yo	soñar (con)	estudiar mucho
mi hermano/a	jugar (al)	cantar (bailar…)
mi mejor amigo/a	recordar	dinero (novio/a)
mis primos	volver (a)	planes para…
mis tíos	querer	todos los días (mañana…)
¿…?	poder	mucho (poco)

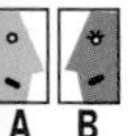

4-11A El/La curioso/a. Take turns asking each other about your family. Use the following questions to get started. Be sure to conjugate the verbs in italics. Student B, please see **Appendix 1,** page A4.

TUS PREGUNTAS

1. ¿Cuándo almuerzas con la familia?
2. ¿Prefieren ustedes comer en casa o en un restaurante?
3. ¿Qué sirven en una cena especial?
4. Después de una cena especial, ¿duermen o ven la televisión?
5. ¿Dónde prefieres vivir, en casa con tu familia o en un apartamento? ¿Por qué?

POSIBLES RESPUESTAS A LAS PREGUNTAS DE TU COMPAÑERO/A

Todos nosotros *dormir* la siesta.

Servir la comida a las seis.

Pensar ir al cine con ellos.

No, *poder* ver siempre mis programas favoritos.

Volver a las…

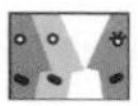 **4-12 Festival de cine.** Take a look at the movies that will be shown during a Latin film festival and decide which of the movies are most popular among your group and why. Below are some of the types of movies.

MODELO: *Quiero ver* Volver *porque prefiero las películas sentimentales.*

PELÍCULAS...
- de acción
- sentimentales
- románticas
- de misterio
- trágicas
- humorísticas
- del director español Almodóvar
- realistas
- peruanas/argentinas/españolas

En el cine

Volver (2006, España) *****

Género: Comedia dramática, sentimental
Director: Pedro Almodóvar
Interpretación: Penélope Cruz, Carmen Maura...

Se basa en la vida y los recuerdos del director sobre su madre y del lugar donde se crió.

Ojos que no ven (2005, Perú) ***

Género: Drama, misterio, suspenso
Director: Francisco José Lombardi
Interpretación: Daniel Hendler

Tiene lugar durante la presidencia de Alberto Fujimori. La política es el contexto en el que se narran historias sobre las personas afectadas por la descomposición moral que inundó la sociedad peruana.

Doble juego (2004, Perú) ****

Género: Comedia dramática
Director: Alberto Durant
Interpretación: Fabrizio Aguilar

Un cineasta *(filmmaker)* es víctima de un doble juego *(scam)*...

El destino no tiene favoritos (2003 Perú) ***

Género: Comedia romántica
Director: Álvaro Velarde
Interpretación: Angélica María Cepeda Jiménez

Ana es una mujer rica que permite que se filme una telenovela en su casa. Ella, junto con todos los que trabajan en su casa, quiere ser parte de la acción.

El fondo del mar (2003, Argentina) ****

Género: Drama psicológico *(thriller)*
Director: Damián Szifrón
Interpretación: Daniel Hendler

1967 – En un país imaginario de América Latina, que vive bajo la dictadura del General Abalorio, Arcibel Alegría, un joven de veintiséis años, sospecha que su novia tiene otro...

2. Direct objects, the personal *a*, and direct object pronouns

4-16 to 4-24

Los complementos directos

- A direct object is the noun that generally follows, and receives the action of, the verb. The direct object is identified by asking *whom* or *what* about the verb. Note that the direct object can either be an inanimate object (**un carro**) or a person (**su amigo Luis**).

Pablo va a comprar **un carro.**	*Pablo is going to buy a car.*
Anita llama **a su amigo Luis.**	*Anita calls her friend Luis.*

La *a* personal

- When the direct object is a definite person or persons, an **a** precedes the noun in Spanish. This is known as the personal **a.** However, the personal **a** is omitted after the verb **tener** when it means *to have* or *possess*.

Quiero mucho **a** mi papá.	*I love my father a lot.*
Julia y Ricardo tienen un hijo.	*Julia and Ricardo have a son.*

- The personal **a** is not used with a direct object that is an unspecified or indefinite person.

Ana quiere un novio inteligente.	*Ana wants an intelligent boyfriend.*

- The preposition **a** followed by the definite article **el** contracts to form **al.**

Alicia visita **al** médico.	*Alicia visits the doctor.*

- When the interrogative **quién(es)** requests information about the direct object, the personal **a** precedes it.

¿**A** quién llama Elisa?	*Whom is Elisa calling?*

- The personal **a** is required before every specific human direct object in a series.

Visito **a** Emilio y **a** Lola.	*I visit Emilio and Lola.*

Los pronombres de complemento directo

A direct object noun is often replaced by a direct object pronoun. The chart below shows the forms of the direct object pronouns.

	Singular		Plural
me	*me*	**nos**	*us*
te	*you* (inf.)	**os**	*you* (inf.)
lo	*him, you, it* (masc.)	**los**	*you, them* (masc.)
la	*her, you, it* (fem.)	**las**	*you, them* (fem.)

- Direct object pronouns are generally placed directly before the conjugated verb. If the sentence is negative, the direct object pronoun goes between **no** and the verb.

¿**Me** esperas?	*Will you wait for me?*
No, no **te** espero.	*No, I won't wait for you.*

- Third-person direct object pronouns agree in gender and number with the noun they replace.

  Quiero **el dinero.** → **Lo** quiero.

  Necesitamos **los cuadernos.** → **Los** necesitamos.

  Llamo **a Mirta.** → **La** llamo.

  Buscamos **a las chicas.** → **Las** buscamos.

- Direct object pronouns are commonly used in conversation when the object is established or known. When the conversation involves first and second persons (*me, we, you*), remember to make the proper transitions.

¿Dónde ves **a Jorge** y **a Sarita**?	*Where do you see Jorge and Sarita?*
Los veo en clase.	*I see them in class.*
¿Visitas **a tu abuela** con frecuencia?	*Do you visit your grandmother often?*
Sí, **la** visito mucho.	*Yes, I visit her a lot.*

In constructions that use the infinitive, direct object pronouns may either precede the conjugated verb or be attached to the infinitive.

Adolfo va a llamar **a Ana.**	*Adolfo is going to call Ana.*
Adolfo va a llamar**la.** Adolfo **la** va a llamar.	*Adolfo is going to call her.*

- In negative sentences, the direct object pronoun is placed between **no** and the conjugated verb. The object pronoun may also be attached to the infinitive in negative sentences.

Adolfo no **la** va a llamar. Adolfo no va a llamar**la.**	*Adolfo is not going to call her.*

Aplicación

4-13 Planes para hacer un viaje a Centroamérica. Match each question with the corresponding response.

1. _____ ¿Dónde compramos los boletos (*tickets*)?
2. _____ ¿Tienes mi pasaporte?
3. _____ ¿A qué hora te busco en el aeropuerto?
4. _____ ¿Vamos a visitar el Museo Popol Vuh?
5. _____ ¿Es necesario cambiar dinero?
6. _____ ¿Quieres invitar a tu hermana también?

a. Sí, ¿quieres llamarla para ver si puede ir?
b. Me puedes buscar a las siete de la mañana.
c. Sí, lo podemos cambiar en el aeropuerto.
d. Los podemos comprar en una agencia de viajes (*travel agency*).
e. No, no lo tengo.
f. Sí, vamos a visitarlo el primer día.

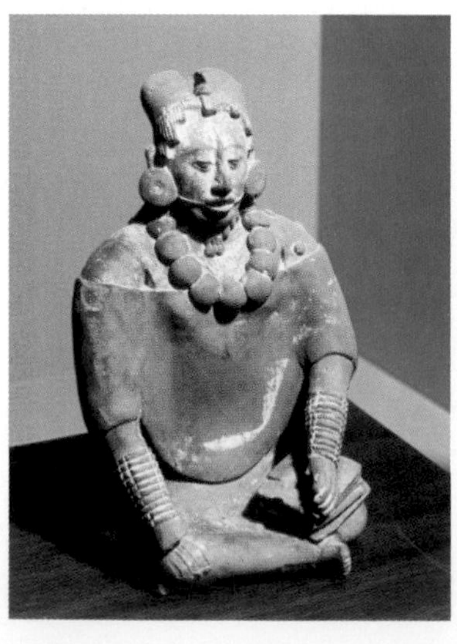

4-14 Una visita al Museo Popol Vuh. This museum houses an impressive collection of art and artifacts. Read about the museum and underline all direct objects.

> El Museo Popol Vuh reúne una de las mejores colecciones de arte prehispánico y colonial de Guatemala. La colección incluye obras maestras del arte maya elaboradas en cerámica, piedra (*stone*) y otros materiales. Además, posee un notable conjunto (*group*) de obras de platería e imaginería (*statuary*) colonial.
>
> El museo está en el Campus Central de la Universidad Francisco Marroquín, en la Ciudad de Guatemala. Este museo ofrece una oportunidad sin igual para apreciar la historia y cultura de Guatemala.
>
> *Dirección:* Avenida La Reforma, 8-60, Zona 9, 6to Piso.
> *Horario:* de lunes a sábado de 9:00 a 16:30 hrs.

4-15 ¿Cómo es el museo? Now answer the following questions based on what you have read about the museum in **4-14.**

1. ¿Dónde está el museo?
2. ¿Qué colecciones tiene?
3. ¿Por qué es importante?
4. ¿Cuándo está abierto?
5. ¿Lo quieres visitar algún (*some*) día?

4-16 En la universidad Francisco Marroquín. Read the conversation between Ana and Carlos, and write the personal **a** (or **al**) wherever necessary.

Ana: Oye, Carlos. ¿(1) _____ quién ves todos los días?

Carlos: Yo siempre veo (2) _____Tomás en la universidad. Tomamos (3) _____ café todas las tardes.

Ana: ¿Ven (4) _____ muchos amigos allí?

Carlos: Sí, claro. Siempre vemos (5) _____ Mercedes y (6) _____ Gustavo. A veces (*Sometimes*) sus compañeros de cuarto toman (7) _____ un refresco con nosotros también.

Ana: ¿Son interesantes sus compañeros de cuarto?

Carlos: Tomás y Gustavo tienen (8) _____ un compañero de cuarto muy simpático y la compañera de cuarto de Mercedes es muy sociable. Esta noche todos, menos Gustavo, vamos a ver (9) _____ una película muy buena. Gustavo no puede ir porque él tiene que visitar (10) _____ padre de su novia.

Ana: ¿Invitas (11) _____ mi amigo Héctor también?

Carlos: ¡Claro que sí!

4-17 Carlos en Tegucigalpa. Complete the exchanges between Carlos and his tour guide in Honduras. Use a direct object pronoun in each answer.

MODELO: GUÍA: ¿Tiene usted su pasaporte?
CARLOS: *Sí, lo tengo.*

Guía: ¿Estudia usted arquitectura colonial? Es muy bonita.

Carlos: 1. ____________

Guía: ¿Quiere usted ver los bailes folklóricos?

Carlos: 2. ____________

Guía: ¿Tiene usted su cámara?

Carlos: 3. ____________

Guía: ¿Ve usted el daño (*damage*) del huracán?

Carlos: 4. ____________

Guía: ¿Desea visitar las ruinas arqueológicas?

Carlos: 5. ____________

Guía: ¿Cuándo quiere visitar las montañas?

Carlos: 6. ____________

Guía: ¿Me llama usted esta noche?

Carlos: 7. ____________

La Iglesia de Nuestra Señora de Los Dolores, Tegucigalpa, Honduras.

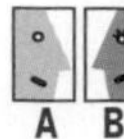
A B

4-18A Una entrevista para *Prensa Libre*. *Prensa Libre* is an independent newspaper from Guatemala. Role-play a reporter to ask your partner—a member of a famous family—questions about the following activities. Your partner will also ask you questions. Student B, please see **Appendix 1,** page A4.

MODELO: E1: *¿Practica usted fútbol?*
E2: *No, no lo practico. Y usted, ¿escribe artículos en inglés también?*
E1: *Sí, los escribo. (No, no los escribo.)*

ACTIVIDADES

leer el periódico todos los días
llamar a su esposo/a todas las noches
preferir la comida guatemalteca
querer mucho a sus hijos
recibir dinero del gobierno
tener muchos parientes en otros países
visitar al presidente de Guatemala
¿...?

4-25 to 4-29

3. The present tense of *poner, salir,* and *traer*

You have already learned some Spanish verbs that are irregular only in the first-person singular form of the present indicative tense **(hacer → hago; ver → veo)**. With these verbs, all other forms follow the regular conjugation patterns.

	poner *(to put; to place)*	salir *(to leave; to go out)*	traer *(to bring)*
yo	**pongo**	**salgo**	**traigo**
tú	pones	sales	traes
él, ella, Ud.	pone	sale	trae
nosotros/as	ponemos	salimos	traemos
vosotros/as	ponéis	salís	traéis
ellos/as, Uds.	ponen	salen	traen

Si **traes** tu libro, te ayudo con la tarea. — *If you bring your book, I'll help you with your homework.*

Siempre **salgo** a las ocho y veo a mis amigos allí. — *I always go out at eight and see my friends there.*

EXPANSIÓN **More on structure and usage**

Salir

Each of the following expressions with **salir** has its own meaning.

salir de: *to leave a place; to leave on a trip*

Salgo de casa a las siete.	*I leave home at seven.*
Salimos de viaje esta noche.	*We leave on a trip tonight.*

salir para: *to leave for (a place); to depart*

Mañana **salen para** Tegucigalpa.	*Tomorrow they leave for Tegucigalpa.*
¿**Sales para** las montañas ahora?	*Are you leaving for the mountains now?*

salir con: *to go out with; to date*

Diana **sale con** Lorenzo.	*Diana goes out with Lorenzo.*
Lucía **sale con** sus amigas esta tarde.	*Lucía is going out with her friends this afternoon.*

salir a (+ infinitive): *to go out (to do something)*

Salen a cenar los sábados.	*They go out to have dinner on Saturdays.*
¿**Sales a** caminar por la mañana?	*Do you go out walking in the morning?*

Aplicación

4-19 Eduardo e Hilda van a San Salvador. Complete the following paragraph using the correct form of a logical verb from the list below.

pone	salgo	salir	traigo
pongo	salimos	trae	veo

Esta tarde mi esposo Eduardo y yo (1) ____________ para la capital de El Salvador. Antes de (2) ____________, (yo) (3) ____________ la guía turística en mi maleta (*suitcase*). Después, (4) ____________ las noticias en la televisión para ver el pronóstico meteorológico para la capital. En mi oficina, mi secretaria me (5) ____________ el itinerario para el viaje. Ella (6) ____________ todos mis papeles en el maletín (*briefcase*). Ahora todo está en orden para el viaje. Mi esposo y yo vamos al aeropuerto dos horas antes del vuelo (*flight*). Desafortunadamente, cuando quiero pagar al taxista, veo que no (7) ____________ dinero. Afortunadamente, mi esposo tiene dinero, y yo después (8) ____________ a buscar un cajero automático.

4-20 En una fiesta familiar. Combine subjects and complements to say what people will do to get ready for the family gathering tonight.

MODELO: *Nosotros ponemos la casa en orden.*

yo	salir a comprar refrescos
nosotros/as	poner la mesa
mis tíos	traer comida
tú	salir a invitar a todos
nuestros padres	**poner la casa en orden**
mi abuela	hacer los sándwiches
mi primo	traer música
mi amigo	salir a buscar más sillas
¿...?	ver que todo está listo para la fiesta

Tegucigalpa
18 de agosto de 2007

Querida Hilda:
Como todos los sábados, tu padre y yo salimos con los señores Ramírez para visitar a tus abuelos en Copán. Tu tía Carlota prepara un pícnic y yo compro los platos y los refrescos. Tu papá lo pone todo en el coche. Salimos de casa a las ocho de la mañana y volvemos a las seis de la tarde. Como siempre, veo que tenemos muchos refrescos, pero poca comida. Por eso, por la noche todos salimos a un restaurante. Creo (I think) que hoy va a ser un día muy lindo.

Un beso y un abrazo,
-Mamá

4-21 Una carta de Mamá. Read the letter that Hilda received from her mother and respond to the questions that follow.

1. ¿Dónde viven los padres de Hilda?
2. ¿Dónde viven sus abuelos?
3. ¿Adónde van esa noche?
4. ¿Cómo va a ser el día?

4-22 ¿Con quién sale...? Take turns asking each other who the following people are dating; you can also add some names. Take note of the responses. Then ask for additional information, such as where they are going, what time they are leaving, and why they are going.

MODELO: Tom Cruise
E1: *¿Con quién sale Tom ahora?*
E2: *Sale con Katie Holmes.*
E1: *¿Adónde van?*
E2: *Van a Miami.*
E1: *¿A qué hora salen? ¿Por qué van?*
E2: *Salen a la medianoche. Van porque quieren hablar con los padres de Katie.*

tú	Juan González	el presidente de Guatemala
John Leguizamo	Alexis Bledel	Wilmer Valderrama
Jamie-Lynn Sigler	ustedes	su esposo/a
nosotros	Rigoberta Menchú	el ministro de cultura de Colombia
Batman	George López	la esposa del presidente de Honduras

4-23 Planes. Take turns finding out about each other's plans.

MODELO: ¿A qué hora salir/tú para...?
E1: *¿A qué hora sales para la casa de tu familia?*
E2: *Salgo para su casa a las diez de la mañana.*

1. ¿A qué hora salir/tú para...?
2. ¿Con quiénes ir/tú a...?
3. ¿Quién hacer...?
4. ¿Dónde poner/tú...?
5. ¿Quién traer...?
6. ¿Qué ver/tú...?

¿Cuánto sabes tú? *Can you...*

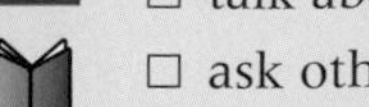
4-30 to 4-33

- ☐ talk about your family?
- ☐ ask others about their families?
- ☐ say what you want to do and make plans?
- ☐ talk about activities that you and others do using a variety of verbs?
- ☐ ask and respond to questions using direct objects and direct object pronouns?

Comparaciones

La familia hispana

4-24 En tu experiencia. ¿A quiénes consideras parte de tu núcleo familiar? ¿Cuántos miembros de tu familia viven en tu casa? ¿Dónde viven los otros miembros de tu familia? Y tú, ¿vives en una residencia estudiantil, en tu casa o en un apartamento? ¿Por qué? En las familias que conoces (*you know*), ¿quién cuida a los niños cuando los padres no están en casa? ¿Quién ayuda a los padres con los quehaceres (*chores*) de la casa? Lee el siguiente (*following*) artículo con esta pregunta en mente: ¿En qué consiste el concepto de familia para muchas personas del mundo hispano?

En los Estados Unidos, el núcleo familiar generalmente incluye sólo a los padres y a los hijos. Pero, el concepto hispano de familia puede incluir también a los abuelos, a los tíos y a los primos. Los miembros de una familia hispana suelen (*tend to*) vivir juntos más tiempo que los miembros de una familia estadounidense o canadiense. Los hijos solteros (*single*) generalmente viven en casa, aun (*even*) cuando trabajan o asisten a la universidad, pero esto está cambiando (*is changing*). En muchas casas hispanas, los padres, los hijos y un abuelo, tío o primo viven juntos. Las familias son muy unidas y forman un sistema de apoyo (*support*). Por ejemplo, un abuelo o abuela puede cuidar a los niños de la casa mientras los padres trabajan. Un tío soltero o una tía viuda (*widowed*) puede ayudar en la casa y formar parte de la familia y el hogar (*home*). Aunque (*Although*) la situación cambia poco a poco, los miembros de la familia que viven fuera de casa (*outside the home*) en muchos casos viven cerca —en la misma ciudad y a menudo (*often*) en el mismo barrio.

4-25 En tu opinión. Take turns reacting to each of the following statements.

Modelo: Me gusta vivir en casa de mis padres.
Estoy de acuerdo (I agree). / *No estoy de acuerdo.* / *No sé* (I don't know).

1. Para mí, el núcleo familiar consiste en los padres, los hijos y los abuelos y toda la familia política (*in-laws*).
2. Me gusta vivir cerca de mi familia.
3. Es bueno tener muchos hijos.
4. Tengo una buena relación con mis primos.
5. Los suegros deben vivir lejos de los recién casados (*newlyweds*).
6. Me gusta ir de fiesta con mis padres.
7. Me gusta la idea de vivir con abuelos, tíos y primos.
8. Me gusta vivir en casa de mis padres.

SEGUNDA PARTE

¡Así lo decimos! Vocabulario

CD 1, Track 26

4-34 to 4-35

¡Así es la vida! Una invitación

Laura: Aló.

Raúl: Sí, con Laura, por favor.

Laura: Habla Laura.

Raúl: Laura, es Raúl. ¿Cómo estás?... Pues, te llamo para ver si quieres ir al cine esta noche.

Laura: ¿Sabes qué película ponen?

Raúl: Sí, en el Cine Rialto ponen una película con John Leguizamo, *Tlatelolco: México 68*. Es a las siete. ¿Vamos?

El ocio

CD 1,
Track 27

4-36 to
4-38

el café al aire libre

el cine

la orquesta

el parque

el teatro

Palabras relacionadas	*Related words*
el centro	*downtown*
el concierto	*concert*
la entrada	*admission ticket*
la función	*show*
el partido	*game*
la película	*movie*

Verbos	*Verbs*
conocer	*to know (someone); to be familiar with (something)*
pasear	*to take a walk*
poner una película	*to show a movie*
saber	*to know (how to do) something*

Hacer una invitación	*Extending invitations*
¿Quieres ir a...?	*Do you want to go to...?*
¿Te gustaría (+ *inf.*)...?	*Would you like (+ inf.)...?*
¿Vamos a...?	*Should we go...?*

Aceptar una invitación	*Accepting invitations*
De acuerdo.	*Fine with me; Okay.*
Me encantaría.	*I would love to.*
Paso por ti.	*I'll come by for you.*
Sí, claro.	*Yes, of course.*
¡Vamos!	*Let's go!*

Rechazar una invitación	*Rejecting invitations*
Estoy muy ocupado/a.	*I'm very busy.*
Gracias, pero no puedo...	*Thanks, but I can't...*
Lo siento, tengo que...	*I'm sorry, I have to...*

EXPANSIÓN | **More on structure and usage**

En el teléfono

Aló **Bueno** (Mexico) **Diga** (Spain)	*Hello* (answering the telephone)

Te invito a . . .

Aplicación

4-26 Una invitación. State whether each statement is **Cierto** or **Falso** or **No se sabe,** based on the conversation between Laura and Raúl in **¡Así es la vida!** Correct any false statements.

1. ____________ Raúl invita a Laura al cine.
2. ____________ Raúl sabe qué película ponen.
3. ____________ Es una película colombiana.
4. ____________ La película es a las siete y media.
5. ____________ Laura pasa por la casa de Raúl.

4-27 Otras actividades. Complete this paragraph stating what each person does by completing the sentences with logical words or expressions from **¡Así lo decimos!**

Raúl y Laura van al (1) ____________ para ver una película. Caminan por (2) ____________ y van al cine, donde tienen que comprar (3) ____________. Después toman refrescos en un café (4) ____________. La música que toca la (5) ____________ es maravillosa. El día siguiente, Laura invita a Raúl a ir a un (6) ____________ de béisbol.

CD 1, Track 28

4-28 Marilú invita a José. Listen as Marilú and José talk on the telephone. Then complete each statement based on their conversation.

1. Marilú invita a José a ____________.
   a. bailar b. comer c. pasear por el parque
2. José acepta la invitación para ____________.
   a. esta noche b. mañana c. las tres de la tarde
3. Los chicos también van a ver ____________.
   a. un partido b. una película c. un programa de televisión
4. Es evidente que los chicos son ____________.
   a. hermanos b. novios c. amigos
5. Marilú y José no tienen que estudiar porque ____________.
   a. mañana no hay clases b. su clase es fácil c. no hay tarea para mañana

4-29 Ahora tú. Take turns inviting each other to do something together. Ask what day, where, what time, etc. Follow the model and complete the following phrases in your conversation.

MODELO: E1: *—Oye, ______. ¿Quieres ir ______?*
E2: *—No sé. ¿A qué hora?*
E1: *—A la/s...*

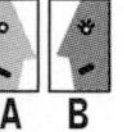

4-30A ¡Estoy aburrido/a! Tell a classmate that you are bored so that he/she will invite you to do something. Accept the invitation, or reject it, making excuses. Student B, please see **Appendix 1,** page A4.

MODELO: E1: *Estoy aburrido/a.*
E2: *¿Quieres ir a bailar?*
E1: *Me encantaría. ¡Vamos! / Gracias, pero no puedo. No tengo dinero.*

ALGUNAS EXCUSAS

estar cansado/a	no tener carro	no tener dinero
tener novio/a	no tener tiempo	tener mucho trabajo

4-31 El fin de semana. Make plans for this weekend. Use the questions below as a guide for your conversation. Prepare a summary for the class.

MODELO: *Vamos a un partido de fútbol el sábado a la una de la tarde. Después vamos a pasear por el centro y ver a nuestros amigos. Los invitamos a tomar un refresco en el Café Luna. Luego, volvemos a casa en autobús. Llegamos a casa a las siete y media.*

¿Adónde quieren ir?	¿Qué necesitan?	¿Con quiénes van?
¿Qué quieren hacer?	¿Qué día?	¿Quién paga?
¿Cómo es?	¿A qué hora empieza?	¿A qué hora vuelven a casa?

4-32 Una película histórica. Read the following movie plot summary and take turns answering the questions.

1. ¿Cómo se llama la película?
2. ¿En qué parte del mundo se produce?
3. ¿De dónde es el periodista?
4. ¿Por qué está en México?
5. ¿Quiénes son los actores?
6. ¿Quieres verla? ¿Por qué?

Tlatelolco: México 68

Género: Drama

Directores: Everardo Valerio Gout, Leopoldo Gout

Interpretación: **John Leguizamo, Vanessa Bauche**

Resumen: Un periodista estadounidense que cubre las Olimpiadas del Verano de 1968 en la Ciudad de México se involucra *(gets involved)* en los actos estudiantiles que llevaron a la masacre por el gobierno de centenares de estudiantes en el campus de Tlatelolco.

CD 1, Track 29

4-39 to 4-40

Letras y sonidos

Word stress and written accent marks in Spanish

Most words in Spanish (for example, all nouns, verbs, adjectives, and adverbs) carry word stress, where one syllable in the word is given special emphasis. It is important to hear and say word stress with accuracy, since it can affect meaning in Spanish, as it does in English: (Eng.) *sub*-ject (noun) versus *sub-ject* (verb); (Sp.) *pa-pa* ("potato") versus *pa-pá* ("dad"). In Spanish, word stress always falls on one of the last three syllables of the word: *tra-ba-ja-dor, in-te-li-gen-te, sim-pá-ti-co*. In some cases, word stress is indicated in writing with an accent mark, or *acento (ortográfico)*, according to the following rules.

1. Usually, words ending in a consonant (except *n* or *s*) are stressed on the *last syllable*.
   a-brir *ins-truc-tor* *es-pa-ñol* *re-loj* *us-ted* *ac-triz*
   Exceptions to this rule require a written accent mark.
   Víc-tor *ú-til* *di-fí-cil* *fút-bol* *lá-piz* *sánd-wich*
2. Usually, words ending in a vowel or the consonants *n* or *s* are stressed on the *second to last syllable.*
   bo-ni-ta *tra-ba-jo* *tra-ba-jan* *jo-ven* *tra-ba-jas* *no-so-tros*
   Exceptions to this rule require a written accent mark.
   es-tá *a-quí* *es-tán* *lec-ción* *es-tás* *in-glés*
3. Words with stress on the *third to last syllable* always require a written accent mark.
   nú-me-ro *mú-si-ca* *bo-lí-gra-fo* *jó-ve-nes* *miér-co-les*
4. Some words are identical in spelling but different in emphasis and meaning. In such cases, words with emphasis are marked with a written accent to differentiate them from the versions without emphasis which have a different meaning.
   él = he *tú* = you *mí* = (to) me *¿Qué?* = What? *¿Có-mo?* = How?
   el = the *tu* = your *mi* = my *que* = that *co-mo* = how, as, like
5. A written accent mark also is used with an *i* or *u* to indicate hiatus (i.e., when these letters, adjacent to another vowel, represent a separate syllable).
   dí-a *grú-a* *pa-ís* *Ra-úl*

¡Así lo hacemos! Estructuras

4. Demonstrative adjectives and pronouns

4-41 to 4-46

Demonstrative adjectives

	Singular	Plural		Related adverbs
masculine	**este**	**estos**	*this/these (close to me)*	aquí (*here*)
feminine	**esta**	**estas**		
masculine	**ese**	**esos**	*that/those (close to you)*	allí (*there*)
feminine	**esa**	**esas**		
masculine	**aquel**	**aquellos**	*that/those (over there; away from both of us)*	allá (*over there*)
feminine	**aquella**	**aquellas**		

- Demonstrative adjectives point out people and objects and the relative position and distance between the speaker and the object or person modified.
- Demonstrative adjectives are usually placed before the modified noun and agree with it in number and gender.

  ¿De quién son **esos** refrescos? — *To whom do those soft drinks belong?*

- Note that the **ese/esos** and **aquel/aquellos** forms, as well as their feminine counterparts, are equivalent to the English *that/those*. In normal, day-to-day usage, these forms are interchangeable, but the **aquel** forms are preferred to point out objects and people that are relatively farther away than others.

  Yo voy a comprar **esa** guitarra y **aquel** trombón. — *I am going to buy that guitar and that trombone (over there).*

- Demonstrative adjectives are usually repeated before each noun in a series.

  Esta película y **estos** actores son mis favoritos. — *This movie and these actors are my favorites.*

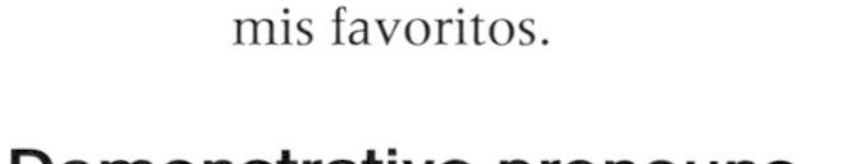

Demonstrative pronouns

	Singular	Plural	
masculine	**éste**	**éstos**	*this one/these ones (close to me)*
feminine	**ésta**	**éstas**	
masculine	**ése**	**ésos**	*that one/those ones (close to you)*
feminine	**ésa**	**ésas**	
masculine	**aquél**	**aquéllos**	*that/those (over there; away from both of us)*
feminine	**aquélla**	**aquéllas**	

- Note that when you omit the noun, the adjective becomes a pronoun and carries a written accent.

  ¿Ves a **ese** hombre alto y misterioso? — *Do you see that tall, mysterious man?*
  ¿Cuál? ¿**Ése** o **aquél**? — *Which one? That one (closer) or that one (farther away)?*

- The neuter forms **esto, eso,** and **aquello** do not take a written accent nor do they have plural forms. They are used to point out ideas, actions, or concepts, or to refer to unspecified objects or things.

Aquello no me gusta.	*I don't like that.*
No dije **eso.**	*I didn't say that.*
Esto está mal.	*This is wrong.*

- These forms are also used to ask for a definition of something.

¿Qué es **eso**?	*What's that?*
Es un teatro.	*It's a theater.*
¿Qué es **esto**?	*What's this?*
Es una fiesta.	*It's a party.*

Aplicación

4-33 De compras en la librería. Read the conversation between Ana and the clerk and underline the demonstrative adjectives and pronouns.

Ana: ¿Qué es esto? ¿Una enciclopedia?
Dependiente: Sí, señorita. Ésta es la mejor que tenemos. ¿La quiere ver?
Ana: No, prefiero ver aquélla que está cerca de la puerta.
Dependiente: ¿Aquélla? Es muy cara.
Ana: Ah, pues entonces voy a comprar estos cuadernos de aquí, en este estante (*bookshelf*). ¿Cuánto cuestan?
Dependiente: ¿Ésos? Son baratos, pero no son muy bonitos. Quizás (*Perhaps*) usted quiere comprar unos más atractivos con el logo de la universidad, ¿no?
Ana: Bueno, tengo que comprar una calculadora. Quiero ésa que tiene usted.
Dependiente: Lo siento, no puede comprar ésta, porque es mía.

4-34 ¿Dónde están? Now draw the objects mentioned in activity **4-33** where you would expect to find them in the illustration.

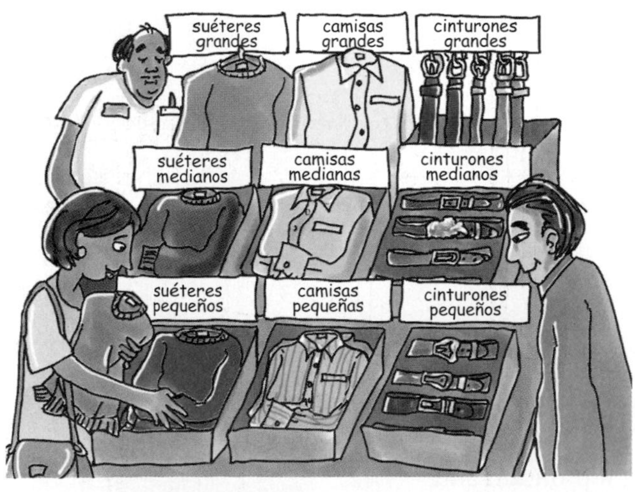

4-35 En un mercado en Tegucigalpa. Use demonstrative adjectives and pronouns to complete the conversation between Carlos, the vendor, and Amanda, the customer. Note that the currency used in Honduras is the *lempira.* ($1.00 US = 19 HNL)

Carlos: Buenas tardes, señorita. ¿Qué desea?
Amanda: Ummm... No sé. Quiero un suéter (*sweater*)... ¿Es de buena calidad (1) ____________ suéter morado que tiene usted? ¿O es mejor (2) ____________ de color azul que tengo yo?
Carlos: ¡Todos (3) ____________ suéteres son buenos! ¿Quiere usted probarse (*try on*) (4) ____________ de aquí?
Amanda: No, no es para mí. Es para mi amiga. ¿Cuánto cuesta?
Carlos: Para usted, 190 lempiras.
Amanda: ¡Es mucho! A ver... Las camisas (*shirts*) de colores de allá. Quiero ver una de (5) ____________ grandes.
Carlos: Sí, las camisas son de primera calidad.

Amanda: Y, ¿cuánto cuesta (6) ___________ camisa pequeña que tengo aquí?

Carlos: (7) ___________ que tiene usted allí… 170 lempiras.

Amanda: ¡Uf! Es mucho también. ¿Qué tal si le doy 300 lempiras por todo (8) ___________ que tengo aquí?

Carlos: ¡Ay, señorita! Pero, ¡la calidad, los colores…! Pero bueno, como usted es tan amable, le puedo dejar todo (9) ___________ que tiene allí en 320 lempiras.

Amanda: Perfecto. ¡Muchas gracias!

4-36 ¿Qué vas a comprar? Imagine that one of you is a vendor and the other a customer in the same market in Tegucigalpa. Use the drawing in activity **4-35** to ask and respond to questions about the merchandise.

MODELO: E1: *¿Vas a comprar esa camisa rosada?*
E2: *No, voy a comprar aquel suéter marrón.*

4-37 ¿Qué es esto? Take turns asking each other to identify classroom objects.

MODELO: E1: (point to table) *¿Qué es esto?*
E2: *Es una mesa. ¿Y esto?*
E1: *Es…*

4-38 Tu familia. Bring in a photo of your family or make a drawing of an imaginary family. Take turns asking about each of the family members.

MODELO: E1: *¿Quién es esa señora?*
E2: *Ésta es mi madre. Es alta y delgada. Tiene… años.*

5. *Saber* and *conocer*

4-47 to 4-51

Although the verbs **saber** and **conocer** can both mean *to know,* they are not interchangeable.

	saber (*to know*)	conocer (*to know*)
yo	**sé**	**conozco**
tú	**sabes**	**conoces**
él, ella, Ud.	**sabe**	**conoce**
nosotros/as	**sabemos**	**conocemos**
vosotros/as	**sabéis**	**conocéis**
ellos/as, Uds.	**saben**	**conocen**

STUDY TIPS

Un resumen de *saber* y *conocer*

Saber

- knowing a fact, skill
- knowing how to do something
- knowing information
- may be followed by an infinitive

Conocer

- knowing people
- knowing a place
- meeting someone for the first time
- may *not* be followed by an infinitive

- The verb **saber** means *to know a fact* or to have knowledge or information about someone or something.

¿**Sabes** dónde está el cine?	*Do you know where the movie theater is?*
No **sé.**	*I don't know.*

- With an infinitive, the verb **saber** means *to know how to do something.*

La tía Berta **sabe** bailar tango.	*Aunt Berta knows how to dance the tango.*

- **Conocer** means *to be acquainted* or *to be familiar* with a person, thing, or place.

Tina **conoce** a mis abuelos.	*Tina knows my grandparents.*
Conozco San Salvador.	*I know (am acquainted with) San Salvador.*

- Use the personal **a** with **conocer** to express that *you know a specific person.*

La profesora **conoce a** mis tíos.	*The professor knows my uncles.*

Aplicación

4-39 Una chica extraordinaria. Read the article about Julia Catalina Flores and answer the questions based on the reading.

Julia Catalina Flores: la charanguista más joven de Progreso

Julia Catalina Flores Ramírez sabe tocar la guitarra y desde la edad de 6 años toca en la banda de su papá. (Foto de Suyapa Carias)

¿Conoces a Julia? Pues si la ves en el grupo de su padre, vas a saber que es una chica extraordinaria. Aunque es pequeña y tímida, es una experta tocando el *charango,* un instrumento similar a la guitarra. Es de una madera hondureña muy rara y especial. Ella dice que conoce su charango como a un miembro de su familia.

Julia vive en el pueblo de El Progreso en el norte de Honduras. Cuando las personas la escuchan tocar, están maravilladas por su talento. Ella quiere tocar con su familia y hacer feliz a la gente. Ya sabe tocar más de 200 canciones. Si la quieres escuchar, el grupo cobra unas 25 lempiras por canción. Pero tienes que viajar a Honduras, porque ella es muy joven para salir de viaje como música profesional.

1. ¿Dónde vive Julia?
2. ¿Cómo es?
3. ¿Qué sabe hacer?
4. ¿Cuántas canciones sabe?
5. ¿La puedes escuchar en tu ciudad?
6. ¿Quieres conocerla algún día? ¿Por qué?

4-40 Una amiga. Complete the following conversation between Marcela and Carmiña with the correct form of **saber** or **conocer.**

MODELO: Yo *conozco* a Julia Catalina Flores.

Marcela: ¿(1) (tú) ____________ a Julia también?
Carmiña: No, yo no la (2) ____________ personalmente pero (3) ____________ que ella es hondureña.
Marcela: Todos (4) ____________ que ella toca muy bien el charango, ese instrumento musical similar a la guitarra.
Carmiña: Ramona (5) ____________ que Julia vive en El Progreso.
Marcela: Sí, es verdad. Su familia es muy famosa. Julio y Ramona (6) ____________ a sus padres, pero no (7) ____________ dónde viven.
Carmiña: Roberto quiere invitarla a una fiesta, pero no (8) ____________ si puede ir. ¿(9) (tú) ____________ a sus padres?
Marcela: Sí, (10) ____________ a los padres, pero no (11) ____________ su número de teléfono.
Carmiña: ¿(12) (tú) ____________ cuántos años tiene Julia?
Marcela: No (13) ____________. Pero (14) ____________ que es muy joven.

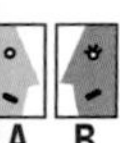

4-41A Entrevista. Read the following profile and answer your partner's questions using that information. Then ask your partner the questions below. Write down his/her answers. Student B, please see **Appendix 1,** page A5.

MODELO: E1: *¿Conoces alguna* (any) *persona famosa?*
E2: *Sí, conozco a Ricky Martin. Soy amigo/a de él.*

Soy intérprete personal del presidente de Honduras.
Juego muy bien al tenis.
Viajo mucho a El Salvador y a Honduras y muy poco a los EE.UU.
Soy amigo/a del actor colombiano John Leguizamo.
Hablo inglés y francés también.
Estudio la política y los gobiernos de Centroamérica.

1. ¿Sabes hablar otros idiomas?
2. ¿Conoces las ruinas de Tikal?
3. ¿Qué instrumento sabes tocar?
4. ¿Sabes jugar bien al béisbol?
5. ¿Conoces alguna persona famosa de Costa Rica?
6. ¿Qué ciudades centroamericanas conoces?

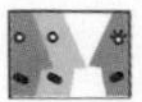

4-42 ¿Quién? Ask as many classmates as possible questions regarding the following. Write the name of each person on the chart, noting his/her answer (as **sí** or **no**).

Modelo: la fecha
E1: *¿Sabes la fecha de hoy?*
E2: *Sí, la sé. Es el 15 de noviembre.*

la fecha de hoy __________	el número de teléfono del/de la profesor/a __________	un restaurante salvadoreño __________	una persona hispana __________
un restaurante español __________	una persona de Centroamérica __________	cuándo hay examen __________	dónde vive el presidente de Guatemala __________
cantar en español __________	jugar al béisbol __________	la capital de Honduras __________	preparar café __________
bailar bien __________	una ciudad interesante __________	un actor __________	mi nombre __________

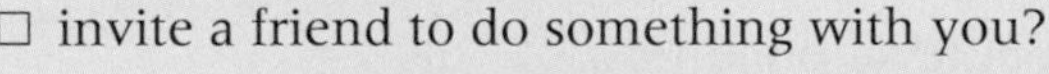

¿Cuánto sabes tú? *Can you…*

4-52 to 4-55

- ☐ invite a friend to do something with you?
- ☐ point out objects that are near, farther away, and very far away by using demonstrative adjectives and pronouns?
- ☐ talk about people and places you know, information you know, and things you know how to do by using **saber** and **conocer**?

Observaciones

¡Pura vida! Episodio 4

Episode 4

4-56 to 4-59

In this episode you'll learn more about Felipe's family and an upcoming wedding.

Antes de ver el video

4-43 Una boda. Marcela explains how weddings are celebrated in her town in Mexico. Read her description and answer the questions that follow in Spanish.

En mi pueblo, cerca de Michoacán, una boda es un evento de tres días o más. Primero, hay fiestas familiares con amigos en las que los novios reciben regalos (*gifts*) para su nuevo hogar (*home*). La boda es muy solemne; generalmente se celebra en una iglesia con una misa (*mass*). Después hay una gran fiesta con música de mariachis, baile y grandes cantidades de comida. Se sirven tamales, mole y muchas cosas más. ¡Y claro, una torta (*cake*)! Esta fiesta dura hasta la madrugada (*dawn*) cuando todos desayunan juntos. Las bodas en México son fiestas alegres (*happy*) en las que todos disfrutan (*enjoy*) mucho.

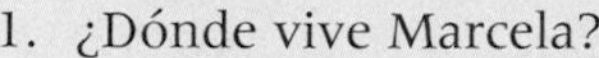

Los mariachis tocan en una boda mexicana.

1. ¿Dónde vive Marcela?
2. ¿Cuántos días dura una boda en su pueblo?
3. ¿Qué pasa después de la ceremonia en la iglesia?

A ver el video

4-44 Hay una boda. Watch the fourth episode of *¡Pura vida!* You will hear Felipe and Marcela discuss an upcoming wedding. Complete the statements that follow.

Felipe recibe un traje *(suit).*

Marcela

Felipe

1. La boda es el ____________.
2. Claudia es la ____________ de Felipe.
3. Marcela tiene una ____________, la hija de la segunda esposa de su papá.
4. En Madrid, Felipe tiene muchos ____________.
5. Elvira es la ____________ de Felipe.

Después de ver el video

WWW

4-45 Los mariachis. Connect with your **¡Arriba!** web site to see more photos of mariachis and to hear their music. What instruments do you hear?

NUESTRO MUNDO

Panoramas

La América Central I: Guatemala, El Salvador, Honduras

Vistas culturales

4-60 to 4-62

4-46 ¿Ya sabes...? How many of the following can you name or answer?

1. las capitales de estos tres países
2. el país que tiene frontera con México
3. un producto agrícola
4. el país más pequeño de los tres
5. una civilización antigua

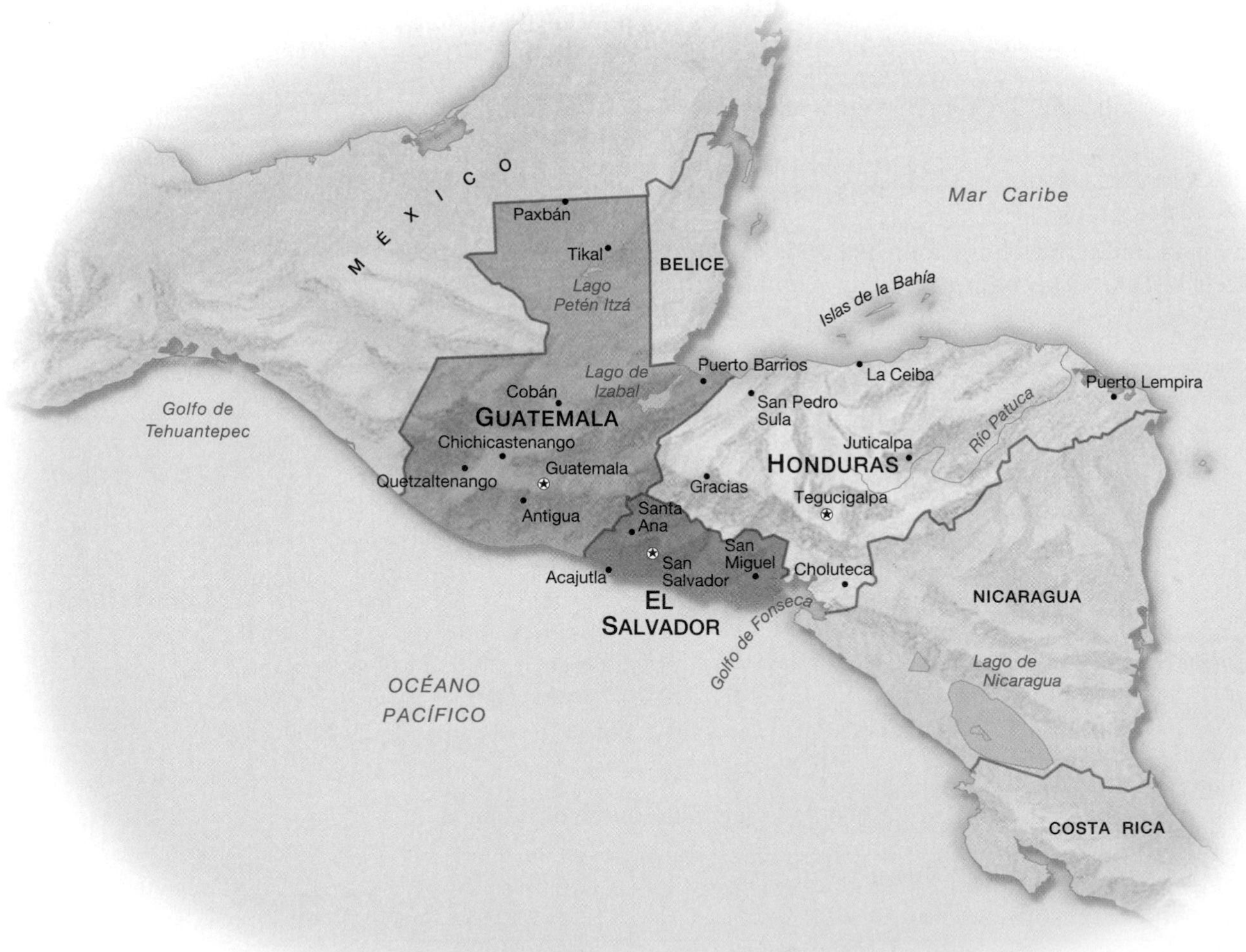

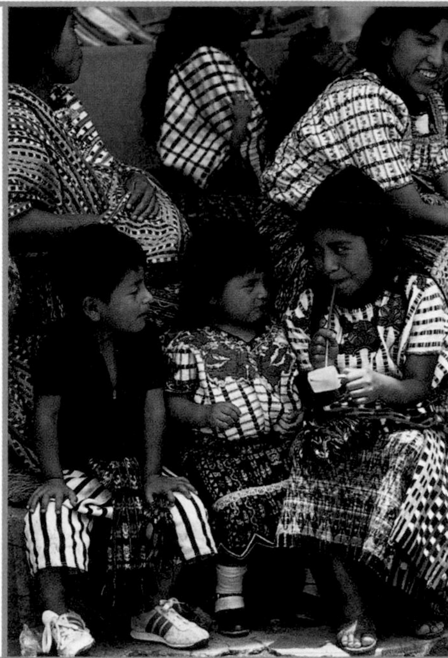

Estos niños indígenas llevan ropa que refleja las antiguas tradiciones artesanales de los tejidos (*woven goods*) guatemaltecos. Los tejidos son también muy populares entre los turistas.

La economía de estos países depende mucho de la agricultura. El café, un producto importante en toda la región, es especialmente susceptible a los cambios climáticos, como (*like*) los huracanes.

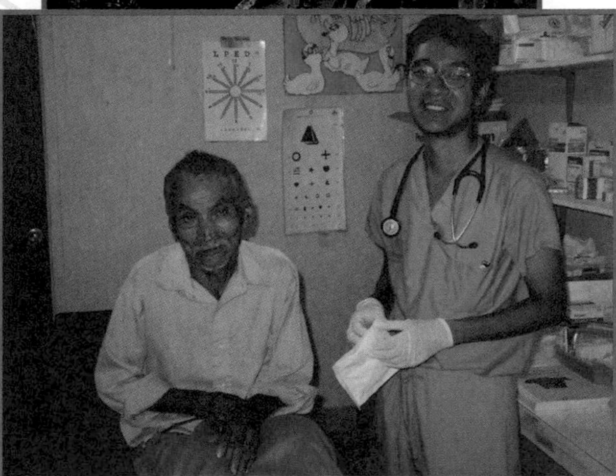

El terreno selvático (*jungle*) y montañoso de gran parte de Centroamérica dificulta la implementación de servicios de salud (*health*). Sin embargo, los gobiernos centroamericanos y las organizaciones internacionales como "Hombro a hombro" (*Shoulder to Shoulder*) hacen grandes esfuerzos para hacer llegar los avances de la medicina.

En el interior de El Salvador, el ecoturismo es una buena manera de conocer el país. En Cerro Verde, por ejemplo, puedes observar una gran variedad de flora y fauna, además del volcán El Izalco. El volcán está activo desde 1722, y en la época de la colonización, los indígenas lo denominaron "el infierno de los españoles".

Después de muchos años de graves problemas militares, políticos y económicos, los países centroamericanos están en un período de paz, con gobiernos democráticos. Este mural conmemora el cese de fuego (*cease-fire*) de 1992 en El Salvador.

La ciudad de Tikal es la más grande y antigua de las ruinas mayas excavadas hasta ahora. Además de algunas de las impresionantes edificaciones de la arquitectura maya, el turista puede admirar el sistema de canales para usar el agua de lluvia (*rain*) que consumían los 40.000 indígenas mayas que vivían allí.

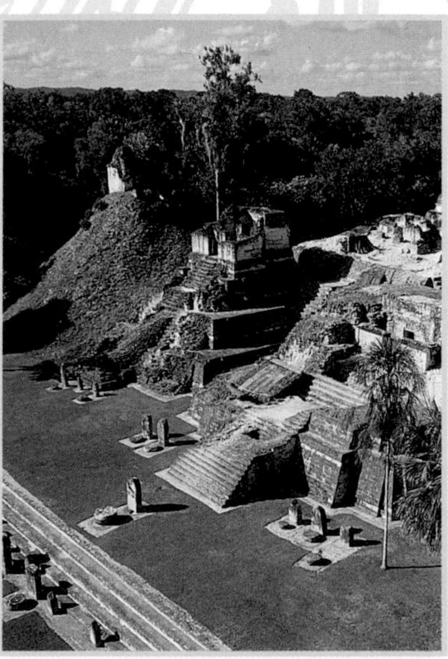

4-47 ¿Cómo son? Complete these statements based on the previous information.

1. Los tres países tienen...
   a. industria. b. desiertos. c. costas.
2. La artesanía incluye...
   a. la platería. b. los tejidos multicolores. c. los suéteres.
3. Tikal es...
   a. una ruina arqueológica.
   b. una maquiladora.
   c. un centro comercial.
4. El sistema del gobierno de los tres países es...
   a. una dictadura. b. comunista. c. democrático.
5. Una de las industrias más importantes es...
   a. la minería. b. los automóviles. c. la agricultura.
6. Uno de los desafíos (*challenges*) más grandes para los gobiernos es...
   a. llevar los servicios de salud a la gente.
   b. establecer una democracia.
   c. excavar los sitios arqueológicos.
7. Muchas ruinas de la antigua civilización de los mayas se encuentran en...
   a. El Salvador. b. Honduras. c. Guatemala.
8. De los tres países, El Salvador es el más...
   a. pequeño. b. rico. c. montañoso.

4-48 Investigar. Connect with your **¡Arriba!** web site to see more images of one of these countries. Choose one and respond to the following questions.

1. ¿Qué es?
2. ¿Dónde está?
3. ¿Cómo es?
4. ¿Lo/La quieres visitar o ver algún día? ¿Por qué?

4-49 Debes conocer... Take turns describing the country that you researched in **4-48** and try to convince each other that it is a good place to visit. Include the cost of airfare and hotel. Decide which country you would both like to visit.

MODELO: *Debes conocer... porque tiene... El vuelo en avión cuesta... y el hotel cuesta...*

Ritmos

4-63

"Marimba con punta" (Los profesionales, Honduras)

"Marimba con punta" combines the marimba, a xylophone-like instrument derived from West Africa, with *punta rock*, a regional dance music that is popular in Central America. Originally, *punta* music was played at wakes by the Garifunas, descendants of West African people.

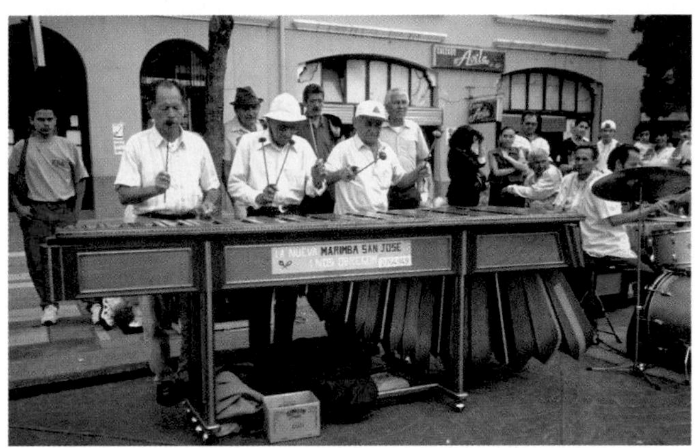

La marimba tiene su origen en África.

Antes de escuchar

4-50 Bailar punta. Complete the following sentences that refer to the song by conjugating the verbs in parentheses. Then rewrite the sentences using the appropriate direct object pronouns.

MODELO: Todo el mundo __________ (poder) bailar punta.
Todo el mundo __*puede*__ *bailar punta.*
Todo el mundo __*la*__ *puede bailar.*

1. También yo __________ (querer) bailar punta...
2. ...pero mis amigos y yo no __________ (saber) bailar punta.
3. Los cantantes (*singers*) __________ (repetir) el coro muchas veces.
4. Uds. __________ (preferir) esta música porque es muy alegre y rápida.
5. ¿__________ (tú) (entender) las palabras de la canción?

A escuchar

4-51 Los amantes de punta rock. What types of people do you think like *punta rock* music? Supply the missing adjectives for the following stanza with the correct word from the list as you listen to the song.

Note: In **Capítulo 2** you learned about diminutives with names (**-ito/-ita**). Diminutives can also be used with adjectives like those listed below: **bajitos** and **gorditos.**

bajitos	altos	gorditos	ricos	pobres

Marimba con punta
Éste es un ritmo sabroso,
que el mundo lo baila ya.
Éste es un ritmo sabroso,
que el mundo entero lo baila ya.

Lo bailan los cocineros,
___________ y ___________, ¡qué rico está!
Bailamos flacos, ___________,
___________, ___________, ¡oye mamá!

Después de escuchar

4-52 Mis amiguitos. What diminutives would you use to describe your family members? Your friends? Using the adjectives in activity **4-51** and others that you know, write five complete sentences describing them.

Páginas

4-64

"Querida Dolores"

Antes de leer

4-53 Pistas extratextuales (*Extra-textual clues*). The publication in which you find an article often gives away its content. Think of what you expect from the financial or sports pages of the newspaper, a handwritten letter on perfumed paper, or a traffic citation left on your windshield. The following selection comes from a bilingual magazine called *Latina*. Think about these clues before you read the selection.

1. ¿Quiénes crees que leen *Latina*?
2. En tu opinión, ¿cuáles de estas secciones **no** aparecen en *Latina*?

moda (*fashion*) deportes cocina (*cuisine*) horóscopo

A leer

4-54 Los consejos (*advice*) sentimentales. Read the following letters from *Latina*.

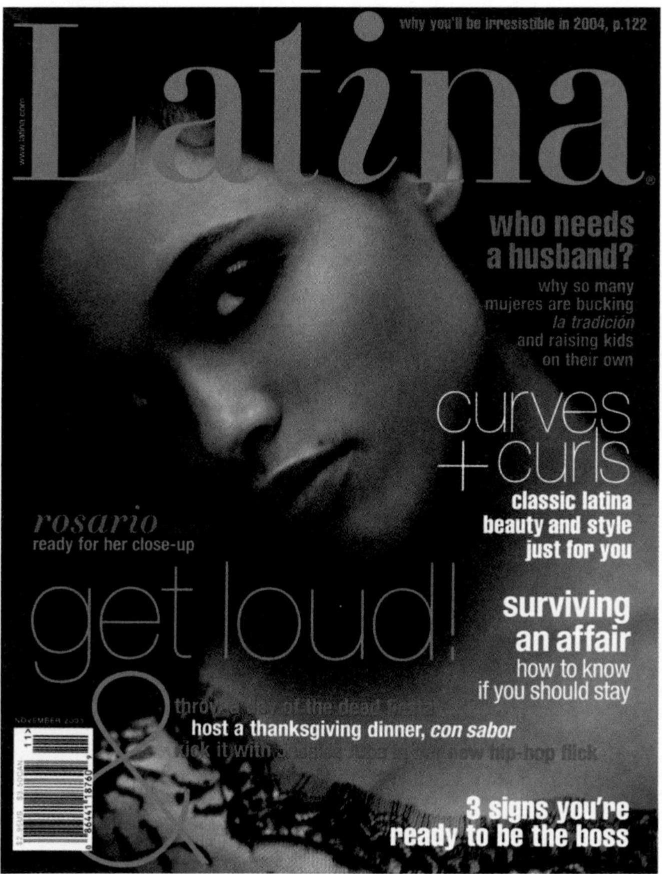

Querida Dolores:

Soy un hombre de 27 años y hace unos siete años que tengo una relación con una mujer. Tenemos dos hijos pero no estamos casados. No he deseado (*I haven't wanted*) dar ese paso porque mis sentimientos han cambiado en los últimos dos años y no estoy seguro de que la amo suficientemente para casarme con ella. Discutimos todo el tiempo y raramente cocina o limpia. Nos llevamos bien (*we get along*) mientras no le mencione ninguna de esas cosas. No quiero dejarla porque no quiero herirla (*hurt her*) o a mis hijos. ¿Qué crees que debo hacer?

—Frustrado.

Querido Frustrado:

Mi hijo, si quieres una sirvienta, pon un anuncio en la sección de clasificados de tu periódico local. Si quieres una esposa, comparte los quehaceres (*chores*) de la casa y no asumas que cocinar (*to cook*) y limpiar (*to clean*) es el deber de las mujeres. Eso pasó de moda con el hula hoop.

—Y no discutan más, D.

Después de leer

4-55 ¿Comprendiste? Complete the following statements logically according to what you have read.

1. El hombre que escribe la carta está...
   a. contento. b. desilusionado. c. casado.
2. Él y su novia...
   a. están separados. b. están divorciados. c. viven juntos.
3. Él cree que los quehaceres de la casa son para...
   a. las mujeres. b. los hombres. c. los niños mayores.
4. Ella...
   a. es de la misma opinión.
   b. no está de acuerdo.
   c. lo deja (*leaves*) por otro.
5. Dolores responde que en una relación...
   a. la mujer debe tener sirvienta para ayudarla.
   b. el hombre es el rey de la casa.
   c. tanto los hombres como las mujeres cooperan.

4-56 En su opinión. Work together to express your opinion about these family issues. Use the following statements in your discussion.

Estoy de acuerdo. No opino. No estoy de acuerdo.

1. El hombre y la mujer deben compartir (*share*) los quehaceres de la casa.
2. Si la mujer trabaja fuera de la casa, necesita tener ayuda doméstica.
3. La mujer que no trabaja fuera de la casa no necesita ayuda de su pareja (*partner*).
4. Los hijos y las hijas deben ayudar con los quehaceres de la casa.
5. En una familia, la mujer generalmente trabaja más.
6. En mi casa, yo soy la persona que trabaja más.

Taller

4-65 to 4-67

4-57 Una invitación. In this activity, you will write a short letter to invite a friend to spend the weekend with you. Follow the steps below and also see the *Ampliación* chart for useful expressions in your letter.

Tegucigalpa, 30 de mayo de 2007

Querida Pilar:

Hola, ¿cómo estás? Estoy aquí en Tegucigalpa para pasar las vacaciones con mi familia. Conoces a mi amigo, Pancho, ¿verdad? Pues, el 27 de junio es su cumpleaños y quiero invitarte a cenar a mi casa...

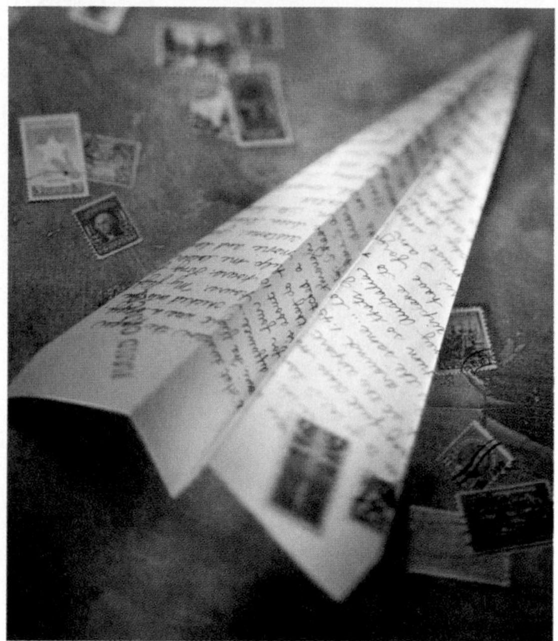

Antes de escribir

- Make a list based on the following information.
  - ☐ lugar, fecha
  - ☐ saludo
  - ☐ presentación
  - ☐ algunas actividades
  - ☐ ¿Con quiénes?
  - ☐ ¿Cuándo?
  - ☐ ¿Por qué?
  - ☐ despedida
  - ☐ ¿Por cuánto tiempo?

A escribir

- **Saludo.** Use the format of the sample letter on page 151, beginning with the place, date, and greeting.
- **Carta.** Incorporate the information from your list above. Use words such as **y, pero,** and **porque** to link your ideas.
- **Respuesta.** Ask for a reply to your letter.
- **Despedida.** Close the letter with a farewell (e.g., **Un abrazo de...,** or **Con todo cariño...,)**

AMPLIACIÓN	
Saludos	***Greetings***
Mi(s) querido/a(s) amigo/a(s):	*My dear friend(s),*
Queridísima familia:	*Dearest family,*
Querido/a(s)...:	*Dear...,*
Despedidas	***Closings***
Responde pronto,	*Respond soon,*
Un abrazo (de),	*A hug (from),*
Un beso (de),	*A kiss (from),*
Cariñosamente,	*Love, Affectionately,*
Con todo (el) cariño,	*With all my love,*

Después de escribir

- **Revisar.** Review the following elements in your letter:
  - ☐ use of stem-changing verbs, **poner, salir,** and **traer**
  - ☐ use of **saber** and **conocer** and the personal **a**
  - ☐ use of direct objects and direct object pronouns
  - ☐ use of demonstratives (**este, ese, aquel,** etc.)
  - ☐ correct spelling, including accents
- **Intercambiar**
  Exchange your letter with a classmate's; make grammatical corrections and content suggestions. Then respond to the letter.
- **Entregar**
  Rewrite your original letter, incorporating your classmate's suggestions. Then turn in your original letter and the response from your classmate to your instructor.

Vocabulario

Primera parte

Miembros de la familia	*Family members*
el/la abuelo/a	*grandfather/grandmother*
el/la cuñado/a	*brother-in-law/sister-in-law*
el/la esposo/a	*husband/wife*
el/la hermanastro/a	*stepbrother/stepsister*
el/la hermano/a	*brother/sister*
el/la hijo/a	*son/daughter*
la madrastra	*stepmother*
la madre	*mother*
el/la nieto/a	*grandson/granddaughter*
el/la novio/a	*boyfriend/girlfriend; groom/bride*
la nuera	*daughter-in-law*
el padrastro	*stepfather*
el padre	*father*
el/la primo/a	*cousin*
el/la sobrino/a	*nephew/niece*
el/la suegro/a	*father-in-law/mother-in-law*
el/la tío/a	*uncle/aunt*
el yerno	*son-in-law*

Verbos	*Verbs*
almorzar (ue)	*to have lunch*
costar (ue)	*to cost*
dormir (ue)	*to sleep*
empezar (ie)	*to begin*
encontrar (ue)	*to find*
entender (ie)	*to understand*
jugar a (ue)	*to play*
pasar	*to spend (time)*
pensar (ie)	*to think*
pedir (i)	*to ask for; to request*
perder (ie)	*to lose*
poder (ue)	*to be able; can*
poner	*to put; to place*
preferir (ie)	*to prefer*
querer (ie)	*to want; to love*
recordar (ue)	*to remember*
repetir (i)	*to repeat*
salir	*to leave; to go out*
servir (i)	*to serve*
soñar (ue) (con)	*to dream (about)*
traer	*to bring*
venir (ie)	*to come*
volver (ue)	*to return*

Adjetivos	*Adjectives*
casado/a	*married*
divorciado/a	*divorced*
mayor	*older*
menor	*younger*
soltero/a	*single; unmarried*
unido/a	*close; close-knit*

Segunda parte

El ocio	*Leisure time*
el café al aire libre	*outdoor café*
el centro	*downtown*
el cine	*movie theatre*
el concierto	*concert*
la entrada	*admission ticket*
la función	*show*
la orquesta	*orchestra*
el parque	*park*
el partido	*game*
la película	*movie*
el teatro	*theatre*

Verbos	*Verbs*
conocer	*to know (someone); to be familiar with (something)*
poner una película	*to show a movie*
pasear	*to take a walk*
saber	*to know (how to do) something*

Hacer una invitación	*Extending invitations*
¿Quieres ir a...?	*Do you want to go to...?*
¿Te gustaría (+ *inf.*)...?	*Would you like (+ inf.)...?*
¿Vamos a...?	*Should we go...?*

Aceptar una invitación	*Accepting invitations*
De acuerdo.	*Fine with me; Okay.*
Me encantaría.	*I would love to.*
Paso por ti.	*I'll come by for you.*
Sí, claro.	*Yes, of course.*
¡Vamos!	*Let's go!*

Rechazar una invitación	*Rejecting invitations*
Estoy muy ocupado/a.	*I'm very busy.*
Gracias, pero no puedo...	*Thanks, but I can't...*
Lo siento, tengo que...	*I'm sorry, I have to...*

Direct object pronouns — *See page 125.*
Demonstrative adjectives and pronouns — *See page 137.*

5 ¿Cómo pasas el día?

PRIMERA PARTE

¡Así lo decimos! Vocabulario Las actividades diarias

¡Así lo hacemos! Estructuras Reflexive constructions: pronouns and verbs

Comparisons of equality and inequality

Comparaciones El ecoturismo en Costa Rica

- Describing your daily routine and habits
- Expressing needs related to personal care
- Expressing emotional states
- Comparing objects and people

SEGUNDA PARTE

¡Así lo decimos! Vocabulario Los quehaceres domésticos

¡Así lo hacemos! Estructuras The superlative

The present progressive

Observaciones ¡Pura vida! Episodio 5

- Talking about what you do around the house
- Describing people or things using superlatives
- Describing what is happening at the moment

NUESTRO MUNDO

Panoramas La América Central II: Costa Rica, Nicaragua, Panamá

Ritmos "Ligia Elena" (Rubén Blades, Panamá)

Páginas Playa Cacao

Taller Vendo casa

Uno de los cantantes más famosos de salsa es Rubén Blades. No sólo se le conoce por su música y por ser un buen actor, sino también por su activismo social y político.

La América Central II: Costa Rica, Nicaragua, Panamá

«Un lugar para cada cosa y cada cosa en su lugar.»*

Al mono aullador (*howler*) se le conoce por sus gritos. La especie vive en los árboles altos de los bosques de la América Central.

*__Refrán:__ A place for everything and everything in its place.

PRIMERA PARTE

¡Así lo decimos! Vocabulario

CD 1, Track 30

5-1 to 5-2

¡Así es la vida! El arreglo personal

Los vecinos (*neighbors*) de la Calle Ricardo Arias en la Ciudad de Panamá.

Son las siete de la mañana y cada vecino tiene que prepararse para este nuevo día.

Antonio, el vecino del cuarto piso, tiene que afeitarse. Janet, la vecina del tercer piso, necesita levantarse para ir a la universidad. Cristina, la vecina del primero, tiene que vestirse y Eduardo, del primero también, debe secarse el pelo porque tiene que salir inmediatamente.

¡Ya empieza otro día!

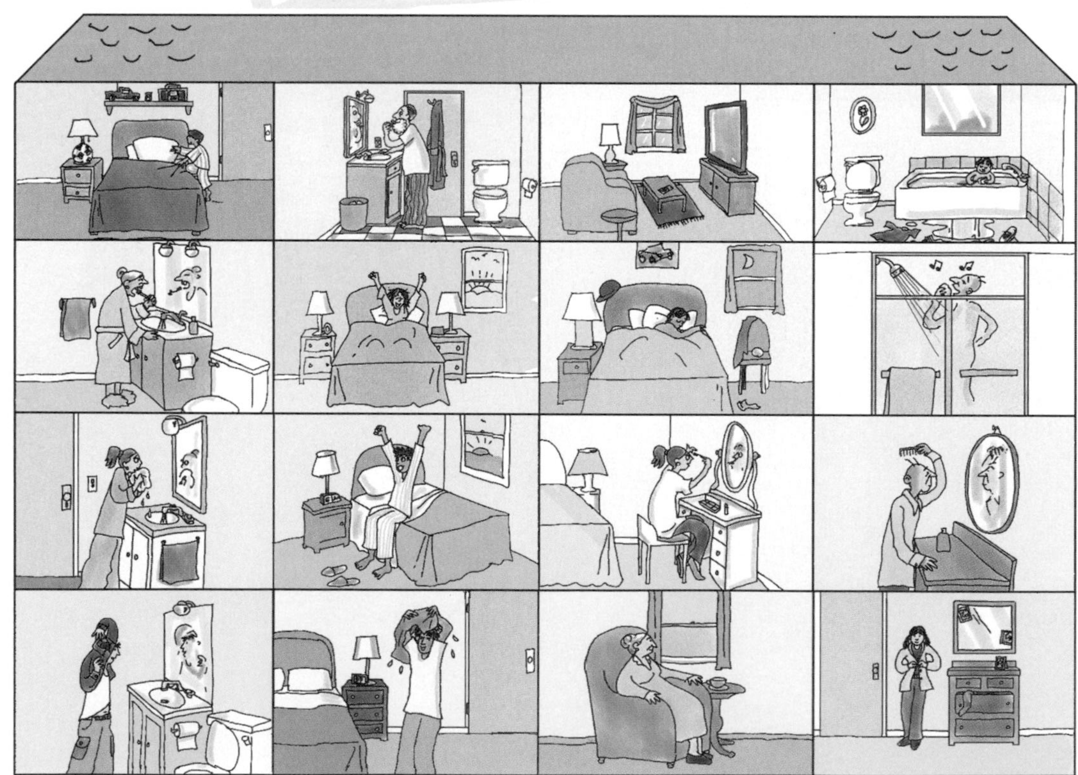

Las actividades diarias

CD 1, Track 31

5-3 to 5-8

acostarse (ue)

afeitarse

bañarse

cepillarse (los dientes)

despertarse (ie)

dormirse (ue, u)

ducharse

lavarse (la cara)

levantarse

maquillarse

peinarse

quitarse (la camisa)

secarse (el pelo)

sentarse (ie)

vestirse (i, i)

Algunas partes del cuerpo	*Some parts of the body*
la cara	*face*
los dientes	*teeth*
la mano	*hand*
la nariz	*nose*
el ojo	*eye*
el pelo	*hair*

Algunas emociones	*Some emotions*
ponerse contento/a	*to become happy*
furioso/a	*angry*
impaciente	*impatient*
nervioso/a	*nervous*
triste	*sad*
reírse (i, i)	*to laugh*
sentirse (ie, i)	*to feel*

Artículos de uso personal	*Personal care items*
el cepillo (de dientes)	*(tooth) brush*
el champú	*shampoo*
la crema (de afeitar)	*(shaving) cream*
el desodorante	*deodorant*
el espejo	*mirror*
el jabón	*soap*
el lápiz labial	*lipstick*
la loción (de afeitar)	*(shaving) lotion*
el maquillaje	*makeup*
la máquina de afeitar	*electric razor*
la navaja de afeitar	*razor*
el peine	*comb*
el secador	*hair dryer*

Aplicación

5-1 ¿Quién es quién? Identifica la persona de **¡Así es la vida!** que probablemente dice lo siguiente.

Antonio (**A**) Janet (**J**) Cristina (**C**) Eduardo (**E**)

1. _____ Prefiero secarme el pelo antes de salir.
2. _____ Necesito levantarme.
3. _____ Todos los días me afeito.
4. _____ Tengo que vestirme.

5-2 ¿Qué asocias con...? Escribe asociaciones con las siguientes actividades.

Modelo: afeitarse
la cara, la crema de afeitar, la máquina de afeitar, la navaja, etcétera.

1. bañarse
2. mirarse
3. secarse
4. peinarse
5. despertarse
6. cepillarse
7. sentarse
8. levantarse
9. ponerse impaciente
10. ponerse nervioso/a

WWW **5-3 El arreglo personal.** Conéctate con la página web de **¡Arriba!** y busca uno de los productos siguientes. Descríbelo e incluye su precio. ¿Es para hombres o mujeres? ¿Te parece un producto bueno? ¿Quieres comprarlo? ¿Por qué?

Modelo: *La crema Toja Sensible es una crema de afeitar para hombres. La compro porque no es cara.*

crema de afeitar	máquina de afeitar	maquillaje
loción	jabón	secador

CD 1, Track 32 **5-4 Los señores Rodríguez.** Escucha la descripción de la rutina diaria de la familia Rodríguez. Indica a quién/es se refiere cada oración a continuación: al señor Rodríguez, a la señora Rodríguez o a los dos.

LA ACTIVIDAD	EL SEÑOR	LA SEÑORA
1. Se levanta temprano todos los días.	________	________
2. Trabaja en una oficina.	________	________
3. Se baña por la mañana.	________	________
4. Se afeita.	________	________
5. Toma café en el desayuno.	________	________
6. Almuerza con otras personas.	________	________
7. Hace ejercicio después de comer.	________	________
8. Prepara la cena.	________	________

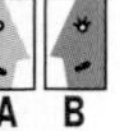

5-5A El monstruo ***(Monster)*****.** Túrnense *(Take turns)* para describir un monstruo mientras su compañero/a lo dibuja (*draw*). Incluyan características físicas. Luego comparen sus descripciones con sus dibujos. Estudiante B, por favor ve al **Apéndice 1,** página A5.

MODELO: El monstruo tiene cuatro ojos, dos dientes, una nariz...

El monstruo tiene...

- tres ojos pequeños
- dos dientes grandes
- no tiene pelo
- dos narices

¡Así lo hacemos! Estructuras

1. Reflexive constructions: pronouns and verbs

5-9 to 5-19

A reflexive construction is one in which the subject is both the performer and the receiver of the action expressed by the verb.

- The drawing on the left depicts a reflexive action (Isabel is combing her own hair); the drawing on the right depicts a nonreflexive action (Isabel is combing her sister's hair).

Isabel **se peina.**
Isabel combs her hair.

Isabel **peina** a su hermana.
Isabel combs her sister's hair.

Los pronombres reflexivos

- Reflexive constructions require reflexive pronouns.

Subject pronouns	Reflexive pronouns	Verb (*lavarse*)
yo	**me** (*myself*)	**lavo**
tú	**te** (*yourself*)	**lavas**
él, ella, Ud.	**se** (*himself, herself, yourself*)	**lava**
nosotros/as	**nos** (*ourselves*)	**lavamos**
vosotros/as	**os** (*yourselves*)	**laváis**
ellos/as, Uds.	**se** (*themselves, yourselves*)	**lavan**

- Reflexive pronouns have the same forms as direct object pronouns, except for the third-person singular and plural. The reflexive pronoun of the third-person singular and plural is **se.**

  Paco **se** baña. — *Paco bathes.*
  Los niños **se** levantan temprano. — *The children get up early.*

- As with object pronouns, reflexive pronouns are placed immediately before the conjugated verb. In Spanish the definite article, not the possessive adjective, is used to refer to parts of the body and articles of clothing.

  Me lavo las manos. — *I wash my hands.*
  Pedro **se** pone el sombrero. — *Pedro puts on his hat.*

- With infinitives, reflexive pronouns are either attached to the infinitive or placed in front of the conjugated verb.

  Sofía **va a maquillarse** ahora.
  Sofía **se va a maquillar** ahora. } *Sofía is going to put her makeup on now.*

- In English, reflexive pronouns are frequently omitted, but in Spanish, reflexive pronouns are required in all reflexive constructions.

Pepe **se afeita** antes de acostarse.	*Pepe shaves before going to bed.*
Marina siempre **se baña** a las ocho.	*Marina always bathes at eight.*

Los verbos reflexivos

- Verbs that describe personal care and daily habits carry a reflexive pronoun if the same person performs and receives the action.

Me voy a acostar temprano.	*I'm going to bed early.*
Mis hermanos se despiertan tarde todas las mañanas.	*My brothers wake up late every morning.*

- Such verbs can also be used nonreflexively when someone other than the subject receives the action.

Elena **acuesta** a su hija menor.	*Elena puts her youngest daughter to bed.*
¿**Despiertas** a tu abuela?	*Do you wake up your grandmother?*

- In Spanish, verbs that express feelings, moods, and conditions are often used with reflexive pronouns. A reflexive pronoun is usually not required in English. Instead, verbs such as *to get, to become*, or nonreflexive verbs, are used.

alegrarse (de)	*to become happy*
divertirse (ie, i)	*to have fun*
enamorarse (de)	*to fall in love (with)*
enfermarse	*to become sick*
enojarse (con)	*to get angry*
olvidarse (de)	*to forget*

Me alegro de ganar.	*I am happy to win.*
Siempre **nos divertimos** en la fiesta.	*We always have fun at the party.*
Luis **va a enamorarse de** Ana.	*Luis is going to fall in love with Ana.*
Jorge **se enoja** si pierde.	*Jorge gets angry if he loses.*
Me olvido de todo cuando la veo.	*I forget everything when I see her.*

- Some verbs have different meanings when used with a reflexive pronoun.

NONREFLEXIVE		REFLEXIVE	
acostar (ue)	*to put to bed*	**acostarse (ue)**	*to go to bed*
dormir (ue, u)	*to sleep*	**dormirse (ue, u)**	*to fall asleep*
enfermar	*to make sick*	**enfermarse**	*to become sick*
ir	*to go*	**irse**	*to go away; to leave*
levantar	*to lift*	**levantarse**	*to get up*
llamar	*to call*	**llamarse**	*to be called*
poner	*to put; to set*	**ponerse**	*to put on*
quitar	*to remove*	**quitarse**	*to take off*
vestir (i, i)	*to dress*	**vestirse (i, i)**	*to get dressed*

Las construcciones recíprocas

- The plural reflexive pronouns **nos, os,** and **se** may be used with verbs that take direct objects to express reciprocal actions. The verbs can be reflexive or nonreflexive verbs, and these actions are conveyed in English by *each other* or *one another*.

Nos queremos mucho.	*We love each other a lot.*
Los novios **se ven** todos los días.	*The sweethearts see one another every day.*

Aplicación

5-6 Mariano Rivera, un panameño en Nueva York. Lee el siguiente párrafo y subraya *(underline)* los verbos reflexivos.

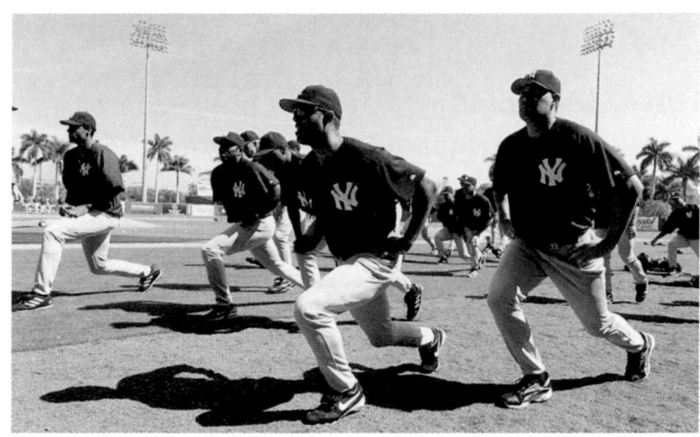

Mariano Rivera es un jugador de los Yankees de Nueva York y lleva años en Manhattan. Su vida es muy activa. Tiene que levantarse temprano porque tiene que practicar béisbol todos los días para estar en buenas condiciones físicas. Después de practicar, se sienta en su estudio para ver la televisión. Por la tarde, se divierte con sus amigos en un café y se pone muy contento cuando tocan música latina. Por la noche, después de hacer ejercicio en un gimnasio, se baña y se acuesta temprano, pues al día siguiente tiene que despertarse a las seis de la mañana porque tiene un juego en Boston esa noche.

5-7 ¿Cómo es su día? Contesta *(Answer)* las preguntas sobre la rutina diaria de Mariano Rivera.

1. ¿Dónde vive?
2. Generalmente, ¿se levanta tarde o temprano? ¿Por qué?
3. ¿Qué hace en su estudio?
4. ¿Cómo se siente cuando está con sus amigos?
5. ¿Qué hace antes de acostarse?
6. ¿Cómo es su día en tu opinión? ¿Interesante? ¿Difícil? ¿Divertido? ¿Por qué?

5-8 ¿En qué orden lo haces? Pon *(Put)* estas actividades en orden lógico según tu rutina diaria.

_____ me duermo	_____ me peino
_____ me lavo	_____ me cepillo los dientes
_____ me afeito	_____ me despierto
_____ me acuesto	_____ me lavo la cara

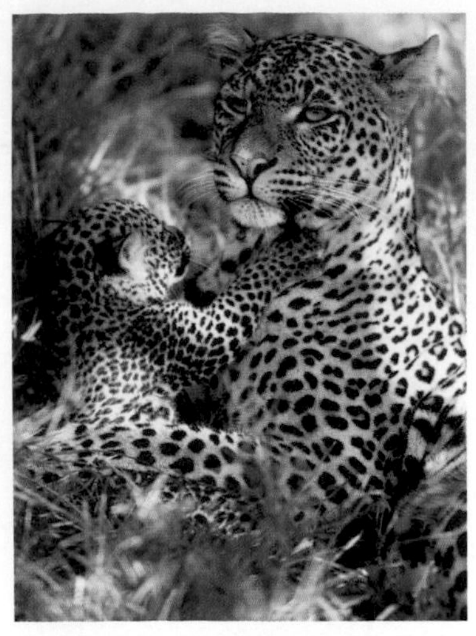

El leopardo y su cachorro se aman mucho.

5-9 Parejas famosas. Explica qué tienen en común las siguientes personas.

MODELO: Romeo y Julieta
Romeo y Julieta se quieren mucho.

ALGUNAS PAREJAS		**ALGUNAS RELACIONES**
Charlie Brown y Snoopy		quererse
Antonio y Cleopatra		llamarse
Antonio Banderas y Melanie Griffith		escribirse
los republicanos y los demócratas		verse
los perros *(dogs)* y los gatos *(cats)*	(no)	besarse
Marc Anthony y Jennifer López		odiarse
Tú y yo		encontrarse
¿...?		tolerarse

5-10 ¿Qué tienen en común? Háganse *(Ask each other)* las siguientes preguntas para comparar sus horarios. Luego, hagan un resumen de lo que tienen en común.

MODELO: despertarse
E1: *¿A qué hora te despiertas?*
E2: *Me despierto a las seis. ¿Y tú?*

Actividad	**La hora que lo hago yo**	**La hora que lo hace mi compañero/a**
dormirse		
levantarse		
bañarse		
vestirse		
acostarse		

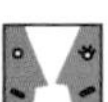

5-11 Las emociones y las reacciones. Túrnense para hacerse preguntas sobre cómo se sienten en las siguientes situaciones.

MODELO: llegas tarde a clase
E1: *¿Qué pasa cuando llegas tarde a clase?*
E2: *Me pongo nervioso/a.*

sacas una "A" en un examen
conoces a una persona importante
pierdes tu libro de texto
el/la profesor/a llega tarde para un examen

5-12 Una relación especial. Túrnense para hacerse preguntas sobre relaciones especiales que tienen con algunas personas. Puede ser con un/a novio/a, un/a amigo/a o un familiar.

MODELO: E1: *¿Se conocen bien?*
E2: *Sí, nos conocemos bastante bien.*

1. ¿Con qué frecuencia se ven?
2. ¿Dónde se encuentran generalmente?
3. ¿Cuántas veces al día se llaman por teléfono?
4. ¿Qué se dicen cuando se ven?
5. ¿Se quieren mucho?
6. ¿Cuándo se dan regalos?
7. ¿Se entienden bien?
8. ¿Se respetan mucho?

2. Comparisons of equality and inequality

5-20 to 5-26

Comparaciones de igualdad

- In Spanish, you may make comparisons of equality with adjectives (e.g., *as good as*) and adverbs (e.g., *as quickly as*) by using the following construction.

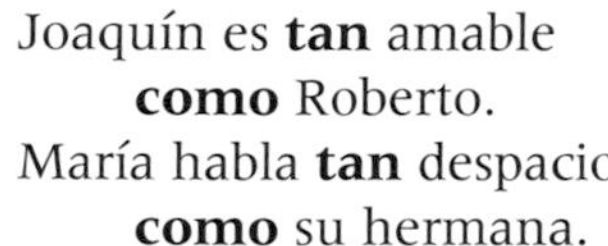

tan + *adjective/adverb* + **como**

Joaquín es **tan** amable **como** Roberto.	*Joaquín is as nice as Roberto.*
María habla **tan** despacio **como** su hermana.	*María speaks as slowly as her sister.*

- Make comparisons of equality with nouns (*e.g., as much money as; as many friends as*) by using the following construction. Note that **tanto** is an adjective and agrees in gender and number with the noun or pronoun it modifies.

tanto/a(s) + *noun* + **como**

Marta tiene **tantos** amigos **como** ustedes.	*Marta has as many friends as you.*
Tú tienes **tanta** paciencia **como** Eugenio.	*You have as much patience as Eugenio.*

- Make comparisons of equality with verbs (e.g., *works as much as*) by using the following construction.

verb + **tanto como**

Mis hermanos se enamoran **tanto como** tú.	*My brothers fall in love as much as you.*

Comparaciones de desigualdad

- A comparison of inequality expresses *more than* or *less than*. Use this construction with adjectives, adverbs, or nouns.

más/menos + *adjective/adverb/noun* + **que**

adjective	
Mercedes es **menos** responsable **que** Claudio.	*Mercedes is less responsible than Claudio.*
adverb	
Yo me visto **más** rápidamente **que** tú.	*I get dressed faster than you.*
noun	
Esta casa tiene **menos** cuartos **que** la otra.	*This house has fewer rooms than the other.*

- Make comparisons of inequality with verbs using the following construction.

verb + **más/menos** + **que**

Estudio **más que** tú. *I study more than you (do).*

- With numerical expressions, use **de** instead of **que.**

Tengo **más de** cinco buenos amigos. *I have more than five good friends.*

Summary of comparisons of equality and inequality	
Equal comparisons	
nouns:	**tanto/a(s)** + *noun* + **como** + *noun* or *pronoun*
adjectives/adverbs:	**tan** + *adj./adv.* + **como** + *noun* or *pronoun*
verbs:	*verb* + **tanto como** + *noun* or *pronoun*
Unequal comparisons	
adj./adv./noun:	**más/menos** + *adj./adv./noun* + **que** + *noun* or *pronoun*
verbs:	*verb* + **más/menos** + **que**
with numbers:	**más/menos** + **de** + *number*

EXPANSIÓN More on structure and usage

Los adjetivos comparativos irregulares

Some Spanish adjectives have both regular and irregular comparative forms:

ADJECTIVE	REGULAR FORM	IRREGULAR FORM	
bueno/a	más bueno/a	mejor	*better*
malo/a	más malo/a	peor	*worse*
viejo/a	más viejo/a	mayor	*older*
joven	más joven	menor	*younger*

The irregular forms **mejor** and **peor** are more commonly used than the regular forms.

Esta casa es **mejor** que ésa. *This house is better than that one.*
Rafael es **peor** que Luis. *Rafael is worse than Luis.*

Mayor, **menor**, and **más joven** are commonly used with people; **más viejo** may be used with inanimate objects.

Manuel es **menor** que Berta y yo soy **mayor** que Manuel. *Manuel is younger than Berta and I am older than Manuel.*
San José, Costa Rica, es **más vieja** que Alajuela. *San José, Costa Rica, is older than Alajuela.*

Aplicación

5-13 Dos chismosas (*gossips*). Subraya las comparaciones de igualdad y de desigualdad en el diálogo entre dos personas chismosas en una fiesta.

Carlota: Creo que el champú que usa Marilú no es tan bueno como el que uso yo.
Ángela: Es verdad que su pelo no es tan bonito como el tuyo (*yours*).
Carlota: ¿Crees que ella es tan rica como dice?

Ángela: No, pero creo que es más rica que nosotras. Sin embargo, es menos rica que su esposo.

Carlota: Pero su esposo no tiene tantos coches como tú.

Ángela: Es verdad, pero mis coches son menos lujosos que los de su esposo.

Carlota: ¿Y quién crees que es mayor? ¿Tú o Marilú?

Ángela: ¡Qué barbaridad! Yo soy mucho menor que ella. Ella tiene más de cincuenta años. Yo tengo menos de cuarenta.

Carlota: Bueno, estoy aburrida. Vamos a casa. No me gusta la comida aquí. En casa la comida es mejor que la que hacen aquí.

Ángela: Tienes razón. ¡Esta comida es peor que la nuestra! ¡Vamos!

Carlota: Buenas noches, Marilú. Esta fiesta es perfecta. ¡La comida está deliciosa!

5-14 Ahora tú. Haz *(Make)* comparaciones para describir a estas personas y cosas en la fiesta de Marilú.

MODELO: Ángela
Ángela es tan chismosa como Carlota.

1. el pelo
2. el champú
3. Marilú
4. los coches
5. la comida
6. Ángela y tú

5-15 Los Óscars. Imagínense que son reporteros/as para la ceremonia de los Óscars en Hollywood y ven llegar a las estrellas *(stars)*. Comparen a las estrellas cuando salen de su carro.

Penélope Cruz

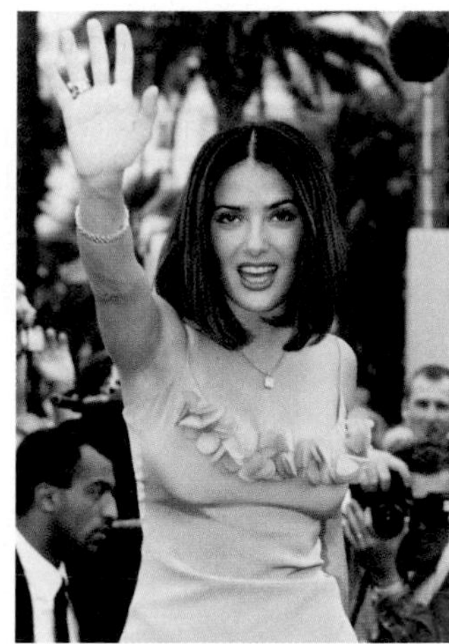

Salma Hayek

MODELO: E1: *Salma Hayek es más alta que Penélope Cruz.*
E2: *Sí, pero Penélope es más guapa que Salma.*

1. Gael García Bernal y Cameron Díaz
2. Ricky Martin y John Travolta
3. Jennifer López y Gloria Estefan
4. Enrique Iglesias y Julio Iglesias (su padre)
5. Benjamín Bratt y Jimmy Smits
6. ¿... y ...?

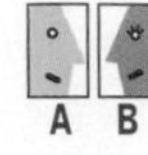

5-16A En la agencia de bienes raíces *(real estate)*. Eres un agente de bienes raíces y tienes que vender *(sell)* dos casas: una, grande y lujosa, y la otra, pequeña y en malas condiciones. Compara las dos casas y usa estos criterios para vendérselas a tu compañero/a. Estudiante B, por favor ve al **Apéndice 1,** página A5.

- grande
- bonito/a
- en buenas condiciones
- en un barrio bueno
- número de dormitorios
- ...

¿Cuánto sabes tú? *Can you...*

5-27 to 5-30

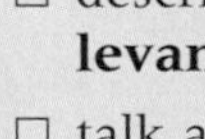

- ☐ describe your daily routine and habits using reflexive verbs such as **me levanto, me visto,** and **me duermo**?
- ☐ talk about your personal care habits, including articles such as **maquillaje** or **crema de afeitar** that you use or do not use?
- ☐ express emotional changes using verbs such as **ponerse**?
- ☐ compare objects and people using **más** or **menos... que** or **tan... como** with adjectives, adverbs, nouns, and verbs?

El ecoturismo en Costa Rica

5-17 En tu experiencia. ¿Hay organizaciones en tu país que se dedican a preservar el medio ambiente (*environment*)? ¿En qué lugares es popular hacer ecoturismo? Para ti, ¿qué diferencias hay entre el turismo y el ecoturismo? ¿Te interesa la naturaleza? ¿Por qué?

Costa Rica es el país centroamericano que más se preocupa de su ecología. El Ministerio de Recursos Naturales colabora con la *Nature Conservancy* y la *Costa Rica-USA Foundation* para establecer programas de conservación en los que voluntarios ayudan a proteger la flora y fauna de los parques nacionales y a limpiar la basura de las playas de las costas de la nación. Además, una comisión nacional de limpieza incluye las ciudades y parques de muchas comunidades de la costa.

La flora y la fauna de Costa Rica han convertido (*have turned*) a este país en uno de los favoritos de los ecoturistas del mundo. Todos los años decenas de miles de turistas visitan sus parques nacionales. Algunos de estos parques aceptan voluntarios por períodos de dos meses, y cientos de turistas trabajan en la construcción de senderos (*trails*) o la investigación sobre la riqueza de la flora y la fauna de este país. En Costa Rica los ecoturistas tienen la oportunidad de ver parte de las 850 variedades de pájaros (*birds*), 35.000 variedades de insectos, entre ellas 3.000 clases de mariposas (*butterflies*), 150 variedades de reptiles y ranas (*frogs*) y 10.000 especies de plantas, entre las cuales hay 1.200 variedades de orquídeas.

5-18 En su opinión. Lean las siguientes oraciones y túrnense para expresar y anotar sus opiniones.

1. ¡Ni modo! No estoy de acuerdo.
2. No es probable.
3. No opino.
4. Es posible.
5. Estoy completamente de acuerdo.

a. Cuando voy de vacaciones, me levanto temprano.
   1 2 3 4 5
b. Me gusta el ecoturismo.
   1 2 3 4 5
c. Prefiero ir donde hay mucha gente.
   1 2 3 4 5
d. No es importante ducharme todos los días cuando estoy de vacaciones.
   1 2 3 4 5
e. Me gusta ir de camping.
   1 2 3 4 5

SEGUNDA PARTE

¡Así lo decimos! Vocabulario

CD 1, Track 33

5-31 to 5-32

¡Así es la vida! Vamos a limpiar

Cristina, una de las vecinas de la Calle Ricardo Arias, tiene dos hijas desastrosas que siempre dejan todo por el piso. Ahora Cristina está enojada y les escribe una nota a sus hijas:

> ***Rosa:*** *Tienes que lavar los platos, lavar y secar la ropa, barrer el piso y sacar la basura.*
>
> ***Paloma:*** *Tú también debes ayudar. Tienes que ordenar la sala, pasar la aspiradora y sacudir el polvo de los muebles.*

¡Qué desastre!

Los quehaceres domésticos

CD 1, Track 34

5-33 to 5-39

ACCESORIOS Y MUEBLES	QUEHACERES	ACCESORIOS Y MUEBLES	QUEHACERES	ACCESORIOS Y MUEBLES	QUEHACERES
 la aspiradora	pasar la aspiradora	 la lavadora	lavar la ropa	 los muebles	sacudir el polvo de los muebles
 el basurero	sacar la basura	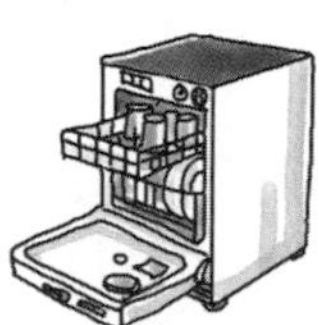 el lavaplatos	lavar los platos	 la plancha	planchar
 la escoba	barrer el piso	 la mesa	poner la mesa/ quitar la mesa	 la secadora	secar la ropa

Más muebles y accesorios	*More furniture and accessories*
la cama	*bed*
la cómoda	*dresser*
el cuadro	*painting*
el estante	*bookcase*
la lámpara	*lamp*
la mesa de noche	*nightstand*
el sillón	*armchair; overstuffed chair*
el sofá	*sofa; couch*

Las partes de una casa	*Parts of a house*
el baño	*bathroom*
la casa	*house*
la cocina	*kitchen*
el comedor	*dining room*
el cuarto	*room; bedroom*
el dormitorio	*bedroom*
el garaje	*garage*
el jardín	*garden*
el pasillo	*hallway*
el patio	*patio; backyard*
el piso	*floor*
la sala	*living room*
la terraza	*terrace*

Los quehaceres domésticos	*Household chores*
barrer el piso	*to sweep the floor*
hacer la cama	*to make the bed*
lavar los platos	*to wash dishes*
lavar la ropa	*to wash clothes*
limpiar/ordenar la casa	*to clean the house*
pasar la aspiradora	*to vacuum*
planchar	*to iron*
poner la mesa	*to set the table*
quitar la mesa	*to clear the table*
sacar la basura	*to take out the garbage*
sacudir el polvo (de los muebles)	*to dust (the furniture)*
secar la ropa	*to dry clothes*

EXPANSIÓN **More on structure and usage**

Preposiciones de lugar

To describe the location of a person or an object, use the following prepositions:

arriba de	*above*
contra	*against*
debajo de	*under; below*
dentro de	*within; inside of*
sobre	*on*

CD 1, Track 35

5-40 to 5-41

Letras y sonidos

The consonants "h, ch" in Spanish

In Spanish, the letter *h* is silent. In other words, it is a letter for which there is no corresponding sound.

ho-la *ha-cer* *hom-bre* *her-mo-sa* *que-ha-ce-res*

In the sequence *ch*, however, the letters *c* and *h* combine to create one single sound *ch*, which is pronounced the same as in English *church*.

mu-cho *no-che* *plan-cha* *cu-chi-lla* *mu-cha-cho*

Aplicación

5-19 En casa de Cristina. Completa las siguientes frases lógicamente.

Modelo: _____ Paloma tiene que pasar... *la aspiradora.*

1. _____ Paloma necesita ordenar...	a. la basura.
2. _____ Rosa tiene que sacar...	b. el piso.
3. _____ Paloma debe sacudir...	c. los platos.
4. _____ Rosa necesita barrer...	d. la sala.
5. _____ Rosa tiene que lavar...	e. los quehaceres.
6. _____ Cristina escribe una lista de...	f. el polvo de los muebles.

5-20 ¡Emparejar! ¿Dónde encuentras las siguientes cosas?

Modelo: _____ el coche
El coche está en el garaje.

1. _____ la bicicleta
2. _____ el sofá
3. _____ la ropa *(clothing)*
4. _____ la cama
5. _____ el lavaplatos
6. _____ la mesa y las sillas

a. el comedor
b. la cocina
c. la sala
d. la cómoda
e. el garaje
f. el dormitorio

5-21 ¿Quién lo hace en tu casa? Túrnense para decir quién hace estos quehaceres en su casa.

Modelo: lavar los platos
Mi hermano los lava.

1. pasar la aspiradora
2. hacer las compras
3. sacudir el polvo de los muebles
4. poner la mesa
5. sacar la basura
6. hacer las camas
7. lavar la ropa
8. ordenar la casa

EXPANSIÓN More on structure and usage

The noun *vez*

The noun **vez** is used in several adverbial expressions.

a veces	*sometimes; at times*
de vez en cuando	*from time to time*
dos (tres, cuatro...) veces (a la semana)	*two (three, four...) times (per week)*
otra vez	*again*
una vez	*one time; once*

Pasa la aspiradora **dos veces** a la semana.	*He vacuums two times a week.*
Limpio el garaje **de vez en cuando.**	*I clean the garage once in a while.*

CD 1, Track 36

5-22 ¡Todo lo que necesita para la casa! Escucha el siguiente anuncio de radio sobre los productos para la casa. Escribe el nombre y el precio de cada producto debajo del dibujo correspondiente.

MODELO: Una silla:
<u>$19</u>

1. 

____

2. 

____

3. 

____

4. 

____

5. 

____

6. 

____

7. 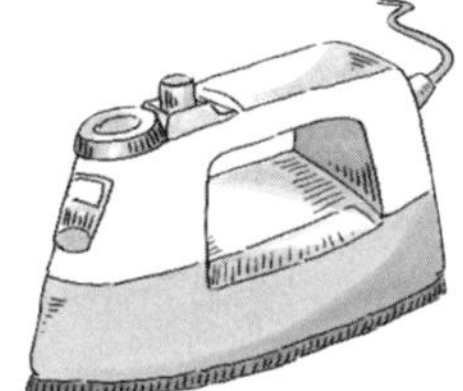

____

8. 

____

5-23 En tu casa. Ustedes tienen un presupuesto (*budget*) de 600 balboas panameños ($1.00 US = 1,00 PAB). Decidan cuáles de los productos de la actividad **5-22** van a comprar y expliquen por qué.

5-24 División de trabajo. Imagínense que son compañeros/as de casa y necesitan ponerse de acuerdo (*to agree*) sobre los quehaceres domésticos de la casa. Hablen de cómo van a dividir el trabajo.

MODELO: poner la mesa
E1: *¿Quieres poner la mesa?*
E2: *Está bien. Pongo la mesa si tú preparas la cena.*
E3: *Yo prefiero preparar la cena.*

limpiar la cocina	lavar la ropa	planchar la ropa
ordenar el baño	lavar los platos	sacar la basura
comprar la comida	ordenar la sala	sacudir el polvo de los muebles
hacer las camas	pasar la aspiradora	secar la ropa

¡Así lo hacemos! Estructuras

3. The superlative

5-42 to 5-44

- A superlative statement expresses the highest or lowest degree of a quality, for example, the most, the greatest, the least, or the worst. To express the superlative in Spanish, the definite article is used with **más** or **menos.** Note that the preposition **de** is the equivalent of *in* or *of* after a superlative.

definite article + **más** or **menos** + *adjective* + **de**

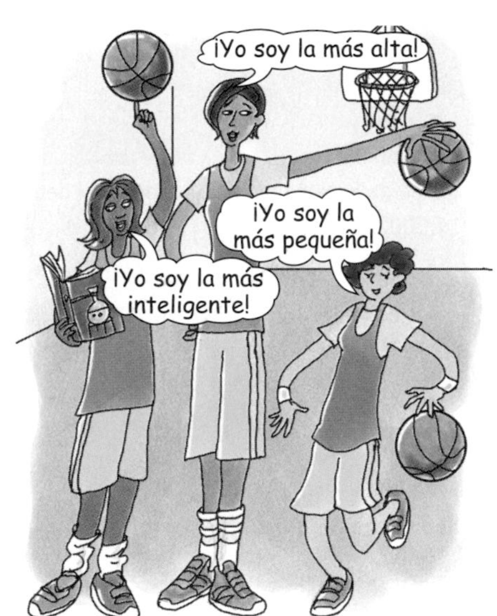

Antonio es **el más alto de** mis hermanos.	*Antonio is the tallest of my brothers.*
Este jabón es **el menos caro de** todos.	*This soap is the least expensive of all.*

- When a noun is used with the superlative, the article precedes the noun in Spanish.

Mi lápiz labial es **el** lápiz labial **más** caro que venden aquí.	*My lipstick is the most expensive lipstick they sell here.*
La casa de Carlos es **la** casa **más** popular **del** barrio.	*Carlos' house is the most popular in the neighborhood.*

- Adjectives and adverbs that have irregular forms in the comparative use the same irregular forms in the superlative.

Juan es el **mejor de** mis amigos.	*Juan is the best of my friends.*
La tía Isabel es **la mayor de** mis tías.	*Aunt Isabel is the oldest of my aunts.*

Aplicación

5-25 El Canal de Panamá. Lee el siguiente párrafo y subraya los superlativos.

La nación de Panamá controla el canal por donde navegan más de 14.000 barcos cada año.

El Canal de Panamá no es el más largo, ni el más ancho (*widest*), ni el más profundo (*deepest*), ni el más antiguo del mundo. Pero sí es el único que conecta dos océanos: el Atlántico y el Pacífico, y aún hoy es la vía de agua navegable más importante del mundo. Al principio, enfermedades como la malaria, la fiebre (*fever*) amarilla y el cólera causaron los problemas más graves de la construcción del canal. De todos los ingenieros, primero los franceses y después los norteamericanos, George Goethals fue el que tuvo más éxito en terminar el proyecto. Cuando completó el canal en 1914, era (*it was*) el peor momento de esa época: el comienzo de la Primera Guerra Mundial. Hoy en día, el canal todavía es una de las obras de ingeniería más impactantes del mundo.

5-26 ¿Cómo es el Canal de Panamá? Contesta las preguntas, basándote en la actividad **5-25.**

1. ¿Qué conecta el canal?
2. ¿Por qué es importante?
3. ¿En qué año se completó?
4. ¿Cuáles eran (*were*) los problemas más graves al principio?
5. ¿Cuál fue el ingeniero que tuvo más éxito de todos?
6. ¿Qué evento importante comenzó en 1914?

5-27 Otros superlativos de Centroamérica. Busca en el mapa de Centroamérica el nombre de estos lugares superlativos.

MODELO: el país de Centroamérica más popular entre los estudiantes
Costa Rica es el país más popular entre los estudiantes.

1. el país más grande de Centroamérica
2. el lago más grande de Nicaragua
3. el país más pequeño de Centroamérica
4. el país más sureño de Centroamérica
5. el país más estrecho (*narrow*) de Centroamérica

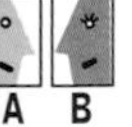

5-28A ¿Cómo son? Túrnense para preguntarse sobre "su familia". Imagínate que eres uno de los personajes *(characters)* de la serie popular, *The Brady Bunch*. Si no conocen a esta familia, pueden usar su familia. Estudiante B, por favor ve al **Apéndice 1,** página A6.

MODELO: más trabajador/a
E1: *¿Quién es el/la más trabajador/a de tu familia?*
E2: *Mi padre, Mike, es el más trabajador de mi familia.*

1. más alegre
2. más alto/a
3. menos responsable
4. menor
5. mayor
6. más simpático/a

 **5-29 Entre todos.** Aquí tienen series de tres cosas o lugares. Túrnense para compararlas, siempre diciendo (*saying*) cuál es el superlativo, en su opinión.

Modelo: Miami – Buenos Aires – Ciudad de Panamá (norteño)
Miami es la ciudad más norteña de las tres.

1. el Canal de Panamá – el Canal de Suez – el Canal de Erie (largo)
2. la Ciudad de Panamá – San José, Costa Rica – Managua (sureño)
3. la Ciudad de Panamá – San José, Costa Rica – Managua (grande)
4. Penélope Cruz – Daisy Fuentes – Mariah Carey (mayor)
5. Andy García – Benjamín Bratt – Rubén Blades (conocido: *well-known*)
6. la civilización de los aztecas – la civilización de los mayas – la civilización de los navajos (civilización antigua)

4. The present progressive

5-45 to 5-48

- The present progressive tense describes an action that is in progress at the time the statement is made. It is formed by using the present indicative of **estar** as an auxiliary verb and the present participle (the **-ando/-iendo** form) of the main verb. The present participle is invariable regardless of the subject. It never changes its ending. Only **estar** is conjugated when using the present progressive forms.

Present progressive of *hablar*			
yo	**estoy hablando**	nosotros/as	**estamos hablando**
tú	**estás hablando**	vosotros/as	**estáis hablando**
él, ella, Ud.	**está hablando**	ellos/as, Uds.	**están hablando**

- To form the present participle of regular **-ar** verbs, add **-ando** to the verb stem:

habl~~ar~~ + -ando → **hablando**

Los niños **están bailando** en la sala. — *The children are dancing in the living room.*

- To form the present participle of **-er** and **-ir** verbs, add **-iendo** to the verb stem:

com~~er~~ + -iendo → **comiendo** escrib~~ir~~ + -iendo → **escribiendo**

El profesor **se está poniendo** impaciente. — *The professor is becoming impatient.*

Estoy escribiendo la composición. — *I'm writing the composition.*

- **Leer** has an irregular present participle. The **i** from **-iendo** changes to **y.**

lee~~r~~ + -iendo → **leyendo**

- **-ir** verbs with a stem change will also have a change in the participle. This change will be indicated when you first encounter the infinitive.

dormir (ue, u)	*to sleep*	→	**durmiendo**	*sleeping*
pedir (i, i)	*to ask for*	→	**pidiendo**	*asking for*
servir (i, i)	*to serve*	→	**sirviendo**	*serving*

- Reflexive pronouns can either precede **estar** or be attached to the participle. Add an accent when the reflexive pronoun is attached to the participle.

Carlos se está vistiendo.
Carlos está vistiéndose. } *Carlos is getting dressed.*

Aplicación

5-30 ¿Qué estamos haciendo? Empareja el lugar donde estamos con lo que estamos haciendo.

Modelo: _____ Estamos en el laboratorio de ciencias.
Estamos estudiando para un examen de biología.

1. _____ Estamos en un café.
2. _____ Estamos en el sofá.
3. _____ Estamos en el parque.
4. _____ Estamos en un concierto.
5. _____ Estamos en clase.
6. _____ Estamos en un partido.
7. _____ Estamos en la biblioteca.
8. _____ Estamos en casa a la medianoche.

a. Estamos viendo la televisión.
b. Estamos escuchando música.
c. Estamos escribiendo apuntes en un cuaderno.
d. Estamos jugando al tenis.
e. Estamos leyendo un libro.
f. Estamos tomando un refresco.
g. Estamos durmiendo.
h. Estamos haciendo un pícnic.

5-31 ¡Imagínate! Escribe lo que imaginas que estas personas están haciendo ahora. Completa las oraciones lógicamente.

Modelo: el presidente de México
El presidente de México está visitando Monterrey.

1. Chef Emeril
2. Joaquín Phoenix
3. Derek Jeter
4. Katie Holmes y Tom Cruise
5. Pedro Almodóvar
6. Carlos Fuentes (autor)
7. Ricky Martin y Shakira
8. el vicepresidente de los EE.UU.

asistir a una fiesta
cantar
dormir
escribir una novela
hablar con…
hacer una película
jugar al béisbol
preparar una comida francesa

5-32 Lo siento, no está aquí. Túrnense para inventar excusas para explicar por qué un amigo no puede hablar por teléfono.

MODELO: E1: *Hola, ¿está Carlos?*
E2: *Lo siento, Carlos está ocupado ahora. Está limpiando el apartamento.*

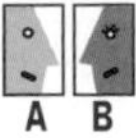

A B

5-33A ¿Qué estoy haciendo? Mientras (*While*) actúas una de las siguientes situaciones, tu pareja trata de adivinar (*guess*) lo que estás haciendo. Túrnense para actuar y adivinar. Estudiante B, por favor ve al **Apéndice 1,** página A6.

MODELO: afeitarse
E1: (act out "shaving") *¿Qué estoy haciendo?*
E2: *Estás afeitándote.*

1. cepillarse los dientes
2. maquillarse
3. bañarse
4. mirarse en el espejo

¿Cuánto sabes tú? *¿Can you…*

5-49 to 5-52

☐ talk about what you do around the house using verbs like **limpiar, ordenar,** and **sacudir**?
☐ describe your house, its rooms, and some of its furniture?
☐ describe people and things as the best, worst, tallest, etc.?
☐ say what people are doing at the moment (**Estoy lavándome el pelo.**)?

Observaciones

Episode 5

¡Pura vida! Episodio 5

En este episodio hay conflicto entre Hermés y Marcela.

5-53 to 5-56

Antes de ver el video

5-34 Los quehaceres de la casa. En muchas familias de clase media es común tener la ayuda de alguien *(someone)* en la casa. Lee la situación de la familia de Silvia y contesta brevemente las siguientes preguntas en español.

Vivimos en Madrid. Como (*Since*) mi padre y mi madre trabajan fuera (*outside*) de casa, tenemos una señora que nos ayuda con los quehaceres. Se llama Ana y viene todos los lunes, miércoles y viernes. Pasa tres o cuatro horas lavando la ropa, ordenando la casa, lavando los platos y limpiando los pisos. Algunas veces, también va al mercado y hace las compras para la cena, pero mi mamá siempre prepara la comida. Con frecuencia, tenemos visita (*guests*) los viernes por la noche: mis abuelos y mis tíos o algunos amigos de la oficina de mis padres. En esas ocasiones, Ana prepara algo especial, como una paella o una torta. Después, el sábado por la mañana tenemos que lavar los platos.

Una casa de apartamentos en Madrid.

1. ¿Dónde vive la familia de Silvia?
2. ¿Por qué necesitan a la señora que les ayuda a mantener la casa?
3. ¿Cuáles son los quehaceres de Ana?
4. ¿Quién normalmente prepara la cena?

A ver el video

5-35 Hay conflicto en casa. Mira el quinto episodio de *¡Pura vida!* para identificar el conflicto entre Marcela y Hermés. Luego, empareja (*pair*) las frases para formar oraciones lógicas.

Marcela

Marcela y Hermés

La lista de quehaceres.

1. _____ Hermés trabaja...
2. _____ A Marcela le molestan...
3. _____ Hermés dice que siempre...
4. _____ Marcela dice que ella siempre...
5. _____ Según Silvia, cada uno...

a. los papeles que están en el piso.
b. saca la basura.
c. plancha su ropa y hace su cama.
d. lavando platos en un restaurante.
e. limpia el baño.

Después de ver el video

WWW

5-36 Servicio de limpieza. Conéctate con la página web de **¡Arriba!** para buscar servicio doméstico. Escoge uno que te guste y anota los servicios y el costo, si se incluye.

NUESTRO MUNDO

Panoramas

La América Central II: Costa Rica, Nicaragua, Panamá

Vistas culturales

5-37 ¿Ya sabes...? Trata *(Try)* de identificar lo siguiente.

5-57 to 5-58

1. las capitales de Costa Rica, Nicaragua y Panamá
2. un huracán que causó (*caused*) daño (*damage*) en gran parte de Centroamérica
3. el nombre de la presidenta de Nicaragua famosa por promover la paz (*peace*)
4. un animal en peligro de extinción

La rana, entre otros animales exóticos, sirve de modelo para los diseños de oro de los indígenas precolombinos de Centroamérica.

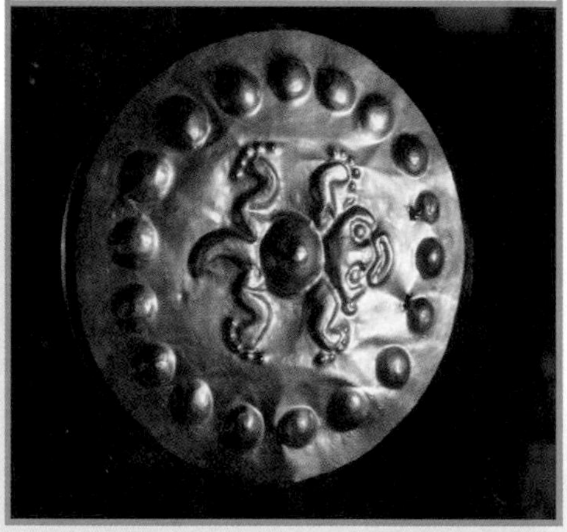

HONDURAS
EL SALVADOR
Río Coco
Puerto Cabezas
Cayos Miskitos
Matagalpa
Río Grande de Matagalpa
Golfo de Fonseca
León
NICARAGUA
Managua
Granada
Bluefields
Lago de Nicaragua
Islas del Maíz
Río San Juan
Mar Caribe
COSTA RICA
Puntarenas
San José
Orosi
Puerto Limón
Puerto Quepos
Golfito
Bocas del Toro
Canal de Panamá
Colón
Panamá
Balboa
David
PANAMÁ
Archipiélago de las Perlas
La Palma
Santiago
Golfo de Panamá
Isla de Coiba
OCÉANO PACÍFICO
AMÉRICA DEL SUR
COLOMBIA

Los desastres naturales son parte de la vida de Centroamérica. Hay volcanes activos, terremotos (*earthquakes*) y huracanes. En el huracán Mitch de 1998, uno de los desastres naturales más destructivos del siglo XX, más de 10.000 personas murieron (*died*) en Centroamérica. Gran parte de la infraestructura, la agricultura y la economía también se perdió (*was lost*) en el huracán.

Hay una gran variedad de ranas en las selvas costarricenses. Algunas segregan (*secrete*) líquidos venenosos (*poisonous*); otras, alucinógenos.

Violeta Chamorro, presidenta de Nicaragua, 1990–96, trabajó para restaurar la estabilidad política y económica del país. Ahora encabeza *La Fundación Violeta Chamorro,* cuya misión es promover la paz, la democracia, la libertad de expresión y la disminución de la pobreza.

La Fundación Pro-Iguana Verde de Costa Rica se dedica a la protección de los animales en peligro de extinción, como la iguana verde y el guacamayo escarlata.

Los indios Kuna, que habitan las islas de San Blas cerca de la costa de Panamá, se conocen por sus bellas molas, textiles que representan la flora y la fauna de la región. Las mujeres usan faldas y blusas de vívidos colores, decoradas en el pecho (*chest*) y la espalda (*back*). La sociedad de los Kuna es un matriarcado; la mujer hereda los bienes de su familia y cuando se casa, su esposo va a vivir en la casa de ella.

5-38 ¿Cierto o falso? Corrige las oraciones falsas.

1. _____ *La Fundación Pro-Iguana Verde* es activa en la conservación del medio ambiente (*environment*) en Costa Rica.
2. _____ El huracán Mitch causó daños (*damages*) en gran parte de Centroamérica.
3. _____ La mola es un ejemplo de artesanía nicaragüense.
4. _____ Violeta Chamorro fue la esposa del presidente de Nicaragua.
5. _____ El guacamayo escarlata es un animal en peligro de extinción.
6. _____ Algunas de las ranas centroamericanas son venenosas.
7. _____ El Canal de Panamá es territorio norteamericano.
8. _____ La sociedad Kuna es un patriarcado.

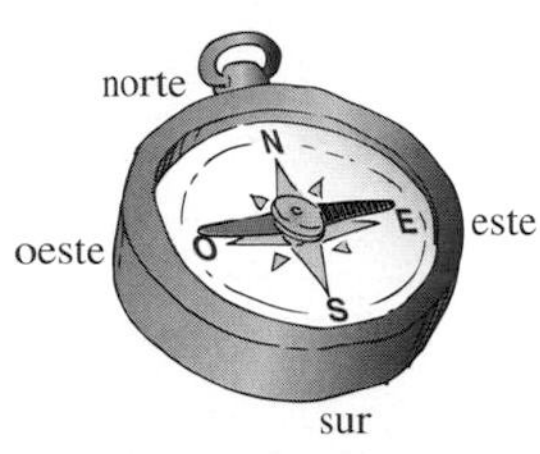

5-39 ¿Dónde? Identifica en el mapa de Centroamérica de este libro, en la página 180, dónde hay las siguientes cosas.

1. playas
2. artesanía
3. comercio marítimo
4. volcanes
5. mucha lluvia
6. cultivo de café

5-40 El mapa. Revisen el mapa de Centroamérica e identifiquen en qué país se encuentran estos sitios, ciudades y países.

Modelo: La Isla de Coiba
La Isla de Coiba está en el Océano Pacífico.

al este de...
al norte de...
al oeste de...
al sur de...
en la costa del Caribe
en la costa del golfo de México
en la costa del Pacífico
en el centro
en la península de...
en la frontera

1. el Lago de Nicaragua
2. el Canal de Panamá
3. Colombia
4. San José
5. el Río Coco
6. el Golfo de Panamá

5-41 Investigar. Conéctate con la página web de **¡Arriba!** y contesta una de estas preguntas.

1. ¿Cuál es la misión de *La Fundación Violeta Chamorro*?
2. ¿Cuáles son algunos de los animales que vas a ver en una visita a Costa Rica?
3. Busca una mola que te gusta y descríbela.
4. ¿Cuáles son algunas de las canciones exitosas (*hits*) de Rubén Blades?
5. ¿Qué hace *La Fundación Pro-Iguana Verde* para proteger los animales en peligro de extinción?

Ritmos

5-59

"Ligia Elena" (Rubén Blades, Panamá)

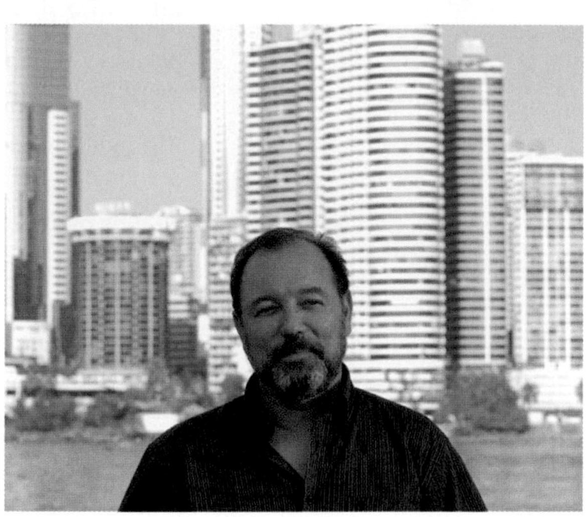

Uno de los temas de esta canción es el amor prohibido. Es un amor entre dos jóvenes de raza y de clase social distintas: Ligia Elena, que es de la alta sociedad, y un trompetista, que es de la vecindad *(neighborhood)*. Ella es blanca y él es afrohispano. Los padres de Ligia Elena están escandalizados por el amor entre su hija y el trompetista.

Ligia Elena la cándida niña de la sociedad,
se ha fugado con un trompetista de la vecindad.
El padre la busca afanosamente,
lo está comentando toda la gente,
y la madre pregunta angustiada ¿en dónde estará?

[...]
Se han mudado a un cuarto chiquito con muy pocos muebles,
y allí viven contentos y llenos de felicidad.
Mientras tristes los padres preguntan, ¿en dónde fallamos?
Ligia Elena con su trompetista amándose está.

Dulcemente se escurren los días en aquel cuartito,
mientras que en las mansiones lujosas de la sociedad,
otras niñas que saben del cuento, al dormir preguntan:
"ay señor, y mi trompetista, ¿cuándo llegará?".

[...]
Ligia Elena está contenta y su familia está asfixiá'.[1]
Ligia Elena está contenta y su familia está asfixiá'.

Antes de escuchar

5-42 Comparaciones. Usando comparaciones de igualdad y de desigualdad, indica tus opiniones sobre los siguientes elementos relacionados con los temas de la canción.

Modelo: El amor es **más** importante **que** el dinero.

el amor	las clases sociales
las relaciones familiares	la amistad
el dinero	la felicidad
el color de la piel *(skin)*	la independencia
las profesiones	el lujo *(luxury)*

5-43 Opiniones. Ahora intercambia *(exchange)* tus comparaciones con las de un/a compañero/a de clase para ver si está de acuerdo *(agrees)* contigo.

[1]asfixiada

A escuchar

5-44 Acciones. Mientras escuchas "Ligia Elena" completa las siguientes oraciones con el presente progresivo para indicar lo que están haciendo las diferentes personas. Luego completa cada oración con tus propias palabras.

Modelo: Rubén Blades / estar / cantar / ____.
Rubén Blades *está cantando* "Ligia Elena".

1. Ligia Elena / estar / hablar ____.
2. El trompetista / estar / tocar ____.
3. Los padres de Ligia Elena / estar / llorar ____.
4. Los estudiantes y yo / estar / tratar de ____.
5. Tú / estar / leer ____.

Después de escuchar

5-45 ¿Cómo se sienten? Usa la construcción reflexiva para formar oraciones que describan cómo Ligia Elena, sus padres u otros pueden sentirse sobre un amor prohibido. Usa los sujetos y verbos siguientes.

Ligia Elena	ponerse (+ adjetivo)	cuando...
los padres	alegrarse	si...
el novio	enamorarse	
yo	enojarse	
mis amigos	divertirse	
la familia	aburrirse	

5-46 Pensamientos. Ahora, habla con tus compañeros/as de clase sobre Rubén Blades y su música, y completen las oraciones según sus opiniones.

Cuando pensamos en...

1. ...los temas de "Ligia Elena", nosotros/as ________.
2. ...la música salsa, nosotros/as ________.
3. ...el activismo político de Rubén Blades y de otros, nosotros/as ________.

Páginas

5-60

Playa Cacao

Antes de leer

5-47 Lo que ya sabes. Lo que ya sabes de algo (*something*) juega un papel (*role*) importante para entender lo que lees. Por ejemplo, en la construcción de una casa, los materiales dependen del clima y de otros factores como el gusto (*taste*), la situación económica, etc. Antes de leer la descripción de la casa que aparece a continuación, piensa en tus preferencias para comprar una casa.

Para mí, la casa debe...

_____ tener muchos dormitorios

_____ respetar el medio ambiente (*environment*)

_____ estar cerca de buenas escuelas

_____ estar en un barrio seguro (*safe*)

_____ tener una cocina bien equipada

_____ costar más (menos) de $150.000

_____ otros requisitos (*requirements*)

A leer

5-48 Esta casa. Mientras lees la descripción de esta casa, compárala con tu casa ideal. ¿Qué tiene la casa que te gusta? ¿Qué tiene la casa que no te gusta?

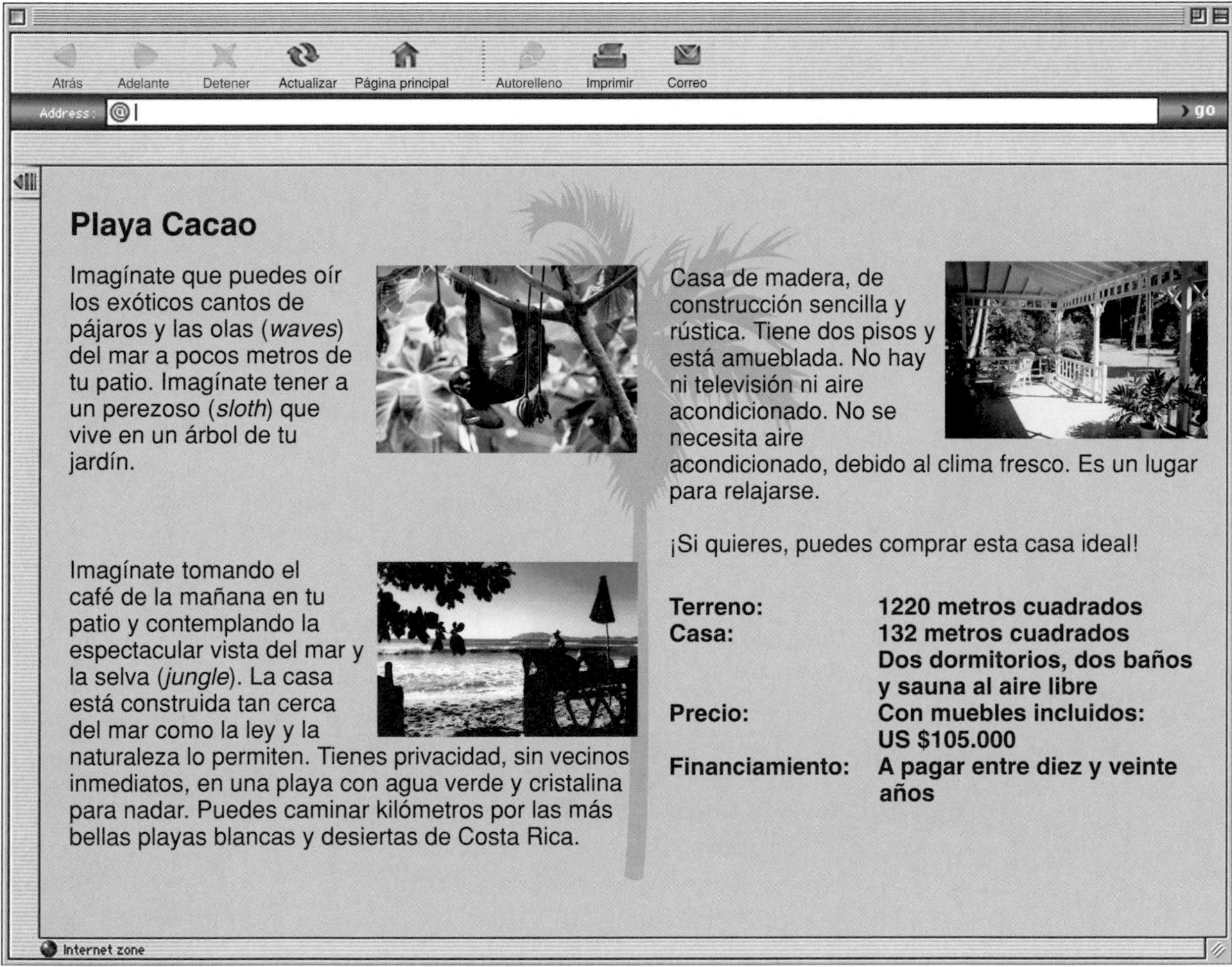

Atrás Adelante Detener Actualizar Página principal Autorelleno Imprimir Correo

Address:

go

Playa Cacao

Imagínate que puedes oír los exóticos cantos de pájaros y las olas (*waves*) del mar a pocos metros de tu patio. Imagínate tener a un perezoso (*sloth*) que vive en un árbol de tu jardín.

Imagínate tomando el café de la mañana en tu patio y contemplando la espectacular vista del mar y la selva (*jungle*). La casa está construida tan cerca del mar como la ley y la naturaleza lo permiten. Tienes privacidad, sin vecinos inmediatos, en una playa con agua verde y cristalina para nadar. Puedes caminar kilómetros por las más bellas playas blancas y desiertas de Costa Rica.

Casa de madera, de construcción sencilla y rústica. Tiene dos pisos y está amueblada. No hay ni televisión ni aire acondicionado. No se necesita aire acondicionado, debido al clima fresco. Es un lugar para relajarse.

¡Si quieres, puedes comprar esta casa ideal!

Terreno:	**1220 metros cuadrados**
Casa:	**132 metros cuadrados** **Dos dormitorios, dos baños y sauna al aire libre**
Precio:	**Con muebles incluidos: US $105.000**
Financiamiento:	**A pagar entre diez y veinte años**

Internet zone

Después de leer

5-49 ¿Comprendiste? Resume *(Summarize)* las características de la casa que aparece en la página web.

1. Ubicación (*Location*) _____________________
2. Número de dormitorios _____________________
3. Accesorios incluidos _____________________
4. Número de pisos _____________________
5. Número de baños _____________________
6. ¿A/C? _____________________
7. Precio *(Price)* _____________________
8. ¿Vista (*View*)? _____________________

5-50 ¿Compras esta casa? Hablen sobre si piensan comprar o no esta casa y por qué.

Modelo: E1: *Compro esta casa porque...*
E2: *Pues, yo no la compro porque...*

Taller

5-61 to 5-62

5-51 Vendo casa. En esta actividad vas a diseñar (*design*) un anuncio o página web para vender una casa como la que aparece en **Páginas.**

Antes de escribir

- Comienza con una lista para dar más información sobre tu casa:
  - ☐ su ubicación (ciudad, país, cerca de...)
  - ☐ los metros cuadrados
  - ☐ los dormitorios y su descripción
  - ☐ los accesorios incluidos
  - ☐ los accesorios extras (*additional*): patio, piscina (*pool*), vista, cancha de tenis, etcétera
  - ☐ las actividades que uno puede hacer en la casa o en la comunidad
  - ☐ el precio
  - ☐ las fotos o dibujos para ilustrar la casa

A escribir

- **Descripción.** Ahora escribe dos párrafos para describir la casa. Recuerda, deseas venderla.

Después de escribir

- **Revisar.** Revisa la descripción para verificar los siguientes puntos:
  - ☐ el uso correcto de los verbos reflexivos
  - ☐ el uso de comparativos y superlativos
  - ☐ el uso del presente progresivo
  - ☐ la ortografía, incluidos los acentos
- **Intercambiar**
  Intercambia tu anuncio con el de un/a compañero/a y comenten sobre el diseño de cada anuncio y si es efectivo.
- **Entregar**
  Revisa tu anuncio, incorporando (*incorporating*) las sugerencias de tu compañero/a. Después, dale el anuncio y las respuestas de tu compañero/a a tu profesor/a.

Vocabulario

Primera parte

Las actividades diarias	*Daily activities*
acostarse (ue)	*to go to bed*
afeitarse	*to shave*
bañarse	*to bathe*
cepillarse	*to brush*
despertarse (ie)	*to wake up*
dormirse (ue, u)	*to fall asleep*
ducharse	*to take a shower*
lavarse	*to wash*
levantarse	*to get up; to stand up*
maquillarse	*to apply makeup*
peinarse	*to comb*
quitarse	*to take off*
secarse	*to dry off*
sentarse (ie)	*to sit down*
vestirse (i, i)	*to get dressed*

Algunas emociones	*Some emotions*
ponerse contento/a	*to become happy*
furioso/a	*angry*
impaciente	*impatient*
nervioso/a	*nervous*
triste	*sad*
reírse (i, i)	*to laugh*
sentirse (ie, i)	*to feel*

Algunas partes del cuerpo	*Some parts of the body*
la cara	*face*
los dientes	*teeth*
la mano	*hand*
la nariz	*nose*
el ojo	*eye*
el pelo	*hair*

Artículos de uso personal	*Personal care items*
el cepillo (de dientes)	*(tooth) brush*
el champú	*shampoo*
la crema (de afeitar)	*(shaving) cream*
el desodorante	*deodorant*
el espejo	*mirror*
el jabón	*soap*
el lápiz labial	*lipstick*
la loción (de afeitar)	*(shaving) lotion*
el maquillaje	*makeup*
la máquina de afeitar	*electric razor*
la navaja de afeitar	*razor blade*
el peine	*comb*
el secador	*hair dryer*

Segunda parte

Los accesorios y los muebles	*Furniture and accessories*
la aspiradora	*vacuum cleaner*
el basurero	*garbage can*
la cama	*bed*
la cómoda	*dresser*
el cuadro	*painting*
la escoba	*broom*
el estante	*bookcase*
la lámpara	*lamp*
la lavadora	*washing machine*
el lavaplatos	*dishwasher*
la mesa	*table*
la mesa de noche	*nightstand*
los muebles	*furniture*
la plancha	*iron*
la secadora	*dryer*
el sillón	*armchair; overstuffed chair*
el sofá	*sofa; couch*

Los quehaceres domésticos	*Household chores*
barrer el piso	*to sweep the floor*
hacer la cama	*to make the bed*
lavar los platos	*to wash dishes*
lavar la ropa	*to wash clothes*
limpiar/ordenar la casa	*to clean the house*
pasar la aspiradora	*to vacuum*
planchar	*to iron*
poner la mesa	*to set the table*
quitar la mesa	*to clear the table*
sacar la basura	*to take out the garbage*
sacudir el polvo (de los muebles)	*to dust (the furniture)*
secar la ropa	*to dry clothes*

Las partes de una casa	*Parts of a house*
el baño	*bathroom*
la casa	*house*
la cocina	*kitchen*
el comedor	*dining room*
el cuarto	*room; bedroom*
el dormitorio	*bedroom*
el garaje	*garage*
el jardín	*garden*
el pasillo	*hallway*
el patio	*patio; backyard*
el piso	*floor*
la sala	*living room*
la terraza	*terrace*

Reflexive pronouns	*See page 159.*
Comparisons of equality and inequality	*See page 163.*
The superlative	*See page 173.*

6 ¡Buen provecho!

PRIMERA PARTE

¡Así lo decimos! Vocabulario	Las comidas y las bebidas
¡Así lo hacemos! Estructuras	The verbs **decir** and **dar**
	Indirect objects and indirect object pronouns
	Gustar and similar verbs
Comparaciones	La compra de la comida y la cocina chilena

- Discussing food, eating preferences, and ordering meals
- Talking about things and expressing to whom or for whom
- Expressing likes and dislikes

SEGUNDA PARTE

¡Así lo decimos! Vocabulario	En la cocina
¡Así lo hacemos! Estructuras	The preterit of regular verbs
	Verbs with irregular forms in the preterit (I)
Observaciones	¡Pura vida! Episodio 6

- Discussing cooking and recipes
- Talking about events in the past

NUESTRO MUNDO

Panoramas	Chile: un país de contrastes
Ritmos	"Tren al sur" (Los prisioneros, Chile)
Páginas	"El Santiago" (Reseña periodística)
Taller	Una reseña de un restaurante

Ajos y col (1984) es una naturaleza muerta (*still life*) por el pintor chileno Claudio Bravo.

Source: Claudio Bravo, "Ajos y Col," 1984, oil on canvas, 52.1 x 65.2 cm. © Claudio Bravo, courtesy, Marlborough Gallery, New York

Chile: un país de contrastes

«Disfruta, come y bebe, que la vida es breve.»*

Isabel Allende es una de las escritoras latinoamericanas contemporáneas más conocidas.

*__Refrán:__ Enjoy, eat, and drink, for life is short.

¡Así lo decimos! Vocabulario

CD 2, Track 1

6-1 to 6-2

¡Así es la vida! ¡Buen provecho!

Arturo: ¡Este bufé es fantástico! ¡Todo es realmente exquisito!
Marta: Sí, mira estos camarones a la parrilla, ¿los quieres probar?
Arturo: Sí, me encantan los camarones.
Marta: ¿Tienen bebidas? No las veo.
Arturo: Sí, aquí. ¿Qué quieres?
Marta: Una limonada, por favor.
Arturo: Ah, pues yo voy a tomar una copa de vino tinto.
Marta: ¿Sabes si además del bufé tienen alguna especialidad de la casa?
Arturo: No sé pero mira, ahí viene el camarero con un menú. Enseguida se lo pregunto...

Las comidas y las bebidas

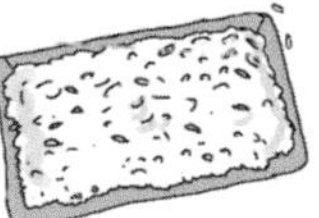
el arroz

el bistec

el café

los camarones

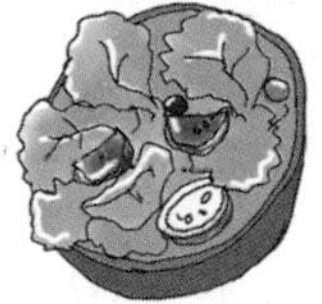
la ensalada

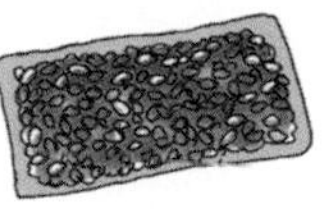
los frijoles

el helado

la langosta

la leche

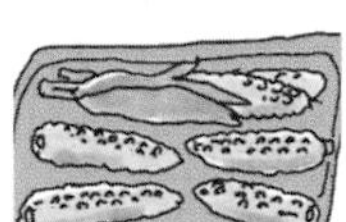
el maíz

las manzanas

el pan

las papas

el pescado

el pollo

el queso

la sopa

la torta de chocolate

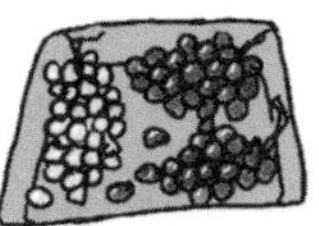
las uvas

el vino

Más comidas y bebidas	*More foods and beverages*
el agua (mineral)	*(mineral) water*
el azúcar	*sugar*
la banana	*banana*
el bocadillo/el sándwich	*sandwich*
las carnes	*meats*
la cerveza	*beer*
el flan	*custard dessert*
las frutas	*fruits*
las galletas	*cookies*
la hamburguesa	*hamburger*
los huevos	*eggs*
el jamón	*ham*
el jugo[1] **(de naranja)**	*(orange) juice*
la lechuga	*lettuce*
la limonada	*lemonade*
la mantequilla	*butter*
los mariscos	*seafood*
la naranja	*orange*
el pastel	*cake; pie*
el pavo	*turkey*
el pimiento	*pepper*
el refresco	*soft drink*
la sal	*salt*
la tarta de limón	*lemon pie*
el té	*tea*
el tomate	*tomato*
la toronja[2]	*grapefruit*
las verduras	*vegetables*
el yogur	*yogurt*
las zanahorias	*carrots*

Las comidas	*Meals*
el almuerzo	*lunch*
la cena	*dinner*
el desayuno	*breakfast*
la merienda	*snack*

En un restaurante	*In a restaurant*
el bufé	*buffet*
el/la camarero/a	*waiter/waitress*
el/la cliente	*client; customer*
la cuenta	*bill*
la especialidad de la casa	*house specialty*
el menú	*menu*
la propina	*tip*
el/la vegetariano/a	*vegetarian*

Expresiones	*Expressions*
¡Buen provecho!	*Enjoy your meal!*
¿Desean algo de tomar/comer?	*Would you like something to drink/eat?*
Enseguida	*Right away*

Adjetivos	*Adjectives*
caliente	*hot*
frío/a	*cold*
picante	*hot (spicy)*
rico/a[3]	*delicious*

Verbos	*Verbs*
almorzar (ue)	*to have lunch*
cenar	*to have dinner*
dar	*to give*
decir	*to say*
desayunar	*to have breakfast*

[1] **el zumo** en España

[2] **el pomelo** en España

[3] Used with **estar, rico/a** means *to taste delicious.* Used with **ser,** it means *wealthy.*

Aplicación

6-1 Arturo y Marta. Indica a quién se refiere cada una de las descripciones a continuación.

1. _____ Le encantan los camarones.
2. _____ Toma vino con la comida.
3. _____ Prefiere tomar limonada.
4. _____ Quiere saber si hay alguna especialidad de la casa.

6-2 ¿Qué es? Empareja la comida con su descripción.

MODELO: Es verde. Forma parte de una ensalada.
la lechuga

1. _____ Es una fruta amarilla.
2. _____ Se comen con el arroz.
3. _____ Es una carne rosada.
4. _____ Es un postre con muchas calorías.
5. _____ Es una bebida con cafeína.
6. _____ Es rojo y se usa mucho en la salsa italiana.
7. _____ Es un postre frío hecho con crema, huevos y azúcar.
8. _____ Se comen y también se usan para hacer vino.

a. el jamón
b. el tomate
c. la banana
d. las uvas
e. el té
f. los frijoles
g. el helado
h. la torta de chocolate

CD 2, Track 3

6-3 ¡Buen provecho! Indica en la cuenta la comida y la bebida que piden Marta y Arturo en el Café El Náufrago con Arturo (**A**) o Marta (**M**).

Avenida Allende 489 • Tel. 311-1539 • Valparaiso

FECHA ___/___/___ MESERO/A ____________ MESA ___

TOTAL

VINO ______ TINTO ______ BLANCO
REFRESCO ______ AGUA MINERAL ______ CERVEZA
JUGO DE MANZANA ______ DE NARANJA ______
DE TORONJA ______

CAMARONES ______
ATÚN ______
FILETE DE PESCADO ______
CALAMARES ______
SALMÓN ______
B. DE CHORIZO ______

ENSALADA MIXTA ______
PAPAS FRITAS ______ TOMATE Y CEBOLLA ______
PAN ______ PAPA AL HORNO ______

HELADO DE LIMÓN ______ DE CHOCOLATE ______
FLAN ______
ENSALADA DE FRUTAS ______
CAFÉ ______ TÉ ______

CUENTA TOTAL
(IVA INCLUIDO)

6-4 Ahora tú. Túrnense para preguntarse qué piden para cada comida del menú del Café El Náufrago.

MODELO: la cena
E1: *¿Qué pides para la cena?*
E2: *Pido una ensalada.*
E1: *¿Es todo?*

1. la cena
2. el desayuno
3. la merienda
4. el almuerzo

6-5 La comida, ¿qué prefieres? En un grupo de tres personas, pregunten qué prefieren comer. Indiquen cuántos de ustedes prefieren lo siguiente.

MODELO: **desayunar** todos los días
E1: *¿Desayunas todos los días? Yo, sí.*
E2: *No, sólo cuando tengo tiempo.*
E3: *Sí, siempre desayuno.*

PREFERENCIAS	NÚMERO DE PERSONAS EN SU GRUPO QUE DICEN QUE SÍ
desayunar todos los días	*3*
cenar a las diez de la noche	____
ser vegetariano/a	____
comer la langosta	____
tomar café con la comida	____
ser alérgico/a a los mariscos	____
almorzar en la universidad	____
preferir la leche en vez de los refrescos	____

6-6 Mi pirámide. En 2005 se introdujo una nueva pirámide de la alimentación. Aquí tienen los resultados para una mujer de veinticinco años. Túrnense para decir si comen más o menos de lo que deben comer de cada grupo, según (*according to*) la pirámide.

MODELO: E1: *Según la pirámide debo comer dos tazas de frutas todos los días. Creo que como más de cuatro.*
E2: *Pues, yo también como muchas frutas…*

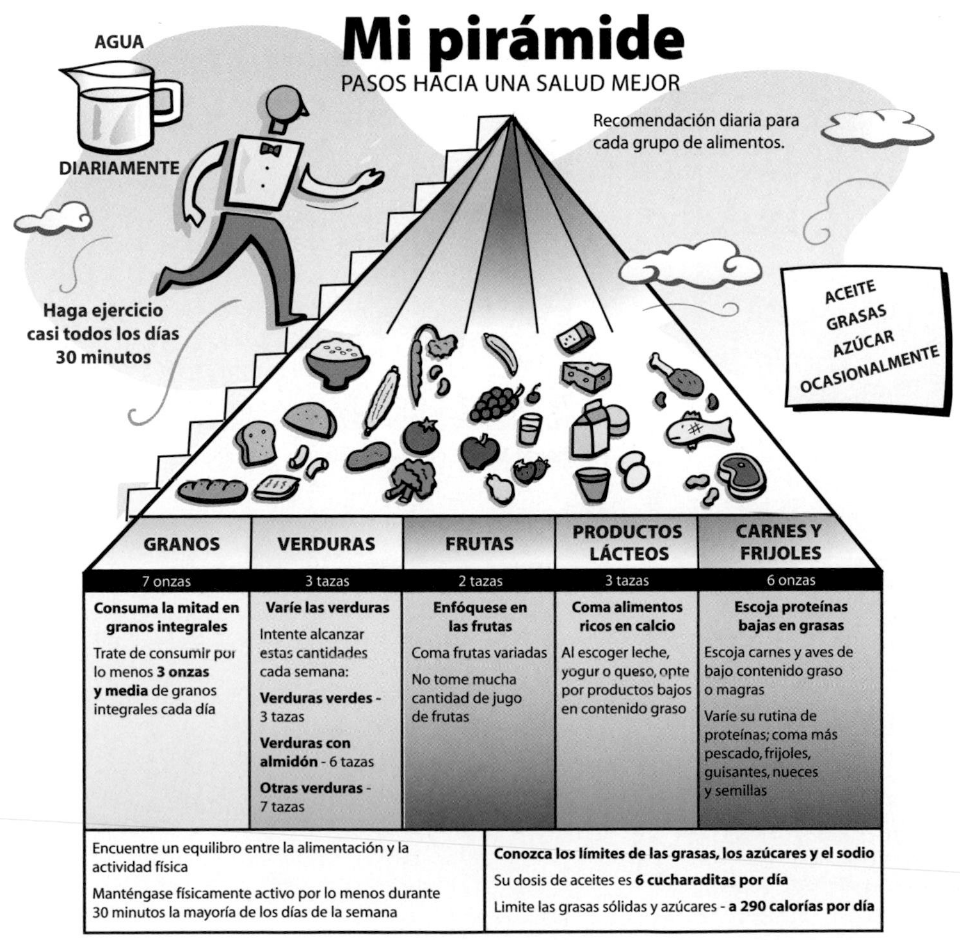

6-7 Tu pirámide. Conéctate con la página web de **¡Arriba!** para hacer un análisis de los alimentos que necesitas. Completa el siguiente cuadro según los resultados.

Edad:	
Sexo:	
Número de calorías diarias:	
Cantidad de productos lácteos:	
Cantidad de aceites:	
Cantidad de carnes y frijoles:	
Límite diario de grasas sólidas y azúcares:	

6-8 ¿Qué compramos para la cena? Refiéranse a la pirámide de la alimentación en la actividad **6-6** y decidan qué van a comprar para la cena. Tengan en cuenta (*Keep in mind*) las siguientes consideraciones.

1. Uno/a de ustedes es vegetariano/a.
2. Uno/a de ustedes está a dieta.
3. Uno/a de ustedes es deportista *(athlete)*.
4. Uno/a de ustedes está muy ocupado/a.

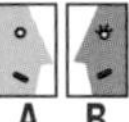

6-9A Cocina Concha. Esta "cocina" (restaurante informal) es una de las muchas que se encuentran por la costa chilena, donde las especialidades son pescados y mariscos. Imagínate que tú eres el cliente. Tienes 27.000 pesos (US $30) para la cena. Decide qué vas a pedir. Estudiante B, por favor ve al **Apéndice 1,** página A6.

Puerto Montt: un paraíso visual y culinario

¡Así lo hacemos! Estructuras

6-9 to 6-16

1. The verbs *decir* and *dar*, indirect objects, and indirect object pronouns

Decir y dar

- **Decir** is an **e → i** stem-changing verb with an irregular first-person singular form (like **tener** and **venir**).

decir *(to say)*			
yo	**dig**o	nosotros/as	decimos
tú	d**i**ces	vosotros/as	decís
él, ella, Ud.	d**i**ce	ellos/as, Uds.	d**i**cen

- **Dar** has an irregular first-person singular form like **ser** and **estar.**

dar *(to give)*			
yo	d**oy**	nosotros/as	damos
tú	das	vosotros/as	dais
él, ella, Ud.	da	ellos/as, Uds.	dan

- The verbs **decir** and **dar** often require indirect object pronouns.

Los pronombres de complementos indirectos

An indirect object indicates to or for whom an action is carried out. In Spanish the indirect object pronoun is also used to indicate from whom something is bought, borrowed, or taken away.

Indirect object pronouns			
	Singular		**Plural**
me	*(to) me*	**nos**	*(to) us*
te	*(to) you*	**os**	*(to) you* (fam. Sp.)
le	*(to) him, her, you* (for.)	**les**	*(to) them, to you*

- The forms of the indirect object pronouns are identical to the direct object pronouns, except for the third-person singular and plural forms.
- Indirect object pronouns agree only in number with the noun to which they refer. There is no gender agreement.

  Le lavo los platos. — *I'll wash the dishes for her.*
  ¿Me preparas arroz para la cena? — *Can you prepare rice for dinner for me?*

- Indirect object pronouns usually precede the conjugated verb.

  Te compramos el almuerzo. — *We'll buy you lunch.*

- In negative sentences the indirect object pronoun is placed between **no** and the conjugated verb.

  No **le** doy mi receta. — *I won't give him my recipe.*

- In constructions with an infinitive, the indirect object pronouns may either precede the conjugated verb or be attached to the infinitive.

  Mamá **nos** quiere enseñar a cocinar.
  Mamá quiere enseñar**nos** a cocinar. } *Mom wants to teach us how to cook.*

- The familiar plural form, **os** (**vosotros**), is used in Spain.

EXPANSIÓN **More on structure and usage**

Redundant indirect objects

When the indirect object refers to a specific person or group of people and is included in the sentence, the corresponding indirect object pronoun is also included. These are called redundant or repetitive indirect object pronouns. They have no English equivalent and are only used with third person nouns. Thus **le** or **les** are the only redundant indirect object pronouns.

Le damos las galletas **a Julia.**	*We give the cookies to Julia.*
Les lavo los platos **a mis amigos.**	*I wash the dishes for my friends.*

Use of prepositional pronouns for emphasis

To emphasize or clarify an indirect object, you can also use the corresponding prepositional pronouns with a prepositional phrase beginning with **a.**

me... a mí	nos... a nosotros/as
te... a ti	os... a vosotros/as
le... a él, a ella, a Ud.	les... a ellos/as, a Uds.

La niña **le** dice su nombre **a él.**	*The girl tells him her name.*
La profesora **me** da los papeles **a mí.**	*The professor gives the papers to me.*

Aplicación

6-10 Michelle Bachelet. La presidenta de Chile tiene muchos planes para el futuro de este país. Lee el párrafo sobre ella y subraya todos los pronombres de complementos indirectos.

Michelle Bachelet fue electa presidenta de Chile en 2006.

Al tomar la presidencia de Chile, Michelle Bachelet les va a explicar a los ciudadanos sus metas (*goals*) para el futuro. Primero, aunque sólo un 34% de las mujeres en Chile trabaja fuera de la casa, piensa nombrar a mujeres para muchos de los puestos *(positions)* de ministros en su gabinete *(cabinet)*. Les va a dar responsabilidad de formar nuevas leyes para el bienestar de la nación. También, les asegura *(assures)* a todos que su gobierno va a respetar a todos los chilenos, hombres y mujeres. Les manifiesta que va a bajar la tasa de desempleo *(unemployment rate)*, mejorar el sistema de seguro social y trabajar para mejorar el sistema de salud *(health)*.

6-11 Michelle Bachelet en Santiago. Contesta las preguntas, basándote en la actividad **6-10.**

1. ¿Cuál es la nacionalidad de Michelle Bachelet?
2. ¿Cuáles son algunas de sus promesas?
3. ¿En qué año fue electa presidenta?
4. En tu opinión, ¿cuál es su meta más importante?

6-12 Más cosas que promete Bachelet. Ahora, escribe en los espacios en blanco los pronombres de complemento indirecto para describir lo que va a hacer Michelle Bachelet como presidenta.

1. _____ va a subir los salarios a los trabajadores.
2. _____ va a explicar a su hija que necesita cambiar de escuela.
3. _____ va a escribir cartas a sus amigos invitándolos a la inauguración.
4. Decide que va a dar _____ a sus padres su apartamento.
5. _____ enseña la oficina a su asesor (*advisor*).
6. _____ va a prometer al público dar conferencias de prensa *(press)* todas las semanas.

6-13 Ahora tú. Imagínate que te vas a Chile por un año. Contesta las siguientes preguntas sobre lo que va a pasar durante tu ausencia.

1. ¿Quién te va a cuidar la casa?
2. ¿Quiénes te van a escribir correos electrónicos?
3. ¿A quién le vas a vender tu coche?
4. ¿Quiénes te desean un buen viaje?

6-14 ¿Qué te hace la familia? Hablen de lo que su familia les hace a ustedes y comparen las cosas que tienen en común.

Modelo: *Mi padre me prepara la comida, pero no me lava los platos.*

6-15 Algo especial. Hablen de lo que ustedes dan o dicen en las siguientes situaciones.

Modelo: a tu hermano en su cumpleaños
Le digo: "Feliz cumpleaños" y le doy un beso.

1. a tu madre el Día de las Madres
2. a tu padre el Día de los Padres
3. a tu esposo/a o novio/a el día de su aniversario
4. a tu profesor/a al final del curso
5. a un/a turista en la calle

2. *Gustar* and similar verbs

6-17 to 6-22 The verb **gustar** is used to express preferences, likes, and dislikes. **Gustar** literally means *to be pleasing*, and the verb is used with an indirect object pronoun.

No me gusta desayunar.	*I don't like to eat breakfast. (Eating breakfast is not pleasing to me.)*
No **le gustan** los restaurantes caros.	*He doesn't like expensive restaurants. (Expensive restaurants are not pleasing to him.)*

- The subject of the verb **gustar** is whatever is pleasing to someone. Because we generally use **gustar** to indicate that something (singular) or some things (plural) are pleasing, **gustar** is most often conjugated in the third-person singular or third-person plural forms, **gusta** and **gustan.** The indirect object pronoun indicates who is being pleased.

Nos gusta la torta de chocolate.	*We like chocolate cake.*
No me gustan los frijoles.	*I don't like beans.*

- To express the idea that one likes to do something, **gustar** is followed by an infinitive. In such cases the third-person singular of **gustar** is used, even when you use more than one infinitive.

Me gusta preparar la cena y lavar los platos.	*I like to prepare dinner and wash the dishes.*

- Some other verbs like **gustar** are listed below. Note that the equivalent expressions in English are not direct translations.

aburrir	*to bore; to tire*	**interesar**	*to be interesting*
encantar	*to like very much; to be extremely pleasing*	**molestar**	*to be a bother; to annoy*
faltar	*to be lacking; absent*	**parecer**	*to seem*
fascinar	*to be fascinating*	**quedar**	*to be left; remaining*

Me molestan las cocinas sucias.	*I am annoyed by dirty kitchens.*
Nos parece caro este vino.	*This wine seems expensive to us.*

- Remember, you can use the prepositional phrase beginning with **a** to emphasize or clarify the indirect object pronoun.

A mí me fascina la cocina, pero **a ella** le parece pequeña.	*I am fascinated by the kitchen, but it seems small to her.*

Aplicación

6-16 A los pingüinos... Lee el siguiente párrafo sobre los pingüinos de la Patagonia chilena y subraya los verbos como **gustar** (**V**), su sujeto (**S**) y su complemento indirecto (**I**).

Modelo: *A mí <u>me</u> <u>interesan</u> <u>los animales marinos</u>.*
I V S

A muchas personas les fascinan los pingüinos que habitan las costas del sur de Chile. Son casi como pequeños seres humanos en la manera en que cuidan a sus bebés. A los pingüinos, también les gusta observar a la gente y no le tienen miedo. Para comer, les encantan los calamares y otros mariscos que pescan del mar. Los pingüinos son protegidos estrictamente por los parques nacionales de Chile y está prohibido darles comida. A mí, me parecen animales preciosos, pero no me interesa tener uno como mascota (*pet*). Prefiero verlos libres.

6-17 ¿Qué les gusta? Ahora, contesta las siguientes preguntas, basándote en la actividad **6-16.**

1. ¿Dónde viven los pingüinos?
2. ¿Qué les gusta hacer?
3. ¿Qué les encanta comer?
4. ¿Por qué nos fascinan?
5. ¿A ti te interesa tener uno como mascota?

6-18 Me interesa(n). Me gusta(n). Me molesta(n). Completa el cuadro con las cosas y actividades de la lista que te interesan, te gustan o te molestan. Incluye unas frases originales.

limpiar la cocina	los restaurantes de cuatro tenedores *(forks)*	una cocina lujosa *(fancy)*	los cafés sencillos
preparar comida complicada	tomar vino con la cena	los vinos chilenos	cocinar
los restaurantes de cocina... (mexicana, china...)	los cocineros egoístas	bailar	las novelas de Isabel Allende

MODELO:

INTERESAR	GUSTAR	MOLESTAR
Me interesan las matemáticas.	*Me gusta bailar.*	*Me molestan los insectos.*

6-19 ¿Y a ti? Túrnense para preguntarse sobre sus intereses y gustos de la actividad **6-18.**

MODELO: E1: *¿Qué te interesa?*
E2: *Me interesan las novelas de Isabel Allende.*

6-20 Una carta de la Patagonia. Usa los pronombres de complemento indirecto y los verbos correspondientes de la lista para completar la carta.

encantar fascinar gustar interesar molestar parecer quedar

El lobo marino habita la costa de Chile.

Querida Isabel:

Te escribo para contarte sobre mi viaje a la Patagonia. Es una región bellísima de Chile que incluye montañas y costas y una gran variedad de animales. Nuestro guía Antonio es muy simpático y nos explica sobre la región. (1.) (a nosotros) ____________ que él conoce bien la flora y la fauna de la región. (2.) (a mí) ____________ las plantas y los animales, pero a Carlos y Ana (3.) ____________ especialmente los lobos marinos (*sea lions*) que llegan todos los años para criar a sus hijos. Están protegidos en toda la costa de Chile, y a muchas personas (4.) ____________ observarlos durante este tiempo. (5.) (A mí) No ____________ mucho la playa porque hace mucho viento para nadar, pero (6.) ____________ observar la vida marina. Todos los días (7.) ____________ salir temprano para ver los pelícanos y otros pájaros que viven en la costa.

Bueno, Isabel, si (8.) (a ti) ____________ la naturaleza, (9.) (a ti) ____________ va a ____________ la Patagonia.

Un abrazo,

Eduardo

6-21 Su opinión. Conversen sobre sus opiniones acerca de los restaurantes.

MODELO: las cafeterías estudiantiles
E1: *¿Te gustan las cafeterías estudiantiles?*
E2: *¡Sí, me encantan porque son económicas!*

1. los restaurantes lujosos (*fancy*)
2. los platos picantes
3. los mariscos
4. las frutas tropicales

6-22 ¿A quién? Entrevístense para saber las opiniones de sus compañeros/as.

MODELO: E1: *¿Te gusta tomar café?*
E2: *Sí, me gusta. / No, no me gusta.*

comer pasteles	comer en restaurantes	comer mariscos
____________	____________	____________
comer frutas	comer en la cafetería	dejarle propina al/a la camarero/a
____________	____________	____________
ser vegetariano	tomar café	comer una merienda todos los días
____________	____________	____________

¿Cuánto sabes tú? *Can you...*

6-23 to 6-26

- ☐ role-play a restaurant scene with a waiter and client; order and/or comment on a meal?
- ☐ talk about what you like to eat (**Me gusta...**) and order a meal (**¿Me trae...?**)?
- ☐ say and give things to people by using the verbs **decir** and **dar** with indirect object pronouns?
- ☐ express and ask about likes and dislikes with verbs such as **gustar, interesar, molestar,** and **parecer**?

Comparaciones

La compra de la comida y la cocina chilena

6-23 En tu experiencia. ¿Cuántas veces vas al supermercado por semana? ¿Compras comidas fáciles de preparar? ¿Compras en tiendas especializadas o en un supermercado grande? ¿Conoces un mercado donde todo está muy fresco (*fresh*)? ¿Tu familia prepara una comida especial en los días festivos?

Aquí tienes una descripción de la rica y variada comida del mundo hispano y, en particular, de la de Chile. Compárala con la comida que comes en tu casa.

La comida tiene un papel muy importante en el mundo hispano. Se puede decir que para los hispanos la comida desempeña (*serves*) una función social crucial. Se dice que en los países hispanos se vive para comer, no se come para vivir.

Aunque los supermercados ya son muy populares, todavía es común ir al mercado dos o tres veces por semana para asegurarse (*to be sure*) de que los productos son frescos. El mercado típico es un edificio enorme y abierto, con tiendas (*shops*) pequeñas donde se vende todo tipo de comestibles (*food*). En el mercado hay tiendas especiales como carnicerías, pescaderías y fruterías. En cada barrio también hay una panadería, una pastelería y una heladería.

Los mercados y las comidas típicas de cada región varían y dependen mucho de los productos disponibles en esa región. La cocina de Chile refleja la variedad topográfica del país. Debido a su enorme costa, en Chile se come mucho marisco y pescado; también carnes diferentes, frutas frescas y verduras. Hay dos especialidades populares: la parrillada, que consiste en distintos tipos de carne, morcilla (*blood sausage*) e intestinos asados a la parrilla; y el curanto, que es un estofado (*stew*) de pescado, marisco, pollo, cerdo, carnero (*lamb*), carne y papas. Además, el vino chileno es de gran calidad.

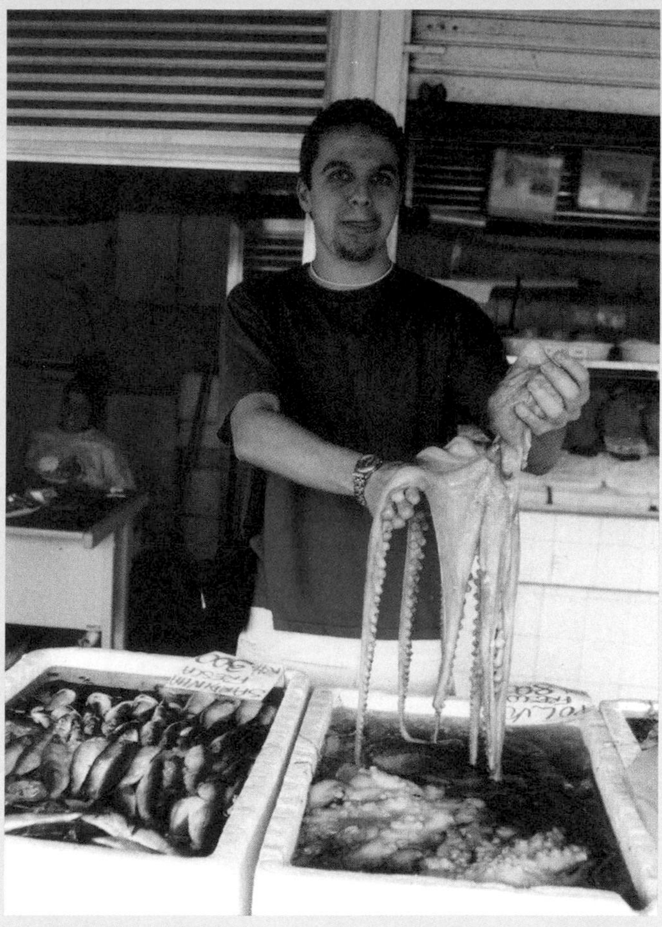

La abundancia de pescados y mariscos en Chile los hace una parte importante de su cocina.

6-24 En tu opinión. Conversen sobre sus gustos culinarios.

	MI OPINIÓN	LA OPINIÓN DE MI COMPAÑERO/A
1. La especialidad de nuestra región...	__________	__________
2. El restaurante más popular...	__________	__________
3. Nuestro restaurante favorito...	__________	__________
4. Nuestro plato favorito...	__________	__________
5. Un plato que detestamos...	__________	__________

SEGUNDA PARTE

¡Así lo decimos! Vocabulario

¡Así es la vida! «La tía Julia cocina»

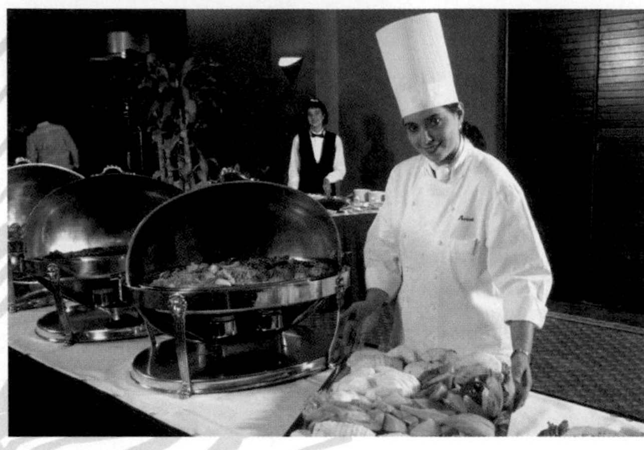

Buenas noches, queridos televidentes. Ayer les enseñé a hacer una paella, un exquisito plato de arroz, mariscos, pollo y otros ingredientes. ¿Prepararon anoche este delicioso plato? ¿Se lo sirvieron a la familia? ¿Les gustó? Bueno, hoy en el programa de **«La tía Julia cocina»** vamos a presentarles otro plato fenomenal: el arroz con pollo…

Para prepararlo, además de los ingredientes, el arroz y el pollo, necesitan una cazuela o una sartén. Este delicioso plato se cocina en la estufa… ¡pero no en el horno!

¡Ahora, todos a la cocina!

En la cocina

CD 2, Track 5

6-29 to 6-32

la cafetera

la cazuela

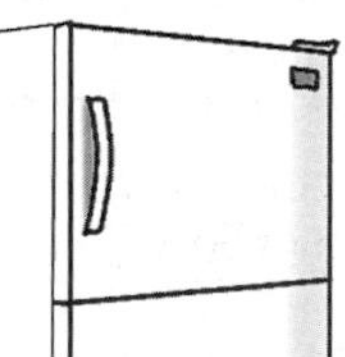

el congelador

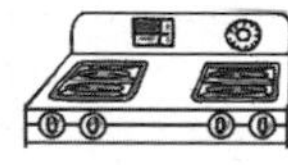

la estufa

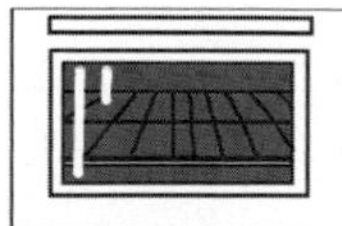

el horno

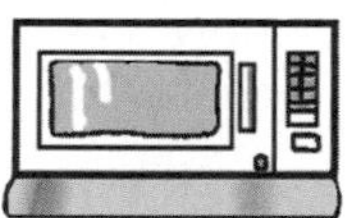
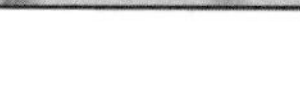

el microondas

el recipiente

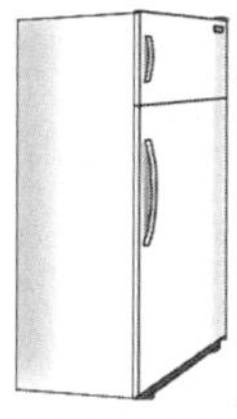

el refrigerador

la sartén

la tostadora

Verbos	*Verbs*
añadir	*to add*
calentar (ie)	*to heat*
cocinar	*to cook*
cortar	*to cut*
echar	*to add; to throw in*
freír (i, i)	*to fry*
guardar	*to save; to keep*
hervir (ie, i)	*to boil*
hornear	*to bake*
mezclar	*to mix*
pelar	*to peel*
tapar	*to cover*
tostar (ue)	*to toast*

Otras palabras y expresiones	*Other words and expressions*
a fuego alto	*on high heat*
mediano	*medium heat*
bajo	*low heat*
la receta	*recipe*

Las medidas	*Measurements*
la cucharada	*tablespoon*
la cucharadita	*teaspoon*
el kilo	*kilogram* (equivalent to 2.2 pounds)
el litro	*liter*
el pedazo	*piece*
la pizca	*pinch (of salt, pepper, etc.)*
la taza	*cup*

Expresiones adverbiales	*Adverbial expressions*
anoche	*last night*
anteayer	*the day before yesterday*
ayer	*yesterday*
el año (lunes, martes, etcétera) pasado	*last year (Monday, Tuesday, etc.)*
el mes pasado	*last month*
la semana pasada	*last week*

Letras y sonidos

CD 2, Track 6

6-33 to 6-36

The sequences "s, z, ce, ci" in Spanish

Generally in Spanish, the letters *s* and *z*, as well as *c* before the vowels *e* and *i*, all correspond to the same sound: the *s* sound in English *sip*. Be careful to avoid the *z* sound in English *zip*, especially where the letter *s* appears between vowels (e.g., *vi-si-tar, pre-si-den-ta*) or where the letter *z* begins or ends a word (e.g., *za-na-ho-ria, diez*).

sal *de-sa-yu-no* *a-zú-car* *ce-na* *ha-cer* *de-cir*

In most parts of Spain, only the letter *s* sounds like the *s* in English *sip*. The other letters treated here (i.e., the letter *z*, as well as *c* before *e* and *i*) are pronounced like the *th* sound in English *thanks*. Keep these differences in mind as you refine your listening skills. Follow the pronunciation of these letters that is consistent with the variety of Spanish that you want to speak, Latin American or Peninsular.

Aplicación

6-25 ¿Qué necesitas para...? Indica un utensilio o aparato que necesitas para hacer lo siguiente.

Modelo: congelar el helado
el congelador

1. _____ freír el pescado
2. _____ calentar la sopa
3. _____ enfriar (*to cool*) el jugo
4. _____ tostar el pan
5. _____ guardar el azúcar
6. _____ preparar el café
7. _____ hornear el pastel

a. la cazuela
b. la cafetera
c. la sartén
d. el recipiente
e. el horno
f. la tostadora
g. el refrigerador

6-26 ¿Qué hacen? Describe lo que hacen las personas en cada dibujo con expresiones de **¡Así lo decimos!**

MODELO:

Mario

Mario pone el pollo en el horno.

1.

Lola

2.

El señor Barroso

3.

Dolores

4.

Diego

5.

Estela

6.

Pilar

CD 2, Track 7

6-27 En la cocina con la tía Julia. Escucha la preparación del flan, un postre muy popular en todo el mundo hispano. Indica con una cruz (**X**) los ingredientes, los utensilios y las acciones que la tía Julia utiliza para preparar esta receta.

INGREDIENTES	**UTENSILIOS**	**ACCIONES**
_____ agua	_____ cucharada	_____ añadir
_____ azúcar	_____ cucharadita	_____ cortar
_____ huevos	_____ licuadora (*blender*)	_____ echar
_____ jugo de limón	_____ molde	_____ hornear
_____ leche condensada	_____ recipiente	_____ mezclar
_____ leche evaporada	_____ sartén	_____ calentar
_____ vainilla	_____ taza	_____ servir

6-28 Una receta tuya. Túrnense para hacer una lista de los ingredientes, utensilios y acciones para una receta popular y para tratar de adivinar para qué plato es la receta.

MODELO: E1: *Necesitas tres limones, un litro de agua, media taza de azúcar, hielo, etcétera.*
E2: *Es una receta para hacer limonada.*

6-29 ¿Qué dicen? Túrnense para explicar o responder a estas situaciones.

MODELO: E1: *La sopa no tiene sabor.*
E2: *La sopa necesita más condimentos. Voy a echarle cebolla, ajo y una pizca de sal.*

1. La carne no tiene sabor.
2. El café tiene un sabor muy malo.
3. Quieres una hamburguesa especial.
4. Siempre preparas un desayuno muy original.
5. La leche está cortada (*sour*).
6. La mesa está llena de platos y utensilios sucios.

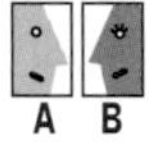

6-30A El arroz con leche. El arroz con leche es un postre muy conocido en todo el mundo hispano. Imagínate que tienes la receta y tu compañero/a tiene algunos de los ingredientes. Decidan qué ingredientes necesitan comprar. Estudiante B, por favor ve al **Apéndice 1,** página A7.

MODELO: E1: *Necesitamos una taza de arroz.*
E2: *No tenemos arroz. Tenemos que comprarlo.*

Ingredientes:	**Preparación**
1 taza de arroz 2 litros de leche 9 cucharadas de azúcar corteza (*peel*) de 1 limón 1 palito (*stick*) de canela (*cinnamon*) canela molida (*ground*) pizca de sal	• Poner* el arroz en una cazuela antiadherente (*nonstick*) y añadir agua fría hasta que lo cubra, junto con una pizquita de sal. Poner al fuego y, cuando empiece a hervir, darle diez minutos, o hasta que se consuma el agua. • Echar en la cazuela leche hasta que cubra el arroz y bajar el fuego al mínimo. Añadir el limón y el palito de canela, y mover todo constantemente mientras el arroz se va poniendo cremoso. • Si no se pone cremoso, seguir cocinando a fuego muy lento, añadiendo de vez en cuando un poco de leche, según se vaya consumiendo. Hay que mover todo a menudo. La operación dura unas dos horas. Cuando ya esté incorporada toda la leche, añadir el azúcar, dar unas vueltas más para que se mezcle bien y retirar del fuego la cazuela. Servir el arroz con leche frío, en recipientes individuales, espolvoreados (*sprinkled*) con canela.

*A common use of the infinitive in Spanish is to convey a command.

¡Así lo hacemos! Estructuras

3. The preterit of regular verbs

6-37 to 6-43

So far you have learned to use verbs in the present indicative tense. In this chapter you will learn about the preterit, one of two simple past tenses in Spanish. In **Capítulo 8** you will be introduced to the imperfect, which is also used to refer to events in the past.

Preterit of regular *-ar*, *-er*, and *-ir* verbs

	-ar	**-er**	**-ir**
	tomar	**comer**	**vivir**
yo	tom**é**	com**í**	viv**í**
tú	tom**aste**	com**iste**	viv**iste**
él, ella, Ud.	tom**ó**	com**ió**	viv**ió**
nosotros/as	tom**amos**	com**imos**	viv**imos**
vosotros/as	tom**asteis**	com**isteis**	viv**isteis**
ellos/as, Uds.	tom**aron**	com**ieron**	viv**ieron**

- The preterit tense is used to report actions completed at a given point in the past and to narrate past events.

Gasté mucho dinero en comida.	*I spent a lot of money on food.*
Ayer **comimos** en la cafetería de la universidad.	*Yesterday we ate at the university cafeteria.*

- The preterit forms for **nosotros** of **-ar** and **-ir** verbs are identical to the corresponding present tense forms. The situation or context of the sentence will clarify the meaning.

Siempre **hablamos** de recetas de cocina.	*We always talk about cooking recipes.*
La semana pasada **hablamos** de tu receta de pollo.	*Last week we talked about your chicken recipe.*
Vivimos aquí ahora.	*We live here now.*
Vivimos allí el año pasado.	*We lived there last year.*

- Always use an accent mark in the final vowel for the first- and third-person singular forms of regular verbs, unless the verb is only one syllable.

Compré aceite de oliva.	*I bought olive oil.*
Ana Luisa **añadió** una pizca de sal.	*Ana Luisa added a pinch of salt.*
Vi una receta interesante en ese libro.	*I saw an interesting recipe in that book.*

EXPANSIÓN **More on structure and usage**

Los verbos que terminan en *-car, -gar* y *-zar*

Verbs that end in **-car, -gar,** and **-zar** have the following spelling changes in the first-person singular of the preterit. All other forms of these verbs are conjugated regularly.

c → qu	buscar	yo **busqué**
g → gu	llegar	yo **llegué**
z → c	almorzar	yo **almorcé**

Bus**qu**é el programa en la tele.	*I looked for the program on the TV.*
Lle**gu**é muy contento ayer.	*I arrived very happy yesterday.*
Almor**c**é poco hoy.	*I had little for lunch today.*

The following verbs follow this pattern as well.

jugar (a)	*to play*	**pagar**	*to pay*
empezar	*to begin*	**practicar**	*to practice*
explicar	*to explain*	**tocar**	*to touch; to play a musical instrument*

Aplicación

6-31 Una entrevista con Isabel Allende. Lee la siguiente entrevista con esta famosa escritora chilena y subraya los verbos en el pretérito.

Entrevistador: Señora Allende, ¿cuándo empezó a escribir?

Isabel: A la edad de trece años. Escribí un cuento para mi tío, Salvador.[1]

Entrevistador: ¿Y a su tío le gustó el cuento?

Isabel: Sí, mucho. Escribí sobre mi familia. Tengo algunos familiares más interesantes que algunos de ficción. Después, empecé a escribir cuentos cortos, como los de mi colección *Eva Luna.* Son cuentos fantásticos, pero siempre basados en Chile.

Entrevistador: Usted publicó varios libros en español y luego recibió una sorpresa. ¿Qué pasó?

Isabel: Bueno, me llamó Billy August, el director de cine norteamericano, y me invitó a hacer una película basada en mi novela, *La casa de los espíritus.*[2] Contrató a varios de mis actores favoritos: Meryl Streep, Jeremy Irons y Antonio Banderas, entre otros. Esto fue (*was*) en 1993.

Entrevistador: ¿Cuál es su obra favorita?

Isabel: La verdad, es *Paula.* La escribí después de la muerte de mi querida hija, Paula. Fue una experiencia muy difícil para mí, pero también la más satisfactoria porque volví a recordar los momentos más importantes de su vida.

[1]Salvador Allende, presidente de Chile hasta que fue asesinado en 1973.

[2]*The House of the Spirits*

6-32 Las experiencias de Isabel. Contesta las siguientes preguntas, basándote en la entrevista anterior.

1. ¿Cuándo empezó a escribir cuentos?
2. ¿Quién leyó su primer cuento?
3. ¿De qué escribió?
4. ¿Quién la llamó para hacer una película?
5. ¿Conoces esa película?
6. ¿Cuál es el tema de *Paula*? ¿Crees que es una historia alegre o triste?

6-33 En tu cocina. Usa estos verbos y otros que aprendiste en el vocabulario para hablar de la última receta que preparaste.

Primero compré...	Cociné...	Eché...
En casa lavé...	Pelé...	Serví...

6-34 Me gustó. / No me gustó. Túrnense para decir si les gustó o no lo siguiente en un restaurante.

Modelo: los camarones
E1: *¿Te gustaron los camarones a la parrilla?*
E2: *Sí, me gustaron. / ¡No, no me gustaron nada!*

1. el vino chileno	5. las papas fritas	9. la sopa
2. las verduras	6. la fruta	10. el pan
3. las ensaladas	7. el café con leche	11. el pescado
4. las tortas	8. el jugo	12. el pollo asado

6-35 Este fin de semana. Describe en un párrafo lo que hiciste (*you did*) durante el fin de semana. Usa verbos de la lista y expresiones como **y, pero, cuando** y **aunque** para unir tus ideas.

Modelo: estudiar
Estudié el sábado todo el día, pero salí con mis amigos el sábado por la noche.

cocinar	comprar	estudiar	llamar	preparar	trabajar
comer	escribir	leer	mirar	salir	ver

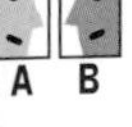

6-36A Charadas. Túrnense para representar éstas y otras acciones en el pasado para ver si el/la otro/a compañero/a puede adivinar la acción. Estudiante B, por favor ve al **Apéndice 1,** página A7.

Modelo: E1: (Act out! *Corté el pan.*)
E2: *Cortaste el pan.*

Comí langosta.	Preparé sopa.
Cocinamos papas fritas.	Encontré una mosca (*fly*) en la sopa.
Mezclaste huevos y sal para la tortilla.	¿...?

 **6-37 Te creo; no te creo.** Escribe tres oraciones ciertas y tres oraciones falsas. Luego reta (*challenge*) a un/a compañero/a para decidir si lo que dices es cierto o falso.

MODELO: E1: *Una vez conocí a Isabel Allende.*
E2: *¿Cuándo?*
E1: *En 2005.*
E2: *Te creo. / No te creo.*

besar (a)	comprar	llevar	trabajar (en)	visitar
comer	conocer (a)	salir con	ver	vivir

4. Verbs with irregular forms in the preterit (I)

6-44 to 6-49

El pretérito de los verbos con cambio radical, e → i, o → u

	pedir (*to ask for*)	dormir (*to sleep*)
yo	pedí	dormí
tú	pediste	dormiste
él, ella, Ud.	p**i**dió	d**u**rmió
nosotros/as	pedimos	dormimos
vosotros/as	pedisteis	dormisteis
ellos/as, Uds.	p**i**dieron	d**u**rmieron

- Stem-changing **-ir** verbs in the present also have stem changes in the preterit. The changes are **e → i** and **o → u** and occur only in the third-person singular and plural.

pedir (i, i)	*to ask for*	**seguir (i, i)**	*to follow; to continue*
preferir (ie, i)	*to prefer*	**sentir (ie, i)**	*to feel; to be sorry for*
repetir (i, i)	*to repeat*	**servir (i, i)**	*to serve*

La camarera **repitió** las especialidades del día. — *The waitress repeated the house specialties of the day.*

Los chicos **durmieron** diez horas anoche. — *The kids slept ten hours last night.*

Verbos que cambian la "i" en "y" en la tercera persona del singular y del plural

	creer (*to believe*)	oír (*to hear*)
yo	creí	oí
tú	creíste	oíste
él, ella, Ud.	**creyó**	**oyó**
nosotros/as	creímos	oímos
vosotros/as	creísteis	oísteis
ellos/as, Uds.	**creyeron**	**oyeron**

- For verbs that end in **-er** and **-ir** preceded by a vowel (for example, **creer, leer,** and **oír**) change the **i → y** in the third-person singular and plural. All forms of these verbs are accented in all persons, except the third-person plural.

Mamá no te **creyó** esta mañana.	*Mother didn't believe you this morning.*
Leyeron la receta con cuidado.	*They read the recipe carefully.*
¿**Oíste** que hay un restaurante chileno en Chicago?	*Did you hear that there is a Chilean restaurant in Chicago?*

Aplicación

6-38 Jumbo. Hoy en día, muchas personas compran en un supermercado o en un hipermercado en vez de ir siempre a las tiendas pequeñas. Jumbo es un ejemplo de un hipermercado enorme en Santiago de Chile. Lee acerca de Concha y su ayudante cuando hicieron sus compras esta semana. Luego, completa las siguientes oraciones.

La semana pasada mi ayudante *(assistant)* y yo decidimos hacer las compras en el súper Jumbo que se abrió recientemente en el Unicentro de Santiago. Cuando llegamos al súper, encontramos una sección grande de frutas y verduras, otras de carnes y pescados, y finalmente toda clase de bebidas. Pero, no sólo compramos comida, sino también artículos para la cocina. ¡Qué tentación! Cuando encontré el departamento de aparatos domésticos, compré una cazuela grande. Mi ayudante compró una sartén de hierro. Después comimos una merienda en el restaurante que tienen en el súper. Mi ayudante pidió pastel de limón y yo pedí pastel de manzana. La camarera nos sirvió café con el pastel. Mi ayudante compró un libro de recetas españolas y las leímos en el restaurante. Cuando regresamos a nuestro estudio, me senté a la mesa a leer, pero me dormí enseguida.

1. En Jumbo, Concha y su ayudante ____________ muchas cosas.
2. Concha y su ayudante ____________ una sección de frutas y verduras.
3. El ayudante ____________ una sartén.
4. Los dos ____________ pastel y ____________ café.
5. Los dos ____________ el libro de recetas.
6. Concha se ____________ a la mesa y ____________ a leer, pero se ____________.

6-39 ¿Y tú? Contesta las preguntas sobre tu última visita a un hipermercado.

1. ¿A qué hora saliste para el hipermercado?
2. ¿Qué viste?
3. ¿Qué encontraste?
4. ¿Qué compraste?
5. ¿A qué hora volviste a casa?

6-40 ¿Qué pasó en Jumbo? Combina elementos de cada columna y forma oraciones para explicar lo que pasó en Jumbo ayer.

Modelo: *Concha pidió leche para su café.*

1. nosotros	oír...
2. los niños	preferir...
3. nuestros amigos	pedir...
4. yo	leer...
5. el ayudante	repetir...
6. tú	sentir...

6-41 Verdadero o falso. Túrnense para contar anécdotas personales que pueden ser verdaderas o falsas.

Modelo: E1: *Una vez pedí camarones con helado.*
E2: *No te creo. No los pediste.*

Una vez...

1. (servir)...
2. (oír)...
3. (pedir)...
4. (preferir)...
5. (leer)...

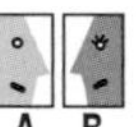

6-42A ¿Qué pasó? Pregúntale a tu compañero/a qué pasó en las siguientes situaciones. Estudiante B, por favor ve al **Apéndice 1,** página A7.

Modelo: en la fiesta familiar
E1: *¿Qué pasó en la fiesta familiar?*
E2: *Mi mamá sirvió nuestra comida favorita.*

SITUACIONES	ALGUNAS ACTIVIDADES
1. en la cafetería estudiantil	1. caerse la comida
2. en una película que viste	2. no haber pescado
3. en clase ayer	3. robar los cuadros

¿Cuánto sabes tú? *Can you...*

6-50 to 6-53

- ☐ put the instructions for preparing a simple recipe in logical order?
- ☐ describe what is needed to prepare a recipe? (**Hay que comprar cebollas, cortarlas, freírlas... etc.**)
- ☐ use a variety of verbs to say what happened and what you did yesterday or once in the past? (**Ayer comí en un restaurante chileno; una vez oí música mexicana.**)

Observaciones

pisode 6

¡Pura vida! Episodio 6

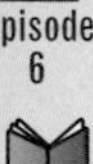
6-54 to 6-57

En este episodio hay una sorpresa (*surprise*) en la comida.

Antes de ver el video

6-43 Las empanadas. Cada país tiene sus especialidades culinarias; en la Argentina, entre otras, son las empanadas. Lee la receta siguiente y haz una lista de los ingredientes.

En la Argentina, la empanada es una de las entradas (*appetizers*) más populares en un restaurante, en un pícnic o como merienda. Se prepara con masa de harina (*flour*) rellena de una mezcla de carne, huevos, aceitunas (*olives*), cebollas y pasas (*raisins*). Se sirve con una salsa que se llama chimichurri. La chimichurri es una mezcla de aceite de oliva, jugo de limón, perejil (*parsley*), ajo, cebolleta (*shallots*), orégano y una pizca de sal y pimienta.

Empanadas argentinas

A ver el video

6-44 Hay una sorpresa en la comida. Mira el sexto episodio de *¡Pura vida!* para identificar la sorpresa que hay en la comida. Luego, completa las oraciones siguientes con palabras lógicas según el video.

El pícnic

La comida

¡Felipe se quedó sin propina!

postre	tacos de pollo	serpiente	tortilla de patatas

1. Silvia preparó una __________, un plato español.
2. Marcela compró unos __________ en un restaurante mexicano.
3. Hermés preparó un __________: arroz con leche de coco.
4. Las empanadas de Felipe llevan un ingrediente sorpresa: carne de __________.

Después de ver el video

WWW

6-45 Los otros platos. Conéctate con la página web de **¡Arriba!** para buscar recetas para los otros platos del pícnic. Escoge una que te guste e indica los ingredientes que ya tienes en casa y los que tienes que comprar para poder preparar el plato.

NUESTRO MUNDO

Panoramas

Vistas culturales

Chile: un país de contrastes

6-46 ¿Ya sabes...? Trata de identificar, describir y/o explicar lo siguiente.

6-58 to 6-59

1. la capital de Chile
2. una cordillera de montañas importantes
3. ciudades en Chile y en Indiana, EE.UU., cuyo nombre significa *Valley of Paradise*
4. un producto agrícola chileno
5. los países en su frontera
6. una industria importante

El clima templado del valle central es ideal para el cultivo de frutas y verduras, muchas de las cuales se exportan a los EE.UU. y al Canadá durante el invierno norteamericano. El vino chileno es uno de los mejores del mundo.

Por sus 10.000 kms. de costas, la industria pesquera es sumamente importante en Chile. La gran variedad de pescados y mariscos de este país no sólo se sirve y se disfruta en los restaurantes chilenos, sino también se exporta a todo el mundo.

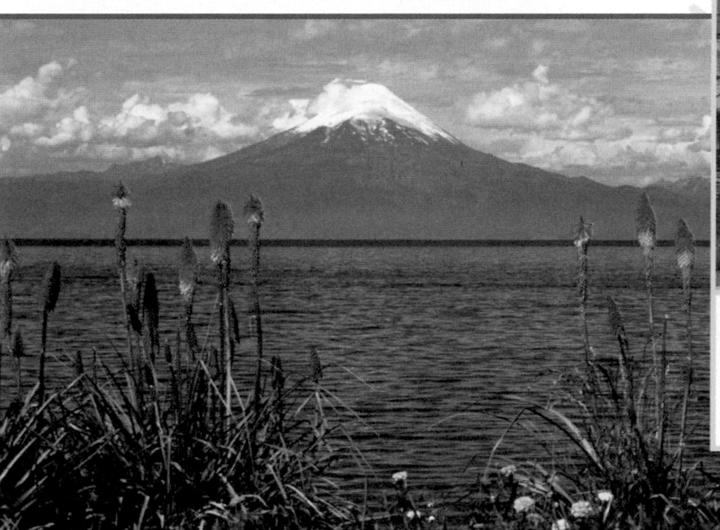

Desde junio hasta octubre se puede disfrutar de los deportes de invierno en los Andes chilenos. El Parque Nacional Vicente Pérez Rosales, dominado por el volcán Osorno, es un lugar popular para hacer excursiones y esquiar.

Se dice que el desierto de Atacama, en el norte de Chile, es el más seco del mundo. Aunque carece de (*it lacks*) vida, la región es rica en minerales, y es aquí donde se mina el nitrato de sodio para la producción de fertilizantes y explosivos. La minería de otros minerales, especialmente la del cobre (*copper*), es importante también.

En el extremo sur del continente americano, en medio de la legendaria Patagonia y junto al Estrecho de Magallanes, se encuentra Punta Arenas, la ciudad más sureña de Chile.

6-47 ¿Cierto o falso? Indica si las siguientes oraciones son ciertas o falsas y si son falsas, explica por qué.

1. En el norte de Chile hay muchos minerales.
2. Punta Arenas se encuentra en el extremo sur del país.
3. En el Parque Nacional Vicente Pérez Rosales puedes nadar en el lago.
4. Una industria importante es la minería.
5. Isabel Allende es pintora.

6-48 ¿Dónde? Identifica un lugar o unos lugares en el mapa donde puedes encontrar las siguientes cosas.

1. industria pesquera
2. desierto
3. producción de vino
4. deportes invernales
5. pingüinos
6. parques nacionales
7. volcanes
8. temperatura baja

6-49 Recomendaciones. Háganles recomendaciones a personas que van a viajar a Chile. Recomiéndenles lugares para visitar según sus intereses.

Modelo: Quiero estudiar mineralogía.
¿Por qué no vas al desierto Atacama? Allí hay minas de cobre y de otros minerales.

1. Quiero estudiar ecología.
2. Me gusta escalar (*hike*) montañas.
3. Quiero observar los pingüinos.
4. Estudio agricultura.
5. Me gustan los mariscos.

6-50 Investigar. Conéctate con la página web de **¡Arriba!** y busca una receta auténtica chilena. Indica los ingredientes y los pasos para prepararla. ¿Quieres probarla? ¿Qué ingredientes no tienes en tu cocina?

Ritmos

6-60

"Tren al sur" (Los prisioneros, Chile)

Esta canción del grupo chileno Los prisioneros, que cuenta de un viaje al sur, también puede ser una alegoría de los cambios que se producen en la vida.

Antes de escuchar

6-51 Los símbolos. "Tren al sur" es un ejemplo de como la letra de una canción se puede considerar poesía. Antes de escuchar la canción, empareja los elementos para ver qué simbolizan o personifican.

1. ____ el sur
2. ____ el tren
3. ____ el corazón (*heart*)
4. ____ el olor (*smell*) de las flores y los animales

a. la libertad
b. la felicidad
c. el paraíso
d. la muerte

A escuchar

6-52 Tren al sur. Ahora escucha la canción y, mientras la escuchas, completa las estrofas (*stanzas*) con las palabras que faltan.

feliz	ferrocarril	alegrías	tierras
olor	contento	mañana	sur

Tren al sur
Siete y media de la (1) __________
mi asiento toca la ventana
estación central segundo carro
del (2) __________ que me llevará al (3) __________.

Ya estos fierros (hierros) van andando
y mi corazón está saltando
porque me llevan a las (4) __________
donde al fin podré de nuevo
respirar adentro y hondo (5) __________ del corazón.
Y no me digas pobre por ir viajando así
no ves que estoy (6) __________
no ves que estoy (7) __________.

Doce y media de la mañana el (8) __________ se mete en la ventana.
Son flores y animales
que me dicen bienvenido al sur
[...]

Después de escuchar

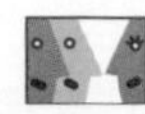

6-53 Significados. En grupos de tres lean cuidadosamente la letra de "Tren al sur" y conversen sobre el significado de la canción.

Páginas

6-61

"El Santiago" (Reseña periodística)

Chile se conoce por su rica gastronomía.

Antes de leer

6-54 ¿Por qué lees? Cuando lees una reseña (*review*) de un restaurante, ¿qué detalles buscas? Haz una lista de la información que esperas sacar del artículo a continuación.

A leer

6-55 Compara. Ahora busca la información que escribiste en la actividad **6-54** para ver si la tiene el artículo. ¿Qué información falta?

El Mercurio

Gastronomía

El Santiago

12 de diciembre de 2007

El ambiente de El Santiago te invita a cenar.

Restaurante de cocina chilena en el centro de la ciudad, cerca de los teatros y la ópera. La carta incluye algunos arroces, pastas y carnes, pero se especializa en pescados y mariscos con unas ofertas únicas. Sus especialidades incluyen el ceviche (pescado crudo "cocido" en jugo de limón); las tapas (tortilla española, queso, calamares), la corvina *(sea bass)* fresca preparada al gusto y los mejores vinos chilenos. De entrada, hay varios pescados a la parrilla de $7.000 a $8.000. Recomendamos la corvina. De postres, hay sorbetes ($2.200), un rico pastel vasco con almendras ($2.900) y una torta de chocolate ($3.700).

Todas las noches a partir de las 9:00, Los Chavales (grupo musical del norte de Chile) tocan música andina. El lugar es hermoso con varios patios y pequeñas mesas alrededor de una fuente *(fountain)* en medio. Las pequeñas luces que decoran los árboles y las plantas contribuyen al ambiente *(atmosphere)* romántico. El servicio es bueno, aunque no excepcional (esperamos media hora para recibir nuestras tapas), pero el ambiente y la música compensaron la demora *(delay)*. Cuando por fin nos llegó la comida, valió la pena esperar *(it was worth waiting for)*. La cuenta para dos personas, que incluyó tapas, comida, una botella de vino tinto, postre y propina, llegó a $35.000. Les recomendamos este lindo restaurante para una ocasión especial, o para una cena después del teatro. Se aceptan reservaciones.

José M. Infante 55, teléfono 3653458 y 3376872, Santiago.

—Mariana Escobar

Después de leer

6-56 Detalles. Completa el cuadro con los detalles de esta reseña.

1. ¿Dónde se encuentra?	
2. ¿Cuáles son algunas de las especialidades?	
3. ¿Qué comes si no te gusta el pescado?	
4. ¿Cómo es el ambiente?	
5. ¿Los platos son caros o económicos?	
6. ¿Qué tipo de música hay?	
7. ¿Recomienda el reseñador el restaurante?	

6-57 El menú. Trabajen juntos para escribir un menú con precios para El Santiago. Incluyan estas categorías y su precio.

Primer plato – Segundo plato – Ensaladas – Postres – Bebidas

6-58 ¡Vamos a comer! Decidan qué van a comer de su menú y cuánto les va a costar. ¿Es una comida cara o económica?

MODELO: E1: *Para el primer plato, voy a pedir ceviche…*
E2: *Pues, yo voy a pedir camarones.*

Taller

6-62 to 6-63

6-59 Una reseña *(review)* de un restaurante. Puedes encontrar reseñas de restaurantes en el periódico, en una revista culinaria o en la Red. La reseña te ayuda a decidir si te interesa visitar el restaurante. Vuelve a leer la reseña en la página 219 para ver la información que se incluye.

Antes de escribir

- Piensa en el nombre de un restaurante, dónde se encuentra y por qué lo recomiendas.
- Contesta las siguientes preguntas para organizar tus ideas:
  - ☐ ¿Cuántos tenedores tiene (de 1: muy económico a 5: muy caro y elegante)?
  - ☐ ¿Dónde está?
  - ☐ ¿Tiene una cocina en especial?
  - ☐ ¿Cuáles son sus especialidades?
  - ☐ ¿Cómo es su ambiente (formal, informal)?
  - ☐ ¿Tiene música?
  - ☐ ¿Cómo es el servicio?
  - ☐ ¿Qué comiste cuando lo visitaste?
  - ☐ ¿Qué te gustó o no te gustó?
  - ☐ ¿Cuánto costó?
  - ☐ ¿Aceptan reservaciones?
  - ☐ ¿Cuál es tu recomendación?

A escribir

- Organiza tus respuestas en un párrafo, siguiendo (*following*) el modelo anterior.

Después de escribir

- **Revisar.** Revisa tu reseña para verificar los siguientes puntos:
  - ☐ el uso del pretérito
  - ☐ la concordancia de adjetivos y sustantivos
  - ☐ alguna frase superlativa (es el restaurante más/menos... de...)
  - ☐ la ortografía (*spelling*)
- **Intercambiar**

  Intercambia tu reseña con la de un/a compañero/a. Mientras leen las reseñas, hagan comentarios y sugerencias sobre el contenido, la estructura y la gramática.
- **Entregar**

  Pasa tu reseña a limpio, incorporando las sugerencias de tu compañero/a. Después, entrégasela a tu profesor/a.

Vocabulario

Primera parte

Las comidas	*Meals*
el almuerzo	*lunch*
la cena	*dinner*
el desayuno	*breakfast*
la merienda	*snack*

Las comidas y las bebidas	*Foods and beverages*
el agua (*mineral*)	*(mineral) water*
el arroz	*rice*
el azúcar	*sugar*
la banana	*banana*
el bistec	*steak*
el bocadillo/ el sándwich	*sandwich*
el café	*coffee*
las carnes	*meats*
los camarones	*shrimp*
la cerveza	*beer*
la ensalada	*salad*
el flan	*custard dessert*
los frijoles	*beans*
las frutas	*fruits*
las galletas	*cookies*
la hamburguesa	*hamburger*
el helado	*ice cream*
los huevos	*eggs*
el jamón	*ham*
el jugo (de naranja)	*(orange) juice*
la langosta	*lobster*
la leche	*milk*
la lechuga	*lettuce*
la limonada	*lemonade*
el maíz	*corn*
la mantequilla	*butter*
la manzana	*apple*
los mariscos	*seafood*
la naranja	*orange*
el pan	*bread*
las papas	*potatoes*
el pastel	*cake; pie*
el pavo	*turkey*
el pescado	*fish*
el pimiento	*pepper*
el pollo	*chicken*
el queso	*cheese*
el refresco	*soft drink*
la sal	*salt*
la sopa	*soup*
la tarta de limón	*lemon pie*
el té	*tea*
el tomate	*tomato*
la toronja	*grapefruit*
la torta de chocolate	*chocolate cake*
las uvas	*grapes*
las verduras	*vegetables*
el vino	*wine*
el yogur	*yogurt*
las zanahorias	*carrots*

En un restaurante	*In a restaurant*
el bufé	*buffet*
el/la camarero/a	*waiter/waitress*
el/la cliente	*client; customer*
la cuenta	*bill*
la especialidad de la casa	*house specialty*
el menú	*menu*
la propina	*tip*
el/la vegetariano/a	*vegetarian*

Expresiones	*Expressions*
¡Buen provecho!	*Enjoy your meal!*
¿Desean algo de tomar/comer?	*Would you like something to drink/eat?*
Enseguida	*Right away*

Adjetivos	*Adjectives*
caliente	*hot*
frío/a	*cold*
picante	*hot (spicy)*
rico/a	*delicious*

Verbos	*Verbs*
almorzar (ue)	*to have lunch*
cenar	*to have dinner*
dar	*to give*
decir	*to say*
desayunar	*to have breakfast*

Segunda parte

Aparatos en la cocina	*Kitchen appliances*
la cafetera	*coffee maker*
la cazuela	*stewpot; casserole dish; saucepan*
el congelador	*freezer*
la estufa	*stove*
el horno	*oven*
el microondas	*microwave*
el recipiente	*container*
el refrigerador	*refrigerator*
la sartén	*skillet; frying pan*
la tostadora	*toaster*

Verbos	*Verbs*
añadir	*to add*
calentar (ie)	*to heat*
cocinar	*to cook*
cortar	*to cut*
echar	*to add; to throw in*
freír (i, i)	*to fry*
guardar	*to save; to keep*
hervir (ie, i)	*to boil*
hornear	*to bake*
mezclar	*to mix*
pelar	*to peel*
tapar	*to cover*
tostar (ue)	*to toast*

Otras palabras y expresiones	*Other words and expressions*
a fuego alto	*on high heat*
mediano	*medium heat*
bajo	*low heat*
la receta	*recipe*

Las medidas	*Measurements*
la cucharada	*tablespoon*
la cucharadita	*teaspoon*
el kilo	*kilogram (equivalent to 2.2 pounds)*
el litro	*liter*
el pedazo	*piece*
la pizca	*pinch*
la taza	*cup*

Expresiones adverbiales	*Adverbial expressions*
anoche	*last night*
anteayer	*the day before yesterday*
ayer	*yesterday*
el año (lunes, martes, etc.) pasado	*last (Monday, Tuesday, etc.) year*
el mes pasado	*last month*
la semana pasada	*last week*

Indirect object pronouns	*See page 195.*
***Gustar* and similar verbs**	*See page 198.*

7 ¡A divertirnos!

Primera parte

¡Así lo decimos! Vocabulario El tiempo libre
¡Así lo hacemos! Estructuras Irregular verbs in the preterit (II)
Indefinite and negative expressions
Comparaciones La vida social de los hispanos

- Talking about activities you like to do in your free time
- Making plans to do something
- Talking about indefinite people and things, and people and things that do not exist

Segunda parte

¡Así lo decimos! Vocabulario Los deportes
¡Así lo hacemos! Estructuras Irregular verbs in the preterit (III)
Double object pronouns
Observaciones ¡Pura vida! Episodio 7

- Talking about different sports
- Reporting past events and activities
- Taking shortcuts in conversation

Nuestro mundo

Panoramas Las islas hispánicas del Caribe
Ritmos "El pregonero" (Tito Nieves, Puerto Rico)
Páginas "Sensemayá" (Nicolás Guillén, Cuba)
Taller Una entrada en tu diario

Celia Cruz nació en Cuba, y desde su infancia la música tropical corrió por sus venas. Durante su vida, recibió muchos honores, entre ellos uno del Museo Smithsonian, que tiene en su colección un vestido (*dress*) y unos zapatos (*shoes*) suyos.

Las islas hispánicas del Caribe

«Dime con quién andas y te diré quién eres.»*

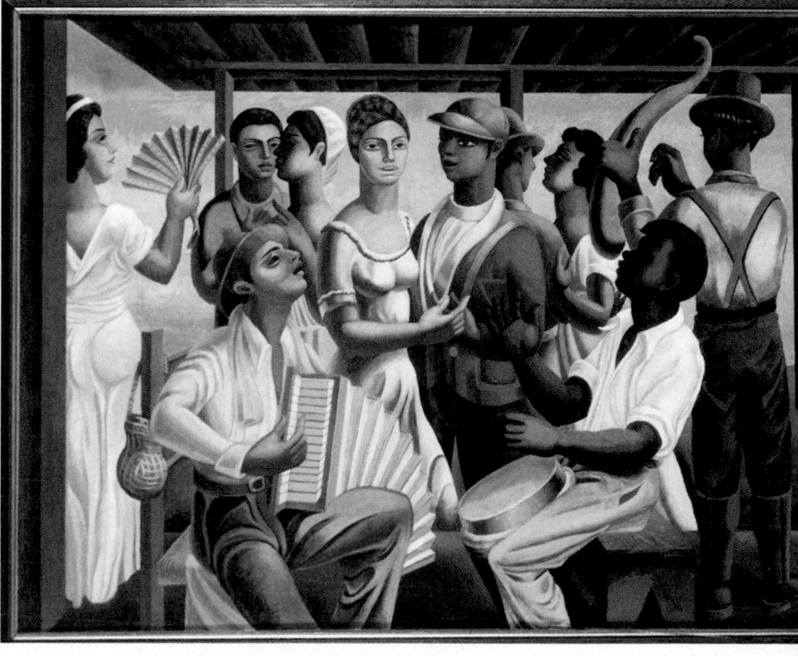

Merengue del artista dominicano Jamie González Colson detalla (*depicts*) los colores y el ritmo de este baile popular de las islas caribeñas.

Source: Jaime Colson, Merengue, 1937. Courtesy of Museo Bellapart, Dominican Republic.

***Refrán:** Tell me who you are with and I'll tell you who you are. *(You are known by the company you keep.)*

PRIMERA PARTE

¡Así lo decimos! Vocabulario

CD 2, Track 8

7-1 to 7-2

¡Así es la vida! El fin de semana

Ricardo: Oye, ¿por qué no vamos al partido de básquetbol?

Susana: No sé. Con este sol tan rico... es un día perfecto para ir a la playa. ¿No crees?

Ricardo: ¡Estupenda idea! ¡Vamos a Luquillo[1] a nadar en el mar y después a hacer un pícnic!

Susana: ¡Perfecto! Voy a llamar a Elena y a Guillermo para ver si también quieren ir.

[1]Luquillo es una de las playas más lindas de Puerto Rico.

CD 2, Track 9

7-3 to 7-8

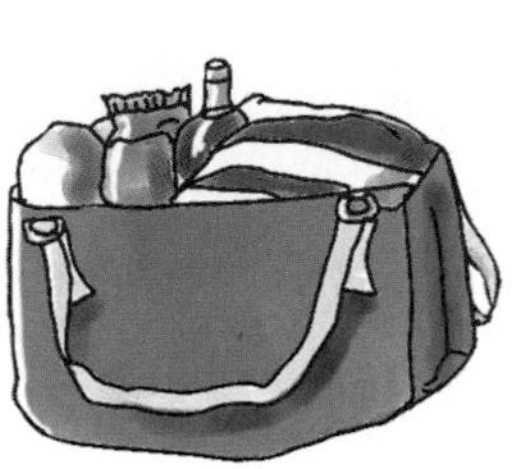

la bolsa

la heladera

el hielo

la sombrilla

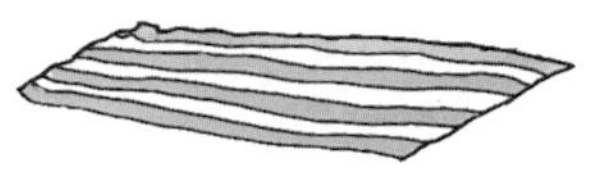
la toalla

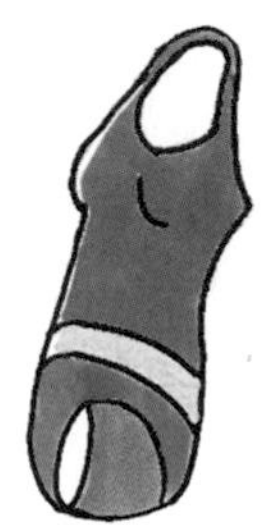
el traje de baño

Los pasatiempos	***Pastimes***
dar un paseo	*to go out; to take a walk*
hacer un pícnic	*to have a picnic*
ir a un concierto	*to go to a concert*
una discoteca	*a nightclub*
un partido	*a game*
leer una novela	*to read a novel*
un periódico	*a newspaper*
nadar en el mar	*to swim in the ocean*
una piscina	*a swimming pool*
ver una película	*to watch a movie*
la televisión	*television*

¿Qué tiempo hace?	***What is the weather like?***
está nublado	*it's cloudy*
hace...	*it's...*
buen/mal tiempo	*good/bad weather*
(mucho) calor	*(very) hot*
(mucho) fresco	*(very) cool*
(mucho) frío	*(very) cold*
(mucha) humedad	*(very) humid*
(mucho) sol	*(very) sunny*
(mucho) viento	*(very) windy*
hay (mucha) contaminación	*there's (a lot of) pollution/smog*
llover (ue)	*to rain*
nevar (ie)	*to snow*

Opiniones y sugerencias	***Opinions and suggestions***
Es un día perfecto para...	*It's a perfect day for...*
¡Oye!	*Listen!*
¿Qué tal si...?	*What if...?*

Reacciones	***Reactions***
¡Estupendo!	*Terrific!*
¡Fabuloso!	*Fabulous!; Great!*
¡Fantástico!	*Fantastic!*
¡Magnífico!	*Great!; Wonderful!*
Me da igual.	*It's all the same to me.*
No te preocupes.	*Don't worry.*
¡Qué mala suerte!	*What bad luck!*

Aplicación

7-1 ¿Qué hacer? Algunos amigos están haciendo planes para el fin de semana. Completa las oraciones con la expresión adecuada de la lista.

Modelo: No quiero quemarme (*get burned*) en el sol.
¿Hay sombrillas en la playa?

1. Queremos ir a escuchar música. Vamos a ____.
2. Hace buen tiempo. ¿Por qué no vamos al parque, llevamos sándwiches y hacemos ____?
3. Hoy hace sol. Vamos a dar ____ por el parque.
4. Los refrescos están en ____.
5. El sábado va a hacer mucho calor. ¿Por qué no vamos a nadar en ____?
6. El domingo hay ____ de básquetbol en el gimnasio.
7. ¡Qué feo! Hace muy mal tiempo: está nublado y hay ____.
8. Si hace mal tiempo, es un día perfecto para ____.

a. un paseo
b. el mar
c. ver una película
d. un concierto
e. un partido
f. un pícnic
g. contaminación
h. la heladera

7-2 ¿Dónde...? Mira este mapa meteorológico y escribe dónde hace el tiempo descrito a continuación.

Modelo: Hay chubascos (*showers*).
Hay chubascos en las Islas Vírgenes.

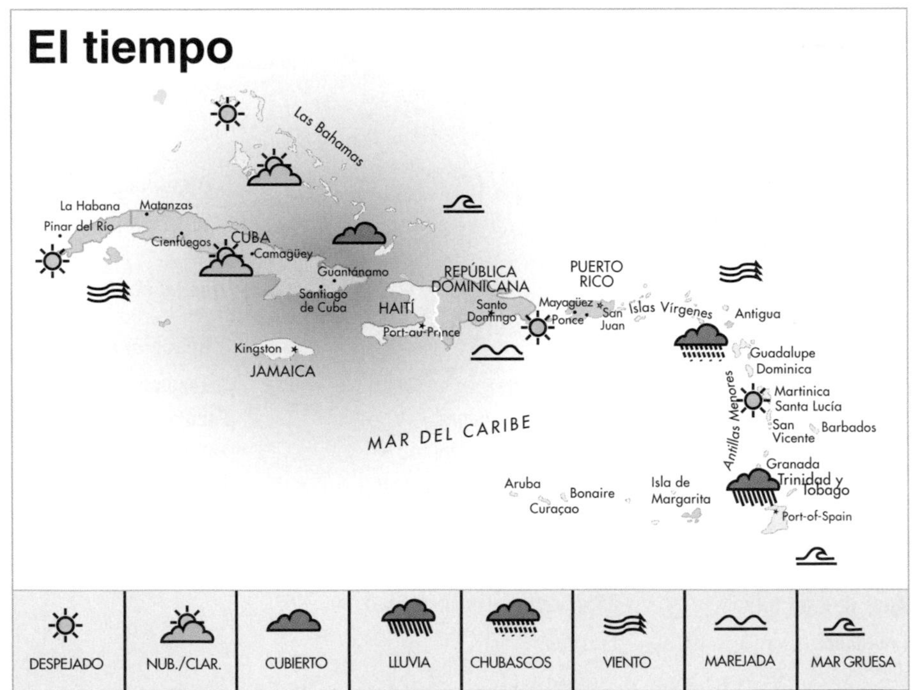

1. Está nublado.
2. Está lloviendo.[1]
3. Hace viento.
4. Hace mucho sol.
5. Está nevando.[2]

[1]Present participle of **llover (ue):** *raining.*

[2]Present participle of **nevar (ie):** *snowing.*

CD 2, Track 10

7-3 El pronóstico (*forecast*) del tiempo. Escucha el pronóstico del tiempo que se da en la radio para esta semana. Luego, completa la siguiente información.

Ciudad: ____________

Siglas (*call letters*) de la emisora de radio: ____________

Fecha: ____________

Estación del año: ____________

Tiempo de ayer: ____________

Pronóstico para hoy: ____________

Pronóstico para mañana: ____________

Una actividad que puedes hacer mañana: ____________

7-4 El clima. Explica los dibujos, diciendo quién es, dónde está, qué tiempo hace y qué tiene.

MODELO:

Ésta es Marta. Vive en Saskatchewan donde hace mucho frío en invierno. Está nevando y Marta tiene mucho frío.

1. 
2. 
3. 
4. 

7-5 ¿Qué te gusta hacer cuando...? Túrnense para contestar las siguientes preguntas.

MODELO: E1: *¿Qué te gusta hacer cuando nieva?*
E2: *Me gusta esquiar.*

ALGUNAS ACTIVIDADES

dar un paseo / una fiesta	ir a un partido /a un concierto
dormir una siesta	leer una novela / el periódico
esquiar en la nieve / en el agua	nadar en la piscina / en el mar
hacer un pícnic	tomar el sol (*sunbathe*) / un refresco
invitar a los amigos	ver una película / la televisión

¿QUÉ TE GUSTA HACER CUANDO...

1. hace calor, pero no tienes aire acondicionado?
2. llueve?
3. hace frío en la playa?
4. hace mucho viento?
5. hace mucho sol?
6. hace buen tiempo, pero tienes que trabajar?

 **7-6 Una entrada (*An admission ticket*).** Aquí tienes una entrada para una función en Puerto Rico. Túrnense para hacer y contestar preguntas sobre la función. Luego decidan si quieren asistir.

Modelo: E1: *¿Dónde es la función?*
E2: *Es en el Auditorio Santa Cruz.*

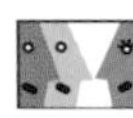 **7-7 Un clima ideal.** Escribe cinco oraciones completas para describir un lugar que para ti tiene un clima ideal. Luego, descríbeselo al resto de la clase. Entre todos, escojan el lugar favorito.

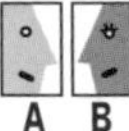 **7-8A Una invitación.** Recibiste dos boletos gratis (*free*) para asistir a un concierto de Ricky Martin. Invita a tu compañero/a a ir contigo. Él/Ella va a hacerte preguntas sobre el concierto. Estudiante B, por favor ve al **Apéndice 1,** página A7.

Modelo: E1: *¿A qué hora empieza el concierto?*
E2: *El concierto empieza a las ocho.*

¡Así lo hacemos! Estructuras

7-9 to 7-13

1. Irregular verbs in the preterit (II)

Irregular preterit forms

	ser/ir	**estar**	**tener**	**dar**	**ver**
yo	fui	estuve	tuve	di	vi
tú	fuiste	estuviste	tuviste	diste	viste
él, ella, Ud.	fue	estuvo	tuvo	dio	vio
nosotros/as	fuimos	estuvimos	tuvimos	dimos	vimos
vosotros/as	fuisteis	estuvisteis	tuvisteis	disteis	visteis
ellos/as, Uds.	fueron	estuvieron	tuvieron	dieron	vieron

- The verbs **ser** and **ir** have the same forms in the preterit. The context of the sentence or the situation will clarify the meaning.

  ¿Sabes?, nuestros abuelos también **fueron** jóvenes. — *You know, our grandparents were also young.*
  Fuimos a dar un paseo al centro. — *We went downtown for a walk.*

- Note that **estar** and **tener** have the same irregularities in the preterit.

  Estuve en la feria internacional. — *I was at the international fair.*
  Gloria **tuvo** que irse temprano del partido. — *Gloria had to leave the game early.*

- **Dar** and **ver** use the same endings as regular **-er** and **-ir** verbs. However, the first and third persons have only one syllable and do not require an accent mark.

  Víctor me **dio** una película excelente. — *Víctor gave me an excellent movie.*
  Los **vi** entrar al teatro. — *I saw them enter the theater.*

Aplicación

7-9 Una fiesta puertorriqueña. Empareja las preguntas con la respuesta más lógica.

1. _____ ¿Dónde fue la fiesta?
2. _____ ¿Quiénes estuvieron?
3. _____ ¿Tuviste que salir temprano?
4. _____ ¿Quién fue con Graciela?
5. _____ ¿Vieron alguna película?
6. _____ ¿Le diste algo al anfitrión (*host*)?

a. Todos nuestros amigos.
b. Sí, una botella de vino.
c. Sí, una de Almodóvar.
d. No, no salí hasta las dos.
e. Su novio, Carlos.
f. En casa de Ramón y Silvia.

7-10 Un concierto de Juan Luis Guerra. Completa el párrafo con la forma correcta del pretérito del verbo entre paréntesis.

Ayer yo (1. ir) __________ a un concierto de Juan Luis Guerra, el famoso cantante dominicano. Mis amigos y yo (2. llegar) __________ allí a las siete. Un agente nos (3. atender) __________ y nos (4. preguntar) __________: "¿Cuántas entradas quieren?" Yo le (5. contestar) __________: "Queremos cuatro, por favor." Él nos (6. dar) __________ los boletos y (7. nosotros: subir) __________ al balcón. (8. Estar) __________ en la octava fila del entresuelo (*mezzanine*). ¡Yo no (9. ver) __________ nada! Pero sí (10. oír) __________ bien la música y (11. sentir) __________ la emoción de un concierto en vivo. (12. Ser) __________ una experiencia estupenda y todos nosotros lo (13. pasar) __________ bien.

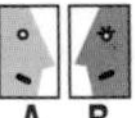

7-11A Chismes (*Gossip*). Alguien encontró unos apuntes del/de la profesor/a sobre la clase de ayer. Hagan y contesten las preguntas sobre lo que ocurrió, basándose en los apuntes. Estudiante B, por favor ve al **Apéndice 1,** página A7.

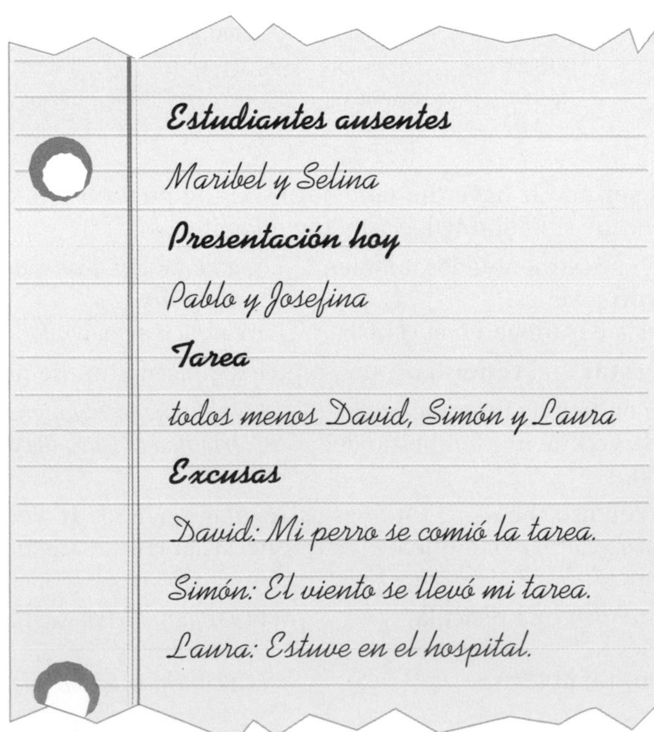

7-12 ¿Quién...? Hazle una pregunta diferente a cada persona sobre lo que hizo la semana pasada y escribe el nombre de la persona que contesta cada pregunta.

MODELO: jugar al béisbol
E1: *¿Jugaste al béisbol?*
E2: *Sí, jugué al béisbol el lunes. (No, no jugué al béisbol.)*

dar un paseo	empezar un trabajo importante	ir a un partido
ver una película	ir a una discoteca	estar en clase
darle un regalo a tu mamá	tener problemas con el coche	jugar al tenis
tener que trabajar mucho	llegar tarde a clase	estar enfermo/a

7-14 to 7-18

2. Indefinite and negative expressions

Afirmativo		Negativo	
algo	*something; anything*	**nada**	*nothing; not anything*
alguien	*someone; anyone*	**nadie**	*nobody; no one*
algún, alguno/a(s)	*any; some*	**ningún, ninguno/a(s)**	*none; not any*
siempre	*always*	**nunca, jamás**	*never*
también	*also; too*	**tampoco**	*neither; not either*
o... o	*either... or*	**ni... ni**	*neither... nor*

- In Spanish, verbs are affirmative unless they are made negative through the use of **no** or a negative expression. There can be more than one negative expression (a double or triple negative) in a single sentence in Spanish. When **no** is used in a sentence, a second negative (e.g., **nada, nadie, ningún**) can either immediately follow the verb or be placed at the end of the sentence.

No fuimos **nunca** a la playa con Lourdes.	*We never went to the beach with Lourdes.*
No le dimos los sándwiches a **nadie.**	*We did not give the sandwiches to anyone.*

- When the negative expression precedes the verb, **no** is omitted.

Nunca fuimos a la playa con Lourdes.	*We never went to the beach with Lourdes.*
A **nadie** le dimos los sándwiches.	*We didn't give the sandwiches to anyone.*

- The expressions **nadie** and **alguien** refer only to persons and require the personal **a** when they appear as direct objects of the verb.

No vi **a nadie** en el agua.	*I didn't see anyone in the water.*
¿Viste **a alguien** especial anoche en la discoteca?	*Did you see someone special last night at the club?*

- The adjectives **alguno** and **ninguno** drop the **-o** before a masculine singular noun in the same way the number **uno** shortens to **un.** Note the use of a written accent when the **-o** is dropped.

Ningún amigo vino al partido.	*No friend came to the game.*
¿Te gusta **algún** tipo de refresco?	*Do you like any type of refreshment?*

- **Ninguno** is almost always used in the singular, not the plural form. The exception would be when used with inherent plural nouns such as things that come in pairs.

¿Quedan **algunas** entradas?	*Are there any tickets left?*
No, no me queda **ninguna** entrada.	*No, there aren't any tickets left.*
¿Encontraste mis gafas?	*Did you find my glasses?*
No, no encontré **ningunas** gafas.	*No, I didn't find any glasses.*

- Once a sentence is negative, all other indefinite words are also negative.

Lucía **no** conoce a **nadie** en la fiesta **tampoco.**	*Lucía doesn't know anybody at the party either.*
No voy a traer **ni** refrescos **ni** sándwiches para **nadie.**	*I am bringing neither refreshments nor sandwiches for anyone.*

Aplicación

7-13 Una entrevista con Celia Cruz.[1] Subraya todas las expresiones indefinidas y negativas en esta entrevista con Celia.

Celia Cruz con el percusionista Tito Puente

Entrevistadora: Señora Cruz, es un placer conocerla y poder hablar con usted hoy. ¿Desea algo de beber? ¿Una botella de agua? ¿Algún refresco?

Celia: No, gracias. No quiero nada por ahora.

Entrevistadora: Bueno. Usted siempre tiene tanta energía. ¿No se cansa (*get tired*) nunca?

Celia: Pues, sí. Algunas veces cuando viajo mucho. Pero mi esposo siempre me acompaña, y eso ayuda.

[1]Celia Cruz murió el 16 de julio de 2003, después de esta entrevista.

Entrevistadora: Usted es famosa como la "reina" (*queen*) de la música salsa. Baila, canta... ¿Toca algún instrumento musical también?

Celia: No, no toco ninguno, pero soy amante de los tambores. Adoro la música de Tito Puente, el gran percusionista (*drummer*) y "rey del mambo" quien murió en 2000. Su muerte fue una gran tragedia para todos.

Entrevistadora: Es verdad. Bueno, señora Cruz, no le voy a preguntar cuántos años tiene, pero ¿nos puede decir cuando empezó su carrera?

Celia: Sí, empecé mis estudios formales de música en 1947.

Entrevistadora: ¿Y cuando piensa jubilarse (*retire*)?

Celia: ¡Nunca!

7-14 ¿Qué sabes de Celia? Contesta las siguientes preguntas basadas en la entrevista anterior.

1. ¿Qué bebida toma Celia en la entrevista?
2. ¿Cuándo se cansa?
3. ¿Cuándo está sola en sus viajes?
4. ¿Qué instrumento toca?
5. ¿Qué tragedia ocurrió en el año 2000?
6. ¿Cuándo dice que va a jubilarse?

WWW

7-15 Celia Cruz, Tito Puente y Juan Luis Guerra. Conéctate con la página web de **¡Arriba!** y busca información sobre uno de estos artistas. Luego, contesta estas preguntas.

1. ¿Dónde y en qué año nació?
2. ¿Por qué es famoso/a?
3. Escucha una selección de su música. ¿Cómo es?
4. ¿Quieres escuchar más? ¿Por qué?

7-16 Una entrevista. Túrnense para preguntarse sobre sus gustos. Usen las expresiones **siempre, algunas veces, casi nunca** y **nunca.**

Modelo: ver películas de ciencia ficción
E1: *¿Te gusta ver películas de ciencia ficción?*
E2: *¡Siempre! Soy muy aficionado/a a las películas de ciencia ficción.*

ALGUNAS ACTIVIDADES				
¿Te gusta...	**Siempre**	**Algunas veces**	**Casi nunca**	**Nunca**
dar paseos en el invierno?				
ir a un partido los sábados?				
ir a una discoteca con los amigos?				
salir con los amigos los viernes?				
ver películas extranjeras (*foreign*)?				
hacer un pícnic en el verano?				
ir a conciertos de música rock?				
¿...?				

7-17 En resumen. Resume *(Summarize)* la información de la entrevista de la actividad **7-16.** Incluye las opiniones de tu compañero/a y las tuyas, también. ¿Son muy diferentes?

¿Cuánto sabes tú? *Can you...*

7-19 to 7-22

- ☐ talk about activities you like to do?
- ☐ make plans to do something this weekend using expressions such as **¿Qué tal si...?** and **¿Qué piensas hacer...?**
- ☐ talk about some activities you completed in the past using a variety of verbs, including **dar, estar,** and **ir**?
- ☐ ask and respond to questions using negative expressions such as **nadie** and **nunca** and with expressions like **alguien** and **siempre**?

Comparaciones

La vida social de los hispanos

7-18 En tu experiencia. ¿Con quién te gusta hacer actividades recreativas? ¿Con tus padres? ¿Con tus hermanos? ¿Con tus amigos? ¿Qué haces para pasar el tiempo? A continuación vas a leer sobre los pasatiempos de muchos jóvenes hispanos. Compáralos con los tuyos.

¿Te gusta jugar canasta?

A los hispanohablantes, como a la mayoría de las personas, les gusta disfrutar de la vida y dedicar mucho tiempo a las actividades recreativas. Generalmente, estas actividades son de tipo social y ocurren por la noche: visitar a la familia y a los amigos íntimos; salir en grupo al cine, al teatro, a un concierto, a dar un paseo; ir a un partido de fútbol, béisbol o básquetbol; o simplemente quedarse (*to stay*) en casa para ver la televisión o para jugar juegos de mesa como canasta o ajedrez (*chess*) con la familia. Durante el fin de semana muchas familias de clase media pasan el día en el club social, donde los padres y los hijos se reúnen (*get together*) con sus respectivos amigos para participar en actividades deportivas o para jugar juegos de azar (*games of chance*). En el club social los jóvenes conocen a sus futuros novios/as, y como los padres de ambos (*the two of them*) generalmente se conocen, son aceptados más fácilmente en el círculo familiar. Varias veces al año en el club hay fiestas a las que también van juntos los padres y los hijos.

7-19 En tu opinión. Pon estas actividades en orden de interés (1 = me interesa más; 10 = me interesa menos) y compara tu lista con la de un/a compañero/a. Si hay diferencias de gustos, expliquen por qué.

_____ dar un paseo
_____ ir a una discoteca
_____ ir al cine
_____ jugar juegos de azar
_____ leer una novela
_____ practicar deportes
_____ salir con la familia
_____ salir con los amigos
_____ ver la televisión
_____ quedarme en casa

Segunda parte

¡Así lo decimos! Vocabulario

CD 2, Track 11

7-23 to 7-24

¡Así es la vida! Actividades deportivas

En el Estadio Francisco Montaner de Ponce, Puerto Rico

Muchas personas practican deportes en este famoso lugar de Ponce. Aquí se puede practicar el atletismo, la gimnasia y se puede correr todos los días. También, se puede jugar al tenis y al vólibol. Algunas personas practican el boxeo, un deporte un poco violento, y todos los sábados se puede asistir a un partido de fútbol americano.

Al igual que en los Estados Unidos, muchas personas practican deportes para mantenerse en forma.

Los deportes

el atletismo

el boxeo

el ciclismo

la gimnasia

el hockey

el vólibol

Más deportes[1]	*More sports*
el esquí	*skiing*
el esquí acuático	*water skiing*
el golf	*golf*
el patinaje	*skating*

Términos deportivos	*Sports terms*
el/la aficionado/a	*fan*
el árbitro	*referee*
el/la campeón/campeona	*champion; winner*
el/la entrenador/a	*coach; trainer*
el equipo	*team; equipment*
la temporada	*season*

Actividades deportivas	*Sporting activities*
animar	*to encourage; to cheer*
batear	*to bat*
correr	*to run*
empatar	*to tie (the score)*
esquiar	*to ski*
ganar	*to win*
gritar	*to shout*
hacer ejercicio	*to exercise*
levantar pesas	*to lift weights*
patear	*to kick*
patinar	*to skate*

[1]See *Capítulo 2* to review other sports.

CD 2, Track 13

7-30 to 7-31

Letras y sonidos

The sequences "ca, co, cu, que, qui, k" in Spanish

As explained in **Chapter 6,** in Spanish the letter *c* before the vowels *e* and *i* sounds like the *s* in English *sip* (in Latin America) or the *th* in English *thanks* (in Spain). When before the vowels *a, o,* and *u,* however, the letter *c* sounds like the *c* in English *scan* in all varieties of Spanish. Avoid the *c* sound made in English *can,* however, where a strong puff of air is expelled from the mouth after the sound. The combinations *que* and *qui* in Spanish, as well as the letter *k,* likewise correspond to the *c* sound in *scan.*

ca-lor *co-mi-da* *cu-bo* *que-rer* *qui-tar-se* *ki-lo*

Be careful not to pronounce the *u* in the sequences *que* and *qui* as a glide. For example, the first syllable in Spanish *qui-tar-se* sounds like English *key,* not *queen.* In sum, the sequences *ca, co, cu, que, qui, k* sound like the *c* in English *scan* in all varieties of Spanish.

Aplicación

7-20 Los deportistas. Generalmente identificamos a la persona que participa en un deporte con el sufijo *(suffix)* **-ista.** Otro sufijo posible es **-dor/a.** Una persona que practica deportes es **deportista** o **jugador/a.** Empareja a los siguientes deportistas con su deporte.

1. _____ baloncestista/basquetbolista	a. el ciclismo
2. _____ nadador/a	b. el patinaje
3. _____ beisbolista	c. el boxeo
4. _____ esquiador/a	d. el fútbol
5. _____ ciclista	e. el baloncesto
6. _____ futbolista	f. la natación
7. _____ boxeador/a	g. el tenis
8. _____ gimnasta	h. el béisbol
9. _____ tenista	i. el esquí
10. _____ patinador/a	j. la gimnasia

7-21 Tany y Eduardo Pérez (padre e hijo). Lee sobre estos dos beisbolistas y contesta las preguntas siguientes.

Se considera a Atanasio "Tany" Pérez uno de los mejores beisbolistas latinos del mundo. Nació en Cuba y a la edad de diecisiete años firmó con los Reds de Cincinnati. Cuando salió de Cuba, le dieron su visa y $250 para hacer el viaje. Pasó su primer invierno en Geneva, Nueva York, en 1960, donde hacía tanto frío que quería volver a Cuba. Sin embargo, se quedó y aprendió a hablar inglés para comprender a los árbitros y a los otros jugadores y para pedir comida en los restaurantes. Conoció a su querida esposa Pituka durante su entrenamiento en Puerto Rico. Se casaron y tuvieron dos hijos, Eduardo y Orlando. En 1975, Tany ayudó a los Reds a ganar la Serie Mundial. Desde el año 2000, está en el *National Baseball Hall of Fame.* Ahora Tany es entrenador de los Marlins y su hijo Eduardo jugó para los Cardenales de St. Louis y Tampa Bay, pero ahora juega para los Indios de Cleveland. Padre e hijo son amantes del béisbol.

1. ¿Qué deporte juega Tany?
2. ¿Dónde nació?
3. ¿A qué edad salió de su país?
4. ¿Por qué aprendió a hablar inglés?
5. ¿Qué le pasó en 2000?
6. ¿Qué tienen en común Tany y su hijo, Eduardo?

CD 2, Track 14

7-22 Los deportes. Escucha a Raquel y a Tomás mientras hablan de sus intereses en los deportes. Indica qué frases le corresponden a cada uno. Si una frase no le corresponde a ninguno, marca **ninguno.**

	Raquel	**Tomás**	**Ninguno**
jugar al béisbol	_____	_____	_____
ver los partidos de fútbol	_____	_____	_____
jugar al tenis	_____	_____	_____
practicar gimnasia	_____	_____	_____
practicar atletismo	_____	_____	_____
ver el boxeo	_____	_____	_____
ser campeón/campeona	_____	_____	_____
ser entrenador/a	_____	_____	_____
esquiar en invierno	_____	_____	_____
ver la natación en los Juegos Olímpicos	_____	_____	_____

7-23 ¿Qué les interesa? Completen estas oraciones y luego comparen sus intereses. ¿Qué tienen en común?

1. Soy aficionado/a al/a la...
2. Mi equipo favorito son los/las...
3. Me gusta practicar...
4. No me gusta practicar / jugar al...

7-24 Un partido. Túrnense para contestar las preguntas sobre el anuncio. Luego, decidan si quieren asistir al partido.

1. ¿Qué pasa hoy?
2. ¿A qué hora es?
3. ¿De dónde son los equipos?
4. ¿Dónde van a jugar los equipos?
5. ¿Quieren ir?

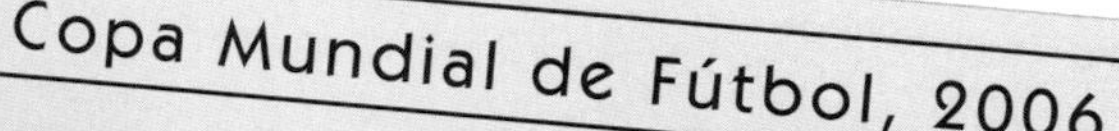

Hora: 7:00 PM
Lugar: Estadio Olímpico de Berlín
Boletos: $125

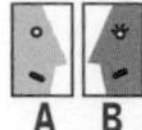

7-25A Consejos. Explíquense cómo se sienten y pidan consejos sobre lo que deben hacer. Pueden aceptar o rechazar (*reject*) los consejos, pero es necesario dar excusas si no los aceptan. Estudiante B, por favor ve al **Apéndice 1,** página A8.

MODELO: E1: *Estoy aburrido/a. ¿Qué hago?*
E2: *¿Por qué no das un paseo?*
E1: *No quiero. No me gusta salir de noche.*
E2: *Bueno, yo voy contigo. ¿Está bien?*

Situaciones	Sugerencias	Reacciones
Estás enfermo/a.	ir a un partido	¡Fabuloso!
Estás cansado/a.	salir con tus amigos	No me gusta(an)...
Necesitas aire fresco.	dar un paseo	¡Ideal!
Tienes mucho trabajo.	jugar al golf	¡Qué buena idea!
No tienes nada que hacer.	trabajar en el jardín	Me da igual.
	hacer las tareas	¡Qué mala idea!
	ir a la playa	No quiero porque...
	jugar al tenis	Tienes razón.
	leer una novela	No puedo porque...
	¿...?	¡Vamos!

7-26 En mi tiempo libre. Escribe un párrafo de por lo menos cinco oraciones. Explica cómo te gusta pasar el tiempo libre. Usa algunas de las siguientes palabras para conectar tus ideas.

pero   porque   cuando   si   y   aunque

MODELO: *Me gusta pasar tiempo con mi amigo Roberto porque él es mi mejor amigo. A Roberto le fascina el tenis, pero él no lo practica mucho. Prefiere verlo en la televisión. Cuando estoy con él, nos gusta ver a Venus y a Serena Williams porque son muy buenas. Mi pasión es el golf, pero no lo juego muy bien.*

¡Así lo hacemos! Estructuras

7-32 to 7-36

3. Irregular verbs in the preterit (III)

Irregular preterit forms

	poder	poner	saber	venir	hacer	querer	decir	traer
yo	**pud**e	**pus**e	**sup**e	**vin**e	**hic**e	**quis**e	**dij**e	**traj**e
tú	**pud**iste	**pus**iste	**sup**iste	**vin**iste	**hic**iste	**quis**iste	**dij**iste	**traj**iste
él, ella, Ud.	**pud**o	**pus**o	**sup**o	**vin**o	**hiz**o	**quis**o	**dij**o	**traj**o
nosotros/as	**pud**imos	**pus**imos	**sup**imos	**vin**imos	**hic**imos	**quis**imos	**dij**imos	**traj**imos
vosotros/as	**pud**isteis	**pus**isteis	**sup**isteis	**vin**isteis	**hic**isteis	**quis**isteis	**dij**isteis	**traj**isteis
ellos/as, Uds.	**pud**ieron	**pus**ieron	**sup**ieron	**vin**ieron	**hic**ieron	**quis**ieron	**dij**eron	**traj**eron

- The preterit forms of **poder, poner,** and **saber** have a **u** in the stem.

  Pude ir a la piscina. — *I was able to go to the pool.*
  ¿Por qué **pusiste** la toalla allí? — *Why did you put the towel there?*
  Supimos quién ganó enseguida. — *We found out (learned about) who won right away.*

- The preterit of **venir, hacer,** and **querer** have an **i** in the stem.

  ¿**Vino** Julio al partido ayer? — *Did Julio come to the game yesterday?*
  ¿Dónde **hicieron** los uniformes? — *Where did they make the uniforms?*
  Quise patear el balón, pero no fue posible. — *I wanted to kick the soccer ball, but it wasn't possible.*

- The preterit form of **hay** (from the verb **haber**) is **hubo** for both singular and plural.

  Ayer **hubo** un partido de fútbol en el estadio. — *Yesterday there was a soccer game in the stadium.*
  Hubo más de 50.000 espectadores. — *There were more than 50,000 spectators.*

- Since the stem of the preterit forms of **decir** and **traer** ends in **j,** the third-person plural form of these verbs ends in **-eron,** not **-ieron.**

  Los beisbolistas di**jeron** cosas buenas del entrenador. — *The ballplayers said good things about the trainer.*
  Tra**jeron** los esquís al comienzo de la temporada. — *They brought their skis at the beginning of the season.*

EXPANSIÓN **More on structure and usage**

Significados especiales en el pretérito

Certain Spanish verbs have different connotations when used in the preterit.

	PRESENT	PRETERIT
conocer	*to know*	*to meet someone (the beginning of knowing)*
poder	*to be able (have the ability)*	*to manage (to do something)*
no poder	*to not be able (without necessarily trying)*	*to fail (after trying) (to do something)*
(no) querer	*to (not) want*	*to try (to refuse)*
saber	*to know*	*to find out, to learn*

Mario **conoció** a una tenista muy buena.	*Mario met a very good tennis player.*
Supo que el boxeador está muy grave.	*He found out that the boxer is in very serious condition.*
No quisimos aprender gimnasia con uno de los mejores entrenadores.	*We refused to learn gymnastics with one of the best trainers.*

Aplicación

LA PRENSA

20-02-2006

Marc Anthony y Jennifer López llegan a Puerto Rico

Las superestrellas de la música *pop* Marc Anthony y Jennifer López, quienes se casaron en 2004, llegaron a San Juan esta semana para filmar escenas de su nueva película sobre la vida del salsero legendario Héctor Lavoe.

Marc Anthony y Jennifer, las co-estrellas de *El Cantante*, decidieron rodar *(shoot)* escenas en el histórico Viejo San Juan y también en la ciudad de Ponce, dijo su publicista. Estuvieron trabajando aquí en el proyecto hasta el 2 de febrero.

El Cantante se basa en la vida de Lavoe, quien ayudó a conocer la música de salsa a los Estados Unidos. Lavoe, cuyo apellido original era *(used to be)* Pérez, recibió el apodo de "la voz" por su lindo canto. Su apellido "Lavoe" se derivó de este apodo. Marc Anthony y Lavoe se conocieron cuando Lavoe estaba *(was)* todavía en el apogeo *(height)* de su carrera musical. Murió en 1993 a la edad de cuarenta y tres años debido a complicaciones del SIDA *(AIDS)*.

7-27 Dos superestrellas están en Puerto Rico. Aquí tienes un artículo publicado en Puerto Rico. Subraya todos los verbos en el pretérito y escribe su infinitivo.

7-28 ¿Por qué estuvieron en Puerto Rico? Contesta las preguntas, basándote en el artículo.

1. ¿Quiénes estuvieron en Puerto Rico? ¿Por qué son "superestrellas"?
2. ¿Qué hicieron allí?
3. ¿Dónde rodaron las escenas de la película?
4. ¿Por qué es famoso Héctor Lavoe?
5. ¿Cuándo y de qué murió?
6. ¿Cómo recibió su apodo y qué ocurrió con su apellido?

7-29 Un concierto memorable. Completa la entrada en el diario de Encarnación, usando el pretérito de los verbos entre paréntesis.

Querido diario:

Anoche Manolo y yo (1. tener) ____________ mucha suerte porque yo (2. poder) ____________ comprar boletos para un concierto de Millie Corretjer. Como sabes, ella es puertorriqueña y una superestrella de música pop latina. El concierto (3. ser) ____________ en el estadio de Mayagüez. Nosotros (4. salir) ____________ de la casa a las 7:30 y (5. llegar) ____________ al estadio a las 8:00 en punto. El concierto no (6. empezar) ____________ hasta las 9:00, pero así Manolo y yo (7. poder) ____________ encontrar unos buenos asientos para el espectáculo. Al entrar en el estadio, Manolo (8. ir) ____________ a comprar un programa y yo le (9. dar) ____________ dinero para comprarme uno también. Cuando Millie (10. salir) ____________ al escenario, todo el mundo (11. aplaudir) ____________. Durante todo el concierto (12. hacer) ____________ mucho calor en el estadio. Todos nosotros (13. bailar) ____________ hasta la medianoche cuando Millie por fin (14. decidir) ____________ dejar de cantar. Después, nosotros (15. andar) ____________ a casa y (16. recordar) ____________ la emoción de esa noche bajo las estrellas con Millie Corretjer.

Bueno, esto es todo por hoy. La semana que viene vamos a un concierto de rock.

7-30 Pero ayer... Completa las oraciones, indicando por qué ayer fue un día excepcional. Usa pronombres de objetos directo cuando sea apropiado.

MODELO: Siempre hago ejercicios antes de salir para la clase, pero ayer...
Siempre hago ejercicios antes de salir para la clase, pero ayer no los hice.

1. Siempre puedo hablar con el entrenador, pero ayer...
2. Todas las mañanas estamos en el estadio, pero ayer...
3. Todos los días mis padres quieren asistir a los partidos, pero ayer...
4. Todas las tardes los deportistas hacen gimnasia, pero ayer...
5. Generalmente, los aficionados se ponen contentos, pero ayer...
6. Casi nunca sé quién gana el partido, pero ayer...

7-37 to 7-41

4. Double object pronouns

Indirect object pronouns	Direct object pronouns
me	me
te	te
le → se	lo/la
nos	nos
os	os
les → se	los/las

- When both a direct and an indirect object pronoun are used together in a sentence, they are usually placed before the verb, and the indirect object pronoun precedes the direct object pronoun.

Julián, ¿**me** traes **la película**?	*Julián, will you bring me the movie?*
Te la traigo en un momento.	*I'll bring it to you in a moment.*

- The indirect object pronouns **le** (*to you, to her, to him*) and **les** (*to you, to them*) change to **se** when they appear with the direct object pronouns **lo, los, la, las.** Rely on the context of the previous statement to clarify the meaning of **se.**

El entrenador **les** trae **el balón** a los jugadores.	*The coach is bringing the ball to the players.*
El entrenador **se lo** trae.	*The coach is bringing it to them.*

- As with single object pronouns, the double object pronouns may be attached to the infinitive. In that case, the order of the pronouns is maintained, and an accent mark is added to the stressed vowel of the verb.

Carlos, ¿puedes **traerme la bolsa**?	*Carlos, can you bring me the bag?*
En un segundo voy a **traértela.**	*I'll bring it to you in a second.*

STUDY TIPS

Para aprender a usar los pronombres de complemento directo e indirecto juntos

Double object pronouns may appear confusing at first because of the number of combinations and positions that are possible in Spanish sentences. Here are a few strategies to help you with this structure.

1. Review the use of pronouns and do the practice activities to reinforce your knowledge of this structure.
2. Also review the use of indirect objects and indirect object pronouns.
3. Learning to use double object pronouns is principally a matter of combining the two pronouns in the right order.
4. Getting used to the way these pronouns sound together will help you make them become second nature to you. Practice repeating out loud phrases such as the ones below. Increase your pronunciation speed as you become more comfortable with verbalizing the double object pronouns.

me lo da	te lo doy	se los da
me las traes	te los traigo	se las traemos
se lo llevo	se las llevamos	se la llevas

Aplicación

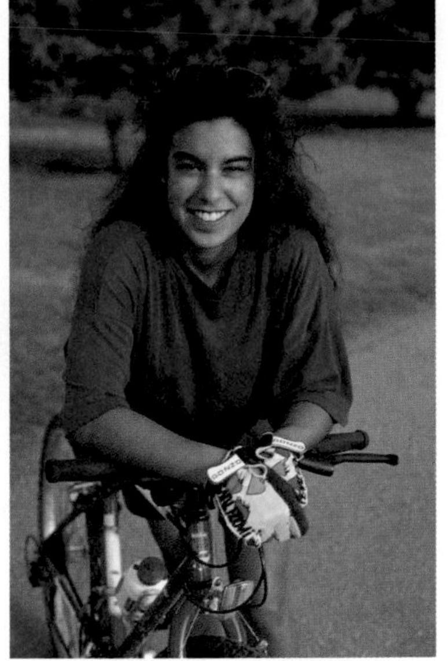

7-31 Antes de la carrera (*race*). Daniela va a competir en una carrera de ciclismo. Lee el diálogo entre Daniela y su entrenador, y subraya los pronombres de complemento directo (**D**) e indirecto (**I**). Indica cuál es cuál.

Modelo: Necesito guantes. ¿A quién se los pido?
I D

Daniela: Sebastián, ¿me pasas la botella de agua, por favor?

Entrenador: Enseguida te la doy, Daniela. ¿Dónde te la pongo?

Daniela: La quiero en mi mochila, Sebastián. Después, ¿me buscas las barras de proteína?

Entrenador: ¿Dónde las busco?

Daniela: Creo que están en el coche. Seguramente mi mamá las tiene. Debes pedírselas a ella. ¿Tienes mis gafas de sol?

Entrenador: Las voy a buscar ahora. ¿Te las traigo?

Daniela: Sí, debes ponérmelas en la cabeza. Y ahora, ¿me compras un jugo de naranja?

Entrenador: Buena idea, Daniela. Te lo compro ahora mismo.

7-32 ¿Quién lo hace? Ahora, contesta las preguntas, basándote en el diálogo anterior. Usa pronombres de complemento directo e indirecto en tus respuestas cuando sea necesario.

1. ¿Quién tiene la botella de agua?
2. ¿A quién se la da?
3. ¿Dónde se la pone?
4. ¿Qué más necesita Daniela?
5. ¿Por qué crees que las quiere?
6. ¿Qué desea tomar antes de la carrera?

7-33 De viaje en la República Dominicana. Haz el papel de turista en la República Dominicana y responde a las preguntas del guía (*guide*), usando los pronombres de complemento indirecto y directo.

Modelo: **GUÍA:** ¿Quiere ver el autobús que tomamos mañana?
TÚ: Sí, *¿me lo* enseña ahora?

1. **GUÍA:** ¿Quiere ver el restaurante donde vamos a cenar?
   TÚ: —Sí, ¿_____ enseña ahora?
2. **GUÍA:** ¿Quiere leer el periódico de ayer?
   TÚ: —Sí, ¿_____ trae ahora?
3. **GUÍA:** ¿Le traigo la información turística?
   TÚ: —No, no es necesario traér _____.
4. **GUÍA:** ¿Quiere ver el primer hospital del Nuevo Mundo?
   TÚ: —¡Sí! ¿_____ muestra ahora?

5. **GUÍA:** ¿Le traigo el refresco?
   TÚ: —No, no tengo sed. No tiene que traér ____.
6. **GUÍA:** ¿Le enseño el Parque Nacional del Este?
   TÚ: —¡Claro! ¿____ enseña mañana?
7. **GUÍA:** ¿Le doy una propina al camarero?
   TÚ: —Buena idea. Debe dár ____ ahora.
8. **GUÍA:** ¿Les preparo un cóctel a ustedes?
   TÚ: —No, gracias. No es necesario preparár ____.

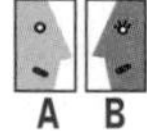
A B

7-34A ¿Tienes? Imagínate que estás muy enfermo/a y tu compañero/a va a traerte unas cosas que necesitas. Pregúntale si tiene las siguientes cosas. Si las tiene, pregúntale si puede traértelas. Si no las tiene, pregúntale si puede comprártelas. Luego, consúltense para hacer una lista de las cosas que tu compañero/a necesita comprar. Estudiante B, por favor ve al **Apéndice 1,** página A8.

MODELO: E1: *¿Tienes naranjas?*
E2: *Sí, tengo naranjas. / No, no tengo naranjas.*
E1: *¿Me las traes? / ¿Me compras unas naranjas?*
E2: *Sí, te las traigo. / Sí, te las compro.*

1. sopa de pollo
2. jugo de tomate
3. té
4. manzanas
5. pan
6. galletas
7. jugo de naranja
8. sopa de tomate

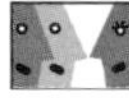

7-35 En el campamento de verano. Hagan los papeles de consejero/a *(advisor)* y campistas en un campamento de verano y pídanle varias cosas al/a la consejero/a. El/La consejero/a debe contestar, usando dos pronombres de complemento directo e indirecto. Pueden usar las sugerencias a continuación.

MODELO: E1: *Consejero, nos trae el bate, por favor.*
E2: *Sí, se lo traigo enseguida...*

el hielo	las toallas	dar
la bolsa	los guantes	pedir
los sándwiches	las raquetas	preparar
los esquís	el chocolate	traer

¿Cuánto sabes tú? *Can you...*

7-42 to 7-45

- ☐ talk about different sports you like to participate in and watch?
- ☐ talk about some activities you completed in the past using a variety of verbs, including **poder, poner, saber, venir, hacer, querer, decir,** and **traer**?
- ☐ use **saber** and **conocer** in the preterit to express *found out* and *met*?
- ☐ recognize the referents for direct and indirect object pronouns and respond to a question such as **¿Me traes el bate?** using two object pronouns (**Sí, te lo traigo.**)?

Observaciones

Episode 7

¡Pura vida! Episodio 7

En este episodio los amigos hablan de los deportes.

7-46 to 7-49

Antes de ver el video

7-36 Un evento histórico. En el mundo hispano el fútbol es el juego que más atrae a los fanáticos. Lee la descripción de los últimos minutos de un partido importante y contesta las siguientes preguntas.

El último partido de la Copa América 2004 tuvo lugar en el Estadio Nacional del Perú en Lima. En un final dramático, que tuvo goles en los últimos minutos, la Argentina y el Brasil empataron dos a dos. Un gol de Adriano Leite Ribeiro, en el último minuto del partido, forzó la decisión de la Copa América a la definición por penales. Desde los doce pasos, Julio César le detuvo el penal a Andrés D'Alessandro y Gabriel Heinze desvió (*deflected*) el suyo, y el Brasil se quedó con la 41ª edición de la Copa América. Ahora la Argentina tiene que esperar hasta 2008 para participar en la próxima Copa América en Venezuela.

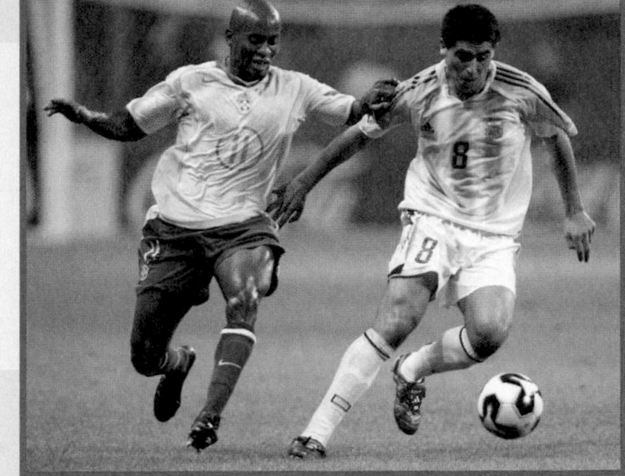
Una rivalidad histórica

1. ¿Dónde fue la competencia?
2. ¿En qué año fue?
3. ¿Qué equipo ganó?

A ver el video

7-37 Los deportes. Mira el séptimo episodio de *¡Pura vida!* para emparejar los intereses y las características de cada personaje según el video.

Marcela

Felipe

Silvia

F: Felipe   **H:** Hermés   **M:** Marcela   **S:** Silvia

1. _____ Le encanta surfear.
2. _____ Está triste porque perdió su equipo favorito.
3. _____ Sale mucho al cine, a conciertos, a bailar y más.
4. _____ Prefiere el boxeo al fútbol.
5. _____ Su hermana tenía un novio futbolista.

Después de ver el video

WWW

7-38 ESPN Deportes. Conéctate con la página web de **¡Arriba!** para buscar una noticia deportiva que te interese. Escribe un párrafo en que incluyas esta información:

- el evento
- dónde tuvo lugar
- los personajes
- el resultado

NUESTRO MUNDO

Panoramas

Vistas culturales

7-50 to 7-51

Las islas hispánicas del Caribe

7-39 ¿Ya sabes...? Trata de identificar, describir y/o explicar lo siguiente.

1. las dos naciones de la isla de la Española (*Hispaniola*)
2. el nombre del explorador europeo de Cuba en 1492
3. la capital de Puerto Rico
4. un atractivo turístico de todas las islas del Caribe
5. la relación política entre Puerto Rico y los Estados Unidos

Puerto Rico es un estado libre asociado (*commonwealth*) de los Estados Unidos. Las relaciones entre Puerto Rico y los EE.UU. no han sido siempre cordiales. Hay algunos puertorriqueños que prefieren que Puerto Rico sea estado de los EE.UU. y otros que quieren que sea un país independiente.

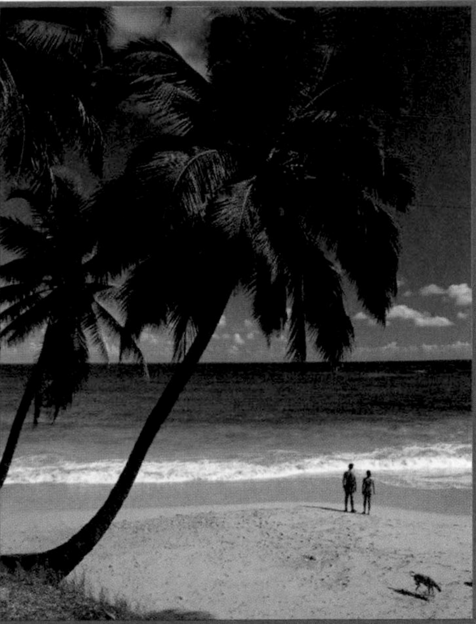

Las aguas cristalinas, el sol, el agua tibia y sus bellas playas atraen a miles de turistas a la República Dominicana todos los años.

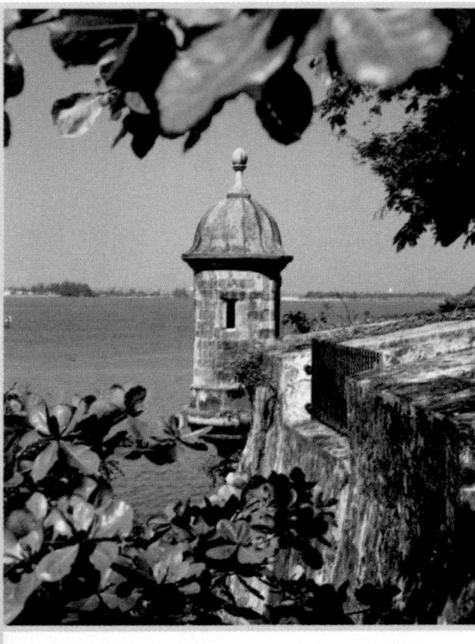

La fortaleza de El Morro rodeó la antigua ciudad de San Juan, Puerto Rico, para protegerla de las invasiones de los piratas de países extranjeros.

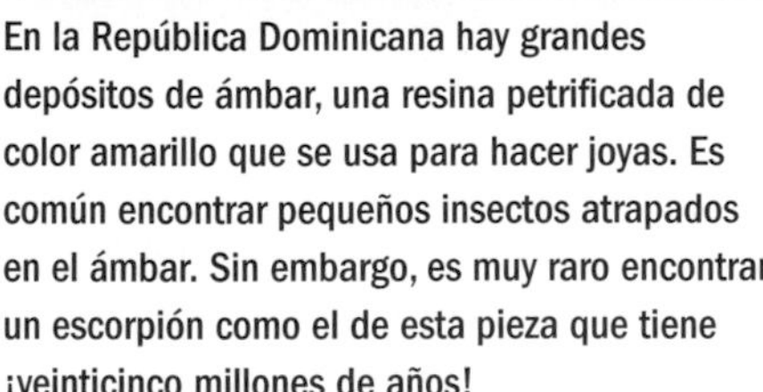

En la República Dominicana hay grandes depósitos de ámbar, una resina petrificada de color amarillo que se usa para hacer joyas. Es común encontrar pequeños insectos atrapados en el ámbar. Sin embargo, es muy raro encontrar un escorpión como el de esta pieza que tiene ¡veinticinco millones de años!

La isla de Cuba, la más grande de las Antillas, es un paraíso visual y cultural. Su rica historia se refleja en su gente, su arquitectura, su música y su arte.

Si quieres ir de un lado al otro de La Habana, ¿por qué no vas en "coco-taxi"? Es una manera rápida y económica de viajar.

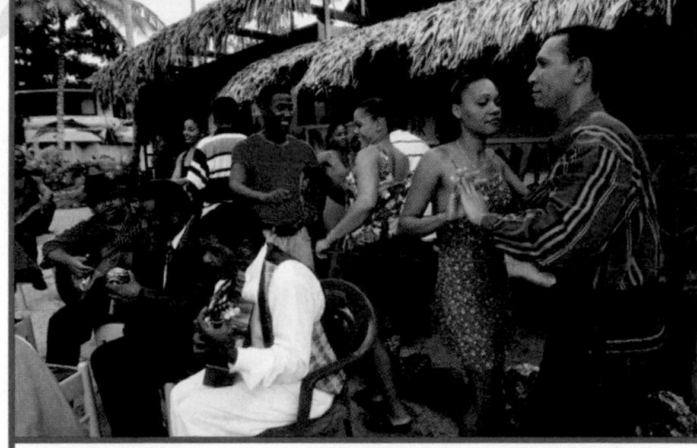

Se siente el ritmo afrocaribeño en la música de la República Dominicana. ¿Sabes por qué este baile se llama "merengue" (*meringue*)?

7-40 ¿Cierto o falso? Indica si las siguientes oraciones son ciertas o falsas. Si son falsas, explica por qué.

1. _____ Cuba es la isla más grande de las Antillas.
2. _____ Cuba tiene una herencia africana y española.
3. _____ El coco-taxi es un modo de transporte en Puerto Rico.
4. _____ El merengue es un baile popular que tiene raíces (*roots*) francesas.
5. _____ Muchos turistas son atraídos a las islas del Caribe por sus montañas.
6. _____ El ámbar es una joya semipreciosa.
7. _____ Puerto Rico fue víctima de invasiones de piratas.
8. _____ Puerto Rico es un estado de los Estados Unidos.

7-41 Asociaciones. Conversen sobre lo que asocian con las islas hispanas del Caribe. Pueden incluir sus ideas y opiniones en las siguientes categorías.

Modelo: la política
Puerto Rico: un estado libre asociado de los EE.UU. Cuba:...

1. la política
2. el clima
3. la música
4. la composición racial
5. la economía

7-42 Recomendaciones. Túrnense para pedir y hacer recomendaciones, según sus intereses.

Modelo: E1: *Quiero escuchar música afrocaribeña.*
E2: *Debes visitar la República Dominicana. Allí puedes bailar merengue.*

1. Quiero comprar ámbar.
2. Quiero ir a la isla más bella de las Antillas.
3. Quiero conocer la isla donde no necesito llevar pasaporte.
4. Deseo hablar francés.

7-43 Un viaje a... En un grupo de tres o cuatro estudiantes, hagan planes para una excursión a una isla caribeña. Escriban una lista de todo lo que deben hacer antes de salir de viaje.

Modelo: *Primero, tenemos que sacar el pasaporte.*

7-44 Más información. Conéctate con la página web de **¡Arriba!** para ver más imágenes de las islas del Caribe. Escoge (*Choose*) una y describe un punto de interés.

Ritmos

7-52

"El pregonero" (Tito Nieves, Puerto Rico)

En esta canción Tito Nieves canta sobre el trabajo del pregonero, un trabajo que hoy en día, en estos tiempos modernos, no existe. En los países hispanos del Caribe los pregoneros iban (*used to go*) de pueblo en pueblo vendiendo (*selling*) sus productos, particularmente frutas y verduras.

Antes de escuchar

7-45 El pregonero. Lee las siguientes estrofas de la canción y con un/a compañero/a busca las frutas que se mencionan en la canción. Hay cuatro frutas diferentes.

El pregonero

Yo soy el pregonero
que pasa por las mañanas;
vendiendo la fruta fresca,
guindando de la vara.

Ay, casera
llevo la piña fresca,
la naranja madura;
llevo la caña dulce
y el coco seco, cáscara dura.
[...]

Casera, así que cómpreme un poco
(*se repite*).
Ay, casera, ven y cómpreme un poco
aquí te traigo un mango y el coco
sabroso;
ay, casera de mi vida aprovecha la
ocasión
le traigo fruta sabrosa de mi pueblo.
Caserita de mi vida no me digas no
casera, así que cómpreme un poco (*se repite*).
Llevo la piña fresca
también te traigo la naranja madura,
tengo la cola de bacalao pa' la fritura.
[...]

A escuchar

7-46 ¿Cómo te parece la canción? Mientras escuchas indica con **R** (ritmo) y con **L** (letra) qué palabras y expresiones caracterizan estos dos elementos de la canción en tu opinión.

_____ triste
_____ alegre
_____ rápido
_____ bueno para bailar
_____ nostálgico
_____ serio
_____ divertido
_____ interesante
_____ melancólico

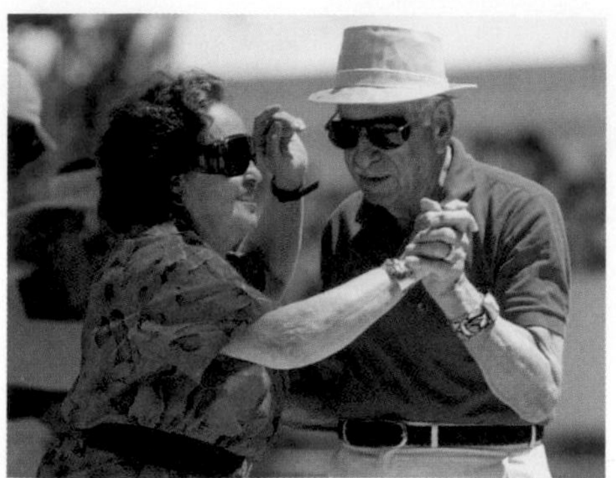

La salsa es popular entre gente de todas las edades.

7-47 ¡Vamos a bailar salsa! "El pregonero" es un ejemplo de música **salsa,** un estilo musical muy popular en las islas hispánicas del Caribe. La salsa tiene un ritmo alegre y muy bailable. No importa si el tema de una canción de salsa es feliz o serio, a todos les gusta bailar salsa. Mira el diagrama de los pasos de salsa y con los compañeros de clase trata de seguirlos con la música.

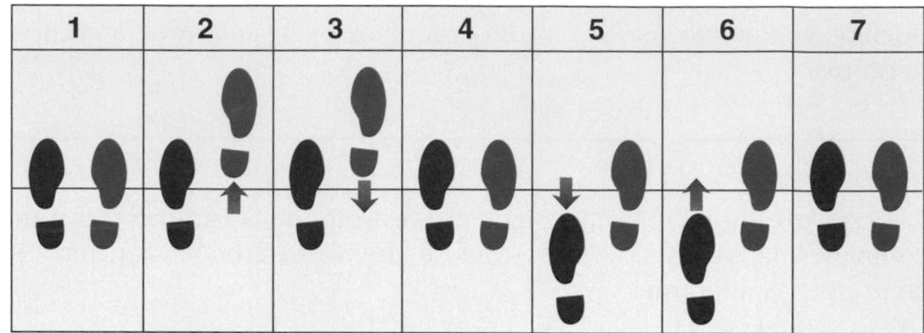

el medio

izquierda (left)

derecha (right)

1. Both feet in middle
2. Right foot forward; left foot in middle
3. Step in place with left foot, then move right foot back to middle
4. Both feet in middle
5. Left foot back; right foot in middle
6. Step in place with right foot, then move left foot back to middle
7. Both feet in middle

Después de escuchar

7-48 ¿Cuántos verbos puedes usar? Usa los verbos de la lista en el pretérito y escribe un breve párrafo sobre un día imaginario en la vida de un pregonero como el de la canción.

MODELO: *El pregonero **fue** al pueblo y **anduvo** por muchas horas.*

ser	ir	dar	ver	tener	estar
poner	poder	saber	venir	hacer	querer

Páginas

7-53

"Sensemayá" (Nicolás Guillén, Cuba)

Nicolás Guillén (1902–1989) nació en Camagüey, Cuba. Este gran escritor mulato (mezcla de africano y español) dedicó su vida a la poesía. Su poesía se caracteriza por su ritmo y belleza, y también por su contenido sociocultural. En su obra, Guillén escribe sobre la experiencia afrocubana, mientras que denuncia la discriminación racial que sufren los negros y los mulatos. Guillén perteneció desde joven al partido Socialista Popular (comunista) y defendió la revolución cubana hasta su muerte en 1989. A continuación tienes el poema "Sensemayá", uno de los más populares por su musicalidad. El poema expresa la creencia afrocubana de que todo ser, aun la culebra (*snake*) tiene un alma (*soul*).

Antes de leer

7-49 ¿Qué representa? Decidan qué representa la culebra para ustedes. Aquí tienen algunas posibilidades.

_____ lo malo	_____ lo peligroso	_____ lo exótico
_____ lo bueno	_____ lo misterioso	_____ lo sensual

A leer

7-50 El ritmo de la música. Este poema tiene un ritmo y un sonido que se parecen a un instrumento musical. Mientras lo lees, decide qué instrumento oyes.

_____ una flauta	_____ un piano	_____ un violín
_____ un tambor	_____ una guitarra	_____ un arpa

"Sensemayá"

¡Mayombe-bombe-mayombé!
¡Mayombe-bombe-mayombé!
¡Mayombe-bombe-mayombé!
La culebra tiene los ojos de vidrio (*glass*);
la culebra viene, y se enreda (*twists around*) en un palo;
con sus ojos de vidrio, en un palo,
con sus ojos de vidrio.
La culebra camina sin patas (*paws*);
la culebra se esconde en la yerba (*grass*)
caminando se esconde en la yerba,
caminando sin patas.
¡Mayombe-bombe-mayombé!
¡Mayombe-bombe-mayombé!
¡Mayombe-bombe-mayombé!
Tú le das con el hacha (*hatchet*), y se muere:
¡dale ya!
¡No le des con el pie (*foot*), que te muerde (*bites*)
no le des con el pie, que se va!
Sensemayá, la culebra,
sensemayá.
Sensemayá, con sus ojos,
sensemayá.
Sensemayá, con su lengua (*tongue*),
sensemayá.
¡Sensemayá, con su boca,
sensemayá!
La culebra muerta no puede correr;
la culebra muerta no puede silbar (*to hiss*);
no puede caminar,
no puede correr.
La culebra muerta no puede beber;
no puede respirar,
no puede morder.
¡Mayombe-bombe-mayombé!
Sensemayá, la culebra…
¡Mayombe-bombe-mayombé!
Sensemayá, no se mueve…
¡Mayombe-bombe-mayombé!
Sensemayá, la culebra…
¡Mayombe-bombe-mayombé!
¡Sensemayá, se murió (*died*)!

Después de leer

7-51 La culebra. Haz una lista de las oraciones del poema que describen a la culebra y di qué cualidades personales te sugieren.

MODELO: *Tiene ojos de vidrio. Tiene una personalidad fría.*

7-52 La música de la poesía. Este poema es un buen ejemplo de la musicalidad de la obra de muchos escritores afrocaribeños. Léelo en voz alta para sentir mejor el ritmo de sus palabras.

Taller

7-54 to 7-55

7-53 Una entrada en tu diario. Cuando escribes en tu diario, relatas algo interesante, curioso o significativo que te ha pasado (*has happened to you*) ese día (por eso se llama **diario**). Contesta las preguntas a continuación para escribir una entrada.

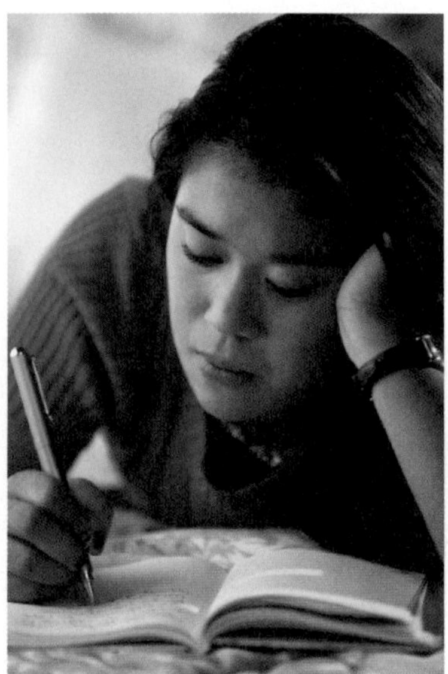

Antes de escribir

- Piensa en lo que hiciste hoy. Escribe una lista de frases para indicar brevemente tus acciones, por ejemplo: **asistir a clase, ver a mis amigos, hablar por teléfono con..., etc.**
- Pon tus acciones en orden cronológico.

A escribir

- Comienza tu entrada con una oración para resumir tu día, por ejemplo:

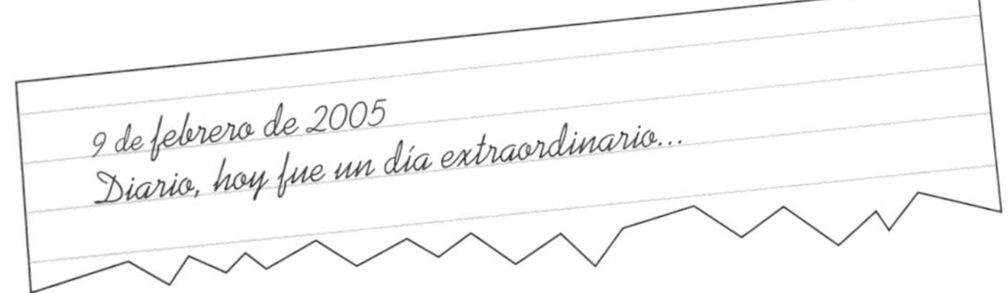

- Escribe sobre cuatro o cinco actividades que hiciste o acontecimientos que ocurrieron.
- Utiliza expresiones de entrada y transición, como **primero, segundo, entonces, después, por eso, aunque,** etc.
- Cierra tu entrada con una oración de despedida.

Después de escribir

- **Revisar.** Revisa tu entrada para ver si fluye bien. Luego revisa la mecánica.
  - ☐ ¿Has incluido una variedad de vocabulario?
  - ☐ ¿Has conjugado bien los verbos en el pretérito?
  - ☐ ¿Has verificado la ortografía y la concordancia?
- **Intercambiar**
  Intercambia tu entrada con la de un/a compañero/a. Mientras leen las entradas, hagan comentarios y sugerencias sobre el contenido, la estructura y la gramática.
- **Entregar**
  Pasa tu entrada a limpio, incorporando las sugerencias de tu compañero/a. Después, entrégasela a tu profesor/a.

Vocabulario

Primera parte

En la playa	*At the beach*
la bolsa	*big bag*
la heladera	*cooler*
el hielo	*ice*
la sombrilla	*umbrella*
la toalla	*towel*
el traje de baño	*swimsuit*

Los pasatiempos	*Pastimes*
dar un paseo	*to go out; to take a walk*
hacer un pícnic	*to have a picnic*
ir a un concierto	*to go to a concert*
ir a una discoteca	*to go to a nightclub*
ir a un partido	*to go to a game*
leer una novela	*to read a novel*
leer un periódico	*to read a newspaper*
nadar en el mar	*to swim in the ocean*
nadar en una piscina	*to swim in a pool*
ver una película	*to watch a movie*
ver la televisión	*to watch television*

¿Qué tiempo hace?	*What is the weather like?*
está nublado	*it's cloudy*
hace...	*it's...*
buen/mal tiempo	*good/bad weather*
(mucho) calor	*(very) hot*
(mucho) fresco	*(very) cool*
(mucho) frío	*(very) cold*
(mucha) humedad	*(very) humid*
(mucho) sol	*(very) sunny*
(mucho) viento	*(very) windy*
hay (mucha) contaminación	*there's (a lot of) pollution/smog*
llover (ue)	*to rain*
nevar (ie)	*to snow*

Opiniones y sugerencias	*Opinions and suggestions*
Es un día perfecto para...	*It's a perfect day for...*
¡Oye!	*Listen!*
¿Qué tal si...?	*What if...?*

Reacciones	*Reactions*
¡Estupendo!	*Terrific!*
¡Fabuloso!	*Fabulous; Great!*
¡Fantástico!	*Fantastic!*
¡Magnífico!	*Great; Wonderful!*
Me da igual.	*It's all the same to me.*
No te preocupes.	*Don't worry.*
¡Qué mala suerte!	*What bad luck!*

Segunda parte

Los deportes	*Sports*
el atletismo	*track and field*
el boxeo	*boxing*
el ciclismo	*cycling*
el esquí	*skiing*
el esquí acuático	*water skiing*
la gimnasia	*gymnastics*
el golf	*golf*
el hockey	*hockey*
el patinaje	*skating*
el vólibol	*volleyball*

Términos deportivos	*Sports terms*
el/la aficionado/a	*fan*
el árbitro	*referee*
el/la campeón/campeona	*champion; winner*
el/la entrenador/a	*coach; trainer*
el equipo	*team; equipment*
la temporada	*season*

Actividades deportivas	*Sporting activities*
animar	*to encourage; to cheer*
batear	*to bat*
correr	*to run*
empatar	*to tie (the score)*
esquiar	*to ski*
ganar	*to win*
gritar	*to shout*
hacer ejercicio	*to exercise*
levantar pesas	*to lift weights*
patear	*to kick*
patinar	*to skate*

Indefinite and negative expressions	*See page 231.*
Double object pronouns	*See page 244.*

8 ¿En qué puedo servirle?

PRIMERA PARTE

¡Así lo decimos! Vocabulario	Las compras y la ropa
¡Así lo hacemos! Estructuras	The imperfect tense of regular and irregular verbs
	Ordinal numbers
Comparaciones	De compras

- Shopping at a department store
- Talking about what used to happen and what you used to do in the past
- Describing a scene in the past

SEGUNDA PARTE

¡Así lo decimos! Vocabulario	Tiendas y artículos personales
¡Así lo hacemos! Estructuras	Preterit versus imperfect
	Impersonal and passive **se**
Observaciones	¡Pura vida! Episodio 8

- Reading and responding to advertisements
- Describing a product
- Contrasting what happened in the past with something else that was going on
- Making general statements about what people do

NUESTRO MUNDO

Panoramas	El reino inca: el Perú y el Ecuador
Ritmos	"Junto a ti" (Yawar, Perú)
Páginas	"Los rivales y el juez" (Ciro Alegría, Perú)
Taller	Una fábula

El ecuatoriano Oswaldo Guayasamín fue uno de los pintores latinoamericanos más importantes del siglo XX. Muchas de sus obras tienen un tema social.

Source: Fundacion Guayasamin

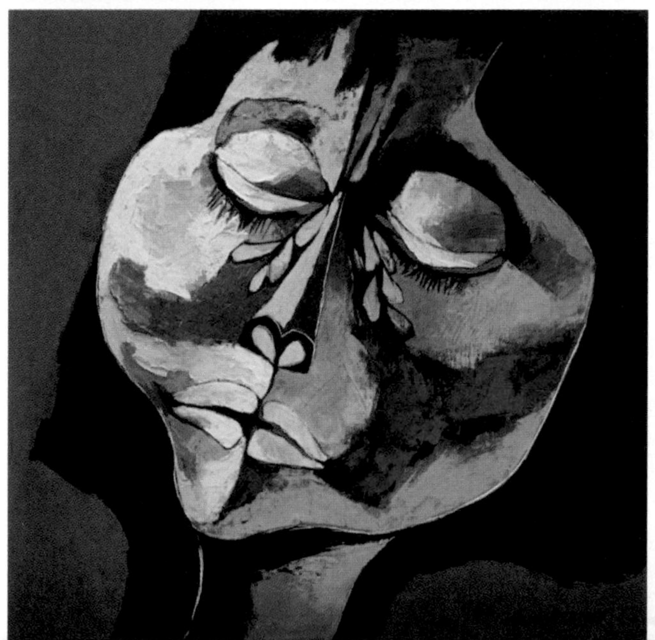

El reino inca: el Perú y el Ecuador

«Quien compra ha de tener cien ojos; a quien vende le basta uno solo.»*

Machu Picchu, la misteriosa ciudad de los incas, estuvo "perdida" hasta que la descubrió un arqueólogo en 1910.

*__Refrán:__ He who buys needs a thousand eyes. He who sells needs only one.

PRIMERA PARTE

¡Así lo decimos! Vocabulario

CD 2, Track 15

8-1 to 8-2

¡Así es la vida! De compras

En el centro comercial "El progreso II" en Lima, Perú

Son las diez de la mañana y empiezan a llegar los clientes.

Dependienta: Buenos días. ¿En qué puedo servirle?

Manuel: Quiero ver las chaquetas y las camisas que están en rebaja.

Dependienta: Muy bien, por aquí por favor, en la sección de caballeros. Las chaquetas están muy bien de precio y las camisas son una verdadera ganga. ¿Qué talla usa?

Manuel: Creo que es la 39. ¿Puedo probarme ésa?

Dependienta: Sí, claro. Allí está el probador.

Caballeros

Señoras

Las compras y la ropa

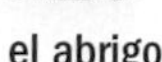

el abrigo

la blusa

el bolso

la camisa

la chaqueta

las corbatas

la falda

los pantalones

el saco

las sandalias

el suéter

el traje

los vaqueros[1]

el vestido

los zapatos

Lugares donde vamos a comprar	***Places where we shop***
el almacén	*department store*
el centro comercial	*shopping center; mall*
la tienda	*store; shop*

En una tienda	***At a store***
la caja	*cash register*
la calidad	*quality*
el/la cliente	*customer*
el/la dependiente/a	*clerk*
el descuento	*discount*
la ganga	*bargain; good deal*
el piso	*floor*
el precio	*price*
el probador	*fitting room*
la rebaja	*sale*
el recibo	*receipt*
la tarjeta de crédito	*credit card*
el/la vendedor/a	*salesperson*
la venta-liquidación	*clearance sale*

Materiales	***Fabrics***
el algodón	*cotton*
el cuero	*leather*
la lana	*wool*
la seda	*silk*

Verbos	***Verbs***
costar (ue)	*to cost*
llevar	*to wear*
pagar (en efectivo)	*to pay (cash)*
probarse (ue)[2]	*to try on*
regatear	*to bargain; haggle over*

Descripciones	***Descriptions***
de cuadros	*plaid*
de manga corta/larga	*short-/long-sleeved*
de moda	*in style*
de rayas	*striped*
sin manga	*sleeveless*

Expresiones para comprar	***Shopping expressions***
¿En qué puedo servirle(s)?	*How may I help you?* (for.)
Está en rebaja.	*It's on sale.*
Le queda muy bien.	*It fits you very well.* (for.)
¿Qué número calza?	*What (shoe) size do you wear?* (for.)
¿Qué talla usa?	*What's your size?* (for.)
Calzo el número...	*I wear a (shoe) size...*
Me queda estrecho/a (grande).	*It's too tight (big).*
¿Qué tal me queda?	*How does it fit me?*

[1]La palabra **vaqueros** se utiliza en España. En Puerto Rico, se llaman **mahones** y en muchos otros países hispanos se llaman **jeans** como en inglés.

[2]In general, **probar** means *to try*. In **Capítulo 6** you learned **probar** in the context of food: *to try* or *to taste food*. In the reflexive construction, **probarse** is used to express *to try something on oneself*, usually referring to clothing.

Aplicación

8-1 ¿Dónde están? Si ves a estas personas vestidas de la manera descrita (*described*) a continuación, ¿dónde están?

1. _____ El Sr. Domínguez lleva un traje azul oscuro, una camisa blanca, una corbata de seda y una billetera (*wallet*) con dinero.
2. _____ Raúl lleva pantalones cortos, una camiseta y unos tenis.
3. _____ Maripaz lleva un vestido blanco largo de seda y un velo.
4. _____ Manolito lleva un traje de baño y sandalias.
5. _____ Carmen lleva vaqueros, un suéter de rayas, una chaqueta de cuero y patines.
6. _____ El Sr. Cisneros lleva muchas bolsas llenas de ropa y la tarjeta de crédito en su billetera.

a. un partido de hockey
b. una boda
c. una playa
d. un banco
e. un partido de tenis
f. un almacén

CD 2, Track 17

8-2 En el almacén. Escucha la conversación entre Manuel y la dependienta del almacén Saga Falabella. Primero, indica los artículos que Manuel decide comprar; luego, escucha otra vez para escribir el precio de cada artículo. Recuerda que en el Perú usan nuevos soles.

	SÍ	NO	ARTÍCULO	PRECIO
1.	☐	☐	calcetines	________
2.	☐	☐	camisa	________
3.	☐	☐	billetera	________
4.	☐	☐	corbata	________
5.	☐	☐	pantalones	________
6.	☐	☐	chaqueta	________
7.	☐	☐	suéter	________
8.	☐	☐	traje	________

8-3 Los amigos de Samuel. Los amigos de Samuel se visten de una manera muy rara (*strange*). Describe qué ropa llevan.

8-4 En un almacén. Contesta las siguientes preguntas, basándote en el dibujo.

1. ¿Qué está comprando la señora?
2. ¿De qué forma paga?, ¿con tarjeta de crédito o en efectivo?
3. ¿Quién está en la caja?
4. ¿Qué miran las dos jóvenes?
5. ¿Qué ropa llevan?

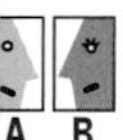

8-5A ¿Tienes? Tienes un recibo para varios artículos, pero falta parte de la información. Túrnense para llenar su recibo con la información que falta. Estudiante B, por favor ve al **Apéndice 1,** página A9.

MODELO: E1: *¿Cuánto cuesta la blusa de manga corta?*
E2: *Cuesta 50 nuevos soles. ¿De qué talla es?*
E1: *Es una...*

Falabella		**00917** **12 diciembre de 2008**
Artículo	Talla	Precio (nuevos soles)
blusa de manga corta	36	NS 50
camiseta de ______	40	NS 20
pantalones de lana		NS 75
blusa de seda	38	
chaqueta de cuero		NS 200
______ de cuero	39	NS 39
falda de algodón	38	

8-6 ¿Están de moda o no? Conversen sobre la ropa que Uds. consideran que está de moda y la que no está de moda. ¿Tienen la misma opinión?

MODELO: E1: *Los vaqueros y los tenis están de moda. Las camisetas sin manga no están de moda.*
E2: *No estoy de acuerdo. Yo creo que las camisetas sin manga sí están de moda.*

8-7 ¿Qué llevas cuando...? Pregúntense qué ropa llevan en diferentes ocasiones.

MODELO: E1: *¿Qué llevas cuando tienes examen?*
E2: *Llevo vaqueros y una camiseta.*
E1: *Pues, yo llevo...*

OCASIÓN	ROPA
1. asistes a un concierto	________
2. te invitan a la casa del rector de tu universidad	________
3. visitas Alaska en enero	________
4. vas a nadar	________
5. invitas a tus compañeros a una fiesta en tu casa	________
6. practicas un deporte	________
7. trabajas como camarero/a	________
8. vas de vacaciones a Macchu Pichu	________

8-8 ¿Quién es? Describe la ropa que lleva otra persona de la clase para ver si tus compañeros/as pueden adivinar quién es.

MODELO: *Lleva una camisa azul de manga larga. Tiene pantalones negros. Tiene zapatos marrones. ¡Está muy elegante! ¿Quién es?*

8-9 En la tienda. Hagan el papel de dependiente/a y el de clientes en una tienda elegante.

MODELO: DEPENDIENTE/A: *Buenas tardes. ¿En qué puedo servirle?*
CLIENTE1: *Quiero ver...*
CLIENTE2: *¿Me puede mostrar...?*

¡Así lo hacemos! Estructuras

1. The imperfect tense of regular and irregular verbs

8-9 to 8-16

El imperfecto de verbos regulares

CAMINÁBAMOS, SUBÍAMOS CERROS
Y NOS SENTÍAMOS LOS DUEÑOS DEL MUNDO.
JEEP.

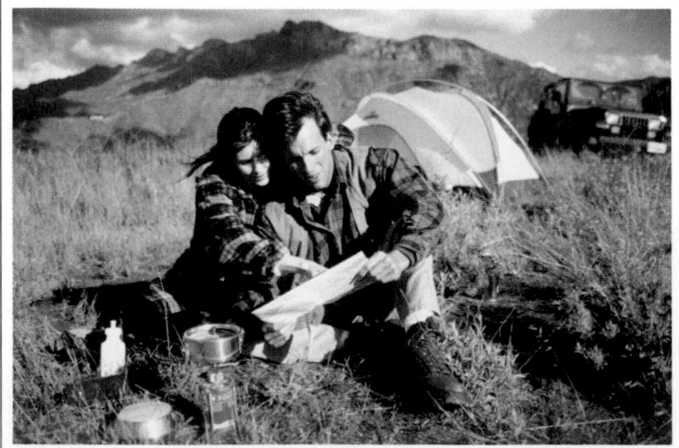

You have already studied the preterit tense in **Capítulos 6** and **7**. Here you will be introduced to the imperfect, the other simple past tense in Spanish.

- The imperfect tense of regular verbs is formed as follows.

	hablar	comer	escribir
yo	habl**aba**	com**ía**	escrib**ía**
tú	habl**abas**	com**ías**	escrib**ías**
él, ella, Ud.	habl**aba**	com**ía**	escrib**ía**
nosotros/as	habl**ábamos**	com**íamos**	escrib**íamos**
vosotros/as	habl**abais**	com**íais**	escrib**íais**
ellos/as, Uds.	habl**aban**	com**ían**	escrib**ían**

- With **-ar** verbs, only the first-person plural form has a written accent mark. The imperfect endings for **-er** and **-ir** verbs are identical, and all forms have a written accent mark.
- The Spanish imperfect has three common English equivalents: the simple past, the past progressive, and the *used to* + infinitive construction.

Rosario **trabajaba** en la tienda.	*Rosario worked at the store.* *Rosario was working at the store.* *Rosario used to work at the store.*

- Use the imperfect to describe repeated, habitual, or continuous actions in the past with no reference to the beginning or ending.

Cuando yo **viajaba** al Ecuador, **volaba** en Zaeta.	*When I traveled to Ecuador, I would fly on Zaeta.*
Susana y Mauricio **leían** la guía todos los días.	*Susana and Mauricio read the guidebook every day.*
Mauricio **pensaba** todo el tiempo en el viaje.	*Mauricio was thinking about the trip all the time.*
Comíamos en el restaurante cerca del centro comercial.	*We used to eat at the restaurant close to the mall.*

- Use the imperfect to describe an event or action in progress when another event or action takes place (in the preterit) or is occurring (in the imperfect).

Estaban en la tienda cuando **llegaron** sus amigas.	*They were in the store when their friends arrived.*
Mientras Rosario **hablaba** con Clara, Mauricio **miraba** los suéteres.	*While Rosario was talking with Clara, Mauricio was looking at the sweaters.*

- The imperfect is used to describe characteristics or states of being (health, emotions, etc.) in the past when no particular beginning or ending is implied in the statement.

Mi abuela **era** muy activa.	*My grandmother was very active.*
Tenía mucha energía.	*She had a lot of energy.*
Mis padres **estaban** muy contentos en Quito.	*My parents were very happy in Quito.*

Verbos irregulares en el imperfecto

There are only three verbs that are irregular in the imperfect tense.

	ir	ser	ver
yo	iba	era	veía
tú	ibas	eras	veías
él, ella, Ud.	iba	era	veía
nosotros/as	íbamos	éramos	veíamos
vosotros/as	ibais	erais	veíais
ellos/as, Uds.	iban	eran	veían

- Only the first-person plural forms of **ir** and **ser** have a written accent mark; all forms of **ver** require a written accent.

Aplicación

8-10 El reino inca. Aquí tienes una descripción de la gran civilización inca, la más importante de Sudamérica, que incluía lo que hoy es el Perú y el Ecuador. Subraya los verbos en el imperfecto e identifica el infinitivo.

Muchas personas consideran Sacsahuamán como un tesoro arquitectónico.

Cuando los españoles llegaron a Sudamérica, se encontraron con el reino inca, una civilización indígena muy avanzada.

El reino inca se extendía desde la región cercana a la línea ecuatorial y a lo largo de la costa del Pacífico, hasta lo que hoy es el norte de Chile. Por el este se extendía a través de los Andes hasta partes de la Argentina y Bolivia. Aquel inmenso imperio se llamaba Tahuantinsuyu en quechua, la lengua de los incas. Su nombre quería decir "las cuatro partes", que representaban los cuatro puntos cardinales: norte, sur, este y oeste. En su capital, Cuzco, ahora una ciudad importante del Perú, los incas construyeron edificios de enormes bloques de piedras que se encajaban (*fitted*) tan perfectamente que no era posible insertar un cuchillo *(knife)* entre ellos. Aunque la arquitectura de los edificios era de aspecto severo, éstos estaban adornados con planchas (*sheets*) y ornamentos de oro. Los incas llamaban a este metal "las lágrimas (*tears*) del sol". (A la plata se le llamaba "las lágrimas de la luna".) En el interior de los templos brillaban esos metales preciosos.

Los incas construyeron un impresionante sistema de regadío (*irrigation*) y terrazas escalonadas (*stair step*) en las faldas de las montañas para cultivar verduras.

8-11 ¿Cómo era el reino inca? Contesta ahora las siguientes preguntas, basándote en la actividad **8-10.**

1. ¿Cómo era el reino inca?
2. ¿Qué países de hoy formaban parte del reino?
3. ¿Qué idioma hablaban?
4. ¿Cuál era su capital?
5. ¿Qué decoraciones usaban en sus edificios?
6. ¿Qué significaba el oro para ellos?
7. ¿Qué significaba la plata para ellos?

8-12 La manera de vestirse. Las mujeres de la foto de la actividad **8-10** se visten de una manera típica de los indígenas del Perú. Describe su ropa, indicando lo que llevaban en la foto. Después usa la imaginación y describe cómo crees que era un día típico para ellas y qué hacían antes de tomar esta foto.

MODELO: *Todas las mujeres llevaban…*

8-13 En el mercado de Otavalo. El mercado del pueblo de Otavalo, Ecuador, es famoso por sus artesanías, su comida típica y los turistas que lo visitan. Usa el imperfecto de los verbos entre paréntesis para completar la entrada que escribió Manuel en su diario cuando él y su hermana Victoria lo visitaron.

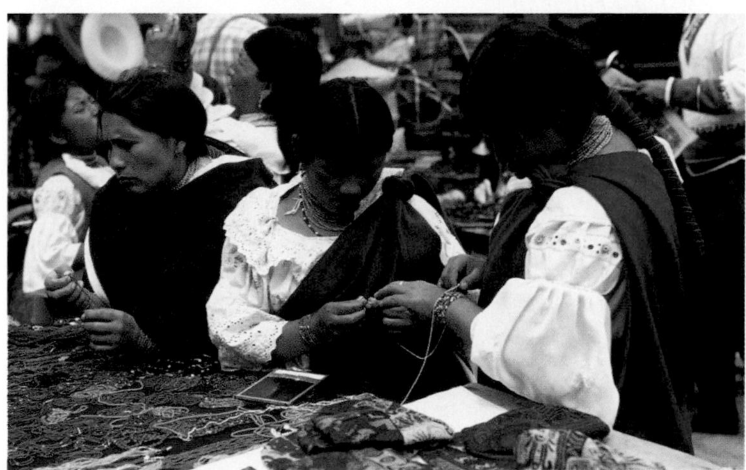

Se puede comprar de todo en el mercado de Otavalo.

El pueblo de Otavalo está situado a tres horas de Quito. Ese día, (1. hacer) ____________ mucho calor y el cielo (2. estar) ____________ despejado *(cloudless)*. El taxista se (3. llamar) ____________ Ramón y (4. ser) ____________ muy simpático. Otavalo (5. parecer) ____________ una ciudad impresionante. (6. Haber) ____________ gente por todas partes vendiendo verduras, pollos, todo tipo de comida, ropa, etcétera. No (7. poder) ____________ creer el espectáculo tan agradable de colores y olores (*smells*). En uno de los puestos, algunas mujeres (8. comprar) ____________ pulseras (*bracelets*); en otro, un hombre (9. vender) ____________ camisas de algodón. Muchas personas (10. comprar) ____________ verduras: cebollas, ajos, etc. En un lugar (11. preparar) ____________ un cochinillo (*young pig*) a la parrilla. Por todas partes los clientes y los vendedores (12. regatear) ____________ el precio de sus cosas. Cuando por fin dejamos Otavalo, (13. ser) ____________ las dos de la tarde, la hora del almuerzo. (14. Estar) ____________ exhaustos, pero contentos.

8-14 ¿Comprendiste? Contesta las siguientes preguntas, basándote en la actividad **8-13.**

1. ¿En qué país está Otavalo?
2. ¿Qué tiempo hacía ese día?
3. ¿Qué se vendía en el mercado?
4. ¿Qué comida había?
5. ¿Cómo se sentían Manuel y Victoria al final del día?
6. ¿Qué crees que compraron en el mercado?

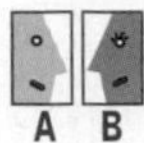

8-15A ¿Qué pasaba? Pregúntale a tu compañero/a qué pasaba en las siguientes situaciones. Estudiante B, por favor ve al **Apéndice 1,** página A9.

Modelo: a la medianoche en la última fiesta que asististe
E1: *¿Qué pasaba a la medianoche en la fiesta?*
E2: *Todos bailaban.*

1. al mediodía en el centro estudiantil
2. anoche en tu cuarto
3. a las diez y media en clase ayer
4. en el almacén la última vez que fuiste
5. ayer en la cena
6. en el mercado de Otavalo

8-17 to 8-19

2. Ordinal numbers

primero/a	*first*	**sexto/a**	*sixth*
segundo/a	*second*	**séptimo/a**	*seventh*
tercero/a	*third*	**octavo/a**	*eighth*
cuarto/a	*fourth*	**noveno/a**	*ninth*
quinto/a	*fifth*	**décimo/a**	*tenth*

- Ordinal numbers in Spanish agree in gender and number with the noun they modify.

  Clarita compró el **segundo** vestido. *Clarita bought the second dress.*
  Éstas son las **primeras** rebajas del año. *These are the first sales of the year.*

- **Primero** and **tercero** are shortened to **primer** and **tercer** before masculine singular nouns.

  La tienda está en el **tercer** piso. *The store is on the third floor.*
  Es el **primer** mostrador a la izquierda. *It's the first counter to the left.*

- In Spanish, ordinal numbers are rarely used after **décimo.** The cardinal numbers are used instead and follow the noun.

  La oficina del gerente está en el piso **doce.** *The manager's office is on the twelfth floor.*

Aplicación

8-16 El almacén La Gran Vía. Usa la guía siguiente para completar las siguientes oraciones.

MODELO: Si quieres comprarle una blusa a tu mamá, la vas a buscar en el *segundo piso.*

	Almacén La Gran Vía
1er piso	Ropa de hombres
	Calzado (zapatos, botas, sandalias...)
	Caja
2do piso	Ropa de mujer
	Oficinas de administración
3er piso	Ropa infantil
	Prendas deportivas
4to piso	Restaurante
	Cambio de moneda
5to piso	Supermercado

1. Si tienes hambre, puedes ir al ____________.
2. Si necesitas ropa para un bebé, vas al ____________.
3. Si buscas zapatos, los compras en el ____________.
4. Si necesitas comprarle una corbata a tu tío, la vas a encontrar en el ____________.
5. Si necesitas aceite de oliva (*olive oil*), lo puedes comprar en el ____________.

8-17 Su orden de importancia. Individualmente, pongan los siguientes artículos en orden de importancia en este momento (de primero a décimo). Luego comparen sus resultados.

MODELO: *Primero, necesito comprar una camisa de manga larga, porque todas mis camisas son viejas. Segundo, . . .*

MI LISTA		**LA LISTA DE MI COMPAÑERO/A**
____________	una corbata de seda	____________
____________	unos zapatos de tacón (*high heels*)	____________
____________	una camiseta de algodón	____________
____________	una falda de lana	____________
____________	un par de tenis	____________
____________	un traje de rayas	____________
____________	un abrigo de lana	____________
____________	unos vaqueros	____________
____________	unas sandalias	____________
____________	¿...?	____________

 **8-18 En la oficina de información.** Uno/a de ustedes trabaja en Información de Saga Falabella. Los otros le piden información. Sigan el modelo a continuación.

MODELO: E1: *Señor/a (Señorita), ¿dónde está la zapatería?*
E2: *Está en el sexto piso.*
E1: *Gracias, ¿y la caja?*

1. ropa para mujer
2. las corbatas de seda
3. artículos deportivos
4. tallas especiales
5. ropa para bebé
6. los probadores
7. suéteres para niños
8. el restaurante
9. comida
10. agencia de viajes
11. ropa para hombres
12. ¿...?

¿Cuánto sabes tú? *Can you...*

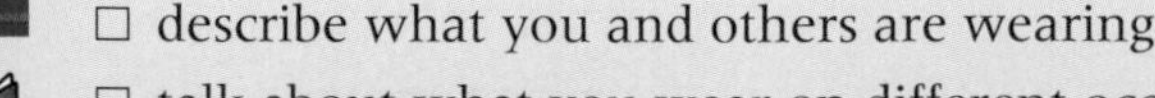

8-20 to 8-23

- ☐ describe what you and others are wearing?
- ☐ talk about what you wear on different occasions?
- ☐ use the imperfect tense to describe a scene in the past?
- ☐ use the imperfect tense to talk about what you used to do in the past?
- ☐ use ordinal numbers to put things in physical order (**primer piso**) or order of importance (**primero, segundo**)?

Comparaciones

De compras

8-19 En tu experiencia. En los EE.UU. y el Canadá, ¿es típico cerrar las tiendas a la hora de almorzar? ¿Por qué? ¿Cuántos días de vacaciones tienen los empleados en las tiendas norteamericanas? ¿Se cierran las tiendas durante las vacaciones? ¿Por qué? A continuación hay un artículo sobre los almacenes y las tiendas de muchos países del mundo hispano. Mientras lees, piensa en las diferencias que existen según tu experiencia.

Las tiendas y los bancos en los países hispanos no tienen los mismos horarios que los de las tiendas y los bancos en los EE.UU. Generalmente, están abiertos menos horas que los de (*those of*) los EE.UU. o el Canadá. En las ciudades principales del Ecuador y el Perú, las tiendas tienen horarios más amplios, pero en las ciudades pequeñas, por ejemplo, las tiendas abren generalmente a las nueve o diez de la mañana y cierran a las dos de la tarde durante dos o tres horas para el almuerzo. Vuelven a abrir a las cinco de la tarde y cierran a las ocho o nueve de la noche. Las tiendas están abiertas de lunes a viernes y los sábados por la mañana. Casi todas las ciudades y los pueblos tienen mercados al aire libre en los que se puede regatear el precio de un artículo. También es posible regatear con los vendedores ambulantes (*street vendors*).

En muchos otros países hispanos los empleados tienen derecho (*the right*) a un mes de vacaciones al año. La mayoría de los empleados prefiere tomar las vacaciones durante el verano y algunos dueños (*owners*) deciden cerrar sus comercios durante ese mes y tomar sus vacaciones al mismo (*the same*) tiempo que sus empleados. El turista que va a estos países en los meses de verano puede encontrar algunas tiendas y restaurantes cerrados.

8-20 En tu opinión. Conversen sobre dónde prefieren comprar los siguientes artículos, por ejemplo: en una tienda especializada, en un almacén grande, en un mercado al aire libre, de un vendedor ambulante, en una tienda de artículos de segunda mano, etc.

EL ARTÍCULO	PREFIERO COMPRARLO EN...
1. unos vaqueros	____________
2. unos tenis	____________
3. un traje de baño	____________
4. una camisa de manga larga	____________
5. unos zapatos de cuero	____________
6. un traje para el trabajo	____________
7. unos calcetines deportivos	____________
8. una gorra (*hat*) de mi equipo preferido	____________

SEGUNDA PARTE

¡Así lo decimos! Vocabulario

CD 2, Track 18

8-24 to 8-25

¡Así es la vida! ¿Qué hiciste hoy?

Lucía: Oye Victoria, llamé tres veces a tu casa, pero no contestó nadie. ¿Qué hiciste hoy? ¿Adónde fuiste?

Victoria: Iba a pasar el día en la biblioteca porque tenía un trabajo que terminar, pero sabía que el almacén se cerraba temprano y decidí ir de compras. Quería comprar una cadena de plata para mi mamá, y estuve en la joyería toda la mañana. Luego fui a la farmacia a comprar unas cosas y eran las dos cuando volví a casa.

En la joyería

En la farmacia

Tiendas y artículos personales

el anillo (de oro)

los aretes (de diamantes)

la cadena (de plata)

el collar (de perlas)

la pulsera

el reloj de pulsera

la colonia

el desodorante

el maquillaje

la pasta de dientes

el perfume

el talco

Más tiendas	*More shops*
la florería[1]	*flower shop*
la heladería	*ice cream shop*
la papelería	*stationery shop*
la perfumería	*perfume shop*
la zapatería	*shoe store*

Verbos	*Verbs*
devolver (ue)	*to return (something)*
gastar	*to spend*
hacer juego (con)	*to match; to go well with*
valer	*to be worth; to cost*

[1]**la floristería** en España

Letras y sonidos

The sequences "j, ge, gi, x" in Spanish

In Spanish, the letter *j*, as well as *g* before the vowels *e* and *i*, all correspond to the same sound: the *h* sound in English *hip* (although in Spain, the corresponding sound is harder and occurs in the back of the throat, where the *k* sound in English *keep* is made).

jo-ya *tra-je* *re-loj* *ge-ne-ro-so* *gim-na-sio*

In some Spanish words, the letter *x* also has the *h* sound, for example, in *México* and *Xavier*. In most cases, however, the letter *x* creates two sounds, *k* and *s*, as in English *extra: exigente* (*e[k-s]i-gen-te*) and *extra* (*e[ks]-tra*). In a few words, the letter *x* even corresponds to the *s* sound in English *sip*, as in the musical instrument *xilófono*.

Aplicación

8-21 Las tiendas especializadas. Aquí tienes unas tiendas especializadas. Emparéjalas con las cosas que venden.

1. _____ la farmacia
2. _____ la joyería
3. _____ la perfumería
4. _____ la florería
5. _____ la zapatería
6. _____ la librería
7. _____ la papelería
8. _____ la heladería

a. un collar de esmeraldas
b. un helado
c. una novela
d. la penicilina
e. las rosas
f. las invitaciones
g. la colonia
h. unas sandalias

CD 2, Track 21

8-22 ¡Yo también fui de compras! Lucía también fue de compras ayer. Escucha e indica las tiendas que visitó, los artículos que compró y los que devolvió.

Tiendas	Compró	Devolvió
______ el almacén	______ una agenda	______
______ la farmacia	______ una blusa	______
______ la joyería	______ unas sandalias	______
______ la papelería	______ una camisa	______
______ la perfumería	______ talco	______
______ la librería	______ desodorante	______
______ el supermercado	______ un té especial	______
______ la zapatería	______ un frasco de colonia	______
______ la tienda pequeña	______ una torta de queso	______
______ la heladería	______ una falda	______
______ la florería	______ un libro de Guayasamín	______
______ la panadería (*bakery*)	______ un reloj	______

¿Qué compró en la florería?

8-23 ¿En qué tiendas compras? Conversen sobre dónde hacen las compras y por qué.

MODELO: *Me gusta comprar helado en la heladería* La Creme *que está en mi ciudad porque tiene veintiún sabores deliciosos.*

Centro Comercial Largo Mar en Miraflores, Lima, Perú

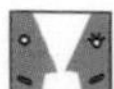

8-24 ¿Hacen juego? Decidan si estos artículos hacen juego. Si no, cámbienlos.

MODELO: traje de baño y zapatos de cuero
No hacen juego. Es mejor llevar sandalias con un traje de baño.

1. una camisa de cuadros y pantalones de rayas
2. un vestido de seda y botas de cuero
3. un collar de oro y aretes de plata
4. sandalias y calcetines
5. vaqueros y tenis
6. ¿...?

WWW

8-25 De compras en Lima. Conéctate con la página web de **¡Arriba!** y busca información acerca de una tienda especializada. Escoge (*Choose*) un artículo que te interese y contesta estas preguntas.

1. ¿Cuál es el artículo? 2. ¿Cómo es? 3. ¿Dónde se vende?

¡Así lo hacemos! Estructuras

8-31 to 8-37

3. Preterit versus imperfect

In Spanish, the use of the preterit and the imperfect reflects the way the speaker views the action or event being expressed. The uses of these two tenses are compared on the following page.

The Preterit...

1. narrates actions or events in the past that the speaker views as completed or finished.

   Victoria y Lucía **hablaron** por teléfono por dos horas. — *Victoria and Lucía talked on the phone for two hours.*

2. expresses the beginning or end of a past event or action.

   El zapatero **llegó** a las tres y cinco. — *The shoemaker arrived at 3:05.*
   La película **terminó** a las ocho de la noche. — *The movie ended at 8:00 P.M.*

3. narrates completed events that occured in a series.

   Carlos **entró** en la farmacia, **vio** a su ex-novia y **salió** inmediatamente. — *Carlos entered the pharmacy, saw his ex-girlfriend, and left immediately.*

4. expresses changes in mental, physical, and emotional conditions or states in the past.

   Alejandra **se puso** furiosa cuando vio el cuarto en desorden. — *Alejandra became furious when she saw the messy room.*
   Estuve nerviosa durante la entrevista. — *I was nervous during the interview (but now I'm not).*

5. describes weather and scenes as events or within specific time parameters.

   Ayer **fue** un día horrible. **Llovió** e **hizo** mucho viento. — *Yesterday was a horrible day. It rained and was very windy.*

The Imperfect...

1. describes what was happening in the past, usually in relation to another event or at a given time, with no reference to the beginning or end of an action.

   Rosa **hablaba** mientras **miraba** las compras. — *Rosa was talking while she was looking at her purchases.*

2. expresses habitual actions or events in the past.

   Pedro **comía** en ese restaurante todos los sábados. — *Pedro used to eat at that restaurant every Saturday.*
   Ana **iba** de compras todo el tiempo. — *Ana used to go shopping all the time.*

3. expresses time in the past.

   Eran las once de la noche. — *It was 11:00 in the evening.*

4. expresses mental, physical, and emotional conditions or states in the past.

   Alicia **estaba** contenta durante el concierto. — *Alicia was happy during the concert.*
   Nos **sentíamos** mal después de comer allí. — *We felt sick after eating there.*

5. sets the scene (weather, activities in progress, etc.) for other actions and events that take place.

   Hacía muy mal tiempo y **llovía.** Yo **leía** en mi cuarto y **esperaba** la llamada. — *The weather was bad and it was raining. I was reading in my room and waiting for the call.*

- The preterit and the imperfect tenses are often used together. In the following examples, the imperfect describes what was happening or in progress when another action (in the preterit) interrupted and took place.

  Conversábamos con el dependiente cuando Lourdes **entró** en la joyería. — *We were talking with the clerk when Lourdes entered the jewelry store.*
  Las chicas **salían** de la tienda cuando Jorge las **vio.** — *The girls were leaving the store when Jorge saw them.*

STUDY TIPS

Para distinguir entre el pretérito y el imperfecto

1. Analyze the context in which the verb will be used and ask yourself, does the verb describe the way things were or does it tell what happened? Use the imperfect to describe and the preterit to tell what happened.

   Era de noche cuando **volvieron** a casa.
   Era: describes → It was nighttime.
   volvieron: tells what happened → They returned.

2. In many instances, both tenses produce a grammatical sentence. Your choice will depend on the message you are communicating.

Así **fue.**	*That's how it happened.*
Así **era.**	*That's how it used to be.*
Ayer **fue** un día horrible.	*Yesterday was a horrible day. (This is the point; it's not background information.)*
Era un día horrible.	*It was a difficult day. (This is background information for the actions that will be narrated.)*

3. Here are some temporal expressions that are frequently (but not always) associated with the imperfect and preterit. Note that the ones that require imperfect generally imply repetition or habit and those that use the preterit refer to specific points in time.

IMPERFECT	**PRETERIT**
a menudo	anoche
con frecuencia	anteayer
de vez en cuando	ayer
muchas veces	esta mañana
frecuentemente	el fin de semana pasado
todos los lunes / martes / etcétera	el mes pasado
todas las semanas	el lunes / martes pasado, etc.
todos los días / meses	una vez
siempre (*when an event is repeated with no particular end point*)	siempre (*when an end point is obvious*)
mientras	

Aplicación

8-26 Guayasamín. Lee esta selección sobre el famoso artista ecuatoriano Oswaldo Guayasamín. Después haz una lista con los verbos en el pretérito y otra lista con los verbos en el imperfecto.

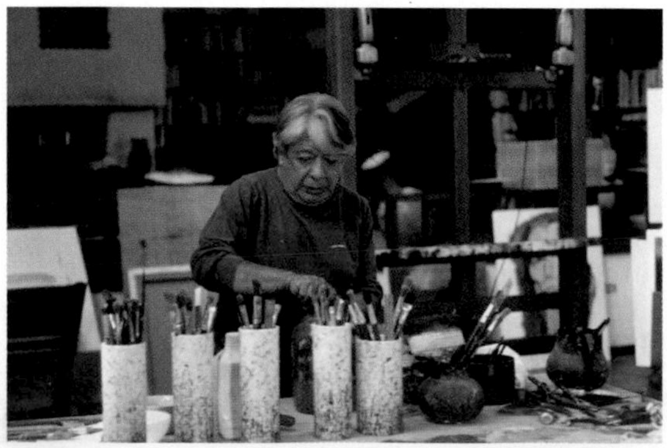

Guayasamín en su estudio

Oswaldo Guayasamín nació en Quito el 6 de julio de 1919. De niño, su familia era muy pobre. Se graduó de pintor y escultor en la Escuela de Bellas Artes de Quito. Realizó su primera exposición cuando tenía veintitrés años, en 1942. Durante su vida, recibió muchos premios (*prizes*) nacionales y varios internacionales. Tuvo una vida artística muy productiva: hizo cuadros, murales, esculturas y monumentos.

Guayasamín era un hombre de izquierdas que, a través de su vida, apoyó (*supported*) causas socialistas. Sin embargo, siempre estuvo en contra de todo tipo de violencia. Su obra humanista quiso reflejar la miseria que sufría la mayor parte de la humanidad.

Murió el 10 de marzo de 1999, a los setenta y nueve años. Hasta poco antes de su fallecimiento estuvo trabajando en la obra que él consideraba más importante: la denominada *La capilla* (chapel) *del hombre.*

8-27 ¿Era o fue? Ahora explica por qué se usa el pretérito versus el imperfecto en la biografía de Guayasamín en la actividad **8-26.**

MODELO: La familia de Oswaldo Guayasamín **era** muy pobre cuando él **nació.**
ERA: *description in the past* (descripción en el pasado)
NACIÓ: *completed event* (evento ocurrido)

8-28 ¿Comprendiste? Contesta las siguientes preguntas basadas en el texto sobre Guayasamín de la actividad **8-26.**

1. ¿Dónde y en qué año nació?
2. ¿Cuántos años tenía cuando murió?
3. ¿Qué honores recibió durante su vida?
4. ¿Qué quiso reflejar Guayasamín en su obra humanista?
5. ¿En qué estuvo trabajando cuando murió?

WWW

8-29 Las obras de Guayasamín. Conéctate con la página web de **¡Arriba!** para ver otras obras de Guayasamín. Describe una de sus obras, contestando estas preguntas.

1. ¿Qué tipo de obra es?
2. ¿Qué colores predominan en la obra?
3. ¿Es una imagen triste o alegre? ¿Optimista o pesimista? ¿Por qué?

8-30 Una escena en el mercado. Completa el párrafo con la forma correcta del verbo entre paréntesis en el pretérito o el imperfecto, según el contexto.

En el mercado (1) ___________ (haber) mucha actividad: un vendedor de fruta (2) ___________ (vender) mangos y plátanos. Una artesana (3) ___________ (mostrar) sus tejidos (*weavings*) de alpaca. Muchos niños (4) ___________ (jugar) en la plaza. De repente, (5) ___________ (llegar) algunas nubes muy oscuras y el cielo se (6) ___________ (poner) muy gris. Luego (7) ___________ (empezar) a llover y el viento (8) ___________ (soplar) (*to blow*) violentamente. Cuando vino la lluvia, los niños (9) ___________ (correr) a casa. Los vendedores (10) ___________ (cerrar) su puesto (*stall*) y los artesanos (11) ___________ (cubrir: *cover*) sus artículos. La tempestad (12) ___________ (durar) media hora y después, todo (13) ___________ (continuar) como antes.

8-31 ¿Cómo era Otavalo? Imagínate que fuiste con unos amigos a Otavalo. Completa las oraciones para describir cómo era la ciudad y lo que pasó. Usa el imperfecto del verbo en la primera columna y el pretérito de otro verbo de la segunda columna.

MODELO: ser temprano cuando
Era temprano cuando llegamos a Otavalo.

1. (nosotros/as) llegar cuando...	decidir ver todos los puestos
2. (nosotros/as) ver las camisas de algodón cuando...	venir a hablarnos la vendedora
3. ser las doce del día cuando...	empezar a llover
4. (nosotros/as) caminar por el mercado cuando...	almorzar con un plato típico
5. (Ana y yo) estar regateando en un puesto cuando...	irse de Otavalo y regresar a casa
6. ser tarde	ofrecernos un precio mucho mejor

 **8-32 Queríamos.** Túrnense para completar las oraciones, indicando lo que querían hacer y lo que hicieron según el contexto. Vean los modelos.

Modelos: Iba a… esta noche pero…
Iba a ver a mi novio esta noche pero me llamó y me dijo que estaba cansado.
Quería… mientras…
Yo quería estudiar mientras escuchaba música.

1. Ayer venía a clase cuando…
2. Una vez el año pasado…
3. Cuando era más joven, frecuentemente…
4. Esta mañana iba a… pero…
5. Muchas veces en el pasado…
6. Ayer tenía ganas de… mientras…

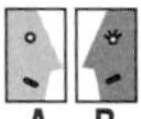 **8-33A Artículo perdido.** Imagínate que eres agente de la oficina de artículos perdidos (*lost and found*) de un almacén y que tu compañero/a viene a buscar un artículo que perdió. Contesta las preguntas de tu compañero/a y hazle las preguntas a continuación para llenar el formulario. Estudiante B, por favor ve al **Apéndice 1,** página A9.

1. ¿Cómo se llama usted?
2. ¿Cuál es su número de teléfono?
3. ¿Cuál es su dirección?
4. ¿Qué perdió?
5. ¿Cómo era? (¿De qué color? ¿Qué talla? ¿Qué número? ¿De qué tela?)

ARTÍCULOS PERDIDOS

Nombre: ____________________

Teléfono: ____________________

Dirección: ____________________

Artículo(s) perdido(s): ____________

Descripción: ____________________

Fecha: ____________________

Artículo encontrado (*Item found*)
Camisa

- Talla: 40
- Tela: Algodón
- Estilo: De cuadros azules y de manga larga con botones *(buttons)* azules

4. Impersonal and passive *se*

8-38 to 8-42

El *se* impersonal

- The pronoun **se** may be used with the third-person singular form of a verb to express an idea without attributing the idea to anyone in particular. These expressions are equivalent to English sentences that have impersonal subjects such as *people, one, we, you,* and *they*.

Se dice que las mejores gangas están en los almacenes.	*People say that you find the best bargains in department stores.*
¿Se permite fumar en esta tienda?	*Can one (Can you) smoke in this shop?*
Se anuncia el resultado de la competición de *Project Runway.*	*They're annnouncing the results of the Project Runway competition.*

- The third-person plural of the verb may be used alone to express these impersonal subjects.

Dicen que Óscar de la Renta es un gran diseñador.	*They say that Óscar de la Renta is a great designer.*

El *se* pasivo

- The pronoun **se** may also be used with the third-person singular or plural form of the verb as a substitute for the passive voice in Spanish. In these expressions, the person who does the action is not identified because in most cases the speaker is making a general reference. Use **se** + the *third-person singular* when the noun acted upon is singular and **se** + the *third-person plural* when the noun is plural.

No se venden entradas para el desfile de moda el domingo.	*Tickets for the fashion show are not sold on Sundays.*
Se encontró el anillo perdido en el probador.	*The lost ring was found in the dressing room.*
Se compran pelotas de golf usadas aquí.	*Used golf balls are bought here.*

Aplicación

8-34 Un concierto al aire libre. Aquí tienes información sobre un concierto de música andina. Subraya el **se** impersonal y el **se** pasivo.

Si usted quiere asistir a un concierto de música andina este fin de semana, le damos la bienvenida a este gran concierto. Se dice que este concierto es uno de los mejores del mundo. La taquilla donde se venden los boletos, se abre a las nueve de la mañana y se cierra a las ocho de la noche. Además se ofrece una gran variedad de precios. Se recibe un descuento si se compran más de cinco boletos. En el concierto se oye la música más típica del Perú y del Ecuador. Además, se venden programas con bellas fotos de los músicos. Después del concierto, se puede pasear por los jardines, tomar una copa de champán y conocer a algunos de los músicos.

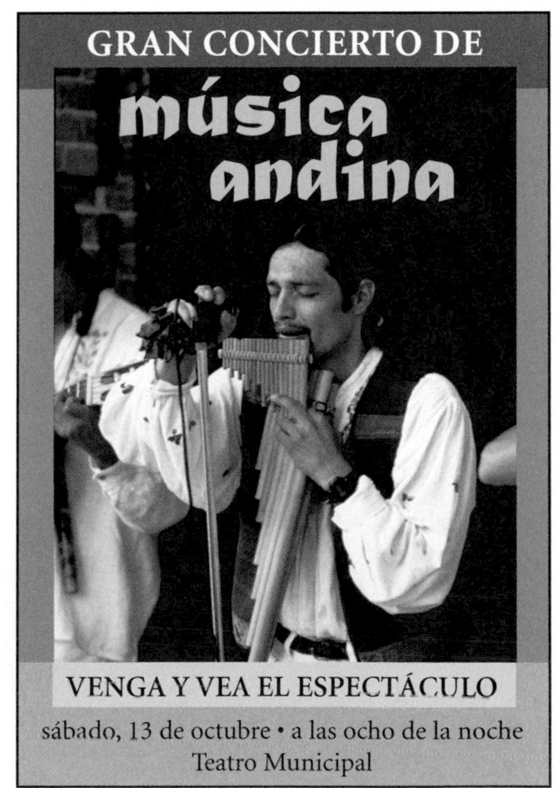

8-35 ¿Cómo es el concierto? Contesta las siguientes preguntas, basándote en la actividad **8-34.**

1. ¿Qué se anuncia?
2. ¿Cuáles son las horas cuando se puede comprar boletos?
3. ¿Cómo son los precios que se ofrecen?
4. ¿Qué tipo de música se oye?
5. ¿Qué más se puede comprar durante el concierto?
6. ¿Qué se hace después del concierto?

8-36 ¿Se permite...? Hablen sobre las siguientes actividades y si se hacen o se permiten en su universidad, ciudad o país. Pídanse detalles.

MODELO: permitir fumar en esta universidad
¿Se permite fumar en esta universidad? ¿Dónde? ¿Por qué? ¿Cuándo?

- permitir fumar en tu apartamento
- comer bien en tu casa
- poder pasear por la noche en esta ciudad sin tener que preocuparse
- decir que es buena la zona cerca de la ciudad
- permitir animales domésticos en tu apartamento

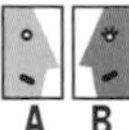

8-37A En una tienda de equipo deportivo. Eres el propietario/a *(owner)* de un nuevo negocio y has puesto (*placed*) un anuncio en el periódico. Tu compañero/a va a preguntarte de qué se trata el negocio. Estudiante B, por favor ve al **Apéndice 1,** página A10.

El Pie Volante

Almacén de zapatos de tenis
Se anuncian ventas especiales de toda clase de zapatos de tenis para hombres, mujeres y niños. Se ofrece todo en liquidación a precios excepcionales.
Se aceptan tarjetas de crédito.

¡No pierda esta oportunidad única de la temporada!

¿Cuánto sabes tú? *Can you...*

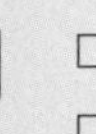

8-43 to 8-46

- ☐ talk about what you are wearing now and what you wear on other occasions?
- ☐ role-play a scene in a department store or a market?
- ☐ talk about activities you used to do in the past using the imperfect tense, such as **iba, veía, quería, compraba**?
- ☐ describe a scene in the past using the imperfect tense, such as **era, estaba, hacía**?
- ☐ narrate an event in the past where you set the scene (imperfect) and relate specific completed events (preterit)?
- ☐ talk about what people say and believe using the impersonal **se** (**se dice que..., se cree que...**)?
- ☐ talk about what is done using the passive **se** (**se venden libros en la librería, se necesita más dinero**)?

Observaciones

Episode 8

¡Pura vida! Episodio 8

En este episodio Silvia y Marcela van de compras.

8-47 to 8-51

Antes de ver el video

8-38 El regateo (*bargaining*) en los mercados. Lee la explicación de cómo es el regateo en Latinoamérica y contesta las siguientes preguntas.

En Costa Rica existe la costumbre de regatear el precio de los productos que se venden en los mercados centrales: hamacas (*hammocks*), zapatos de cuero, platos de cerámica, sombreros, joyas, ropa y hasta verduras y comida. El regateo es especialmente intenso en las tiendas de artesanías (*crafts*), en las que se venden pequeñas carretas pintadas de colores vivos y otros objetos de madera (*wood*). Es importante no mostrar mucho interés en el producto que deseas comprar y ofrecer un precio bajo para negociar con el vendedor el precio del producto. El precio final depende de la habilidad de cada cliente.

En Costa Rica se pintan las carretas (*oxcarts*) de colores vivos.

1. ¿Qué se regatea en Costa Rica?
2. ¿Qué productos se regatean?
3. ¿Qué es importante hacer cuando se regatea?

A ver el video

8-39 Las compras. Mira el octavo episodio de *¡Pura vida!* para identificar qué compran Silvia y Marcela y para quién lo compran, según el video.

El artículo	¿Lo compra?	¿Para quién?
un arco y una flecha	sí no	
unos aretes	sí no	
una pieza de madera	sí no	
sandalias de cuero	sí no	
una blusa	sí no	

La vendedora

De compras

Marcela y Silvia

Después de ver el video

WWW

8-40 Los mercados. Conéctate con la página web de **¡Arriba!** para ver imágenes de mercados en el Ecuador y Costa Rica. Escribe un párrafo de por lo menos siete líneas en que describas los artículos que veas.

NUESTRO MUNDO

Panoramas

El reino inca: el Perú y el Ecuador

Vistas culturales

8-52 to 8-53

8-41 ¿Ya sabes? Trata de identificar o explicar lo siguiente.

1. la capital del Perú y la del Ecuador
2. el científico inglés que hizo investigaciones en las Islas Galápagos
3. una civilización antigua de la América del Sur
4. un producto agrícola importante del Ecuador
5. los países en las fronteras del Perú y del Ecuador

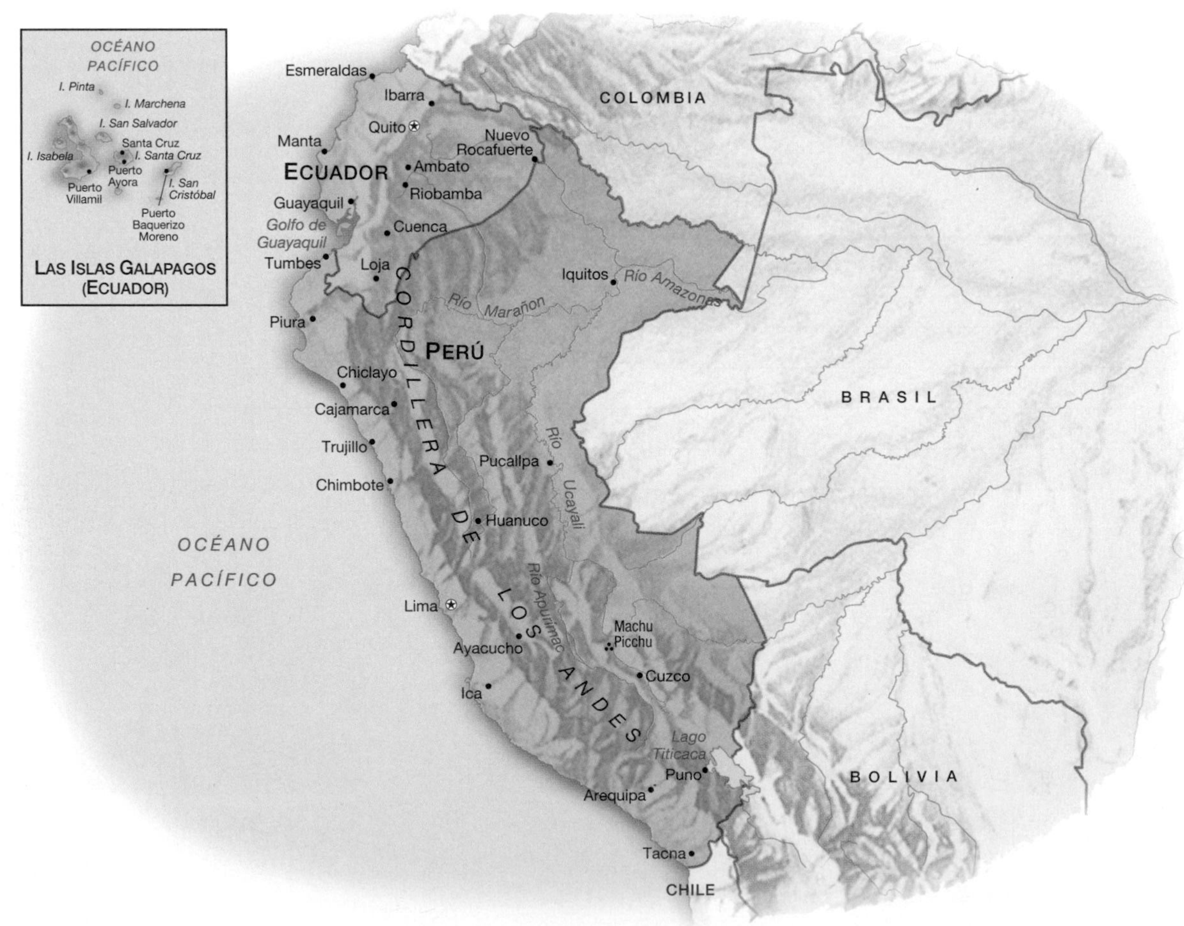

Se conoce el archipiélago de las Islas Galápagos por su exquisita variedad de vida marítima y terrestre. Aquí también se encuentra el Centro de Investigación Charles Darwin, nombrado en honor del famoso científico inglés que visitó las islas y formuló allí su teoría sobre la evolución de las especies. Hoy en día, el gobierno ecuatoriano coopera con el movimiento ecológico para estudiar y proteger las especies únicas, como el galápago (*giant tortoise*), el booby con patas azules (*blue-footed booby*) y la iguana marina.

Según la leyenda, el Padre Sol (que se llamaba Inti Tayta) creó la civilización inca en el lago Titicaca. Los habitantes de esta región conservan sus antiguas tradiciones.

Los Andes, con sus altas montañas y activos volcanes, dominan el paisaje del Ecuador.

La alpaca es un precioso animal camélido (*of the camel family*) que vive en las altas sierras de Sudamérica. La alpaca era importante en la civilización inca. Se usaba su lana en las ceremonias religiosas y para hacer tejidos (*weavings*). La lana de la alpaca es más fuerte y mucho más calurosa que la de la oveja, y se produce en 22 colores naturales distintos.

Si quieres tener una experiencia inolvidable, debes seguir el Camino Inca por el Perú en un viaje de cuatro días. La mejor estación del año para hacer esta excursión es durante la temporada seca: de mayo a octubre. Antes de empezar la excursión, es importante acostumbrarte a la altura de 2.380 metros.

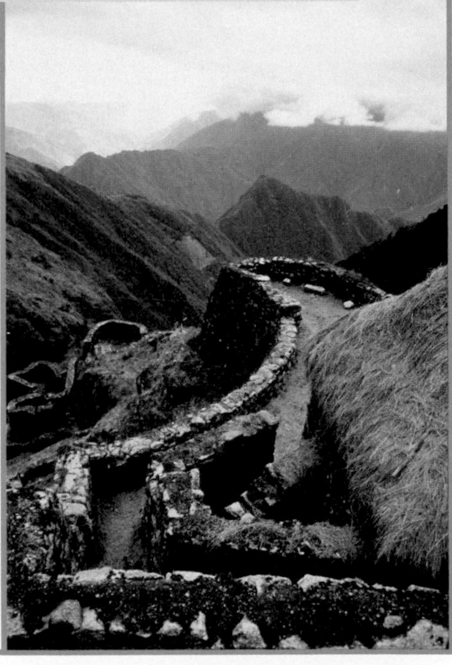

8-42 ¿Qué es? Empareja las expresiones de la columna de la izquierda con las de la derecha.

1. _____ la alpaca
2. _____ el lago Titicaca
3. _____ el Camino Inca
4. _____ los Andes
5. _____ Charles Darwin
6. _____ el galápago
7. _____ Inti Tayta
8. _____ las Islas Galápagos

a. el Padre Sol de los incas
b. una tortuga gigantesca en peligro de extinción
c. el científico inglés conocido por su teoría de la evolución de las especies
d. un antiguo sendero (*trail*) por las montañas del Perú
e. lugar de la creación de la civilización inca
f. el archipiélago donde viven muchas especies únicas
g. un animal del altiplano que produce lana
h. dominan el paisaje del Ecuador

8-43 ¿Dónde? Identifica los lugares en el mapa, en la página 282, donde puedes encontrar las siguientes cosas.

1. industria pesquera (del pescado)
2. investigación ecológica
3. deportes invernales
4. la sede del gobierno
5. volcanes

8-44 Recomendaciones. Háganles recomendaciones a estas personas que van a hacer un viaje al Perú y al Ecuador. Recomiéndenles lugares para visitar, según sus intereses.

MODELO: E1: Quiero estudiar civilizaciones antiguas.
E2: *¿Por qué no vas a Machu Picchu? Allí puedes estudiar el centro ceremonial de los incas.*

1. Quiero estudiar ecología.
2. Me gusta escalar montañas.
3. Estudio agricultura.
4. Me gustan los mariscos.
5. Quiero observar las alpacas.
6. Quiero observar las antiguas tradiciones.

8-45 Más información. Conéctate con la página web de **¡Arriba!** para ver más imágenes del Ecuador y del Perú. Escoge una y descríbela. Aquí tienes algunas posibilidades.

- la música
- la comida
- la civilización inca
- los mercados
- las Islas Galápagos
- la agricultura

Ritmos

8-54

"Junto a ti" (Yawar, Perú)

Este grupo musical, conocido por todo el Perú y Bolivia, toma su nombre *Yawar* de una antigua tradición de los incas. Una vez al año, los descendientes de este gran pueblo suben los altos picos de los Andes para cazar *(hunt)* un cóndor. Lo atan (*tie*) a un toro durante la celebración de su independencia. El grupo Yawar se conoce por su original mezcla de ritmos andinos y contemporáneos, en los cuales predominan instrumentos como la zampoña (*panpipe*) y la quena (tipo de flauta).

Antes de escuchar

8-46 ¿Qué género? Al ver el título de la canción, escoge el género que crees que representa.

_____ rock _____ rap _____ clásica _____ romance (*ballad*) _____ jazz

A escuchar

8-47 "Junto a ti". Mientras escuchas la canción, completa las oraciones con las palabras de la lista siguiente.

amor feliz labios llegar río nubes

Busco siempre en tus (1.) ___________
un gesto y una sonrisa
que siembre en este instante
la palabra (2) ___________.
Juntos ayer crecimos
jugando cerca del (3) ___________
y ya veo tus trenzas (tu pelo)
seguir al viento.
Siempre te tuve
cerca a las (4) ___________
hoy volé junto a ti.
Cuando soñamos
(5) ___________ a los cielos
soy (6) ___________ junto a ti.

La quena y la zampoña se originaron en los pueblos indígenas de los Andes. Son los instrumentos típicos de toda la música andina.

Después de escuchar

8-48 Una excursión inolvidable. Usa el pretérito y el imperfecto para completar la siguiente carta de la persona que escribió la canción:

Amor:

Ayer cuando nosotros nos (1. encontrar) ___________, me (2. poner) ___________ muy contento. (3. Ser) ___________ un lugar donde sólo (4. estar) ___________ nosotros, el aire, el viento y el sol. Los pájaros (5. cantar) ___________. El sol se (6. reflejar) ___________ en el agua y me (7. sentir) ___________ en paz. Miré tus ojos negros, tus trenzas lindas y tu sonrisa angelical y (8. saber) ___________ en ese instante que te quería. (9. Ir) ___________ a declararte mi amor, pero me faltaron las palabras. Luego te levantaste y te (10. ir) ___________. Ya no estoy junto a ti.

Tu admirador

Páginas

8-55

"Los rivales y el juez" (Ciro Alegría, Perú)

Ciro Alegría nació en Huamachuco, Perú, en 1909 y murió en 1967. Vivió muchos años entre los indígenas y sus obras dan vida y validez a sus tradiciones y a su folklore. "Los rivales y el juez" es una fábula.

Antes de leer

8-49 El género de la obra. Si sabes el género (*genre*), puedes anticipar el estilo. Sabiendo que ésta es una fábula, ¿qué te hace saber antes de leerla? ¿Cuáles de estas características se aplican a una fábula?

_____ Tiene una lección.

_____ Es algo que realmente pasó.

_____ Los personajes son dioses.

_____ Los personajes son animales generalmente.

8-50 ¿Quiénes son? Aquí tienes los personajes de esta fábula. Empareja el personaje con su descripción.

El sapo

La cigarra

La garza

1. _____ el sapo
2. _____ la cigarra
3. _____ la garza

a. pequeña, negra, seis patas
b. alta, gris, elegante, pico largo
c. bajo, verde o pardo, cuatro patas, feo

8-51 Para pensar. Piensa en una fábula en inglés y da la información a continuación.

1. el nombre de un escritor de fábulas: ___________
2. el nombre en inglés de una fábula famosa: ___________
3. el nombre de un personaje ufano (*conceited*): ___________

A leer

8-52 La historia. Lee la siguiente fábula para saber qué les pasó al sapo, a la cigarra y a la garza.

"Los rivales y el juez (*judge*)"

Un sapo estaba muy ufano (*conceited*) de su voz y toda la noche se la pasaba cantando: toc, toc, toc...

Y una cigarra estaba más ufana de su voz, y se pasaba toda la noche y también todo el día cantando: chirr, chirr, chirr...

Una vez se encontraron y el sapo le dijo: "Mi voz es mejor".

Y la cigarra contestó: "La mía es mejor".

Se armó una discusión que no tenía cuándo acabar (*had no end*).

El sapo decía que él cantaba toda la noche.

La cigarra decía que ella cantaba día y noche.

El sapo decía que su voz se oía a más distancia y la cigarra que su voz se oía siempre.

Se pusieron a cantar alternándose: toc, toc, toc...; chirr, chirr, chirr... y ninguno se convencía.

Y el sapo dijo: "Por aquí a la orilla (*bank*) de la laguna, se para (hay) una garza. Vamos a que haga de juez".

Y la cigarra dijo: "Vamos". Saltaron y saltaron hasta que vieron a la garza...

Y la cigarra gritó: "Garza, queremos únicamente que nos digas cuál de nosotros dos canta mejor".

La garza respondió: "Entonces acérquense (vengan cerca) para oírlos bien"...

El sapo se puso a cantar, indiferente a todo... y mientras tanto la garza se comió a la cigarra.

Cuando el sapo terminó, dijo la garza: "Ahora seguirá la discusión en mi buche (*belly*)", y también se lo comió. Y la garza, satisfecha de su acción, encogió una pata (*drew up a leg*) y siguió mirando tranquilamente el agua.

Después de leer

8-53 ¿En qué orden? Pon estos eventos en orden cronológico.

_____ ¡La garza se los comió!

_____ El sapo cantaba "toc, toc, toc".

_____ La garza fue juez.

_____ El sapo y la cigarra estaban ufanos.

_____ La cigarra cantaba "chirr, chirr, chirr".

_____ Toda la noche se oía "toc, chirr, toc, chirr, toc, chirr".

8-54 ¿Comprendiste? Contesta brevemente en español.

1. ¿Quiénes son los tres personajes de esta fábula?
2. ¿Cuál de los personajes canta mejor?
3. ¿Cuál es el más inteligente?
4. En tu opinión, ¿cuál es la moraleja (*moral*) de esta fábula?
5. Compara la moraleja de esta fábula con la de otra que conoces.

8-55 Sus animales favoritos. Hablen de los animales que les gustan y de los que no les gustan. Luego expliquen por qué.

Taller

8-56 to 8-57

8-56 Una fábula. En esta actividad vas a escribir una fábula. Recuerda que los personajes son animales y que hay una moraleja explícita o implícita.

MODELO: *En la alta sierra del Perú vivían una alpaca y un águila. La alpaca se creía la criatura más bella de todo el mundo. El águila también se creía muy, muy bella, aún más bella que la alpaca...*

Antes de escribir

- **Descripción.** Escribe una breve descripción de dos o tres personajes. Incluye sus aspectos físicos y personales.

ALGUNOS ANIMALES

el águila	*eagle*	**el gato**	*cat*
la alpaca	*alpaca*	**la iguana**	*iguana*
la araña	*spider*	**el mapache**	*raccoon*
la ardilla	*squirrel*	**el pato**	*duck*
la culebra	*snake*	**el perro**	*dog*
el galápago	*giant tortoise*	**el zorro**	*fox*

A escribir

- Escribe dos o tres oraciones para describir el lugar. Usa el imperfecto.
- Escribe dos o tres oraciones para explicar el problema o el conflicto entre los personajes. Usa el imperfecto.
- Escribe de dos a tres oraciones, describiendo su encuentro (*encounter*) y los resultados. Usa el pretérito.
- Escribe la moraleja (*moral of the story*) para resumir la fábula. La moraleja empieza con esta frase: *(No) hay que...*

Después de escribir

- **Revisar.** Revisa tu fábula para verificar los siguientes puntos:
  el uso del imperfecto (la escena)
  el uso del pretérito (los acontecimientos [*events*])
  la ortografía y la concordancia
- **Intercambiar**
  Intercambia tu fábula con la fábula de otro/a compañero/a para hacer correcciones y sugerencias, y para comentar sobre el mensaje (*message*) de la fábula.
- **Entregar**
  Pasa tu fábula a limpio, incorporando las sugerencias de tu compañero/a. Después, entrégasela a tu profesor/a.

Vocabulario

Primera parte

La ropa y los accesorios	*Clothing and accessories*
el abrigo	*coat*
la blusa	*blouse*
el bolso	*bag; purse*
la camisa	*shirt*
la chaqueta	*jacket*
la corbata	*tie*
la falda	*skirt*
los pantalones	*pants*
el saco	*blazer*
las sandalias	*sandals*
el suéter	*sweater*
el traje	*suit*
los vaqueros	*jeans*
el vestido	*dress*
los zapatos	*shoes*

Lugares donde vamos a comprar	*Places where we shop*
el almacén	*department store*
el centro comercial	*shopping center; mall*
la tienda	*store; shop*

En una tienda	*At a store*
la caja	*cash register*
la calidad	*quality*
el/la cliente	*customer*
el/la dependiente/a	*clerk*
el descuento	*discount*
la ganga	*bargain; good deal*
el piso	*floor*
el precio	*price*
el probador	*fitting room*
la rebaja	*sale*
el recibo	*receipt*
la tarjeta de crédito	*credit card*
el/la vendedor/a	*salesperson*
la venta-liquidación	*clearance sale*

Materiales	*Fabrics*
el algodón	*cotton*
el cuero	*leather*
la lana	*wool*
la seda	*silk*

Verbos	*Verbs*
costar (ue)	*to cost*
llevar	*to wear*
pagar (en efectivo)	*to pay (cash)*
probarse (ue)	*to try on*
regatear	*to bargain; haggle over*

Descripciones	*Descriptions*
de cuadros	*plaid*
de manga corta/larga	*short-/long-sleeved*
de moda	*in style*
de rayas	*striped*
sin manga	*sleeveless*

Expresiones para comprar	*Shopping expressions*
¿En qué puedo servirle(s)?	*How may I help you?* (for.)
Está en rebaja.	*It's on sale.*
Le queda muy bien.	*It fits you very well.* (for.)
¿Qué número calza?	*What (shoe) size do you wear?* (for.)
¿Qué talla usa?	*What's your size?* (for.)
Calzo el número...	*I wear a (shoe) size...*
Me queda estrecho/a (grande).	*It's too tight (big).*
¿Qué tal me queda?	*How does it fit me?*

Segunda parte

En la joyería	*At the jewelry store*
el anillo (de oro)	*(gold) ring*
los aretes (de diamantes)	*(diamond) earrings*
la cadena (de plata)	*(silver) chain*
el collar (de perlas)	*(pearl) necklace*
la pulsera	*bracelet*
el reloj de pulsera	*wristwatch*

En la farmacia	*At the pharmacy*
la colonia	*cologne*
el desodorante	*deodorant*
el maquillaje	*makeup*
la pasta de dientes	*toothpaste*
el perfume	*perfume*
el talco	*talcum powder*

Tiendas	*Shops*
la farmacia	*pharmacy*
la florería	*flower shop*
la heladería	*ice cream shop*
la joyería	*jewelry store*
la papelería	*stationery shop*
la perfumería	*perfume shop*
la zapatería	*shoe store*

Verbos	*Verbs*
devolver (ue)	*to return (something)*
gastar	*to spend*
hacer juego (con)	*to match; to go well with*
valer	*to be worth; to cost*

Ordinal numbers See page 266.

9 Vamos de viaje

PRIMERA PARTE

¡Así lo decimos! Vocabulario	En el aeropuerto
¡Así lo hacemos! Estructuras	**Por** or **para**
	Adverbs ending in **-mente**
Comparaciones	El turismo en los países hispanos

- Requesting travel-related information
- Making travel arrangements

SEGUNDA PARTE

¡Así lo decimos! Vocabulario	Los viajes
¡Así lo hacemos! Estructuras	The Spanish subjunctive: An introduction
	The subjunctive to express volition
Observaciones	¡Pura vida! Episodio 9

- Describing travel experiences
- Trying to influence another person
- Giving advice

NUESTRO MUNDO

Panoramas	Los países caribeños de Sudamérica: Venezuela y Colombia
Ritmos	"Tu ausencia" (Los Tupamaros, Colombia)
Páginas	Un folleto turístico
Taller	Un folleto turístico

Fernando Botero, pintor y escultor colombiano, es conocido por sus figuras voluptuosas. Esta pintura se llama *La familia presidencial.*

Los países caribeños de Sudamérica: Venezuela y Colombia

«Allá donde fueres, haz como vieres.»*

Shakira ha ganado varios Grammys Latinos. Hoy día es mundialmente conocida por su talento como cantante y también por sus obras caritativas. En 2003, UNICEF la nombró Embajadora para el Bienestar Global por su importante ayuda a los niños necesitados.

***Refrán:** When in Rome, do as the Romans do. *(Wherever you go, do as you see.)*

PRIMERA PARTE

¡Así lo decimos! Vocabulario

CD 2, Track 22

9-1 to 9-2

¡Así es la vida! De vacaciones

Susana y su novio, Mauricio, dos jóvenes universitarios venezolanos, se toman unas vacaciones a Colombia entre semestres. Ahora llegan al aeropuerto internacional de Caracas, Venezuela.

Susana: ¡Ah! ¡Toda una semana sin clases! ¡Qué maravilla!

Mauricio: Sí, la oferta que nos dio la agencia fue una ganga: pasaje de ida y vuelta, hospedaje, comidas y excursiones por tres días y dos noches a la Isla de San Andrés, que tiene una playa fabulosa. Además cinco días y cuatro noches en la maravillosa ciudad colonial de Cartagena de Indias. ¡Todo esto por sólo 800 dólares por persona!

Susana: ¿No te dije? La agencia López tiene las mejores ofertas de Venezuela.

En el aeropuerto

CD 2, Track 23

9-3 to 9-7

la asistente de vuelo

el avión

el inspector de aduanas

las maletas

el piloto

Más vocabulario del aeropuerto	*More airport vocabulary*
la aduana	*customs*
la demora	*delay*
la puerta de embarque	*boarding gate*
la sala de espera	*waiting area*
la sala de reclamación de equipaje	*baggage claim area*
la tarjeta de embarque	*boarding pass*
el vuelo	*flight*

En la agencia de viajes	*At the travel agency*
el/la agente de viajes	*travel agent*
el boleto	*ticket*
el folleto	*brochure*
el/la guía	*tour guide*
la guía turística	*guide book*
el hospedaje	*lodging*
el pasaje (de ida y vuelta)	*(roundtrip) fare; ticket*
la reserva	*reservation*
el/la viajero/a	*traveler*

En el avión	*On the plane*
la altura	*altitude*
el asiento de pasillo	*aisle seat*
de ventanilla	*window seat*
la clase turista	*coach class*

Verbos	*Verbs*
abordar	*to board*
aterrizar	*to land*
bajarse (de)	*to get off (of); to get down (from)*
despegar	*to take off*
facturar el equipaje	*to check luggage*
hacer cola	*to stand in line*
hacer la(s) maleta(s)	*to pack the suitcase(s)*
hacer un viaje	*to take a trip*
viajar por barco	*to travel by ship*
tren	*train*
carro	*car*
autobús	*bus*

Aplicación

9-1 En el aeropuerto. Indica si estas declaraciones son ciertas o falsas según la información de **¡Así es la vida!** y corrige las falsas.

1. Susana y Mauricio son agentes de viaje.
2. Tienen dos meses de vacaciones entre semestres.
3. En el aeropuerto hablan de una oferta para un viaje a Colombia.
4. El viaje es muy caro.
5. El viaje incluye todo menos pasaje en avión.

9-2 ¿Adónde van Mauricio y Susana? Mira el siguiente mapa y traza la ruta entre Caracas, San Andrés y Cartagena de Indias. ¿Cuántos kilómetros hay en total?

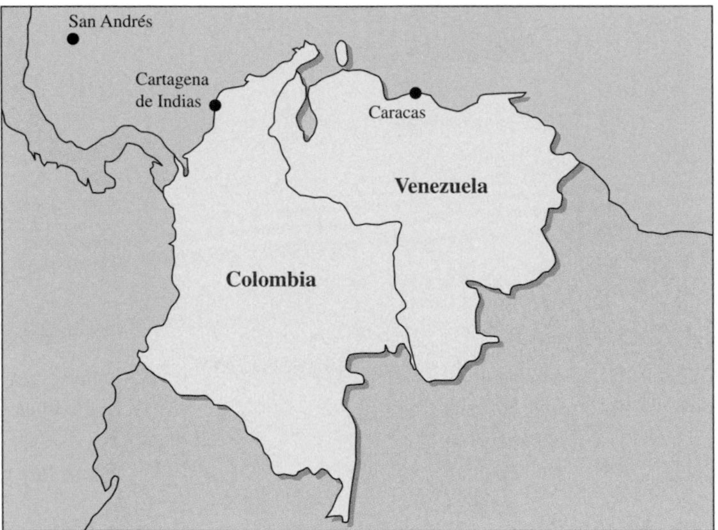

Cartagena de Indias – San Andrés: 827 kms.
Cartagena de Indias – Caracas: 944 kms.

9-3 Planes para un viaje. Tú también quieres ir a Colombia. Imagínate que vas a acompañar a Mauricio y a Susana. Pon en orden las siguientes acciones para poder hacer el viaje.

VOY A...

_____ pedir dos semanas de vacaciones
_____ bajarme del avión
_____ comprar una guía turística y mapas
_____ abrirle la maleta al aduanero
_____ hacer cola para abordar el avión
_____ hacer la maleta
_____ hablar con un agente de viajes
_____ pedir un taxi para el aeropuerto
_____ darle la tarjeta de embarque al asistente de vuelo
_____ hacer las reservas del avión

9-4 Un vuelo en avión. Parece que Susana y Mauricio se equivocaron de vuelo. Escucha el anuncio que ellos oyen en el avión. Indica la información correcta del vuelo.

1. aerolínea:	a. IBERIA	b. AVENSA	c. LACSA
2. número:	a. 895	b. 985	c. 995
3. destino:	a. San Juan	b. San José	c. San Andrés
4. comida:	a. almuerzo	b. merienda	c. desayuno
5. película:	a. cubana	b. venezolana	c. colombiana
6. temperatura:	a. 30° C	b. 30° F	c. 32° C
7. hora de llegada:	a. 2:30 A.M.	b. 3:30 P.M.	c. 2:30 P.M.

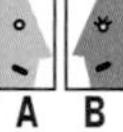

9-5A En el mostrador de AVIANCA. Hagan el papel (*role*) de agente de viajes y de viajero/a en el mostrador (*counter*) de la aerolínea AVIANCA (aerolínea colombiana). Incluyan la siguiente información. Estudiante B, por favor ve al **Apéndice 1,** página A10.

MODELO: (el saludo) *Buenas tardes. ¿En qué puedo ayudarle?*

PREGUNTAS PARA EL/LA VIAJERO/A	INFORMACIÓN
el saludo	el número del vuelo = Av402
el destino	el número de la puerta de embarque = G26
fecha de vencimiento (*expiration*) del pasaporte	la hora de salida = 17:30
su preferencia para sentarse	
el equipaje	

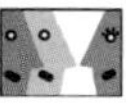

9-6 Especiales de viaje desde Caracas. Lean el aviso de Viajes venezolanos y decidan adónde desean viajar. Incluyan la siguiente información.

1. el país (ciudad) que quieren visitar
2. el número de días de la excursión
3. el tipo de ropa que van a llevar
4. los precios y cuánto quieren gastar
5. algunas actividades que van a hacer

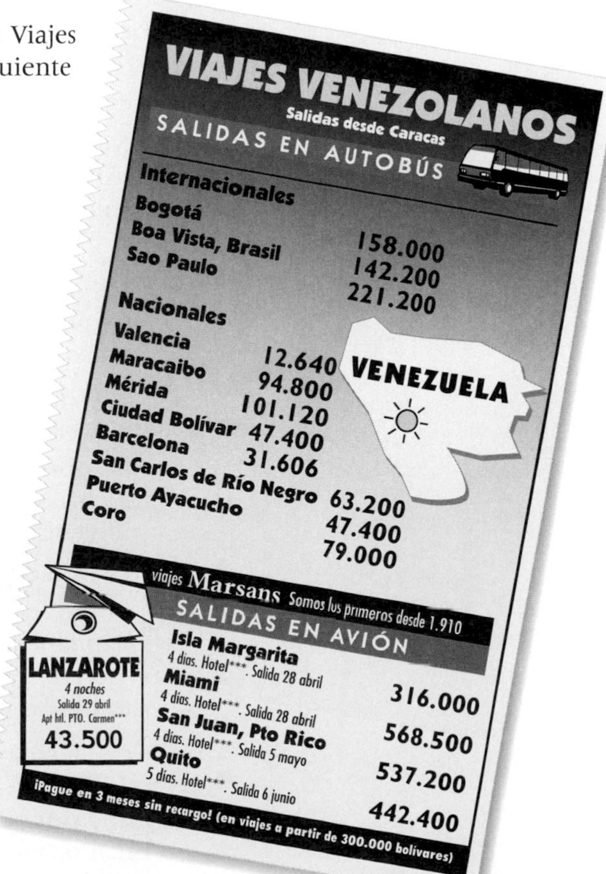

¡Así lo hacemos! Estructuras

1. *Por* or *para*

9-8 to 9-13

Although the prepositions **por** and **para** may both be translated as *for* in English, they are not interchangeable. Each word has a distinctly different use in Spanish, as outlined below.

Por...

- expresses the time during which an action takes place or its duration (*during, for*).

Vamos al aeropuerto **por** la tarde.	*We are going to the airport during the afternoon.*
Pienso estudiar en Caracas **por** un semestre.	*I am planning to study in Caracas for a semester.*

- expresses *because of, in exchange for,* or *on behalf of.*

Tuve que cancelar el vuelo **por** una emergencia.	*I had to cancel the flight because of an emergency.*
¿Quieres $10 **por** esa guía?	*Do you want $10 for that guidebook?*
¿Lo hiciste **por** mí?	*Did you do it for me?*

- expresses the object/goal of an action or a person being sought after (*for*).

Venimos **por** usted a las dos.	*We'll come by for you at two.*
Los estudiantes fueron **por** el equipaje.	*The students went for their luggage.*

- expresses motion (*through, by, along, around*).

Pasé **por** la agencia ayer.	*I went by the agency yesterday.*
Las chicas entraron **por** la puerta de embarque.	*The girls came in through the boarding gate.*

- expresses the means by or manner in which an action is accomplished (*by, for*).

¿Mandaste los pasajes **por** correo aéreo?	*Did you send the tickets by airmail?*
Hicimos las reservaciones **por** teléfono.	*We made the reservations by telephone.*

- **Estar por** + *infinitive* expresses readiness (*to be about to do something*).

Estoy **por** salir.	*I am about to leave.*
Estamos **por** visitar la tumba de Bolívar en el centro de Caracas.	*We are about to visit Bolívar's tomb in downtown Caracas.*

- is used in many common idiomatic expressions.

por ahora	*for now*
por aquí	*around here*
por Dios	*for God's sake*
por eso	*that's why*
por ejemplo	*for example*
por favor	*please*
por fin	*finally*
por lo general	*in general*
por supuesto	*of course*
por último	*finally*

Para...

- expresses the purpose of an action (*in order to* + infinitive) or of an object (*for*).

Vamos a Colombia **para** conocer el país.	*We're going to Colombia in order to get to know the country.*
La cámara es **para** sacar fotos.	*The camera is for taking pictures.*

- expresses destination (*a place or a recipient*).

Mañana salimos **para** Maracaibo.	*Tomorrow we're leaving for Maracaibo.*
Este pasaje es **para** ti.	*This ticket is for you.*

- expresses work objective.

Ana estudia **para** piloto.	*Ana is studying to be a pilot.*

- expresses time limits or specific deadlines (*by, for*).

Necesito el pasaporte **para** esta tarde.	*I need the passport for this afternoon.*
Pienso estar en Cartagena **para** las tres de la tarde.	*I plan to be in Cartagena by three in the afternoon.*

- expresses comparison with others (*stated or implicit*).

Para diciembre, hace buen tiempo.	*For December, the weather is nice.*
Para ser tan joven, la agente da buenas recomendaciones.	*For being so young, the agent gives good recommendations.*

EXPANSIÓN More on structure and usage

Para usar *por* y *para*

The uses of **por** and **para** have apparent similarities, which sometimes cause confusion. In some cases it may be helpful to link their uses to the questions **¿para qué?** (*for what purpose?*) and **¿por qué?** (*for what reason?*).

—**¿Por qué** viniste?	*Why (For what reason) did you come?*
—Vine porque necesitaba los boletos.	*I came because I needed the tickets.*
—**¿Para qué** viniste?	*For what purpose did you come?*
—Vine **para** pedirte un favor.	*I came (in order) to ask a favor of you.*

In many instances the use of either **por** or **para** will be grammatically correct, but the meaning will be different. Compare the following sentences.

Mario viaja **para** Cartagena.	*Mario is traveling to (toward) Cartagena.* (destination)
Mario viaja **por** Cartagena.	*Mario is traveling through (in) Cartagena.* (motion)

Aplicación

Fernando Botero delante de una de sus esculturas en la Quinta Avenida de Nueva York.

9-7 Una entrevista con Fernando Botero. Lee esta entrevista y subraya las preposiciones **por** y **para.** A continuación explica el uso de cada una.

MODELO: ¿Por qué no se quedó en Medellín?
reason or cause

Entrevistadora: Buenas tardes, señor Botero. Usted nació en Medellín pero después se mudó a Bogotá. ¿Por qué no se quedó en Medellín?

Botero: Me mudé por todas las oportunidades que se ofrecían en la capital. Mi primera exposición de pinturas fue en Bogotá cuando tenía veinte años. Después, gané varios premios y decidí ir a Europa.

Entrevistadora: ¿Y qué hizo allí?

Botero: Primero, viajé por Francia, España e Italia para conocer las grandes obras maestras de los museos europeos. Estudié por varios meses en cada lugar, y luego me fui para México.

Entrevistadora: ¿Y por qué fue a México?

Botero: Fui para conocer mejor el arte mexicano, y allí pinté varios cuadros. Luego, salí para Nueva York y en esa ciudad pinté mi *Mona Lisa, 12 años de edad,* que ahora está en el Museo de Arte Moderno.

Entrevistadora: Y, ahora ¿qué hace?

Botero: Me interesa el arte colonial y monumental, especialmente en la escultura. Vivo en París, Nueva York y Bogotá. Para mí, es una vida muy satisfactoria.

9-8 ¿Botero? Ahora contesta las preguntas siguientes basadas en la entrevista.

1. ¿Cuál es la nacionalidad de Botero?
2. ¿Por qué se mudó a Bogotá?
3. ¿Qué hizo en Europa?
4. Después, ¿adónde fue? ¿Por qué?
5. ¿Dónde está uno de sus cuadros en los EE.UU.?
6. ¿Qué tipo de arte hace hoy en día?
7. ¿Cómo encuentra su vida ahora?
8. ¿Cuál es tu opinión de su escultura?

9-9 Planes para un viaje al Salto Ángel. Completa el párrafo con **por** o **para.**

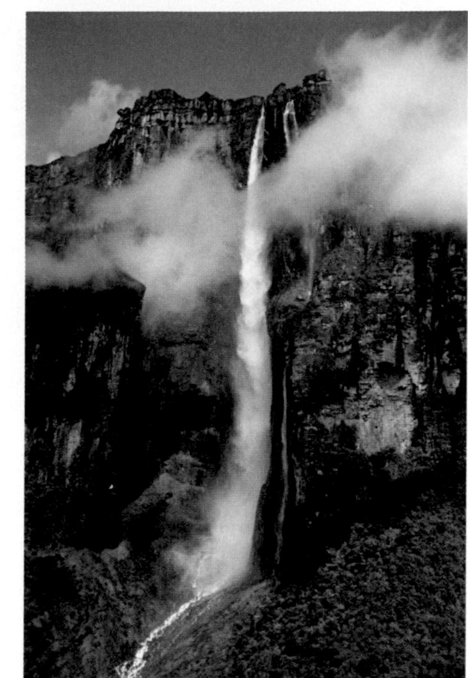

En enero Carmen y yo decidimos hacer un viaje al Salto Ángel en Venezuela. Queríamos ir (1) ___________ Semana Santa, que es en la primavera. El día que hicimos los planes, yo pasé (2) ___________ Carmen y luego nosotras salimos (3) ___________ la agencia de viajes. Carmen y yo caminamos (4) ___________ el parque Central, (5) ___________ Times Square y, (6) ___________ fin, (7) ___________ Grand Central Station. En la agencia le dijimos a la directora que (8) ___________ nosotras la primavera era la mejor estación del año. (9) ___________ eso, queríamos hacer el viaje en abril. Con la agente hicimos los planes. Íbamos a pescar (10) ___________ el río. Íbamos a hacer una excursión (11) ___________ el parque nacional. Íbamos a pasar quince días recorriendo (*traveling through*) toda la región. ¿Cuánto pagamos (12) ___________ un viaje tan bonito? ¡Sólo $850! ¡(13) ___________ mí era una ganga!

La agente dijo: "Está bien. Estos boletos de avión son (14) ___________ ustedes (15) ___________ el viaje. Pero tienen que pasar (16) ___________ la librería (17) ___________ comprar una guía turística". También teníamos que ir al banco (18) ___________ comprar cheques de viajero. Y entonces, con todo listo, ¡sólo teníamos que esperar tres meses!

9-10 Un viaje a un lugar interesante. Ustedes piensan visitar un lugar interesante este verano. Háganse preguntas para planear el viaje y después hagan un resumen de sus planes.

1. ¿Para qué hacemos el viaje?
2. ¿Salimos por la mañana o por la tarde?
3. ¿Cuánto dinero vamos a necesitar para el viaje?
4. ¿Por cuánto tiempo vamos?
5. ¿Es necesario cambiar dólares para pagar en ese lugar?

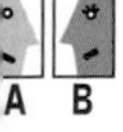

9-11A ¡Explícate! Hablen sobre los viajes que van a hacer, usando las categorías del modelo. Luego, háganse las preguntas siguientes e intenta convencer *(convince)* al otro/a la otra para ir juntos. Estudiante B, por favor ve al **Apéndice 1,** página A10.

	Modelo	**Tu compañero/a**
Destino:	*Washington, D.C.*	
Ruta:	*Pennsylvania*	
Transporte:	*motocicleta*	
Fecha de llegada:	*el 24 de mayo*	
Duración del viaje:	*cuatro días*	
Propósito:	*visitar a mi tía*	

1. ¿A dónde vas?
2. ¿Cómo vas a llegar?
3. ¿Cómo vas a viajar, por tren, por carro, por...?
4. ¿Para cuándo es el viaje?
5. ¿Por cuánto tiempo vas?
6. ¿Para qué vas?

2. Adverbs ending in *-mente*

9-14 to 9-17

In Spanish many adverbs are formed by adding **-mente** to the feminine singular form of the adjectives that end in **-o** or **-a.** Adjectives that have only one form simply add **-mente.** Note that the ending **-mente** is equivalent to the English ending *-ly*. Also note that if the adjective requires an accent mark, the accent remains on the adverb.

Se quieren enormemente.

lento	→	lentamente	rápido	→	rápidamente
alegre	→	alegremente	fácil	→	fácilmente

Teresa canceló el viaje **inmediatamente.**	*Teresa canceled the trip immediately.*
Esteban habla **lentamente.**	*Esteban speaks slowly.*

Aplicación

9-12 En el Museo del Oro de Bogotá. Lee el párrafo sobre una visita al Museo del Oro de Bogotá e identifica los adverbios que terminan en **-mente.** Después, escribe oraciones originales usando cinco de ellos.

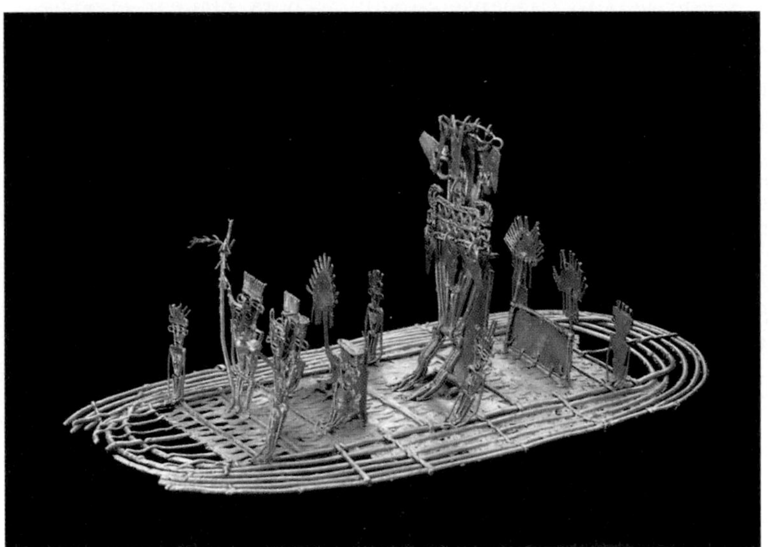

Según la leyenda, los muiscas cubrían (*used to cover*) de oro a su cacique (*chief*).

Source: Gold Museum—Banco de la República—Bogota—Columbia

Cuando Alida y José vivían en Bogotá, iban frecuentemente al Museo del Oro. Para llegar al museo normalmente pasaban por el parque, especialmente cuando hacía buen tiempo. A José siempre le gustaba caminar lentamente, pero Alida tenía más prisa y caminaba rápidamente. En el museo, José se sentaba en los bancos y tranquilamente leía todos los letreros (*signs*) sobre las piezas, pero Alida solamente sacaba fotos de ellas. Generalmente, después de visitar el museo, iban a una heladería donde se sentaban a tomar un refresco y conversar animadamente sobre la visita. Siempre lo pasaban maravillosamente bien.

9-13 La visita al museo. Contesta ahora las siguientes preguntas sobre el texto que acabas de leer.

1. ¿Cuántas veces iban Alida y José al Museo del Oro?
2. ¿Cómo iban normalmente?
3. ¿Cómo caminaba José?
4. ¿Qué hacía José en el museo? ¿Y Alida?
5. ¿Qué hacían después de visitar el museo?

WWW

9-14 El Museo del Oro. Conéctate con la página web de **¡Arriba!** y visita el Museo del Oro. Identifica un objeto que te parezca (*seems*):

MODELO: especialmente bello
Los ídolos de los muiscas me parecen especialmente bellos.

1. enormemente importante
2. elegantemente diseñado (*designed*)
3. particularmente original
4. increíblemente detallado
5. especialmente bello

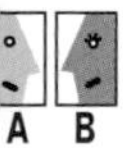
A B

9-15A El robo en el museo. Cada uno/a de ustedes encontró un objeto del Museo del Oro. Túrnense para hacerse preguntas y ver qué objeto encontró cada uno. Contesten cada pregunta con un adverbio que termina en **-mente,** formado con un adjetivo de la lista. Estudiante B, por favor ve al **Apéndice 1,** página A11.

enorme	especial	increíble	inmediato
maravilloso	tranquilo	particular	fácil

1. ¿Cómo es?
2. ¿Cómo lo encontraste?
3. ¿Quién crees que robó el objeto?
4. ¿Qué valor crees que tiene?
5. ¿Qué vas a hacer con el objeto?

Una pintura

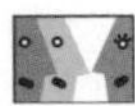

9-16 Charadas. Formen dos equipos para actuar y adivinar actividades con adverbios que terminan en **-mente.** A continuación tienen algunas actividades y algunos adjetivos.

MODELO: *Viajo frecuentemente a lugares interesantes.*

salir con	alegre	elegante
abordar	amable	fácil
comprar	animado/a	frecuente
escribir	ansioso/a	lento/a
salir de	brutal	maravilloso/a
viajar	cómodo/a	rápido/a
ver	cuidadoso/a	raro/a
trabajar	difícil	tranquilo/a

¿Cuánto sabes tú? *Can you...*

9-18 to 9-21

- ☐ make plans for a trip?
- ☐ role-play conversations in a travel agency and at an airport?
- ☐ talk about going to and through places distinguishing between **por** and **para**? (**Antes de salir para el aeropuerto, tenía que pasar por la agencia de viajes para pagar el pasaje.**)
- ☐ use a variety of adverbs to modify adjectives that describe people, places, things, and activities? (**Vancouver es increíblemente bella. Caminamos rápidamente por el museo.**)

Comparaciones

El turismo en los países hispanos

9-17 En tu experiencia. ¿Sabes cuál es la ciudad norteamericana más popular entre los visitantes hispanoamericanos a los EE.UU. y al Canadá? ¿Qué ciudades hispanas visitan más los norteamericanos? Aquí tienes información sobre los lugares más populares. A ver si tenías razón.

Millones de turistas, especialmente los estadounidenses de todas las regiones de los EE.UU., visitan países hispanos todos los años. Ciertos países son más populares que otros. Aquí tienes una pequeña descripción de los cuatro países más populares.

MÉXICO: Más de 16 millones de norteamericanos visitan México todos los años. Las ciudades preferidas son Acapulco, Cancún, Guadalajara y la Ciudad de México. Como México está cerca y tiene un clima cálido (*warm*) en las costas, es un sitio ideal para escaparse de las incomodidades del invierno. Tanto en las costas del Mar Caribe como en las del Pacífico, México tiene centros turísticos de gran belleza, dedicados casi exclusivamente a satisfacer a los turistas norteamericanos.

ESPAÑA: Más de un millón de norteamericanos visitan España todos los años. Las ciudades más populares son Madrid, Barcelona, Sevilla y Málaga. Durante los veranos, miles de estudiantes norteamericanos participan en programas de verano auspiciados (*sponsored*) por universidades españolas.

PUERTO RICO Y LA REPÚBLICA DOMINICANA: Por su ubicación en el Mar Caribe, estas dos islas reciben anualmente a cientos de miles de turistas de los EE.UU. Entre los atractivos principales de las islas están no sólo sus hermosos balnearios (*beach resorts*), sino también las ciudades coloniales de San Juan y Santo Domingo, consideradas las capitales más antiguas del Nuevo Mundo.

¿En qué país está esta ruta turística?

9-18 ¡Vamos a conversar! Pongan en orden de preferencia estos aspectos de sus vacaciones y comparen sus gustos. Luego, decidan qué país hispano prefieren visitar y por qué.

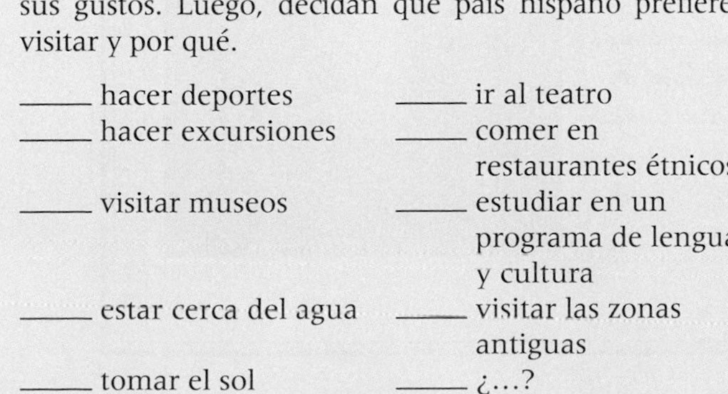

_____ hacer deportes	_____ ir al teatro
_____ hacer excursiones	_____ comer en restaurantes étnicos
_____ visitar museos	_____ estudiar en un programa de lengua y cultura
_____ estar cerca del agua	_____ visitar las zonas antiguas
_____ tomar el sol	_____ ¿...?

¡Así lo decimos! Vocabulario

CD 2, Track 25

9-22 to 9-23

¡Así es la vida! Un correo electrónico de Susana

¡Saludos desde Cartagena, Colombia!

enviar | enviar más tarde | guardar | añadir ficheros | firma | contactos | nombres de control

A: rmejias@yahoo.col.com
De: schavez@yahoo.col.com
Asunto: ¡Saludos desde Cartagena, Colombia!
Fecha: 25 de junio de 2007

tamaño medio

Hola, Raquel:

¡Saludos desde Cartagena, Colombia!

Llegamos aquí ayer después de tres días en la Isla de San Andrés, donde lo pasamos maravillosamente bien. Nuestro hotel era grande y hermoso, verdaderamente de lujo. Nos quedamos en un cuarto muy grande, con una cama grande, jacuzzi y vista al mar. Todos los días salíamos para hacer esquí acuático y bucear en las aguas cristalinas del Caribe. El último día, recorrimos la isla en bicicleta.

En Cartagena nos quedamos en la ciudad antigua en un hotel colonial con un jardín tropical divino. El hotel es más antiguo que el hotel de San Andrés. No hay jacuzzi, pero sí tenemos una vista impresionante.

Te mando una foto digital que saqué de San Andrés.
¡Ojalá que la recibas bien!

CD 2, Track 26

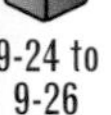
9-24 to 9-26

el bosque

las flores

la isla

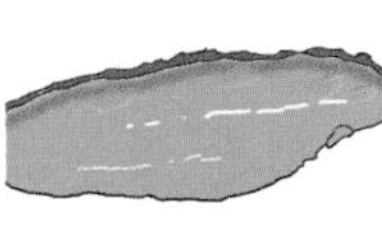
el lago

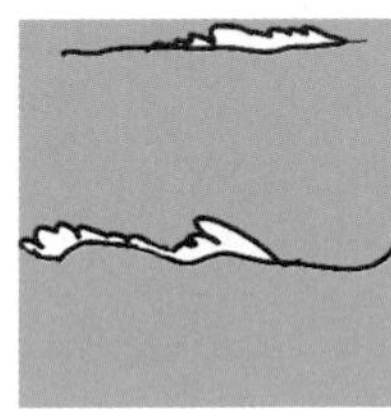
el mar

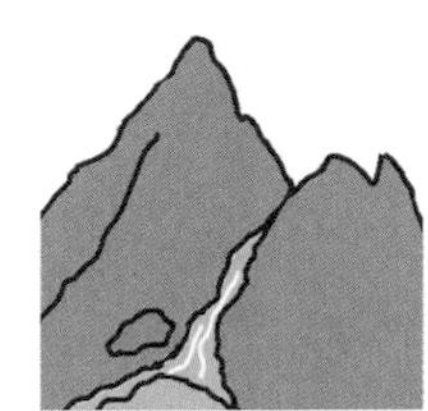
las montañas

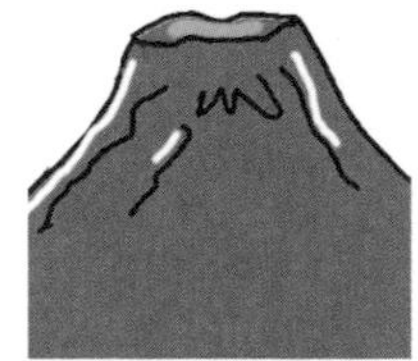
el volcán

Accesorios para viajar	*Travel accessories*
la cámara	*camera*
la cámara de video	*video camera*
las gafas de sol	*sunglasses*
el mapa	*map*
el rollo de película	*film*
la tarjeta de memoria	*memory card*
la tarjeta postal	*postcard*

En el hotel	*At the hotel*
el cuarto doble[1]	*double room*
la estadía[2]	*stay*
el hostal	*inn*
el hotel (de lujo)	*(luxury) hotel*
la vista	*view*

Actividades típicas de los viajeros	*Typical activities for travelers*
bucear	*to scuba dive*
comprar recuerdos	*to buy souvenirs*
ir de excursión	*to go on an outing; to tour*
montar a caballo	*to go horseback riding*
en bicicleta	*bicycle riding*
pasarlo bien	*to have a good time*
mal	*bad time*
de maravilla	*wonderful time*
pescar	*to fish*
quedarse	*to stay (somewhere)*
recorrer	*to go round; to travel through/across*

Atracciones turísticas	*Tourist attractions*
la catedral	*cathedral*
el convento	*convent*
la estatua	*statue*
el monumento	*monument*
el salto de agua/la catarata	*waterfall*

[1] **la habitación doble** en España
[2] **la estancia** en España

CD 2, Track 27

9-27 to 9-28

LETRAS Y SONIDOS

The letter "g" in sequences other than "ge, gi" in Spanish

As explained in **Chapter 8,** in Spanish the letter *g* before the vowels *e* and *i* sounds like the *h* in English *hip* (although in Spain, the sound is somewhat harder). In all other sequences, however, such as *ga, go, gu, gue, gui, gr,* and *gl,* the letter *g* creates one of two sounds, depending on the context. After a pause or the letter *n,* the letter *g* sounds like the *g* in English *good.* In all other positions, especially between vowels, the sound is softer, similar to the *g* in English *sugar.*

Hard *g*:	*ga-lle-ta*	*gus-to*	*guí-a*	*gra-cias*	*ten-go*
Soft *g*:	*la-ga-lle-ta*	*mu-cho-gus-to*	*ha-go*	*ham-bur-gue-sa*	

Note that the letter *u* in the sequences *gue* and *gui* is silent. For the letter *u* to create a glide sound in these sequences (as in, for instance, the name *Guido* in English), two dots (or *diéresis*) are written above it (e.g., *bi-lin-güe, pin-güi-no*). Furthermore, if the letter *u* is inserted with *ga* and *go,* a glide likewise is created (e.g., *a-gua, an-ti-guo*).

Aplicación

WWW

9-19 El pronóstico del tiempo de San Andrés y Cartagena. Conéctate con la página web de **¡Arriba!** y busca el pronóstico del tiempo hoy en San Andrés y en Cartagena. Completa las frases a continuación.

1. Hoy en San Andrés el cielo está... Hace... La temperatura mínima es... La máxima es... Mañana va a...
2. Hoy en Cartagena...
3. Prefiero visitar... porque...

9-20 Una tarjeta postal desde Venezuela. Aquí tienes una tarjeta postal de la isla Margarita, cerca de la costa de Venezuela. Completa la tarjeta con las palabras siguientes.

excursión	mar	película	tarjeta
flores	pasamos	sol	vista

Queridos papás:

Ésta es una (1) ____________ con foto de la Isla Margarita desde nuestro hotel. Desde la ventana tenemos una (2) ____________ impresionante del (3) ____________ y la montaña. En el jardín hay unas (4) ____________ preciosas. Tuvimos que comprar muchos rollos de (5) ____________ para nuestra cámara. Por la tarde, fuimos de (6) ____________ a varios lugares. Nadamos y buceamos en el agua azul verdosa del Caribe. Siempre vamos por la mañana para no tomar demasiado (7) ____________. En fin, lo (8) ____________ maravillosamente bien.

9-21 ¿Cómo reaccionan? Túrnense para contar cómo reaccionan o qué hacen cuando les pasa lo siguiente en un viaje.

Modelo: Hay una demora larga en la salida del vuelo.
E1: *Cuando hay una demora, me pongo impaciente.*
E2: *Pues, yo leo una novela o una revista.*

1. Llego tarde y pierdo el avión.
2. No hay agua caliente en el baño del hotel.
3. El hotel no tiene mi reserva.
4. Mi equipaje no llega conmigo.
5. No hay vista desde el cuarto del hotel.
6. La cama del hotel es incómoda *(uncomfortable)*.

CD 2, Track 28

9-22 El viaje de Carlota y Alex. Escucha a Carlota cuando ella le cuenta a su mamá de su viaje con Alex. Después completa las siguientes oraciones.

1. Regresaron del viaje...
   a. hoy. b. ayer. c. la semana pasada.
2. Fueron a...
   a. Colombia. b. Chile. c. Venezuela.
3. Estuvieron allí por...
   a. ocho días. b. una semana. c. un mes.
4. Una actividad que *no* hicieron allí fue...
   a. nadar. b. montar a caballo. c. escalar montañas.
5. Compraron...
   a. unos rollos de película. b. unas fotos. c. gafas para el sol.
6. Les impresionó especialmente...
   a. el volcán. b. el museo de arte. c. el salto.
7. Llegaron al Salto Ángel...
   a. por las montañas. b. a caballo. c. en helicóptero.
8. Carlota le dice a su mamá que un día todos van a
   a. visitar Venezuela.
   b. montar a caballo.
   c. un lugar más económico.

9-23 Sus gustos. Túrnense para comparar cómo prefieren pasar sus vacaciones. ¿Qué tienen en común y cómo se diferencian?

	Me gusta o no...		A mi compañero/a le gusta o no...	
Actividad	**Sí**	**No**	**Sí**	**No**
escalar montañas				
visitar museos				
bucear				
comprar recuerdos				
montar a caballo				
montar en bicicleta				
pescar				
nadar en el mar				
¿...?				

9-24 Vacaciones caribeñas. Lean el siguiente anuncio y luego háganse preguntas sobre la información.

Modelo: *¿Cómo se llama el lugar? ¿Sabes dónde está?*

9-25 Un folleto turístico de Venezuela. Lean la información que se incluye en el folleto sobre la cadena de saltos por el río Carrao en Venezuela. Ustedes tienen la oportunidad de viajar a este lugar. Hagan una lista de lo que van a llevar en su viaje y otra lista sobre lo que van a hacer allí.

Cuando usted visita el pueblo de Canaima en el río Carrao, vuelve al paraíso. Allí puede observar una gran variedad de flora y fauna, hacer deportes acuáticos en el río y visitar la cadena de siete saltos. En un tributario del río va a experimentar el gozo de su vida viendo el espectáculo del Salto Ángel, el salto más alto del mundo (¡16 veces más alto que las cataratas de Niágara!). ¡Conozca la naturaleza más prístina por el río Carrao, Venezuela!

¡Así lo hacemos! Estructuras

3. The Spanish subjunctive: An introduction

9-29 to 9-36 Until now, you have been using verb tenses (present, preterit, and imperfect) in the indicative mood. The indicative is used to express real, definite, or factual actions or states of being.

In this chapter you will learn about the subjunctive mood. It is used to express the hypothetical or subjective, such as a speaker's attitudes, wishes, feelings, emotions, or doubts. Unlike the indicative that states facts, the subjunctive describes reality subjectively.

Creo que Luis **va** a Cartagena.	*I believe that Luis is going to Cartagena.* (Certainty: indicative)
No creo que Luis **vaya** a San Andrés.	*I don't think that Luis is going to San Andrés.* (Uncertainty: subjunctive)

Los verbos regulares del presente de subjuntivo

- The following chart shows the present subjunctive forms of regular verbs. Note that the endings of **-er** and **-ir** are identical.

	hablar	comer	vivir
yo	habl**e**	com**a**	viv**a**
tú	habl**es**	com**as**	viv**as**
él, ella, Ud.	habl**e**	com**a**	viv**a**
nosotros/as	habl**emos**	com**amos**	viv**amos**
vosotros/as	habl**éis**	com**áis**	viv**áis**
ellos/as, Uds.	habl**en**	com**an**	viv**an**

- Verbs that are irregular in the **yo** form of the present indicative will use the same spelling changes in the present subjunctive. These are not considered irregular in the subjunctive.

Infinitive	Present indicative First-person singular	Present subjunctive
decir	digo	diga, digas, diga, digamos, digáis, digan
hacer	hago	haga, hagas, haga, hagamos, hagáis, hagan
oír	oigo	oiga, oigas, oiga, oigamos, oigáis, oigan
poner	pongo	ponga, pongas, ponga, pongamos, pongáis, pongan
tener	tengo	tenga, tengas, tenga, tengamos, tengáis, tengan
traer	traigo	traiga, traigas, traiga, traigamos, traigáis, traigan
venir	vengo	venga, vengas, venga, vengamos, vengáis, vengan
ver	veo	vea, veas, vea, veamos, veáis, vean

- The following spelling changes occur in all forms of the present subjunctive with infinitives that end in **-car, -gar,** and **-zar.**

-car:	c → qu	buscar	busque, busques, busque, busquemos, busquéis, busquen
-gar:	g → gu	llegar	llegue, llegues, llegue, lleguemos, lleguéis, lleguen
-zar:	z → c	empezar	empiece, empieces, empiece, empecemos, empecéis, empiecen

- The subjunctive forms of **-ar** and **-er** stem-changing verbs have the same pattern of the present indicative.

pensar (ie)		devolver (ue)	
p**ie**nse	pensemos	dev**ue**lva	devolvamos
p**ie**nses	penséis	dev**ue**lvas	devolváis
p**ie**nse	p**ie**nsen	dev**ue**lva	dev**ue**lvan

- **-Ir** stem-changing verbs reflect the stem changes of both the present indicative and the preterit. The preterit stem changes occur in the **nosotros/as** and **vosotros/as** forms, where unstressed **-e-** changes to **-i-,** and the unstressed **-o-** changes to **-u-.** The other persons follow the present-tense pattern.

sentir (ie, i)		pedir (i, i)		dormir (ue, u)	
s**ie**nta	s**i**ntamos	p**i**da	p**i**damos	d**ue**rma	d**u**rmamos
s**ie**ntas	s**i**ntáis	p**i**das	p**i**dáis	d**ue**rmas	d**u**rmáis
s**ie**nta	s**ie**ntan	p**i**da	p**i**dan	d**ue**rma	d**ue**rman

Los verbos irregulares del presente de subjuntivo

- The following verbs are irregular in the present subjunctive.

dar	estar	haber	ir	saber	ser
dé	esté	haya	vaya	sepa	sea
des	estés	hayas	vayas	sepas	seas
dé	esté	haya	vaya	sepa	sea
demos	estemos	hayamos	vayamos	sepamos	seamos
deis	estéis	hayáis	vayáis	sepáis	seáis
den	estén	hayan	vayan	sepan	sean

El subjuntivo en cláusulas nominativas

- A noun clause is a clause that is used as the direct object, subject of the verb, or object of a preposition.

  Necesito **un mapa de Colombia.** (noun—direct object)

  Necesito **que usted me dé un mapa de Colombia.** (noun clause—direct object)

- Noun clauses are also dependent clauses—they depend on the main clause for meaning and structure. The noun clause has its own subject and verb and, in Spanish, is often connected to the main clause with **que.**

Quiero que el guía **hable** despacio.	*I want the guide to speak slowly.*
Nadia desea que Paco **vaya** al río con nosotros.	*Nadia wishes that Paco go to the river with us.*
Esperamos que nuestro abuelo **vaya** a Cartagena.	*We hope (that) our grandfather will go to Cartagena.*
Juan quiere que yo **me quede** con él en la isla.	*Juan wants me to stay on the island with him.*

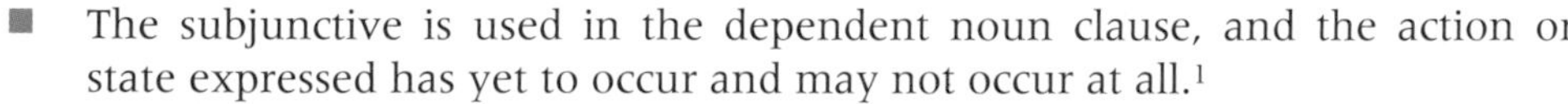

- The subjunctive is used in the dependent noun clause, and the action or state expressed has yet to occur and may not occur at all.[1]

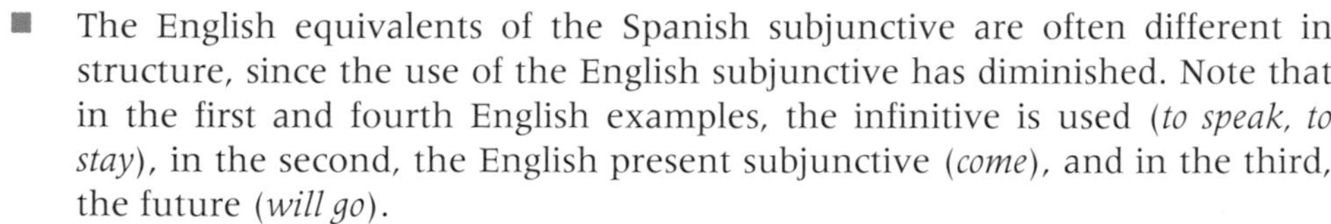

- The English equivalents of the Spanish subjunctive are often different in structure, since the use of the English subjunctive has diminished. Note that in the first and fourth English examples, the infinitive is used (*to speak, to stay*), in the second, the English present subjunctive (*come*), and in the third, the future (*will go*).

Aplicación

9-26 Botero en el MOMA. Lee la conversación entre Fernando Botero y su agente en el Museo de Arte Moderno de Nueva York. Subraya los verbos en el subjuntivo e identifica el infinitivo.

Modelo: Quiero que me traigan un refresco. (traer)

Naturaleza muerta con sopa verde

Source: Fernando Botero. "Nauturaleza muerta con sopa verde" (Still Life with Green Soup). 1972. © Fernando Botero, courtesy, Marlborough Gallery, New York.

Botero: ¡Oye, Ramón! Veo que no hay un salón especial para mis obras. Insisto en que haya un "Salón Botero" como es natural para todos los grandes artistas.

Agente: Tienes razón, Fernando. Voy a hablar con el gerente (*manager*) y decirle que establezca un salón con tu nombre.

Botero: Perfecto. Y en ese salón, vamos a pedir que traigan sillones cómodos para los visitantes.

Agente: ¡Buena idea! Espero que pongan flores y refrescos también.

Botero: No, refrescos no. Es mejor que los visitantes tomen refrescos en la cafetería. Pero me gusta la idea de las flores.

Agente: Y es importante que esté presente un guardia de seguridad y una persona experta en tu obra.

Botero: Espero que no tengan que pagarles extra.

Agente: No sé. ¿Quieres que hable con el gerente sobre eso, también?

Botero: Sí, y deseo que me dé un contrato especial para esta exposición.

Agente: De acuerdo.

---

[1]In the first example, *I want the guide to speak slowly,* but *I have no guarantees that he will.* By the same token, *Luis has no guarantee that Paco will go to the river with us, we cannot be sure that our grandfather will go to Cartagena,* and *many factors can interfere with Juan's desire for me to stay with him on the island.*

9-27 ¿Qué desea Botero? Haz una lista de lo que pide Botero en la actividad **9-26.**

Modelo: *1. un salón especial*

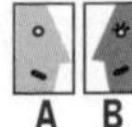

A B

9-28A Desafío (*Challenge*). Cada uno/a de ustedes tiene una lista de verbos diferentes en el indicativo y el subjuntivo. Dile a tu compañero/a el indicativo del verbo, y él/ella debe darte el presente de subjuntivo de ese verbo. Estudiante B, por favor ve al **Apéndice 1,** página A11.

Modelo: E1: *Indicativo: tomamos*
E2: *Subjuntivo: tomemos*
E1: *Correcto.*

MI LISTA			
Indicativo	**Subjuntivo**	**Correcto**	**Incorrecto**
tomamos	**tomemos**	✓	
tengo	*tenga*		
hablo	*hable*		
haces	*hagas*		
pedimos	*pidamos*		
salen	*salgan*		
escribe	*escriba*		

9-37 to 9-38

4. The subjunctive to express volition

- Verbs of volition express the wishes, preferences, suggestions, requests, and implied commands of the speaker. When the verb in the main clause expresses volition, the verb of the noun clause is expressed in the subjunctive mood. The following are verbs of volition.

aconsejar	*to advise*	**pedir (i, i)**	*to ask*
decir	*to tell*	**permitir**	*to permit*
desear	*to wish*	**prohibir**	*to prohibit*
insistir (en)	*to insist*	**querer (ie)**	*to want*
mandar	*to order*	**recomendar (ie)**	*to recommend*
necesitar	*to need*	**sugerir (ie, i)**	*to suggest*

- The subject of the verb in the main clause tries to influence the subject of the dependent noun clause.

Carmen (querer) + yo (ir) ➔	
Carmen **quiere** que yo **vaya** con ella de vacaciones.	*Carmen wants me to go with her on vacation.*
ustedes (necesitar) + yo (llevar) ➔	
¿**Necesitan** que los **lleve** a las montañas?	*Do you need (for) me to take you to the mountains?*
mi novia (desear) + yo (recoger) ➔	
Mi novia **desea** que **recoja** las maletas.	*My girlfriend wants me to pick up the luggage.*

- When there is no change of subject for the two verbs, there is no noun clause. Use the infinitive.

Sofía (desear) + Sofía (ir) ➔	
Sofía **desea** ir a pescar.	*Sofía wants to go fishing.*
yo (querer) + yo (montar) ➔	
Yo **quiero** montar a caballo.	*I want to go horseback riding.*

- Sentences using verbs such as **aconsejar, decir, pedir, recomendar,** and **sugerir** require an indirect object pronoun. This indirect object refers to the subject of the dependent clause.

Le aconsejo que nade más.	*I advise you to swim more.* (Literally, *I advise that you swim more.*)
Nos piden que hagamos más ejercicio.	*They ask us to exercise more.* (Literally, *They ask that we exercise more.*)

- When verbs of communication such as **decir** and **escribir** are used in the main clause and the subject of the verb is simply reporting information (telling someone something), the indicative is used in the dependent clause. If the verb in the main clause is used in the sense of a command (telling someone to do something), the subjunctive is used.

INFORMATION

Julia le **dice** a Juan que **llegamos** mañana.	*Julia tells Juan that we are arriving tomorrow.*
Les **escribo** que **volvemos** el sábado.	*I'm writing them that we're returning on Saturday.*

COMMAND

Julia le **dice** a Juan que **llegue** mañana.	*Julia tells Juan to arrive tomorrow.*
Les **escribo** que **vuelvan** el sábado.	*I'm writing for them to return on Saturday.*

Aplicación

9-29 Shakira. Shakira, la primera colombiana en ganar un Grammy Latino, es ahora una estrella internacional. Lee la entrada que hizo en su diario y haz una lista de qué esperan de ella las personas en su vida.

18 de septiembre de 2007

Querido diario:

¡Hoy fue el mejor día de mi vida! ¡Me nominaron para cinco Grammys y gané dos! Ahora, tengo que pensar en el futuro, pero tengo muchas decisiones que hacer. Mis padres quieren que vuelva a Colombia y que pase más tiempo con ellos. Mi agente sugiere que haga más grabaciones, que viaje por los Estados Unidos y el Canadá, y que vaya a Europa. Mis admiradores insisten en que dé más conciertos. Mis amigos colombianos esperan que dedique más tiempo a obras caritativas (**charitable**) *en Colombia. Mi novio me pide que me case con él y que me convierta en ama de casa. ¿Y yo? ¿Qué quiero yo? Pues, deseo que todo el mundo viva en paz y, especialmente, que disfrute de la música. Ése es mi sueño, pero por ahora, soy feliz.*

LISTA

1. Sus padres:
2. Su agente:
3. Sus admiradores:
4. Sus amigos:
5. Su novio:
6. Ella misma:
7. ¿Tú?:

WWW

9-30 ¿Conoces la música de Shakira? Conéctate con la página web de **¡Arriba!** para ver más imágenes de Shakira y escuchar su música.

9-31 En la agencia de viajes. Completa los consejos que la agente de viajes les da a sus clientes, usando el subjuntivo de los verbos de la lista.

comprar	dejar	fumar	llegar	pedir
dar	dormir	ir	llevar	poner

—Sr. López, es necesario que usted (1) ____________ su pasaje con dos semanas de anticipación. Necesito que usted me (2) ____________ su número de tarjeta de crédito.

—Juan y Carlos, ustedes saben que ahora las aerolíneas no permiten que los pasajeros (3) ____________ en el avión. Si quieren fumar, es mejor que (4) ____________ al restaurante antes de abordar.

—Doña María, sugiero que usted (5) ____________ las recetas (*prescriptions*) en su bolsa y que (6) ____________ una copia de las recetas en la maleta.

—Lupe, es importante que (tú) (7) ____________ con dos horas de anticipación antes de tu vuelo. Los agentes de seguridad insisten en que los pasajeros (8) ____________ los objetos puntiagudos (*sharp*) en su casa.

—Señores Echevarría, les recomiendo que ustedes (9) ____________ en el avión porque si no, van a estar muy cansados después de más de siete horas de viaje. Por eso, les sugiero que le (10) ____________ café descafeinado al asistente de vuelo.

9-32 Un viaje al Salto Ángel. El Salto Ángel, en Venezuela, atrae a muchos turistas todos los años.

El salto tiene ese nombre, en honor al hombre que lo descubrió en 1937, el aventurero y aviador norteamericano Jimmy Angel. Sin embargo, los indígenas de la zona, ya conocían el salto desde antes, y lo llamaban Churún Merú. Completa los consejos que te da una agente de viajes con la forma correcta de uno de los verbos siguientes.

ayudar	entrar	pagar	comprar	ir	tener

Primero, le aconsejo que (1) ____________ listo el pasaporte para poder visitar Venezuela. Segundo, le sugiero que (2) ____________ una buena guía turística. La puede comprar en cualquier (*any*) librería. Ahora, no se permite que los viajeros (3) ____________ al país con frutas u otros comestibles. Una vez en Venezuela, le recomiendo que (4) ____________ al salto en helicóptero. Es un viaje inolvidable. También, le sugiero que (5) ____________ su viaje al Salto antes de salir del país porque muchas veces cuesta menos desde aquí. Si quiere que le (6) ____________ con el viaje, lo hago con mucho gusto.

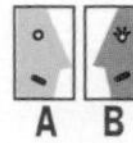

9-33A ¿Qué hacer? Imagínate que necesitas pedirle consejos a tu compañero/a. Explícale tu problema y luego expresa tu reacción a la recomendación que él/ella te dé. Estudiante B, por favor ve al **Apéndice 1,** página A11.

MODELO: E1: *Tengo un examen de química mañana.*
E2: *Te recomiendo que estudies mucho.*
E1: *Buena idea. / No tengo tiempo.*

1. Necesito dinero.
2. Tengo un problema con mi novio/a (mi esposo/a, mi hermano/a).
3. Mi trabajo no me da tiempo para estudiar.
4. Quiero un trabajo más interesante.
5. Mi casa está en desorden y tengo invitados este fin de semana.
6. Quiero ir de vacaciones, pero no tengo dinero.

9-34 ¿Cuáles son tus deseos? Escribe cinco deseos que tienes para el futuro. Expresa los deseos con verbos de voluntad (**querer, desear, preferir,** etc.), usando el subjuntivo cuando haya cambios de sujeto en la oración.

MODELO: *Deseo que mis padres vivan muchos años y que siempre tengamos una buena relación. Espero que mis amigos consigan un buen trabajo y que ganen mucho dinero. Prefiero viajar después de terminar mis estudios.*

¿Cuánto sabes tú? *Can you...*

9-39 to 9-42

- ☐ talk about a vacation you took and one you plan to take?
- ☐ talk about vacation-related activities?
- ☐ try to convince someone to go on a trip with you or do something else for you using expressions such as **quiero que..., deseo que..., espero que...**?
- ☐ give advice to someone by using expressions such as **Te aconsejo que..., te recomiendo que...**?

Observaciones

Episode 9

9-43 to 9-46

¡Pura vida! Episodio 9

En este episodio Patricio les sirve de guía a Felipe, a Silvia y a David Ortiz-Smith.

Antes de ver el video

9-35 En peligro de extinción. Lee el siguiente artículo y escribe cinco características del guacamayo.

El guacamayo es un pájaro de hermoso plumaje. La belleza (*beauty*) de sus plumas (*feathers*) lo ha puesto en peligro de extinción durante años. Sus colores predominantes, azul, rojo y amarillo, atraen la admiración de todos los que lo ven. Estos bellos animales, que pasan la mayor parte del día comiendo y tomando el sol, son los loros (*parrots*) más grandes y los más coloridos.

Su hábitat en la América tropical se extiende desde el sur de México hasta el Paraguay. Algunas de sus características físicas más sobresalientes, además de su bello plumaje, son su enorme pico (*beak*) largo y curvado, y sus ojos redondos y negros.

En particular, las plumas de los guacamayos eran unos de los objetos más apreciados por las culturas indígenas, ya que las utilizaban para adornar sus vestimentas y accesorios. Incluso, las usaban para comerciar o como regalo de amistad.

El *ara macao* habita las selvas de México al Paraguay.

A ver el video

9-36 La excursión. Mira el noveno episodio de *¡Pura vida!* y completa cada oración con la expresión más lógica, según el video.

Patricio

David Ortiz-Smith

Felipe y Silvia

los guacamayos	El Niño	la puerta de embarque	jaguar

1. Cuando tiene lugar (*occurs*) _____, ciertos lugares reciben más lluvia; otros reciben menos.
2. El señor David Ortiz-Smith casi pierde el vuelo porque cambiaron _____.
3. Panchito es un joven _____ que duerme en los árboles durante el día.
4. Al final, todos observan _____.

Después de ver el video

WWW

9-37 Un centro de rescate (rescue). Conéctate con la página web de **¡Arriba!** para aprender más sobre un centro de rescate. Luego escribe una carta al centro en que expreses tu interés en ser voluntario/a en ese centro.

NUESTRO MUNDO

Panoramas

Los países caribeños de Sudamérica: Venezuela y Colombia

9-38 ¿Ya sabes...? Trata de identificar lo siguiente.

1. la capital de Colombia y la de Venezuela
2. una bebida popular colombiana
3. el color de una esmeralda
4. un país importante por su petróleo
5. el país que tiene costas en el Mar Caribe y en el Océano Pacífico
6. un metal precioso que se mina en Colombia

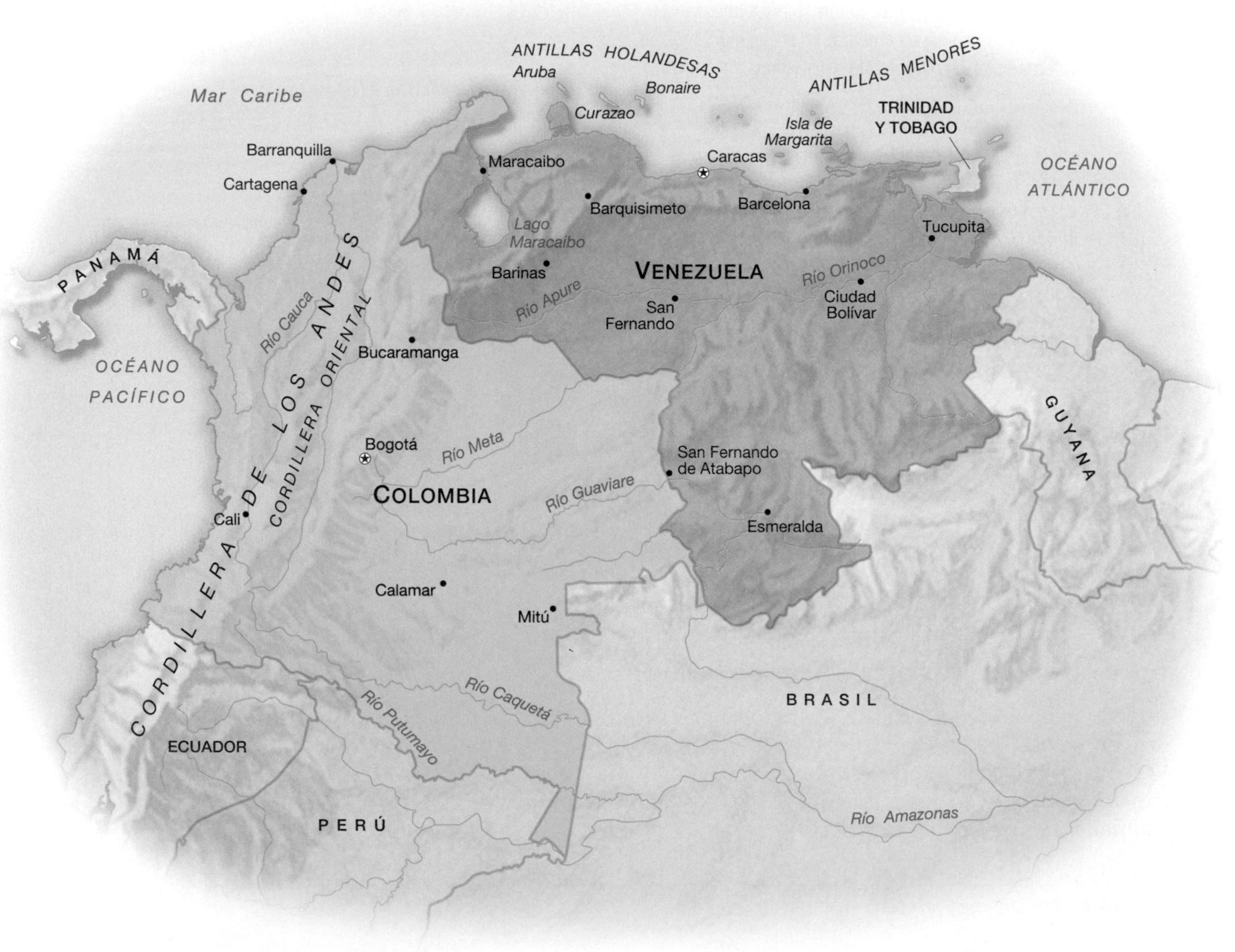

ANTILLAS HOLANDESAS
Aruba
Bonaire
Curazao
ANTILLAS MENORES
Mar Caribe
TRINIDAD Y TOBAGO
Isla de Margarita
Barranquilla
Cartagena
Maracaibo
Caracas
OCÉANO ATLÁNTICO
Barquisimeto
Barcelona
Lago Maracaibo
Tucupita
PANAMÁ
Barinas
VENEZUELA
Río Orinoco
Río Apure
San Fernando
Ciudad Bolívar
Río Cauca
Bucaramanga
OCÉANO PACÍFICO
CORDILLERA DE LOS ANDES
CORDILLERA ORIENTAL
GUYANA
Bogotá
Río Meta
San Fernando de Atabapo
COLOMBIA
Río Guaviare
Cali
Esmeralda
Calamar
Mitú
Río Caquetá
Río Putumayo
BRASIL
ECUADOR
Río Amazonas
PERÚ

En Colombia, tanto como en el Brasil, hay vastos depósitos de oro y piedras preciosas, especialmente de esmeraldas. Estas riquezas figuran en las prendas que llevaban los caciques (*chiefs*) de los indígenas. Los conquistadores españoles sacaron y se llevaron muchas de estas riquezas.

Gabriel García Márquez (1928–) es uno de los mejores escritores del siglo XX. En 1982 ganó el Premio Nobel de Literatura por sus novelas y cuentos. *Cien años de soledad* (1969), la novela que inició su fama, es una de sus novelas más populares e importantes, y uno de los mejores ejemplos del realismo mágico latinoamericano.

Cartagena de Indias fue fundada en 1531. En pocos años su excelente puerto se convirtió en el más importante para España en el Nuevo Mundo. Cartagena llegó a ser una de las ciudades más ricas del Imperio Español. Hoy en día esta acogedora (*cozy*) ciudad colonial, situada en la costa del Caribe, es el centro turístico más importante de Colombia.

El petróleo es un producto importante para la economía de Venezuela, con el que llegó a tener el PIB (*GNP*) más alto de la Hispanoamérica.

La Isla Margarita, de 920 kilómetros de extensión, es la más grande de las islas que bordean Venezuela y que forman lo que muchos llaman un bello collar de perlas en el mar Caribe. Margarita, con su zona franca (*duty-free zone*), magníficos hoteles y restaurantes y espléndidas playas, es un paraíso tropical para el turista. En las playas de Margarita se practican varios deportes acuáticos como el *jet ski,* el *surf,* el buceo, la pesca y, por supuesto, el *windsurf.*

Caracas es una ciudad moderna con grandes autopistas y centros comerciales tan bellos como los de cualquier otra ciudad del mundo.

9-39 ¿Dónde? Identifica un lugar o lugares donde puedes encontrar lo siguiente.

1. industria petrolera
2. museos
3. arquitectura colonial
4. un buen precio para la gasolina
5. muchas autopistas modernas

9-40 Recomendaciones. Háganles recomendaciones a las personas que piensan hacer un viaje a Colombia y a Venezuela. Recomiéndenles algunos lugares según sus intereses.

MODELO: Quiero buscar El Dorado.
¿Por qué no vas a Colombia? Allí puedes buscarlo en los Andes.

1. Me gusta visitar lugares de belleza natural.
2. Deseo visitar una ciudad grande.
3. Me gusta nadar en el mar y tomar el sol.
4. Me interesa visitar la casa donde nació García Márquez.
5. Quiero conocer una ciudad colonial.
6. Me interesan los cuadros de Botero.

WWW

9-41 Investigar. Conéctate con la página web de **¡Arriba!** para ver más imágenes de Colombia y de Venezuela. Escoge una y descríbela.

Ritmos

9-49

"Tu ausencia" (Los Tupamaros, Colombia)

En esta canción del famoso grupo colombiano Los Tupamaros, un hombre lamenta la partida de su novia y pregunta por qué se fue.

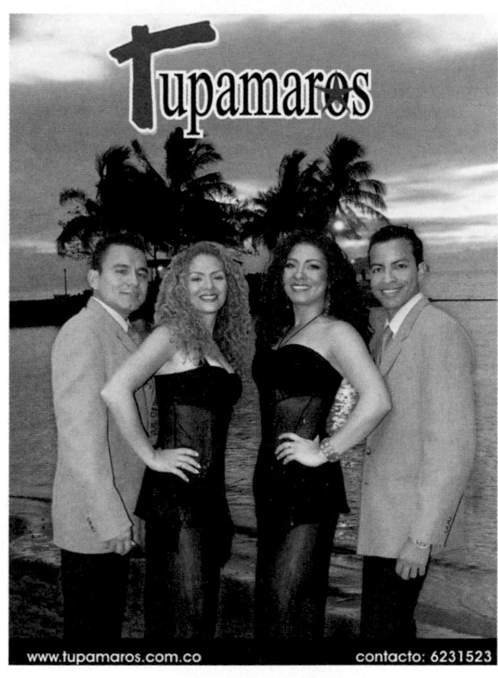

Antes de escuchar

9-42 Por qué y para qué. Lee las siguientes estrofas de "Tu ausencia" para familiarizarte con el tema de la canción, y luego completa los espacios en blanco con **por** o **para** según el caso.

Tu ausencia
No soporto ya tu ausencia,
me destroza el corazón.
Son tan lindos tus recuerdos,
me hacen perder la razón.
Pasan y pasan los días,
y no sé nada de ti.
Lloro y lloro tu partida,
siento que voy a morir.
[...]
Vuelve ya mi vida,
calma mi dolor.
Me duele tu ausencia,
me duele tu amor.

1. El novio quiere saber __________ qué se marchó su novia.
2. __________ él es triste la ausencia de su novia.
3. Él canta __________ decirle a su novia que está triste.
4. Su novia se marchó y, __________ eso, él está triste.
5. ¡__________ Dios, se fue la novia!
6. Ella era muy importante __________ él.

A escuchar

9-43 El ritmo. Compara el ritmo de esta canción con otros estilos que conozcas (salsa, pop rock, etc). ¿Es más rápido? ¿Más bailable? ¿Más divertido?

Después de escuchar

9-44 Los consejos. Trabajando con un/a compañero/a hagan el papel del novio de la canción y el papel de un/a amigo/a de él. El/La amigo/a debe responder a lo que dice el novio, completando las oraciones con el presente de subjuntivo.

NOVIO	**AMIGO/A**
1. Estoy muy triste sin mi novia.	Te sugiero que...
2. Estoy mal y me siento enfermo.	Insisto en que...
3. Tengo el corazón roto *(broken)*.	Te aconsejo que...
4. ¿Qué debo hacer?	Te recomiendo que...

Páginas

Antes de leer

9-50

9-45 Un folleto turístico. De estas actividades, ¿cuáles normalmente encuentras en un folleto turístico? ¿Cuáles son importantes para conocer la cultura de otro lugar?

Normal (N)	Importante (I)
_____ actividades deportivas	_____ comida
_____ fiestas y ferias	_____ excursiones
_____ compras	_____ economía

De estas cosas, ¿cuáles te interesan más a ti? ¿Cuáles son las menos importantes?

A leer

9-46 Los folletos. Los folletos dan información para que puedas decidir si quieres saber más acerca de determinado lugar. Las imágenes son para estimularte la imaginación. Pueden ser exóticas, hermosas o simplemente diferentes. Ve las imágenes en el folleto y trata de identificar de qué se trata sin leer el texto.

Después de leer

9-47 Lo normal y lo exótico. Da tus impresiones sobre la información contenida en el folleto.

1. ¿Cuáles imágenes te parecen más exóticas?
2. ¿Cuáles imágenes te parecen iguales a celebraciones que ya conoces?
3. ¿Cuáles de las fiestas celebras tú?
4. ¿En qué aspectos son parecidas? ¿En qué aspectos son diferentes?
5. ¿Si algún día visitas Colombia, ¿cuál prefieres conocer?

9-48 En su experiencia. Las fiestas reflejan la cultura de la gente. Por ejemplo, mucha gente de origen irlandés celebra el día de San Patricio. Hay desfiles, fiestas, comida, bebidas verdes, etc. Escojan una fiesta que se celebre en su ciudad o su pueblo y expliquen el origen de la fiesta, cuándo y cómo se celebra. ¿Participan ustedes en la celebración? ¿Cómo?

WWW

9-49 Las fiestas y las comidas. Es común tener comida especial en días festivos. Si te encuentras en Colombia o en Venezuela para la Nochevieja, vas a probar comida muy diferente a la que conoces. Conéctate con la página web de **¡Arriba!** para ver ejemplos de comida típica. Escribe un párrafo, describiendo la comida y sus ingredientes.

Taller

9-51 to 9-52

9-50 Un folleto turístico. En esta actividad vas a crear un folleto turístico.

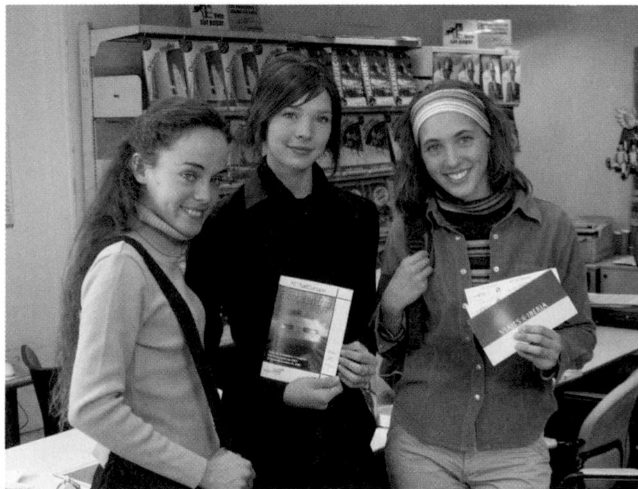

Antes de escribir

- **Ideas.** Piensa en un lugar en el mundo hispano que no conozcas. Haz una lista de lo que quieres saber de este lugar para incluir en el folleto.
- **Investigar.** Busca información e imágenes del lugar en la Red.

A escribir

- Escribe descripciones cortas de las imágenes para el folleto. Incluye puntos interesantes sobre la cultura, la historia, el clima, la comida, fechas importantes, etc.
- Ordena las imágenes y las descripciones en un papel grande.
- Dale un título al folleto.
- Para un modelo, consulta el folleto en la página 324.

Después de escribir

- **Revisar.** Revisa tu entrada para verificar los siguientes puntos:
  - ☐ la concordancia de nombres y adjetivos
  - ☐ el uso de **por** y **para**
  - ☐ el uso de adverbios que terminan en **-mente** (**Originalmente queríamos ir a...**)
  - ☐ el uso del subjuntivo (**Espero que...; Quiero que...**)
- **Intercambiar**
  Intercambia tu folleto con el de un/a compañero/a para hacer correcciones y sugerencias y para decidir si quieren visitar el lugar.
- **Entregar**
  Pasa tu folleto a limpio, incorporando las sugerencias de tu compañero/a. Después, entrégaselo a tu profesor/a.

Vocabulario

Primera parte

En el aeropuerto	*At the airport*
la aduana	*customs*
el/la asistente de vuelo	*flight attendant*
el avión	*plane*
la demora	*delay*
el/la inspector/a de aduanas	*customs inspector*
las maletas	*suitcases; luggage*
el/la piloto	*pilot*
la puerta de embarque	*boarding gate*
la sala de espera	*waiting area*
la sala de reclamación de equipaje	*baggage claim area*
la tarjeta de embarque	*boarding pass*
el vuelo	*flight*

En la agencia de viajes	*At the travel agency*
el/la agente de viajes	*travel agent*
el boleto	*ticket*
el folleto	*brochure*
el/la guía	*tour guide*
la guía turística	*guide book*
el hospedaje	*lodging*
el pasaje (de ida y vuelta)	*(roundtrip) fare; ticket*
la reserva	*reservation*
el/la viajero/a	*traveler*

En el avión	*On the plane*
la altura	*altitude*
el asiento de pasillo	*aisle seat*
de ventanilla	*window seat*
la clase turista	*coach class*

Verbos	*Verbs*
abordar	*to board*
aterrizar	*to land*
bajarse (de)	*to get off (of); to get down (from)*
despegar	*to take off*
facturar el equipaje	*to check luggage*
hacer cola	*to stand in line*
hacer la(s) maleta(s)	*to pack the suitcase(s)*
hacer un viaje	*to take a trip*
viajar por barco	*to travel by ship*
tren	*train*
carro	*car*
autobús	*bus*

Segunda parte

Los viajes	*Trips*
el bosque	*forest*
las flores	*flowers*
la isla	*island*
el lago	*lake*
el mar	*sea*
las montañas	*mountains*
el volcán	*volcano*

Accesorios para viajar	*Travel accessories*
la cámara	*camera*
la cámara de video	*video camera*
las gafas de sol	*sunglasses*
el mapa	*map*
el rollo de película	*film*
la tarjeta de memoria	*memory card*
la tarjeta postal	*postcard*

En el hotel	*At the hotel*
el cuarto doble	*double room*
la estadía	*stay*
el hostal	*inn*
el hotel (de lujo)	*(luxury) hotel*
la vista	*view*

Actividades típicas de los viajeros	*Typical activities for travelers*
bucear	*to scuba dive*
comprar recuerdos	*to buy souvenirs*
ir de excursión	*to go on an outing; to tour*
montar a caballo	*to go horseback riding*
en bicicleta	*bicycle riding*
pasarlo bien	*to have a good time*
mal	*bad time*
de maravilla	*wonderful time*
pescar	*to fish*
quedarse	*to stay (somewhere)*
recorrer	*to go round; to travel through/across*

Atracciones turísticas	*Tourist attractions*
la catedral	*cathedral*
el convento	*convent*
la estatua	*statue*
el monumento	*monument*
el salto de agua/la catarata	*waterfall*

10 ¡Tu salud es lo primero!

Objetivos comunicativos

Primera parte

¡Así lo decimos! Vocabulario	Las partes del cuerpo humano
¡Así lo hacemos! Estructuras	**Nosotros** commands
	Indirect commands
Comparaciones	El ejercicio y la dieta

- Talking about your health and explaining what part of your body hurts
- Inviting others to do something
- Making suggestions indirectly

Segunda parte

¡Así lo decimos! Vocabulario	Los alimentos
¡Así lo hacemos! Estructuras	The subjunctive to express feelings and emotions
	The subjunctive to express doubt and denial
Observaciones	¡Pura vida! Episodio 10

- Talking about how to stay fit
- Expressing emotions
- Giving your opinion about something

Nuestro mundo

Panoramas	Los países sin mar: Bolivia y el Paraguay
Ritmos	"Sol de primavera" (Inkuyo, Bolivia)
Páginas	"El ñandutí" (Leyenda paraguaya)
Taller	Un artículo sobre la salud

En el Paraguay, *el ñandutí* es una artesanía popular.

Los países sin mar: Bolivia y el Paraguay

«Comamos manzanas todo el año y la enfermedad sufrirá un desengaño.»*

En la cultura aymara de Bolivia y del Perú, el dios creador se llamaba Viracocha. Cerca de la Paz, Bolivia, se encuentran los restos de la ciudad Tiahuanaco y su famosa Puerta del Sol, con una imagen del dios creador.

*__Refrán:__ Let's eat apples all year long and illness will be deceived. *(An apple a day keeps the doctor away.)*

PRIMERA PARTE

¡Así lo decimos! Vocabulario

¡Así es la vida! En el consultorio del médico

Dra. Estrada: Buenas tardes, don Rafael. ¿Cómo se siente? ¿Qué tiene? ¿Qué le duele hoy?

Don Rafael: Me duele mucho la garganta y me duelen también el pecho y el estómago.

Dra. Estrada: Vamos a ver… Pues, lo que usted tiene es una infección en la garganta. Empecemos con antibióticos.

Don Rafael: Bueno, pero espero que las pastillas no me molesten el estómago, ¿eh?

Dra. Estrada: No tiene que preocuparse. Ahora, quiero que vuelva a casa y que guarde cama. Le garantizo que se va a sentir mejor, pero si tiene cualquier problema, espero que me llame inmediatamente.

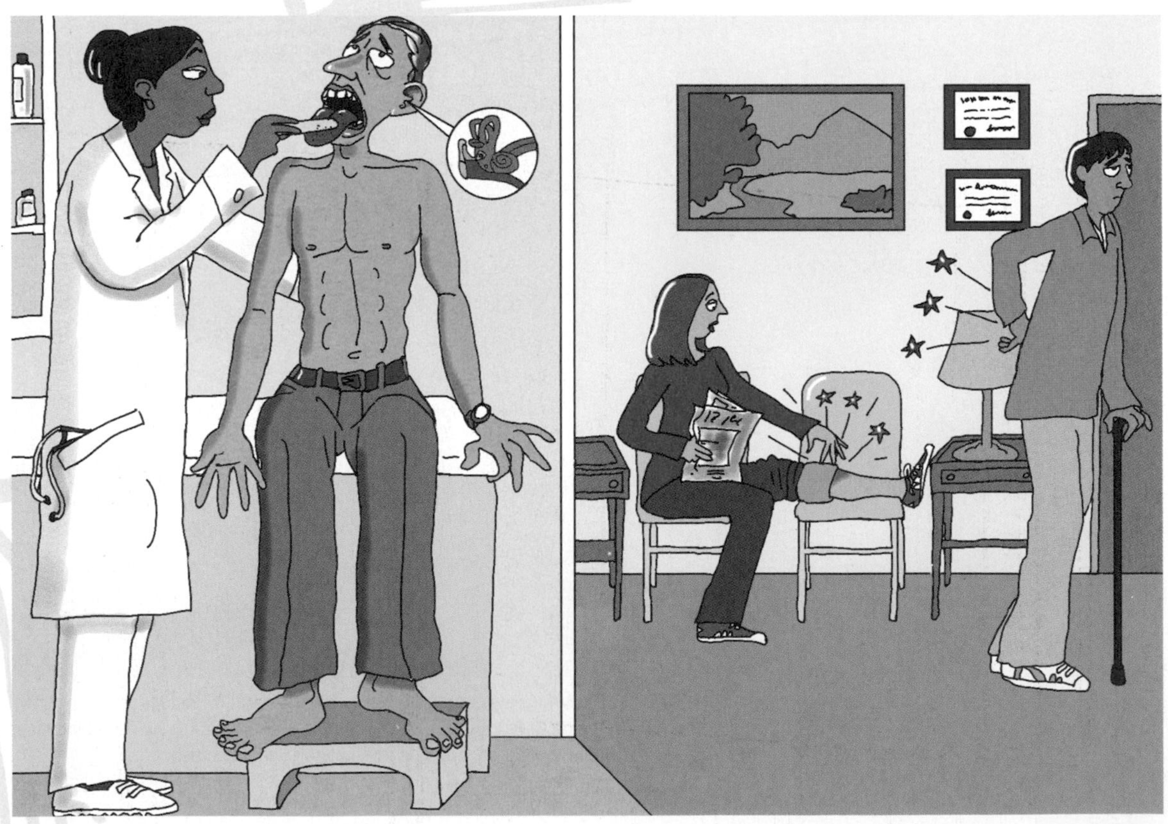

Las partes del cuerpo humano

CD 10, Track 30

10-3 to 10-7

la boca

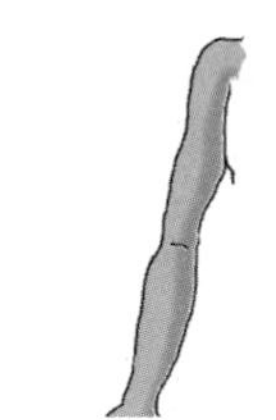
el brazo

la cabeza

el dedo (de la mano)

el diente

la garganta

la mano

la nariz

el oído

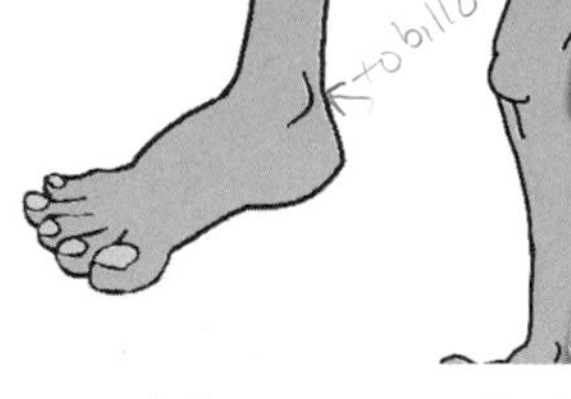
el pie

la pierna

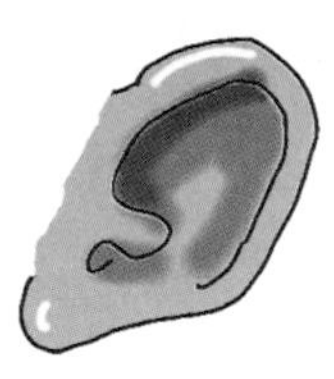
la oreja

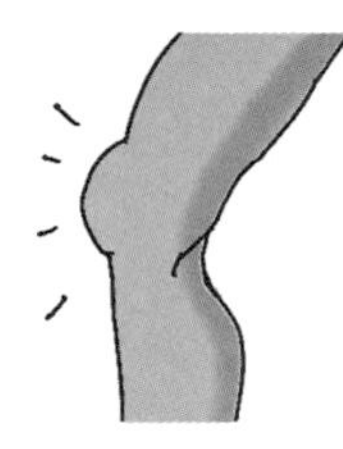
la rodilla

Más partes del cuerpo humano	*More body parts*
el corazón	*heart*
la espalda	*back*
el estómago	*stomach*
la lengua	*tongue*
el pecho	*chest*
los pulmones	*lungs*

Problemas de salud	*Health problems*
doler (ue)	*to hurt*
lastimarse	*to hurt oneself*
romperse (un hueso)	*to break (a bone)*
tener (ie) alergia(s) a	*to be allergic to*
tener (ie) (una) fiebre	*to have a fever*
(un) dolor de cabeza	*a headache*
(la) gripe	*the flu*
(una) infección	*an infection*
(un) resfriado	*a cold*
(una) tos	*a cough*
torcer (ue)	*to twist*
toser	*to cough*

Sugerencias y remedios médicos	*Medical advice and remedies*
dejar de fumar cigarrillos[1]	*to quit smoking cigarettes*
guardar cama	*to stay in bed due to sickness*
hacer una cita	*to make an appointment*
mejorarse	*to get better; to get well*
operar	*to operate*
recetar	*to prescribe*
respirar	*to breathe*
tomarse la presión[2]	*to take one's blood pressure*
la temperatura	*temperature*

Medicinas comunes	*Common medicines*
el antiácido	*antacid*
el antibiótico	*antibiotic*
la aspirina	*aspirin*
el calmante	*tranquilizer*
el jarabe	*cough syrup*
la pastilla	*pill; lozenge*

En el consultorio del médico	*At the doctor's office*
el diagnóstico	*diagnosis*
el dolor	*pain; ache*
la enfermedad	*illness*
el examen físico	*checkup*
la inyección	*shot*
el/la paciente	*patient*
la radiografía	*X-ray*
el síntoma	*symptom*

[1] **Dejar de** is followed by an infinitive in Spanish, whereas the present participle (*-ing*) is used after *to quit* in English. **Fumar** means *to smoke*.

[2] **tomarse la tensión** in Spain

Aplicación

10-1 Categorías. Clasifica las siguientes partes del cuerpo y añade una más al final.

Parte del cuerpo	Tienes uno	Tienes dos	Tienes más de dos	Órgano interno
el dedo			X	
el corazón				
la nariz				
el ojo				
el pulmón				
la oreja				
el brazo				
el estómago				
la pierna				
el diente				
¿...?				

10-2 ¿Qué le pasa? Describe lo que les pasa a estas personas y da una posible causa de su problema.

MODELO:

Alicia

A Alicia le duele el estómago porque comió dos hamburguesas.

1.

Alberto

2.

Ana María

3.

Samuel y Ricardo

4.

Carlos

5.

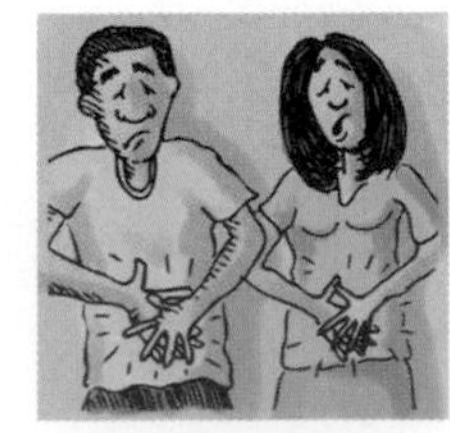

Ramiro y Marta

CD 2, Track 31

10-3 ¡Qué mal me siento! Escucha la conversación entre doña Carmen y su médico; anota sus síntomas, un diagnóstico lógico y el consejo del médico.

SÍNTOMA	DIAGNÓSTICO	CONSEJO
_____ tos	_____ alergias	_____ tomar aspirina
_____ fiebre	_____ presiones del trabajo	_____ descansar
_____ dolor de cabeza	_____ resfriado	_____ comer sopa
_____ dolor de estómago	_____ gripe	_____ comer mejor
_____ dolor de garganta	_____ úlceras	_____ hacer ejercicio
_____ dolor en un diente	_____ mala dieta	_____ tomar antibióticos

10-4 ¿Cuándo consultas al médico? Pregúntense si consultan al médico en las siguientes situaciones.

MODELO: Te duele la cabeza.
E1: *¿Consultas al médico si te duele la cabeza?*
E2: *No. Por lo general tomo dos aspirinas y me siento mejor. ¿Y tú?*

1. Tienes tos.
2. Tienes una fiebre alta.
3. Te duele la espalda.
4. Te rompes un hueso.
5. Necesitas un examen físico para el trabajo.
6. Tienes náuseas.
7. Te duele la garganta.
8. Tienes resfriado.

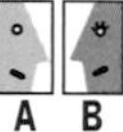
A B

10-5A Consejos médicos. Habla con tu compañero/a para que te dé consejos sobre los siguientes síntomas. Estudiante B, por favor ve al **Apéndice 1,** página A12.

MODELO: E1: *Me duelen los pulmones.*
E2: *Debes dejar de fumar.*

SÍNTOMAS	CONSEJOS PARA EL/LA ESTUDIANTE B
1. Me duelen las piernas.	1. comer carne
2. Creo que tengo fiebre.	2. beber un refresco
3. No tengo energía.	3. tomar aspirinas
4. No me siento bien.	4. descansar mucho y no ir a clase
5. Tengo un resfriado terrible.	5. beber mucha cafeína
6. Me duele el estómago.	6. tomar jarabe

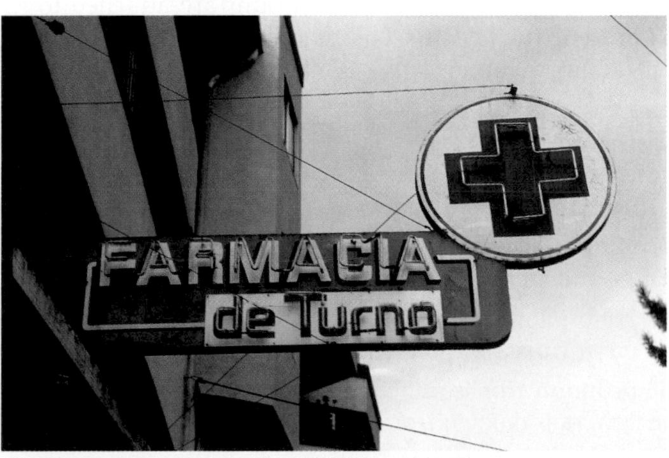

En muchos países hispanos es posible pedirle antibióticos directamente a un farmacéutico.

¡Así lo hacemos! Estructuras

10-8 to 10-13

1. *Nosotros* commands

- There are two ways to give a direct command to a group of persons that includes yourself: **vamos a** + *infinitive* or the **nosotros/as** form of the present subjunctive. As you know, **vamos a...** is also used to express a simple statement or to ask a question. The interpretation of *Let's...* results from intonation and context.

¿**Vamos a** llamar al médico?	*Shall we call the doctor?*
Sí, **vamos a** llamarlo.	*Yes, let's call him.*

- With the present subjunctive form of **nosotros/as,** the command is clearly stated.

Hablemos con la enfermera.	*Let's talk with the nurse.*
No miremos la radiografía ahora.	*Let's not look at the X-ray now.*

- As with all command forms, object pronouns are attached to the affirmative forms and precede the negative commands. In affirmative commands with an attached pronoun, an accent mark is added to maintain the original stress.

Busquemos al enfermero.	*Let's look for the nurse.*
Busquémoslo.	*Let's look for him.*
No molestemos a la paciente.	*Let's not bother the patient.*
No la molestemos.	*Let's not bother her.*

- To express *Let's go,* use the indicative **vamos.** For the negative *Let's not go ...,* however, you must use the subjunctive form.

Vamos al hospital a visitar a Linda.	*Let's go to the hospital to visit Linda.*
No, no vayamos al hospital ahora.	*No, let's not go to the hospital now.*

- When the pronoun **nos** is attached to the affirmative command of reflexive verbs, the final **-s** is deleted from the verb ending.

Vámonos.	*Let's leave.*
Levantémonos.	*Let's get up.*
Durmámonos.	*Let's fall asleep.*

Aplicación

10-6 Benjamín y Talisa. Benjamín Bratt y Talisa Soto se conocieron un poco antes de hacer la película *Piñero,* y un año después, se casaron. Lee la conversación entre los dos actores y subraya los mandatos con la forma de **nosotros.**

Benjamín: ¡Oye, Talisa! Hagamos otra película juntos.

Talisa: Buena idea, pero ¿una película seria o cómica?

Benjamín: Una seria. Veamos este guión (*script*) de León Ichaso que se llama *Piñero*. Se trata de un poeta de Nueva York que muere muy joven. Se dice que su poesía es la precursora del *rap*.

Talisa: Me parece interesante, pero miremos otros guiones menos serios. Leamos, por ejemplo, el guión para *Señorita Congeniality.*

Benjamín: ¡Ay, Talisa! ¡Ya es tarde! Sandra Bullock y yo vamos a hacer esa película.

Talisa: Bueno, hagamos *Piñero*. Después vamos a ver qué pasa.

Benjamín: De acuerdo, Talisa.

10-7 ¿Comprendiste? Ahora contesta las preguntas, basándote en la conversación anterior.

1. ¿Qué quieren hacer Benjamín y Talisa?
2. ¿Qué tipo de película le interesa más a Benjamín? ¿Y a Talisa?
3. ¿Quién es Piñero?
4. ¿Por qué no van a colaborar en *Señorita Congeniality*?

10-8 El doctor Chiringa. El doctor Chiringa es una persona que siempre se incluye en las órdenes que les da a las otras personas. Completa la conversación que tiene con sus pacientes Roberto y Tomás Cruz, usando los mandatos en la forma de **nosotros.**

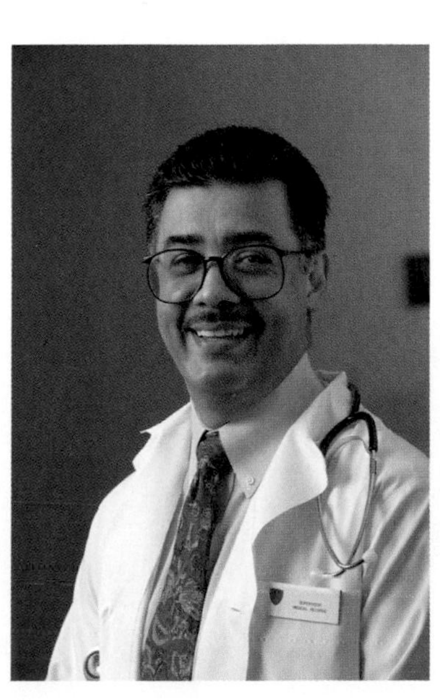

Dr. Chiringa: Señores Cruz, tenemos que hacer algo por nuestra salud. No (1. cenar) ________ tan tarde y no (2. acostarse) ________ todos los días después de las doce de la noche.

Roberto: Sí, doctor, pero es que llegamos del trabajo muy tarde.

Dr. Chiringa: Sí, pero (3. tener) ________ más cuidado, no (4. trabajar) ________ tanto. (5. Llegar) ________ a casa más temprano; (6. descansar) ________ más y (7. cuidarse) ________ un poco más.

Tomás: Doctor, pero es que tenemos muchos problemas. Trabajamos en una panadería por la noche, y sólo tenemos tiempo para comer y dormir porque por la mañana tenemos otro trabajo en un restaurante.

Dr. Chiringa: Bueno, no (8. enfadarse) ________. (9. Seguir) ________ estos consejos y, si es posible, (10. cambiar) ________ de trabajo.

Roberto: No es fácil, doctor, siempre estamos buscando un trabajo mejor.

Dr. Chiringa: Sí, lo sé. Pero nuestra salud es lo primero.

Tomás: ¡De acuerdo, doctor!

10-9 Los enfermeros. Imagínense que ustedes son enfermeros/as y trabajan para el equipo de rescate (*rescue*). Acaban de recibir una llamada del hospital pidiéndoles que atiendan a las víctimas de un accidente. Túrnense para completar la conversación con verbos en el presente y con mandatos con la forma de **nosotros.**

Modelo: (ponerse) los uniformes
E1: *¿Nos ponemos los uniformes?*
E2: *¡Sí, pongámonoslos!*

1. (levantarse) rápidamente
2. (vestirse) ahora mismo
3. (poner) todo el equipo de emergencia en la ambulancia
4. (buscar) la ruta más rápida en el mapa
5. (salir) en la ambulancia ahora mismo
6. (hacer) todo lo posible para ayudar a los heridos (*wounded*)
7. (llenar) el tanque de oxígeno
8. (volver) al hospital rápidamente

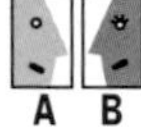

10-10A En la sala de urgencias. Imagínense que ustedes tienen que decidir qué deben hacer en situaciones urgentes. Un/a estudiante presenta unas situaciones. El otro/la otra responde con instrucciones lógicas de su lista, usando un mandato de **nosotros.** Túrnense, cambiando de papel. Estudiante B, por favor ve al **Apéndice 1,** página A12.

Modelo: E1: *El niño tiene gripe.*
E2: *Démosle vitamina C.*

ACCIONES

buscarle un calmante	darle té con limón	recetarle pastillas
darle dos aspirinas	hacerle una radiografía	¿...?

SITUACIONES URGENTES

1. El paciente necesita oxígeno.
2. A la niña le duele el estómago.
3. El bebé está tosiendo mucho.
4. La señora tiene una infección en el brazo.
5. El Sr. Pérez tiene una fiebre muy alta.
6. ¿...?

2. Indirect commands

10-14 to 10-17

Commands may be expressed indirectly, either to the person with whom you are speaking or to express what a third party should do.

- The basic format of an indirect command is as follows.

Que + *subjunctive verb* (+ *subject*)

Que **llames** al Dr. Estrada.	*Call Dr. Estrada.*
Que lo **haga** ella.	*Let (Have) her do it.*
Que no me **moleste** más el enfermero.	*Have the nurse not bother me anymore.*

- This construction is also used to express your wishes for someone else.

¡Que no **te duela** la garganta mañana!	*I hope that your throat doesn't hurt you tomorrow!*

- Object and reflexive pronouns always precede the verb. In a negative statement, **no** also precedes the verb.

¡Que **se** vayan!	*Let them leave!*
¡Que papá **no se** tome la presión después de comer!	*Don't let dad take his blood pressure after eating!*

- When a subject is expressed, it generally follows the verb.

¡Que lo hagas **tú**!	*You do it!*
¿La inyección? Que se la ponga **la enfermera.**	*The shot? Let the nurse give it to him.*

Aplicación

10-11 Viracocha, el dios creador. Lee el monólogo de Viracocha y subraya todos sus deseos expresados con mandatos indirectos. Luego escribe el infinitivo del verbo.

Modelo: ¡Que haya luz!
haber

Hoy voy a crear el mundo y a sus habitantes. Que se abran las aguas y que surjan (*rise*) montañas además de los llanos (*plains*). Que aparezcan los pájaros en el aire, los animales en la tierra y toda clase de insectos. Que se creen el sol y la luna, el hombre y la mujer, y que ellos procreen niños. Que salga el sol, que llueva mucho y que crezcan los alimentos en abundancia. Que no haya guerra y que reine la paz por todo el mundo.

Observatorio, Tiahuanacu, Bolivia

10-12 ¿Qué desea el dios creador? Ahora, escribe cuatro de los deseos de Viracocha.

MODELO: Quiere que se abran las aguas.

10-13 ¿Y tú? Escribe cinco mandatos indirectos que representen tus deseos para el futuro.

MODELO: *Que tenga éxito en los exámenes.*

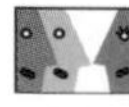

10-14 Un viaje a Bolivia o al Paraguay. Hagan una lista de lo que necesitan para realizar un viaje a Bolivia o al Paraguay. Luego, expresen sus deseos con mandatos indirectos.

MODELO: dinero
E1: *Que la universidad nos dé una beca (*scholarship*).*
E2: *Que nuestros padres...*

¿Cuánto sabes tú? *Can you...*

10-18 to 10-21

- ☐ talk about your health and how you feel using **me siento...**?
- ☐ explain what part of your body hurts using **me duele(n)...**?
- ☐ invite others to do something with you using **nosotros** commands such as **¡Veamos una película! ¡No nos durmamos en clase!**?
- ☐ suggest indirectly that someone do something using indirect commands such as **Que lo haga Juan**?
- ☐ wish something to happen using indirect commands such as **¡Qué esté bien mi mamá!**?

Comparaciones

El ejercicio y la dieta

10-15 En tu experiencia.

1. ¿Se preocupan mucho por mantenerse en forma tus amigos?
2. ¿Siguen ustedes una dieta especial?
3. Tus amigos y tú ¿caminan o hacen algún tipo de ejercicio? ¿Qué ejercicio?
4. Compara tu rutina con la de tus padres o la de tus abuelos. ¿Cuáles de ustedes son más activos?
5. ¿Cómo son las comidas más populares en los EE.UU.? ¿Cuáles son los postres preferidos en los EE.UU.? ¿Son comidas saludables (*healthy*)?

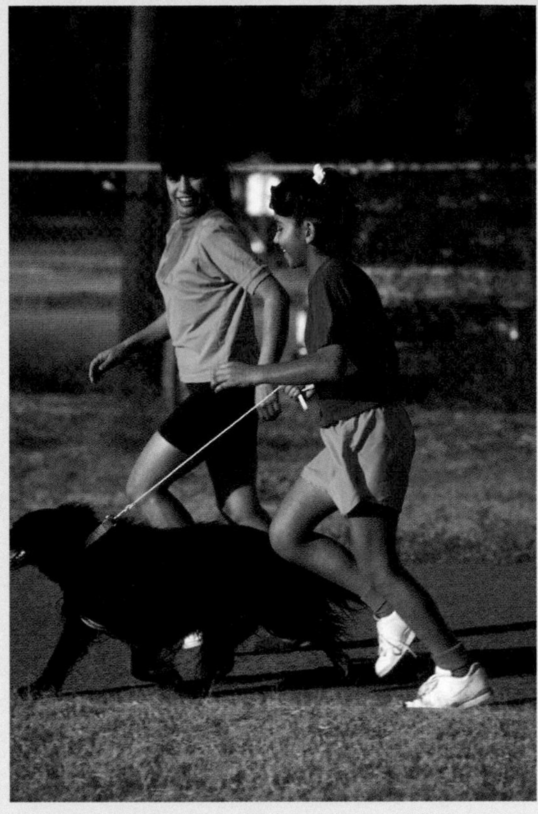

La preocupación por seguir una dieta saludable y por mantenerse en forma (*to stay in shape*) es un fenómeno reciente en los países hispanos. Muchos de los platos tradicionales de la cocina hispana tienen generosas cantidades de azúcar o un alto contenido de grasa animal, como la carne de cerdo y la carne de res. Afortunadamente, muchos hispanos preparan sus comidas con ingredientes naturales y frescos. En esto hay un gran contraste con los EE.UU., donde es muy frecuente que los alimentos se empaquen en fábricas (*factories*) y contengan conservantes (*preservatives*). Según los expertos, los alimentos naturales son mucho más saludables y su consumo resulta en menos casos de cáncer y otras enfermedades. Otro beneficio de la dieta hispana es el equilibrio de platos. Típicamente una comida incluye legumbres, algún tipo de arroz y distintas variedades de frijoles. El postre puede ser alguna fruta, y hoy en día los hispanos comen menos carne de res que antes. Un delicioso y saludable aspecto de la comida hispana es el uso de aceite de oliva, que no contiene colesterol.

En los restaurantes hispanos en los EE.UU. hay una gran variedad de comida y ésta se ha norteamericanizado para complacer el gusto de los clientes de este país. Por ejemplo, los restaurantes mexicanos ofrecen diferentes tipos de tacos y frijoles, pero raramente platos más elaborados como el mole poblano.

Los hispanos tienen la costumbre de caminar mucho todos los días, una actividad excelente para mantenerse en forma. Sin embargo, muchos hispanos no suelen tener un régimen de ejercicio ni se preocupan por mantenerse en forma como los norteamericanos. Esto va cambiando entre los jóvenes de las ciudades que hoy en día hacen footing (*jog*) por los parques o van a clases de ejercicio aeróbico en los gimnasios.

10-16 En tu opinión. Primero, hagan una lista de las ventajas y desventajas de cada sugerencia o de cada tratamiento. Luego, comparen su opinión sobre la utilidad de estos tratamientos.

Modelo: una copa de vino diaria para proteger el corazón

E1: *Creo que es una buena idea tomar una copa de vino todos los días para proteger el corazón. Me parece muy saludable.*

E2: *No estoy de acuerdo. No me gusta el vino y creo que la gente toma demasiado.*

1. la quiropráctica para aliviar el dolor de espalda
2. el té de hierbas para dar energía
3. la acupuntura para aliviar el dolor del tobillo
4. los calmantes para combatir el estrés
5. los antibióticos para el dolor de garganta
6. la aspirina para proteger el corazón

SEGUNDA PARTE

¡Así lo decimos! Vocabulario

CD 2, Track 32

10-22 to 10-23

¡Así es la vida! Mejora tu salud

Bienvenidos a Hacienda La Fortuna

Spa-Hotel, Lago Titicaca, Bolivia

La Hacienda La Fortuna le ofrece un servicio único y personal. Nuestro spa-hotel tiene todo lo que pueda desear en un solo lugar con un ambiente de total relajamiento. Cuenta con 23 habitaciones de lujo con vistas espectaculares, así como jacuzzi y piscina con agua de manantiales (*spring*) termales.

Contamos con el ambiente perfecto para que sus vacaciones sean inolvidables y muy saludables. Nuestros paquetes le ofrecen planes de adelgazamiento, antiestrés, tratamiento para las enfermedades crónicas, clases de cocina y todo tipo de actividades para que usted pueda olvidarse del estrés.

La variedad de servicios le deja crear su propia experiencia....

las bebidas alcohólicas

los carbohidratos

el colesterol

las grasas

los productos lácteos

las proteínas

Las enfermedades y el bienestar	*Illnesses and well-being*
la diabetes	*diabetes*
los ejercicios aeróbicos	*aerobics*
el estrés	*stress*
el peso	*weight*
el sobrepeso	*excess weight; obesity*

Tu línea y tu salud	*Your weight and your health*
adelgazar; bajar de peso	*to lose weight*
cuidar(se)	*to take care (of oneself)*
estar a dieta	*to be on a diet*
guardar la línea	*to stay trim; to watch one's figure*
hacer jogging/footing	*to jog*
mantenerse (ie) en forma	*to stay in shape*
padecer (zc) (de)	*to suffer (from)*
ponerse en forma	*to get in shape*
subir de peso	*to gain weight*

CD 3, Track 34

10-29 to 10-30

Letras y sonidos

The consonants "r, rr" in Spanish

In Spanish, there are two *r* sounds: a flap (or tap) and a trill. A flap involves one quick touch of the tongue tip against the alveolar ridge, located behind the upper front teeth. This sound is similar to the English flap made for the letters *tt* in *butter* and *dd* in *ladder*. A Spanish trill is a rapid series of two or more flaps, where the tongue vibrates from air passing through the mouth. English has no trill, but this sound is approximated when one imitates the sound of a galloping horse or a racecar revving up its engine, or when one says the phrase *edited it* quickly, since it contains four successive flaps.

The difference between a flap and a trill in Spanish is crucial between vowels, the only context where *r* and *rr* contrast meaning, e.g., *pe-ro* ("but") versus *pe-rro* ("dog"). A double *rr* always requires a trill sound.

Trill for *rr*: *pe-rro* *pi-za-rra* *a-bu-rri-do* *a-te-rri-za-mos*

A single *r*, however, is sometimes a flap and sometimes a trill. It is a flap between vowels, in a consonant cluster after *p, b, t, d, c, g,* or *f*, or at the end of a syllable.

Flap for *r*: *pe-ro* *o-pe-rar* *es-trés* *gra-sa* *tor-cer*

A single *r* is a trill at the beginning of a word, or after *l, n,* or *s*. Also, a trill may be used at the end of a syllable instead of a flap.

Trill for *r*: *re-ce-ta* *ra-dio-gra-fí-a* *En-ri-que* *Is-ra-el* *tor-cer*

Aplicación

10-17 Un chequeo para la salud. Completa el cuestionario sobre la diabetes y decide si tienes riesgo.

CHEQUEO PARA SU SALUD...

Los hispanos son más propensos a sufrir diabetes... ¿por qué correr este riesgo sin necesidad?

En honor a la "Semana de Alerta a la Diabetes", hágase una simple prueba. Este servicio es **gratis** para la comunidad. A continuación tiene unas preguntas, solamente necesita responder SÍ o NO y debe anotar 10 puntos por cada respuesta afirmativa.

Estoy sintiendo los siguientes síntomas con regularidad:	SÍ	NO
Sed excesiva	❑	❑
Orino (*I urinate*) con frecuencia	❑	❑
Mucho cansancio	❑	❑
Pérdida de peso inexplicable	❑	❑
Vista nublada a veces	❑	❑
Tengo más de 40 años:	❑	❑
Según las tablas de peso, tengo más peso del debido:	❑	❑
Soy mujer y he tenido niños que han pesado más de 9 lbs al nacer:	❑	❑
Mi madre/padre es diabético/a:	❑	❑
Mi gemelo/a tiene diabetes:	❑	❑
Mi hermano/a tiene diabetes:	❑	❑

Si su total es de 20 o de más de 20 puntos, le recomendamos que se haga una prueba de diabetes, absolutamente gratis.

LAS PRUEBAS SE EFECTUARÁN:

Martes, 19 de marzo—8:00 am -11:00 am
Vestíbulo del Hospital San Vicente
Calle Reina del Río
Asunción

Las personas que deseen hacerse esta prueba no deben comer dos horas antes del examen.

Contaremos con una dietista que podrá informarle sobre las comidas y contestar cualquier pregunta que pueda tener.

Para más información o si quiere recibir nuestra revista gratis, llame al

5-56-68-50

Hospital San Vicente
Calle Reina del Río, Asunción, Paraguay

WWW

10-18 ¿Qué pueden hacer? Conversen entre ustedes para identificar lo que pueden hacer para prevenir *(prevent)* la diabetes. Van a encontrar consejos si se conectan a la página web de **¡Arriba!**

MODELO: *Es importante hacer ejercicio todos los días.*

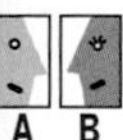
A B

10-19A Te recomiendo que... Un/a estudiante presenta los siguientes problemas mientras el otro/la otra ofrece recomendaciones. Túrnense, cambiando de papel. Pueden usar el verbo **recomiendo** con una cláusula nominativa en el subjuntivo. Estudiante B, por favor ve al **Apéndice 1,** página A12.

MODELO: E1: *Estoy muy flaco/a.*
E2: *Te recomiendo que comas tres comidas completas todos los días.*

PROBLEMAS	RECOMENDACIONES PARA EL ESTUDIANTE B
1. Quiero bajar de peso.	1. tomar leche
2. Necesito bajar mi nivel de azúcar.	2. (no) tomar bebidas alcohólicas
3. Fumo más de un paquete de cigarrillos todos los días.	3. tomar pastillas para el colesterol.
4. Mi hermano tiene dolor de cabeza.	4. tomar antiácidos
5. Mi tío padece de alzheimer.	5. tomar una bebida llena de vitaminas

10-20 Sus preocupaciones sobre la salud. Conversen entre ustedes para poner estas enfermedades y condiciones en orden de importancia para ustedes y para la sociedad.

MODELO: E1: *¿Cuál de las enfermedades es más terrible para ti?*
E2: *Para mí es el cáncer, para la sociedad es...*

	PARA MÍ	PARA MI COMPAÑERO/A	PARA LA SOCIEDAD
el cáncer	_____	_____	_____
la diabetes	_____	_____	_____
las enfermedades del corazón	_____	_____	_____
el SIDA (*AIDS*)	_____	_____	_____
las enfermedades del pulmón	_____	_____	_____
la artritis	_____	_____	_____
el alcoholismo	_____	_____	_____
el SRAS (*SARS*)	_____	_____	_____
¿otra...?	_____	_____	_____

CD 2, Track 35

10-21 Una encuesta (*poll*) médica. Escucha y completa la siguiente encuesta telefónica. Después de completarla, compara tus respuestas con las de un/a compañero/a.

MODELO: ¿Cuántos cigarrillos fuma usted al día?
a. ni uno b. de cinco a diez c. más de un paquete
a. ni uno

1. a. 0 mg	b. 300 mg	c. 600 mg
2. a. muchos	b. algunos	c. ni uno
3. a. mucho	b. un poco	c. nada
4. a. de oliva	b. de maíz	c. de animal
5. a. 80%	b. 50–60%	c. 30%
6. a. menos de una vez	b. dos o tres veces	c. todos los días

10-22 ¿Cómo se comparan? Ahora, conversen entre ustedes y decidan cuál goza de mejor salud, según los siguientes aspectos.

MODELO: comer comida rápida
Mi compañero/a come menos comida rápida que yo. Él/Ella goza de mejor salud que yo.

1. hacer ejercicio
2. comer poca grasa animal
3. mantenerse en forma
4. fumar
5. tomar mucha cafeína
6. tomar bebidas alcohólicas

¡Así lo hacemos! Estructuras

3. The subjunctive to express feelings and emotions

10-31 to 10-37

- The subjunctive is used in noun clauses after verbs that express emotions such as hope, fear, surprise, regret, pity, anger, joy, and sorrow.

alegrarse (de)	*to be glad*
enojar	*to anger; to make angry*
esperar	*to hope*
estar contento/a (de)	*to be happy*
lamentar	*to regret*
molestar	*to bother*
sentir (ie, i)	*to regret*
sorprender (se)	*to surprise*
temer	*to fear*
tener (ie) miedo (de)	*to be afraid*

Talisa **lamenta** que Carlos **esté** enfermo.	*Talisa regrets that Carlos is sick.*
Espero que **hagas** más ejercicio esta semana.	*I hope that you exercise more this week.*
Juana **teme** que su madre **padezca** de diabetes.	*Juana fears that her mother will suffer from diabetes.*

- As with the verbs of volition, verbs that express feelings and emotions require the subjunctive in the dependent clause if the subject is different from that of the main clause. If there is only one subject, the infinitive is used in the dependent clause.

Carlos **lamenta estar** enfermo.	*Carlos regrets being sick.*
Esperamos hacer más ejercicio esta semana.	*We hope to exercise more this week.*
Juana **teme padecer** de diabetes.	*Juana fears suffering from diabetes.*

El subjuntivo con *Ojalá*

- The expression **¡Ojalá!** entered the Spanish language during the Arab occupation of Spain. It comes from an Arabic expression meaning *God (Allah) willing* and is used in Spanish as the equivalent of *I hope that.* **¡Ojalá!** may be used with or without **que** and is followed by the subjunctive.

¡Ojalá (que) nos mantengamos en forma!	*I hope that we stay in shape!*
¡Ojalá (que) visites el spa en Bolivia!	*I hope you visit the spa in Bolivia!*

Aplicación

10-23 Las grasas transformadas (*transfatty acids*). Aquí tienes un artículo sobre un cambio de reglamento para las etiquetas (*labels*) de la comida. Lee el artículo y subraya las formas del subjuntivo. Explica por qué se usa el subjuntivo en esos casos.

Diario ABC de Asunción

lunes, 3 de enero de 2007

Las grasas nocivas en las etiquetas de los alimentos

Desde 2006, el gobierno de los EE.UU. insiste en que la descripción de todos los alimentos incluya la proporción exacta de las grasas transformadas, una de las principales causantes de la obstrucción arterial.

Las papas fritas, las galletas, el pollo frito, los pasteles y los donuts (o donas) son algunos de los alimentos más populares y deliciosos que incluyen grasas transformadas. Sin embargo, esas grasas son tan peligrosas para el corazón y las arterias como las grasas saturadas –y muchos médicos las consideran aún peor.

Las normas de la Agencia de Drogas y Alimentos (FDA) ahora piden que las etiquetas sobre nutrición de los alimentos empaquetados incluyan la cantidad de grasas transformadas, bajo de las grasas saturadas.

El secretario de Salud Michael O. Leavitt afirma: "Queremos que el consumidor sea más inteligente a la hora de adquirir alimentos. Deseamos que lea la etiqueta y encuentre alimentos no dañinos (*harmful*) al corazón". Añadió que 13 millones de norteamericanos sufren de problemas cardiacos y que las grasas transformadas agravan el mal.

10-24 ¿Comprendiste? Ahora, contesta las preguntas siguientes sobre el artículo.

1. ¿En qué insiste el gobierno de los EE.UU.?
2. ¿Qué tipo de comida contiene estas grasas?
3. ¿Por qué es bueno saber el contenido?
4. A partir de ahora, ¿vas a leer bien las etiquetas de las comidas? ¿Por qué?

10-25 ¡Ojalá! Vuelve a leer el artículo y ofrece tus opiniones y deseos, usando las siguientes expresiones.

Modelo: Lamento que...
haya grasas transformadas en mis comidas favoritas.

1. Siento que...
2. Espero que...
3. Temo que...
4. Ojalá que...

10-26 Un examen médico. Completa la conversación entre el médico y el paciente con la forma correcta del verbo entre paréntesis, usando el indicativo, el subjuntivo o dejando el infinitivo.

Paciente: Buenos días, doctor. Me siento muy mal.
Médico: A ver ¿qué le (1. doler) __________?
Paciente: No me duele nada pero yo (2. sentirse) __________ mal.
Médico: Bueno, quiero escucharle el corazón. Deseo que (3. quitarse) __________ la camisa y que (4. respirar) __________ profundamente.
Paciente: Espero que no (5. ser) __________ nada serio.
Médico: No, pero temo que su comida (6. contener) __________ demasiado colesterol y grasas transformadas.
Paciente: Me sorprende que (7. decir) __________ eso. Soy vegetariano.
Médico: Mmmm... Me alegro de (8. saber) __________ eso. ¿Qué come para el desayuno?
Paciente: Donuts, galletas y queso.
Médico: Ah... ¡Ahora entiendo!

10-27 ¡Mejoremos nuestra salud! Hablen de lo que esperan hacer para mejorar la salud durante los próximos meses y reaccionen a los comentarios que escuchen.

Modelo: E1: *Espero bajar tres kilos en un mes.*
E2: *Espero que hagas ejercicio todos los días.*

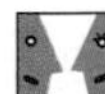

10-28 ¿Qué te molesta? Túrnense para hablar de cosas que les molestan. Pueden inventar cosas que realmente no les molesten.

Modelo: *Me molesta que la gente fume.*

4. The subjunctive to express doubt and denial

10-38 to 10-44 The subjunctive is used in noun clauses after expressions of doubt, uncertainty, or denial. The following verbs can express doubt and denial. Unlike the verbs that express volition and emotion, these verbs do not require a change in subject in the dependent clause in order to use the subjunctive.

dudar	*to doubt*	**no creer**	*to not believe*
negar (ie)	*to deny*	**no estar seguro/a (de)**	*to not be sure (of)*
no pensar (ie)	*to not to think*		

Dudo que Camilo **padezca** de artritis.	*I doubt that Camilo suffers from arthritis.*
No creo que el médico **sepa** el diagnóstico.	*I don't believe that the doctor knows the diagnosis.*
No estamos seguros de que las grasas transformadas **sean** nocivas.	*We're not sure that transfatty acids are harmful.*
Mi padre **niega** que **tenga** un nivel alto de colesterol.	*My father denies that he has a high cholesterol level.*

- When there is no doubt, uncertainty, or disbelief about an action or event, and when the subject appears certain of the facts, the indicative is used in the noun clause. For most expressions of doubt or uncertainty, the indicative will be used for the opposing expression (**dudar** versus **no dudar; no creer** versus **creer**).

No dudo que Camilo **padece** de artritis.	*I don't doubt that Camilo suffers from arthritis.*
Creo que el médico **sabe** el diagnóstico.	*I believe that the doctor knows the diagnosis.*
Estamos seguros de que las grasas transformadas **son** nocivas.	*We're sure that transfatty acids are harmful.*
Mi padre **no niega** que **tiene** un nivel muy alto de colesterol.	*My father does not deny that he has a very high cholesterol level.*

- When the verb **creer** is used in a question, it can imply doubt in the mind of the speaker, thereby triggering the subjunctive in the dependent clause. If the speaker expresses no opinion or does not anticipate a negative response, the indicative is preferred.

¿**Crees** que el alcohol **dañe** el corazón?	*Do you believe (think) that alcohol damages the heart?* (speaker implies doubt)
¿**Crees** que el alcohol **daña** el corazón?	*Do you believe (think) that alcohol damages the heart?* (speaker has no opinion)

El subjuntivo con *tal vez* y *quizá(s)*

- The expressions **tal vez** and **quizá(s)**, meaning *perhaps* or *maybe*, are followed by the subjunctive when the speaker wishes to convey uncertainty or doubt. Both expressions are used without **que.**

Tal vez funcione no comer tanta grasa.	*Perhaps not eating so much fat will work.*
Quizás el ejercicio me **alivie** la artritis.	*Maybe exercise will alleviate my arthritis.*

- When **tal vez** or **quizá(s)** follows the verb, the indicative is used.

Vamos a fumar menos, **tal vez.**	*We're going to smoke less, perhaps.*
Bajo de peso, **quizás.**	*I'll lose weight, maybe.*

Aplicación

10-29 Una entrevista con Raquel Welch. Raquel (Tejada) Welch es de ascendencia inglesa y boliviana. Aunque nació en 1940, todavía se le considera una de las actrices más bellas del cine norteamericano. En esta conversación con la prensa (*press*), habla un poco sobre su carrera. Léela y subraya los verbos en el subjuntivo. Explica por qué se usa el subjuntivo en cada caso.

Raquel Welch y Héctor Elizondo en *Tortilla Soup.*

Periodista: Buenas tardes, señorita Welch. Ojalá que se encuentre bien.

Raquel: Perfectamente bien, gracias. Tal vez usted quiera hacerme algunas preguntas sobre mi carrera, ¿no?

Periodista: ¡Sin duda! Quizás usted pueda hablarme un poco sobre su película favorita.

Raquel: Pues, no creo que pueda limitarme a una sola, pero quizás usted conozca *Tortilla Soup*. Me gustó mucho porque es una comedia con un mensaje serio, y me divertí mucho.

Periodista: Usted también actuó en la televisión.

Raquel: Es verdad. Estoy segura de que mi parte en *American Family* en PBS es una de mis favoritas. Dudo que se repita tal oportunidad en el futuro.

Periodista: ¿Cómo se mantiene tan bien?

Raquel: Niego que esté en perfecta forma, pero es verdad que voy al gimnasio todos los días. Para mí, la buena salud es muy importante.

Periodista: Bueno, señorita Welch. Muchas gracias, y que tenga mucho éxito en el futuro.

Raquel: Gracias a usted.

10-30 La entrevista de Raquel Welch. Vuelve a leer la entrevista con Raquel Welch y contesta las siguientes preguntas.

1. ¿Quién es Raquel Welch?
2. ¿Por qué le gustó mucho la película *Tortilla Soup*?
3. ¿Qué oportunidad tuvo en la televisión?
4. ¿Cuántos años tiene ahora?
5. ¿Cómo se mantiene en forma?
6. ¿Conoces algunas de sus películas? ¿Crees que tiene mucho talento?

10-31 En el Spa-Hotel Hacienda La Fortuna. Imagínate que estás planeando una visita al Spa-Hotel Hacienda La Fortuna. Contesta las preguntas siguientes, usando expresiones de duda, negación y emoción.

Modelo: ¿Vas a bañarte en las aguas termales?
Dudo que me bañe.

1. ¿Vas por más de una semana?
   Quizás…
2. ¿Vas a seguir los consejos del entrenador personal?
   Creo que…
3. ¿Vas a hacer una excursión a los sitios arqueológicos?
   Estoy seguro/a de que…
4. ¿Tienes una cita para hacerte la pedicura?
   Dudo que…
5. ¿Vas a seguir una dieta baja en grasas?
   No creo que…
6. ¿Vas a caminar o hacer otro ejercicio?
   Niego que…
7. ¿Me llevas contigo?
   Dudo que…
8. ¿Vas a divertirte mucho?
   Ojalá…

WWW

10-32 Un spa para ti. Conéctate con la página web de **¡Arriba!** para visitar un spa. Completa las siguientes oraciones, dando tu opinión sobre el lugar.

Modelo: Creo que… *tienen planes muy interesantes.*

1. Dudo que…
2. Quizás…
3. No creo que…
4. Estoy seguro/a que…
5. Ojalá que…

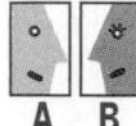

10-33A *Termas Bolivia.* Estás trabajando en el spa, *Termas Bolivia.* Tu compañero/a necesita relajarse y quiere ir a tu spa. Él/Ella va a hacerte preguntas y tú necesitas darle consejos, usando las siguientes palabras de la lista. Estudiante B, por favor ve al **Apéndice 1,** página A13.

(no) creo	(no) dudo
(no) estoy seguro/a	(no) niego
quizás	tal vez

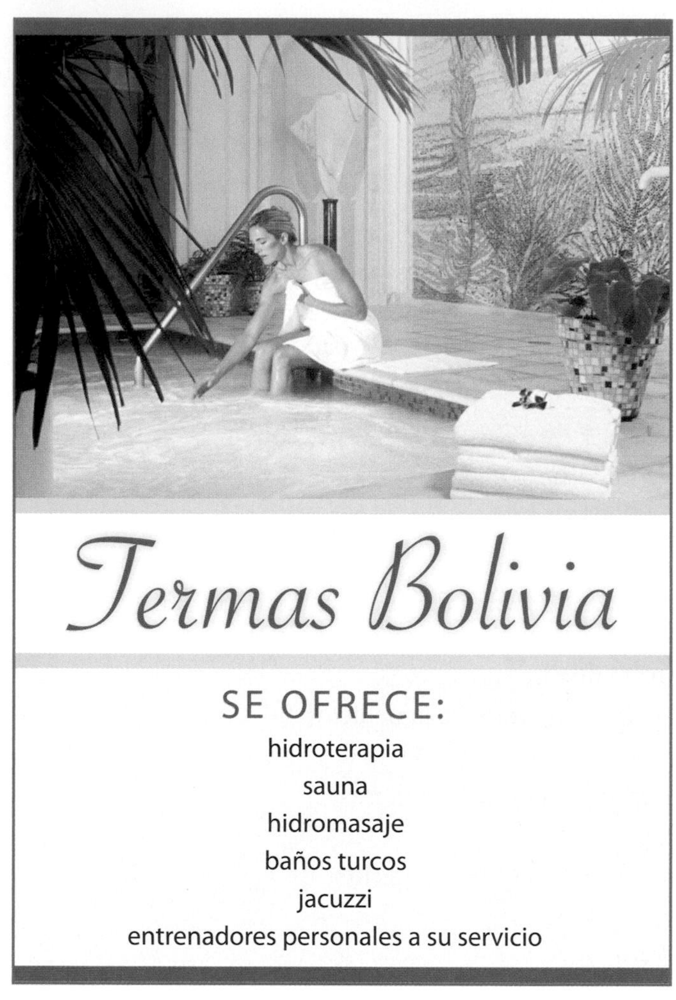

Source: Sri Maiava Rusden / PacificStock.com

¿Cuánto sabes tú? *Can you...*

10-45 to 10-48

- ☐ say what you do to stay fit such as **hago jogging, levanto pesas, guardo la línea**?
- ☐ talk about foods and habits that are good or bad for your health?
- ☐ express emotions using the subjunctive such as **Lamento que no te sientas bien** and **Ojalá te cuides mucho**?
- ☐ give your opinion about something using expressions such as **Creo que el aceite de oliva es bueno para la salud** or **No creo que haya colesterol en los productos vegetales**?

Episode 10

10-49 to 10-53

¡Pura vida! Episodio 10

En este episodio doña María y Marcela atienden a Patricio porque no se siente bien.

Antes de ver el video

10-34 ¿Tengo gripe o resfriado? Lee el artículo para ver cómo se diferencian los síntomas del resfriado y de la gripe y después haz una lista de los síntomas de cada uno.

El resfriado y la gripe pueden tener muchos de los mismos síntomas. Pero un resfriado generalmente es leve, mientras que la gripe es mucho más intensa.

Con frecuencia, con un resfriado comienzas sintiéndote cansado, estornudando (*sneezing*), tosiendo y con la nariz tapada (*stuffy nose*). Si tienes fiebre, es baja: sólo uno o dos grados más de lo normal. Es probable que te duelan los músculos y la garganta, y que tengas los ojos llorosos y dolor de cabeza.

La gripe comienza de repente (*suddenly*) y es más fuerte. Es probable que te sientas débil y cansado, y que tengas fiebre alta, tos seca, la nariz tapada, escalofríos (*chills*), dolores musculares, dolor de cabeza intenso, dolor en los ojos y dolor de garganta. Generalmente, toma más tiempo mejorarse de la gripe que de un resfriado. La mejor manera de evitar la gripe es ponerte una vacuna cada otoño.

¿Qué tomas cuando tienes gripe?

A ver el video

10-35 Lo que tiene Patricio. Mira el décimo episodio de *¡Pura vida!* para identificar la enfermedad que tiene Patricio.

Patricio está enfermo.

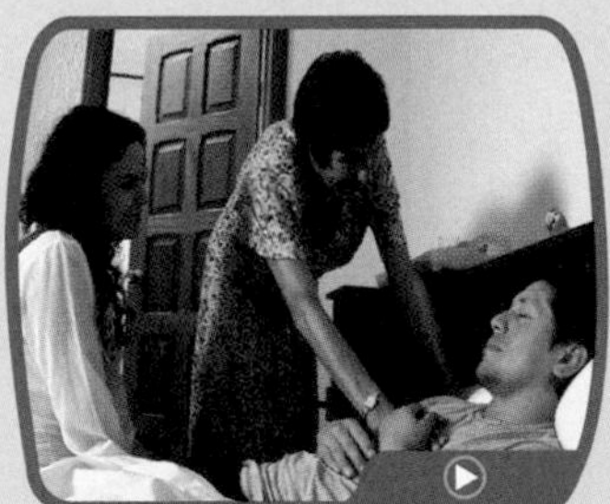
Doña María y Marcela con Patricio

Marcela va a la farmacia.

Según los síntomas, es probable que Patricio tenga...

_____ resfriado _____ diabetes _____ gripe _____ gastritis

Después de ver el video

WWW

10-36 ¿Qué puedo hacer para sentirme mejor? Conéctate con la página web de **¡Arriba!** y lee algunos consejos para sentirte mejor si tienes un resfriado o una gripe. Escribe por lo menos cinco consejos.

NUESTRO MUNDO

Panoramas

Los países sin mar: Bolivia y el Paraguay

Vistas culturales

10-37 ¿Ya sabes...? Trata de identificar o explicar lo siguiente.

10-54 to 10-55

1. la capital de Bolivia y la del Paraguay
2. la altura de La Paz
3. la importancia de Itaipú
4. el país cuyos productos principales son minerales
5. para qué se usa la *quena*
6. el país que tiene una cadena de misiones de los siglos XVII y XVIII

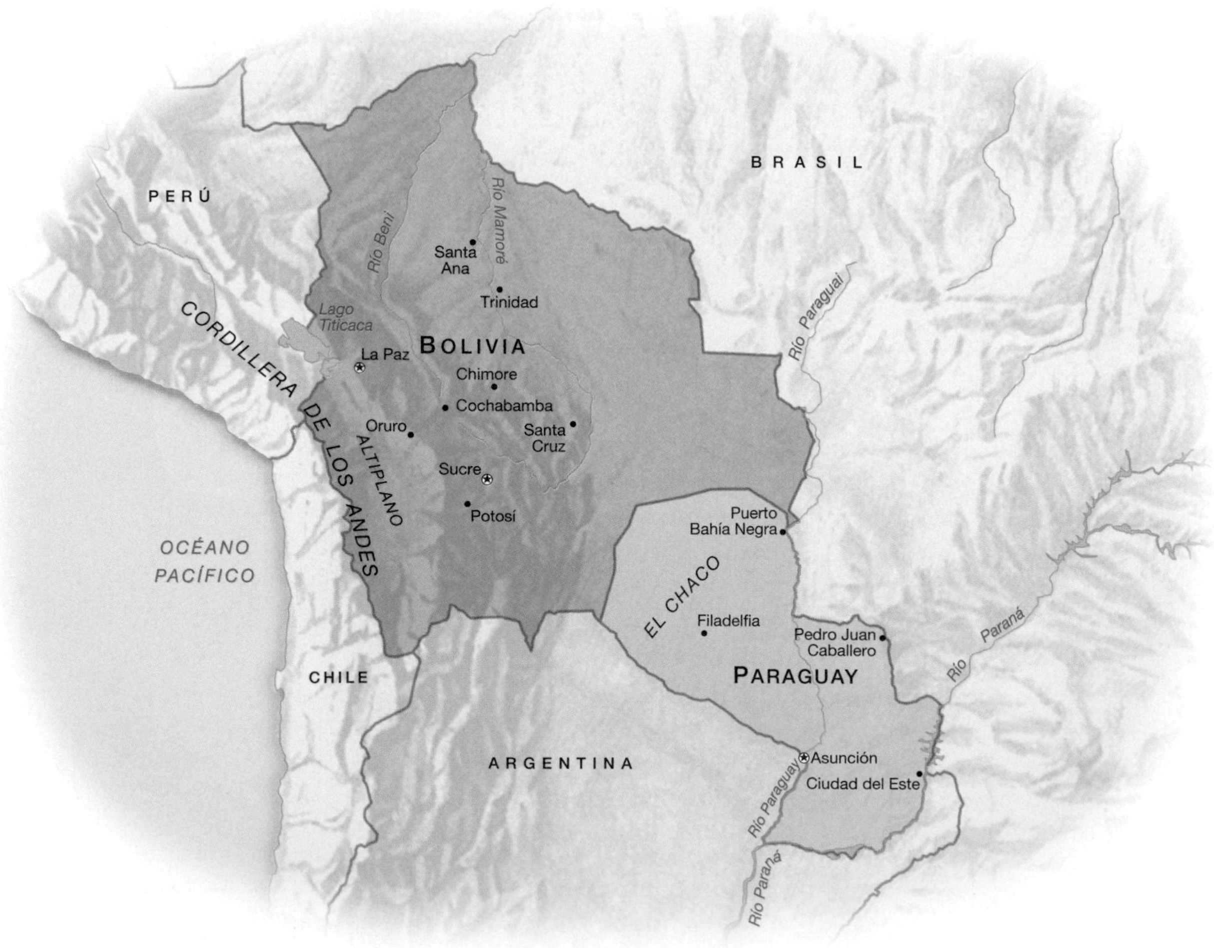

El embalse (*dam*) de Itaipú en el río Paraná proporciona toda la electricidad que necesita el Paraguay y el 25% de la electricidad que usa el Brasil. La construcción del embalse les costó más de 20 mil millones de dólares a los dos países.

Durante los siglos XVII y XVIII, los jesuitas españoles construyeron una cadena de misiones en el Paraguay para educar y cristianizar a los indígenas. La Santísima Trinidad de Paraná se considera "la más grande y la mejor de todas las misiones". Ahora es parte del patrimonio mundial de las Naciones Unidas.

Bolivia tiene ricos depósitos de estaño (*tin*), plata, cinc y cobre (*copper*). Desgraciadamente, la vida de los mineros es sumamente dura.

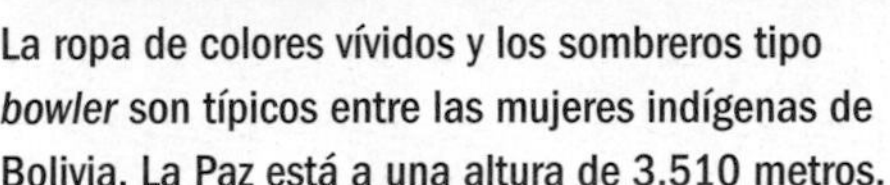

La ropa de colores vívidos y los sombreros tipo *bowler* son típicos entre las mujeres indígenas de Bolivia. La Paz está a una altura de 3.510 metros.

La cría de ganado es importante para la gente que vive en el altiplano (*high plateau*) de Bolivia.

La quena es un instrumento importante para la música andina.

10-38 ¿Cierto o falso? Indica si las siguientes oraciones son ciertas o falsas. Corrige las oraciones falsas.

1. La presa de Itaipú está en el río Amazonas.
2. La extracción de minerales es importante en el Paraguay.
3. El clima del altiplano de Bolivia es bastante templado (*temperate*).
4. Los jesuitas españoles exploraron y construyeron misiones por muchas partes del Paraguay.
5. La *quena* es un instrumento musical típico de los Andes.
6. El embalse de Itaipú le proporciona electricidad al Paraguay.
7. El *bowler* es un sombrero típico de los paraguayos.
8. La vida de los mineros bolivianos es alegre.

WWW

10-39 Más sobre Bolivia y el Paraguay. Conéctate con la página web de **¡Arriba!** para ver más imágenes de Bolivia y el Paraguay. Escribe un párrafo para describir uno de los lugares. Incluye esta información.

- el lugar
- la escena (montañas, planos, agua, etcétera)
- la gente (si la hay)
- el clima

10-40 Guía turística. Prepara un folleto turístico para Bolivia o el Paraguay. Incluye sitios de interés, clima, cambio de moneda, costo de viaje, etcétera.

Ritmos

10-56

"Sol de primavera" (Inkuyo, Bolivia)

Esta canción es representativa del ritmo *taquirari,* que se originó en el oriente de Bolivia y es el resultado de la mezcla de las culturas y tradiciones musicales indígenas y españolas. En las festividades, las mujeres llevan vestidos con colores brillantes y se adornan la cabeza con flores para bailar este tipo de música.

Antes de escuchar

10-41 Preferencias musicales. Aunque muchas canciones de *taquirari* tratan del tema del amor, "Sol de primavera" es una canción instrumental que no tiene letra. En parejas hagan y contesten las siguientes preguntas.

1. ¿Qué estilos de música típicamente no tienen letra y son instrumentales?
2. ¿Cómo se llaman tus grupos y artistas musicales favoritos?
3. ¿Qué prefieres, música con letra o música instrumental?
4. ¿En qué ocasiones te gusta escuchar música con letra? ¿Y música instrumental? ¿Por qué?

A escuchar

10-42 Asociación libre. Ahora escucha la canción. ¿En qué piensas o qué te hace sentir "Sol de primavera"? Escribe por lo menos cinco palabras o expresiones en español que se te ocurren mientras escuchas la canción. Después compara tu lista con las de tus compañeros/as.

Después de escuchar

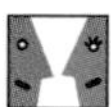

10-43 Sentimientos. Léele a un/a compañero/a de clase lo que escribiste en la actividad **10-42.** Luego intercambia tu trabajo con él/ella y escribe oraciones completas, usando el presente de subjuntivo para responder a lo que escribió. Puedes usar los verbos de la lista y otros verbos para empezar tus oraciones. Luego, comparte tus sugerencias y reacciones con tu compañero/a.

esperar dudar tal vez ojalá alegrarse de sorprenderse no creer

Modelo: E1: *Tal vez la música instrumental no* **sea** *interesante para ti.*
E2: *No creo que la canción te* **haga** *pensar en la comida.*

10-44 Terapia musical. Se dice que la música nos afecta emocionalmente y que puede funcionar como terapia para las personas que padecen de una enfermedad o de un problema emocional o físico. En tu opinión, ¿qué tipos de música pueden ayudar a las siguientes personas? Responde a sus problemas, usando el presente de subjuntivo.

Modelo: E1: *Me duele la cabeza.*
E2: *No creo que la música rock te* **ayude** *a sentirte mejor.*

1. Me duelen los músculos porque caminé mucho ayer.
2. Mis abuelos tienen la presión alta.
3. Mi madre tiene mucha tensión y estrés por su trabajo.
4. Quiero dejar de fumar, pero es difícil.

Páginas

10-57

"El ñandutí" (Leyenda paraguaya)

Antes de leer

La tela de la araña es a la vez artística y funcional.

10-45 ¿Qué es una leyenda? Lee la introducción a continuación e indica si las siguientes afirmaciones son ciertas o falsas. Corrige las falsas.

Las leyendas como tradición oral son populares en todo el mundo hispano. Sirven para transmitir la historia, la cultura y los valores de una generación a la siguiente. Aunque la leyenda se basa en un evento histórico, se hace propiedad de la persona que la cuenta. Por eso, existen muchas versiones de la misma leyenda, y puede transformarse a través de los años hasta que haya poca relación entre la original y la actual. Lo mismo pasa con leyendas que tú conoces, por ejemplo, la de Pocahontas o la de Davy Crockett. A continuación tienes una leyenda paraguaya que se originó durante la colonia española. Representa una mezcla (*blending*) de la cultura indígena y la española. Explica el origen del encaje (*lace*) especial llamado *ñandutí*, una palabra guaraní. Esta versión la cuenta Aitor Bikandi-Mejías, un joven español.

1. Una leyenda tiene base histórica.
2. "Pocahontas" es un ejemplo de una leyenda canadiense.
3. Las leyendas no tienen valor (*value*) cultural.
4. La leyenda de "El ñandutí" se originó durante la época de los incas en Bolivia.

10-46 Anticipa. Ahora, escribe tres preguntas que quieres contestar con relación con esta leyenda.

Modelo: *¿Quiénes son los personajes?*

A leer

10-47 La leyenda. Lee ahora la siguiente leyenda hispana. A ver si puedes contestar las preguntas que escribiste en la actividad **10-46.**

"El ñandutí"

Antes de partir para América —en la época de la colonia—, Manuela, la esposa de un joven oficial del ejército español destinado al Paraguay, fue a decir adiós a su madre. El encuentro fue muy doloroso (*painful*), pues no sabían cuándo iban a verse en vida. Entre las muchas cosas que la madre le dio en aquella ocasión para su nuevo hogar (casa), había una de especial belleza: una mantilla de un encaje (*lace*) exquisito.

—Cuídala (*Take care of it*), porque es mi regalo para ti —le dijo su madre abrazándola—. Si así lo haces, vas a tener abundantes años de felicidad y prosperidad.

Manuela prometió cuidar de la mantilla, besó a su madre y se despidió de ella, tal vez para siempre. Ella y su marido abandonaron (salieron de) España al día siguiente.

Una vez en América, la joven pareja se estableció en el pueblecito de Itaguá. Vivían en una casa grande en el centro del pueblo. Poco después, empezó a vivir con ellos una muchacha guaraní, Ibotí. Ibotí ayudaba a Manuela con las tareas de la casa. Pronto nació entre ellas una amistad sincera y un cariño profundo. Se sentaban las dos en el patio por la tarde y Manuela le confesaba a Ibotí sus recuerdos de su casa en España. Le hablaba a Ibotí de su patria y de su madre. ¡Qué gran consuelo (*consolation*) era para ella poder hablarle a Ibotí!

En cierta ocasión, el marido de Manuela tuvo que irse del hogar, con motivo de una expedición militar. La casa ahora parecía más grande y vacía (sin gente). Como no tenía mucho que hacer, un día Manuela decidió revisar (inspeccionar) todo lo que había traído (*had brought*) de España. Ibotí participaba en esta labor. Muchas cosas hermosas salieron a la luz: tejidos (*weavings*), vestidos, manteles, cubiertos, candelabros, joyas. Entre tantos objetos bellos, el recuerdo más íntimo, era la mantilla de su mamá.

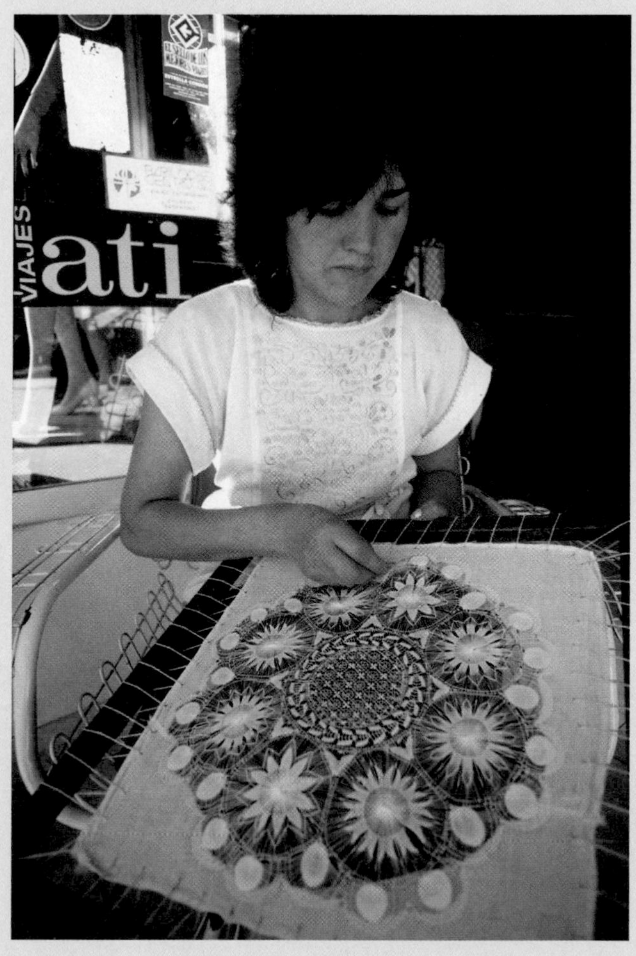

Sin embargo, por el tiempo la mantilla estaba amarilla y un poco gastada (*worn*). Manuela le pidió a Ibotí que la lavara con agua y jabón, recomendándole que fuera muy cuidadosa. La muchacha la lavó cuidadosamente; sin embargo, al sacarla del agua, vio que la mantilla estaba completamente deshecha (*unraveled*). Cuando Manuela supo lo ocurrido, sintió que una parte de su memoria se había perdido (*had been lost*) y lloró con angustia. Esa noche soñó que su mamá estaba muerta. Pasaron muchos días en que tampoco recibió noticias de su esposo. Ibotí trataba de animar (*to comfort*) a su señora. Era imposible.

Una noche, Ibotí soñó con el encaje de la mantilla. Se despertó agitada. —¡Voy a tejer (*weave*) una mantilla igual que la de la señora!—, se dijo esperanzada (*full of hope*).

Empezando esa misma noche, Ibotí se dedicó a tejer una nueva mantilla. Pero cada mañana estaba desilusionada. Nada de lo que hacía era como la mantilla original. Y Manuela estaba más y más triste, más y más enferma.

Una noche de hermosa luna, Ibotí salió al patio a calmar su pena (*sorrow*). Ya no sabía qué hacer. De pronto, por la luz de la luna vio la tela que una arañita (*small spider*) hacía. El corazón de la buena Ibotí palpitó violentamente. ¡Las líneas que aquella araña dibujaba eran como las de la mantilla de Manuela! Durante las siguientes semanas, todas las tardes Ibotí salía al patio y observaba la tela de la araña (*spider's web*). Tan pronto como llegaba la noche, corría a su habitación y se ponía a tejer la mantilla. Tejía y tejía, y no conocía el cansancio (*fatigue*). Por fin, una madrugada, poco antes del alba (*daybreak*), el trabajo estuvo completo.

Aquella mañana, cuando despertó Manuela, vio ante sus ojos una mantilla prácticamente idéntica a la que se había perdido. Creía estar soñando.

—¡Ibotí!, ¿qué es esto? —preguntó asombrada—. ¿De dónde ha salido esta mantilla?

—Es "ñandutí", tela de araña. La tejí yo misma —contestó Ibotí sonriendo.

Manuela recuperó gran parte de su alegría. Se sentía casi feliz. Y aquella misma tarde su felicidad fue completa, pues tuvo noticias de su querido esposo: estaba bien y pronto vendría a casa.

Ibotí, por su parte, encontró su camino. Siguió tejiendo y fabricó otras muchas mantillas maravillosas. También enseñó a hacerlas a las jóvenes guaraníes del lugar. Desde entonces, el pueblo de Itaguá es conocido por sus bellos tejidos de ñandutí, o "tela de araña".

Después de leer

10-48 ¿Quién lo habrá dicho? (*Who might have said...?*) Después de leer la narración, indica quién habrá dicho cada oración.

M: Manuela **MA:** la mamá **I:** Ibotí **E:** el esposo

1. _____ No quiero irme de España, pero tengo que seguir a mi esposo.
2. _____ No se preocupe, señora, yo le lavo la mantilla.
3. _____ Aquí tienes una bella mantilla que te va a traer buena suerte.
4. _____ Tengo que irme del pueblo por algunos días pero voy a volver pronto.
5. _____ ¡Espero que vuelvas pronto a España!
6. _____ La mantilla me hace pensar en mi familia.
7. _____ Voy a tejer como la araña.
8. _____ Aquí tienes tu nueva casa. Ibotí va a ser tu compañera cuando no esté contigo.

10-49 ¿En qué orden? Pon las oraciones en el orden cronológico de la leyenda. Luego, termina la historia.

_____ Le dijo: "Guárdala bien y siempre serás feliz".

_____ Se hizo amiga de Ibotí, una joven guaraní que vivía en su casa.

_____ Antes de irse de su casa, su mamá le dio una bella mantilla de encaje.

_____ Una joven señorita vivía en España durante la época de la colonia.

_____ En su nueva casa, Manuela se sentía muy sola.

_____ Manuela e Ibotí decidieron lavar la mantilla que había traído (*had brought*) Manuela de España.

_____ Se casó con un joven militar, quien la iba a llevar a las Américas.

_____ Un día su esposo se fue en una expedición militar.

A ver si ahora puedes terminar la historia...

10-50 Valores. Las leyendas transmiten los valores de una sociedad. ¿Cuáles de éstos figuran en esta leyenda? Explica por qué.

1. la amistad
2. el amor
3. la diligencia (*industriousness*)
4. la fidelidad

10-51 Entrevista. Divídanse en dos grupos. Un grupo representa a Manuela y el otro representa a Ibotí. Preparen preguntas para entrevistar al otro grupo, luego entrevístense.

MODELO: GRUPO 1: *Manuela, ¿por qué fue usted al Paraguay?*
GRUPO 2: *Fui porque mi esposo consiguió un puesto en el Paraguay.*
GRUPO 2: *Ibotí, ¿por qué quieres tejer una mantilla nueva?*
GRUPO 1: *Porque siento que la señora Manuela esté triste.*

Taller

10-58 to 10-59

10-52 Un artículo sobre la salud. En la prensa popular es común encontrar artículos que dan consejos sobre la salud. En este taller vas a escribir un artículo al estilo de esta prensa.

MODELO: ***Las enfermedades respiratorias***

Se dice que en el mundo más de 300.000.000 personas sufren de alguna enfermedad respiratoria como el asma. Para muchas de ellas, la causa es genética. Para otras, es ambiental, o una combinación de los dos factores. ¿Qué se puede hacer si se sufre de una enfermedad respiratoria?

Antes de escribir

- **Ideas.** Piensa en un problema o en una condición que quieres tratar, por ejemplo, la falta de ejercicio, el sobrepeso, los efectos del sol en la piel (*skin*), etcétera.

A escribir

- **El problema.** Escribe un párrafo en que expliques el problema. Indica a cuánta gente afecta y por qué es importante hacer algo para solucionarlo.
- **Estrategias.** Haz una lista de tres a cinco estrategias o consejos que ayuden al lector/a la lectora a seguir tus consejos.
- **Conclusión.** Concluye el artículo de una manera positiva, explicando cómo el lector/la lectora va a sentirse mejor si sigue tus consejos.
- **Ilustrar.** Agrega alguna foto o algún dibujo que ilustre el problema.

Después de escribir

- **Revisar.** Revisa tu artículo para verificar los siguientes puntos.
  - ☐ los diferentes usos del subjuntivo
  - ☐ el uso de mandatos en la forma de nosotros
  - ☐ la ortografía y la concordancia
- **Intercambiar**
  Intercambia tu artículo con el de un/a compañero/a para hacer correcciones y sugerencias, y para comentar sobre el contenido.
- **Entregar**
  Pasa tu artículo a limpio, incorporando las sugerencias de tu compañero/a. Después entrégaselo a tu profesor/a.

Vocabulario

Primera parte

Las partes del cuerpo humano	*Parts of the human body*
la boca	*mouth*
el brazo	*arm*
la cabeza	*head*
el corazón	*heart*
el dedo	*finger*
el diente	*tooth*
los dientes	*teeth*
la espalda	*back*
el estómago	*stomach*
la garganta	*throat*
la lengua	*tongue*
la mano	*hand*
la nariz	*nose*
el oído	*inner ear*
la oreja	*outer ear*
el pecho	*chest*
el pie	*foot*
la pierna	*leg*
los pulmones	*lungs*
la rodilla	*knee*

Problemas de salud	*Health problems*
doler (ue)	*to hurt*
lastimarse	*to hurt oneself*
romperse (un hueso)	*to break (a bone)*
tener (ie) alergia(s) a	*to be allergic to*
tener (ie) (una) fiebre	*to have a fever*
... (un) dolor de cabeza	*... a headache*
... (la) gripe	*... the flu*
... (una) infección	*... an infection*
... (un) resfriado	*... a cold*
... (una) tos	*... a cough*
torcer (ue)	*to twist*
toser	*to cough*

Sugerencias y remedios médicos	*Medical advice and remedies*
dejar de fumar	*to quit smoking cigarettes*
guardar cama	*to stay in bed*
hacer una cita	*to make an appointment*
mejorarse	*to get better; to get well*
operar	*to operate*
recetar	*to prescribe*
respirar	*to breathe*
tomarse la presión	*to take one's blood pressure*
... la temperatura	*... temperature*

Medicinas comunes	*Common medicines*
el antiácido	*antacid*
el antibiótico	*antibiotic*
la aspirina	*aspirin*
el calmante	*tranquilizer*
el jarabe	*cough syrup*
la pastilla	*pill; lozenge*

En el consultorio del médico	*At the doctor's office*
el diagnóstico	*diagnosis*
el dolor	*pain; ache*
la enfermedad	*illness*
el examen físico	*checkup*
la inyección	*shot*
el/la paciente	*patient*
la radiografía	*X-ray*
el síntoma	*symptom*

Segunda parte

Los alimentos	*Foods*
las bebidas alcohólicas	*alcoholic beverages*
los carbohidratos	*carbohydrates*
el colesterol	*cholesterol*
las grasas	*fats*
los productos lácteos	*dairy products*
las proteínas	*proteins*

Las enfermedades y el bienestar	*Illnesses and well-being*
la diabetes	*diabetes*
los ejercicios aeróbicos	*aerobics*
el estrés	*stress*
el peso	*weight*
el sobrepeso	*excess weight; obesity*

Tu línea y tu salud	*Your weight and your health*
adelgazar; bajar de peso	*to lose weight*
cuidar(se)	*to take care (of oneself)*
estar a dieta	*to be on a diet*
guardar la línea	*to stay trim; to watch one's figure*
hacer jogging/footing	*to jog*
mantenerse (ie) en forma	*to stay in shape*
padecer (zc) (de)	*to suffer (from)*
ponerse en forma	*to get in shape*
sublr de peso	*to gain weight*

11 ¿Para qué profesión te preparas?

Objetivos comunicativos

Primera parte

¡Así lo decimos! Vocabulario Los oficios y las profesiones

¡Así lo hacemos! Estructuras The subjunctive with impersonal expressions

Comparaciones Los empleos y las relaciones personales

- Describing professions and occupations using work-related terms
- Talking about the advantages of different professions
- Persuading others and expressing your opinion

Segunda parte

¡Así lo decimos! Vocabulario La búsqueda de empleo

¡Así lo hacemos! Estructuras Formal commands

The subjunctive and the indicative with adverbial conjunctions

Observaciones ¡Pura vida! Episodio 11

- Reading the want ads
- Writing a brief business letter
- Interviewing for a job
- Giving and following instructions and commands

Nuestro mundo

Panoramas El virreinato de la Plata: la Argentina y el Uruguay

Ritmos "Todo cambia" (Mercedes Sosa, Argentina)

Páginas "No hay que complicar la felicidad" (Marco Denevi, Argentina)

Taller Un *currículum vitae* y una carta de presentación para solicitar trabajo

Las cataratas de Iguazú son cuatro veces más grandes que las del Niágara. Sus 275 cascadas son el resultado de una erupción volcánica. Ahora las cataratas son parte del patrimonio de la humanidad de la UNESCO.

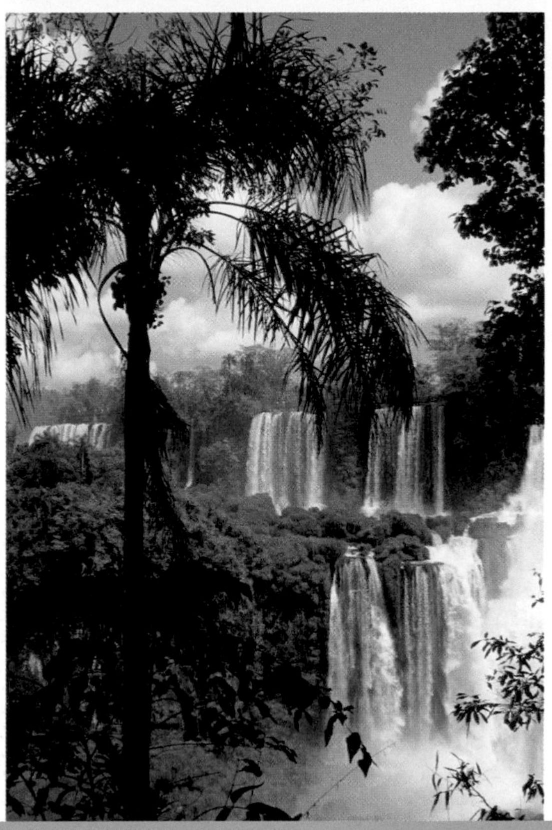

El virreinato de la Plata: la Argentina y el Uruguay

«El trabajo no deshonra, dignifica.»*

*__Refrán:__ Work doesn't bring you dishonor, but dignity.

Source: © Sophie Bassouls/CORBIS Sygma.

Jorge Luis Borges (1899–1986), escritor y poeta argentino, fue perenne candidato al Premio Nobel de Literatura.

¡Así lo decimos! Vocabulario

CD 3, Track 1

11-1 to 11-2

¡Así es la vida! El mundo del trabajo

En el barrio de La Recoleta, en la ciudad de Buenos Aires, hay muchos negocios. En el edificio Gardel, todos están ya en sus trabajos. María, la dentista, tiene muchos pacientes hoy y Angelita, la peluquera, ya empezó a trabajar con su primera cliente. En este edificio se vende un local, el que dos personas, un ingeniero industrial y una psicóloga quieren comprar para abrir aquí su negocio.

¡Qué edificio tan ocupado!

Rafael Betancourt Rosas
Ingeniero industrial

Edificio Díaz de Solís, Gral. Rivera 32
Montevideo, Uruguay
Teléfono 283-1520
Fax 283-9831

Dra. Mercedes Fernández de Robles

Psicóloga clínica
Hospital del Instituto Nacional de la Salud
Paseo de la Reforma 345
México, Distrito Federal
Teléfonos 367-78-12
367-54-34

Los oficios y las profesiones

CD 3, Track 2

11-3 to 11-7

la bombera

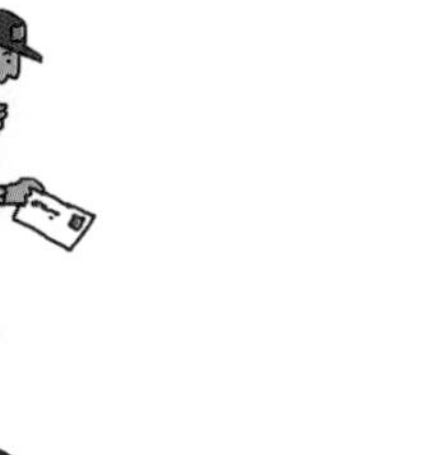
el cartero

el cocinero

la dentista

la electricista

el enfermero

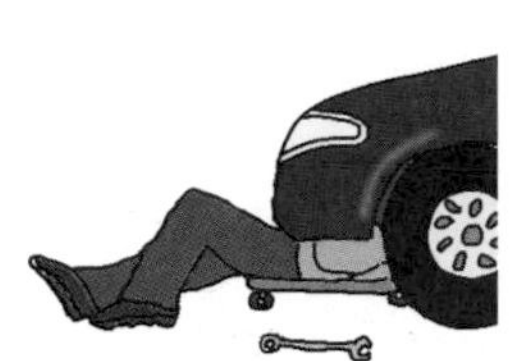
el mecánico

la peluquera

Más oficios y profesiones	*More occupations and professions*
el/la analista de sistemas	*systems analyst*
el/la arquitecto/a	*arquitect*
el/la carpintero/a	*carpenter*
el/la contador/a[1]	*accountant*
el/la ingeniero/a	*engineer*
el/la intérprete	*interpreter*
el/la periodista	*journalist*
el/la plomero/a[2]	*plumber*
el/la psicólogo/a	*psychologist*
el/la secretario/a	*secretary*
el/la veterinario/a	*veterinarian*
el/la viajante	*traveling salesperson*

Términos y expresiones de trabajo	*Work-related terms and expressions*
las calificaciones	*qualifications*
el desempleo	*unemployment*
el entrenamiento	*training*
la formación	*education*
el horario de trabajo	*work schedule*
la meta	*goal*
el puesto	*position (job)*
las responsabilidades	*responsibilities*
el salario/el sueldo	*salary; wages*

Cargos	*Positions*
el/la coordinador/a	*coordinator*
el/la empleado/a	*employee*
el/la gerente	*manager*
el/la jefe/a	*boss*
el/la supervisor/a	*supervisor*

¡Manos a la obra!	*Let's get to work!*
apagar (fuegos/incendios)	*to put out; extinguish (fires)*
curar	*to cure*
diseñar	*to design*
estar en paro (sin trabajo)	*to be out of work*
reparar	*to repair*
repartir	*to deliver; to distribute*
trabajar a comisión	*to work on commission*

[1]**el/la contable** en España

[2]**el/la fontanero/a** en España

Aplicación

11-1 ¿A quién llamas? ¿A qué profesionales llamas en cada una de las siguientes situaciones? Empareja las descripciones con la profesión u oficio. Luego, explica tu selección.

Modelo: Tienes el pelo muy largo y necesitas un corte nuevo.
Llamo a mi peluquera. Siempre voy a "Supercorte" donde no tengo que pagar mucho.

1. ______ No hay agua en el baño.
2. ______ Quieres una entrevista para un artículo en el periódico (*newspaper*).
3. ______ Necesitas resolver algunos problemas emocionales.
4. ______ Tu carro hace un ruido (*noise*) extraño.
5. ______ Tu perro está enfermo.
6. ______ Quieres hacer unos muebles nuevos para tu casa.
7. ______ Es hora de preparar los formularios para pagar los impuestos *(taxes).*
8. ______ Quieres diseñar una casa nueva.
9. ______ No hay luz en tu sala.
10. ______ No recibiste ninguna carta ni ningún otro correo (*mail*) esta semana.

a. carpintero/a
b. plomero/a
c. cartero/a
d. periodista
e. psicólogo/a
f. contador/a
g. arquitecto/a
h. veterinario/a
i. electricista
j. mecánico/a

11-2 ¿Qué es lo que hace? Identifica la profesión u oficio que corresponde a cada persona a continuación. Luego explica algunas de sus responsabilidades y características.

Modelo:

Pilar

Pilar es bombera. En su trabajo, apaga incendios. Su trabajo es difícil y emocionante.

1. 

Don Lucas

2. 

el señor Castillo

3. 

Rafael

4. 

Doña Maruja

5. 

la doctora Fernández

11-3 Un aviso clasificado para el periódico. Contesta las preguntas a continuación, basándote en los siguientes avisos.

1. ¿Cuál/es de estos avisos tiene/n puestos para hombres y mujeres?
2. ¿Qué empresa necesita una persona que sepa cocinar?
3. ¿Cuál/es paga/n salario y comisión?
4. ¿Cuál/es paga/n los gastos de viaje?
5. ¿Cuál/es puesto/s está/están en el Uruguay?

CASALINDA

EMPRESA DE ÁMBITO NACIONAL QUE FABRICA CASAS MODULARES PRECISA PARA SU DELEGACIÓN EN MONTEVIDEO

ARQUITECTO TÉCNICO

- Con experiencia mínima de un año para incorporarse a empresa líder en el sector.
- Responsabilidades: realizar proyectos de producto, nuevos diseños de casas y promoción de productos.
- Cualidades necesarias: iniciativa, facilidad de trabajo con la gente, facilidad para convencer, capacidad de trabajo y espíritu competitivo.
- Salario mínimo inicial 52.000 pesos uruguayos al mes.
- Gastos de kilometraje y comida.

Interesados enviar C.V., con carta de presentación escrita a mano y fotografía reciente, al apartado de Correos 20-037, Montevideo.

Se necesita cocinero y ayudante para restaurante argentino. Preguntar por Julia. Tardes. (4153 2112)

LA TIENDA DE COCINAS Y BAÑOS

necesita

VENDEDORES

–ambos sexos–

SE REQUIERE:

- Experiencia en venta de servicios.
- Capacidad de trabajo y ganas de superación.

SE OFRECE:

- Integración en la primera empresa del sector.
- Incorporación inmediata.
- Ingresos superiores a 13.000 pesos argentinos, entre sueldo fijo y comisiones.

Para entrevista personal, llamar al teléfono **4978 0875.**

11-4 Más preguntas. Túrnense para retarse (*challenge each other*) con más preguntas basadas en los avisos de la actividad **11-3.**

CD 3, Track 3

11-5 Las profesiones y los oficios. Escucha a las siguientes personas e indica la profesión u oficio que le interesa a cada una.

MODELO: Soy bilingüe. Me gusta trabajar en la computadora y contestar el teléfono.
secretario/a

a. analista de sistemas	c. cocinero/a	e. dentista	g. peluquero/a
b. arquitecto/a	d. contador/a	f. mecánico/a	h. periodista

1. ________
2. ________
3. ________
4. ________
5. ________
6. ________
7. ________
8. ________

11-6 ¿En qué orden? Pongan individualmente las siguientes cosas en orden de importancia. Luego comparen la lista. Cuando no estén de acuerdo, explíquense su punto de vista.

MODELO: E1: *Quiero un trabajo que sea interesante porque no quiero estar aburrido/a.*
E2: *Bueno, para mí el sueldo es lo más importante. Si gano suficiente, me divierto cuando no estoy trabajando.*

_____ un trabajo interesante	_____ la oportunidad de aprender más
_____ el sueldo	_____ las responsabilidades
_____ la seguridad	_____ los compañeros
_____ el/la jefe/a	_____ el horario de trabajo
_____ el seguro médico	_____ el número de días de vacaciones
_____ la independencia en el trabajo	_____ trabajar a comisión
_____ trabajar a sueldo fijo *(fixed)*	_____ el número de empleados

11-7 Ahora eres el/la jefe/a de personal. Escribe un aviso clasificado para el periódico para anunciar un puesto en tu compañía. Luego, muéstraselo a un/a compañero/a para ver si quiere solicitar el trabajo y por qué.

11-8 En la oficina de empleos. Imagínense que uno/a de ustedes es consejero/a en una oficina de empleos. El/La otro/a es un/a cliente/a que busca trabajo. Representen una escena en que incluyan la información a continuación.

MODELO: CONSEJERO/A: *¿Qué tipo de trabajo le interesa?*
CLIENTE/A: *Soy cocinero/a. Me interesa trabajar en un restaurante italiano.*
CONSEJERO/A: *¿Por qué?*
CLIENTE/A: *Porque me encanta la comida italiana y sé preparar salsas muy buenas.*

1. su nombre, sus estudios, sus intereses
2. si tiene trabajo ahora
3. el sueldo que busca
4. si quiere trabajar a comisión
5. el horario de trabajo que prefiere
6. si tiene carro

¡Así lo hacemos! Estructuras

1. The subjunctive with impersonal expressions

11-8 to 11-15

- The subjunctive is used in noun clauses after impersonal expressions of necessity, doubt, frequency, probability, denial, opinion, pity, and uncertainty when the dependent clause has an expressed subject.

Es bueno	*It's good*	**Es indispensable**	*It's indispensable*
Es común	*It's common*	**Es (una) lástima**	*It's a pity*
Es difícil	*It's difficult*	**Es malo**	*It's bad*
Es dudoso	*It's doubtful*	**Es mejor**	*It's better*
Es extraño	*It's strange*	**Es necesario**	*It's necessary*
Es fácil	*It's easy*	**Es posible**	*It's possible*
Es importante	*It's important*	**Es preciso**	*It's essential*
Es imposible	*It's impossible*	**Es probable**	*It's probable*
Es increíble	*It's incredible*	**Es urgente**	*It's urgent*

Es importante que ustedes **recomienden** a la aspirante.	*It is important that you recommend the applicant.*
Es imposible que el jefe **ascienda** al secretario.	*It is impossible for the boss to promote the secretary.*

- The indicative is used when the impersonal expression conveys certainty or conviction on the part of the speaker. Some common impersonal expressions of certainty are:

Es verdad	*It's true*	**Es seguro**	*It's certain*
Es cierto	*It's true*	**Es obvio**	*It's obvious*
Es evidente	*It's evident*	**No es dudoso**	*It's not doubtful*

Es verdad que Carlota **es** muy honrada.	*It's true that Carlota is very honest.*
Es evidente que el jefe no **está** aquí.	*It's evident that the boss is not here.*
Es seguro que el electricista **viene** a reparar el problema.	*It's certain that the electrician is coming to repair the problem.*

- Use the infinitive with impersonal expressions when there is no expressed subject in the dependent clause.

Es difícil conseguir trabajo.	*It's hard to get work.*
Es necesario apagar el fuego.	*It's necessary to extinguish the fire.*

Aplicación

11-9 Jorge Luis Borges y el Comité Nobel. Lee el discurso sobre los méritos de este autor argentino y subraya todas las expresiones impersonales. Luego explica por qué se usa el subjuntivo o el indicativo con cada expresión.

Miembros del Comité Nobel:

Estamos aquí hoy para hablar sobre los méritos del gran poeta y cuentista Jorge Luis Borges. Es verdad que es uno de los autores más importantes del mundo. Es cierto que se leen sus obras no sólo en español, sino también en muchos otros idiomas. Pero es dudoso que él reciba el honor de este comité que tanto merece. ¿Por qué año tras año ignoramos a esta figura? Es posible que haya otros autores este año que debemos considerar. Es fácil decir que podemos esperar otro año para premiar a Borges. Pero es preciso que lo honremos antes de su muerte. Por eso, colegas, insisto en que lo consideremos seriamente este año. No queremos esperar más. Su salud no es buena. Les repito que es urgente que este año reciba el Premio Nobel. Gracias por su atención.

11-10 Más sobre Jorge Luis Borges. Además de ser autor, Borges era bibliotecario. Su pasión eran los libros. Desafortunadamente, cuando ya era mayor, se quedó ciego (*blind*). Completa estas frases para expresar tu opinión sobre su condición.

Modelo: *Es probable que Borges necesite mucha ayuda.*

1. Es una lástima...
2. Es cierto...
3. Es necesario...
4. Es posible...

11-11 En el despacho *(office)* de la directora de personal. Completa la siguiente conversación con la forma correcta del subjuntivo o indicativo de los verbos de la lista.

completar	contratar	hablar	saber	volver
conocer	dar	ir	tener	

Ligia Gómez: Buenos días. Soy Ligia Gómez y vengo a solicitar el puesto de analista de sistemas.

Sra. Méndez: Mucho gusto. Soy la señora Méndez, la directora de personal. Bueno, es importante que usted (1) ______ esta solicitud de empleo. ¿Es verdad que usted (2) ______ experiencia de trabajo con computadoras?

Ligia Gómez: Sí, usted va a notar en mi *currículum vitae* que es evidente que (3) ______ mucho de informática. Tengo cuatro años de estudios universitarios y cuatro más en un banco internacional. Es posible que usted (4) ______ a mi antiguo jefe, el señor Martínez.

Sra. Méndez: Sí, lo conozco bien. Es importante que yo (5) ______ con él sobre sus calificaciones. Es mejor que usted (6) ______ mañana. Es probable que nosotros la (7) ______.

Ligia Gómez: Es magnífico que ustedes me (8) ______ una oportunidad en su empresa. ¡Muchísimas gracias!

Sra. Méndez: ¡No hay de qué! Es seguro que el puesto le (9) ______ a gustar.

11-12 Tu opinión. Túrnense para expresar sus opiniones sobre el mercado de trabajo y sus oportunidades. Usen expresiones impersonales para expresar sus opiniones y respondan de una manera apropiada.

MODELO: E1: *Es importante que yo busque trabajo.*
E2: *Es verdad que tienes que trabajar.*

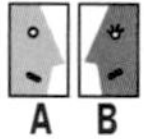

11-13A Consejos. Túrnense para contarse sus problemas y darse consejos, usando expresiones impersonales. Estudiante B, por favor ve al **Apéndice 1,** página A13.

MODELO: un/a amigo/a enojado/a
E1: *Mi amigo/a está enojado/a conmigo.*
E2: *Es indispensable que lo/la llames y que ustedes hablen del problema.*

PROBLEMAS

padres exigentes
una entrevista importante
un/a profesor/a difícil
un carro viejo
un problema con su novio/a o esposo/a
¿...?

CONSEJOS

1. llamar al analista de sistemas
2. cambiar de trabajo
3. estudiar toda la noche
4. pedir un préstamo (*loan*) al banco
5. comprar otro

11-16 to 11-19

¿Cuánto sabes tú? *Can you...*

- ☐ describe different professions and jobs?
- ☐ talk about the advantages of different professions and jobs?
- ☐ persuade others or express an opinion using impersonal expressions such as **Es importante que...** and **Es dudoso que...**?

Comparaciones

Los empleos y las relaciones personales

11-14 En tu experiencia. Contesta las siguientes preguntas dando tu opinión.

1. ¿Tienes un trabajo en este momento?
2. ¿Qué hiciste para conseguirlo?
3. ¿Fue importante para ti conocer a alguien en la empresa para conseguir tu puesto?
4. En tu opinión, ¿son más importantes las relaciones personales que la experiencia en el trabajo?

Las relaciones personales son muchas veces la clave (*key*) para obtener un puesto en los países hispanos. Éste es un factor más importante en el mundo hispano que en los EE.UU. o el Canadá, donde es mucho más frecuente obtener un puesto a través de agencias de empleos o de avisos clasificados.

Para obtener un trabajo, los hispanos típicamente acuden (*turn to*) a sus familiares o a sus amigos íntimos cuando saben que uno de ellos los puede ayudar. Los amigos íntimos o familiares se ayudan porque es parte de la ética (*ethics*) de la familia hispana, y a los amigos íntimos se les considera parte de la familia. Es costumbre que las personas que ocupan puestos importantes ayuden a los jóvenes que están dentro de su círculo de amistades. Una vez que los jóvenes hayan obtenido su puesto y estén establecidos, estos jóvenes van a tener que pagar el favor, haciendo algo similar por otros miembros de la familia.

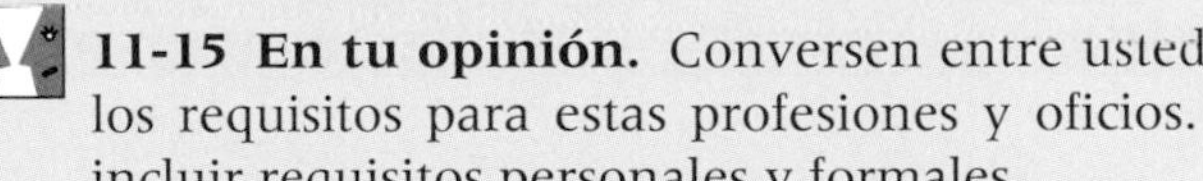

11-15 En tu opinión. Conversen entre ustedes sobre los requisitos para estas profesiones y oficios. Pueden incluir requisitos personales y formales.

Modelo: veterinario

E1: *Para ser veterinario se requieren cuatro años de estudios en ciencias y cuatro años en la Facultad de Medicina Veterinaria.*

E2: *Además, debes querer trabajar con los animales. Y si son animales grandes, como los caballos, tienes que ser bien fuerte.*

1. trabajador/a social
2. pediatra
3. maestro/a
4. ingeniero/a eléctrico/a
5. plomero/a
6. bombero/a
7. analista de sistemas
8. psiquiatra

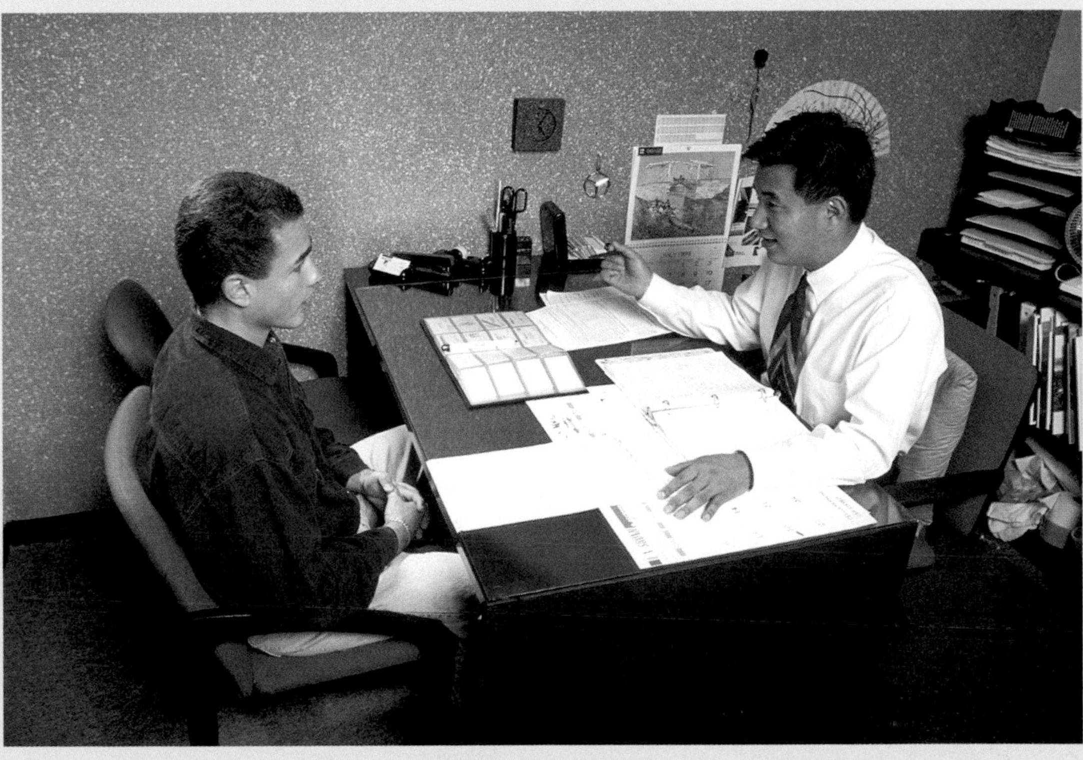

Segunda parte

¡Así lo decimos! Vocabulario

CD 3, Track 4

11-20 to 11-21

¡Así es la vida! En busca de empleo

Sra. Posada: Pase, señor. Siéntese, por favor.

Juan López: Muchas gracias.

Sra. Posada: Acabo de examinar su *currículum vitae*. Para nosotros es bueno que tenga experiencia en contabilidad. Dígame, ¿por qué quiere trabajar en nuestra empresa?

Juan López: Porque es una empresa que realmente se interesa por el bienestar de sus empleados.

Sra. Posada: Muy bien. Me gusta su respuesta. Antes de que se vaya, voy a presentarle al jefe de personal. Si le ofrecemos el puesto, ¿cuándo puede comenzar a trabajar?

La búsqueda de empleo

el aspirante

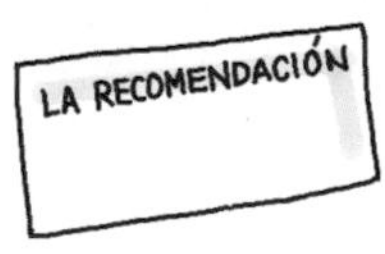

la carta de recomendación

el contrato

la directora

la solicitud de empleo

Más sobre la búsqueda de empleo	*More on job searching*
los anuncios/avisos clasificados	*want ads*
la carta de presentación	*cover letter*
el *currículum vitae*	*resumé*
el despacho	*office*
la empresa	*company; firm*
la entrevista	*interview*
el expediente	*dossier*
el formulario	*form; application*
la vacante	*vacancy*

Los beneficios	*Benefits*
el aumento	*raise*
la bonificación anual	*yearly bonus*
el plan de retiro	*retirement plan*
el seguro médico	*health insurance*

Verbos	*Verbs*
acabar de (+ *infinitive*)	*to have just (done something)*
ascender (ie)	*to promote; to move up*
contratar	*to hire*
dejar	*to quit*
despedir (i, i)	*to fire*
jubilarse/retirarse	*to retire*
rellenar[1]	*to fill completely; to fill out*

Adjetivos	*Adjectives*
capaz	*capable*
entusiasta	*enthusiastic*
honrado/a, honesto/a	*honest*
justo/a	*just; fair*

Una carta comercial	*A business letter*
Saludos	*Salutations; greetings*
Estimado/a señor/a:	*Dear Sir/Madam:*
Despedidas	*Closings*
Atentamente,	*Sincerely yours,*
Cordialmente,	*Cordially yours,*
Lo(s)/La(s) saludo/a atentamente,	*Very truly yours,*

[1]Also: **completar, llenar** *to fill out*

CD 3, Track 6

11-26 to 11-27

LETRAS Y SONIDOS

The consonants "b, v" in Spanish

In Spanish, the letters *b* and *v* sound identical. There is no distinction between them, as there is in English, where *b* involves a tight, bilabial closure between the lips, *v* involves contact between the lower lip and the upper front teeth, and contrasts in meaning exist, e.g., *base* versus *vase*. While *b* and *v* are identical in Spanish, two different sounds correspond to them, depending on the context. After a pause or the letters *m* or *n*, the sound for *b* and *v* is like the *b* in English *base*, where a tight closure between the lips momentarily stops the flow of air out of the mouth.

Hard bilabial: *bús-que-da* *ve-te-ri-na-rio* *bom-be-ro* *con-ven-to*

In all other positions, especially between vowels, the sound for *b* and *v* is softer. There is a loose closure between the lips that allows air to flow through them. English has no sound similar to soft, bilabial *b* and *v* but this sound is approximated when one imitates the steady murmur of a motor boat in the distance.

Soft bilabial: *la-bús-que-da* *el-ve-te-ri-na-rio* *con-ta-ble* *a-vión*

Aplicación

11-16 En busca de empleo. Empareja las siguientes definiciones con la expresión más lógica.

MODELO: Tienes que rellenar este formulario.
la solicitud de empleo

1. ______ Tu último jefe escribió excelentes comentarios.
2. ______ Rellenas tu solicitud de empleo y hablas con el jefe de personal en este lugar.
3. ______ Firmas este documento. Los términos son por un año, pero el documento es renovable (*renewable*).
4. ______ Incluyes los nombres y números de teléfono de personas que te van a recomendar favorablemente.
5. ______ Este beneficio es importante si tienes hijos pequeños.
6. ______ Esta persona necesita buenas calificaciones; debe ser entusiasta y capaz.
7. ______ Después de trabajar bien por unos años en una empresa, tu sueldo cambia.
8. ______ Debes indicar todas las cosas que sabes hacer y que son pertinentes al puesto que buscas.

a. las referencias
b. el seguro médico
c. el contrato
d. la oficina de empleo
e. las calificaciones
f. el aumento
g. la recomendación
h. el/la aspirante

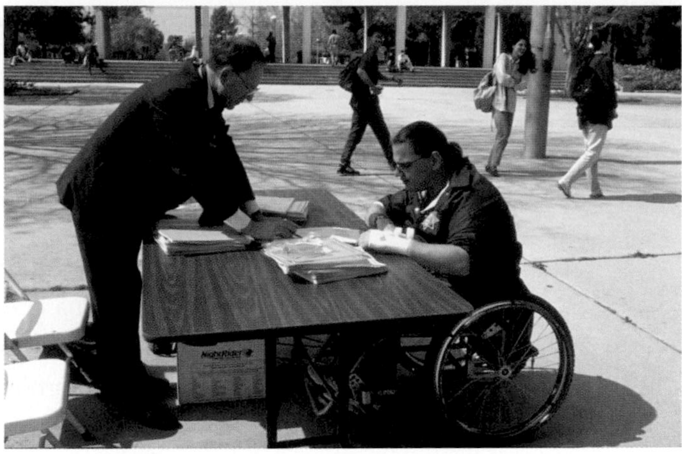

11-17 ¿En qué orden? Indica el orden en que completas estos pasos para conseguir un puesto.

_____ llamar para hacer una cita con el/la jefe de personal
_____ volver a casa y esperar una llamada
_____ leer los avisos clasificados en el periódico
_____ rellenar la solicitud de empleo
_____ ir al despacho de personal
_____ hacer preguntas sobre los beneficios del trabajo
_____ tener la entrevista
_____ contestar las preguntas sobre mi formación y experiencia
_____ vestirme bien
_____ preguntar sobre el sueldo

CD 3, Track 7

11-18 La solicitud de empleo. Imagínate que trabajas en una agencia de empleos y Alejandra es una clienta. Escucha a Alejandra mientras explica su formación y experiencia. Luego completa su solicitud de empleo. ¡Ojo! Alejandra no da toda la información necesaria.

Solicitud de empleo

Fecha: __________ Referido por: __________

Información personal

Apellidos: __________ Nombre: __________

Dirección: __________ Teléfono: __________

Fecha de nacimiento: __________

Empleo deseado

Puesto: __________ Fecha de comienzo: __________

¿Actualmente empleado/a? __________ Sueldo deseado: __________

¿Permiso para ponernos en contacto con jefe actual? __________

Educación

	Nombre de la institución	Lugar
Primaria:		
Secundaria:		
Universidad:		

Idiomas: __________ Otras habilidades: __________

Empleos anteriores

Fechas	Compañía	Puesto	Sueldo	Jefe

Referencias

Nombre	Teléfono

11-19 Una llamada por teléfono. Escriban por lo menos cinco preguntas que les gustaría (*you would like*) hacerle a un/a jefe/a de personal, luego túrnense para hacer y responder las preguntas.

MODELO: *Buenos días. Soy... ¿Tiene usted vacantes en...?*

11-20 ¿A qué empresa deseas solicitar? Conéctate con la página web de **¡Arriba!** para ver una selección de empresas argentinas. Escoge una que te interese y contesta estas preguntas sobre tu selección.

1. ¿Cómo se llama la empresa?
2. ¿Dónde tiene su sede (*head office*)?
3. ¿Qué vende o produce?
4. ¿Por qué te parece interesante?
5. ¿Hay información para solicitar un puesto?

11-21 Una carta de recomendación. Escribe una carta de recomendación para una persona que conoces. Incluye tu relación con la persona, sus cualidades y tu evaluación de su futuro en el trabajo.

MODELO:

9 de agosto de 2007
Vancouver, B.C.

A quién le pueda interesar:

***Asunto:** Eduardo Mazuecos Villar*
El señor Mazuecos es un empleado en esta oficina donde trabaja como asistente del director de personal. Es una persona muy entusiasta y honrada, trabaja bien con los otros empleados y . . .

Atentamente,
Ana María del Val
Supervisora
Editorial Pilar

11-22 Ensayar (*rehearse*) la entrevista. Representen al/a la aspirante y al/a la jefe/a de personal para dramatizar una búsqueda de empleo.

MODELO: E1: *Buenas tardes. Soy... Quiero solicitar el puesto de...*
E2: *Sí, señor/a. ¿Qué experiencia tiene usted?*

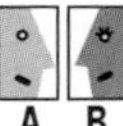

11-23A La despedida. Eres el/la director/a de la sección de finanzas de tu empresa. Encuentras que hay una discrepancia en las cuentas (*accounts*) y sospechas (*suspect*) que uno/a de tus empleados no ha sido (*has been*) honrado/a. Explícale tus sospechas y despídelo/la con dos semanas de sueldo. Estudiante B, por favor ve al **Apéndice 1,** página A13.

LAS CUENTAS DE ABRIL

- COMPRAS: $100.000,00
- VENTAS: $345.000,00
- GASTOS: $200.000,00

¡Así lo hacemos! Estructuras

11-28 to 11-34

2. Formal commands

We use commands to give instructions or to ask people to do things. In Spanish, commands have different forms to distinguish between formal (**usted/ustedes**) and informal (**tú/vosotros**) address. **Formal commands** use subjunctive forms, with the implied meaning that the speaker is trying to influence the listener to do something.

Infinitive	Subjunctive	Formal commands	
		Ud.	**Uds.**
hablar	hable	hable	hablen
pensar	piense	piense	piensen
comer	coma	coma	coman
saber	sepa	sepa	sepan
escribir	escriba	escriba	escriban
ir	vaya	vaya	vayan
pedir	pida	pida	pidan

Hable con su gerente. — *Speak to your manager.*
Despida a ese empleado, Sr. Ruiz. — *Fire that employee, Mr. Ruiz.*
Salgan pronto de la oficina. — *Leave the office soon.*
Piensen antes de hablar. — *Think before speaking.*

- Negative commands are formed by placing **no** in front of the command form.

  No llegue tarde. — *Don't arrive late.*
  No asciendan a todos los empleados. — *Don't promote all of the employees.*

- Subject pronouns may be used with commands for emphasis or clarification. As a rule, they are placed after the verb.

  Piense **usted.** — ***You** think.*
  No griten **ustedes** en el trabajo. — *Don't **you** shout at work.*

- Object pronouns are attached to affirmative commands and precede negative commands. Affirmative commands with pronouns attached require a written accent.

  ¡**Váyase** de aquí! — *Leave here!*
  Tráiganmelo, por favor. — *Bring it to me, please.*
  No se levante, señorita. — *Don't get up, miss.*
  No se lo den al jefe. — *Don't give it to the boss.*

Aplicación

11-24 Un viaje a las cataratas de Iguazú. El año pasado, Daniela visitó las cataratas de Iguazú. Ahora les recomienda a sus padres que también las visiten. Lee sus recomendaciones y subraya todos los mandatos formales.

Papá y mamá, tienen que visitar las cataratas de Iguazú. Vayan primero a Buenos Aires y desde allí tomen un vuelo a Foz Iguazú en el Brasil. Hagan una reserva en el hotel Das Cataratas. Pidan una habitación doble con vista a las cataratas. Si van en invierno (julio-agosto), no se olviden de llevar ropa de abrigo porque hace frío. Y lleven también una sombrilla porque hay mucha bruma (*mist*). En el hotel, coman en el restaurante, que es estupendo. Al día siguiente, hagan una gira en bicicleta. Los guías los van a llevar en minibús a la Argentina. En el parque del lado argentino, alquilen bicicletas y paseen por los bosques tropicales del parque. Vean las cataratas y también la linda flora y la fauna de la región. Admiren, por ejemplo, los tucanes de picos grandes. De regreso al hotel, pasen por el lado paraguayo. Allí tienen una zona franca (*duty-free zone*) donde pueden comprar todo tipo de artículos sin tener que pagar impuestos. Finalmente, saquen muchas fotos y regresen sanos y salvos a casa.

11-25 ¿Qué desea Daniela? Escribe una lista de seis sugerencias que les hace a sus padres. Usa el subjuntivo con verbos de voluntad.

MODELO: *Desea que sus padres vayan primero a Buenos Aires.*

11-26 Prohibido fumar. Es común ver anuncios con mandatos que usan el infinitivo o el "se impersonal" en vez del subjuntivo. Primero, empareja el mandato con el lugar donde aparece; luego, escribe un mandato formal.

MODELO: prohibido fumar
en un teatro: ¡No fume!

1. _____ prohibido estacionar (*to park*)
2. _____ prohibido pisar la hierba (*to step on the grass*)
3. _____ prohibido traer comida o bebida
4. _____ prohibido hablar alto
5. _____ no tocar música después de la medianoche
6. _____ prohibido tomar bebidas alcohólicas
7. _____ prohibido tocar (*to touch*)
8. _____ prohibido entrar después de empezar la función

a. a un restaurante elegante
b. en un museo
c. en un teatro
d. en un parque
e. enfrente de una estación de policía
f. en una casa de apartamentos
g. en un convento
h. en un coche

¿Por qué fue necesario poner este aviso en la puerta de un garaje?

11-27 La carta para Eulalia. Túrnense para responder a la carta que recibió Eulalia. Usen por lo menos tres mandatos formales.

El Salvador, 2 de noviembre de 2007

¡Necesito su ayuda! Acabo de dejar mi puesto como viajante porque no me gusta pasar tanto tiempo en el camino. Tengo título en administración de empresas y dos años de experiencia vendiendo productos para limpiar la casa, como detergentes y jabones. Soy una persona sociable. Me gusta conocer a gente nueva y ayudarla. Pero no sé qué tipo de trabajo buscar. Por favor, Eulalia, aconséjeme sobre lo que debo hacer.

Un saludo cordial de,
—Manolo

11-35 to 11-41

3. The subjunctive and the indicative with adverbial conjunctions

Conjunciones que siempre requieren el subjuntivo

- Certain conjunctions are always followed by the subjunctive when they introduce a dependent clause because they express purpose, intent, condition, or anticipation. The use of these conjunctions presupposes that the action described in the dependent clause is uncertain or has not yet taken place. The following are some of these conjunctions.

a fin de que	*in order that*	**en caso de que**	*in case*
a menos (de) que	*unless*	**para que**	*in order that; so that*
antes (de) que	*before*	**sin que**	*without*
con tal (de) que	*provided (that)*		

Déle la recomendación **para que** la **lea.**	*Give him the recommendation so that he can read it.*
Carmen no va a aceptar el trabajo **a menos que** le **suban** el sueldo.	*Carmen is not going to accept the job unless they raise the salary.*
No me enojo **con tal que** el jefe me **dé** una bonificación.	*I will not get angry provided that the boss gives me a bonus.*
Lleve la evaluación **en caso** que la **necesitemos.**	*Take the evaluation in case we need it.*
Le recomiendo que visite el museo **antes de que** lo **cierren.**	*I recommend that you visit the museum before they close it.*

Conjunciones que siempre requieren el indicativo

- A few conjunctions always use the indicative because they convey that the action in the subordinate clause is within our experience.

ahora que / ya que	*now that*
desde que	*since*
porque	*because*

Srta. Martínez, le ofrezco el trabajo **ahora que** la **necesito.**	*Miss Martínez, I'm offering you the job now that I need you.*
El plan de retiro es más atractivo **desde que incluimos** más incentivos.	*The retirement plan is more attractive since we included more incentives.*
El jefe le dio el trabajo a Pedro **porque** lo **impresionó** mucho.	*The boss gave the job to Pedro because he impressed him a lot.*

Conjunciones que se usan con el subjuntivo y el indicativo

- The subjunctive is used after some conjunctions that introduce time clauses referring to an action that has not yet taken place. Since the action has yet to take place, we cannot speak with certainty about it. The main clause may be in the future tense, the present indicative (with future meaning), or the imperative (direct command).

cuando	*when*	**hasta que**	*until*
después (de) que	*after*	**luego que**	*as soon as*
donde	*where*	**mientras que**	*as long as*
en cuanto	*as soon as*	**tan pronto como**	*as soon as*

José, hable con el gerente **cuando él llegue** a la oficina.	*José, talk to the manager when he arrives at the office.*
Le voy a explicar el plan de retiro **en cuanto llene** la solicitud de empleo.	*I'm going to explain the retirement plan to you as soon as you fill out the job application.*
No puedo hacer nada **mientras que no me den** la respuesta.	*I can't do anything as long as they don't give me the answer.*
No van a hablar con el empleado problemático **hasta que se vaya** su amigo.	*They won't talk to the problematic employee until his friend leaves.*
Cuando la supervisora **se jubile,** se va a sentir mejor.	*When the supervisor retires, she's going to feel better.*

- However, if the action referred to in the time clause is habitual or has already taken place, the present or past indicative is used after these conjunctions because we can speak with certainty about things that have already occurred or that occur regularly.

Ana pregunta por el seguro médico **cuando tiene** una entrevista.	*Ana asks about the medical insurance whenever she has an interview.* (habit)
Isabel pidió un aumento **en cuanto** el jefe le **dio** la oportunidad.	*Isabel asked for a raise as soon as the boss gave her the opportunity.* (past)
Nunca despido a nadie **mientras que se lleva** bien con los otros empleados.	*I never fire anybody as long as he/she gets along with the other employees.* (habit)
Hablaron con la aspirante **hasta que se fue.**	*They talked with the candidate until she left.* (past)
Cuando voy a la agencia de empleo, me atienden enseguida.	*When I go to the employment agency, they assist me right away.* (habit)

- When there is no change in subject, the following prepositions are used with the infinitive: **antes de, después de, para,** and **sin.**

Van a comprar un teléfono móvil **después de hablar con el** dependiente.	*They are going to buy a cellular phone after talking to the clerk.*
No puedes preparar un contrato **sin usar** una computadora.	*You can't prepare a contract without using a computer.*
Trabajo mucho en la empresa **para ascender** rápido.	*I work a lot at the firm in order to move up quickly.*

Aunque

- The conjunction **aunque** (*although, even though, even if*) is followed by the subjunctive when the speaker wishes to convey uncertainty. If the speaker wants to express certainty or refer to a completed event, the indicative is used.

Subjunctive

Aunque haga todo bien, no va a ascender fácilmente.	*Even if she does everything right, she's not going to be promoted easily.* (uncertainty)
Aunque no la **necesites,** compra la impresora.	*Even though you don't need it, buy the printer.* (uncertainty)

Indicative

Aunque hay poco trabajo, no me molesta.	*Although there's little work, it doesn't bother me.* (certainty)
Miraste los avisos clasificados, **aunque tenías** un buen empleo.	*You looked at the classified ads even though you had a good job.* (certainty)

Aplicación

11-28 El gaucho. El gaucho es una figura popular que se asocia con las pampas argentinas y uruguayas. Lee la descripción de su vida diaria y subraya todas las conjunciones subordinadas. Identifica si se usa el subjuntivo, el indicativo o el infinitivo y explica por qué.

Soy Juan Ramón Soldado y soy "gaucho" de profesión. Todos los días, antes de que salga el sol, me levanto, me visto y preparo mi yerba mate. Caliento el agua hasta que está por hervir. Luego la echo en una calabaza (*gourd*) con la yerba mate. Machaco (*I mash*) las hojas (*leaves*) en el agua caliente hasta que está lista. Es una bebida sabrosa y saludable (y además, ¡tiene mucha cafeína!). Después de tomar el mate, le doy agua y heno (*hay*) a Diablo, mi caballo. En la estancia (el rancho) donde trabajo, tenemos cinco mil ovejas (*sheep*) y hoy es el día para llevarlas al mercado. Le pongo la silla a mi caballo y la ajusto para que esté cómodo. Lo monto (*ride*) y me dirijo hacia las pampas donde encuentro las ovejas. Aunque puedo agarrar (*grab*) muchas de ellas, es imposible atraparlas a todas. Pero al final del día, mis compañeros y yo preparamos una parrillada (una barbacoa) y nos acostamos temprano a fin de que al día siguiente podamos levantarnos de nuevo antes del amanecer y volver a nuestro trabajo.

11-29 ¿Cuándo? ¿Qué? ¿Por qué? Vuelve a leer el párrafo sobre el gaucho y contesta las siguientes preguntas.

1. ¿Cuándo se levanta Juan Ramón?
2. ¿Qué hace primero? ¿Qué hace después?
3. ¿Qué necesita para preparar su yerba mate?
4. ¿Por qué le gusta tomar yerba mate?
5. ¿Cuántas ovejas hay en la estancia donde trabaja?
6. ¿Qué hace al final del día?
7. ¿Cuándo se acuesta?

11-30 En la oficina de Mundiplásticos. El director de una compañía que fabrica artículos de plástico espera piratear a algunos ingenieros de una empresa rival. Escoge la conjunción más lógica entre paréntesis.

Hoy es 17 de mayo, y (1. aunque/sin que) no sé cómo voy a hacerlo, mi plan es piratear a cinco ingenieros de la empresa Plásticos, S.A. (2. para que/tan pronto como) pueda. He estudiado todos los documentos (3. para/sin) entender bien su organización. Quiero hablar con todos los empleados (4. en cuanto/a menos que) me lo impidan. Quiero invitarlos a mi fábrica (5. a fin de que/cuando) vean las máquinas modernas. ¡Estoy decidido! Voy a aumentar el número de empleados de mi empresa (6. aunque/cuando) me cueste una fortuna.

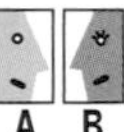
A B

11-31A Dos empresas. Eres el/la directora/a de la empresa Plásticos, S.A. y tu compañero/a es el/la directora/a de la empresa Mundiplásticos. Túrnense para hacer y contestar las siguientes preguntas con la información de tu empresa. Usen el subjuntivo o el indicativo con la lista de conjunciones, según sea necesario. Estudiante B, por favor ve al **Apéndice 1,** página A14.

cuando	tan pronto como	hasta (que)
para (que)	después de (que)	donde

PLÁSTICOS, S.A.

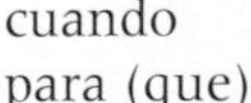

- ORGANIZACIÓN: 200 ingenieros/100 empleados
- EQUIPO: 10 máquinas nuevas
- PUESTOS NUEVOS: 3 ingenieros
- FECHA DE SOLICITUD: 30 de mayo
- DECISIÓN PARA: 1 de julio

PREGUNTAS:

1. ¿Cuándo vas a contratar más empleados?
2. ¿Cuántos empleados vas a contratar?
3. ¿Hasta cuándo vas a aceptar candidatos?
4. ¿Cuándo vas a tomar la decisión?

11-32 En la oficina de empleo. Aquí tienes algunos consejos de la directora de empleo. Complétalos con la forma correcta del verbo entre paréntesis.

1. Te voy a enseñar los avisos clasificados para que (tú: ver) ___________ los nuevos empleos que publicamos hoy.
2. Ayer recibimos avisos nuevos después de que tú (salir) ___________ de la oficina.
3. Voy a obtenerte una entrevista tan pronto como (yo: hablar) ___________ con el jefe de personal.
4. Debes hacer copias de tu *currículum vitae* antes de (ir) ___________ a la entrevista.
5. Vamos a ensayar (*rehearse*) tu entrevista para que (tú: sentirse) ___________ cómodo/a.
6. Aunque te (costar) ___________ más, debes ir a la entrevista en taxi en vez de ir en autobús.
7. Vas a conocer a la supervisora cuando te (ellos: enseñar) ___________ la línea de producción.
8. Vas a tener éxito porque (tener) ___________ buena preparación y mucha experiencia.

11-33 Excusas. Escríbanse un mensaje por correo electrónico en el que se expliquen cuándo van a cumplir sus obligaciones. Usen expresiones como **después de que, tan pronto como, hasta que, en cuanto, mientras que** y **aunque.** Luego, contesten el mensaje que reciban.

Modelo: *Querido Miguel:*
Te prometo que voy a terminar el trabajo para la clase de español en cuanto…

¿Cuánto sabes tú? *Can you…*

11-42 to 11-45

- ☐ get information from the want ads?
- ☐ write a brief business letter?
- ☐ interview for a job?
- ☐ give and follow instructions and commands?
- ☐ recognize when to use the subjunctive or indicative after conjunctions such as **cuando** and **para que**?

Observaciones

Episode 11

1-46 to 11-49

¡Pura vida! Episodio 11

En este episodio David le ofrece trabajo a Patricio.

Antes de ver el video

11-34 El pluriempleo. En Latinoamérica es muy común que la gente tenga más de un empleo. A continuación tienes un aviso que una persona puso en la Red informática para buscar trabajo. Lee el aviso y escríbele una carta para recomendarle el tipo de trabajo que debe buscar. Explica tus razones para darle la recomendación.

Busco pluriempleo

Tengo mucho tiempo libre durante la semana ya que sólo trabajo dos días. Busco pluriempleo en algo serio. Tengo experiencia como ayudante administrativo y ayudante clínico. Ahora, trabajo como operador de comunicaciones. Soy muy hábil con las manos. Tengo licencia de conducir y tengo un carro grande.

MODELO: *Le recomiendo que…*

Busco pluriempleo.

A ver el video

11-35 Las características del trabajo. Mira el episodio número once de *¡Pura vida!* para identificar las características del trabajo que David le ofrece a Patricio.

La oficina de CREFASI

David Ortiz-Smith

Patricio

Características	Sí	No
1. salario mínimo		
2. bonificación anual		
3. oficina con ventana		
4. plan de retiro		
5. seguro médico		
6. una beca universitaria		
7. un mes de vacaciones al año		
8. secretaria		
9. supervisión de cinco empleados		
10. camioneta		

Después de ver el video

WWW

11-36 Busco empleo. Conéctate con la página web de **¡Arriba!** para ver avisos clasificados. Escoge uno y escribe por lo menos cinco razones por las que te interesa el trabajo.

NUESTRO MUNDO

Panoramas

Vistas culturales

11-50 to 11-51

El virreinato de la Plata: la Argentina y el Uruguay

11-37 ¿Ya sabes...? Trata de identificar o explicar lo siguiente.

1. la capital de la Argentina y la del Uruguay
2. dónde trabajan los gauchos
3. el deporte que apasiona a los uruguayos y a los argentinos
4. el pico más alto de los Andes
5. un baile popular argentino

La Argentina y el Uruguay tienen mucha variedad topográfica y climática: la Patagonia, los Andes, las pampas, los bosques, los ríos, las cataratas y las costas.

Bariloche, Patagonia, tiene bellas vistas que atraen a turistas y a aficionados a los deportes de todo el mundo.

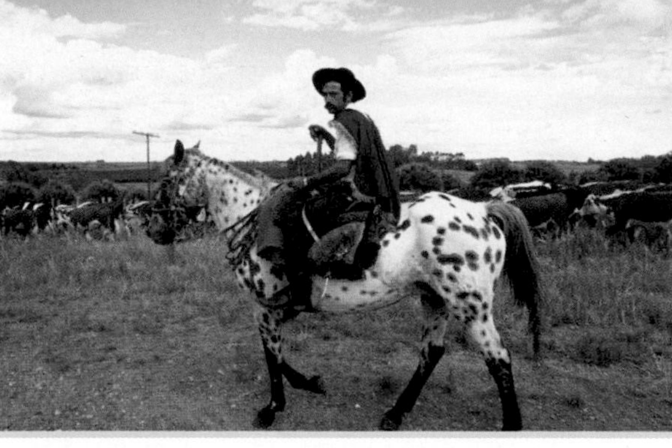

El gaucho que vive en las pampas de la Argentina y el Uruguay lleva una vida que parece romántica, pero en verdad es solitaria. La producción de carne es sumamente importante en los dos países. En la Argentina se consume más carne por persona que en cualquier otro país del mundo.

Tanto en el Uruguay como en la Argentina, el fútbol es una pasión nacional.

El tango, música y baile popular, se originó en las calles de Buenos Aires a fines del siglo XIX.

El pico Aconcagua es el más alto de los Andes.

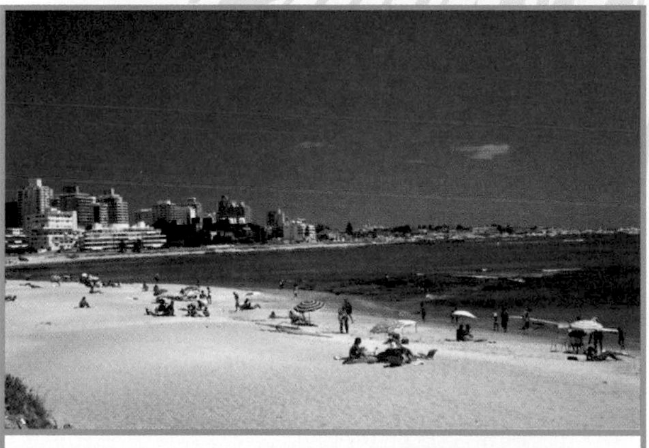

Punta del Este, Uruguay, es un lugar muy apreciado por los turistas que gozan del sol y de sus bellas playas.

11-38 Para buscar. ¿Ahora puedes identificar...?

1. el país que produce y consume más carne del mundo
2. un atractivo del Uruguay
3. un lugar popular entre los aficionados de deportes de invierno
4. dónde se encuentran las pampas
5. un *cowboy* argentino o uruguayo
6. una ciudad argentina cosmopolita

WWW

11-39 El tango, música de la calle. Conéctate con la página web de **¡Arriba!** para obtener más información y escuchar música de tango.

- Identifica los instrumentos que se usan en la selección.
- ¿Cómo caracterizas el tango? ¿Alegre? ¿Melancólico? ¿Animado? ¿Romántico?
- ¿Dónde se originó?

WWW

11-40 La diversidad de la Argentina y el Uruguay. Conéctate con la página web de **¡Arriba!** para ver más imágenes de la Argentina y el Uruguay. Escoge una región: la Patagonia, las pampas, los Andes o la costa. Después descríbela según los siguientes criterios.

- sitios de interés
- deportes
- gastronomía
- productos
- clima
- artes

Ritmos

11-52

"Todo cambia" (Mercedes Sosa, Argentina)

Esta canción es un ejemplo de la nueva canción latinoamericana, una forma artística musical en la cual el/la cantante expresa los sentimientos por su país y también sus opiniones políticas. La nueva canción no se interesa por lo comercial ni lo material, sino que muestra respeto por la cultura tradicional de la gente, especialmente la de los pobres y los trabajadores de un país.

Antes de escuchar

11-41 Los cambios de la vida. Haz una lista de las cosas que te gustaría cambiar en este mundo. Después intercambia tu lista con la de un/a compañero/a. ¿Qué tienen en común? ¿Qué les gustaría hacer de manera diferente? ¿Qué cambios no harían nunca?

A escuchar

11-42 La canción. Mientras escuchas "Todo cambia" completa los espacios en blanco de la letra con las palabras de la lista que indican qué cosas cambian y qué cosas no cambian según Mercedes Sosa.

amor	recuerdo	superficial	clima
todo	dolor	profundo	yo (la narradora)

Todo cambia

1. Cambia lo ___________,
cambia también lo ___________,
cambia el modo de pensar
cambia ___________ en este mundo.
Cambia el ___________ con los años
cambia el pastor su rebaño,
y así como todo cambia,
que yo cambie no es extraño [...]
2. Cambia, todo cambia, cambia, todo cambia. [...]
3. Pero no cambia mi ___________,
por más lejos que me encuentre.
Ni el ___________ ni el
___________,
de mi pueblo, de mi gente.
4. Y lo que cambió ayer
tendrá que cambiar mañana.
Así como cambio ___________
en esta tierra lejana. [...]

Después de escuchar

11-43 Mi gente, mi país. Al escuchar las dos últimas estrofas de "Todo cambia" es evidente que Mercedes Sosa no quiere olvidar ni a su pueblo ni a su gente, aunque ella está lejos. Imagínate que tienes unos amigos o familiares lejos de tu familia o de tu país. Dales mandatos formales para que no se olviden de ti.

Modelo: *Piensen en mí, por favor.*

11-44 Reacciones. Ahora intercambia tu lista de mandatos con la de un/a compañero/a, y usa expresiones impersonales (con el subjuntivo, el indicativo o el infinitivo, según el caso) para parafrasear lo que escribió él/ella.

Modelo: *No se olviden de nosotros.*
Es importante que nuestros primos no se olviden de nosotros.

Páginas

11-53

"No hay que complicar la felicidad" (Marco Denevi, Argentina)

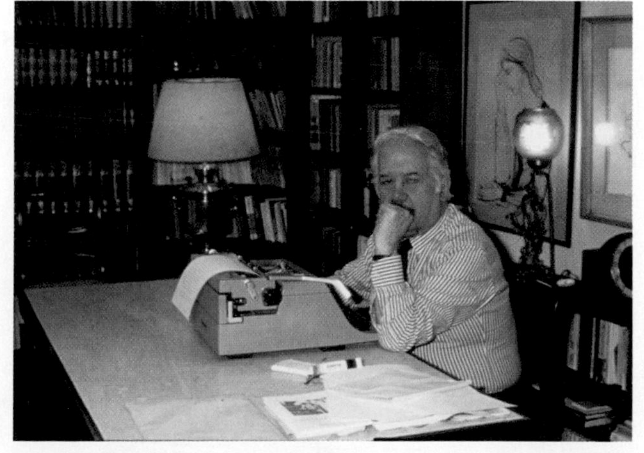

Marco Denevi (1922–1998) es uno de los cuentistas latinoamericanos más conocidos. Escribió varias novelas, incluyendo *Rosaura a las diez* (1955) y *Ceremonia secreta* (1960). Ésta última fue convertida en una película estadounidense con Mia Farrow de protagonista. Denevi es conocido por sus narrativas, minidramas y minicuentos, los cuales comentan verdades humanas y sociológicas.

En "No hay que complicar la felicidad", hay dos novios sin nombre que no están satisfechos con su felicidad. La conclusión es a la vez sorprendente (*surprising*) y misteriosa.

Antes de leer

11-45 El poder de la imaginación. En la literatura, puede haber varios niveles de interpretación. Esto ocurre especialmente cuando es necesario imaginarnos los motivos de un personaje o adivinar (*guess*) el final de una historia. Muchas veces el autor nos deja con la sensación de ambigüedad o de misterio. Lee las primeras diez líneas de este minidrama y escribe tres preguntas que se te ocurran. Al final, vuelve a tus preguntas para ver si las puedes contestar.

Modelo: *¿Quién es Él?*

1. ______________________________
2. ______________________________
3. ______________________________

11-46 A buscar. Busca esta información en la ilustración.

1. Aquí vemos a dos _____.
   a. amigos c. novios
   b. enemigos d. hermanos
2. Están en _____.
   a. una iglesia c. una casa
   b. una clase d. un parque
3. Según la ilustración, están muy _____.
   a. impacientes c. enojados
   b. enamorados d. aburridos

11-47 Anticipación. En este drama los protagonistas realizan (*carry out*) acciones recíprocas. ¿Cuáles de estas acciones crees que se hacen?

_____ Se miran.
_____ Se besan.
_____ Se aman (quieren).
_____ Se gritan.
_____ Se detestan.
_____ Se matan (*kill each other*).

A leer

11-48 Una historia de... Lee ahora la siguiente historia de Marco Denevi.

"No hay que complicar la felicidad"

Un parque. Sentados bajo los árboles, Ella y Él se besan.

Él: Te amo.
Ella: Te amo.

Vuelven a besarse.

Él: Te amo.
Ella: Te amo.

Vuelven a besarse.

Él: Te amo.
Ella: Te amo.

Él se pone violentamente de pie.

Él: ¡Basta! (*Enough!*) ¿Siempre lo mismo? ¿Por qué, cuando te digo que te amo no contestas que amas a otro?

Ella: ¿A qué otro?

Él: A nadie. Pero lo dices para que yo tenga celos (*jealousy*). Los celos alimentan (*nourish; add spice*) el amor. Despojado de este estímulo, el amor languidece (*languishes*). Nuestra felicidad es demasiado simple, demasiado monótona. Hay que complicarla un poco. ¿Comprendes?

Ella: No quería confesártelo porque pensé que sufrirías (*you would suffer*). Pero lo has adivinado (*you've guessed it*).

Él: ¿Qué es lo que adiviné?

Ella se levanta, se aleja (gets up, moves away) *unos pasos.*

Ella: Que amo a otro.

Él: Lo dices para complacerme (*please me*). Porque te lo pedí.

Ella: No. Amo a otro.

Él: ¿A qué otro?

Ella: No lo conoces.

Un silencio. Él tiene una expresión sombría (somber).

Él: Entonces, ¿es verdad?

Ella: (*Dulcemente*) Sí, es verdad. Está allí.

*Él se pasea haciendo ademanes (*gestures*) de furor.*

Él: Siento celos. No finjo (*I'm not faking*), créeme. Siento celos. Me gustaría matar a ese otro.

Ella: (*Dulcemente*) Está allí.

Él: ¿Dónde?

Ella: Nos espía. También él es celoso.

Él: Iré en su busca (*I'll look for him*).

Ella: Cuidado. Quiere matarte.

Él: No le tengo miedo.

Él desaparece entre los árboles. Al quedar sola ella se ríe.

Ella: ¡Qué niños son los hombres! Para ellos hasta el amor es un juego.

Se oye el disparo de un revólver. Ella deja de reír.

Ella: Juan.

Silencio.

Ella: (*Más alto*) Juan.

Silencio.

Ella: (*Grita.*) ¡Juan!

Silencio. Ella corre y desaparece entre los árboles. Después de unos instantes se oye el grito desgarrador (heartrending cry) *de ella.*

Ella: ¡Juan!

Silencio. Después desciende el telón (curtain).

Después de leer

11-49 La cronología. Pon en orden las siguientes acciones de la historia.

_____ La novia no lo toma en serio (*doesn't take him seriously*).
_____ La novia dice que ama a otro.
_____ La novia grita.
_____ Los novios se besan.
_____ El novio quiere tener celos.
_____ El novio desaparece.

11-50 ¿Comprendiste? Contesta brevemente en español las siguientes preguntas.

1. Según él, ¿por qué es importante tener celos?
2. ¿Tiene ella la misma opinión?
3. ¿Por qué dice ella que tiene otro novio?
4. ¿Qué busca él entre los árboles?
5. ¿Qué hace ella cuando él sale de la escena?
6. ¿Qué se oye desde los árboles?
7. ¿Qué se oye al final?

11-51 Imagínate. Imagínate lo que pasa después. ¿Cuál de estos desenlaces (*conclusions*) te parece la más posible? ¿Por qué?

_____ Todo es una broma (*joke*) del novio.
_____ El segundo amante sale de los árboles. Besa a la novia.
_____ Un policía llega y detiene (*arrests*) a la novia.
_____ El novio mata al segundo amante por celos.
_____ ¿...?

11-52 Una carta para pedir consejos. Asume el punto de vista de uno de los personajes (Él, Ella o el otro) y escribe una carta para pedirle consejos a doña Eulalia.

MODELO: *lunes, el 30 de abril de 2007*
Querida doña Eulalia:
¡Necesito sus consejos! Mi novio, Juan,...

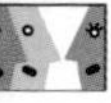

11-53 ¿Cuál es tu opinión? Hablen en español de las siguientes cuestiones de amor.

MODELO: A los hombres les gusta tener celos.
E1: *Estoy de acuerdo. Los hombres son mucho más celosos que las mujeres.*
E2: *No estoy de acuerdo. Soy hombre y no tengo celos de mi novia...*
E3: *Bueno, depende de...*

Sí, estoy de acuerdo porque...
No estoy de acuerdo porque...
No estoy seguro/a. Depende de...

1. Los celos alimentan el amor.
2. El amor lo vence (*conquers*) todo.
3. Es bueno confesárselo todo a tu novio/a o esposo/a.
4. Los novios deben siempre complacerse (*please each other*).
5. En el amor, todos somos niños.
6. Es imposible ser feliz en el amor.

Taller

11-54 to 11-56

11-54 Un *currículum vitae* y una carta de presentación para solicitar trabajo. En esta actividad, vas a escribir tu *currículum vitae* y una carta para solicitar un puesto.

MODELO:

Manuel Martínez Gil
48 Calle Ocho
Miami, FL 32819
Tel. (305) 555-1950

27 de abril de 2007
José Sánchez García
Director de Recursos Humanos
Microduro, S.A.
Montevideo, Uruguay

Estimado señor Sánchez García:

En respuesta al anuncio publicado en el *New York Times* de fecha 25 de abril en el que solicitan programadores, me gustaría ser considerado como candidato. Como verá en el *currículum vitae* que adjunto, tengo cinco años de experiencia trabajando...

Muy atentamente,
Manuel Martínez Gil
Manuel Martínez Gil

Anexo: *Currículum vitae*

Antes de escribir

- **El puesto.** Primero, inventa el puesto que vas a solicitar. ¿Qué tipo de empresa es? ¿Qué tipo de trabajo?
- **Tus datos personales y tu experiencia.** Escribe una lista de tus experiencias académicas y laborales con la fecha de cada una.

A escribir

- **El *currículum vitae*.** Escribe tu *currículum vitae* en una hoja de papel aparte. Usa la información a continuación como guía. La información que incluyas (especialmente las aficiones) debe reflejar de alguna manera el tipo de puesto que solicitas.

  DATOS PERSONALES

  (FOTO)

  Nombre y apellidos:
  Fecha de nacimiento:
  Lugar:
  Estado civil:
  Domicilio actual:
  Teléfono: Teléfono móvil:
  Correo electrónico:
  DATOS ACADÉMICOS (en orden cronológico inverso)
  (fechas) (títulos)
  EXPERIENCIA PROFESIONAL (en orden cronológico inverso)
  (fechas) (títulos)
  PUBLICACIONES, COLABORACIONES, HONORES (en orden cronológico inverso)
  IDIOMAS
  AFICIONES (por ejemplo, viajar, jugar al tenis, nadar)
  REFERENCIAS

- **La carta de presentación.** Incluye esta información:

Nombre	Presentación
Dirección	Trabajo que solicitas
Fecha	Breve resumen de tus calificaciones
Destinatario	Despedida formal
Saludo formal	Firma

Después de escribir

- **Revisar.** Revisa tu *currículum vitae* y la carta para verificar los siguientes puntos.
  - ☐ las expresiones impersonales
  - ☐ la ortografía y la concordancia
- **Intercambiar**
  Intercambia tu trabajo con el de un/a compañero/a para hacer correcciones y sugerencias y para comentar sobre el contenido.
- **Entregar**
  Pasa tu trabajo a limpio, incorporando los comentarios de tu compañero/a. Después, entrégaselo a tu profesor/a.

Vocabulario

Primera parte

Oficios y profesiones	*Occupations and professions*
el/la analista de sistemas	*systems analyst*
el/la arquitecto/a	*arquitect*
el/la bombero/a	*firefighter*
el/la carpintero/a	*carpenter*
el/la cartero/a	*mail carrier*
el/la cocinero/a	*chef*
el/la contador/a	*accountant*
el/la dentista	*dentist*
el/la electricista	*electrician*
el/la enfermero/a	*nurse*
el/la ingeniero/a	*engineer*
el/la intérprete	*interpreter*
el/la mecánico/a	*mechanic*
el/la peluquero/a	*hairstylist*
el/la periodista	*journalist*
el/la plomero/a	*plumber*
el/la psicólogo/a	*psychologist*
el/la secretario/a	*secretary*
el/la veterinario/a	*veterinarian*
el/la viajante	*traveling salesperson*

Términos y expresiones de trabajo	*Work-related terms and expressions*
las calificaciones	*qualifications*
el desempleo	*unemployment*
el entrenamiento	*training*
la formación	*education*
el horario de trabajo	*work schedule*
la meta	*goal*
el puesto	*position (job)*
las responsabilidades	*responsibilities*
el salario/el sueldo	*salary; wages*

Cargos	*Positions*
el/la coordinador/a	*coordinator*
el/la empleado/a	*employee*
el/la gerente	*manager*
el/la jefe/a	*boss*
el/la supervisor/a	*supervisor*

¡Manos a la obra!	*Let's get to work!*
apagar (fuegos/ incendios)	*to put out; extinguish (fires)*
curar	*to cure*
diseñar	*to design*
estar en paro (sin trabajo)	*to be out of work*
reparar	*to repair*
repartir	*to deliver; to distribute*
trabajar a comisión	*to work on commission*

Segunda parte

La búsqueda de empleo	*Job searching*
el/la aspirante	*job candidate*
los avisos clasificados	*want ads*
la carta de presentación	*cover letter*
la carta de recomendación	*letter of recommendation*
el contrato	*contract*
el *currículum vitae*	*resumé*
el despacho	*office*
el/la director/a	*director*
la empresa	*company; firm*
la entrevista	*interview*
el expediente	*dossier*
el formulario	*form; application*
la solicitud de empleo	*job application*
la vacante	*vacancy*

Los beneficios	*Benefits*
el aumento	*raise*
la bonificación anual	*yearly bonus*
el plan de retiro	*retirement plan*
el seguro médico	*health insurance*

Verbos	*Verbs*
acabar de (+ *infinitive*)	*to have just (done something)*
ascender (ie)	*to promote; to move up*
contratar	*to hire*
dejar	*to quit*
despedir (i, i)	*to fire*
jubilarse/retirarse	*to retire*
rellenar	*to fill completely; to fill out*

Adjetivos	*Adjectives*
capaz	*capable*
entusiasta	*enthusiastic*
honrado/a, honesto/a	*honest*
justo/a	*just; fair*

Una carta comercial	*A business letter*
Saludos	*Salutations, greetings*
Estimado/a señor/a:	*Dear Sir/Madam:*
Despedidas	*Closings*
Atentamente,	*Sincerely yours,*
Cordialmente,	*Cordially yours,*
Lo(s)/La(s) saluda atentamente,	*Very truly yours,*

12 El futuro es tuyo

PRIMERA PARTE

¡Así lo decimos! Vocabulario	La computadora y otros aparatos electrónicos
¡Así lo hacemos! Estructuras	The past participle and the present perfect indicative
	The present perfect subjunctive
	The future and the future of probability
Comparaciones	La tecnología y el idioma

- Discussing technology
- Talking about what will happen and what has happened

SEGUNDA PARTE

¡Así lo decimos! Vocabulario	El medio ambiente
¡Así lo hacemos! Estructuras	The conditional and the conditional of probability
	Tú commands
Observaciones	¡Pura vida! Episodio 12

- Talking about the environment
- Talking about what could happen
- Giving and following instructions and commands

NUESTRO MUNDO

Panoramas	Los hispanos en los Estados Unidos
Ritmos	"Caminando" (Millo Torres y El Tercer Planeta, Puerto Rico)
Páginas	*La casa en Mango Street* (fragmento) (Sandra Cisneros, EE.UU.)
Taller	Un relato personal

El cuadro *Paisajes humanos No. 95* de Melesio Casas representa a trabajadores mexicoamericanos en un campo estadounidense con el logotipo del sindicato (el águila) del *United Farm Workers* en el fondo.

Source: "Humanscape 65," Mel Casas, Acrylic, 72" x 96", Collection of Jim & Ann Harithas, New York, New York.

Los hispanos en los Estados Unidos

«Hay tres cosas que el ser humano necesita en su vida: alguien a quien amar, algo que hacer y una esperanza para el futuro.»*

En el año 2005 Antonio Villaraigosa fue electo alcalde de Los Ángeles, llegando a ser así, el primer alcalde hispano desde 1872. Ha prometido plantar un millón de árboles, construir un metro que llegue al mar y reformar el sistema escolar de la ciudad.

*__Refrán:__ There are three things that human beings need in their lives: someone to love, something to do, and hope for the future.

Primera parte

¡Así lo decimos! Vocabulario

CD 3, Track 8

12-1 to 12-2

¡Así es la vida! El impacto de la tecnología

Buenos días a todos. Bienvenidos al "Tercer encuentro sobre la tecnología". Como todos ustedes ya saben, la tecnología ha revolucionado el mundo en que vivimos así como sus carreras. En la universidad ustedes hacen todos sus diseños en computadora. Usan hojas electrónicas para mantener tablas de estadísticas. Asisten a reuniones internacionales a distancia por videoconferencias como ésta. Asimismo, escuchan conferencias en sus *iPods* y buscan los recursos de la biblioteca en la Red informática desde sus casas. ¿Y en el futuro? ¿Cómo será el futuro de la tecnología?...

La computadora y otros aparatos electrónicos

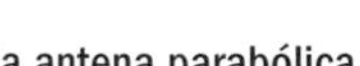
la antena parabólica

la computadora portátil

el disco duro

el disquete

el DVD

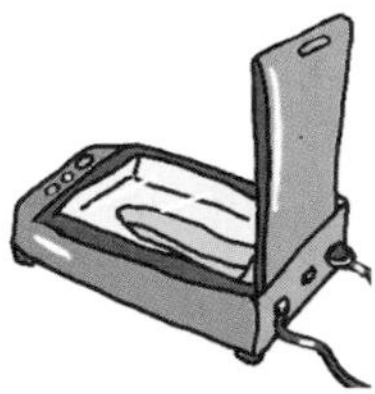
el escáner

la fotocopiadora

la impresora

el lector de CD/DVD

la pantalla

el ratón

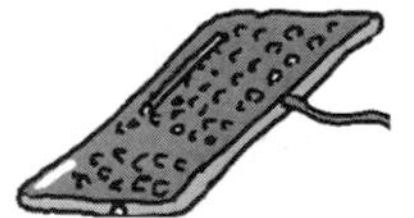
el teclado

el teléfono móvil/celular

la videograbadora

Otros aparatos electrónicos	*Other electrical appliances*
el cajero automático	*ATM machine*
el contestador automático	*answering machine*
el teléfono inalámbrico	*cordless phone*

Recursos en la computadora	*Resources on the computer*
el correo electrónico	*e-mail*
la hoja electrónica	*spreadsheet*
el hipervínculo/el enlace	*hyperlink*
el juego electrónico	*computer (electronic) game*
la Red informática	*Internet*
el sitio web/la página web	*web site/web page*

Verbos	*Verbs*
apagar	*to turn off*
archivar	*to file; to save*
borrar	*to erase*
encender (ie)	*to turn on*
fotocopiar	*to photocopy*
funcionar	*to function; to work*
grabar	*to record*
imprimir[1]	*to print*
instalar	*to install*
programar	*to program*

Adjetivos	*Adjectives*
electrónico/a	*electronic*
tecnológico/a	*technological*

Otras palabras y expresiones	*Other words and expressions*
el diseño	*design*
la marca	*brand*

[1]The past participle is **imprimido. He imprimido el documento.** With the verb **estar** the part participle is irregular: **impreso. El documento está impreso** but **está imprimido** is also acceptable. The form **impreso/a** functions as an adjective in general: **los documentos impresos, la carta impresa,** etc.

Aplicación

12-1 ¿Para qué se usa? Empareja los aparatos con sus usos.

1. _____ la videograbadora
2. _____ el teléfono móvil
3. _____ la antena parabólica
4. _____ la computadora portátil
5. _____ el cajero automático
6. _____ la pantalla
7. _____ la Red informática
8. _____ el contestador automático

a. para tomar apuntes en clase
b. para ver un documento en la computadora
c. para buscar información
d. para hacer llamadas, estando fuera de casa
e. para recibir mensajes cuando no estás en casa
f. para grabar un programa de televisión
g. para sacar dinero en efectivo
h. para recibir programas internacionales

12-2 En la oficina. Completa la conversación con los verbos de la lista siguiente.

apagar	borrar	imprimir	programar
archivar	fotocopiar	instalar	

Sra. Molina: ¡Ay! Otro día más. Son las seis de la tarde. Voy a (1) ____________ estos documentos en un CD antes de irme. No quiero (2) ____________ ninguno porque todos son muy importantes.

Rafael: Sí, y además los debo (3) ____________, pero la fotocopiadora no funciona. Necesitamos una copia. La impresora todavía funciona. Si usted quiere, los puedo (4) ____________ en color.

Sra. Molina: Buena idea. ¿Mañana vas a (5) ____________ el *software* en mi computadora?

Rafael: Claro. Pero primero tengo que (6) ____________ la computadora. Quiero que se apague automáticamente.

Sra. Molina: Bueno, eso es para otro día. No te olvides de (7) ____________ la computadora antes de irte esta noche.

Rafael: De acuerdo. ¡Buenas noches!

12-3 El *Gigabeat S*. Lee el anuncio y contesta las preguntas que siguen.

1. ¿Cuál es la marca del aparato?
2. ¿Para qué sirve?
3. ¿Cuáles son sus características?
4. ¿Qué tipo de persona busca un aparato como éste?
5. ¿Te interesa este producto? ¿Por qué?

CD 3, Track 10

12-4 Compre.com. Se puede encontrar cualquier aparato electrónico en Compre.com. Escucha la descripción de uno de ellos y completa las siguientes oraciones.

1. El anuncio es para un sistema de...
   a. audio.
   b. computadora personal.
   c. videocámara digital.
2. No incluye...
   a. lector de CD.
   b. receptor.
   c. televisor.
3. A la persona que compre este sistema, le gusta(n)...
   a. la fotografía.
   b. los juegos electrónicos.
   c. la música.
4. Puedes comprar este sistema en...
   a. seis meses.
   b. un año.
   c. un año y medio.
5. Se compra este sistema...
   a. directamente de la fábrica.
   b. en la Red informática.
   c. en tiendas especializadas.

12-5 ¿Qué aparato quieres comprar? Conéctate con la página web de **¡Arriba!** y busca un aparato electrónico que te interese comprar. Contesta las siguientes preguntas para explicar por qué lo quieres comprar.

- ¿Qué tipo de aparato es?
- ¿Cuál es la marca?
- ¿Cuánto cuesta?
- ¿Cuáles son algunas de sus características?

12-6 ¿Quién...? Hazles preguntas a tus compañeros/as para saber quién tiene más experiencia con la tecnología. Pregúntales qué pasó.

Modelo: perder un documento en la computadora
¿Alguna vez perdiste un documento en la computadora?

borrar un documento sin querer	usar la computadora para calcular los impuestos (*taxes*)	trabajar con una supercomputadora
programar una computadora	usar el escáner	participar en una videoconferencia
apagar la computadora sin archivar el documento	usar un *Gigabeat* o un *iPod*	comprar un aparato en un sitio web

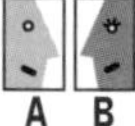

12-7A Una encuesta de Harris. Haz el papel de entrevistador/a para hacer esta encuesta de Harris. Empieza con esta presentación. Estudiante B, por favor ve al **Apéndice 1,** página A14.

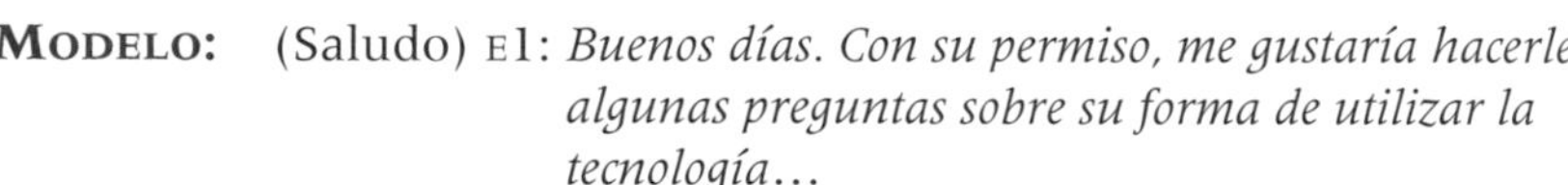

Modelo: (Saludo) E1: *Buenos días. Con su permiso, me gustaría hacerle algunas preguntas sobre su forma de utilizar la tecnología...*
E2: *Bueno, no tengo mucho tiempo pero...*

Saludo

1. si tiene computadora	sí no
2. la frecuencia con que la usa	los fines de semana una hora o más al día a todas horas, todos los días ¿otro? ____________
3. los programas que usa con más frecuencia	una hoja electrónica el correo electrónico editar fotos juegos ¿otro? ____________
4. la memoria que tiene	512 K 1 gigabyte más de 1 gigabyte ¿otro? ____________
5. la pantalla que tiene	pequeña grande plana (*flat*)
6. los problemas que tiene	un virus la falta de memoria es lenta ¿otro? ____________

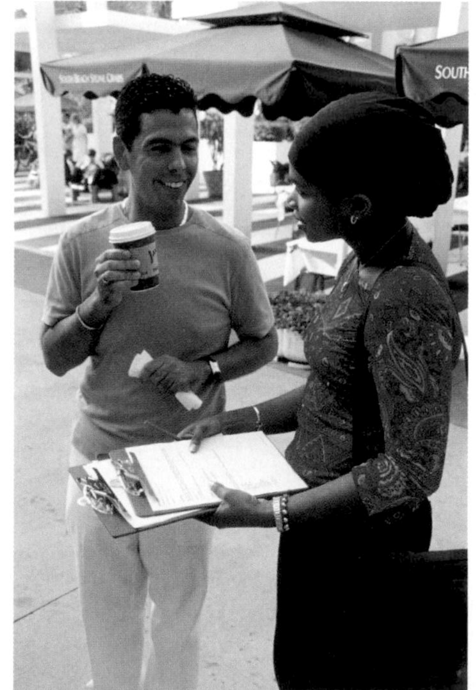

Con su permiso, me gustaría hacerle algunas preguntas...

¡Así lo hacemos! Estructuras

12-8 to 12-15

1. The past participle and the present perfect indicative

El participio pasado

The past participle is used in Spanish and English as an adjective or as part of the perfect tenses. In English, it is usually the *-ed* or *-en* form of the verb.

Hemos **archivado** los documentos.	*We have filed/saved the documents.*
Los programas están **instalados.**	*The programs are installed.*

- In Spanish the regular participle is formed by adding **-ado** to the stem of **-ar** verbs and **-ido** to the stem of **-er** and **-ir** verbs.

tomar	**comer**	**vivir**
tom**ado** (*taken*)	com**ido** (*eaten*)	viv**ido** (*lived*)

- An accent mark is used when a past participle has the combination of vowels **ai, ei,** or **oi.**

creer	**creído**	*believed*	oír	**oído**	*heard*
leer	**leído**	*read*	traer	**traído**	*brought*

- The following verbs have irregular past participles.

abrir	**abierto**	*opened*	ir	**ido**	*gone*
cubrir	**cubierto**	*covered*	morir	**muerto**	*dead*
decir	**dicho**	*said*	poner	**puesto**	*put*
descubrir	**descubierto**	*discovered*	romper	**roto**	*broken*
escribir	**escrito**	*written*	ver	**visto**	*seen*
hacer	**hecho**	*done; made*	volver	**vuelto**	*returned*

El presente perfecto de indicativo

The present perfect in English and Spanish is considered a compound tense because its forms require two verbs. In English, the present perfect is formed with the present tense of the auxiliary verb *to have* + past participle. In Spanish, the present perfect is formed with the present tense of the auxiliary verb **haber** + past participle.

	haber	Past participle	*to have*	Past participle
yo	he		*I have*	
tú	has	**tomado**	*you have*	*taken*
él, ella, Ud.	ha	**comido**	*he, she has, you have*	*eaten*
nosotros/as	hemos	**vivido**	*we have*	*lived*
vosotros/as	habéis		*you* (pl.) *have*	
ellos/as, Uds.	han		*they, you* (pl.) *have*	

- In general, the present perfect is used to refer to a past action or event that is perceived as having some bearing on the present.

  ¿Ya **has usado** la impresora? — *Have you already used the printer?*

  Estoy buscando el cajero automático. ¿Lo **has visto**? — *I'm looking for the automatic teller. Have you seen it?*

- The auxiliary verb **haber** agrees with the subject of the sentence. The past participle, however, is invariable when used in the perfect tense.

  Mi jefe me **ha dado** un teléfono móvil muy bueno. — *My boss has given me a very good cellular telephone.*

  Marisa **ha preparado** la hoja electrónica. — *Marisa has prepared the spreadsheet.*

- The auxiliary verb **haber** and the past participle cannot be separated by another word. Object pronouns and negative words are always placed before **haber.**

  No la he preparado. — *I haven't prepared it.*

  ¿La has abierto? — *Have you opened it?*

- The verb **haber** is not interchangeable with **tener. Haber** means *to have* only when used as an auxiliary verb with the past participle. **Tener** means *to have* or *to own* in the sense of possession.

  Julia **tiene** muchos amigos en esa empresa. — *Julia has many friends in that company.*

  ¿**Has tenido** experiencia en hacer diseños? — *Have you had experience in doing designs?*

Acabar de + *infinitive*

You can use the present tense of **acabar**[1] **de** + infinitive in order to describe an event that has just happened.

Acabamos de ver la videoconferencia. — *We have just seen the videoconference.*

Acaban de borrar el archivo. — *They have just erased the file.*

---

[1]**Acabar** means *to finish.*

El participio pasado usado como adjetivo

- In both English and Spanish, the past participle may be used as an adjective to modify a noun. In Spanish, when the past participle is used as an adjective, it agrees in gender and number with the noun it modifies.

Vimos las conferencias **grabadas** por nuestro supervisor.	*We saw the conferences recorded by our supervisor.*
Hay muchos programas **escritos** en *Visual Basic.*	*There are many programs written in Visual Basic.*

- The verb **estar** may be used with the past participle to describe a state or condition that is the result of a previous action. In this resultant condition, the past participle is an adjective and agrees in gender and number with the noun it modifies.

La carta **está impresa;** la secretaria la ha imprimido.	*The letter is printed; the secretary has printed it.*
El contestador automático **está roto;** lo rompió el estudiante que nos ayudaba.	*The answering machine is broken; the student who was helping us broke it.*

Aplicación

12-8 Sandra Cisneros. Lee el párrafo sobre la escritora chicana Sandra Cisneros, subraya los tiempos perfectos e identifica el infinitivo. Luego, expresa la misma acción en el pretérito.

MODELO: Ha tenido que cambiar muchas veces de casa.
Tener: Tuvo que cambiar muchas veces de casa.

Sandra Cisneros, de padres mexicanos, nació en 1954 en Chicago, pero ahora vive en San Antonio donde dice que se siente "en casa". En su juventud, tuvo muchas experiencias que han influido en sus cuentos. Por ejemplo, ha tenido que cambiar muchas veces de casa. Ha tenido que vivir en apartamentos y casas pequeñas con pocas comodidades modernas. Ha ayudado a su mamá con sus hermanos más pequeños. Ha asistido a escuelas donde todos los muchachos son de familias pobres y hay pocos recursos educativos. Sin embargo, ha superado las dificultades de su juventud y ha ganado mucha fama por sus colecciones de cuentos cortos como *La casa en Mango Street* y *El Arroyo de La Llorona* (*Woman Hollering Creek*) y por sus colecciones de poesía. Si has leído uno de sus cuentos, has visto su manera única de narrar. Además de recibir varios premios del *National Endowment for the Arts*, en 1996, fue honrada por *La Fundación MacArthur* con su *Genius Award.* En los últimos años, su casa de San Antonio se ha vuelto polémica (*controversial*) porque a los vecinos no les gusta la manera en que Sandra la ha pintado.

La casa de Sandra Cisneros en San Antonio

12-9 Más sobre Sandra Cisneros. Contesta ahora las preguntas sobre el texto que acabas de leer.

1. ¿Cuántos años tiene Sandra Cisneros?
2. ¿Cuál es su nacionalidad?
3. ¿Dónde ha vivido?
4. ¿Qué dificultades ha tenido en la escuela?
5. ¿Cómo ha ganado fama?
6. ¿Por qué ha sido tan polémica su casa de San Antonio?

12-10 Preguntas para Sandra Cisneros. Escriban individualmente tres preguntas que les gustaría hacerle a Sandra Cisneros y túrnense para hacérselas y contestárselas. Usen el presente perfecto.

MODELO: E1: *Señorita Cisneros, ¿ha vivido en otras casas en San Antonio?*
E2: *No. Ésta es mi primera casa en San Antonio.*

12-11 Elena Ochoa, primera astronauta latina. Completa la entrevista a Elena Ochoa con las preguntas que le hace la periodista. Usa el presente perfecto del verbo entre paréntesis en tu pregunta.

MODELO: (viajar) *¿Ha viajado a la luna?*
No, no conozco todavía la luna, pero algún día...

Periodista: ¿...? (vivir)
Elena Ochoa: En varios lugares, pero he pasado más tiempo en San Diego.
Periodista: ¿...? (estudiar)
Elena Ochoa: He estudiado mucha física, especialmente física óptica.
Periodista: ¿...? (tener)
Elena Ochoa: Sí, he tenido varias oportunidades para viajar en naves espaciales.
Periodista: ¿...? (impresionarle)
Elena Ochoa: ¡La vista de la tierra!
Periodista: ¿...? (hablar)
Elena Ochoa: Sí, he pasado mucho tiempo en las escuelas hablando con los jóvenes sobre la importancia de completar su educación.
Periodista: Gracias, señorita Ochoa... (ser)
Elena Ochoa: De nada. Para mí también.

12-12 La Calle Ocho. La Calle Ocho está en el centro de la Pequeña Habana en Miami. Completa la conversación entre dos turistas cubanas que están visitando esta calle. Usa la forma correcta del participio pasado.

abrir	dormir	perder	poner	vestir
cansar	hacer	pintar	preparar	

Rosa: Me gusta el aire fresco. Deja la ventana (1) __________.

Flor: Cómo no. Te la abro enseguida.

Rosa: ¡Dios mío! ¡Las llaves del carro están (2) __________ otra vez!

Flor: No te preocupes. Creo que las tienes en tu bolso.

Rosa: ¿Qué te parece ese mural (3) __________ en la pared?

Flor: Es lindo, pero no muy original. Prefiero los murales de Los Ángeles.

Rosa: Tu nieta estaba muy bien (4) __________ ayer en la fiesta. Y su familia es preciosa.

Flor: Es verdad. Su hija es un encanto. No hay nada más tranquilo que un bebé (5) __________.

Rosa: Mira la guayabera[1] blanca que lleva ese señor. Esas camisas son típicas del trópico, pero las guayaberas (6) __________ en Panamá son más baratas.

Flor: Es verdad, pero prefiero las guayaberas de *La casa de las guayaberas*, que está aquí en la Calle Ocho porque son más elegantes.

Rosa: Mira, allí hay un restaurante cubano. ¿Entramos? Es la una y estoy (7) __________ de tanto caminar.

Flor: ¡Bueno! Las mesas ya están (8) __________ y la comida está (9) __________. Sentémonos a almorzar.

12-13 ¿Cómo te sentías cuando...? Imagínate que has estado varios días en Miami. Usa participios pasados para expresar cómo te sentías en estas situaciones.

MODELO: ¿Cómo te sentías cuando llegaste a Miami?
Me sentía emocionado/a.

(bien/mal) atender (*attended to*)	encantar	preparar
cansar	enojar	sorprender
decidir (a ir a...)	interesar	(bien/mal) vestir
desilusionar	preocupar	¿...?

¿Cómo te sentías...

1. cuando volviste del banco?
2. cuando perdiste tu billetera (*wallet*)?
3. después de ver un concierto de Gloria Estefan?
4. en la fiesta para tus amigos cubanos?
5. cuando te perdiste en la Pequeña Habana?
6. cuando cenaste en el restaurante cubano?

---

[1]Men's shirt typical of the Caribbean, usually long-sleeved and with four pockets in front.

12-14 Recuerdos. Túrnense para hablar de experiencias que han tenido y también de experiencias que no han tenido, pero que desean tener.

MODELO: ver películas
E1: *¿Qué películas has visto este año?*
E2: *Esta semana he visto* Volver, *una película de Almodóvar.*
E1: *¿Has visto muchas películas españolas?*

comer...	escribir...	hacer...	leer...	trabajar...	visitar...
conocer...	estudiar...	ir...	salir...	ver...	volver...

12-15 Diez preguntas. Formen dos o más grupos para tratar de adivinar lo que han hecho. Pueden hacerse diez preguntas que puedan contestarse con **sí** o **no,** hasta que adivinen la respuesta. Deben usar el presente perfecto de indicativo en sus preguntas y en sus respuestas.

MODELO: E1: *He hecho un viaje interesante.*
E2: *¿Has viajado a algún país de habla española?*
E1: *No, no he viajado a ningún país de habla española.*
E3: *¿Has visitado...?*

2. The present perfect subjunctive

12-16 to 12-20

- The present perfect subjunctive is formed with the present subjunctive of the auxiliary verb **haber** + the past participle.

	Present subjunctive of *haber*	Past participle
yo	**haya**	**tomado**
tú	**hayas**	**comido**
él, ella, Ud.	**haya**	**vivido**
nosotros/as	**hayamos**	
vosotros/as	**hayáis**	
ellos/as, Uds.	**hayan**	

- The present perfect subjunctive, like the present subjunctive, is used when the main clause expresses a wish, emotion, doubt, denial, etc., pertaining to the subject of another clause. Generally, the verb in the main clause is in the present tense.

Dudamos que Antonio Villaraigosa **haya sido** nominado para gobernador.	*We doubt that Antonio Villaraigosa has been nominated for governor.*
Espero que el teléfono móvil **haya funcionado** bien.	*I hope that the cellular phone has worked well.*

Aplicación

12-16 Un comité de búsqueda (*search*). La empresa Ecomundo fabrica (*manufactures*) productos para conservar el medio ambiente. Cuatro ejecutivos de la empresa conversan sobre los candidatos al puesto de ingeniero del medio ambiente que necesitan. Primero subraya los verbos en el presente perfecto y luego explica por qué se usa el indicativo o el subjuntivo.

MODELO: Espero que hayamos recibido suficientes solicitudes para el puesto.
Se usa el subjuntivo después de un verbo de emoción cuando hay un cambio de sujeto en los verbos.

Ramón: Aquí tienen todas las solicitudes que han llegado hasta hoy. Ojalá que hayan solicitado buenos candidatos.

Caridad: Hemos recibido más de 20 solicitudes. ¿Quiénes han tenido tiempo para leerlas todas?

Ramón: Yo las he leído todas, pero hay pocos que me han impresionado tanto como la que leí ayer por la tarde de Gabriela González.

Clemencia: Yo creo que Gabriela González es un buen ejemplo. Es una ingeniera que ha sobresalido (*excelled*) en sus estudios y ha tenido mucho éxito en su carrera. Pero ya tiene un buen trabajo y realmente dudo que ella haya solicitado este puesto en serio.

Urbano: Bueno, vamos a entrevistar a los cinco mejores candidatos, a menos que ustedes hayan identificado a otros.

Caridad: De acuerdo. Creo que los mejores ya han presentado su solicitud. Vamos a cerrar la búsqueda para identificar a los finalistas. ¿Les parece bien?

12-17 Gabriela decide solicitar el puesto. Aunque Gabriela ya tiene un buen puesto con otra empresa, ha decidido solicitar el puesto de ingeniero del medio ambiente. Esa noche, Gabriela le cuenta a su amigo sobre la entrevista con Ecomundo. Empareja las frases para completarlas de una manera lógica.

MODELO: Gabriela: *Espero que les haya gustado mi currículum vitae.*

Saúl:	No hay duda que...	he aprendido mucho en esta entrevista.
Gabriela:	Ojala que...	les has impresionado favorablemente.
Saúl:	Es bueno que...	hayan pasado varios días.
Gabriela:	No los llamo hasta que...	no te hayan avisado de inmediato.
Saúl:	Es una lástima que...	no hayan contratado a otro candidato.
Gabriela:	Es cierto que...	hayas tenido mucha experiencia.

12-18 Gabriela González revive su experiencia. A continuación tienes la entrevista de Gabriela González con Ecomundo. Completa el diálogo con el presente perfecto de indicativo o subjuntivo del verbo entre paréntesis.

Ramón: Buenos días, señorita González. ¿Cómo (1. oír) __________ usted acerca de esta empresa?

Gabriela: La empresa Ecomundo (2. recibir) __________ mucha atención estos días en la prensa y en otros medios de comunicación. Creo que su trabajo con los pingüinos en la Patagonia la (3. hacer) __________ muy popular.

Caridad: Es verdad que nosotros (4. tener) __________ mucho éxito en el área de conservación de las especies. Y creo que usted (5. estudiar) __________ sobre este tema también, ¿no?

Gabriela: Sí, espero que Uds. (6. recibir) __________ mi *currículum vitae*. Allí explico que (7. trabajar) __________ varios años con Paz Verde.

Ramón: ¿Quiere ver nuestra planta y conocer a los demás ingenieros?

Gabriela: Me encantaría.

Caridad: Perfecto. Y después de que nosotros (8. ver) __________ la planta, hablaremos de su contrato.

12-19 En su experiencia. Usen expresiones tales como: **es necesario, es bueno, es malo, es lógico** o **es excepcional,** para decir algo que hayan hecho antes de su primera entrevista para un trabajo.

Modelo: Es bueno que... (yo) *haya investigado sobre esa empresa.*

1. Es obvio que...
2. Es malo que...
3. Es cierto que...
4. Es necesario que...
5. Es verdad que...

3. The future and the future of probability

El futuro

- The Spanish future tense is formed with only one set of endings for the **-ar, -er,** and **-ir** verbs. For regular verbs, the endings are attached to the infinitive (do not drop the **-ar, -er,** or **-ir**). Note that all endings, except for the **nosotros/as** forms, have a written accent mark.

	tomar	**comer**	**vivir**
yo	tomar**é**	comer**é**	vivir**é**
tú	tomar**ás**	comer**ás**	vivir**ás**
él, ella, Ud.	tomar**á**	comer**á**	vivir**á**
nosotros/as	tomar**emos**	comer**emos**	vivir**emos**
vosotros/as	tomar**éis**	comer**éis**	vivir**éis**
ellos/as, Uds.	tomar**án**	comer**án**	vivir**án**

Mañana **hablaremos** con la programadora. — *Tomorrow we will talk with the programmer.*

¿**Verás** el programa por satélite conmigo? — *Will you see the satellite program with me?*

- As in English, the Spanish future tense expresses what will happen in the future. The English equivalent is *will* + verb.

Estudiaré informática en la universidad.	*I will study computer science at the university.*
Ustedes **comprarán** pronto otro disco duro.	*You will buy a new hard drive soon.*

- Remember that the present tense is often used to express immediate future in Spanish.

El técnico **viene** para arreglar mi computadora hoy.	*The technician will come (is coming) to fix my computer today.*
Termino mi trabajo esta tarde.	*I will finish my paper this afternoon.*

- The future may also be conveyed with the present tense of **ir a** + *infinitive*.

Voy a arreglar la computadora.	*I am going to fix the computer.*
¿**Vas a archivar** ese documento?	*Are you going to save that document?*

- The idea of willingness, sometimes expressed with the English future, cannot be expressed with the Spanish future tense. Use verbs like **querer** or simple present tense to express willingness.

¿**Quieres** ayudarme con la impresora?	*Will you help me with the printer?*
¿Me **traes** el otro programa?	*Will you bring me the other program?*

- The irregular verbs in the future are formed by adding the future endings to an irregular stem. The irregular stems can be grouped into three categories.

1. Drop two letters to form the stem of the future.

decir	**dir-**	diré, dirás,...
hacer	**har-**	haré, harás,...

2. The **e** of the infinitive ending is dropped to form the stem of the future.

haber	**habr-**	habré, habrás,...
poder	**podr-**	podré, podrás,...
querer	**querr-**	querré, querrás,...
saber	**sabr-**	sabré, sabrás,...

3. The **e** or the **i** of the infinitive ending is replaced by **d** to form the stem of the future.

poner	**pondr-**	pondré, pondrás,...
salir	**saldr-**	saldré, saldrás,...
tener	**tendr-**	tendré, tendrás,...
venir	**vendr-**	vendré, vendrás,...

El programa **hará** todos los cálculos.	*The program will make all the calculations.*
El técnico **vendrá** a las ocho.	*The technician will come at eight.*

El futuro y la probabilidad

- Probability or conjecture in the present is often expressed in Spanish with the future tense. This use of the future has many equivalents in English, for example, *probably, may, I wonder,* etc.

¿Dónde **estará** Antonio?	*I wonder where Antonio is?*
Estará jugando juegos electrónicos.	*He's probably playing computer games.*
¿Qué hora **será**?	*What time must it be?*
Serán las seis.	*It must be six.*

Aplicación

12-20 Antonio Villaraigosa. Lee la entrevista con Antonio Villaraigosa. Subraya los verbos en el futuro y da el infinitivo. Luego expresa la misma acción, usando la expresión **ir a...**

MODELO: **sabrá**
saber ¿Cuándo va a saber si...?

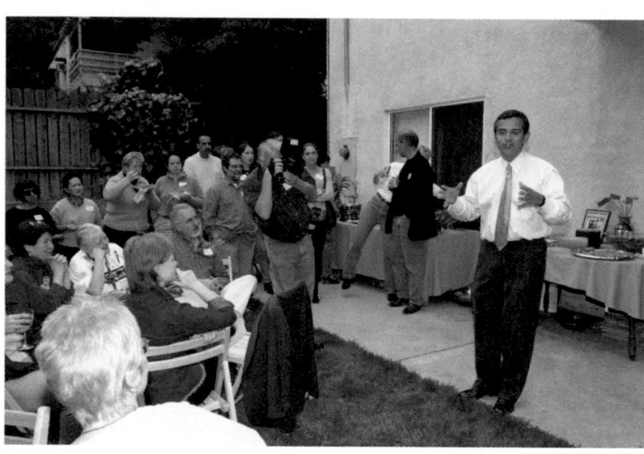

Periodista: Sr. Villaraigosa, ¿cuándo sabrá si será candidato para gobernador de California?

Villaraigosa: Bueno, no se lo puedo decir. No es sólo decisión mía. Será importante conversarlo con mi esposa, pues ella querrá participar en cualquier decisión. Por ahora, seguiré trabajando por el bien de la gente de Los Ángeles.

Periodista: De acuerdo, pero ¿habrá debates políticos entre usted y sus contrincantes (*opponents*)?

Villaraigosa: Pondré esa decisión en manos de las personas encargadas de la campaña política.

Periodista: Y si gana las elecciones, ¿qué hará?

Villaraigosa: Para empezar, me reuniré con mis asesores y les pediré que me acompañen a Sacramento. Pero esto es pura conjetura (*guess*). Ya veremos qué pasa en el futuro.

12-21 El futuro de Antonio Villaraigosa. Contesta ahora las preguntas sobre el texto que acabas de leer.

1. Según esta entrevista, ¿es Villaraigosa candidato para gobernador?
2. ¿Cuándo sabrá si será candidato?
3. ¿Quién participará en su decisión?
4. ¿Para qué o para quién seguirá trabajando Villaraigosa?
5. ¿Quiénes decidirán si habrá debates?
6. En tu opinión, ¿será Villaraigosa candidato?

12-22 La empresa MicroDuro. Isela tiene una entrevista con la empresa MicroDuro. Completa la conversación entre ella y el director de personal de una manera lógica, usando el futuro de los verbos a continuación.

conocer	decir	informar	poder	responder	tener
dar	escribir	llamar	recibir	ser	trabajar

Isela: Señor Mejías, ¿(1. yo) __________ desde las nueve hasta las cinco?

Director: No. Los nuevos programadores trabajan desde las tres hasta las once.

Isela: ¿(2. yo) __________ trabajar con un programador veterano?

Director: Sí, usted puede trabajar con varias personas con experiencia.

Isela: ¿(3. yo) __________ muchas oportunidades para ser creativa?

Director: Bueno, los nuevos tienen que ayudar a los veteranos.

Isela: ¿(4. yo) __________ programas para juegos electrónicos?

Director: No. Es más probable que usted escriba manuales para *software*. También, usted (5) __________ el correo electrónico de los clientes.

Isela: ¿Usted me (6) __________ cuánto me van a pagar?

Director: Sí, le (7) __________ sobre su sueldo antes de que se vaya hoy.

Isela: ¿Cuándo (8. yo) __________ el primer aumento?

Director: Normalmente los empleados lo reciben después del primer año de servicio.

Isela: ¿(9. yo) __________ a gente importante?

Director: Sí. Usted va a tener muchas oportunidades de conocer a gente importante.

Isela: ¿Cuándo me (10) __________ usted su decisión?

Director: La (11) __________ por teléfono mañana por la mañana.

Isela: Gracias, señor Mejías. (12) __________ muy interesante trabajar en esta empresa.

12-23 ¿Por qué será? Usa las ideas de la lista siguiente en el futuro para hacer una conjetura *(guess)* sobre cada situación.

MODELO: Recibes una llamada por teléfono a las siete de la mañana.
Será algo urgente.

estar contaminado	la fotocopiadora estar rota
haber problemas con la antena parabólica	ser mi jefe

1. Hay peces (*fish*) muertos en el lago.
2. Hay un mensaje en el contestador automático.
3. No podemos ver la película.
4. La secretaria no ha hecho las fotocopias.

12-24 El/La adivino/a. Túrnense para ser el/la adivino/a (*fortune-teller*) y el/la cliente que quiere saber su futuro. Háganse tres preguntas originales.

MODELO: E1: *¿Dónde voy a trabajar el año que viene?*
E2: *Trabajarás en alguna parte de la universidad.*

1. ¿Dónde voy a estar este verano?
2. ¿Qué voy a hacer después de graduarme?
3. ¿Con quién voy a pasar el resto de mi vida?
4. ¿Cuántos hijos voy a tener?
5. ¿Dónde voy a vivir? ¿En una finca *(farm)*?
6. ¿Cómo voy a ser? ¿Feliz? ¿Infeliz?

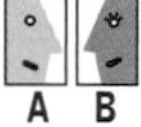

12-25A ¿Qué harás? Túrnense para preguntarse qué harán en estas circunstancias. Estudiante B, por favor ve al **Apéndice 1,** página A14.

MODELO: Ni el fax ni la conexión a la Red informática funcionan.
Llamaré a un técnico o compraré un módem nuevo.

CIRCUNSTANCIAS	SOLUCIONES
1. El cajero automático no tiene dinero.	1. ir a la Red informática
2. Se rompe tu computadora.	2. borrar los que no son importantes
3. Borras un trabajo importante en tu computadora.	3. comprar uno nuevo
4. Tu escáner no funciona.	4. bajarlo (*download*) del Internet

¿Cuánto sabes tú? *Can you...*

12-27 to 12-30

- ☐ talk about electronic gadgets that you use?
- ☐ identify the parts of a computer?
- ☐ say what you and others have done in the past using the present perfect and present perfect subjunctive? **(He visitado Los Ángeles; Ojalá que el técnico haya reparado mi computadora.)**
- ☐ describe people and things using past participles as adjectives? **(Estamos cansados; Mi impresora está rota.)**
- ☐ say what will happen using the future tense? **(Algún día viviremos en la luna.)**

Comparaciones

La tecnología y el idioma

12-26 En tu experiencia. ¿Puedes nombrar algunas palabras que se usan en inglés que vienen de otros idiomas? ¿Cuáles vienen del español? Por ejemplo: siesta (*español*); coup d'état (*francés*), etc.

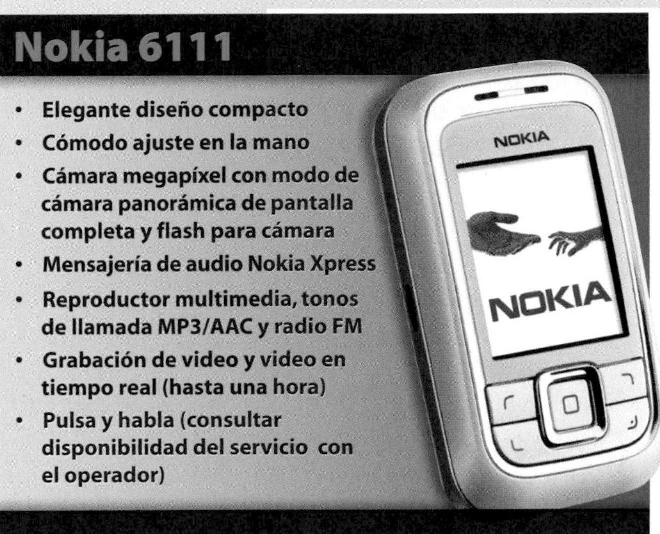

La tecnología avanza a un ritmo muy acelerado, pero el idioma, que tiene que adaptarse constantemente a los inventos que surgen todos los días, sigue un ritmo más lento. La mayoría de los nuevos productos electrónicos viene de los países industrializados. Por eso, muchas palabras relacionadas con la tecnología en español son anglicismos (palabras derivadas del inglés) y extranjerismos (palabras de otros idiomas). En esta lección ya hemos presentado palabras como **fax** y **disquete.** A continuación hay una lista de palabras tecnológicas que vienen del inglés.

el casete	el escáner	el home page	el módem	el shareware
el chip	el formato MP3	el/la Internet	el monitor	la página web
el DVD	hacer clic	el láser	el PDA	el software

Entre los países hispanohablantes, algunos aparatos electrónicos varían de nombre. En España, por ejemplo, se dice **el ordenador** para referirse a **la computadora.** En ciertos países de Hispanoamérica también se dice **el computador** o **el microcomputador.**

12-27 En tu opinión. Hagan una lista de cinco problemas que se nos presentan cuando nos falla (*fails*) la tecnología.

Modelo: *Si el módem no funciona, no podemos mandar información a otros lugares tan rápidamente.*

SEGUNDA PARTE

¡Así lo decimos! Vocabulario

CD 3, Track 11

12-31 to 12-32

¡Así es la vida! El medio ambiente: ¿El problema de los más jóvenes?

Entre los jóvenes hispanos de hoy hay una preocupación por la protección del medio ambiente. Ellos saben que, aunque sus países de origen tienen grandes recursos naturales, el desarrollo industrial y la falta de preocupación de los gobiernos por proteger estos valiosos recursos naturales, hacen que el medio ambiente se deteriore.

En muchas grandes ciudades, como la Ciudad de México, el gran problema es la contaminación del aire. En la capital hay más de 18 millones de habitantes y la contaminación que producen los carros y camiones es algo serio. Asimismo, otros problemas como el humo que producen las fábricas, las plantas nucleares y otros factores contaminantes están poniendo en peligro la vida de todos, no sólo la de los más jóvenes. Obviamente, todos tendremos que cooperar para tratar de resolver estos problemas.

El medio ambiente

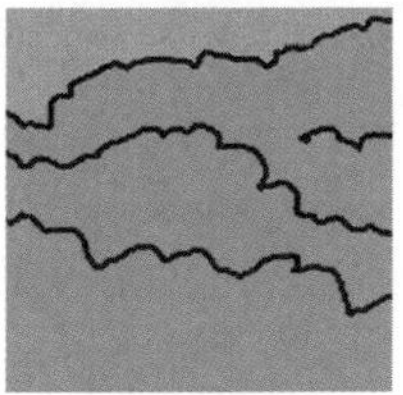
el bosque

la fábrica

el humo

el petróleo

la planta nuclear

Nuestro mundo y el medio ambiente	*Our world and the environment*
la deforestación[1]	*deforestation*
los desechos	*waste*
la energía	*energy*
el envase (de aluminio)	*(aluminum) container*
la escasez	*shortage*
la medida	*measure*
el medio ambiente	*environment*
la multa	*fine*
la naturaleza	*nature*
los pesticidas	*pesticides*
la radioactividad	*radioactivity*
el recurso natural	*natural resource*
el reciclaje	*recycling*
la reforestación[2]	*reforestation*

Verbos	*Verbs*
arrojar	*to throw out*
conservar	*to conserve; to preserve*
consumir	*to consume*
contaminar	*to contaminate; to pollute*
echar	*to throw out*
proteger (j)	*to protect*
reciclar	*to recycle*

Adjetivos	*Adjectives*
dispuesto/a	*willing; ready; disposed*
obligatorio/a	*mandatory*

[1]**la despoblación** en España

[2]**la repoblación forestal** en España

LETRAS Y SONIDOS

The consonants "t, d" in Spanish

In Spanish, the letter *t* sounds like the *t* in English *stop*, except in Spanish, the tongue tip forms a closure behind the upper front teeth instead of against the alveolar ridge (located just beyond the teeth). Avoid, however, the *t* sound made in English *top*, where a strong puff of air is expelled after the sound.

Hard *t*: *te-lé-fo-no* *tra-í-do* *vuel-to* *au-to-má-ti-co*

The letter *d* in Spanish creates one of two sounds, depending on the context. After a pause or the letters *n* or *l*, the letter *d* sounds like the *d* in English *den*. In all other contexts, especially between vowels, the sound is softer, like the *th* in English *then* or *father*. While in English the sound for *d* is made with the tongue tip against the alveolar ridge, and the sound for *th* is made with the tongue tip placed between the upper and lower front teeth, both sounds for Spanish *d*, like *t*, are formed behind the upper front teeth. The hard *d* involves a tight closure that momentarily stops the flow of air, while the soft *d* involves a partial closure that allows the air to flow but creates friction.

Hard *d*: *dis-co* *di-se-ño* *un-di-se-ño* *don-de* *el-di-se-ño* *suel-do*
Soft *d*: *los-di-se-ños* *me-di-da* *le-í-do* *ver-dad* *la Red*

In sum, Spanish has the same three sounds found at the beginning of the English words *ten* (but with less air expelled), *den* (hard *d*), and *then* (soft *d*). However, in Spanish, all three of these sounds are created with the tongue tip behind the upper front teeth only.

Aplicación

12-28 ¿Qué solución hay? Empareja cada problema con la solución correspondiente.

1. ____ la contaminación del aire
2. ____ la deforestación
3. ____ arrojar envases a la calle
4. ____ los desechos industriales
5. ____ la escasez de energía
6. ____ la escasez de agua
7. ____ echar basura en el parque

a. usar basureros en el parque
b. ahorrar agua
c. conservar electricidad
d. multar las fábricas
e. establecer programas de reciclaje
f. plantar más árboles
g. usar un programa de inspección de las emisiones de automóviles

12-29 En las noticias. Completa cada titular con el verbo correspondiente.

arroje consume contaminó conservar multa protege

1. **Accidente del Exxon Valdez ______ el agua de la costa de Alaska**
2. **No ______ los artículos de plástico, recíclelos**
3. **NIÑOS COSTARRICENSES APRENDEN A ______ ENERGÍA**
4. **El gobierno de la India ______ a la Dow Chemical por un accidente de pesticidas**
5. **La EPA regula y ______ el medio ambiente**
6. **Los EE.UU. ______ más energía que cualquier otro país del mundo**

CD 3, Track 14

12-30 Un anuncio público. Escucha el anuncio de la radio y completa las afirmaciones que siguen.

1. El anuncio habla de un programa...
   a. del gobierno.
   b. de una organización no gubernamental.
   c. de la ONU.
2. Los participantes son...
   a. niños y jóvenes.
   b. ancianos.
   c. amas de casa.
3. Van a trabajar en la limpieza y...
   a. el control de los pesticidas.
   b. el reciclaje.
   c. la reforestación.
4. El trabajo será durante...
   a. las vacaciones.
   b. el año escolar.
   c. la Semana Santa.

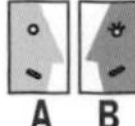

12-31A ¿Cuál es tu opinión? Túrnense para hacer y responder a preguntas sobre el medio ambiente. Usa expresiones como: **¿Cuál es tu opinión sobre...? ¿Qué podemos hacer para...?,** etc. Estudiante B, por favor ve al **Apéndice 1,** página A15.

Modelo: la contaminación del medio ambiente
E1: *¿Crees que la contaminación es un problema grave?*
E2: *En mi opinión, es el problema más grave que tenemos.*

PREGUNTAS	**RESPUESTAS**
1. la escasez de agua	la única respuesta
2. la conservación de energía	leyes más fuertes
3. la energía nuclear	hacer todo lo posible
4. el sistema de transporte público en tu ciudad	nuestro futuro

12-32 ¡Salve nuestro paraíso! Refiéranse a la siguiente tarjeta que se encontró en la habitación de un hotel y hagan por lo menos cinco afirmaciones para explicar el problema y las posibles soluciones.

Modelo: *Estamos en una región que tiene escasez de agua. Tendremos que...*

12-33 Debate. Formen dos equipos para debatir algunos de los siguientes asuntos (*issues*). Usen las frases a continuación para expresar sus opiniones.

En mi opinión...	No estoy de acuerdo...
Estás equivocado/a...	Para mí lo más importante es...
Creo que...	Desde mi punto de vista...

1. las ventajas y desventajas de la tecnología moderna
2. las plantas nucleares y el peligro para el medio ambiente
3. la destrucción de la selva (*jungle*) del Amazonas
4. el exceso de población en Latinoamérica

¡Así lo hacemos! Estructuras

12-39 to 12-45

4. The conditional and the conditional of probability

El condicional

In Spanish, the conditional of regular verbs is formed by adding the imperfect ending for **-er** and **-ir** verbs to the infinitive. The same endings are used for **-ar, -er,** and **-ir** verbs.

	tomar	comer	vivir
yo	tomar**ía**	comer**ía**	vivir**ía**
tú	tomar**ías**	comer**ías**	vivir**ías**
él, ella, Ud.	tomar**ía**	comer**ía**	vivir**ía**
nosotros/as	tomar**íamos**	comer**íamos**	vivir**íamos**
vosotros/as	tomar**íais**	comer**íais**	vivir**íais**
ellos/as, Uds.	tomar**ían**	comer**ían**	vivir**ían**

- The conditional expresses what you would do under certain circumstances.

  ¿Reciclarías envases de aluminio? — *Would you recycle aluminum cans?*

  Consumiríamos menos agua. — *We would consume less water.*

- The conditional is also used when the speaker is referring to an event that is future to another past event.

  Creíamos que **habría** más gente protestando enfrente de la planta nuclear. — *We thought there would be more people protesting in front of the nuclear plant.*

  Nos dijo que no **contaminarían** el agua. — *He told us they wouldn't pollute the water.*

- The verb **deber,** when used in the conditional tense, is equivalent to the English *should* + infinitive.

  Deberías conservar recursos. — *You should conserve resources.*

- The conditional has the same irregular stems as the future.

decir	**dir-**	diría, dirías,...	saber	**sabr-**	sabría, sabrías,...
hacer	**har-**	haría, harías,...	poner	**pondr-**	pondría, pondrías,...
haber	**habr-**	habría, habrías,...	salir	**saldr-**	saldría, saldrías,...
poder	**podr-**	podría, podrías,...	tener	**tendr-**	tendría, tendrías,...
querer	**querr-**	querría, querrías,...	venir	**vendr-**	vendría, vendrías,...

EXPANSIÓN **More on structure and usage**

Conjetura con el condicional

Probability or conjecture in the past is often expressed in Spanish with the conditional.

—¿A qué hora **sería** la conferencia de prensa?	*I wonder at what time the press conference was.*
—**Sería** a las cuatro.	*It was probably at four.*

Aplicación

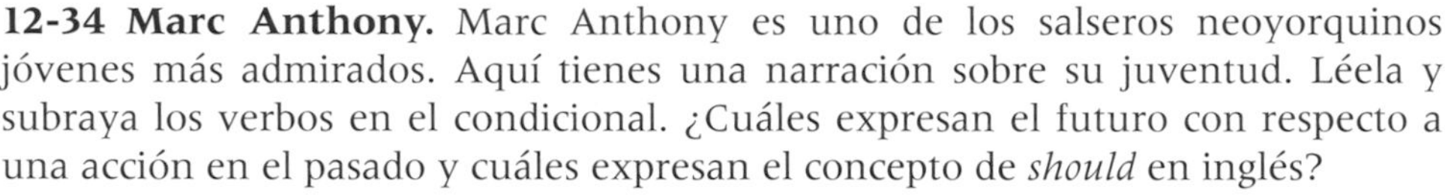

12-34 Marc Anthony. Marc Anthony es uno de los salseros neoyorquinos jóvenes más admirados. Aquí tienes una narración sobre su juventud. Léela y subraya los verbos en el condicional. ¿Cuáles expresan el futuro con respecto a una acción en el pasado y cuáles expresan el concepto de *should* en inglés?

Cuando tenía diez años sabía que sería cantante de salsa. Mis padres siempre me decían que tendría éxito, porque me gustaba bailar y cantar los ritmos de las islas del Caribe. Cuando era niño, cantaba con mi padre, quien tocaba la guitarra. Fue él quien me enseñó todo lo que sabía sobre la música puertorriqueña y quien me decía que algún día yo daría conciertos por todo el mundo. En 1990, conocí a Little Louis Vega, otro músico. Él me dijo que debería producir un álbum de mis canciones. En ese álbum, también tocó Tito Puente, el gran percusionista puertorriqueño y otro modelo importante en mi vida. Tito y Celia Cruz me animaron y me guiaron mucho. De joven soñaba con crear música, pero nunca me imaginé que trabajaría al lado de estas dos leyendas del mundo hispano.

12-35 Más sobre Marc Anthony. Contesta las preguntas siguientes sobre el texto que acabas de leer.

1. ¿Quién es Marc Anthony?
2. ¿Qué hacía de joven?
3. ¿Quiénes le sirvieron de modelo?
4. ¿Qué sabía él de joven?
5. ¿Qué no sabía?

WWW **12-36 ¿Conoces su música?** Conéctate con la página web de **¡Arriba!** para ver más imágenes de Marc Anthony y escuchar su música. Escribe un párrafo en el que describas al artista o su música.

12-37 Lo que haría Cristina Saralegui. Cristina Saralegui es una presentadora de la cadena hispana Univisión. En un programa reciente, dijo que el próximo año haría lo siguiente. Completa cada promesa con la forma correcta del verbo correspondiente en el condicional.

MODELO: Dijo que *trabajaría* para aumentar su influencia en la comunidad hispana.

añadir	buscar	entrevistar	ser
atraer	combatir	poder	tener

1. Prometió que ___________ a un político hispano.
2. Dijo que no ___________ candidata para el congreso.
3. Nos aseguró que ___________ a más televidentes.
4. Creía que ___________ más éxito con los patrocinadores (*sponsors*).
5. Prometió que ___________ los estereotipos.
6. Dijo que ___________ diferentes maneras para informar mejor al público hispano.
7. Creía que ___________ ayudar a la mujer latina.
8. Prometió que ___________ otra hora a su programa.

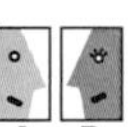

12-38A Geraldo. Imagínate que eres entrevistador/a para un programa de investigación en la televisión. Hazle preguntas al/a la jefe/a de una planta nuclear y contesta las suyas. Siempre insiste en que te dé respuestas directas. Estudiante B, por favor ve al **Apéndice 1,** página A15.

MODELO: limpiar los desechos
E1: *Usted dijo que limpiaría los desechos de su planta, pero…*
E2: *Es verdad. Pero eso toma tiempo. Usted dijo que no me haría preguntas indiscretas.*
E1: *Es verdad, pero…*

PREGUNTAS DEL/DE LA ENTREVISTADOR/A

Usted dijo que…

1. proteger la naturaleza alrededor de la planta
2. reciclar los desechos nucleares
3. pagar las multas de la EPA
4. no contaminar el agua del río
5. trabajar en la reforestación de las montañas

12-39 Diferentes situaciones. Túrnense para contar lo que harían en estas situaciones para mejorar el medio ambiente.

MODELO: en la playa
E1: *¿Qué harías en la playa?*
E2: *Recogería la basura y los envases. ¿Y tú? ¿Qué harías?*
E1: ...

1. con un millón de dólares
2. en una organización benéfica
3. en un comité sobre el medio ambiente en el congreso o el parlamento
4. en un editorial para el periódico
5. en un bosque
6. en tu coche para conservar gasolina
7. en tu casa para conservar energía
8. en tu vida para conservar el medio ambiente

5. *Tú* commands

12-46 to 12-50

In **Capítulo 11** you learned that formal commands used the forms of the subjunctive. Here are the informal (**tú**) commands, which we use in the directions for the activities. Note how they compare with the subjunctive as well.

Infinitive	Affirmative	Negative	(Subjunctive)
comprar	**compra**	**no compres**	(compres)
comer	**come**	**no comas**	(comas)
escribir	**escribe**	**no escribas**	(escribas)
pensar	**piensa**	**no pienses**	(pienses)
dormir	**duerme**	**no duermas**	(duermas)
pedir	**pide**	**no pidas**	(pidas)
traer	**trae**	**no traigas**	(traigas)

- Regular affirmative **tú** commands have the same form as the third-person singular of the present indicative.

  Recicla los platos de papel. — *Recycle the paper plates.*
  Protege nuestros bosques. — *Protect our forests.*

- Negative **tú** commands use the subjunctive.

  No cortes los árboles pequeños. — *Don't cut the small trees.*
  No cierres la fábrica todavía. — *Don't close the factory yet.*

- Remember that irregularities in the subjunctive will also appear in the negative **tú** command.

  No conduzcas tan rápido. — *Don't drive so fast.*
  No te vayas. — *Don't leave.*

Mandatos irregulares e informales de la forma *tú*

- The following verbs have irregular **affirmative** command forms.

decir	di	**Di** por qué.	*Tell (Say) why.*
hacer	haz	**Haz** la inspección.	*Do the inspection.*
ir	ve	**Ve** a la selva.	*Go to the jungle.*
poner	pon	**Pon** la basura en el basurero.	*Put the trash in the trash can.*
salir	sal	**Sal** de ese aire contaminado.	*Get out of that contaminated air.*
ser	sé	**Sé** amable con los voluntarios.	*Be nice to the volunteers.*
tener	ten	**Ten** paciencia con el gobierno.	*Be patient with the government.*
venir	ven	**Ven** a la sierra conmigo.	*Come to the mountain range with me.*

- As with the formal commands, attach pronouns to the affirmative command and place them in front of the negative command. Remember to place an accent on the next-to-last syllable of the verb in the affirmative command form.

Recíclala mañana.	*Recycle it tomorrow.*
No le pongas la multa a la estudiante.	*Don't give the fine to the student.*

Aplicación

12-40 En la oficina del alcalde Antonio Villaraigosa. Cuando el alcalde Villaraigosa habla con su personal en su oficina, le pide que le haga muchas cosas. ¿Cuáles de estos favores crees que **no** le pediría? Explica por qué.

MODELO: María, tráeme los documentos de mi escritorio, por favor.
Sí.
María, prepárame una tortilla española, por favor.
No, porque no se cocina en una oficina.

1. Tomás, no trabajes más de cinco horas diarias.
2. Clarisa, escribe este informe en latín.
3. Ramón, ve a la piscina y nada por tres horas.
4. Josefina, búscame el informe de Sacramento.
5. Raúl, llama al jefe de la EPA.
6. Concha, sé amable con los visitantes.
7. Eduardo, pon las sillas alrededor de la mesa para la reunión.
8. Julia, descansa. No hagas tu trabajo.

12-41 Tú eres el alcalde. Imagina que tú eres el alcalde. ¿Qué mandatos darías tú en la oficina? Combina elementos de las dos columnas para formar mandatos lógicos.

MODELO: poner—los papeles en la mesa
Sandra, pon los papeles en la mesa, por favor.

(no) buscar	una impresora para tu oficina
(no) comprar	al banco a depositar dinero
(no) salir	a trabajar el sábado
(no) decirle	la verdad al público
(no) venir	información en la Red informática

12-42 Alex Rodríguez, una gran estrella del béisbol. Alex Rodríguez nació en los EE.UU. de padres dominicanos. Imagínense que son amigos de él y que le pueden pedir lo que quieran. Túrnense para darle mandatos.

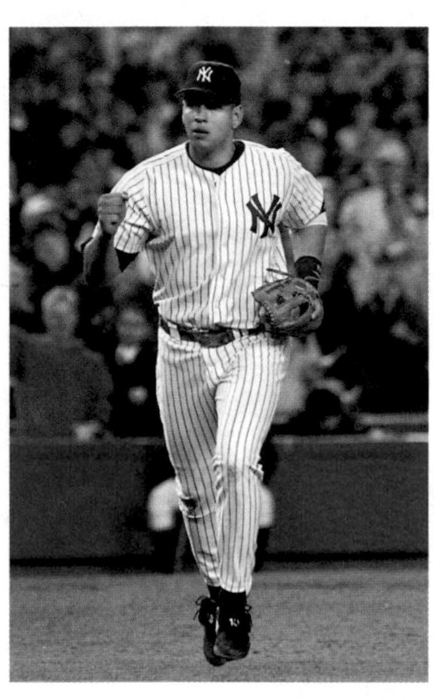

MODELO: *Alex, ven a mi casa a cenar esta noche.*

beber	comer	hacer	jugar	salir
buscar	decir	ir	practicar	ser

12-43 Consejos. Túrnense para darse consejos sobre el medio ambiente.

MODELO: E1: *Hay mucha contaminación del aire.*
E2: *No uses tu coche.*

ALGUNOS PROBLEMAS

1. Mi coche no es muy económico.
2. Hay mucha contaminación en la ciudad.
3. Algunas empresas no procesan sus desechos.
4. Me interesa la ecología.
5. El humo de algunas fábricas causa la lluvia ácida.
6. La deforestación es un problema crítico para muchos países.

¿Cuánto sabes tú? *Can you…*

12-51 to 12-54

- ☐ talk about environmental issues?
- ☐ say what you would do to help the environment, using the conditional tense, such as **Le escribiría una carta al editor del periódico; Protestaría en contra de las empresas que contaminan**?
- ☐ give a friend advice using **tú** commands such as **Camina más; no vayas siempre en coche**?

Observaciones

Episode 12

12-55 to 12-58

¡Pura vida! Episodio 12

En este episodio Felipe busca una camioneta nueva.

Antes de ver el video

12-44 Vehículos usados en Costa Rica. Cuando Felipe va a la Red informática encuentra una página web con camionetas a la venta. Lee sus características y explícale a Felipe por qué crees que la debe comprar o no.

MODELO: *En mi opinión,…*

MODELO:	Chevrolet S10
AÑO:	1995
AIRE ACONDICIONADO:	✗
VIDRIOS ELÉCTRICOS :	✗
TRANSMISIÓN:	Manual
MOTOR:	2500 cc diesel
DIRECCIÓN HIDRÁULICA:	✓
CIERRE CENTRAL:	✗
KILOMETRAJE:	224.000 km
COLOR:	blanco y azul
PRECIO:	US $ 8.000

Vehículos usados.

A ver el video

12-45 Felipe en la Red informática. Mira el episodio número doce de *¡Pura vida!* para ver cómo Felipe busca otra camioneta. Luego, indica si las afirmaciones siguientes son ciertas o falsas.

Felipe

Felipe en la Red informática

Los amigos ayudan a Felipe.

1. Felipe se ha conectado a su correo electrónico.	cierto	falso
2. Recibe un mensaje que dice que ha ganado la lotería.	cierto	falso
3. El mecánico ha reparado su camioneta.	cierto	falso
4. Imprime la dirección de la agencia.	cierto	falso
5. Busca una camioneta en **Terra.es.**	cierto	falso
6. El teléfono de Marcela no manda mensajes instantáneos.	cierto	falso
7. A Marcela le interesan más los trajes de baño.	cierto	falso
8. Felipe le pide la moto a Patricio para ir a ver la camioneta.	cierto	falso

Después de ver el video

WWW

12-46 www.Terra.es. Terra.es es un buscador (*search engine*) muy popular en España. Conéctate con la página web de **¡Arriba!** para ver qué se ofrece en **Terra.es** y anota qué hay en alguna de sus secciones.

NUESTRO MUNDO

Panoramas

Vistas culturales

12-59 to 12-60

Los hispanos en los Estados Unidos

12-47 ¿Ya sabes...? Trata de identificar o explicar lo siguiente.

1. el número de hispanos en los EE.UU.
2. el nombre de algunos hispanoamericanos importantes
3. un canal de televisión que sirve al público hispano
4. el nombre de un negocio hispano
5. el tema de un mural mexicoamericano

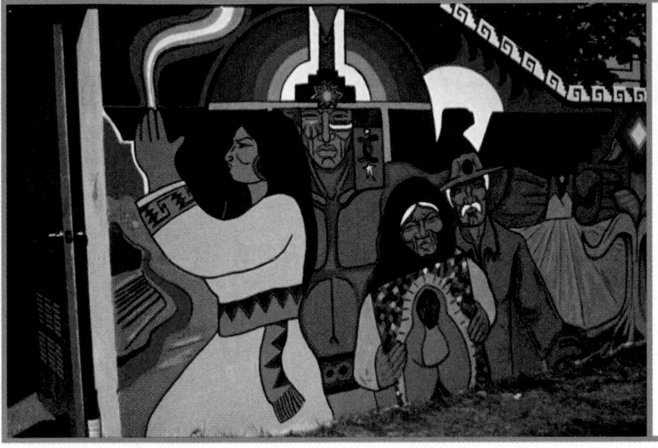

Los murales, hechos por artistas mexicoamericanos, ilustran la conexión entre el pasado y el presente del pueblo. Éste, por Juanishi Orosco, es parte de una colección llamada *Idaho Migrant Council Murals (1978).* Su tema es la leyenda de "Nuestra Raza" desde los aztecas hasta los campesinos de hoy en día.

Source: Juanishi Orosco V. and Esteban Villa, "Idaho Migrant Council Murals," 1978, one shot enamel paints on concrete wall. Dimension: stairway 20' x 14'. Idaho Migrant Council, Burley, Idaho Art Center. Courtesy of the California Ethnic and Multicultural Arch.

Cheech Marín es más conocido como actor de películas y programas de televisión, pero también es director, escritor y músico.

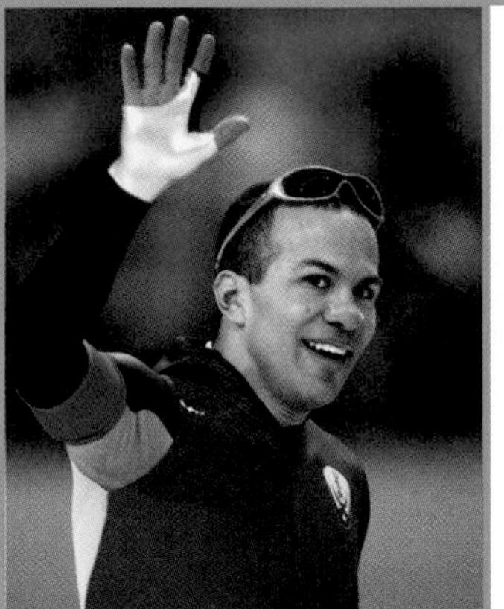

El mexicoamericano Derek Parra ganó la medalla de oro de patinaje de velocidad en los Juegos Olímpicos del año 2002.

La cubanoamericana Gloria Estefan ha popularizado la música y el baile de las islas del Caribe.

Hoy en día más de 42 millones de hispanos viven en los EE.UU., un gran número de los cuales habla español en casa y en el trabajo. Por eso, los EE.UU. constituye la cuarta nación hispanohablante. Esta presencia es evidente en los medios de comunicación, como en los canales de televisión Univisión y HBO en Español, en revistas populares como *Vanidades* y *People en español* y en periódicos como *La Opinión* y *El Nuevo Herald.*

La puertorriqueña Esmeralda Santiago es conocida por sus novelas, las cuales retratan la difícil transición que tuvo cuando se mudó de Puerto Rico a Nueva York. Entre sus novelas, se destacan *Cuando era puertorriqueña* y *El sueño de América.*

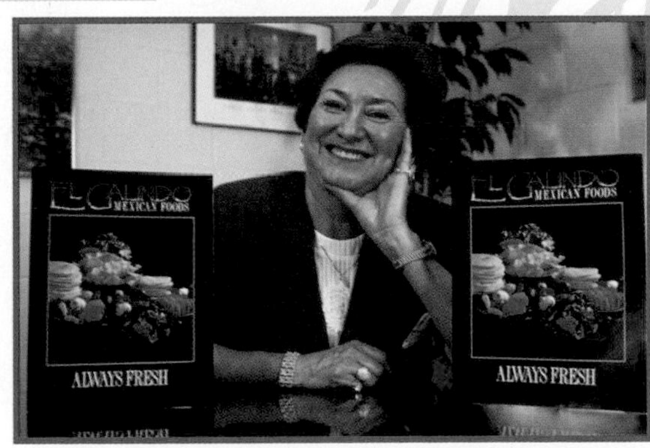

No es de extrañar que hoy en día haya miles de negocios hispanos que sirven a clientes de cualquier origen étnico.

12-48 A ver si puedes identificar a estas personalidades. Empareja a las siguientes personas con su profesión.

1. _____ Roberto Clemente
2. _____ Gloria Estefan
3. _____ Jennifer López
4. _____ Esmeralda Santiago
5. _____ Derek Parra
6. _____ Ricky Martin
7. _____ Cheech Marín
8. _____ Óscar de la Hoya

a. actor mexicoamericano
b. beisbolista puertorriqueño
c. escritora puertorriqueña
d. actriz y cantante puertorriqueña
e. patinador de velocidad mexicoamericano
f. boxeador mexicoamericano
g. cantante cubanoamericana
h. cantante puertorriqueño

12-49 Figuras conocidas. Conéctate con la página web de **¡Arriba!** para buscar más información sobre una persona hispana importante. Escribe un párrafo en el que incluyas esta información:

- su nombre completo
- sus raíces
- su edad
- por qué es conocido/a
- unas obras o reconocimientos

12-50 Entrevistas. Asuman el papel de la personalidad que investigaron en la actividad **12-49** y entrevístense para tener más información.

Ritmos

"Caminando" (Millo Torres y El Tercer Planeta, Puerto Rico)

La música de Millo Torres y El Tercer Planeta, un grupo puertorriqueño, es conocida por la mezcla de varias influencias musicales: rock, reggae, música ska (parecida al reggae pero más rápida y con muchos más instrumentos) y ritmos afrocaribeños. Los problemas sociales frecuentemente aparecen como tema principal en sus canciones.

Antes de escuchar

12-51 El futuro. En esta canción, el autor canta sobre el porvenir y la necesidad de seguir adelante en la vida. Las siguientes oraciones vienen de la canción. Cambia los verbos entre paréntesis al tiempo futuro para indicar lo que pasará o lo que hará el narrador.

1. Mi alma __________ (sonreír).
2. (Yo) __________ (tener) que seguir.
3. (Nosotros) __________ (navegar) con el viento y __________ (buscar) un porvenir (*future*).
4. El tiempo __________ (pasar).
5. (Yo) __________ (seguir) caminando.
6. __________ (hacerse) camino al andar.
7. Cada huella (*trace*) __________ (ser) un impreso de enseñanza.
8. Tropezando (*stumbling*) (yo) __________ (aprender) a caminar.
9. Alegría (yo) __________ (encontrar).
10. __________ (Llegar) un cambio.

A escuchar

12-52 Palabras clave. Completa la letra de "Caminando" con las siguientes palabras clave.

alegría	alma	cambio	enseñanza
esperanza	porvenir	seguir	vivir

Caminando
No hay segundo que detenga la __________,
mi __________ quiere sonreír.
Si entre ruegos y súplicos y alabanzas (*praise*),
anda y busca un trago lleno de __________.
Que estoy sediento (*thirsty*) y tengo que __________.
Navegamos con el viento,
sí buscando un __________.
Y el tiempo pasa.

Yo sigo caminando...
No hay camino que se pierda en la distancia,
se hace camino al andar.
Cada huella es un impreso de __________ y
tropezando es que se aprende a caminar.

Yo sigo caminando, ya tengo que llegar,
__________ estoy buscando sí, la tengo que encontrar.
Ya tengo que llegar a un __________,
y el tiempo pasa.
Yo sigo caminando...

Después de escuchar

12-53 El mensaje. En parejas, hablen de cuál es el mensaje (o mensajes) de "Caminando". Compartan sus opiniones y escriban una lista de posibles mensajes para esta canción. Refiéranse a las palabras clave con las cuales completaron la letra de la canción.

12-54 Experiencias. Trabajando con las mismas parejas, contesten las siguientes preguntas y compartan sus opiniones: ¿Cómo se relacionan los mensajes de "Caminando" con las experiencias de los hispanos en los EE.UU.? ¿Con las experiencias de sus antepasados (*ancestors*) o de los antepasados tuyos y de tu compañero/a?

Páginas

12-62

La casa en Mango Street (fragmento) (Sandra Cisneros, EE.UU.)

Sandra Cisneros (1954–), EE.UU.

La escritora Sandra Cisneros es chicana (mexicoamericana). Durante su vida se ha dedicado a mejorar y a enriquecer el futuro de los jóvenes. La novela *La casa en Mango Street* fue escrita originalmente en inglés y luego traducida al español por Elena Poniatowska, una importante figura literaria mexicana.

Antes de leer

12-55 Dialectos. El dialecto que se habla entre los mexicoamericanos ha sido influenciado por el español mexicano y el inglés norteamericano. Una característica del mexicano es usar el diminutivo para comunicar que algo es pequeño, querido o, a veces, sin importancia. Por ejemplo, **una cosita** es una cosa pequeña. El sufijo **-ito/a, -illo/a** puede extenderse. Por ejemplo, **chiquitito** significa aún más pequeño que **chiquito.** A ver si puedes adivinar qué significan los diminutivos que describen la casa en Mango Street.

1. Es pequeña y roja, con escalones (*stair steps*) apretados al frente y unas **ventanitas** tan chicas que parecen guardar su respiración.
2. No hay jardín al frente sino cuatro olmos (*elms*) **chiquititos** que la ciudad plantó en la banqueta.
3. Afuera, atrás hay un garaje **chiquito** para el carro que no tenemos todavía, y un **patiecito** que luce todavía más **chiquito** entre los edificios de los lados.
4. El **modito** en que lo dijo me hizo sentirme una nada.

A leer

12-56 La casa en Mango Street. Lee ahora la lectura para conocer esta famosa obra de Cisneros.

La casa en Mango Street (fragmento)

No siempre hemos vivido en Mango Street. Antes vivimos en el tercer piso de Loomis, y antes de allí vivimos en Keeler. Antes de Keeler fue en Paulina y de más antes, ni me acuerdo, pero de lo que sí me acuerdo es de un montón de mudanzas (*moves*). Y de que en cada una éramos uno más. Ya para cuando llegamos a Mango Street éramos seis: Mamá, Papá, Carlos, Kiki, mi hermana Nenny y yo.

La casa de Mango Street es nuestra y no tenemos que pagarle renta a nadie, ni compartir el patio con los de abajo, ni cuidarnos de hacer mucho ruido, y no hay propietario que golpee (golpear: *to pound*) el techo (*ceiling*) con una escoba. Pero aún así no es la casa que hubiéramos querido.

Tuvimos que salir volados (*in a rush*) del departamento (apartamento) de Loomis. Los tubos del agua se rompían y el casero (dueño) no los reparaba porque la casa era muy vieja. Salimos corriendo. Teníamos que usar el baño del vecino y acarrear (*carry*) agua en botes lecheros de un galón. Por eso Mamá y Papá buscaron una casa, y por eso nos cambiamos a la de Mango Street, muy lejos, del otro lado de la ciudad.

Siempre decían que algún día nos mudaríamos (nos... *we would move*) a una casa, una casa de verdad, que fuera nuestra para siempre, de la que no tuviéramos que salir cada año, y nuestra casa tendría agua corriente y tubos que sirvieran. Y escaleras interiores propias, como las casas de la tele. Y tendríamos un sótano, y por lo menos tres baños para no tener que avisarle a todo el mundo cada vez que nos bañáramos. Nuestra casa sería blanca, rodeada de árboles, un jardín enorme y el pasto creciendo sin cerca (*fence*). Ésa es la casa de la que hablaba Papá cuando tenía un billete de lotería y ésa es la casa que Mamá soñaba en los cuentos que nos contaba antes de dormir.

Pero la casa de Mango Street no es de ningún modo como ellos la contaron. Es pequeña y roja, con escalones apretados (escalones... *small and narrow steps*) al frente y unas ventanitas tan chicas que parecen guardar su respiración (parecen... *seem to be holding their breath*). Los ladrillos (*bricks*) se hacen pedazos en algunas partes y la puerta del frente se ha hinchado (hinchar: *to swell*) tanto que uno tiene que empujar fuerte para entrar. No hay jardín al frente sino cuatro olmos (*elms*) chiquititos que la ciudad plantó en la banqueta. Afuera, atrás hay un garaje chiquito para el carro que no tenemos todavía, y un patiecito que luce todavía más chiquito entre los edificios de los lados. Nuestra casa tiene escaleras pero son ordinarias, de pasillo, y tiene solamente un baño. Todos compartimos recámaras (dormitorios), Mamá y Papá, Carlos y Kiki, yo y Nenny.

Una vez, cuando vivíamos en Loomis, pasó una monja (*nun*) de mi escuela y me vio jugando enfrente. La lavandería (*laundry*) del piso bajo había sido cerrada con tablas (*boards*) arriba por un robo dos días antes, y el dueño había pintado en la madera SÍ, ESTÁ ABIERTO, para no perder clientela.

—¿Dónde vives?—preguntó.

—Allí—dije señalando arriba, al tercer piso.

—¿Vives *allí*?

Allí. Tuve que mirar a donde ella señalaba. El tercer piso, la pintura descarapelada (*peeling*), los barrotes (*bars*) que Papá clavó en las ventanas para que no nos cayéramos. ¿Vives *allí*? El modito (*manner*) en que lo dijo me hizo sentirme una nada. *Allí.* Yo vivo *allí.* Moví la cabeza asintiendo.

Desde ese momento supe que debía tener una casa. Una que pudiera señalar. Pero no esta casa. La casa de Mango Street no. Por mientras (*for the time being*), dice Mamá. Es temporario, dice Papá. Pero yo sé cómo son esas cosas.

Después de leer

12-57 ¿Probable o improbable? Lee las siguientes oraciones e indica si cada una es probable (**P**) o improbable (**I**) según el fragmento que has leído.

1. ______ La joven tenía doce años cuando se mudaron a Mango Street.
2. ______ Dejaron su antigua casa porque estaba en muy malas condiciones.
3. ______ Antes de Mango Street vivían en el campo.
4. ______ La casa de Mango Street era para dos familias.
5. ______ La familia compró la casa, no la alquiló.
6. ______ El jardín tenía espacio para plantar lechugas, tomates y otras verduras.
7. ______ Cada niño tenía su propio dormitorio.

12-58 ¿Es ésa su casa? Compara la casa de los sueños de la narradora con la que encontraron en Mango Street. ¿Era mejor o peor?

MODELO:

La de sus sueños	La de la calle Mango
era blanca	*era roja*

12-59 Resumir. Trabajen juntos para resumir el contentido de la lectura. Pueden usar las preguntas a continuación como guía.

1. ¿Quién narra la selección?
2. ¿Cómo era su familia?
3. ¿Qué quería? ¿Por qué?
4. ¿Por qué se desilusionó?
5. ¿Por qué dice que se sintió como una "nada" cuando le habló la monja?
6. ¿Crees que algún día la casa de Mango Street será la casa de sus sueños? ¿Por qué?

12-60 La casa de sus sueños. Túrnense para describir la casa de sus sueños. ¿Cómo se compara con la de la narradora del cuento?

MODELO: E1: *La casa de mis sueños tiene un jardín grande y una piscina. La de la joven no tenía jardín, ni piscina...*

Taller

12-63 to 12-64

12-61 Un relato personal. En este taller, vas a narrar alguna experiencia que hayas tenido con la tecnología o con el medio ambiente en el pasado. Si no has tenido ninguna, puedes inventarla. Puedes incluir también un diálogo entre los personajes para explicar si el conflicto ha sido resuelto.

MODELO: *En 2004 mi familia se mudó a San Antonio. Éramos cinco personas, mi madre, mis tres hermanas y yo. Para mí fue difícil el cambio. No conocía a nadie y me sentía fuera de lugar, pero luego conocí a una chica por la Red, y...*

Antes de escribir

- **El escenario.** Piensa en el lugar, las personas, la situación y tus impresiones.

A escribir

- **Introducción.** Abre el relato con una oración para describir el contexto y el evento.
- **Anzuelo (*Hook*).** Escribe cuatro o cinco oraciones que piquen (*spark*) el interés del lector.
- **Conflicto.** Presenta algún conflicto psicológico o personal.
- **Diálogo.** Escribe dos o tres líneas de diálogo entre los personajes.
- **Conclusión.** Resume o cierra el relato.

Después de escribir

- **Revisar.** Revisa tu relato para verificar los siguientes puntos:
  - ☐ el uso del pretérito, del imperfecto y del presente perfecto
  - ☐ el uso del futuro y del condicional
  - ☐ la concordancia y la ortografía
- **Intercambiar**
  Intercambia tu relato con el de un/a compañero/a. Mientras leen los relatos, hagan comentarios y sugerencias sobre el contenido, la estructura y la gramática. Reaccionen también a los relatos.
- **Entregar**
  Pasa tu relato a limpio, incorporando las sugerencias de tu compañero/a. Después, entrégaselo a tu profesor/a.

Vocabulario

Primera parte

La computadora y otros aparatos electrónicos	The computer and other electronic appliances
la antena parabólica	*satellite dish*
el cajero automático	*ATM machine*
la computadora portátil	*laptop computer*
el contestador automático	*answering machine*
el disco duro	*hard drive*
el disquete	*computer disc*
el DVD	*DVD*
el escáner	*scanner*
la fotocopiadora	*photocopier*
la impresora	*printer*
el lector de CD/DVD	*CD/DVD player*
la pantalla	*screen*
el ratón	*mouse*
el teclado	*keyboard*
el teléfono inalámbrico	*cordless phone*
el teléfono móvil/celular	*cellular phone*
la videograbadora	*VCR*

Recursos en la computadora	Resources on the computer
el correo electrónico	*e-mail*
la hoja electrónica	*spreadsheet*
el hipervínculo / el enlace	*hyperlink*
el juego electrónico	*computer (electronic) game*
la Red informática	*Internet*
el sitio web/la página web	*web site/web page*

Verbos	Verbs
apagar	*to turn off*
archivar	*to file; to save*
borrar	*to erase*
encender (ie)	*to turn on*
fotocopiar	*to photocopy*
funcionar	*to function; to work*
grabar	*to record*
imprimir	*to print*
instalar	*to install*
programar	*to program*

Adjetivos	Adjectives
electrónico/a	*electronic*
tecnológico/a	*technological*

Otras palabras y expresiones	Other words and expressions
el diseño	*design*
la marca	*brand*

Segunda parte

Nuestro mundo y el medio ambiente	Our world and the environment
el bosque	*forest*
la deforestación	*deforestation*
los desechos	*waste*
la energía	*energy*
el envase (de aluminio)	*(aluminum) container*
la escasez	*shortage*
la fábrica	*factory*
el humo	*smoke*
la medida	*measure*
el medio ambiente	*environment*
la multa	*fine*
la naturaleza	*nature*
el petróleo	*oil*
los pesticidas	*pesticides*
la planta nuclear	*nuclear plant*
la radioactividad	*radioactivity*
el recurso natural	*natural resource*
el reciclaje	*recycling*
la reforestación	*reforestation*

Verbos	Verbs
arrojar	*to throw out*
conservar	*to conserve; to preserve*
consumir	*to consume*
contaminar	*to contaminate; to pollute*
echar	*to throw out*
proteger (j)	*to protect*
reciclar	*to recycle*

Adjetivos	Adjectives
dispuesto/a	*willing; ready; disposed*
obligatorio/a	*mandatory*

Appendix 1

B Activities

Capítulo 1

1-6B ¿Cómo está usted? Your partner will assume the role of instructor; you are his/her student. Greet each other and ask how things are. Use the following information about yourself and the day.

- Answer your instructor. Then ask him/her how he/she feels.
- Respond and say good-bye to you instructor.
- Tell your instructor you will see him/her later.

1-10B Otra vez, por favor (*please*). Take turns spelling out your words to each other. Be sure to say what category they are in. If you need to hear the spelling again, ask your partner to repeat by saying, **Otra vez, por favor.**

Modelo: cosa (*thing*) (enchilada)
e- ene - ce - hache - i - ele - a - de - a

YOU SPELL...	**YOU WRITE...**
1. persona famosa (Salma Hayek)	1. persona famosa: ____________
2. ciudad (Tampa)	2. ciudad (*city*): ____________
3. cosa (café)	3. cosa: ____________
4. ciudad (Quito)	4. ciudad: ____________

1-24B Necesito... Below is a list of items you have. Your classmate will tell you what he/she needs. Tell him/her if you have each item or not. Circle the items you have that your classmate needs. When you finish, compare your lists.

Modelo: E1: *Necesito ochenta bolígrafos. ¿Tienes ochenta?*
E2: *Sí, tengo bolígrafos.*
E1: *Necesito treinta y tres libros. ¿Tienes treinta y tres libros?*
E2: *Sólo* (only) *veintidós.*

Tengo...

80 bolígrafos	30 lápices	14 cuadernos	22 libros
17 mochilas	95 mapas	15 diccionarios	100 papeles
25 pizarras	11 sillas	7 puertas	1 mesa

Capítulo 2

Hora	Actividad
	la clase
11:30	la conferencia (*lecture*)
	la reunión
13:45	el examen
	el partido de fútbol
19:00	el programa "Amigos" en la televisión
20:30	la fiesta

2-10B ¿A qué hora? Complete your calendar by asking your partner when the events with times missing take place.

Modelo: la fiesta (20:30)
E1: *¿A qué hora es la fiesta?*
E2: *Es a las ocho y media de la noche.*

2-23B ¿Dónde estoy? Take turns identifying the country where you speak the language.

Modelo: E1: Hablo italiano.
E2: Estás en Italia.

HABLO...	TU COMPAÑERO/A ESTÁ EN...
1. español	Corea
2. japonés	Inglaterra
3. chino	Portugal
4. alemán	Rusia

2-34B Entrevistas. Ask each other questions to obtain information. Be prepared to report back to the class.

Modelo: E1: *¿A qué hora llegas a clase?*
E2: *Llego a las dos.*

1. ¿Dónde estudias?
2. ¿Aprendes mucho en clase?
3. ¿Qué música (popular, clásica, de rock) escuchas?
4. ¿Bailas en una fiesta?
5. ¿Qué programa ves en la televisión?

2-39B ¿Tienes? Take turns asking each other if you have the items on your list. If your partner has the item you want, you make a pair. The first person who has five pairs of items wins.

Modelo: ☐ un libro de historia
E1: *¿Tienes un libro de historia?*
E2: *Sí, tengo. (No, no tengo.)*

☐ un cuaderno verde
☐ una mochila negra
☐ un libro de francés
☐ una pintura de Dalí
☐ una novela de Hemingway
☐ un reloj grande
☐ un lápiz rojo
☐ un cuaderno viejo
☐ un examen difícil
☐ un/a profesor/a inteligente
☐ un libro viejo
☐ un buen amigo

Capítulo 3

3-9B Inventario. Take turns dictating your inventory numbers to each other in Spanish. Which items do you have in common? **¡Ojo! (*Watch out!*)** Watch for agreement.

MODELO: 747 mesas
setecientas cuarenta y siete mesas

1. 202 diccionarios
2. 5.002 escritorios
3. 816 pizarras
4. 52 mapas
5. 1.326 libros
6. 2.700.000 calculadoras
7. 110.000 sillas
8. 762 computadoras

3-26B Las materias, la hora, el lugar. Take turns asking and answering questions in order to complete the missing information on your class schedules.

MODELO: E1: *¿A qué hora es la clase de...?*
E2: *¿Qué clase es a la/s...?*
E1: *¿Dónde es la clase de...?*
E2: *¿Quién es el/la profesor/a de...?*

Hora	Clase	Lugar	Profesor/a
8:30	*cálculo*	*Facultad de Informática*	
9:00			*Ramón Sánchez Guillón*
	biología	*Facultad de Medicina*	
12:00	*lingüística*	*Facultad de Letras*	*Juan Ramón Jiménez*
1:55		*Facultad de Ingeniería*	*Carlos Santos Pérez*

3-37B ¿Dónde estoy? Take turns acting out your situations while your partner tries to guess where you are.

MODELO: E1: (act out reading a book) *¿Dónde estoy?*
E2: *Estás en la biblioteca.*

1. (feeling very sick)
2. (playing tennis)
3. (painting a picture)
4. (playing basketball)
5. ¿...?

3-43B Dibujos (*Drawings*). Take turns describing a person using the following information while your classmate tries to draw the person described. Then compare your drawings with the descriptions.

MODELO: chica: dieciocho años, alta, bonita, triste, oficina
E1: *Es una chica. Tiene dieciocho años. Es alta y bonita. Está triste y está en la oficina.*
E2: *Es un hombre...*

1. chico, veinte años, delgado, bajo, enamorado, cafetería
2. mujer, cuarenta años, alta, gorda, cansada, gimnasio
3. mujer, noventa años, delgada, pequeña, ocupada, biblioteca

Capítulo 4

4-11B El/La curioso/a. Take turns asking each other about your family. Use the following questions to get started. Be sure to conjugate the verbs in italics.

TUS PREGUNTAS	POSIBLES RESPUESTAS A LAS PREGUNTAS DE TU COMPAÑERO/A
1. ¿Sirven las comidas en tu casa temprano o tarde?	*Preferir* vivir en un apartamento.
2. ¿Quiénes duermen la siesta en tu familia?	*Almorzar* con ellos siempre que estoy en casa.
3. ¿A qué hora vuelven tus padres (hijos) a casa durante la semana?	*Servir* platos especiales.
4. ¿Qué piensas hacer con tu familia este fin de semana?	*Preferir* comer en casa porque la comida es mejor.
5. ¿Puedes ver la televisión todas las noches en casa?	*Dormir* la siesta.

4-18B Una entrevista para *Prensa Libre*. *Prensa Libre* is an independent newspaper from Guatemala. Role-play a member of a famous family as your partner—a reporter—asks you questions. After the interview, ask the reporter questions based on the following information. Write down his/her answers.

MODELO: E1: *¿Practica usted fútbol?*
E2: *No, no lo practico. Y usted, ¿escribe artículos en inglés también?*
E1: *Sí, los escribo. (No, no los escribo.)*

ACTIVIDADES

escribir muchos artículos
hablar inglés en su trabajo
visitar El Salvador
preferir los periódicos norteamericanos
siempre escribir la verdad
ver a muchas personas famosas
necesitar mi fotografía
¿...?

4-30B ¡Estoy aburrido/a! Your partner is bored. Invite him/her to do something that he/she might enjoy.

MODELO: E1: *Estoy aburrido/a.*
E2: *¿Quieres ir a bailar?*
E1: *Me encantaría. ¡Vamos! / Gracias, pero no puedo. No tengo dinero.*

ALGUNAS ACTIVIDADES

conversar con...
correr por el parque
hacer ejercicio
dar una fiesta
ir al cine / a la playa
pasear por el centro
tomar un café
visitar a amigos / la familia

4-41B Entrevista. Read the following profile and answer your partner's questions using this information. Then ask your partner the questions below. Write down his/her answers.

Modelo: E1: *¿Conoces alguna* (any) *persona famosa?*
E2: *Sí, conozco a Ricky Martin. Soy amigo/a de él.*

Soy amigo/a del presidente de Costa Rica.
Toco el piano muy bien.
No practico mucho los deportes.
Vivo y trabajo en la Ciudad de Guatemala.
Hablo español y una lengua maya.
Soy arqueólogo/a y estudio las pirámides mayas.

1. ¿Conoces un político importante?
2. ¿Qué actores famosos conoces?
3. ¿Qué idiomas sabes hablar?
4. ¿Qué países conoces muy bien?
5. ¿Estudias la biología?
6. ¿Juegas bien al fútbol?

Capítulo 5

5-5B El monstruo (*Monster*). Túrnense (*Take turns*) para describir un monstruo mientras su compañero/a lo dibuja (*draw*). Incluyan características físicas. Luego comparen sus descripciones con sus dibujos.

Modelo: El monstruo tiene cuatro ojos, dos dientes, una nariz...

El monstruo tiene...

- un ojo grande
- cinco dientes pequeños
- pelo largo
- tres narices

5-16B En la agencia de bienes raíces (*real estate*). Buscas una casa en una agencia de bienes raíces. Quieres comprar una casa pequeña, pero por un precio razonable. En la agencia hay dos casas. Escucha las descripciones del agente y después hazle preguntas. Decide cuál de las dos casas quieres comprar.

5-28B ¿Cómo son? Túrnense para preguntarse sobre "su familia". Imagínate que eres uno de los personajes (*characters*) de la serie popular, *The Simpsons*. Si no conocen a esta familia, pueden usar su familia.

Modelo: más trabajador/a
E1: *¿Quién es el/la más trabajador/a de tu familia?*
E2: *Mi padre, Mike, es el más trabajador de mi familia.*

1. menor
2. más imaginativo/a
3. peor cantante (*singer*)
4. más atractivo/a
5. más activo/a
6. mayor

5-33B ¿Qué estoy haciendo? Mientras (*While*) actúas una de las siguientes situaciones, tu pareja trata de adivinar (*guess*) lo que estás haciendo. Túrnense para actuar y adivinar.

Modelo: afeitarse
E1: (act out "shaving") *¿Qué estoy haciendo?*
E2: *Estás afeitándote.*

1. secarse el pelo
2. ponerse el desodorante
3. levantarse de la cama
4. lavarse las manos

Capítulo 6

6-9B Cocina Concha. Esta "cocina" (restaurante informal) es una de las muchas que se encuentran por la costa chilena, donde las especialidades son pescados y mariscos. Imagínate que tú eres un/a camarero/a que atiende a un/a turista. Trata de convencerlo/a de que pida los platos más caros, para luego recibir una propina más grande. Puedes utilizar expresiones como **exquisito, fenomenal, delicioso, rico,** etcétera.

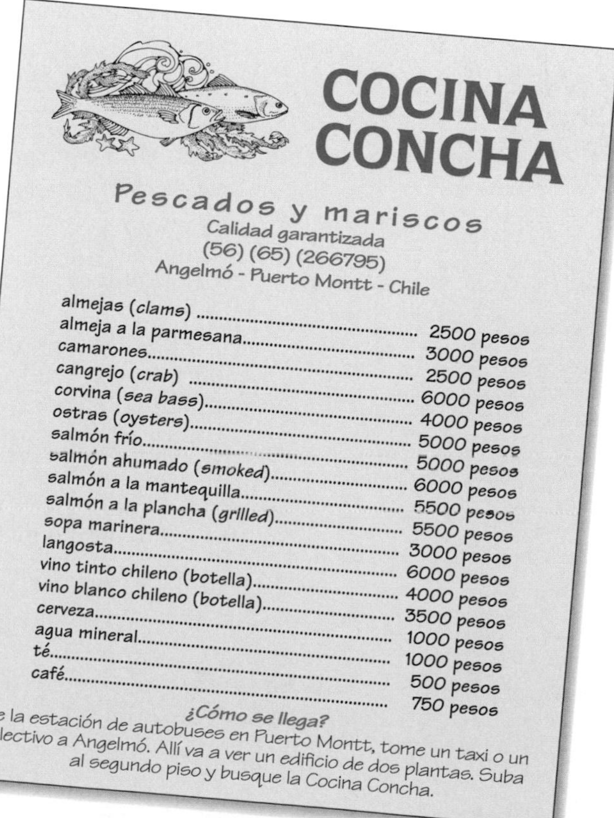

6-30B El arroz con leche. El arroz con leche es un postre muy conocido en todo el mundo hispano. Imagínate que tu compañero/a tiene la receta y tú tienes algunos de los ingredientes. Decidan qué ingredientes necesitan comprar.

Modelo: E1: *Necesitamos una taza de arroz.*
E2: *No tenemos arroz. Tenemos que comprarlo.*

EN TU COCINA, TIENES...

1 litro leche

½ taza de azúcar

1 limón viejo

canela molida (*ground cinnamon*)

sal

6-36B Charadas. Túrnense para representar éstas y otras acciones en el pasado para ver si el/la otro/a compañero/a puede adivinar la acción.

Modelo: E1: (Act out: *Corté el pan.*)
E2: *Cortaste el pan.*

El/La profesor/a peló las zanahorias.

Comí un huevo crudo.

Volteé la tortilla en el plato.

Cortamos el bistec.

Tomaste café con leche.

¿...?

6-42B ¿Qué pasó? Tu compañero/a te va a preguntar qué pasó en algunas situaciones. Contesta usando actividades lógicas de la lista.

Modelo: en la fiesta familiar
E1: *¿Qué pasó en la fiesta familiar?*
E2: *Mi mamá sirvió nuestra comida favorita.*

SITUACIONES

1. en el restaurante el sábado
2. en el museo
3. en el mercado

ALGUNAS ACTIVIDADES

1. dormirse
2. no saber el pretérito
3. servir bebidas alcohólicas

Capítulo 7

7-8B Una invitación. Responde a la invitación de tu compañero/a. Pídele (*Ask him/her for*) detalles. Puedes usar preguntas de la lista.

- ¿Qué día?
- ¿Dónde?
- ¿A qué hora volvemos?
- ¿A qué hora?

7-11B Chismes (*Gossip*). Alguien encontró unos apuntes del/de la profesor/a sobre la clase de ayer. Hagan y contesten las preguntas sobre lo que ocurrió, basándose en los apuntes.

1. ¿Quiénes no estuvieron en clase?
2. ¿Quiénes tuvieron que hacer presentaciones?
3. ¿Quiénes no hicieron la tarea?
4. ¿Qué excusas le dieron al/a la profesor/a?

7-25B Consejos. Explíquense cómo se sienten y pidan consejos sobre lo que deben hacer. Pueden aceptar o rechazar (*reject*) los consejos, pero es necesario dar excusas si no los aceptan.

MODELO: E1: *Estoy aburrido/a. ¿Qué hago?*
E2: *¿Por qué no das un paseo?*
E1: *No quiero. No me gusta salir de noche.*
E2: *Bueno, yo voy contigo. ¿Está bien?*

Situaciones	Sugerencias	Reacciones
Me siento muy solo/a.	hacer un pícnic	¡Fabuloso!
Estoy en la oficina todo el día sin salir.	jugar al tenis	No me gusta(an)...
Quiero conocer a Tiger Woods.	escuchar música	¡Ideal!
Tengo mucho calor.	trabajar en la biblioteca	¡Qué buena idea!
Compré una raqueta nueva.	ver la televisión	Me da igual.
	visitar una librería	¡Qué mala idea!
	ir a un concierto	No quiero porque...
	¿...?	Tienes razón.
		No puedo porque...
		¡Vamos!

7-34B ¿Tienes? Imagínate que tu compañero/a está muy enfermo/a y quiere saber si le puedes traer algunas cosas. Contesta las preguntas para decidir qué puedes traerle de casa y qué necesitas comprar.

MODELO: E1: *¿Tienes naranjas?*
E2: *Sí, tengo naranjas. / No, no tengo naranjas.*
E1: *¿Me las traes? / ¿Me compras unas naranjas?*
E2: *Sí, te las traigo. / Sí, te las compro.*

EN TU COCINA, TIENES...

azúcar	jugo de limón	manzanas	sopa de tomate	sal
café	jugo de naranja	pan	lechuga	tomates
naranjas	leche	papas	pollo	zanahorias

Capítulo 8

8-5B ¿Tienes? Tienes un recibo para varios artículos, pero falta parte de la información. Túrnense para llenar su recibo con la información que falta.

Modelo: E1: *¿Cuánto cuesta la blusa de manga corta?*
E2: *Cuesta 50 nuevos soles. ¿De qué talla es?*
E1: *Es una...*

Falabella		**00917** **12 diciembre de 2008**
Artículo	Talla	Precio (nuevos soles)
blusa de manga corta		NS 50
camiseta de algodón	40	
_____ de lana	81	NS 75
blusa de seda		NS 58
chaqueta de _____	42	NS 200
sandalias de cuero	39	
falda de _____		NS 49

8-15B ¿Qué pasaba? Tu compañero/a te va a preguntar qué pasaba en algunas situaciones. Contesta, usando actividades lógicas de la lista.

Modelo: a la medianoche en la última fiesta que asististe
E1: *¿Qué pasaba a la medianoche en la fiesta?*
E2: *Todos bailaban.*

ALGUNAS ACTIVIDADES

1. todos *divertirse* mucho
2. los turistas *preferir* comprar...
3. yo *dormir* como un ángel
4. el profesor *repetir* la lección
5. los estudiantes *pedir* refrescos
6. todos *ver* el maniquí (*mannequin*)

8-33B Artículo perdido. Imagínate que perdiste un artículo que compraste y que lo vas a buscar en la oficina de artículos perdidos (*lost and found*) de un almacén. Di lo que perdiste y contesta las preguntas que te hace tu compañero/a mientras completa el formulario necesario. Después, hazle las siguientes preguntas al agente.

Artículo perdido (*Item lost*)
Camisa

- Talla: 40
- Tela: Algodón
- Estilo: De cuadros azules y de manga larga con botones (*buttons*) blancos

8-37B En una tienda de equipo deportivo. Tu compañero/a es propietario/a (*owner*) de un nuevo negocio (*business*) y tú estás interesado/a en descubrir de qué se trata. Hazle las siguientes preguntas.

1. ¿Qué se vende?
2. ¿Qué se anuncia?
3. ¿Qué se ofrece?
4. ¿Cómo se paga?

Capítulo 9

9-5B En el mostrador de AVIANCA. Hagan el papel *(role)* de agente de viajes y viajero/a en el mostrador (*counter*) de la aerolínea AVIANCA (aerolínea colombiana). Incluyan la siguiente información.

Modelo: (el destino) *Quiero comprar un boleto para Bogotá.*

PREGUNTAS PARA EL/LA AGENTE	INFORMACIÓN
la hora de salida	destino = Bogotá
el número del vuelo	equipaje = dos maletas
el número de la puerta de embarque	fecha de vencimiento *(expiration)* del pasaporte = 17-04-09
	el asiento = de ventanilla

9-11B ¡Explícate! Hablen sobre los viajes que van a hacer, usando las categorías del modelo. Luego, háganse las preguntas siguientes e intenta convencer (*convince*) al otro/a la otra para ir juntos.

	Modelo	Tu compañero/a
Destino:	*Miami*	
Ruta:	*Carolina del Norte*	
Transporte:	*avión*	
Fecha de llegada:	*el 27 de mayo*	
Duración del viaje:	*una semana*	
Propósito:	*divertirme en South Beach, ir de compras y nadar en la playa*	

1. ¿A dónde vas?
2. ¿Cómo vas a llegar?
3. ¿Cómo vas a viajar, por tren, por carro, por...?
4. ¿Para cuándo es el viaje?
5. ¿Por cuánto tiempo vas?
6. ¿Para qué vas?

Una escultura

9-15B El robo en el museo. Cada uno/a de ustedes encontró un objeto del Museo del Oro. Túrnense para hacerse preguntas y ver qué objeto encontró cada uno. Contesten cada pregunta con un adverbio que termina en **-mente,** formado con un adjetivo de la lista.

enorme	especial	increíble	inmediato
maravilloso	tranquilo	particular	fácil

1. ¿Cómo es?
2. ¿Cuál es el origen del objeto?
3. ¿Dónde lo encontraste?
4. ¿Qué valor crees que tiene?
5. ¿Vas a llamar a la policía?

9-28B Desafío (*Challenge*). Cada uno/a de ustedes tiene una lista de verbos diferentes en el indicativo y el subjuntivo. Dile a tu compañero/a el indicativo del verbo, y él/ella debe darte el presente de subjuntivo de ese verbo.

Modelo: E1: *Indicativo: tomamos*
E2: *Subjuntivo: tomemos*
E1: *Correcto.*

MI LISTA			
Indicativo	**Subjuntivo**	**Correcto**	**Incorrecto**
tomamos	**tomemos**	✔	
vemos	*veamos*		
voy	*vaya*		
lees	*leas*		
dormimos	*durmamos*		
ponen	*pongan*		
quiere	*quiera*		

9-33B ¿Qué hacer? Imagínate que tu compañero/a te pide consejos. Después de escuchar cada problema, ofrécele un consejo. Usa verbos de la lista para tus recomendaciones. Escucha su reacción.

Modelo: E1: *Tengo un examen de química mañana.*
E2: *Te recomiendo que estudies mucho.*
E1: *Buena idea. / No tengo tiempo.*

te aconsejo	te digo	mando	te pido	te recomiendo
deseo	insisto en	permito	te prohíbo	te sugiero

Capítulo 10

10-5B Consejos médicos. Habla con tu compañero/a para que te dé consejos sobre los siguientes síntomas.

MODELO: E1: *Me duelen los pulmones.*
E2: *Debes dejar de fumar.*

SÍNTOMAS	CONSEJOS PARA EL/LA ESTUDIANTE A
1. Tengo gripe.	1. tomar más café
2. Tengo náuseas.	2. no caminar tanto y usar más el coche
3. Tengo un dolor de cabeza terrible.	3. ir de vacaciones
4. Toso mucho.	4. tomar antiácidos
5. No tengo energía.	5. ponerse el termómetro
6. Soy alérgico/a a los mariscos.	6. comprar *Kleenex*

10-10B En la sala de urgencias. Imagínense que ustedes tienen que decidir qué deben hacer en situaciones urgentes. Un/a estudiante presenta unas situaciones. El otro/la otra responde con instrucciones lógicas de su lista, usando un mandato de **nosotros.** Túrnense, cambiando de papel.

MODELO: E1: *El niño tiene gripe.*
E2: *Démosle vitamina C.*

ACCIONES

buscar el tanque de oxígeno	darle un jarabe	tomarle la temperatura
darle un antiácido	ponerle una inyección de penicilina	¿...?

SITUACIONES URGENTES

1. La paciente en la silla se rompió una pierna.
2. El señor viejo está muy ansioso.
3. La niña está resfriada.
4. La señora tiene dolor de cabeza.
5. Al joven le duele un diente.
6. ¿...?

10-19B Te recomiendo que... Un/a estudiante presenta los siguientes problemas mientras el otro/la otra ofrece recomendaciones. Túrnense, cambiando de papel. Pueden usar el verbo **recomiendo** con una cláusula nominativa en el subjuntivo.

MODELO: E1: *Estoy muy flaco/a.*
E2: *Te recomiendo que comas tres comidas completas todos los días.*

PROBLEMAS	RECOMENDACIONES PARA EL ESTUDIANTE A
1. Mi jefe/a padece de úlceras.	1. tomar una aspirina
2. A mi abuelo/a le preocupa su alto nivel de colesterol.	2. practicar juegos de memoria
3. A mi amigo/a le falta energía.	3. no comer postres
4. No quiero engordar cuando voy de vacaciones.	4. hacer jogging
5. Me duele el estómago.	5. no fumar

10-33B *Termas Bolivia.* Tienes mucho estrés y quieres ir a un spa. Tu compañero/a trabaja en *Termas Bolivia*. Explícale tus problemas para ver si es el spa apropiado para ti.

PROBLEMAS

1. Necesito perder 15 kilos.
2. Tengo que dejar de fumar.
3. Tengo mucho estrés.
4. Me duelen los músculos.
5. Necesito hacer yoga.

Capítulo 11

11-13B Consejos. Túrnense para contarse sus problemas y darse consejos, usando expresiones impersonales.

MODELO: un/a amigo/a enojado/a
E1: *Mi amigo/a está enojado/a conmigo.*
E2: *Es indispensable que lo/la llames y que ustedes hablen del problema.*

PROBLEMAS

no tener dinero	un examen difícil
un virus en tu computadora	un reloj que no funciona *(broken)*
un/a jefe/a imposible	¿…?

CONSEJOS

1. vestirse bien
2. hablar con él/ella y explicar el problema
3. comprar un carro nuevo
4. hacerle preguntas para comprender el tema
5. obedecerles

11-23B La despedida. Eres un/a empleado/a de veinte años en la sección de finanzas de tu empresa. Siempre has sido (*have been*) muy honrado/a, pero ahora hay una discrepancia en las cuentas. Explícale a tu director/a por qué mereces (*deserve*) quedarte en tu trabajo. Si hay un error, no fue tu culpa (*not your fault*), trabajas mucho y largas horas, etc.

LAS CUENTAS DE ABRIL

- COMPRAS: $125.000,00
- VENTAS: $305.000,00
- GASTOS: $250.000,00

11-31B Dos empresas. Eres el/la directora/a de la empresa Mundiplásticos y tu compañero/a es el/la directora/a de la empresa Plásticos, S.A. Túrnense para hacer y contestar las siguientes preguntas con la información de tu empresa. Usen el subjuntivo o el indicativo con la lista de conjunciones, según sea necesario.

cuando	tan pronto como	hasta (que)
para (que)	después de (que)	donde

MUNDIPLÁSTICOS

- ORGANIZACIÓN: 10 ingenieros/50 empleados
- EQUIPO: 2 máquinas nuevas
- NUEVOS PUESTOS: 2 ingenieros
- FECHA DE SOLICITUD: 3 de mayo
- DECISIÓN PARA: 12 de agosto

PREGUNTAS:

1. ¿Cuándo vas a contratar más empleados?
2. ¿Cuántos empleados vas a contratar?
3. ¿Hasta cuando vas a aceptar candidatos?
4. ¿Cuándo vas a tomar la decisión?

Capítulo 12

12-7B Una encuesta de Harris. Haz el papel de una persona que contesta las preguntas para una encuesta de Harris.

MODELO: (Saludo) E1: *Buenos días. Con su permiso, me gustaría hacerle algunas preguntas sobre su forma de utilizar la tecnología...*
E2: *Bueno, no tengo mucho tiempo pero...*

- Usa la computadora para sus estudios y en su trabajo. Tienes una pantalla grande.
- Usa una variedad de programas pero no es muy artístico/a.
- En casa tiene una computadora con poca memoria; en la oficina tiene una más rápida.
- En la oficina tiene alguien que le ayuda con cualquier problema técnico.

12-25B ¿Qué harás? Túrnense para preguntarse qué harán en estas circunstancias.

MODELO: Ni el fax ni la conexión de la Red informática funcionan.
Llamaré a un técnico o compraré un módem nuevo.

CIRCUNSTANCIAS

1. Necesitas información para un trabajo sobre un país hispano.
2. Recibes cien mensajes en tu correo electrónico.
3. No funciona tu contestador automático.
4. Hay un disco compacto nuevo que te interesa oír.

SOLUCIONES

1. llamar un/a analista de sistemas
2. comprar otro/a
3. usar una tarjeta de crédito
4. escribir otro trabajo

12-31B ¿Cuál es tu opinión? Túrnense para hacer y responder a preguntas sobre el medio ambiente. Usa expresiones como: **¿Cuál es tu opinión sobre...? ¿Qué podemos hacer para...?,** etc.

MODELO: la contaminación del medio ambiente
E1: *¿Crees que la contaminación es un problema grave?*
E2: *En mi opinión, es el problema más grave que tenemos.*

PREGUNTAS

1. los coches pequeños
2. el deber del gobierno de proteger el medio ambiente
3. la energía solar
4. nuestro deber como seres humanos

RESPUESTAS

la mejor solución

peligroso/a

importante hacer más

todo lo necesario para no gastarla

12-38B Geraldo. Imagínate que eres jefe/a de una planta nuclear y tu compañero/a es entrevistador/a para un programa de investigación en la televisión. Contesta sus preguntas, pero siempre con respuestas indirectas y excusas.

MODELO: limpiar los desechos
E1: *Usted dijo que limpiaría los desechos de su planta, pero...*
E2: *Es verdad. Pero eso toma tiempo. Usted dijo que no me haría preguntas indiscretas.*
E1: *Es verdad, pero...*

RESPUESTAS DEL/DE LA JEFE/A

Usted dijo que...

1. no sacarle fotos a mi familia
2. ayudarme a mejorar mi imagen en su artículo
3. ser un artículo favorable
4. no hacerme preguntas difíciles
5. escuchar mi punto de vista

Appendix 2

Verb Charts

Regular Verbs: Simple Tenses

Infinitive Present Participle Past Participle	Indicative					Subjunctive		Imperative
	Present	Imperfect	Preterit	Future	Conditional	Present	Imperfect	
hablar hablando hablado	hablo hablas habla hablamos habláis hablan	hablaba hablabas hablaba hablábamos hablabais hablaban	hablé hablaste habló hablamos hablasteis hablaron	hablaré hablarás hablará hablaremos hablaréis hablarán	hablaría hablarías hablaría hablaríamos hablaríais hablarían	hable hables hable hablemos habléis hablen	hablara hablaras hablara habláramos hablarais hablaran	habla tú, no hables hable usted hablemos hablen Uds.
comer comiendo comido	como comes come comemos coméis comen	comía comías comía comíamos comíais comían	comí comiste comió comimos comisteis comieron	comeré comerás comerá comeremos comeréis comerán	comería comerías comería comeríamos comeríais comerían	coma comas coma comamos comáis coman	comiera comieras comiera comiéramos comierais comieran	come tú, no comas coma usted comamos coman Uds.
vivir viviendo vivido	vivo vives vive vivimos vivís viven	vivía vivías vivía vivíamos vivíais vivían	viví viviste vivió vivimos vivisteis vivieron	viviré vivirás vivirá viviremos viviréis vivirán	viviría vivirías viviría viviríamos viviríais vivirían	viva vivas viva vivamos viváis vivan	viviera vivieras viviera viviéramos vivierais vivieran	vive tú, no vivas viva usted vivamos vivan Uds.

Vosotros Commands					
hablar	hablad, no habléis	comer	comed, no comáis	vivir	vivid, no viváis

Regular Verbs: Perfect Tenses

Indicative										Subjunctive			
Present Perfect		Past Perfect		Preterit Perfect		Future Perfect		Conditional Perfect		Present Perfect		Past Perfect	
he		había		hube		habré		habría		haya		hubiera	
has	hablado	habías	hablado	hubiste	hablado	habrás	hablado	habrías	hablado	hayas	hablado	hubieras	hablado
ha	comido	había	comido	hubo	comido	habrá	comido	habría	comido	haya	comido	hubiera	comido
hemos	vivido	habíamos	vivido	hubimos	vivido	habremos	vivido	habríamos	vivido	hayamos	vivido	hubiéramos	vivido
habéis		habíais		hubisteis		habréis		habríais		hayáis		hubierais	
han		habían		hubieron		habrán		habrían		hayan		hubieran	

Irregular Verbs

Infinitive Present Participle Past Participle	Indicative					Subjunctive		Imperative
	Present	Imperfect	Preterit	Future	Conditional	Present	Imperfect	
andar	ando	andaba	anduve	andaré	andaría	ande	anduviera	anda tú,
andando	andas	andabas	anduviste	andarás	andarías	andes	anduvieras	no andes
andado	anda	andaba	anduvo	andará	andaría	ande	anduviera	ande usted
	andamos	andábamos	anduvimos	andaremos	andaríamos	andemos	anduviéramos	andemos
	andáis	andabais	anduvisteis	andaréis	andaríais	andéis	anduvierais	anden Uds.
	andan	andaban	anduvieron	andarán	andarían	anden	anduvieran	
caer	caigo	caía	caí	caeré	caería	caiga	cayera	cae tú,
cayendo	caes	caías	caíste	caerás	caerías	caigas	cayeras	no caigas
caído	cae	caía	cayó	caerá	caería	caiga	cayera	caiga usted
	caemos	caíamos	caímos	caeremos	caeríamos	caigamos	cayéramos	caigamos
	caéis	caíais	caísteis	caeréis	caeríais	caigáis	cayerais	caigan Uds.
	caen	caían	cayeron	caerán	caerían	caigan	cayeran	
dar	doy	daba	di	daré	daría	dé	diera	da tú,
dando	das	dabas	diste	darás	darías	des	dieras	no des
dado	da	daba	dio	dará	daría	dé	diera	dé usted
	damos	dábamos	dimos	daremos	daríamos	demos	diéramos	demos
	dais	dabais	disteis	daréis	daríais	deis	dierais	den Uds.
	dan	daban	dieron	darán	darían	den	dieran	

Irregular Verbs (continued)

Infinitive Present Participle Past Participle	Indicative					Subjunctive		Imperative
	Present	Imperfect	Preterit	Future	Conditional	Present	Imperfect	
decir diciendo dicho	digo dices dice decimos decís dicen	decía decías decía decíamos decíais decían	dije dijiste dijo dijimos dijisteis dijeron	diré dirás dirá diremos diréis dirán	diría dirías diría diríamos diríais dirían	diga digas diga digamos digáis digan	dijera dijeras dijera dijéramos dijerais dijeran	di tú, no digas diga usted digamos decid vosotros, no digáis digan Uds.
estar estando estado	estoy estás está estamos estáis están	estaba estabas estaba estábamos estabais estaban	estuve estuviste estuvo estuvimos estuvisteis estuvieron	estaré estarás estará estaremos estaréis estarán	estaría estarías estaría estaríamos estaríais estarían	esté estés esté estemos estéis estén	estuviera estuvieras estuviera estuviéramos estuvierais estuvieran	está tú, no estés esté usted estemos estad vosotros, no estéis estén Uds.
haber habiendo habido	he has ha hemos habéis han	había habías había habíamos habíais habían	hube hubiste hubo hubimos hubisteis hubieron	habré habrás habrá habremos habréis habrán	habría habrías habría habríamos habríais habrían	haya hayas haya hayamos hayáis hayan	hubiera hubieras hubiera hubiéramos hubierais hubieran	
hacer haciendo hecho	hago haces hace hacemos hacéis hacen	hacía hacías hacía hacíamos hacíais hacían	hice hiciste hizo hicimos hicisteis hicieron	haré harás hará haremos haréis harán	haría harías haría haríamos haríais harían	haga hagas haga hagamos hagáis hagan	hiciera hicieras hiciera hiciéramos hicierais hicieran	haz tú, no hagas haga usted hagamos haced vosotros, no hagáis hagan Uds.
ir yendo ido	voy vas va vamos vais van	iba ibas iba íbamos ibais iban	fui fuiste fue fuimos fuisteis fueron	iré irás irá iremos iréis irán	iría irías iría iríamos iríais irían	vaya vayas vaya vayamos vayáis vayan	fuera fueras fuera fuéramos fuerais fueran	ve tú, no vayas vaya usted vamos, no vayamos id vosotros, no vayáis vayan Uds.

Irregular Verbs (continued)

Infinitive Present Participle Past Participle	Indicative					Subjunctive		Imperative
	Present	Imperfect	Preterit	Future	Conditional	Present	Imperfect	
oír oyendo oído	oigo oyes oye oímos oís oyen	oía oías oía oíamos oíais oían	oí oíste oyó oímos oístes oyeron	oiré oirás oirá oiremos oiréis oirán	oiría oirías oiría oiríamos oiríais oirían	oiga oigas oiga oigamos oigáis oigan	oyera oyeras oyera oyéramos oyerais oyeran	oye tú, no oigas oiga usted oigamos oigan Uds.
poder pudiendo podido	puedo puedes puede podemos podéis pueden	podía podías podía podíamos podíais podían	pude pudiste pudo pudimos pudisteis pudieron	podré podrás podrá podremos podréis podrán	podría podrías podría podríamos podríais podrían	pueda puedas pueda podamos podáis puedan	pudiera pudieras pudiera pudiéramos pudierais pudieran	
poner poniendo puesto	pongo pones pone ponemos ponéis ponen	ponía ponías ponía poníamos poníais ponían	puse pusiste puso pusimos pusisteis pusieron	pondré pondrás pondrá pondremos pondréis pondrán	pondría pondrías pondría pondríamos pondríais pondrían	ponga pongas ponga pongamos pongáis pongan	pusiera pusieras pusiera pusiéramos pusierais pusieran	pon tú, no pongas ponga usted pongamos pongan Uds.
querer queriendo querido	quiero quieres quiere queremos queréis quieren	quería querías quería queríamos queríais querían	quise quisiste quiso quisimos quisisteis quisieron	querré querrás querrá querremos querréis querrán	querría querrías querría querríamos querríais querrían	quiera quieras quiera queramos queráis quieran	quisiera quisieras quisiera quisiéramos quisiérais quisieran	quiere tú, no quieras quiera usted queramos quieran Uds.
saber sabiendo sabido	sé sabes sabe sabemos sabéis saben	sabía sabías sabía sabíamos sabíais sabían	supe supiste supo supimos supisteis supieron	sabré sabrás sabrá sabremos sabréis sabrán	sabría sabrías sabría sabríamos sabríais sabrían	sepa sepas sepa sepamos sepáis sepan	supiera supieras supiera supiéramos supiérais supieran	sabe tú, no sepas sepa usted sepamos sepan Uds.
salir saliendo salido	salgo sales sale salimos salís salen	salía salías salía salíamos salíais salían	salí saliste salió salimos salisteis salieron	saldré saldrás saldrá saldremos saldréis saldrán	saldría saldrías saldría saldríamos saldríais saldrían	salga salgas salga salgamos salgáis salgan	saliera salieras saliera saliéramos salierais salieran	sal tú, no salgas salga usted salgamos salgan Uds.

Irregular Verbs (continued)

Infinitive Present Participle Past Participle	Indicative					Subjunctive		Imperative
	Present	Imperfect	Preterit	Future	Conditional	Present	Imperfect	
ser siendo sido	soy eres es somos sois son	era eras era éramos erais eran	fui fuiste fue fuimos fuisteis fueron	seré serás será seremos seréis serán	sería serías sería seríamos seríais serían	sea seas sea seamos seáis sean	fuera fueras fuera fuéramos fuerais fueran	sé tú, no seas sea usted seamos sed vosotros, no seáis sean Uds.
tener teniendo tenido	tengo tienes tiene tenemos tenéis tienen	tenía tenías tenía teníamos teníais tenían	tuve tuviste tuvo tuvimos tuvisteis tuvieron	tendré tendrás tendrá tendremos tendréis tendrán	tendría tendrías tendría tendríamos tendríais tendrían	tenga tengas tenga tengamos tengáis tengan	tuviera tuvieras tuviera tuviéramos tuvierais tuvieran	ten tú, no tengas tenga usted tengamos tened vosotros, no tengáis tengan Uds.
traer trayendo traído	traigo traes trae traemos traéis traen	traía traías traía traíamos traíais traían	traje trajiste trajo trajimos trajisteis trajeron	traeré traerás traerá traeremos traeréis traerán	traería traerías traería traeríamos traeríais traerían	traiga traigas traiga traigamos traigáis traigan	trajera trajeras trajera trajéramos trajerais trajeran	trae tú, no traigas traiga usted traigamos traed vosotros, no traigáis traigan Uds.
venir viniendo venido	vengo vienes viene venimos venís vienen	venía venías venía veníamos veníais venían	vine viniste vino vinimos vinisteis vinieron	vendré vendrás vendrá vendremos vendréis vendrán	vendría vendrías vendría vendríamos vendríais vendrían	venga vengas venga vengamos vengáis vengan	viniera vinieras viniera viniéramos vinierais vinieran	ven tú, no vengas venga usted vengamos venid vosotros, no vengáis vengan Uds.
ver viendo visto	veo ves ve vemos véis ven	veía veías veía veíamos veíais veían	vi viste vio vimos visteis vieron	veré verás verá veremos veréis verán	vería verías vería veríamos veríais verían	vea veas vea veamos veáis vean	viera vieras viera viéramos vierais vieran	ve tú, no veas vea usted veamos ved vosotros, no veáis vean Uds.

Stem-Changing and Orthographic-Changing Verbs

Infinitive Present Participle Past Participle	Indicative					Subjunctive		Imperative
	Present	Imperfect	Preterit	Future	Conditional	Present	Imperfect	
dormir (ue, u) durmiendo dormido	duermo duermes duerme dormimos dormís duermen	dormía dormías dormía dormíamos dormíais dormían	dormí dormiste durmió dormimos dormisteis durmieron	dormiré dormirás dormirá dormiremos dormiréis dormirán	dormiría dormirías dormiría dormiríamos dormiríais dormirían	duerma duermas duerma durmamos durmáis duerman	durmiera durmieras durmiera durmiéramos durmierais durmieran	duerme tú, no duermas duerma usted durmamos dormid vosotros, no dormáis duerman Uds.
incluir (y) incluyendo incluido	incluyo incluyes incluye incluimos incluís incluyen	incluía incluías incluía incluíamos incluíais incluían	incluí incluiste incluyó incluimos incluisteis incluyeron	incluiré incluirás incluirá incluiremos incluiréis incluirán	incluiría incluirías incluiría incluiríamos incluiríais incluirían	incluya incluyas incluya incluyamos incluyáis incluyan	incluyera incluyeras incluyera incluyéramos incluyerais incluyeran	incluye tú, no incluyas incluya usted incluyamos incluid vosotros, no incluyáis incluyan Uds.
pedir (i, i) pidiendo pedido	pido pides pide pedimos pedís piden	pedía pedías pedía pedíamos pedíais pedían	pedí pediste pidió pedimos pedisteis pidieron	pediré pedirás pedirá pediremos pediréis pedirán	pediría pedirías pediría pediríamos pediríais pedirían	pida pidas pida pidamos pidáis pidan	pidiera pidieras pidiera pidiéramos pidierais pidieran	pide tú, no pidas pida usted pidamos pedid vosotros, no pidáis pidan Uds.
pensar (ie) pensando pensado	pienso piensas piensa pensamos pensáis piensan	pensaba pensabas pensaba pensábamos pensabais pensaban	pensé pensaste pensó pensamos pensasteis pensaron	pensaré pensarás pensará pensaremos pensaréis pensarán	pensaría pensarías pensaría pensaríamos pensaríais pensarían	piense pienses piense pensemos penséis piensen	pensara pensaras pensara pensáramos pensarais pensaran	piensa tú, no pienses piense usted pensemos pensad vosotros, no penséis piensen Uds.

Stem-Changing and Orthographic-Changing Verbs (continued)

Infinitive Present Participle Past Participle	Indicative					Subjunctive		Imperative
	Present	Imperfect	Preterit	Future	Conditional	Present	Imperfect	
producir (zc) produciendo producido	produzco produces produce producimos producís producen	producía producías producía producíamos producíais producían	produje produjiste produjo produjimos produjisteis produjeron	produciré producirás producirá produciremos produciréis producirán	produciría producirías produciría produciríamos produciríais producirían	produzca produzcas produzca produzcamos produzcáis produzcan	produjera produjeras produjera produjéramos produjerais produjeran	produce tú, no produzcas produzca usted produzcamos pruducid vosotros, no produzcáis produzcan Uds.
reír (i, i) riendo reído	río ríes ríe reímos reís ríen	reía reías reía reíamos reíais reían	reí reíste rio reímos reísteis rieron	reiré reirás reirá reiremos reiréis reirán	reiría reirías reiría reiríamos reiríais reirían	ría rías ría riamos riáis rían	riera rieras riera riéramos rierais rieran	ríe tú, no rías ría usted riamos reíd vosotros, no riáis rían Uds.
seguir (i, i) (ga) siguiendo seguido	sigo sigues sigue seguimos seguís siguen	seguía seguías seguía seguíamos seguíais seguían	seguí seguiste siguió seguimos seguisteis siguieron	seguiré seguirás seguirá seguiremos seguiréis seguirán	seguiría seguirías seguiría seguiríamos seguiríais seguirían	siga sigas siga sigamos sigáis sigan	siguiera siguieras siguiera siguiéramos siguierais siguieran	sigue tú, no sigas siga usted sigamos seguid vosotros, no sigáis sigan Uds.
sentir (ie, i) sintiendo sentido	siento sientes siente sentimos sentís sienten	sentía sentías sentía sentíamos sentíais sentían	sentí sentiste sintió sentimos sentisteis sintieron	sentiré sentirás sentirá sentiremos sentiréis sentirán	sentiría sentirías sentiría sentiríamos sentiríais sentirían	sienta sientas sienta sintamos sintáis sientan	sintiera sintieras sintiera sintiéramos sintierais sintieran	siente tú, no sientas sienta usted sintamos sentid vosotros, no sintáis sientan Uds.
volver (ue) volviendo vuelto	vuelvo vuelves vuelve volvemos volvéis vuelven	volvía volvías volvía volvíamos volvíais volvían	volví volviste volvió volvimos volvisteis volvieron	volveré volverás volverá volveremos volveréis volverán	volvería volverías volvería volveríamos volveríais volverían	vuelva vuelvas vuelva volvamos volváis vuelvan	volviera volvieras volviera volviéramos volvierais volvieran	vuelve tú, no vuelvas vuelva usted volvamos volved vosotros, no volváis vuelvan Uds.

APPENDIX 3

Spanish–English Vocabulary

A

a tiempo on time (3)
a través along (8)
abajo below (12)
abandonar to abandon (10)
abarcar to extend to (14)
abatido/a dejected (15)
abierto/a open (2)
abolición, la abolition (15)
abolir to abolish (**15**)
abordar to board (**9**)
abrazar to embrace (10)
abrazo, el hug; embrace (4)
abrigo, el coat (**8**)
abril April (**1**)
abrir to open (**2**)
abstener to abstain (9)
abuelita, la grandma (*diminutive*) (4)
abuelo/a, el/la grandfather/grandmother (**4**)
abundancia, la abundance (10)
abundante abundant (10)
abundar to abound (15)
aburrido/a boring (**1**)
aburrir to bore; to tire (**6**)
acabar (de) to finish; to have just (*done something*) (8, **11**)
académico/a academic (3)
acarrear to carry (12)
accesorio, el accessory (5)
acción, la action (2)
aceite (de oliva), el (olive) oil (2)
aceituna, la olive (2)
acelerado/a accelerated (12)
acelerar to accelerate (15)
aceptado/a accepted (7)
acerca de about (6)
acercarse to approach (8)
aclarar to clarify (15)
acompañar to accompany (15)
acorde, el chord (15)
acordeón, el accordion (1, **14**)
acostarse (ue) to go to bed (2, **5**)
acostumbrar to be accustomed to (10, 13)
acostumbrarse to become accustomed (8)
activismo, el activism (5)
activista, el/la activist (**15**)
acto, el act (legal) (15)
actor, el actor (**1**)
actriz, la actress (**1**)
actual current (10)
actuar to act (5, **13**)
acuático/a aquatic (9)
acudir to present oneself (11)
acuerdo, el accord (15)
acupuntura, la acupuncture (10)
acusación, la accusation (13)
adaptarse to adapt (12)
adecuado/a adequate (7)
adelanto, el advance (15)
adelgazar to lose weight (**10**)
ademán, el gesture (11)
además in addition (6)
adentro inside (6)
Adiós. Good-bye. (**1**)
adivinar to guess (5)
adivino/a, el/la fortune teller (12)
administración de empresas, la business administration (**3**)
administración, la administration (8)
admirador/a, el/la admirer (8)
admirar to admire (15)
adoptivo/a adoptive (14)
adorar to adore (14)
adornado/a adorned (8)
adornar to adorn (10)
adquirir (ie, i) to acquire (14)
aduana, la customs (**9**)
advertir (ie, i) to warn (14)
aeróbico/a aerobic (10)
aeropuerto, el airport (**9**)
afanosamente laboriously (5)
afeitarse to shave (**5**)
aficionado/a, el/la fan (**7**)
afirmación, la statement (12)
afrocaribeño/a Afro-Caribbean (7)
afrontar to face (**15**)
agarrar to grab (11)
agencia de viajes, la travel agency (**9**)
agente de viajes, el/la travel agent (**9**)
agitado/a agitated (10)
agosto August (**1**)
agradecido/a thankful (13)
agrandar to enlarge (15)
agravar to aggravate (10)
agregar to add; to gather (15)
agrícola agricultural (4)
agricultura, la agriculture (8)
agua (mineral), el (*fem.*) (mineral) water (**6**)
águila, el (*fem.*) eagle (8)
ahora now (**2**)
ajedrez, el chess (7)
ajo, el garlic (6)
ajustar to adjust (11)
ajuste, el fit (12)
al igual the same as (15)
alabanza, la praise (12)
alambrada, la wire (15)
albergar to house (3)
alcalde/sa, el/la mayor (12, **15**)
alcantarilla, la sewer (13)
alcanzar reach, to (2)
alcohol, el alcohol (13)
alegoría, la allegory (6)
alegre cheerful (4)
alegría, la happiness (2)
alejarse to go away (11)
alejar to move away (13)
alemán, el German (**2**)
alergia, la allergy (**10**)
alergia(s) a, tener to be allergic to (**10**)
alérgico/a allergic (6)
álgebra, el (*fem.*) algebra (**3**)
algo something (3, **6**)
algodón, el cotton (**8**)
alguien someone (**7**)
alguno/a/os/as some (**7**)
alhajas, las jewels (13)
alimentación, la nutrition (6)
alimentar to feed (11)
alimentos, los foods (**10**)
aliviado/a alleviated (14)
aliviar to alleviate (10)
allá there (9)
alma, el (*fem.*) soul (2)
almacén, el department store (**8**)
almendra, la almond (6)
almorzar (ue) to have lunch (**4**)
almuerzo, el lunch (2, **6**)
alquilar to rent (11)
alquiler, de for rent (14)
alternarse to alternate (8)
altiplano, el high plateau (10)
alto/a tall (**2**)
altura, la altitude (8, **9**)
alucinógeno/a hallucinogenic (5)
alumbrarse to light up (15)
ama de casa, el (*fem.*) housewife (12)
amable amiable (4)
amanecer, el dawn (11)
amante, el/la lover (7)
amarillo/a yellow (**1**)
ámbar, el amber (7)
ambiental environmental (10)
ambiente, el atmosphere; surroundings (3, 6)
ambigüedad, la ambiguity (11)
ambos/as both (7)
ambulancia, la ambulance (10)
amigo/a, el/la friend (1, **2**)
amistad, la friendship (5)
amor, el love (2)
amplio/a wide (8)
amueblado/a furnished (5)
analista (de sistemas), el/la systems analyst (**11**)
anaranjado/a orange (**1**)
ancho/a wide (5)
anciano/a, el/la old person (12)
andar to walk (6)
andén, el platform (13)
andino/a Andean (8)
anfitrión/anfitriona, el/la host/hostess (7, **13**)
angelical angelical (8)
anglicismo, el Anglicism (12)
angustia, la anguish (10)
angustiado/a anguished (5)
anillo de oro, el gold ring (**8**)
animado/a animated (9)
animal, el animal (3)
animar to encourage; to cheer (**7**, 10)
aniversario, el anniversary (6)
anoche last night (**6**)
anochecer to get dark (15)
ansiado/a long-awaited (15)
ansioso/a anxious (9)
anteayer the day before yesterday (**6**)
antena parabólica, la satellite dish (**12**)
antepasado/a, el/la ancestor (12)
antes (de) before (2)
antiácido, el antacid (**10**)
antibiótico, el antibiotic (**10**)
anticipación, de in advance (14)
anticipación, la anticipation (9)
anticipar to anticipate (8)
anticuado/a antiquated (3)
antiguo/a old (2)
antropología, la anthropology (**3**)
anual annual (9)
anudado/a knotted (15)
anunciar to announce (8)
anuncio, el announcement (15)
anuncios clasificados, los classified ads (13)
añadir to add (15)
año, el year (**1**)
años, tener... to be... years old (**3**)
apagar to turn off (**12**)
apagar (fuegos/incendios) to put out; to extinguish (fires) (**11**)
aparato, el appliance (**6**)
aparecer appear, to (4)
aparente apparent (15)
apartamento, el apartment (3)
apartar to separate (15)
apasionado/a passionate (9)
apasionar to impassion (11)
apellido, el surname (2)
apilar to pile (15)
aplaudir to clap (**14**)
apodo, el nickname (2)
apogeo, el apogee (15)
apoyar to support (8, **15**)
apoyo, el support (4)
apreciado/a appreciated (11)
apreciar appreciate, to (4)
aprender to learn (**2**)
apretado/a tight (12)
aprobar (ue) to pass (*a test*); to approve (13, 15)
aprovechar to take advantage of (7)
apunte, el note (5)
apurado/a hurried (14)
aquel/la that (*over there*) (**4**)
aquél/la that one (*over there*) (**4**)
aquello that (neuter) (*over there*) (**4**)

aquellos/as those (*over there*) (**4**)
aquéllos/as those ones (*over there*) (**4**)
aquí here (**1**)
árabe, el Arabic (**3**)
araña, la spider (8)
arañita, la little spider (10)
árbitro, el referee (**7**)
árbol, el tree (4)
archipiélago, el archipelago (8)
archivar to file; to save (**12**)
arco, el bow (8)
arder to burn (10)
ardilla, la squirrel (8)
aretes de diamantes, los diamond earrings (**8**)
argentino/a Argentine (**2**)
argumento, el argument (15)
aria, el (*fem.*) aria (14)
arma, el (*fem.*) weapon (**15**)
armado/a armed (15)
armar to assemble; to furnish (8, 15)
armario, el wardrobe (5)
arpa, el (*fem.*) harp (7, **14**)
arqueólogo, el archeologist (8)
arquitecto/a, el/la architect (2, **11**)
arquitectónico/a architectural (8)
arquitectura, la architecture (2, **3**)
arrastrar to drag (15)
arreglar to arrange; to fix (12)
arriba de above (**5**)
arrodillarse to kneel down (15)
arrojar to throw out (**12**)
arroz, el rice (**6**)
arte, el art (**3**)
artes plásticas, las plastic arts (14)
artesanal artisan (4)
artesanía, la handicraft (3)
artesano/a, el/la artisan (3)
artículo, el article (8, **13**)
artritis, la arthritis (10)
ascendencia, la ancestry (10)
ascender (ie) to promote; to move up (**11**)
asegurar to assure (2)
asentir (ie, i) to agree (12)
asesinado/a assassinated (6)
asesinar assassinate (13)
asesor/a, el/la consultant; advisor; counselor (6, **15**)
asfixiado/a asphyxiated (5)
asiento (de ventanilla / de pasillo), el (window/aisle) seat (6, **9**)
asistente de vuelo, el/la flight attendant (**9**)
asistente, el/la helper (3)
asistir (a) to attend (**2**)
asma, el (*fem.*) asthma (10)
asociación, la association (10)
asociar to associate (2)
aspecto, el aspect (8)
aspiradora, la vacuum cleaner (**5**)
aspirante, el/la job candidate (**11**)
aspirina, la aspirin (**10**)
asumir assume, to (4)
asustado/a frightened (13)
asustar to frighten (11)
atar to tie (8)
atasco, el traffic jam (14)
atención, la attention (3)
atender (ie) to tend to; to assist (7)
atentamente sincerely yours (**11**)
aterrizar to land (**9**)
atletismo, el track and field (**7**)
atracción, la attraction (5)
atractivo/a attractive (4)
atraer to attract (7)
atrapado/a trapped (7)
atrapar to trap (11)
atrás behind (15)
audición, la audition (**14**)
auditorio, el auditorium (**3**)
auge, el peak (15)
aullador/a howling (5)
aumentar to increase (13, **15**)
aumento, el raise (**11**)
aun still; even (4)
auriculares, los earbuds (12)
ausencia, la absence (9)
auspiciado/a auspicious (9)
autobiografía, la autobiography (3)
autobús, el bus (9)
automóvil, el automobile (2)
autónomo/a autonomous (13)
autopista, la highway (9)
avance, el advance (4)
avanzado/a advanced; advancing (3, 4)
avenida, la avenue (13)
aventurero/a, el/la adventurer (9)
averiado/a damaged (13)
avión, el plane (**9**)
avisos clasificados, los classified ads (13)
ayer yesterday (**6**)
ayudante, el/la assistant (6)
ayudar to help (**2**)
ayuntamiento, el city council (1)
azar, el chance (7)
azúcar, la sugar (**6**)
azul blue (**1**)

B

bacalao, el cod (7)
bailable danceable (9)
bailar to dance (**2**)
bailarín/a, el/la dancer (14)
bajar to download; to lower (6)
bajar de peso to lose weight (**10**)
bajarse (de) to get off (of); to get down (from) (**9**)
bajo lower; below (12)
bajo, el bass (3, **14**)
bajo/a short (*in stature*) (**2**)
bala, la bullet (15)
balboa, el monetary unit of Panama (5)
ballet, el ballet (1)
balneario, el spa (9)
baloncesto, el basketball (**2**)
banana, la banana (**6**)
banco, el bank (8); bench (13)
banda, la band (**14**)
bandera, la flag (1)
banjo, el banjo (1)
banqueta, la sidewalk (12)
bañarse to bathe (**5**)
baño, el bathroom (**5**)
barato/a cheap; inexpensive (**1**)
barbaridad, la outrage (5)
barco, el boat (**9**)
barra, la bar (12)
barrer to sweep (**5**)
barrio, el neighborhood (3)
basado/a based (6)
basalto, el basalt (15)
básquetbol, el basketball (**2**)
bastante quite; fairly (**3**)
bastantes quite a few (13)
bastar to be enough (8)
basurero, el garbage can (**5**)
batalla, la battle (1)
batear to bat (**7**)
batería, la drums (**14**)
bebé, el/la baby (6)
beber to drink (**2**)
bebida, la beverage (**6**)
bebidas alcohólicas, las alcoholic beverages (**10**)
beca, la scholarship (10)
béisbol, el baseball (**2**)
beisbolista, el baseball player (7)
bélico/a war-like (13)
belleza, la beauty (9)
bellísimo/a really beautiful (6)
bendito/a blessed (6)
beneficiar to benefit (15)
beneficio/s, el/los benefit/s (10, **11**)
benéfico/a charitable (14)
besar to kiss (10)
beso, el kiss (4)
biblioteca, la library (**3**)
bibliotecario/a, el/la librarian (11)
bien well (**1**)
bien hecho/a well made (**14**)
bienes raíces, los real estate (5)
bienes, los goods (5)
bienestar, el well-being (**10**)
bienvenida, la welcome (8)
bilingüe bilingual (13)
billete, el bill (12)
billetera, la billfold (12)
biografía, la biography (2)
biología, la biology (**3**)
bistec, el steak (**6**)
blanco/a white (**1**)
bloque, el block (8)
blusa, la blouse (**8**)
boca, la mouth (7, **10**)
bocadillo, el sandwich (**6**)
boda, la wedding (3)
boleto, el ticket (4, **9**)
bolígrafo, el pen (**1**)
bolsa, la (big) bag (**7**, 15)
bolso, el bag; purse (**8**)
bombardear to bomb (14)
bombero/a, el/la firefighter (**11**)
bondad, la kindness (15)
bonificación anual, la yearly bonus (**11**)
bonito/a pretty; cute (**2**)
bordear to border (9)
borrar to erase (**12**)
bosque, el forest (5, **9**, **12**)
bote, el can (12)
botella, la bottle (7)
botellita , la little bottle (13)
boxeo, el boxing (**7**)
brazo, el arm (**10**)
breve brief (6)
brillante bright (10)
brillar to shine (8)
broma, la joke (11)
bronce, el bronze (15)
bruma, la mist (11)
bucear to scuba dive; snorkel (**9**)
buche, el belly (8)
¡Buen provecho! Enjoy your meal! (1, **6**)
Buenas noches. Good evening. (**1**)
Buenas tardes. Good afternoon. (**1**)
bueno/a good (**1**)
Buenos días. Good morning. (**1**)
bufé, el buffet (**6**)
buitre, el vulture (14)
buscador, el search engine (12)
buscar to look for (**2**)
búsqueda, la search (**11**)
buzón, el mailbox (2)

C

caballero, el gentleman (2)
cabeza, la head (**10**)
cabrón, el rascal (13)
cachorro, el cub (13)
cachucha, la cap (15)
cacique, el chief (9)
cadáver, el cadaver (14)
cadena de plata, la silver chain (**8**)
cadencia, la rhythm (15)
caerse to fall down (12)
café, el coffee (**6**)
café (al aire libre), el outdoor café (**4**)
cafecito, el little cup of coffee; little café (7)
cafeína, la caffeine (6)
cafetera, la coffee maker (**6**)
cafetería, la cafeteria (2, **3**)
caja, la box; cash register (6, **8**)
cajero automático, el ATM (automatic teller machine) (4, **12**)
cajuela, la trunk (15)
calabaza, la squash (11)
calamar, el squid (6)
calavera, la skull (15)
calculadora, la calculator (**1**)
cálculo, el calculus (**3**)
calentar (ie) to heat (**6**)
calidad, la quality (4, **8**)
cálido/a hot; warm (9)
caliente hot (**6**)
calificaciones, las qualifications (**11**)
calle, la street (2)
calma, la calm (9)
calmante, el tranquilizer (**10**)
calor, hace it is hot (**7**)
calor, tener to be hot (**3**)
caloría, la calorie (6)
caluroso/a warm (8)
calzado, el footwear (8)
calzar to wear a shoe size (**8**)
cama, (hacer la) (to make the) bed (**5**)
cámara de video, la video camera (**9**)
cámara, la camera (4, 9, **13**)
camarero/a, el/la waiter/waitress (**6**)
camarones, los shrimp (**6**)
cambiar change, to (4)
cambio, el exchange (8)
camélido/a camel-like (8)

caminar to walk (**2**)
camino, el road (8)
camión, el truck; bus (*Mexico*) (15)
camioneta, la pickup truck (1)
camisa, la shirt (4, **8**)
campamento, el camp (15)
campaña, la campaign (13, **15**)
campeón/campeona, el/la champion (7)
canadiense Canadian (**2**)
canal, el canal; channel (4, **13**)
canas, tener to be grey-haired (13)
cáncer, el cancer (10)
cancha de tenis, la tennis court (**3**)
cancha, la court (2)
canción, la song (3)
candidato/a, el/la candidate (3, **15**)
cansado/a tired (4)
cansancio, el fatigue (10)
cansar to tire (7)
cantante, el/la singer (1)
cantar to sing (8)
cantar, el poem (15)
cantero de jardín, el flower bed (14)
cantidad, la quantity (6)
caña, la cane (7)
capacidad, la capacity (12)
capataz, el foreman (15)
capaz capable (**11**)
capilla, la chapel (8)
capital, la capital city (1, **2**)
capitán, el captain (3)
cara, la face (**5**)
carácter, el character (13)
característica, la characteristic (5)
caramba gosh (7)
carbohidratos, los carbohydrates (**10**)
cárcel, la jail (15)
carecer de to lack (6)
cargo político, el political post (**15**)
cargo, el position (**11**)
caribeño/a Caribbean (7)
caricia, la caress (2)
cariño, el affection (2)
cariñosamente affectionately (4)
caritativo/a charitable (9)
carnaval, el Mardi Gras (9)
carne de res, la beef (10)
carnero, el mutton (6)
caro/a expensive (**1**)
carpa, la tent (15)
carpintero/a, el/la carpenter (**11**)
carrera, la career (3)
carretera, la highway (14)
carro, el car (3, **9**)
carta de presentación, la cover letter (**11**)
carta (de recomendación), la letter (of recommendation) (1, **11**)
cartelera, la entertainment section (**13**)
cartera, la wallet (15)
cartero/a, el/la mail carrier (**11**)
casa, en in the house; at home (2)
casa, la house (**5**)
casado/a married (**4**)
casarse to marry (4)
cascadas, las cascades (11)
cáscara, la shell; peel (*fruit*) (7)
casco, el helmet (12)
casera, la housewife (7)
casero/a, el/la landlord/lady (12)
caso, hacer to pay attention (13)
castillo, el castle (13)
cataratas, las falls (11)
catedral, la cathedral (**9**)
caudillo, el leader (15)
causa, la cause (8)
cavar to dig (14)
cazar to hunt (8)
cazuela, la stewpot; casserole dish; saucepan (**6**)
celebración, la celebration (3)
celebrar to celebrate (9)
celos, los jealousy (11)
celoso/a jealous (11)
celta Celtic (13)
cementerio, el cemetery (14)
cena, la dinner (**6**)
cenar to have dinner (**6**)
censo, el census (15)
censurar to censure (13)
centenares, los hundreds (4)
céntimo, el cent (2)
centro comercial, el shopping center; mall (**8**)
centro estudiantil, el student union (**3**)
centro, el downtown (3, **4**)
cepillarse to brush (5)
cepillo (de dientes), el (tooth) brush (**5**)
cerámica, la ceramic (4)
cerca (de) nearby; close (to) (**3**)
cerca, la fence (12)
cercano/a nearby (8)
cerdo, el pork (10)
ceremonia, la ceremony (4)
cerveza, la beer (**6**)
cese de fuego, el ceasefire (4)
ceviche, el raw fish with lemon (6)
champán, el champagne (8)
champú, el shampoo (**5**)
chaqueta, la jacket (**8**)
charada, la charade (6)
charango, el guitar-like instrument (4)
chicano/a Mexican-American (12)
chicle, el chewing gum (15)
chico/a, el/la boy/girl (**3**)
chileno/a Chilean (**2**)
chimichurri, la sauce popular in Argentina (6)
chinchilla, la chinchilla (14)
chino, el Chinese (**2**)
chiquito/a very small (5, 15)
chismoso/a gossipy (5)
chiste, el joke (15)
chocar to crash (15)
chocita, la little hut (15)
chorro, el stream (15)
chubasco, el heavy rain; shower (7)
cibernético/a cybernetic (2)
cicatriz, la scar (13)
ciclismo, el cycling (**7**)
ciego/a blind (11)
cielo, el heaven; sky (2, 8)
ciencia ficción, la science fiction (7)
ciencias políticas, las political science (**3**)
ciencias sociales, las social science (**3**)
científico/a, el/la scientist (1)
cierto/a true; certain (2)
cigarra, la cricket (8)
cinc, el zinc (10)
cine, el movie theater (2, **4**)
cineasta, el/la filmmaker (4)
cinematografía, la cinematography (**13**)
cinta, la film (*tape*) (**13**)
ciprés, el cypress (14)
círculo, el circle (7)
cita, (hacer una) to make an appointment (**10**, 11)
ciudad, la city (1, **2**)
ciudadano/a, el/la citizen (6, **15**)
cívico/a civil (15)
civilización, la civilization (5)
clandestinidad, la secrecy (13)
clarinete, el clarinet (1, **14**)
claro of course (**4**)
clase turista, la coach class (**9**)
clase, la class (1, 2, **3**)
cliente, el/la client; customer (**6, 8**)
clientela, la clientele (12)
clima, el climate (5)
coactor/a, el/la co-actor (13)
cobre, el copper (6)
coca, la coca (15)
coche, el car (5)
cochinillo, el suckling pig (8)
cocina, la cuisine; kitchen (4, **5, 6**)
cocinar to cook (4, **6**)
cocinero/a, el/la chef; cook (6, **11**)
coco, el coconut (6)
cocodrilo, el crocodile (9)
código, el code (15)
cognado, el cognate (2)
coincidir to coincide (15)
cojo/a lame (13)
col, la cauliflower (6)
cola, hacer to stand in line (**9**)
cola, la tail (7)
colaborar to collaborate (5)
colchón, el mattress (13)
colección, la collection (4)
colega, el/la colleague (11)
cólera, el cholera (5)
colesterol, el cholesterol (**10**)
colgar (ue) to hang (13)
colibrí, el hummingbird (9)
collar (de perlas), el (pearl) necklace (7, **8**)
colombiano/a Colombian (**2**)
colonia, la colony; cologne (3, **8**)
colonizador/a, el/la colonizer (9)
coloradito/a blushing (3)
colorido/a brightly colored; coloring (9)
comal, la griddle (15)
combatir to combat (10, **15**)
combinación, la combination (10)
comedia musical, la musical comedy (**14**)
comedia, la comedy (**13**)
comedor, el dining room (**5**)
comentar to comment (5)
comentarista deportivo/a, el/la sportscaster (**13**)
comentarista, el/la newscaster; commentator (**13**)
comer to eat (**2**)
comercio, el commerce (3)
comestibles, los provisions; groceries (6)
cometer to commit (14)
comida, la meal (2, **6**)
comienzo, el beginning (5)
comisión, la commission (5)
comité, el committee (4)
cómo how; what (**1, 2**)
¿Cómo está usted? How are you? (*for.*) (**1**)
¿Cómo estás? How are you? (*inf.*) (**1**)
¿Cómo se llama usted? What's your name? (*for.*) (**1**)
¿Cómo te llamas? What's your name? (*inf.*) (**1**)
cómoda, la dresser (**5**)
comodidades, las comforts (9)
cómodo/a comfortable (9)
compañía, la company (14)
comparación, en comparison, in (2)
comparar to compare (5)
compartir share, to (4)
compatible compatible (12)
competir (i) to compete (15)
complacer to please (11)
complejo, el complex (14)
complejo/a complex (15)
complicado/a complicated (**3**)
complicar to complicate (11)
componer to compose (**14**, 15)
composición, la composition (2)
compositor/a, el/la composer (**14**)
comprar to buy (**2**)
comprender to understand (**2**)
comprobar (ue) to prove (15)
compromiso, el obligation (11)
compuesto/a composed (15)
computación, la computer science (**3**)
computadora, la computer (1, **3**)
común common (1)
comunicaciones, las communications (**3**)
comunidad, la community (3)
con with (**1**)
concierto, (ir a un) (to go to a) concert (3, **4, 7**)
concurso, el contest; game show; pageant (**13**)
condenado/a condemned (13)
condominio, el condominium (5)
cóndor, el condor (8)
conducir to conduct; to drive (15)
conductora, el/la conductor (15)
conectar connect (5)
conexión, la connection (13)
confeccionar to make up (15)
conferencia de prensa, la press conference (6)
conferencia, la lecture (3)
confesar (ie) to confess (10)

conflicto, el conflict (8, **15**)
conforme in agreement (15)
confundir to confuse (14)
congelador, el freezer (**6**)
conjetura, la conjecture (12)
conjunto, el outfit; group (4, **14**)
conmemorar commemorate, to (4)
conocer to know (*someone*); to be familiar with (**4**)
conocido/a known (6)
conocimiento, el knowledge (15)
conquista, la conquest (3)
consecuencias, las consequences (15)
conseguir (i, i) to get (9)
consejo, el advice (4)
conservación, la conservation (5)
conservador/a conservative (13)
conservante, el preservative (10)
conservar to conserve; to preserve (8, **12**)
considerado/a considered; considerate (9, 15)
considerar to consider (3)
constante constant (14)
constantemente constantly (12)
constituir to constitute (12)
construcción, la construction (5)
construir to construct (10)
consuelo, el consolation (10)
consultar to consult (10)
consultorio sentimental, el advice column (**13**)
consultorio, el doctor's office (**10**)
consumidor/a, el/la consumer (1)
consumir to consume (4, **12**)
consumo, el consumption (10)
contabilidad, la accounting (**3**)
contactar to contact (6)
contador/a, el/la accountant (**11**)
contaminación, hay there is pollution; there is smog (**7**)
contaminar to contaminate; to pollute (**12**)
contar (ue) to tell (*a story*) (10)
contemporáneo/a contemporaneous (6)
contenedor, el container (13)
contener (ie) to contain (10)
contenido, el content (10)
contento/a happy (**5**)
contestador automático, el answering machine (**12**)
continuación, a following (6)
continuar to continue (14)
contra, (en) against (**5**, 8)
contraste, el contrast (6)
contratar to hire (**11**)
contrato, el contract (**11**)
contrincante, el/la opponent (12, **15**)
controlar to control (**15**)
convencer to convince (2)
convencional conventional (13)
convento, el convent (**9**)
conversar to converse (**2**)
convertido/a converted (5)
convertir (ie, i) to convert (9)
cooperar to cooperate (8)
coordinador/a, el/la coordinator (**11**)
copia, la copy (5)
corazón, el heart (2, **10**)
corbata, la tie (**8**)
cordial cordial (7)
cordialmente cordially yours (**11**)
coreano, el Korean (**2**)
coreógrafo/a, el/la choreographer (14)
corneta, la cornet (**14**)
corpulento/a corpulent (15)
correo electrónico, el email (6, **12**)
correo, el mail (2)
correr run, to (2, **7**)
corresponsal, el/la correspondent (13)
corriente, la electric current (9)
corrupción, la corruption (**15**)
cortado/a cut (6)
corto/a short (6)
corvina, la sea bass (6)
cosa, la thing (**1**)
costa, la coast (2)
costar (ue) to cost (2, **4**, **8**)
costumbre, la custom (3)
costura, la alta high fashion (**14**)
creación, la creation (15)
creador/a, el/la creator (10)
crear to create (8)
creativo/a creative (12)
crecer to grow (8)
creer to believe (**2**)
crema (de afeitar), la (shaving) cream (**5**)
cría, la raising; chick (10, 13)
criarse to grow up (4)
crimen, el crime (14)
criollo/a creole (6)
crisis, la crisis (15)
cristalino/a clear; crystalline (5)
cristianizar to christianize (10)
cristiano/a Christian (14)
crítico/a, el/la critic (**13**)
crónica social, la social page (**13**)
cronológico/a chronological (11)
crucial crucial (6)
cruzar to cross (14)
cuaderno, el notebook (**1**)
cuadra, la block (3)
cuadrado/a square (5)
cuadro, el picture; painting (2, **5**)
cuadros, de plaid (**8**)
cual/es which (one/s) (**2**)
cualquier/a any/one (9)
cuando when (**2**)
cuanto/a how much/many (**1**)
Cuaresma, la Lent (9)
cuarteto, el quartet (**14**)
cuartito, el little room (5)
cuarto, el room (**5**)
cuarto/a fourth (**8**)
cubano/a Cuban (**2**)
cubierto/a covered (10)
cubismo, el cubism (2)
cucharada, la tablespoon (**6**)
cucharadita, la teaspoon (**6**)
cuchillo, el knife (8)
cuenta, la bill; account; bead (**6**, 7, 15)
cuenta, por su on your own (11)
cuentista, el/la storyteller (11)
cuerda, la cord (15)
cuero, el leather (**8**)
cuerpo, el body (**5**)
cuestas, a on the back (14)
cuestionario, el questionnaire (10)
cuidado, tener to be careful (**3**)
cuidadoso/a careful (9)
cuidar(se) to take care (of oneself) (6, **10**)
culebra, la snake (7)
culinario/a culinary (6)
culpa, la blame (13)
cultivo, el cultivation (2)
cumpleaños, el birthday (1)
cumplir (con) to make good (*on a promise*); to fulfill (*a promise*) (**15**)
cuna, la cradle (1)
cuñado/a, el/la brother-in-law/sister-in-law (3, **4**)
curanto, el Chilean stew (6)
curar to cure (**11**)
curioso/a curious (7)
currículo, el curriculum (14)
currículum vitae, el résumé (**11**)
curso, el course (3)
cuyo/a/os/as whose (5)

D

danza, la dance (14)
dañar to damage (*not work*) (10, **12**)
dañino/a harmful (10)
daño, el damage; harm (4, 15)
dar igual to be the same (7)
dar un paseo to go out; to take a walk (**7**)
datar to date from (15)
dato, el data; information (1)
de acuerdo fine with me; okay; in agreement; agreed (3, **4**)
de nada you're welcome (**1**)
de verdad really (**1**)
debajo (de) under; below (**5**)
debate, el debate (15)
deber, el duty (4, **15**)
debido a owing to (5)
debut, el debut (14)
decenas, las tens (5)
decidir to decide (**2**)
décimo tenth (**8**)
decir (i) to say (**6**)
decoración, la decoration (8)
dedicación, la dedication (14)
dedicado/a dedicated (9)
dedicar to dedicate (7)
dedo, el finger (10)
defender (ie) to defend (7)
defensa propia, la self-defense (14)
definir to define (14)
deforestación, la deforestation (**12**)
dejar (de fumar) to leave; to quit (smoking cigarettes) (4, **10**, **11**)
delante de in front of (2, **3**)
delgado/a thin (**2**)
delicioso/a delicious (2)
delincuencia, la delinquency (15)
demagogo/a, el/la demagogue (15)
demasiado too much (9)
democracia, la democracy (**15**)
democrático/a democratic (4)
demográfico/a demographic (13)
demora, la delay (6, **9**)
demostrar (ue) to demonstrate (14)
denominar to designate (4)
dentista, el/la dentist (3, **11**)
dentro de within; inside of (**5**)
denunciar denounce (7)
depender de to depend on (5)
deporte, el sport (1, **7**)
deportiva, la sección sports section (**13**)
deportivo/a sporting (7)
depósito, el deposit (10)
derecha, a la to/on the right (**3**)
derecho, el law; right (**3**, 8, **15**)
derechos humanos, los human rights (4)
derivado/a derived (12)
derribar to tear down (13)
desafío, el challenge (4)
desaparecer to disappear (11)
desaparecido/a disappeared (15)
desarmar to disarm (15)
desarme, el disarmament (**15**)
desastre, el disaster (5)
desayunar to have breakfast (**6**)
desayuno, el breakfast (**6**)
descafeinado/a decaffeinated (3)
descansar to rest (12)
descarapelado/a peeling (12)
descender (ie) to descend (11)
descendiente, el/la descendant (8)
descomposición, la decomposition (4)
desconocido/a unknown (15)
describir to describe (2)
descubierto/a discovered (13)
descubrimiento, el discovery (14)
descuento, el discount (**8**)
desde from; since (2)
deseado/a desired (4)
desechos, los waste (**12**)
desempeñar to carry out (6)
desempleo, el unemployment (6, **11**)
desengaño, el disillusionment (10)
desfile, el parade (9)
desgarrador/a heartrending (11)
desgraciadamente unfortunately (10)
desgranar to shell (15)
deshecho/a unraveled (10)
deshonesto/a dishonest (15)
deshonrar to dishonor (11)
desierto, el desert (4)
desierto/a deserted (5)
desigualdad, la inequality (5)
desilusionado/a disillusioned (4)
desnudo/a nude (15)
desodorante, el deodorant (**5**, **8**)

desorden, el disorder (8)
desorganizado/a disorganized (15)
despacho, el office (**11**)
despacio slowly (5)
despedida, la farewell (1, **4**)
despedidas, las closings (**11**)
despedir (i, i) to fire (**11**)
despegar to take off (**9**)
despejado/a clear (sky) (8)
despertarse (ie) to wake up (**5**)
después de after (**3**)
destacar to stand out (12)
destinado/a destined (10)
destinatario/a, el/la addressee (11)
destino, el destination (9)
destreza, la skill (15)
destrozado/a destroyed (9)
destrozar to destroy (9)
destructivo/a destructive (5)
desventaja, la disadvantage (10)
detallar to detail (7)
detalle, el detail (6)
detener (ie) to detain (11)
deteriorar to deteriorate (12)
determinado/a determined (9)
detestar to detest (11)
detrás (de) behind (**3**)
devolver (ue) to return (*something*) (**8**)
día, el day (**1**)
diabetes, la diabetes (**10**)
diabólico/a diabolical (14)
diagnóstico, el diagnosis (**10**)
diagrama, el diagram (7)
diario/a daily (2)
dibujar to draw (10)
dibujo, el drawing (5)
diccionario, el dictionary (**1**)
diciembre December (**1**)
dictador/a, el/la dictator (**15**)
dictadura, la dictatorship (**15**)
dientes, los teeth (**5, 10**)
dieta, estar a to be on a diet (**10**)
dieta, la diet (10)
diferente different (6, 8)
difícil difficult (**2**)
dificultar to make difficult (4)
difunto/a dead (15)
dignidad, la dignity (13)
dignificar to dignify (11)
diminutivo/a diminutive (12)
dinero, el money (4)
dios, el god (9)
diplomático/a, el/la diplomat (3)
director/a, el/la director; conductor (9, 11, 14)
dirigido/a directed (13)
dirigir to conduct (14)
discapacitado/a handicapped (3)
disco duro, el hard drive (**12**)
discoteca, ir a una to go to a nightclub (**7**)
discrepancia, la discrepancy (11)
disculparse to apologize (15)
discurso, el speech (**15**)
discusión, la argument (8)
discutir to argue (4)
diseñador/a, el/la designer (**14**)
diseñar to design (2, **11**)
diseño, el design (2, **3, 12**)
disfraz, el disguise; costume (**14**)
disfrutar de to enjoy (6)
disimular to cover up; to feign (13)
disminución, la decrease (5)
disminuir to diminish; to lessen (13, 15)
disparar to shoot (11)
dispuesto/a willing; ready; disposed (**12**)
disquete, el computer disc (**12**)
distancia, la distance (8)
distinguir to distinguish (15)
distinto/a different (6, 8)
distraer to entertain; to distract (15)
distribuir to distribute (13)
diva, la diva (**14**)
divertido/a fun (9)
división, la division (5)
divorciado/a divorced (**4**)
doble cuarto, el double room (**9**)
doble juego, el scam (4)
doctorado, el doctorate (3)
doler (ue) to hurt (9, **10**)
dolor de cabeza, el headache (10)
dolor, el pain; ache (**10**)
doloroso/a painful (10)
doméstico/a domestic (3)
dominado/a dominated (6)
dominar to dominate (8)
domingo, el Sunday (**1**)
dominicano/a Dominican (**2**)
donar to donate (14)
donde where (**2**)
dormir (ue, u) to sleep (**4**)
dormirse (ue, u) to fall asleep (**5**)
dormitorio, el bedroom (**5**)
dote, el dowry (15)
drama, el drama (**13**)
dramático/a dramatic (13)
dramatización, la dramatization (13)
dramaturgo/a dramatist (13)
drogadicción, la drug addiction (**15**)
dueño/a, el /la owner (5)
dulcemente softly (5)
dulces, los sweets (15)
durabilidad, la durability (14)
duradero/a lasting (15)
durante during (2)
durar to last (8)
durazno, el peach (14)
duro/a hard (10)
DVD, el DVD (**12**)

E

echar to add; to throw in (**6, 12**)
echar de menos to miss (2)
ecología, la ecology (5)
ecológico/a ecological (8)
económico/a economical (2)
ecoturismo, el ecotourism (4, 5)
ecuatoriano/a Ecuadorian (**2**)
edificación, la building (4)
edificio, el building (8)
editar to edit (12)
editorial, el editorial (page) (**13**)
educación física, la physical education (**3**)
educar to educate (10)
efectivo, en cash (5)
efímero/a ephemeral (13)
ejecución, la execution (14)
ejecutivo/a, el/la executive (3)
ejemplo, el example (9)
ejercer to exercise (15)
ejercicio, hacer to exercise (**7**)
ejercicios aeróbicos, los aerobics (**10**)
ejército, el army (5, **15**)
el the (**1**)
él he (**1**)
elaboración, la elaboration (15)
elaborado/a elaborated (4)
elaborar to elaborate (15)
elástico, el elastic (**14**)
electo/a elected (6)
electricidad, la electricity (10)
electricista, el/la electrician (**11**)
eléctrico/a electric (3)
electrónico/a electronic (2, **12**)
elegible eligible (13)
elegir (i, i) to elect (14, **15**)
elemento, el element (14)
eliminar to end (**15**)
ella she (**1**)
ellos/as they (**1**)
embajador/a, el/la ambassador (9)
embalse, el dam (10)
emisora, la radio station (*business entity*) (7, **13**)
emocional emotional; exciting (11)
emocionante exciting (2)
emocionarse to get excited (15)
empacar to pack (10)
empanada (empanadilla), la turnover (6)
empaquetado/a packaged (10)
emparejar to match (*pair up*) (6)
empatar to tie (*the score*) (**7**)
empezar (ie) to begin (3, **4**)
empleado/a, el/la employee (8, **11**)
empresa, la company; firm (**11**)
en demanda in/on demand (14)
en directo live (*on television*) (**13**)
encajar to fit (8)
encaje, el lace (10)
Encantado/a. Delighted.; Pleased to meet you. (**1**)
encantador/a enchanting; delightful (**14**)
encantar to delight; to be extremely pleasing (**6**)
encanto, el delight (12)
encargar to take on (14)
encender (ie) to turn on (**12**)
encima on top (13)
enclavado/a nailed (15)
encoger draw up (8)
encogerse to shrink (15)
encontrar (ue) to find (**4**)
encuentro, el encounter (8)
encuesta, la survey (10)
enemigo/a, el/la enemy (11)
energía, la energy (3, **12**)
enero January (**1**)
enfermedad, la illness (5, **10**)
enfermero/a, el/la nurse (**11**)
enfrente in front (12)
enfrente de facing; across from (**3**)
engañar to deceive (13)
enlace, el hyperlink (**12**)
enojarse to get angry (14)
enorme enormous (6)
enredar to twist around (7)
enriquecer to enrich (12)
ensalada, la salad (**6**)
ensamblar assemble (3)
ensartar to string (15)
ensayar to rehearse (11, **14**)
enseguida right away (**6**)
enseñanza, la teaching (12)
enseñar to teach (**2**)
entender (ie) to understand (**4**)
enterarse to become aware (15)
entero/a entire (4)
enterrar (ie) to bury (14)
entonación, la intonation (14)
entrada, la admission ticket; entrance (**4**, 8)
entre between (**3**)
entregar to deliver (8)
entrenador/a, el/la trainer (**7**)
entrenamiento, el training; entertainment (7, **11**)
entresuelo, el mezzanine (7)
entretener (ie) to entertain (9)
entretenimiento, el entertainment (7)
entrevista, la interview (2, **11**)
entusiasta enthusiastic (**11**)
envase (de aluminio), el (aluminum) container (**12**)
época, la epoch (4)
equilibrio, el equilibrium (10)
equipo, el team; equipment (**7**)
equivocado/a mistaken (15)
erradicar to eradicate (15)
erupción, la eruption (11)
escalar to climb (8)
escaleras, las stairs (12)
escalonada, la stair step (8)
escandalizado/a scandalized (5)
escáner, el scanner (**12**)
escarlata scarlet (5)
escasez, la shortage (**12**)
escaso/a scarce (15)
escenario, el stage (**14**)
esclavo/a, el/la slave (9)
escoba, la broom (**5**)
escolar scholastic (12)
esconder to hide (7)
escorpión, el scorpion (7)
escribir to write (**2**)
escritor/a, el/la writer (6)
escuchar to listen (**2**)
escuela, la school (5)
escultor/a, el/la sculptor (8)
escurrir to drain (5)
ese/a that (**4**)
ése/a that one (**4**)
esencia, la essence (14)
esfuerzo, el effort (4, **15**)
esmeralda, la emerald (9)
esmoquin, el tuxedo (**14**)
eso that (neuter) (**4**)
esos/as those (**4**)
ésos/as those ones (**4**)
espalda, la back (**10**)
español, el Spanish (**2**)
español/a Spanish (**2**)
especialidad de la casa, la house specialty (**6**)
especie, la species (5)
espectacular spectacular (2, 5)
espectáculo, el spectacle (8)
espectador/a, el/la spectator (**13**)

especular to speculate (13)
espejo, el mirror (**5**)
esperanza, la hope (12)
esperanzado/a hopeful (10)
espeso/a thick (15)
espiar to spy (11)
esposo/a, el/la husband; wife (3, **4**)
esquela funeraria, la obituary (**13**)
esquí (acuático), el (water) skiing (**7**)
esquiar to ski (**7**)
esquina, la corner (3)
establecer establish (4)
estación de radio, la radio station (13)
estación, la season; station (**1, 13**)
estacionar to park (11)
estadía, la stay (**9**)
estadio, el stadium (**3**)
estadísticas, las statistics (**3**)
estado libre asociado, el commonwealth (7)
estado, el state (7)
estadounidense American (US) (**2**)
estampado/a stamped (14)
estancia, la ranch (11)
estante, el bookcase (3, **5**)
estaño, el tin (10)
estar to be (**3**)
estatua, la statue (**9**)
este/a this (**4**)
éste/a this one (**4**)
estereotipo, el stereotype (12)
estilo, el style (2, **14**)
estimado/a señor/a dear sir/madam (**11**)
estimularse to stimulate (9)
estímulo, el stimulus (11)
esto this (neuter) (**4**)
Estocolmo Stockholm (4)
estofado, el stew (6)
estómago, el stomach (**10**)
estos/as these (**4**)
éstos/as these ones (**4**)
estrecho/a tight (*clothing*) (**8**)
estrenar to debut (13)
estrés, el stress (**10**)
estrofa, la stanza (11)
estudiante, el/la student (**1**)
estudiantil student (*adj.*) (6)
estudiar to study (**2**)
estudio, el studio; study (3, **13**)
estudios, los studies (2)
estufa, la stove (**6**)
estufita, la little stove (15)
estupendo/a terrific (**7**)
etapa, la stage (3)
ética, la ethic (11)
etiqueta, la label (10)
étnico/a ethnic (12)
eucalipto, el eucalyptus (15)
Europa Europe (2)
euskera, el Basque language (13)
evento, el event (3)
evolución, la evolution (8)
examen físico, el medical checkup (**10**)
examen, el exam (3)
excavar to excavate (4)
excelente excellent (2)
excepción, la exception (15)
excepcional exceptional (7)
exclusivo/a exclusive (9)
excursión, ir de to go on an outing; to tour (**9**)
excursión, la excursion (6)
exento/a exempt (3)
exhausto/a exhausted (8)
exhibir to exhibit (15)
exigente challenging; demanding (**3**)
existir to exist (8)
éxito, el success (11)
exótico/a exotic (5)
expedición, la expedition (10)
expediente, el dossier (**11**)
experimentado/a experienced (15)
experto/a, el/la expert (9)
explicar to explain (5)
explícito/a explicit (13)
explorar explore (10)
explosivo/a explosive (6)
explotar to exploit (15)
exportar to export (6)
exposición, la exposition; show (3, 8)
expresar to express (15)
expresivo/a expressive (14)
expreso/a expressed (15)
exquisito/a exquisite (6)
extender (ie) to extend (8)
extensión, la extension (9)
extinción, la extinction (5)
extracción, la extraction (10)
extranjerismo, el foreign expression (12)
extranjero/a foreign (13)
extranjero/a, el/la foreigner (7)
extrañar to miss (someone); seem strange (3, 12)
extraño/a strange (11)
extraordinario/a extraordinary (4)
extratextual extratextual (2)
extremo/a extreme (6)
extrovertido/a outgoing (1)

F

fábrica, la factory (2, **12**)
fabricación, la manufacture (2)
fabricar to manufacture (12)
fábula, la fable (8)
fabuloso/a fabulous; great (**7**)
fácil easy (**2**)
factor, el factor (10)
facturar el equipaje to check luggage (**9**)
Facultad de Arte, la School of Art (**3**)
Facultad de Ciencias, la School of Science (**3**)
Facultad de Derecho, la School of Law (**3**)
Facultad de Filosofía y Letras, la School of Humanities (**3**)
Facultad de Ingeniería, la School of Engineering (**3**)
Facultad de Matemáticas, la School of Mathematics (**3**)
Facultad de Medicina, la School of Medicine (**3**)
falda, la skirt; slope (**8**)
fallar to fail (5)
fallecimiento, el death (8)
falso/a false (2)
falta, la lack (12)
faltar to be lacking; to be in need of (**6**)
fama, la fame (9)
familia, la family (3, **4**)
familiar family (*adj.*) (4)
familiares, los family members (11)
fanático/, el/la fan(atic) (2)
fantasía, la fantasy (14)
fantástico/a fantastic (3, **7**)
farmacia, la pharmacy (**8**)
fascinante fascinating (1)
fascinar to be fascinating (**6**)
fascista, el/la fascist (14)
febrero February (**1**)
fecha, la date (**1**)
felicidad, la happiness (6)
femenino/a feminine (15)
feminidad, la femininity (14)
fenomenal phenomenal (6)
fenómeno, el phenomenon (10)
feo/a ugly (**2**)
feria, la fair (9)
ferrocarril, el railroad (6)
fertilidad, la fertility (15)
fertilizante, el fertilizer (6)
fibra, la fiber (15)
fiebre, la fever (5, **10**)
fiesta, la party; celebration (1)
figura, la figure (9)
fíjese look (*for. command*) (9)
fila, la row (7)
filarmónico/a philharmonic (14)
filmación, la filming (13)
filmar to film (**13**)
final, el end (**13**)
financiera, la sección business section (**13**)
financiero/a financial (15)
finanzas, las finance (**3**)
finca, la farm (12)
fines, a toward the end (11)
fingir to pretend (11)
fino/a delicate (13)
firma, la signature (11)
firmar to sign (*a letter, a treaty, etc.*) (7, **15**)
física, la physics (**3**)
físico/a physical (5)
flaco/a skinny (**2**)
flamenco/a flamenco (2)
flan, el custard dessert (**6**)
flanquear to flank (15)
flauta, la flute (1, **14**)
flor, la flower (2, **9**)
florería, la flower shop (**8**)
fluvial river (*adj.*) (9)
folklórico/a folkloric (3)
folleto, el brochure (**9**)
fondo, el bottom; background (12, 14)
fondos, los funds (14)
footing, hacer to jog (**10**)
forma, en in shape (10)
forma, la form (4)
formación, la education (**11**)
formar to form (8)
formular to formulate (8)
formulario, el form (**11**)
foro, el forum (14)
fortalecer to strengthen; to fortify (**15**)
fotocopia, la photocopy (12)
fotocopiadora, la photocopier (**12**)
fotocopiar to photocopy (**12**)
fotógrafo/a, el/la photographer (1)
fracasar to fail (13)
fragmento, el fragment (13)
francés, el French (**2**)
frecuencia, con frequently (8)
frecuente frequent (11)
frecuentemente frequently (8)
freír (i, i) to fry (**6**)
fresa, la strawberry (15)
fresco, hace it is cool (**7**)
fresco/a fresh (6)
frijoles, los beans (**6**)
frío, hace it is cold (**7**)
frío, tener to be cold (**3**)
frío/a cold (**6**)
fritura, la fried snack (7)
frontera, la frontier; border (3)
frotar to rub (15)
frustrado/a frustrated (4)
fuego alto/mediano/bajo high/ medium/low heat (**6**)
fuego, el fire (11)
fuegos artificiales, los fireworks (9)
fuente, la fountain (6)
fuera (de) outside (4)
fuera de lugar out of place (12)
fueres, si if you were (9)
fuerza, la force (15)
fumar to smoke (8, **10**)
función, la show; function; event (**4**)
funcional functional (10)
funcionar to function; to work (10, **12**)
fundación, la founding; foundation (13, 15)
fundado/a founded (9)
fundar to found (14)
furibundo/a raging (14)
furioso/a angry (**5**)
furor, el furor (11)
fusión, la fusion (14)
fútbol, el soccer (**2**)
fútbol americano, el football (**2**)

G

gabardina, la gabardine (*lightweight wool*) (**14**)
gabinete, el cabinet (6)
gafas de sol, las sunglasses (7, **9**)
gafas, las glasses (15)
gaita, la bagpipe (13)
galán, el leading man (**13**)
galápago, el tortoise (8)
galletas, las cookies (**6**)
gallina, la hen (15)
ganador/a, el/la winner (15)
ganar to earn; to win (2, **7**)
ganga, la bargain, good deal (**8**)
garaje, el garage (**5**)
garganta, la throat (**10**)
garza, la crane (8)
gastado/a worn out (10)
gastar to spend (**8**)
gasto, el expense (11)
gastronomía, la gastronomy (2)
gato/a, el/la cat (5)
gaucho, el Argentine cowboy (11)
genealógico/a genealogical (4)
generación, la generation (10)
general general (9)

generar to generate (15)
género, el genre (8)
generosidad, la generosity (15)
generoso/a generous (10)
genético/a genetic (10)
genial of genius (7)
genovés/-esa Genoese (7)
gente, la people (8)
geografía, la geography (**3**)
geología, la geology (**3**)
gerente, el/la manager (9, **11**)
gesto, el gesture (8)
gigante, el giant (6)
gigantesco/a gigantic (15)
gimnasia, la gymnastics (**7**)
gimnasio, el gymnasium (2, **3**)
gira, la outing; tour (11, **14**)
glifo, el glyph (15)
gobernador/a, el/la governor (**15**)
gobierno, el government (2)
golf, el golf (2, **7**)
golpear to pound (12)
gordo/a chubby (**2**)
gorra, la cap (8)
gozar de to enjoy (11)
grabación, la recording (12)
grabado/a recorded (13)
grabar to record (**12, 13**)
Gracias. Thank you. (**1**)
graduarse to graduate (12)
Gran Depresión, la Great Depression (3)
grande big (1, **2**)
grasa, la fat (6, **10**)
grasas transformadas, las fatty acids (10)
gratis free of charge (7)
grave serious (sickness) (5)
gripe, la flu (**10**)
gris grey (**1**)
gritar to shout (**7**)
grito, el cry; shout (5, 11)
grúa, la tow truck (4)
guacamayo, el macaw (5)
guapo/a good-looking (**2**)
guaraní, el Guarani language (10)
guardar to save; to keep (**6,** 10)
guardar cama to stay in bed (**10**)
guardar la línea to stay trim; to watch one's figure (**10**)
guardia, el/la guard (9)
guayaba, la guava (1)
gubernamental governmental (12)
Guerra Civil, la Civil War (3)
guerra, la war (5)
guerrero, el warrior (3)
guía, el/la tour guide (**9**)
guía, la guide book (**9**)
guiar to guide (12)
guindando hanging (7)
guión, el script (10, **13**)
guionista, el/la script writer (13)
guitarra, la guitar (1, **14**)
gustar to like (**6**)
gusto, el taste (5)

H

ha de one must (8)
habitante, el/la inhabitant (8)
habitar to inhabit; to live (6)
hablar to speak (**2**)
hacer to do; to make (2, **3**)
hacer la(s) maleta(s) to pack the suitcase(s) (**9**)
hacer juego (con) to match; to go well with (**8**)
hacha, el hatchet (7)
hambre, tener to be hungry (**3**)
hamburguesa, la hamburger (**6**)
hasta luego see you later (**1**)
hasta mañana see you tomorrow (**1**)
hasta pronto see you soon (**1**)
hay there is/are (**1**)
hay que one must (8)
haz do; make (*inf. command*) (9)
hectárea, la hectare (15)
heladera, la cooler (**7**)
heladería, la ice cream shop (**8**)
helado, el ice cream (**6**)
helicóptero, el helicopter (13)
heno, el hay (11)
heredar to inherit (5)
herencia, la heritage (7)
herido/a injured; wounded (9)
herir (ie, i) to wound (4)
hermanastro/a, el/la stepbrother/stepsister (**4**)
hermano/a, el/la brother/sister (3, **4**)
hervir (ie, i) to boil (**6**)
hidromasaje, el hydromassage (10)
hidroterapia, la hydrotherapy (10)
hielo, el ice (**7**)
hierba, la herb (10)
hierro, el iron (6)
hijo/a, el/la son/daughter (**4**)
hinchar to swell (12)
hipermercado, el hypermarket (6)
hipervínculo, el hyperlink (**12**)
hipótesis, la hypothesis (15)
hispano/a Hispanic (1)
histérico/a hysterical (13)
historia, la history (**3**)
hockey, el hockey (**7**)
hogar, el home (4)
hoja electrónica, la spreadsheet (**12**)
hoja, la leaf (15)
hola hello; hi (**1**)
hombre, el man (**1**)
hondo/a deep (6)
honestidad, la honesty (**15**)
honesto/a honest (**11**)
honradez, la honesty (**15**)
honrado/a honest; honored (**11, 14**)
horario (de clases), el (class) schedule (**3,** 8)
horario de trabajo, el work schedule (**11**)
horno, el oven (**6**)
horóscopo, el horoscope (4, **13**)
horrorizado/a horrified (14)
hospedaje, el lodging (**9**)
hospital, el hospital (3)
hostal, el inn (**9**)
hotel (de lujo), el (luxury) hotel (**9**)
hoy en día nowadays (3)
hoyo, el hole (15)
huella, la trace (12)
huérfano/a, el/la orphan (9)
huevos, los eggs (**6**)
humanidad, la humanity (11)
humanista humanistic (8)
húmedo/a wet (13)
humo, el smoke (**12**)
humorístico/a humoristic (4)
huracán, el hurricane (4)

I

ida y vuelta roundtrip (**9**)
ideal ideal (1)
idéntico/a identical (10)
idioma, el language (**2**)
ignorar to be ignorant of (11)
igualmente likewise (**1**)
iluminación, la illumination (15)
ilusión, la illusion (6)
ilustre illustrious (10)
imagen, la image (8)
imaginería, la statuary (4)
impaciente impatient (**5**)
impactante stunning (5)
impacto, el impact (15)
imperio, el empire (8)
impresionante impressive (2)
impresionar to impress (9)
impreso/a printed (12)
impresora, la printer (**12**)
imprimir to print (**12**)
improvisado/a improvised (15)
improvisar to improvise (**14**)
impuestos, los taxes (11, **15**)
inacabado/a unfinished (13)
inalámbrico, el teléfono cordless phone (12)
inauguración, la inauguration (6)
inaugurado/a inaugurated (3)
inca Inca (15)
incendio, el fire (**11**)
incentivo, el incentive (11)
incitar to incite (13)
incluir to include (2)
inclusive including (5)
incomodidad, la discomfort (9)
incómodo/a uncomfortable (9)
incorporar incorporate (6)
increíblemente incredibly (15)
indefinido/a indefinite (7)
indicar to indicate (8)
indiferente indifferent (8)
indígena indigenous (4)
indiscreto/a indiscrete (13)
industria, la industry (4)
infantil childish (8)
infección, la infection (**10**)
inferior lesser (3)
infidelidad, la infidelity (13)
infiel unfaithful (13)
infierno, el inferno; hell (4)
inflación, la inflation (**15**)
influido/a influenced (12)
influyente influential (13)
informal informal (3)
informar to report (**13**)
informática, la computer science (**3**)
infraestructura, la infrastructure (5)
ingeniería (eléctrica), la (electrical) engineering (2, **3**)
ingeniero/a, el/la engineer (**11**)
inglés, el English (**2**)
ingrediente, el ingredient (6)
iniciado/a initiated (9)
iniciar to begin (9)
inmediato, de immediately (15)
inmediato/a immediate (9)
inmenso/a immense (8)
inmigración, la immigration (15)
inmigrante, el/la immigrant (13)
inmunología, la immunology (1)
innato/a innate (14)
innovador/a innovative (14)
inolvidable unforgettable (8)
inquietud, la uneasiness (13)
insecto, el insect (5)
insertar to insert (8)
inspeccionar to inspect (14)
inspector/a de aduanas, el/la customs inspector (**9**)
instalación, la equipment (3)
instalar to install (**12**)
instante, el instant (8)
instrumento, el instrument (2)
insurrecto/a, el/la insurrectionist (13)
inteligente intelligent (**1**)
intercambiar to exchange (5)
intercambio, el exchange (3)
interesante interesting (**1**)
interesar to be interesting (**6**)
internacional international (2)
intérprete, el/la interpreter (4, **11**)
interrumpir to interrupt (15)
intervención, la intervention (15)
intestino, el intestine (6)
íntimo/a intimate (10)
inundar to flood (4)
inútil useless (15)
invasión, la invasion (7)
inventar to invent (15)
invernal (*adj.*) wintertime (6)
investigación, la research; investigation (3, 14)
investigador/a, el/la researcher (1)
invierno, el winter (**1**)
invitar to invite (3)
involucrar to involve (4)
inyección, la shot (**10**)
ir to go (**3**)
irlandés/esa, el/la Irish (9)
irónico/a ironic (14)
irrigación, la irrigation (15)
isla, la island (2, **9**)
italiano, el Italian (**2**)
itinerario, el itinerary (4)
izquierda (de), a la to/on the left (of) (**3**)
izquierdas, de leftist (8)

J

jabón, el soap (**5**)
jade, el jade (15)
jaguar, el jaguar (9)
jamón, el ham (**6**)
japonés, el Japanese (**2**)
jarabe, el cough syrup (**10**)
jardín, el garden (5)
jefe/a, el/la boss (**11**)
jeroglífico, el hieroglyphic (15)
jesuita, el Jesuit (10)
jogging, hacer to jog (**10**)
joven young (**2**)
joya, la jewel (7)
joyería, la jewelry store (**8**)
jubilarse to retire (7, **11**)
judío/a Jewish (14)

juego electrónico, el computer (electronic) game (**12**)
Juegos Olímpicos, los Olympic Games (3)
jueves, el Thursday (**1**)
juez/a, el/la judge (8, **15**)
jugador/a, el/la player (2)
jugar (ue) a to play (2, **4**)
jugo, el juice (**6**)
julio July (**1**)
junio June (**1**)
junto a next to (8)
juntos/as together (4)
jurado, el jury (14)
justamente exactly (15)
justificar to justify (14)
justo/a just (**11**)
juventud, la youth (12)

K

kilo, el kilogram (*= 2.2 pounds*) (**6**)

L

la the (**1**)
labio, el lip (8)
labor, la work (10)
laboratorio (de lenguas/de idiomas), el (language) laboratory (2, **3**)
lácteo/a milky (10)
lado (de), al next to (**3**)
lado, el side (11)
ladrillo, el brick (12)
lago, el lake (**9**)
lágrima, la tear (8)
lámpara, la lamp (**5**)
lana, la wool (**8**)
langosta, la lobster (**6**)
languidecer to languish (11)
lápida, la tomb stone (14)
lápiz labial, el lipstick (**5**)
lápiz, el pencil (**1**)
las the (**1**)
lastimarse to hurt oneself (**10**)
lavadora, la washing machine (**5**)
lavandería, la laundry (12)
lavaplatos, el dishwasher (**5**)
lavar la ropa to wash clothes (**5**)
lavar los platos to wash dishes (**5**)
lavarse to wash (**5**)
lección, la lesson; moral (**1**, 8)
leche, la milk (**6**)
lechuga, la lettuce (**6**)
lector de CD/DVD, el CD/DVD player (**12**)
lector/a, el/la reader (12, **13**)
leer to read (**2**)
legendario/a legendary (6)
lejano/a faraway (11)
lejos (de) far (from) (**3**)
lema publicitario, el slogan (13)
lema, el motto (**15**)
lengua, la tongue (7, **10**)
lentejuelas, las sequins (**14**)
lento/a slow (9)
letra, la lyrics (3)
letrero, el sign (9)
levantar pesas weightlifting (**7**)
levantarse to get up; to stand up (**5**)
léxico, el lexicon (15)
ley, la law (6, **15**)
liberar to liberate (9)
libertad, la liberty (5)
libre free (6)
librería, la bookstore (1, **3**)
libro, el book (**1**)
líder, el/la leader (15)
liderazgo, el leadership (9)
ligero/a light (13)
limitar to limit (10)
límite, el limit (6)
limón, el lemon (6)
limonada, la lemonade (4, **6**)
limosina, la limousine (14)
limpiar (la casa) to clean (the house) (4, **5**)
limpio/a clean (8)
lindo/a pretty (8)
línea ecuatorial, la equator (8)
lingüístico/a linguistic (13)
líquido, el liquid (5)
literatura, la literature (**3**)
litro, el liter (**6**)
llamamiento, el call (15)
llano, el plain (10)
llave, la key (12)
llegada, la arrival (3)
llegar to arrive (**2**)
llegar a ser to become (12)
lleno/a full (8)
llevar to wear (**8**)
llevarse bien to get along (4)
llorar to cry (9)
llover (ue) to rain (**7**)
lluvia, la rain (4)
lo que that which (5)
lobo marino, el sea lion (6)
loción (de afeitar), la (shaving) lotion/cream (**5**)
locutor/a, el/la announcer (**13**)
logotipo, el emblem (12)
lograr to achieve (**15**)
loma, la hill (15)
los the (**1**)
lucha, la struggle (15)
luchar to fight (13)
lucir to shine (14)
lujo, el luxury (5)
lujoso/a luxurious (3)
luna, la moon (8)
lunes, el Monday (**1**)

M

machacar to crush (11)
madera, la wood (3)
madrastra, la stepmother (**4**)
madre, la mother (**4**)
madrugada, la daybreak (10)
madrugar to get up early (13)
magia, la magic (14)
magnífico/a great; wonderful (**7**)
maíz, el corn (**6**)
mal bad (**1**)
mala pinta bad appearance (13)
maldito/a damned (13)
maleta(s), hacer la(s) to pack the suitcase(s) (**9**)
maleta, la suitcase (4)
maletín, el briefcase (4)
malo/a bad (**1**)
mandato, el command (11)
manejar to manage; to drive (12)
manera, la way (6)
manga corta/larga, de short-/long-sleeved (**8**)
manga, sin sleeveless (**8**)
manifestar (ie) manifest (6)
mano, la hand (**5**, **10**)
mansión, la mansion (5)
mantener (ie) to support (*a family, etc.*) (**15**)
mantenerse (ie) en forma to stay in shape (**10**)
mantequilla, la butter (**6**)
mantilla, la mantilla (10)
manzana, la apple; block (*Spain*) (3, **6**)
mañana, la tomorrow (**2**)
mapa, el map (**1**, **9**)
mapache, el raccoon (8)
Mapoma Marathon in Madrid (1)
maquiladora, la assembly plant (3)
maquillaje, el makeup (**5**, **8**)
maquillarse to apply makeup (**5**)
máquina de afeitar, la electric razor (**5**)
mar, el sea; ocean (2, **7**, **9**)
maracas, las maracas (**14**)
maravillado/a surprised (4)
maravilloso/a marvelous (4)
marca, la brand (**12**)
marcharse to go away (9)
marcial martial (13)
marearse to become seasick (13)
mariachi, el (*Mexico*) mariachi musician (3)
marinero/a, el/la sailor (3)
marino/a marine (6)
mariposa, la butterfly (5)
mariscos, los seafood (**6**)
marítimo/a maritime (5)
martes, el Tuesday (**1**)
marzo March (**1**)
más o menos so, so (**1**)
más… que more… than (**5**)
masacre, el massacre (4)
mascota, la pet (6)
matar to kill (11)
matemáticas, las mathematics (2, **3**)
materia, la academic subject; course (**3**)
material, el material (5)
matriarcado, el matriarchy (5)
máximo/a maximum (9)
mayo May (**1**)
mayor older (**4**)
mayoría, la majority (8)
mazorca de maíz, la ear of corn (15)
Me da igual. It's all the same to me. (**7**)
Me encantaría. I would love to. (**4**)
Me llamo… My name is… (**1**)
mecánico/a, el/la mechanic (**11**)
medicina, la medicine (**3**)
medida, la measurement; measure (**6**, **12**)
medio ambiente, el environment (5, **12**)
medio/a half (2)
medios, los means (14)
medir (i, i) to measure (6)
mejor better (3)
mejorar to improve (6, **15**)
mejorarse to get better; to get well (**10**)
melancólico/a melancholic (7)
melodía, la melody (14)
mencionado/a mentioned (15)
mencionar to mention (4)
menor younger (**4**)
menos… que less… than (**5**)
mensaje, el message (8)
mensajería, la voicemail (12)
mentado/a named (15)
menú, el menu (**6**)
menudo (*slang*) real
menudo, a often (2)
mercado, el market (4)
merengue, el Caribbean dance (7)
merienda, la snack (**6**)
mérito, el merit (11)
mes, el month (**1**)
mesa de noche, la nightstand (**5**)
mesa, la table (**1**, **5**)
meta, la goal (6, **11**)
meteorológico/a meteorological (4)
meteorólogo/a, el/la weatherman/woman (**13**)
meter to put (6)
metro, el meter (8)
mexicano/a Mexican (**2**)
mezclar to mix (8)
Mi nombre es… My name is… (**1**)
mi/s my (**1**, **3**)
mi'jo my son (*slang*) (15)
micrófono, el microphone (15)
microondas, el microwave (**6**)
microscopio, el microscope (1)
miedo, tener (ie) to be afraid (**3**)
miembro, el member (4)
mientras while (4)
miércoles, el Wednesday (**1**)
migra, la immigration (*slang*) (15)
migratorio/a migrant (15)
milenio, el millennium (3)
militar military (4)
milla, la mile (15)
millón/millones, el/los million/s (2)
mina, la mine (6)
mineralogía, la mineralogy (6)
minería, la mining (4)
minero/a, el/la miner (10)
mínimo/a minimum (9)
ministro/a, el/la minister (4, **15**)
minoría, la minority (13)
mío/a/os/as mine (**13**)
mirada, la glance (13)
mirar to look at (**2**)
misa, la Mass (15)
misceláneo/a miscellaneous (1)
miseria, la misery (8)
misión, la mission (5)
mismo/a same (8)
misterio, el mystery (4)
misterioso/a mysterious (11)
mochila, la backpack (**1**)
moda, de in style (**8**)
moda, la fashion (4, **14**)
modelo, el/la model (**14**)
moderado/a moderate (15)
moderno/a modern (3)
modo (de vestir), el way/ manner (of dressing) (11, **14**)

mojar to wet (14)
mola, la Panamanian embroidery (5)
mole poblano, el Mexican chicken dish (10)
molestar to be a bother; to annoy (**6**)
monarca, el/la monarch (13)
monarquía, la monarchy (**15**)
moneda, la coin (8)
monja, la nun (12)
monjita, la little nun (14)
mono, el monkey (5)
monótono/a monotonous (11)
monstruo, el monster (5)
montaña, la mountain (2, **9**)
montañoso/a mountainous (4)
montar to ride (11)
montar a caballo to go horseback riding (**9**)
montar en bicicleta bicycle riding (**9**)
montón, el pile (12)
montuno/a wild (14)
monumento, el monument (**9**)
morado/a purple (**1**)
moraleja, la moral (8)
morcilla, la sausage (blood) (6)
morder (ue) to bite (7)
moreno/a brunette (**2**)
morir (ue, u) to die (9)
moro/a, el/la Moor (Arab) (13)
mostrar (ue) to show (8)
motivo, el motive (10)
movimiento, el movement (8)
muchacho/a, el/la boy/girl (**2**)
Mucho gusto. Pleased to meet you. (**1**)
mudanza, la move (12)
mudarse to move (5)
muebles, los furniture (**5**)
muerte, la death (6)
muerto/a dead (7)
muestra, la sample (15)
mujer, la woman (**1**)
mulato/a mulatto (7)
multa, la fine (**12**)
multinacional multinational (15)
mundial world (15)
mundo, el world (1)
mural, el mural (12)
muralista, el/la muralist (3)
músculo, el muscle (10)
musculoso/a muscular (13)
museo, el museum (2, **3**)
música, la music (**3**)
músico/a, el/la musician (8, **14**)
musulmán/ana Moslem (14)
muy very (**1**)

N

nacer to be born (2)
nacionalidad, la nationality (2)
nada nothing (**7**)
nadar (en el mar/en una piscina) to swim (in the ocean/in a pool) (**2, 7**)
nadie no one (**7**)
naranja, la orange (**6**)
nariz, la nose (**5, 10**)
narrador/a, el/la narrator (11, 14)
narrar to narrate (4)
narrativo/a story; narrative (*adj.*) (14)
natación, la swimming (**2**)
naturaleza muerta, la still life (6)
naturaleza, la nature (5, **12**)
navaja de afeitar, la razor blade (**5**)
navegable navigable (5)
navegante, el/la navigator (7)
navegar to navigate; to sail (12, 14)
necesitado/a in need (9)
necesitar to need (1, **2**)
negativo/a negative (7)
negocio, el business (8)
negro/a black (**1**)
neoyorquino/a New Yorker (12)
nervioso/a nervous (3, **5**)
nevar (ie) to snow (**7**)
ni modo no way (3)
ni... ni neither... nor (**7**)
nido, el nest (11)
niebla, la fog (9)
nieto/a, el/la grandson/granddaughter (**4**)
nilón, el nylon (**14**)
ningún/ninguna none (**7**)
ninguno/a no one (**7**)
niños/as, los/las children (1)
nitrato de sodio, el sodium nitrate (6)
nivel, el level (10)
No te preocupes. Don't worry. (**7**)
noble noble (15)
nobleza, la nobility (15)
noche, la night (**2**)
Nochevieja, la New Year's Eve (9)
nocivo/a harmful (10)
nomás only (*slang*) (15)
nombrar to name (6)
nombre, el name (**1**)
nominación, la nomination (13)
nominado/a nominated (12)
norteamericano/a American (US) (**2**)
nosotros/as we (**1**)
nostálgico/a nostalgic (7)
nota, la grade (3)
noticias, las news (**13**)
noticiero, el newscast (**13**)
notificar to notify (14)
novela, la novel (2, **7**)
novelista, el/la novelist (2)
noveno/a ninth (**8**)
noviembre November (**1**)
novio/a, el/la boyfriend/girlfriend; groom/bride (3, **4**)
nube, la cloud (8)
nublado/a cloudy (**7**)
núcleo, el nucleus (4)
nuera, la daughter-in-law (**4**)
nuestro/a/os/as our/s (**3, 13**)
nuevo/a new (**2**)
nunca never (2, **7**)

Ñ

ñandutí, el cloth woven with a spider web pattern (10)

O

o or (**1**)
o... o either... or (**7**)
objeto, el object (9)
obligación, la obligation (15)
obligatorio/a mandatory (**12**)
obra work (*art*); play (*theater*) (2, **13**)
obra maestra, la masterpiece (9)
observar to observe (8)
observatorio, el observatory (**3**)
obstrucción, la obstruction (10)
obtener (ie) to obtain (11)
octavo/a eighth (7, **8**)
octubre October (**1**)
ocupar to occupy (2)
ocurrir to occur (3)
oferta, la offer (1)
oficial official (13)
oficina, la office (2)
oficio, el trade (**11**)
ofrecer to offer (9)
oído, el inner ear (**10**)
oír to hear (8)
ojo, el eye (**5**)
ola, la wave (5)
olmo, el elm (12)
olor, el perfume; odor; smell (6, **8**)
ONU, la UN (12)
ópera, la opera (1, **14**)
operar to operate (**10**)
opinar to express an opinion (5)
oprimido/a oppressed (15)
oración, la sentence (7)
orden, el order (4)
ordenar to order (15)
ordenar la casa to clean the house (**5**)
ordeñar to milk (15)
ordinario/a ordinary (12)
oreja, la outer ear (10)
oriente, el east (10)
origen, el origin (3)
originalidad, la originality (13)
originar to originate (8)
orilla, la river bank (8)
ornamento, el ornament (8)
orquesta (sinfónica), la (symphony) orchestra (**4, 14**)
orquídea, la orchid (5)
oscuro/a dark (8)
otoño, el fall (*season*) (**1**)
oveja, la sheep (8)
oxígeno, el oxygen (10)
Oye. (*command*) Listen. (**7**)
oyeres whatever you hear (13)

P

paciente, el/la patient (**10**)
pacífico/a peaceful (15)
pacifista, el/la pacifist (**15**)
padecer (de) to suffer (from) (**10**)
padrastro, el stepfather (**4**)
padre, el father (**4**)
padres, los parents (**2**)
pagar (en efectivo) to pay (cash) (**8**)
página Web, la web page (**12**)
país (en desarrollo), el (developing) country (**2, 15**)
paisaje, el landscape (8)
paja, la straw (**14**)
pájaro, el bird (5)
palacio, el palace (3)
palillo, el drum stick; toothpick (14)
palo, el stick (7)
palpitar to beat (10)
pampas, las plains of Argentina (11)
pan, el bread (**6**)
panameño/a Panamanian (**2**)
pantalla, la screen (**12**)
pantalones, los pants (**8**)
papas, las potatoes (**6**)
papel, el paper; role (**1**, 12)
papelería, la stationery shop (**8**)
parada, la stop (15)
parado/a standing (15)
paraíso, el paradise (6)
pararse to stand up (8)
pardo/a brown (8)
parecer to seem (**6**)
parecido/a similar (12)
pareja, la couple; partner (4)
pariente, el/la relative (*family*) (4)
paro, estar en el to be out of work (**11**)
parque, el park (1, **4**)
párrafo, el paragraph (5)
parrilla, la grill (6)
parrillada, la barbecue (*Chile, Argentina*) (6)
parte, la part (3)
participante, el/la participant (1)
participar to participate (3)
particularmente particularly (2)
partida, la parting (9)
partido, (ir a un) (to go to a) game (2, **4, 7**)
partir de, a from then on (10)
partitura, la score (14)
pasado, el past (15)
pasado/a last (6)
pasaje (de ida y vuelta), el (roundtrip) fare; ticket (**9**)
pasar (por) to spend (*time*); pass (by) (**4**)
pasar la aspiradora to vacuum (**5**)
pasarlo bien/mal/de maravilla to have a good/bad/wonderful time (**9**)
pasatiempo, el pastime (7)
pasear to take a walk (**4**)
paseo, el stroll (1)
pasillo, el hallway; aisle (1, **9**)
pasión, la passion (13)
paso, el step (4)
Paso por ti. I'll come by for you. (**4**)
pasta de dientes, la toothpaste (**8**)
pastel, el cake; pie (**6**)
pastilla, la pill; lozenge (**10**)
pasto, el grass (12)
pata, la paw; foot (*animal*) (7, 8)
patear to kick (**7**)
patiecito, el small patio (12)
patinador/a, el/la skater (12)
patinaje, el skating (**7**)
patinar to skate (**7**)
patio, el yard; patio (**5**)
pato, el duck (8)
patria, la homeland (10)
patriarca, el patriarch (14)
patriarcado, el patriarchy (5)
patrimonio mundial, el world heritage (10)
patrocinador/a, el/la sponsor (12, **13**)
patrocinar to sponsor (**13**)

patronato, el board of trustees (1)
pavo, el turkey (**6**)
Paz Verde, la Green Peace (12)
paz, la peace (4)
pecho, el chest (**10**)
pedagogía, la teaching (**3**)
pedazo, el piece (6)
pedicura, la pedicure (10)
pedir (i, i) to ask for; to request; to order (**4, 6**)
peinarse to comb one's hair (2, **5**)
peine, el comb (**5**)
pelar to peel (**6**)
pelícano, el pelican (6)
película, la movie; film (**4, 13**)
peligro, el danger (5)
peligroso/a dangerous (2)
pelo, el hair (**5**)
pelón/pelona barren (15)
peluquería, la hair salon (13)
peluquero/a, el/la hairstylist (**11**)
pena, la pity; sorrow (2, 10)
penales, los (*Latin America*) penalties (7)
penaltis, los (*Spain*) penalties (7)
pensamiento, el thought (3)
pensar (ie) to think (3, **4**)
pequeño/a small (1, **2**)
percusionista, el/la percussionist (7)
perder (ie) to lose (**4**)
perdurar to last (14)
perenne perennial (11)
perezoso/a lazy (2)
perezoso, el sloth (5)
perfecto/a perfect (2)
perfil, el profile (11)
perfume, el perfume (**8**)
perfumería, la perfume shop (**8**)
periódico, el newspaper (**7, 13**)
periodista, el/la journalist (4, **11, 13**)
periodístico/a journalistic (15)
período, el period (2)
perlas, las pearls (**8**)
permanecer to remain (14)
permanente permanent (3)
permiso, el permission (15)
pero but (**2**)
perpetuarse to perpetuate (15)
perro/a, el/la dog (**4**)
perseverancia, la perseverance (13)
persona, la person (**1**)
personaje, el character (8)
personal, el personnel (11)
personalidad, la personality (7)
personificar to personify (6)
pertinente pertinent (11)
peruano/a Peruvian (**2**)
pesca, la fishing (2)
pescado, el fish (**6**)
pescar to fish (**9**)
peso, el weight (**10**)
pesquero/a fishing (6)
pesticidas, los pesticides (**12**)
petrificado/a petrified (7)
petróleo, el oil (9, **12**)
pez, el fish (12)
piano, el piano (1, **14**)
PIB, el GNP (9)
picante spicy (**6**)
pícnic, hacer un to have a picnic (**7**)
pico, el peak (8)
pie, el foot (7, **10**)
piedra, la stone (4)
piel, la skin; leather; fur (5, **14**)
pierna, la leg (**10**)
pieza (musical), la (musical) piece (3, **14**)
pila, la battery (12)
piloto, el/la pilot (**9**)
pimiento, el pepper (**6**)
pingüino, el penguin (6)
pintado/a painted (3)
pintor/a, el/la artist; painter (1)
pintura, la painting (2)
pirámide, la pyramid (3)
pirata, el pirate (7)
piratear to pirate (11)
pisar to step on (11)
piscina, la swimming pool (5, 7, **9**)
piso, el floor (5, **8**)
pista, la clue (2)
pizarra, la blackboard (**1**)
pizca, la pinch (**6**)
pizcar to pick (*Mexico*) (15)
placa, la license plate (12)
placer, el pleasure (7)
plan de retiro, el retirement plan (**11**)
plancha, la iron; metal sheet (**5**, 8)
planchar to iron (**5**)
planear to plan (14)
plano/a flat (10)
planta nuclear, la nuclear plant (**12**)
plantar to plant (12)
plantear to pose (15)
plástico, el plastic (3)
plataforma, la platform (15)
plátano, el banana (8)
platería, la silverware (3)
plato, el dish; plate (2, 15)
playa, la beach (2, **7**)
plomero/a , el/la plumber (**11**)
población, la population (2)
pobre poor (**2**)
pobreza, la poverty (5, **15**)
poder (ue) to be able; can (**4**)
poder, el power (15)
poesía, la poetry (6)
poeta, el/la poet (2)
polémica, la controversy (12)
poliéster, el polyester (**14**)
política, la politics (15)
político, el politician (15)
político/a political (15)
pollo, el chicken (**6**)
poner to put (**4**)
poner la mesa to set the table (**5**)
poner una película to show a movie (**4**)
ponerse to become (**5**)
ponerse en forma to get in shape (**10**)
por eso therefore (2)
por qué why (**2**)
porque because (**2**)
portátil, la computadora laptop computer (**12**)
portugués, el Portuguese (**2**)
porvenir, el future (12)
posado/a posed (14)
posar to pose (model) (14)
posible possible (3)
posiblemente possibly (2)
postor/a, el/la bidder (13)
pozo, el well (*of water*) (15)
practicar to practice; to play (*a sport*) (**2**)
precio, el price (5, **8**)
precioso/a precious (6)
precolombino/a pre-Colombian (5)
precursor/a precursor (10)
predecir (i) predict (15)
predominar to predominate (8)
preferencia, la preference (5)
preferido/a preferred (9)
preferir (ie, i) to prefer (**4**)
pregonero, el town crier (7)
pregunta, la question (**1**)
prehispánico/a prehispanic (3)
prehistórico/a prehistoric (3)
premiar to reward (11)
premio, el prize (8)
prenda, la accessory; garment (8, **14**)
prensa, la press (4)
preocupación, la preoccupation (10)
preocuparse to worry (8)
preparar to prepare (**2**)
presa, la dam (10)
presentador/a, el/la moderator (12, **13**)
preservar to preserve (5)
presidencia, la presidency (15)
presidente/a, el/la president (**15**)
presidir to preside (15)
presión, la blood pressure (**10**)
préstamo, el loan (11)
prestar to lend (12)
prestar atención to pay attention (13)
prestigio, el prestige (14)
prestigioso/a prestigious (2)
presupuesto, el budget (5)
primavera, la spring (**1**)
primer/o/a first (2, **8**)
primera actriz, la leading lady (**13**)
primera plana, la front page (**13**)
primo/a, el/la cousin (**4**)
príncipe, el prince (2)
principiante, el/la beginner (3)
principio, al at first (5)
principio, el beginning (**13**)
principios, a at the beginning (15)
prioridad, la priority (15)
prisa, tener (ie) to be in a hurry (**3**)
prisionero/a, el/la prisoner (15)
privacidad, la privacy (5)
probador, el fitting room (**8**)
probar (ue) to try (6)
probarse (ue) to try on (4, **8**)
procesar to process (12)
procesión, la procession (1)
proceso, el process (15)
procrear to procreate (10)
producir to produce (8)
producto, el product (2)
productor/a, el/la producer (**13**)
productos lácteos, los dairy products (**10**)
profesor/a, el/la professor (**1**)
profundamente profoundly (10)
profundo/a deep; profound (5)
programador/a programmer (12)
programar to program (**12**)
programas sociales, los social welfare programs (**15**)
progreso, el progress (15)
prohibido/a prohibited (6)
prohibir to prohibit (15)
prolífico/a prolific (2)
promesa, la promise (6)
prometer to promise (6)
promover (ue) to promote (*an idea*) (14, **15**)
pronóstico, el forecast (4)
pronto soon (10)
propiedad, la property (10)
propietario/a, el/la owner (8)
propina, la tip (*monetary*) (**6**)
propio/a own (13)
proponer to propose (15)
proporcionar to proportion; to provide (1)
prosperidad, la prosperity (10)
próspero/a prosperous (6)
protagonista, el/la protagonist; star (**13**)
proteger to protect (5, **12**)
protegido/a protected (6)
proteínas, las proteins (**10**)
proveniente originating (14)
provisión, la provision (15)
próximo/a next (6)
proyecto, el project (5)
psicología, la psychology (**3**)
psicológico/a psychological (14)
psicólogo/a, el/la psychologist (3, **11**)
púas, las barbs (15)
publicar to publish (6)
publicitario/a publicity (*adj.*) (13)
público, el public; audience (**13**)
pueblecito, el small town (10)
pueblo, el town; the people; the masses (8, **15**)
puente, el bridge (13)
puerta, la door (**1**)
puerto, el port (2)
puertorriqueño/a Puerto Rican (**2**)
pues well; because (**3, 5**)
puesto, el place; stall; position (*job*) (5, 6, **11**)
pulmones, los lungs (**10**)
pulsar to dial (12)
pulsera, la bracelet (**8**)
punta, la tip (4)
puntiagudo/a sharp (9)
punto (de vista), el point (of view) (1, 13)
punto, en on the dot (2)

Q

que that which (5)
qué what (1, **2**)
qué padre great (*Mexico*) (7)
¿Qué pasa? What's happening?; What's up? (**1**)
¿Qué tal? What's up? (**1**)
quedar to be left; to be remaining; to fit (6, **8**)
quedarse to stay (*somewhere*); to remain (**9**)
quehaceres, los chores (4, **5**)

quemar to burn (10)
quena, la Andean flute (8)
querer (ie) to want; to love (**4**)
queso, el cheese (**6**)
quien who (**2**)
¿Quieres ir a...? Do you want to go to...? (**4**)
química, la chemistry (**3**)
quinto/a fifth (**8**)
quipu, el knotted string (*Inca*) (15)
quiropráctico/a, el/la chiropractor (10)
quitar la mesa to clear the table (**5**)
quitarse to take off (**5**)
quizás perhaps (4)

R

radioactividad, la radioactivity (**12**)
radiografía, la X-ray (**10**)
radioyente, el/la radio listener (**13**)
rana, la frog (5)
ranchito, el small ranch (15)
rápido/a rapid (2)
raramente rarely (4)
ratito, el a little while (15)
rato, el short time; while (13)
ratón, el mouse (**12**)
rayas, de striped (**8**)
rayón, el rayon (**14**)
raza, la race (5)
razón, la reason (2)
razón, no tener to be wrong (**3**)
razón, tener to have a point; to be right (**3**)
reaccionar to react (10)
real royal (14)
realista realistic (4)
realizar to achieve (8)
rebaja, en on sale (**8**)
rebaja, la sale (**8**)
recámara, la bedroom (12)
recargable rechargeable (12)
receptor, el receiver (12)
receta, la recipe (**6**)
recetar to prescribe (**10**)
rechinar to squeak (15)
recibir to receive (**2**)
recibo, el receipt (**8**)
reciclaje, el recycling (**12**)
reciclar to recycle (**12**)
recientemente recently (6)
recipiente, el container (**6**)
recoger to pick up (9)
recomendar (ie) to recommend (9)
reconocimiento, el recognition (12)
reconquista, la reconquest (13)
reconstruir to reconstruct (15)
recordar (ue) to remember (**4**)
recorrer to go round; to travel through/across (**9**)
recreativo/a recreational (7)
recto, todo straight ahead (3)
rector/a, el/la president (*of a university*) (8)
rectoría, la president's office (**3**)
recuerdo, el souvenir; memory (4, **9**)
recuperación, la recovery (9)
recuperar to recuperate (10)
recurso (natural), el (natural) resource (5, **12**)
Red informática, la Internet (**12**)
redondo/a round (15)
reducir to reduce (15)
reflejar to reflect (8)
reforestación, la reforestation (**12**)
reformar to reform (12)
reforzar (ue) to reinforce (15)
refrescante refreshing (9)
refresco, el refreshment; soft drink (3, **6**)
refrigerador, el refrigerator (**5**)
regadío, el irrigated land (8)
regatear to bargain; to haggle over (**8**)
régimen, el diet (10)
reglamento, el ruling (10)
regordete chubby (15)
regresar to return (**2**)
regreso, de on return (11)
reina, la queen (7, **15**)
reinar to reign (10)
reino, el kingdom (8)
reírse (i, i) to laugh (**5**)
relación, la relation (4)
relajarse to relax (10)
relatar to relate (7)
relativo/a relative (15)
relato, el story (12)
religioso/a religious (15)
rellenar to fill out/completely (**11**)
reloj, el clock; watch (**1**)
reloj de pulsera, el wristwatch (**8**)
remediar to remedy (13)
remedio, el remedy (**10**)
remover (ue) to remove (14)
rendir (i, i) to defeat (13)
renombre, el renown (14)
renovable renewable (11)
renta, la rent (*Mexico*) (12)
reparar to repair (**11**)
repartir to deliver; to distribute (2, **11**)
repaso, el review (13)
repertorio, el repertoire (**14**)
repetir (i, i) to repeat (**4**)
reportar report (13)
reportero/a, el/la (television) reporter (4, **13**)
representación, la presentation (14)
representante, el/la representative (**15**)
representar to perform; to represent (2, 13, **14**)
representativo/a representative (3)
república, la republic (15)
requerir (ie) to require (11)
requisito, el requirement (5)
res, la beef (10)
reseña, la review (*article*) (6)
reserva, la reservation (**9**)
reservación, la reservation (6)
resfriado, el cold (*illness*) (**10**)
residencia, la residence (2)
resina, la resin (7)
resolver (ue) to resolve; to solve (12, **15**)
respectivo/a respective (7)
respetable respectable (14)
respetar to respect (15)
respiración, la breathing (12)
respirar to breathe (6, **10**)
respiratorio/a respiratory (10)
responsabilidades, las responsibilities (**11**)
responsabilizar to take responsibility (1)
responsable responsible (3)
respuesta, la answer; response (**1, 5**)
restaurán, el restaurant (13)
restaurante, el restaurant (**6**)
restaurar to restore (5)
restos, los remains; leftovers (10)
resultado, el result (6)
resumen, el summary (5)
resumir to summarize (7)
retar to challenge (11)
retirarse to retire; to withdraw (**11**, 15)
retrasar to detain; to be behind (11, 13)
retrato, el portrait (14)
revelar to reveal (15)
reverenciado/a venerated (15)
revisar to check (**13**)
revolucionado/a revolutionized (12)
revólver, el revolver (11)
rey, el king (2, **15**)
rezar to pray (15)
rico/a rich; delicious (**2, 6**)
riel, el rail (15)
riesgo, el risk (10)
río, el river (2)
riqueza, la wealth; richness (5)
risa, la laughter (13)
ritmo, el rhythm (1)
ritual, el ritual (3)
rival, el rival (8)
robar to steal; to rob (6)
robo, el theft (11)
rodaje, el filming (13)
rodeado/a surrounded (12)
rodilla, la knee (**10**)
rojo/a red (**1**)
rollo de película, el film (**9**)
romance, el ballad (8)
romántico/a romantic (4)
romperse (un hueso) to break (a bone) (**10**)
ropa, la clothing (**8**)
rosado/a pink (**1**)
rubio/a blond (**2**)
ruido, el noise (11)
ruina, la ruin (4)
rumor, el rumor (13)
ruso, el Russian (**2**)
ruta, la route (10)
rutina, la routine (5)

S

sábado, el Saturday (**1**)
saber to know (**4**)
sabor, el flavor (1)
sabroso/a tasty (4)
sacar to take out; to get (*a grade*) (5, 9)
sacar fotos to take pictures (9)
sacar la basura to take out the garbage (**5**)
saco, el blazer (**8**)
sacrificado/a sacrificed (15)
sacudir to shake (15)
sacudir el polvo (de los muebles) to dust (the furniture) (**5**)
sagrado/a sacred (13)
sal, la salt (**6**)
sala de espera, la waiting area (**9**)
sala de reclamación de equipaje, la baggage claim area (**9**)
sala de urgencias, la emergency room (10)
sala, la living room (3, **5**)
salario, el salary (**11**)
saldo, el balance (13)
salir to leave; to go out (**4**)
salón, el room (9)
salsero/a, el/la salsa performer (12)
saltar to leap (8)
salto, el waterfall (**9**)
salud, la health (4, **10**)
saluda atentamente, lo(s)/la(s) very truly yours (**11**)
saludable healthy (10)
saludo/s, el/los greeting/s; salutation/s (**1, 11**)
salvadoreño/a Salvadorian (**2**)
salvar to save (12)
sandalias, las sandals (**8**)
sándwich, el sandwich (3, **6**)
sanfermines, los Sanfermín festival (2)
sanidad, la sanitation; public health (15)
sano/a y salvo/a safe and sound (11)
santo/a holy (14)
sapo, el toad (8)
sartén, la skillet; frying pan (**6**)
satélite, la televisión por satellite TV (**13**)
satisfacer to satisfy (9)
satisfactorio/a satisfactory (6)
satisfecho/a satisfied (8)
saturado/a saturated (10)
saxofón, el saxophone (**14**)
sé I know (4)
secador, el hair dryer (**5**)
secadora, la dryer (**5**)
secar la ropa to dry clothes (**5**)
secarse to dry (*oneself*) (**5**)
seco/a dry (6)
secretario/a, el/la secretary (1, **11**)
sed, tener (ie) to be thirsty (**3**)
seda, la silk (**8**)
sede, la seat of government (8)
sediento/a thirsty (12)
segregar to secrete (5)
segundo/a second (**8**)
seguramente surely (3)
seguridad, la security (9)
seguro médico, el health insurance (**11**)
seguro social, el social security (6)
seguro/a sure (4)
selección, la selection (7)
seleccionar to select (15)
sello, el stamp (2)
selva, la jungle (5)
selvático/a jungle (4)
Semana Santa, la Holy Week (1)

semana, la week (**1**)
sembrar (ie) to sow (8)
semejante similar (14)
semestre, el semester (**3**)
senador/a, el/la senator (**15**)
sencillez, la simplicity (**14**)
sendero, el path (5)
sensacionalista sensationalist (13)
sensual sensuous (7)
sentarse (ie) to sit (**5**)
sentimental sentimental (4)
sentimiento, el feeling (4)
sentirse (ie, i) to feel (**5**)
señalar to point out (12)
señor, el (Sr.) Mr. (**1**)
señora, la (Sra.) Mrs. (**1**)
señorita, la (Srta.) Miss (**1**)
separado/a separated (13)
septiembre September (**1**)
séptimo/a seventh (**8**)
sepulcro, el grave (14)
ser to be (**1**)
ser, el being (3)
serenata, la serenade (3)
serie mundial, la World Series (4)
serio/a serious (7)
servicio, el service (2)
servir (i, i) to serve (**4**)
severo/a severe (8)
sexo, el sex (13)
sexteto, el sextet (**14**)
sexto/a sixth (**8**)
SIDA, el AIDS (10)
siempre always (2, **3**, **7**)
siglas, las call letters (7)
siglo, el century (3)
significante significant (13)
significativo/a significant (7)
siguiente following (4)
silbato, el whistle (15)
silla, la chair (**1**)
sillón, el armchair; overstuffed chair (**5**)
simbolizar symbolize (6)
simpático/a nice (**1**)
sin embargo nevertheless (3)
sindicato, el union (12)
sinfonía, la symphony (**14**)
sinfónica, la symphonic (14)
síntesis, la synthesis (9)
sintético/a synthetic (14)
síntoma, el symptom (**10**)
sinvergüenza, el/la shameless (person) (13)
siquiera, ni not even (15)
sirviente/a, el/la servant (4)
sistema, el system (4)
sitio Web, el web site (**12**)
sitio, el place (10)
situación, la situation (5)
situado/a situated (3)
sobre on (**5**)
sobre, el envelope (2)
sobrepeso, el excess weight; obesity (**10**)
sobrepoblación, la overpopulation (13)
sobresalir to excel (12)
sobresalto, el shock (13)
sobrino/a, el/la nephew/niece (**4**)
socialista, el/la socialist (8)
sociedad, la society (5)
socio/a, el/la colleague (11)
sociología, la sociology (**3**)
sofá, el sofa; couch (**5**)
sofisticación, la sophistication (14)
sofisticado/a sophisticated (14)
sol, hace it is sunny (**7**)
solamente only (**3**)
solar solar (15)
soler (ue) to tend to; to be accustomed to (4, 10, 13)
solicitud de empleo, la job application (**11**)
sólido/a solid (6)
solista, el/la soloist (**14**)
solitario/a solitary (11)
sólo only (**3**)
soltar (ue) to let go (2)
soltero/a single; unmarried (**4**)
solución, la solution (2)
solucionar to solve (15)
sombrilla, la umbrella (**7**)
son, el musical rhythm (14)
sonido, el sound (14)
sonoro/a loud (14)
sonreír (i, i) to smile (10)
sonrisa, la smile (2)
soñar (ue) (con) to dream (about) (**4**)
sopa, la soup (**6**)
sopita, la a bit of soup (10)
soplar to blow (8)
soportar to endure (9)
sorbete, el sorbet (6)
sorprendente surprising (11)
sorpresa, la surprise (6)
sospecha, la suspicion (11)
sostén, el bra (13)
sostener (ie) to hold that (13)
sótano, el basement (12)
soy I am (**1**)
SRAS, el SARS (10)
su/s your (*for. sing./pl.*); his; her; their (**3**)
suave soft (8)
subir to raise; to go up; to climb (6, 8)
subir de peso to gain weight (**10**)
subrayar to underscore (5)
sucio/a dirty (6)
suegro/a, el/la father-in-law/mother-in-law (**4**)
sueldo, el wages (3, **11**)
suelo, el ground (13)
sueño, el dream (12)
sueño, tener to be sleepy (**3**)
suerte, la luck (**7**)
suéter, el sweater (4, **8**)
suficiente sufficient (11)
suficientemente sufficiently (4)
sufrir (de) to suffer (from) (3)
sugerencia, la suggestion (8)
sugerir (ie, i) to suggest (9)
sumamente very (10)
sumario, el summary (2)
superar to overcome (12)
superficial superficial (11)
supermercado, el supermarket (6)
supervisor/a, el/la supervisor (**11**)
supuesto, por of course (14)
supuesto/a supposed (9)
surfear to surf (7)
surgir to rise up; emerge (10)
surrealista surrealist (13)
susceptible susceptible (4)
sustancia, la substance (15)
suyo/a/os/as his; her/s; your/s (*for.*); their/s (7, **13**)

T

tabla, la board (12)
tacto, el touch (13)
tal/es como such as (4)
talco, el talcum powder (**8**)
talento, el talent (9)
talentoso/a talented (**14**)
talla, la clothing size (8)
tamaño, el size (14)
también also (**2**)
tambor, el drum (7, **14**)
tan... como as... as (**5**)
tanque, el tank (10)
tanto/a como as much as (**5**)
tantos/as como as many as (**5**)
tapar to cover (**6**)
tapas, las appetizers (6)
taquilla, la box office (8)
taquillero/a, el/la (box office) clerk (13)
tardar to be late (13)
tarde late (**2**)
tarde, la afternoon (**2**)
tarea, la homework; task (2)
tarjeta de crédito, la credit card (**8**)
tarjeta de embarque, la boarding pass (**9**)
tarjeta de memoria, la memory card (**9**)
tarta de limón, la lemon pie (**6**)
tasa (de desempleo), la rate (of unemployment) (6, **15**)
tatuaje, el tattoo (13)
taxista, el/la taxi driver (4)
te gustaría would you like (**4**)
té, el tea (3, **6**)
teatro, el theatre (**3**, **4**)
techo, el ceiling (12)
teclado, el keyboard (**12**)
técnica, la technique (14)
tecnológico/a technological (**12**)
tejer to weave (10)
tejido, el weaving (4)
tela de la araña, la spider web (10)
tela, la cloth (8)
telefónico/a telephone (*adj.*) (3)
teléfono móvil/celular, el cellular phone (4, **12**)
telenovela, la soap opera (**13**)
televidente, el/la viewer (**13**)
televisión, la television (**7**)
televisión por cable, la cable TV (**13**)
telón, el curtain (11)
tema actual, el current topic (**15**)
tema, el theme (7)
temblor, el tremor (14)
temperatura, la temperature (6, **10**)
tempestad, la storm (8)
templado/a temperate (6)
templo, el temple (8)
temporada, la season (**7**)
temporal temporary (3)
temporario/a temporary (12)
temprano/a early (**2**)
tendencia, la tendency (14)
tener (ie) to have (1, **2**)
tengo I have (**1**)
tenis, el tennis (**2**)
tensión, la tension (13)
tenso/a tense (14)
tentación, la temptation (6)
teoría, la theory (8)
terapia, la therapy (3)
tercer/o/a third (**8**)
terciopelo, el velvet (**14**)
termal thermal (10)
términos, los terms (11)
ternura, la tenderness (14)
terraza, la terrace (**5**)
terremoto, el earthquake (5)
terreno, el land; terrain (4)
terrestre terrestrial (8)
territorio, el territory (13)
tesoro, el treasure (8)
tibio/a lukewarm (7)
tiempo, el time; weather (**1**, **7**)
tienda, la store (**8**)
tienda especializada, la specialty shop (6)
tierra, la earth; land (2)
tímido/a shy; timid (**1**)
tío/a, el/la uncle/aunt (**4**)
típico/a typical (8)
tirar to throw (15)
tiras cómicas, las comics (**13**)
titular, el headline (**13**)
título, el title (2)
toalla, la towel (**7**)
tobillo, el ankle (10)
tocar to play (*an instrument*) (4)
todavía still (3)
todo/a/os/as all; everyone (**3**)
tolerancia, la tolerance (15)
tomar to drink; to take (**2**)
tomarse la presión to take one's blood pressure (**10**)
tomate, el tomato (**6**)
tonto/a stupid (13)
toque, el touch (6)
tórax, el thorax (13)
torcer (ue) to twist (**10**)
torneo, el tournament (2)
torno a, en around (3)
toro, el bull (2)
toronja, la grapefruit (**6**)
torta de chocolate, la chocolate cake (**6**)
tortilla, la omelet (*Spain*) (6)
tos, la cough (**10**)
toser to cough (**10**)
tostadora, la toaster (**6**)
tostar (ue) to toast (**6**)
trabajador/a hard-working (**1**)
trabajador/a, el/la worker (1)
trabajar (a comisión) to work (on commission) (**2**, **11**)
trabajo, estar sin to be out of work (**11**)
tradición, la tradition (3)
traducir to translate (15)
traductor/a, el/la translator (15)
traer to bring (**4**)
traficar to traffic (13)
tráfico, el traffic (15)
tragedia, la tragedy (7)
trágico/a tragic (4)
trago, el drink (12)

traje, el suit (**8**)
traje de baño, el swimsuit (**7**)
tranquilamente calmly (8)
tranquilo/a calm (5)
transacción, la transaction (15)
transformar to transform (10)
transición, la transition (12)
transmitir to transmit (10, **13**)
tras behind (15)
tratamiento, el treatment (10)
tren, el train (6, **9**)
trenzas, las braids, tresses (*of hair*) (8)
trilogía, la trilogy (13)
trimestre, el quarter; trimester (3)
triste sad (**5**)
trombón, el trombone (2, **14**)
trompeta, la trumpet (1, **14**)
trompetista, el/la trumpeter (5)
tropezar (ie) to trip (12)
tú you (**1**)
tu/s your (*inf.*) (**1, 3**)
tubo, el pipe (12)
tucán, el toucan (11)
tul, el tulle (*silk or nylon net*) (**14**)
tumba, la tomb (15)
turco/a Turkish (10)
turismo, el tourism (5)
turista, el/la tourist (2)
turístico/a touristy (9)
turnarse to take turns (5)
tuyo/a/os/as yours (*inf.*) (13)

U

ubicación, la location (5)
ubicado/a located (8)
ufano/a conceited (8)
últimamente lately (15)
último/a last (2)
un/o/a a; one (**1**)
único/a unique (8)
unido/a close (*close-knit*) (**4**)
uniforme, el uniform (7)
unir to unite (15)
universidad, la university (**1**)
uña, la fingernail (13)
usar to use (11)
usted/es you (*for.*) (**1**)
utensilio, el utensil (6)
útil useful (15)
utilidad, la utility (10)
utilizar to use (14)
uvas, las grapes (**6**)

V

vaca, la cow (15)
vacaciones, las vacation (8)
vacante, la vacancy (**11**)
vacío/a empty (10)
valer to be worth; to cost (2, **8**)
valioso/a useful (12)
valor, el value (1)
vamos let's go (**4**)
vamos a should we go (**4**)
vapor, el steam (9)
vaqueros, los jeans (**8**)
vara, la stick (7)
variar to vary (6)
variedad, la variety (5)
varios/as several; various (9)
vasco/a Basque (13)
vecindad, la neighborhood (5)
vecino/a, el/la neighbor (5)
vegetación, la vegetation (13)
vegetariano/a, el/la vegetarian (**6**)
vela, la candle (15)
velocidad, la speed (12)
vencimiento, el conquest (9)
vendedor/a ambulante, el/la street vendor (8)
vender to sell (**2**)
venenoso/a venomous (5)
venezolano/a Venezuelan (**2**)
venir (ie) to come (**4**)
ventaja, la advantage (10)
venta-liquidación, la clearance sale (**8**)
ventanilla, la window (**9**)
ver to see (**2**)
ver (la televisión/una película) to watch (television/a movie) (**7**)
verano, el summer (**1**)
verdad, la truth (8)
verde green (**1**)
versión, la version (10)
vespertino/a evening (13)
vestido, el dress (7, **8**)
vestirse (i, i) to get dressed (3, **5**)
veterano/a veteran (12)
veterinaria, la veterinary science (**3**)
veterinario/a, el/la veterinarian (**11**)
vez en cuando, de from time to time (2)
vía, la way (5)
viajante, el/la traveling salesperson (**11**)
viajar to travel (**2, 9**)
viaje, (hacer un) to take a trip (**9**)
viajero/a, el/la traveler (**9**)
vías de desarrollo, en developing (15)
vibrar to vibrate (15)
víctima, la victim (7)
vida, la life (2)
videograbadora, la VCR (**12**)
videopirata, el/la video pirate (13)
vidrio, el glass (7)
viejo/a old (**2**)
viento, el wind (6)
viento, hace it is windy (**7**)
vieres whatever you see (9)
viernes, el Friday (**1**)
vigilar to watch (15)
villa, la town (15)
vino, el wine (**6**)
viola, la viola (**14**)
violar to violate; to rape (**15**)
violencia, la violence (13)
violento/a violent (14)
violín, el violin (1, **14**)
virreinato, el viceroyalty (11)
visión, la vision (3)
visitante, el/la visitor (9)
vista, la view (5, **9**)
vistoso/a showy (9)
vitamina, la vitamin (10)
viudo/a, el/la widow/er (4)
vívido/a vivid (10)
vivienda, la housing (15)
vivir to live (**2**)
vivo/a alive (3)
volado/a in a hurry (12)
volar (ue) to fly (8)
volcán, el volcano (5, **9**)
vólibol, el volleyball (**7**)
voluntad, la will (15)
voluntario/a voluntary (5)
voluntario/a, el/la volunteer (2)
voluptuosidad, la voluptuousness (14)
voluptuoso/a voluptuous (9)
volver (ue) to return (**4**)
vosotros/as (*Spain*) you (*inf. pl.*) (**1**)
votante, el/la voter (13)
votar (por) to vote (for) (**15**)
voto, el vote (13)
voz, la voice (8)
vuelo, el flight (4, **9**)
vuestro/a/os/as your; yours (*inf. pl.*) (**3, 13**)

Y

y and (**1**)
yerba mate, la tea (*Argentina, Paraguay, Uruguay*) (11)
yerno, el son-in-law (**4**)
yo I (**1**)
yogur, el yogurt (**6**)

Z

zampoña, la panpipe (8)
zanahoria, la carrot (**6**)
zapatería, la shoe store (**8**)
zapatos, los shoes (7, **8**)
zona, la zone (8)
zorro, el fox (8)

Appendix 4

English–Spanish Vocabulary

A

a un/a (**1**)
abandon, to abandonar (10)
able, to be poder (ue) (**4**)
abolish, to abolir (**15**)
abolition la abolición (15)
abound, to abundar (15)
about acerca de (6)
above arriba de (**5,** 15)
absence la ausencia (9)
abstain, to abstenerse (9)
abundance la abundancia (10)
abundant abundante (10)
academic académico/a (3)
accelerate, to acelerar (15)
accelerated acelerado/a (12)
accepted aceptado/a (7)
accessory el accesorio; la prenda (5, 8)
accompany, to acompañar (15)
accord el acuerdo (15)
accordion el acordeón (1, **14**)
account la cuenta (15)
accountant el/la contador/a (**11**)
accounting la contabilidad (**3**)
accusation la acusación (13)
accustomed to, to be soler (ue); acostumbrar (10, 13)
accustomed, to become acostumbrarse (8)
ache el dolor (**10**)
achieve, to realizar; lograr (8, **15**)
acquire, to adquirir (ie, i) (14)
across from enfrente de (**3**)
act el acto (*legal*) (15)
act, to actuar (5, **13**)
action la acción (2)
activism el activismo (5)
activist el/la activista (**15**)
actor el actor (1)
actress la actriz (1)
acupuncture la acupuntura (10)
adapt, to adaptarse (12)
add, to agregar; echar; añadir (**6,** 15)
addition, in además (6)
addressee el/la destinatario/a (11)
adequate adecuado/a (7)
adjust, to ajustar (11)
administration la administración (8)
admire, to admirar (15)
admirer el/la admirador/a (8)
admission ticket la entrada (**4**)
adoptive adoptivo/a (14)
adore, to adorar (14)
adorn, to adornar (10)
adorned adornado/a (8)
advance el avance; el adelanto (4, 15)
advance, in de anticipación (14)
advanced avanzado/a (3)
advancing avanzado/a (4)
advantage la ventaja (10)
adventurer el/la aventurero/a (9)
advice el consejo (4)
advice column el consultorio sentimental (**13**)
advisor el/la asesor/a (6, **15**)
aerobic aeróbico/a (10)
aerobics los ejercicios aeróbicos (**10**)
affection el cariño (2)
affectionately cariñosamente (4)
afraid, to be tener (ie) miedo (**3**)
Afro-Caribbean afrocaribeño/a (7)
after después de (**3**)
afternoon la tarde (**2**)
against contra (**5**); en contra (8)
aggravate, to agravar (10)
agitated agitado/a (10)
agree, to asentir (ie, i) (12)
agreement, in conforme; de acuerdo (3, 15)
agricultural agrícola (4)
agriculture la agricultura (8)
AIDS el SIDA (10)
airplane el avión (**9**)
airport el aeropuerto (**9**)
aisle el pasillo (**9**)
alcohol el alcohol (13)
alcoholic beverages las bebidas alcohólicas (**10**)
algebra el álgebra (*fem.*) (**3**)
alive vivo/a (3)
all todos/a/os/as (**3**)
allegory la alegoría (6)
allergic alérgico/a (6)
allergic to, to be tener alergia(s) a (**10**)
allergy la alergia (**10**)
alleviate, to aliviar (10)
alleviated aliviado/a (14)
almond la almendra (6)
along a través (8)
also también (**2**)
alternate, to alternarse (8)
altitude la altura (8, **9**)
always siempre (2, **3, 7**)
ambassador el/la embajador/a (9)
amber el ámbar (7)
ambiguity la ambigüedad (11)
ambulance la ambulancia (10)
American (US) estadounidense; norteamericano/a (**2**)
amiable amable (4)
analyst, (systems) el/la analista (de sistemas) (**11**)
ancestor el/la antepasado/a (12)
ancestry la ascendencia (10)
and y (**1**)
Andean andino/a (8)
angelical angelical (8)
Anglicism el anglicismo (12)
angry furioso/a (**5**)
angry, to get enojarse (14)
anguish la angustia (10)
anguished angustiado/a (5)
animal el animal (3)
animated animado/a (9)
ankle el tobillo (10)
anniversary el aniversario (6)
announce anunciar (8)
announcement el anuncio (15)
announcer el/la locutor/a (**13**)
annoy, to molestar (**6**)
annual anual (9)
answer la respuesta (**1**)
answering machine el contestador automático (**12**)
antacid el antiácido (**10**)
anthropology la antropología (**3**)
antibiotic el antibiótico (**10**)
anticipate, to anticipar (8)
anticipation la anticipación (9)
antiquated anticuado/a (3)
anxious ansioso/a (9)
any/one cualquier/a (9)
apartment el apartamento (3)
apogee el apogeo (15)
apologize, to disculparse (15)
apparent aparente (15)
appear, to aparecer (zc) (4)
appetizers las tapas (6)
apple la manzana (**6**)
appliance el aparato (**6**)
apply makeup, to maquillarse (**5**)
appointment, (to make an) (hacer una) cita (**10,** 11)
appreciate, to apreciar (4)
appreciated apreciado/a (11)
approach, to acercarse (8)
approve, to aprobar (ue) (15)
April abril (**1**)
aquatic acuático/a (9)
Arabic el árabe (**3**)
archeologist el/la arqueólogo/a (8)
archipelago el archipiélago (8)
architect el/la arquitecto/a (2, **11**)
architectural arquitectónico/a (8)
architecture la arquitectura (2, **3**)
Argentine argentino/a (**2**)
argue, to discutir (4)
argument la discusión (8); el argumento (15)
aria el aria (*fem.*) (14)
arm el brazo (**10**)
armchair el sillón (**5**)
armed armad/o/a (15)
army el ejército (5, **15**)
around en torno a (3)
arrange, to arreglar (12)
arrival la llegada (3)
arrive, to llegar (**2**)
art el arte (**3**)
arthritis la artritis (10)
article el artículo (8, **13**)
artisan el/la artesano/a/la; artesanal (3, 4)
artist el/la pintor/a (1)
as many as tantos/as como (**5**)
as much as tanto/a como (**5**)
as... as tan... como (**5**)
ask for, to pedir (i,i) (**4, 6**)
aspect el aspecto (8)
asphyxiated asfixiado/a (5)
aspirin la aspirina (**10**)
assassinate asesinar (13)
assassinated asesinado/a (6)
assemble ensamblar (3); armar (8)
assembly plant la maquiladora (3)
assist, to atender (ie) (7)
assistant el/la ayudante (6)
associate, to asociar (2)
association la asociación (10)
assume, to asumir (4)
assure, to asegurar (2)
asthma el asma (*fem.*) (10)
ATM (automated teller machine) el cajero automático (4, **12**)
atmosphere el ambiente (3, 6)
attend, to asistir (a)(**2**)
attention la atención (3)
attention, to pay hacer caso; prestar atención (13)
attract, to atraer (7)
attraction la atracción (5)
attractive atractivo/a (4)
audience el público (**13**)
audition la audición (**14**)
auditorium el auditorio (**3**)
August agosto (**1**)
aunt la tía (**4**)
auspicious auspiciado/a (9)
autobiography la autobiografía (3)
automobile el automóvil (2)
autonomous autónomo/a (13)
avenue la avenida (13)
aware, to become enterarse (15)

B

baby el/la bebé (6)
back la espalda (**10**)
background el fondo (14)
backpack la mochila (**1**)

bad mal; malo/a (**1**)
bad appearance la mala pinta (13)
bag, (big) la bolsa; el bolso (**7, 8,** 15)
baggage claim area la sala de reclamación de equipaje (**9**)
bagpipe la gaita (13)
balance el saldo (13)
ballad el romance (8)
ballet el ballet (1)
banana la banana; el plátano (**6**, 8)
band la banda (**14**)
banjo el banjo (1)
bank el banco (8)
bar/s la barra; los barrotes (12)
barbecue la parrillada (*Chile, Argentina*) (6)
barbs las púas (15)
bargain la ganga (**8**)
bargain, to regatear (**8**)
barren pelón/pelona (15)
basalt el basalto (15)
baseball el béisbol (**2**)
baseball player el beisbolista (7)
based basado/a (6)
basement el sótano (12)
basketball el básquetbol; el baloncesto (**2**)
Basque vasco/a (13)
Basque language el euskera (13)
bass el bajo (3, **14**)
bat, to batear (**7**)
bathe, to bañarse (**5**)
bathroom el baño (**5**)
battery la pila (12)
battle la batalla (1)
be, to ser; estar (**1, 3**)
beach la playa (2, **7**)
bead la cuenta (7)
beans los frijoles (**6**)
beat, to palpitar (10)
beautiful, really bellísimo/a (6)
beauty la belleza (9)
because porque; pues (**2**, 5)
become, to ponerse; llegar a ser (**5**, 12)
bed, (to make the) (hacer la) cama (**5**)
bedroom el dormitorio; la recámara (**5**, 12)
beef la carne de res (10)
beer la cerveza (**6**)
before antes (de) (2)
begin, to empezar (ie); iniciar (3, **4**, 9)
beginner el/la principiante (3)
beginning el comienzo; el principio (5, **13**)
beginning, at the a principios de (15)
behind detrás (de); atrás; tras (**3**, 15)
behind, to be retrasar (13)
being el ser (3)
believe, to creer (**2**)
belly el buche (8)
below abajo; bajo; debajo (de) (**5**, 12, 15)
bench el banco (13)
benefit, to beneficiar (15)
benefit/s el/los beneficio/s (10, **11**)
better mejor (3)
better, to get mejorarse (**10**)
between entre (**3**)
beverage la bebida (**6**)
bicycle riding, to go montar en bicicleta (**9**)
bidder el/la postor/a (13)
big grande (1, **2**)
bilingual bilingüe (13)
bill la cuenta; el billete (**6**, 12)
billfold la billetera (12)
biography la biografía (2)
biology la biología (**3**)
bird el pájaro (5)
birthday el cumpleaños (1)
bite, to morder (ue) (7)
black negro/a (**1**)
blackboard la pizarra (**1**)
blame la culpa (13)
blazer el saco (**8**)
blessed bendito/a (6)
blind ciego/a (11)
block la cuadra; la manzana (*Spain*); el bloque (3, 8)
blond rubio/a (**2**)
blood pressure la presión (**10**)
blouse la blusa (**8**)
blow, to soplar (8)
blue azul (**1**)
blushing coloradito/a (3)
board la tabla (12)
board of trustees el patronato (1)
board, to abordar (**9**)
boarding pass la tarjeta de embarque (**9**)
boat el barco (**9**)
body el cuerpo (**5**)
boil, to hervir (ie, i) (**6**)
bomb, to bombardear (14)
bonus, yearly la bonificación anual (**11**)
book el libro (**1**)
bookcase el estante (3, **5**)
bookstore la librería (1, **3**)
border la frontera (3)
border, to bordear (9)
bore, to aburrir (**6**)
boring aburrido/a (**1**)
born, to be nacer (2)
boss el/la jefe/a (**11**)
both ambos/as (7)
bother, to be a molestar (**6**)
bottle la botella (7)
bottle, little la botellita (13)
bottom el fondo (12)
bow el arco (8)
box la caja (6)
boxing el boxeo (**7**)
box office la taquilla (8)
boy el muchacho; el chico (**2, 3**)
boyfriend el novio (3, **4**)
bra el sostén (13)
braids las trenzas (8)
bracelet la pulsera (**8**)
brand la marca (**12**)
bread el pan (**6**)
break (a bone), to romperse (un hueso) (**10**)
breakfast el desayuno (**6**)
breakfast, to have desayunar (**6**)
breathe, to respirar (6, **10**)
breathing la respiración (12)
brick el ladrillo (12)
bride la novia (**4**)
bridge el puente (14)
brief breve (6)
briefcase el maletín (4)
bright brillante (10)
bring, to traer (**4**)
brochure el folleto (**9**)
bronze el bronce (15)
broom la escoba (**5**)
brother el hermano (3, **4**)
brother-in-law el cuñado (**4**)
brown pardo/a (8)
brunette moreno/a (**2**)
brush el cepillo (**5**)
brush, to cepillarse (**5**)
budget el presupuesto (5)
buffet el bufé (**6**)
building la edificación; el edificio (4, 8)
bull el toro (2)
bullet la bala (15)
burn, to arder; quemar (10)
bury, to enterrar (ie) (14)
bus el autobús; el camión (*Mexico*) (**9**, 15)
business el comercio; el negocio; la empresa (8, 13)
business administration la administración de empresas (**3**)
business section la sección financiera (**13**)
but pero (**2**)
butter la mantequilla (**6**)
butterfly la mariposa (5)
buy, to comprar (**2**)

C

cabinet el gabinete (6)
cable TV la televisión por cable (**13**)
cadaver el cadáver (14)
café, (outdoor) el café (al aire libre) (**4**)
cafeteria la cafetería (2, **3**)
caffeine la cafeína (6)
cake el pastel (**6**)
calculator la calculadora (**1**)
calculus el cálculo (**3**)
call el llamamiento (15)
call letters las siglas (7)
calm tranquilo/a; la calma (5, 9)
calmly tranquilamente (8)
calorie la caloría (6)
camel-like camélido/a (8)
camera la cámara (4, **9, 13**)
camp el campamento (15)
campaign la campaña (13, **15**)
can poder (ue) (*to be able*); el bote (**4**, 12)
Canadian canadiense (**2**)
canal el canal (4)
cancer el cáncer (10)
candidate el/la candidato/a (3, **15**)
candle la vela (15)
cane la caña (7)
cap la gorra; la cachucha (8, 15)
capable capaz (**11**)
capacity la capacidad (12)
capital city la capital (1, **2**)
captain el capitán (3)
car el carro; el coche (3, 5, **9**)
carbohydrates los carbohidratos (**10**)
career la carrera (3)
careful cuidadoso/a (9)
careful, to be tener cuidado (**3**)
caress la caricia (2)
Caribbean caribeño/a (7)
Caribbean dance el merengue (7)
carpenter el/la carpintero/a (**11**)
carrot la zanahoria (**6**)
carry out, to desempeñar (6)
carry, to acarrear (12)
cascades las cascadas (11)
cash en efectivo (5)
cash register la caja (**8**)
casserole dish la cazuela (**6**)
castle el castillo (13)
cat el/la gato/a (5)
cathedral la catedral (**9**)
cauliflower la col (6)
cause la causa (8)
CD/DVD player el lector de CD/DVD (**12**)
ceasefire el cese de fuego (4)
ceiling el techo (12)
celebrate, to celebrar (9)
celebration la celebración; la fiesta (1, 3)
cellular phone el teléfono móvil/celular (4, **12**)
Celtic celta (13)
cemetery el cementerio (14)
censure, to censurar (13)
census el censo (15)
cent el céntimo (2)
century el siglo (3)
ceramic la cerámica (4)
ceremony la ceremonia (4)
certain cierto/a (2)
chain, silver la cadena de plata (**8**)
chair la silla (**1**)
chair, overstuffed el sillón (**5**)
challenge el desafío (4)
challenge, to retar (11)
challenging exigente (**3**)
champagne el champán (8)
champion el/la campeón/campeona (7)
chance el azar (7)
change, to cambiar (4)
channel el canal (**13**)
chapel la capilla (8)
character el carácter; el personaje (*in a story*) (8, 13)
characteristic la característica (5)
charade la charada (6)
charitable benéfico/a; caritativo/a (9, 14)
cheap barato/a (**1**)
check luggage, to facturar el equipaje (**9**)
check, to revisar (**13**)
checkup, medical el examen físico (**10**)
cheer, to animar (**7**)
cheerful alegre (4)
cheese el queso (**6**)
chef el/la cocinero/a (**11**)
chemistry la química (**3**)
chess el ajedrez (7)
chest el pecho (**10**)
chewing gum el chicle (15)
chick la cría (13)
chicken el pollo (**6**)
chief el cacique (9)
childish infantil (8)
children los/las niños/as (1)
Chilean chileno/a (**2**)
chinchilla la chinchilla (14)
Chinese el chino (**2**)

chiropractor el/la quiropráctico/a (10)
chocolate cake la torta de chocolate (**6**)
cholera el cólera (5)
cholesterol el colesterol (**10**)
chord el acorde (15)
choreographer el/la coreógrafo/a (14)
chores los quehaceres (4, **5**)
Christian cristiano/a (14)
christianize, to cristianizar (10)
chronological cronológico/a (11)
chubby gordo/a; regordete (**2**, 15)
cinematography la cinematografía (**13**)
circle el círculo (7)
citizen el/la ciudadano/a (6, **15**)
city la ciudad (1, **2**)
city council el ayuntamiento (1)
civil cívico/a (15)
Civil War la Guerra Civil (3)
civilization la civilización (5)
clap, to aplaudir (**14**)
clarify, to aclarar (15)
clarinet el clarinete (1, **14**)
class la clase (1, 2, **3**)
classified ads los anuncios/avisos clasificados (**13**)
clean limpio/a (8)
clean (the house), to limpiar; ordenar (la casa) (4, **5**)
clear cristalino/a; despejado/a (*sky*) (5, 8)
clear the table, to quitar la mesa (**5**)
clearance sale la venta-liquidación (**8**)
clerk, box office el/la taquillero/a (13)
client el/la cliente (**6, 8**)
clientele la clientela (12)
climate el clima (5)
climb, to escalar; subir (8)
clock el reloj (**1**)
close (*close-knit*) unido/a (**4**)
close (to) cerca (de) (**3**)
closings las despedidas (**11**)
cloth la tela (8)
cloth woven with a spider web pattern el ñandutí (10)
clothing la ropa (**8**)
cloud la nube (8)
cloudy nublado/a (**7**)
clue la pista (2)
coach class la clase turista (**9**)
co-actor el/la coactor/a (13)
coast la costa (2)
coat el abrigo (**8**)
coca la coca (15)
coconut el coco (6)
cod el bacalao (7)
code el código (15)
coffee el café (**6**)
coffee, little cup of el cafecito (7)
coffee maker la cafetera (**6**)
cognate el cognado (2)
coin la moneda (8)
coincide, to coincidir (15)
cold frío/a; el resfriado (*illness*) (**6, 10**)
cold, it is hace frío (**7**)
cold, to be tener frío (**3**)
collaborate, to colaborar (5)
colleague el/la colega; el/la socio/a (11)
collection la colección (4)
cologne la colonia (**8**)
Colombian colombiano/a (**2**)
colonizer el/la colonizador/a (9)
colony la colonia (3)
colored, brightly colorido/a (14)
coloring colorido/a (14)
comb el peine (**5**)
comb one's hair, to peinarse (2, **5**)
combat, to combatir (10, **15**)
combination la combinación (10)
come, to venir (ie) (**4**)
comedy la comedia (**13**)
comfortable cómodo/a (9)
comforts las comodidades (9)
comics las tiras cómicas (**13**)
command el mandato (11)
commemorate, to conmemorar (4)
comment, to comentar (5)
commentator el/la comentarista (**13**)
commerce el comercio (3)
commission la comisión (5)
commit, to cometer (14)
committee el comité (4)
common común (1)
commonwealth el estado libre asociado (7)
communications las comunicaciones (**3**)
community la comunidad (3)
company la empresa; la compañía (**11**, 14)
compare, to comparar (5)
comparison, in en comparación (2)
compatible compatible (12)
compete, to competir (i) (15)
complex el complejo; complejo/a (14, 15)
complicate, to complicar (11)
complicated complicado/a (**3**)
compose, to componer (**14**, 15)
composed compuesto/a (15)
composer el/la compositor/a (**14**)
composition la composición (2)
computer la computadora (1, **3**)
computer (electronic) game el juego electrónico (**12**)
computer disc el disquete (**12**)
computer science la informática; la computación (**3**)
conceited ufano/a (8)
concert, (to go to a) (ir a un) concierto (3, **4, 7**)
condemned condenado/a (13)
condominium el condominio (5)
condor el cóndor (8)
conduct, to conducir; dirigir (14, 15)
conductor el/la directora/a; el/la conductora (**14,** 15)
confess, to confesar (ie) (10)
conflict el conflicto (8, **15**)
confuse, to confundir (14)
conjecture la conjetura (12)
connect, to conectar (5)
connection la conexión (13)
conquest la conquista; el vencimiento (3, 9)
consequences las consecuencias (15)
conservation la conservación (5)
conservative conservador/a (13)
conserve, to conservar (**12**)
consider, to considerar (3)
considerate considerado/a (15)
considered considerado/a (9)
consolation el consuelo (10)
constant constante (14)
constantly constantemente (12)
constitute, to constituir (12)
construct, to construir (10)
construction la construcción (5)
consult, to consultar (10)
consultant el/la asesor/a (**15**)
consume, to consumir (4, **12**)
consumer el/la consumidor/a (1)
consumption el consumo (10)
contact, to contactar (6)
contain, to contener (ie) (10)
container, (aluminum) el recipiente; el envase (de aluminio); el contenedor (**6, 12,** 13)
contaminate, to, contaminar (**12**)
contemporaneous contemporáneo/a (6)
content el contenido (10)
contest el concurso (13)
continue, to continuar (14)
contract el contrato (**11**)
contract, to contratar (11)
contrast el contraste (6)
control, to controlar (**15**)
controversy la polémica (12)
convent el convento (**9**)
conventional convencional (13)
converse, to conversar (**2**)
convert, to convertir (ie,i) (9)
converted convertido/a (5)
convince, to convencer (2)
cook el/la cocinero/a (6, **11**)
cook, to cocinar (4, **6**)
cookies las galletas (**6**)
cool, it is hace fresco (**7**)
cooler la heladera (**7**)
cooperate, to cooperar (8)
coordinator el/la coordinador/a (**11**)
copper el cobre (6)
copy la copia (5)
cord la cuerda (15)
cordial cordial (7)
cordially yours cordialmente (**11**)
cordless phone el teléfono inalámbrico (**12**)
corn el maíz (**6**)
corner la esquina (3)
cornet la corneta (**14**)
corpulent corpulento/a (15)
correspondent el/la corresponsal (13)
corruption la corrupción (**15**)
cost, to costar (ue); valer (2, **4, 8**)
costume el disfraz (**14**)
cotton el algodón (**8**)
couch el sofá (**5**)
cough la tos (**10**)
cough, to toser (**10**)
cough syrup el jarabe (**10**)
counselor el/la asesor/a (12)
country (developing) el país (en desarrollo) (**2, 15**)
couple la pareja (4)
course el curso; la materia (3)
court la cancha (2)
cousin el/la primo/a (**4**)
cover letter la carta de presentación (**11**)
cover, to tapar (**6**)
cover up, to disimular (13)
covered cubierto/a (10)
cow la vaca (15)
cowboy, Argentine el gaucho (11)
cradle la cuna (1)
crane la garza (8)
crash, to chocar (15)
cream, (shaving) la crema (de afeitar) (**5**)
create, to crear (8)
creation la creación (15)
creative creativo/a (12)
creator el/la creador/a (10)
credit card la tarjeta de crédito (**8**)
creole criollo/a (6)
cricket la cigarra (8)
crime el crimen (14)
crisis la crisis (15)
critic el/la crítico/a (13)
crocodile el cocodrilo (9)
cross, to cruzar (14)
crucial crucial (6)
crush, to machacar (11)
cry el grito (5)
cry, to llorar (9)
crystalline cristalino/a (7)
cub el cachorro (13)
Cuban cubano/a (**2**)
cubism el cubismo (2)
cuisine la cocina (4)
culinary culinario/a (6)
cultivation el cultivo (2)
cure, to curar (**11**)
curious curioso/a (7)
current actual (10)
current, electric la corriente (9)
curriculum el currículo (14)
curtain el telón (11)
custard dessert el flan (**6**)
custom la costumbre (3)
customer el/la cliente (**6, 8**)
customs la aduana (**9**)
customs inspector el/la inspector/a de aduanas (**9**)
cut cortado/a (6)
cute bonito/a (**2**)
cybernetic cibernético/a (2)
cycling el ciclismo (**7**)
cypress el ciprés (14)

D

daily diario/a (2)
dairy products los productos lácteos (**10**)
dam el embalse; la presa (10)
damage el daño (4)
damage, to (*not work*) dañar (10, **12**)
damaged averiado/a (13)
damned maldito/a (13)
dance la danza (14)
dance, to bailar (**2**)
danceable bailable (9)

dancer el/la bailarín/a (14)
danger el peligro (5)
dangerous peligroso/a (2)
dark oscuro/a (8)
dark, to get anochecer (15)
data el dato (1)
date la fecha (**1**)
date from, to datar (15)
daughter la hija (**4**)
daughter-in-law la nuera (**4**)
dawn el amanecer (11)
day el día (**1**)
day before yesterday, the anteayer (**6**)
daybreak la madrugada (10)
dead muerto/a; difunto/a (7, 15)
deal, good la ganga (**8**)
dear sir/madam estimado/a señor/a (**11**)
death la muerte; el fallecimiento (6, 8)
debate el debate (15)
debut el debut (14)
debut, to estrenar (13)
decaffeinated descafeinado/a (3)
deceive, to engañar (13)
December diciembre (**1**)
decide, to decidir (**2**)
decomposition la descomposición (4)
decoration la decoración (8)
decrease la disminución (5)
dedicate, to dedicar (7)
dedicated dedicado/a (9)
dedication la dedicación (14)
deep profundo/a; hondo/a (5, 6)
defeat, to rendir (i, i) (13)
defend, to defender (7)
define, to definir (14)
deforestation la deforestación (**12**)
dejected abatido/a (15)
delay la demora (6, **9**)
delicate fino/a (13)
delicious delicioso/a; rico/a (2, **6**)
delight el encanto (12)
delight, to encantar (**6**)
Delighted. Encantado/a. (**1**)
delightful encantador/a (**14**)
delinquency la delincuencia (15)
deliver, to entregar; repartir (2, 8, **11**)
demagogue el/la demagogo/a (15)
demanding exigente (**3**)
democracy la democracia (**15**)
democratic democrático/a (4)
demographic demográfico/a (13)
demonstrate, to demostrar (ue) (14)
denounce denunciar (7)
dentist el/la dentista (3, **11**)
department store el almacén (**8**)
depend on, to depender de (5)
deposit el depósito (10)
derived derivado/a (12)
descend, to descender (ie) (11)
descendant el/la descendiente (8)
describe, to describir (2)
desert el desierto (4)
deserted desierto/a (5)
design el diseño (2, **3**, **12**)
design, to diseñar (2, **11**)
designate, to denominar (8)
designer el/la diseñador/a (**14**)
desired deseado/a (4)
destination el destino (9)
destined destinado/a (10)
destroy, to destrozar (9)
destroyed destrozado/a (9)
destructive destructivo/a (5)
detail detalle (6)
detail, to detallar (7)
detain, to detener (ie); retrasar (11)
deteriorate, to deteriorar (12)
determined determinado/a (9)
detest, to detestar (11)
developing en vías de desarrollo (15)
diabetes la diabetes (**10**)
diabolical diabólico/a (14)
diagnosis el diagnóstico (**10**)
diagram el diagrama (7)
dial, to pulsar (12)
diamond earrings los aretes de diamantes (**8**)
dictator el/la dictador/a (**15**)
dictatorship la dictadura (**15**)
dictionary el diccionario (**1**)
die, to morir (ue,u) (9)
diet la dieta; el régimen (10)
diet, to be on a estar a dieta (**10**)
different distinto/a; diferente (6, 8)
difficult difícil (**2**)
difficult, to make dificultar (4)
dig, to cavar (14)
dignify, to dignificar (11)
dignity la dignidad (13)
diminish, to disminuir (13)
diminutive diminutivo/a (12)
dining room el comedor (**5**)
dinner la cena (**6**)
dinner, to have cenar (**6**)
diplomat el/la diplomático/a (3)
directed dirigido/a (13)
director el/la director/a (9, **11**)
dirty sucio/a (6)
disadvantage la desventaja (10)
disappear, to desaparecer (11)
disappeared desaparecido/a (15)
disarm, to desarmar (15)
disarmament el desarme (**15**)
disaster el desastre (5)
discomfort la incomodidad (9)
discount el descuento (**8**)
discovered descubierto/a (13)
discovery el descubrimiento (14)
discrepancy la discrepancia (11)
disguise el disfraz (**14**)
dish el plato (2)
dishonest deshonesto/a (15)
dishonor, to deshonrar (11)
dishwasher el lavaplatos (**5**)
disillusioned desilusionado/a (4)
disillusionment el desengaño (10)
disorder el desorden (8)
disorganized desorganizado/a (15)
disposed dispuesto/a (**12**)
distance la distancia (8)
distinguish, to distinguir (15)
distract, to distraer; entretener (15)
distribute, to repartir; distribuir (**11**, **13**)
diva la diva (**14**)
division la división (5)
divorced divorciado/a (**4**)
Do you want to go to...? ¿Quieres ir a...? (**4**)
do haz (*inf. command*) (9)
do, to hacer (2, **3**)
doctor's office el consultorio (**10**)
doctorate el doctorado (3)
dog el/la perro/a (**4**)
domestic doméstico/a (3)
dominate, to dominar (8)
dominated dominado/a (6)
Dominican dominicano/a (**2**)
Don't worry. No te preocupes. (**7**)
donate, to donar (14)
door la puerta (**1**)
dossier el expediente (**11**)
download, to bajar (de la Red) (12)
downtown el centro (3, **4**)
dowry el dote (15)
drag, to arrastrar (15)
drain, to escurrir (5)
drama el drama (**13**)
dramatic dramático/a (13)
dramatist dramaturgo/a (13)
dramatization la dramatización (13)
draw, to dibujar (10)
draw up, to encoger (8)
drawing el dibujo (5)
dream el sueño (12)
dream (about), to soñar (con) (ue) (**4**)
dress el vestido (7, **8**)
dressed, to get vestirse (i, i) (3, **5**)
dresser la cómoda (**5**)
drink el trago (12)
drink, to beber; tomar (**2**)
drive, to manejar; conducir (12, 15)
drug addiction la drogadicción (**15**)
drum el tambor (7, **14**)
drum stick el palillo (14)
drums la batería (**14**)
dry seco/a (6)
dry (oneself), to secarse (**5**)
dry clothes, to secar la ropa (**5**)
dryer la secadora (**5**)
duck el pato (8)
durability la durabilidad (14)
during durante (2)
dust (the furniture), to sacudir el polvo (de los muebles) (**5**)
duty el deber (4, **15**)
DVD el DVD (**12**)

E

eagle el águila (*fem.*) (8)
ear of corn la mazorca de maíz (15)
ear, inner el oído **outer** la oreja (**10**)
earbuds los auriculares (12)
early temprano/a (**2**)
earn, to ganar (2)
earth la tierra (2)
earthquake el terremoto (14)
east el oriente (10)
easy fácil (**2**)
eat, to comer (**2**)
ecological ecológico/a (8)
ecology la ecología (5)
economical económico/a (2)
ecotourism el ecoturismo (4, 5)
Ecuadorian ecuatoriano/a (**2**)
edit, to editar (12)
editorial (page) el editorial (13, 15)
educate, to educar (15)
education la formación (**11**)
effect, in en efectivo (5)
effort el esfuerzo (4, **15**)
eggs los huevos (**6**)
eighth octavo/a (7, **8**)
either... or o... o (**7**)
elaborate, to elaborar (15)
elaborated elaborado/a (4)
elaboration la elaboración (15)
elastic el elástico (**14**)
elect, to elegir (i,i) (14, 15)
elected electo/a (6)
electric eléctrico/a (3)
electric current la corriente (9)
electric razor la máquina de afeitar (**5**)
electrician el/la electricista (**11**)
electricity la electricidad (10)
electronic electrónico/a (2, **12**)
element el elemento (14)
eligible elegible (13)
elm el olmo (12)
email el correo electrónico (6, **12**)
emblem el logotipo (12)
embrace el abrazo (4)
embrace, to abrazar (10)
emerald la esmeralda (9)
emerge, to surgir (12)
emergency room la sala de urgencias (10)
emotional emocional (11)
empire el imperio (8)
employee el/la empleado/a (8, **11**)
empty vacío/a (10)
enchanting encantador/a (**14**)
encounter el encuentro (8)
encourage, to animar (**7**, 10)
end el final (**13**)
end, toward the a fines (15)
end, to eliminar (**15**)
endure, to soportar (9)
enemy el/la enemigo/a (11)
energy la energía (3, **12**)
engineer el/la ingeniero/a (**11**)
engineering, (electrical) la ingeniería (eléctrica) (2, **3**)
English el inglés (**2**)
Enjoy your meal! ¡Buen provecho! (1, **6**)
enjoy, to disfrutar de; gozar de (6, 11)
enlarge, to agrandar (15)
enormous enorme (6)
enough, to be bastar (8, 11)
enrich, to enriquecer (12)
entertain, to distraer; entretener (ie) (9, 15)
entertainment el entrenamiento (7)
entertainment section la cartelera (**13**)

enthusiastic entusiasta (**11**)
entire entero/a (4)
entrance la entrada (8)
envelope el sobre (2)
environment el medio ambiente (5, **12**)
environmental ambiental (10)
ephemeral efímero/a (13)
epoch la época (4)
equator la línea ecuatorial (8)
equilibrium el equilibrio (10)
equipment la instalación; el equipo (3, **7**)
eradicate, to erradicar (15)
erase, to borrar (**12**)
eruption la erupción (11)
essence la esencia (14)
establish, to establecer (4)
ethic la ética (11)
ethnic étnico/a (12)
eucalyptus el eucalipto (15)
Europe Europa (2)
even aun (8)
evening (*adj.*) vespertino/a (13)
event el evento; la función (3, 7)
everyone todos/a/os/as (**3**)
evolution la evolución (8)
exactly justamente (15)
exam el examen (3)
example el ejemplo (9)
excavate, to excavar (4)
excel, to sobresalir (12)
excellent excelente (2)
exception la excepción (15)
exceptional excepcional (7)
excess weight el sobrepeso (**10**)
exchange el intercambio; el cambio (3, 8)
exchange, to intercambiar (5)
excited, to get emocionarse (15)
exciting emocional; emocionante (2, 11)
exclusive exclusivo/a (9)
excursion la excursión (6)
execution la ejecución (14)
executive el/la ejecutivo/a (3)
exempt exento/a (3)
exercise, to ejercer; hacer ejercicio (**7**, 15)
exhausted exhausto/a (8)
exhibit, to exhibir (15)
exist, to existir (8)
exotic exótico/a (5)
expedition la expedición (10)
expense el gasto (11)
expensive caro/a (**1**)
experienced experimentado/a (15)
expert el/la experto/a (9)
explain, to explicar (5)
explicit explícito/a (13)
exploit, to explotar (15)
explore explorar (10)
explosive explosivo/a (6)
export, to exportar (6)
exposition la exposición (3)
express, to expresar (15)
expressed expreso/a (15)
expressive expresivo/a (14)
exquisite exquisito/a (6)
extend to, to abarcar (14)
extend, to extender (ie) (8)
extension la extensión (9)
extinction la extinción (5)
extinguish (fires), to apagar (fuegos/incendios) (**11**)
extraction la extracción (10)
extraordinary extraordinario/a (4)
extratextual extratextual (2)
extreme extremo/a (6)
extremely pleasing, to be encantar (**6**)
eye el ojo (**5**)

F

fable la fábula (8)
fabulous fabuloso/a (**7**)
face la cara (**5**)
face, to afrontar (**15**)
facing enfrente de (**3**)
factor el factor (10)
factory la fábrica (2, **12**)
fail, to fallar; fracasar (5, 13)
fair la feria (9)
fairly bastante (**3**)
fall (*season*) el otoño (**1**)
fall asleep, to dormirse (ue,u) (5)
fall down, to caerse (12)
falls las cataratas (11)
false falso/a (2)
fame la fama (9)
familiar with, to be conocer (**4**)
family la familia; familiar (*adj.*) (3, **4**)
family members los familiares (11)
fan(atic) el/la aficionado/a; el/la fanático/a (2, **7**)
fantastic fantástico/a (3, **7**)
fantasy la fantasía (14)
far (from) lejos (de) (**3**)
faraway lejano/a (11)
fare, (roundtrip) el pasaje (de ida y vuelta) (**9**)
farewell la despedida (1)
farm la finca (12)
fascinating fascinante (1)
fascinating, to be fascinar (**6**)
fascist el/la fascista (14)
fashion la moda (4, **14**)
fashion, high la alta costura (**14**)
fat la grasa (6, **10**)
father el padre (**4**)
father-in-law el suegro (**4**)
fatigue el cansancio (10)
fatty acids las grasas transformadas (10)
February febrero (**1**)
feed, to alimentar (11)
feel, to sentirse (ie, i) (5)
feeling el sentimiento (4)
feign, to disimular (13)
feminine femenino/a (15)
femininity la feminidad (14)
fence la cerca (12)
fertility la fertilidad (15)
fertilizer el fertilizante (6)
fever la fiebre (5, **10**)
fiber la fibra (15)
fifth quinto/a (**8**)
fight, to luchar; combatir (13, **15**)
figure la figura (9)
file, to archivar (**12**)
fill out/completely, to rellenar (**11**)
film (el rollo de) película; la cinta (*tape*) (**9, 13**)
film, to filmar (**13**)
filming la filmación; el rodaje (13)
filmmaker el/la cineasta (4)
finance las finanzas (**3**)
financial financiero/a (15)
find, to encontrar (ue) (**4**)
fine la multa (**12**)
fine with me de acuerdo (**4**)
finger el dedo (**10**)
fingernail la uña (13)
finish, to acabar (8)
fire el fuego; el incendio (**11**)
fire, to despedir (i, i) (**11**)
firefighter el/la bombero/a (**11**)
fireworks los fuegos artificiales (9)
firm la empresa (**11**)
first primer/o/a (2, **8**)
first, at al principio (5)
fish el pescado; el pez (**6**, 12)
fish, to pescar (**9**)
fishing la pesca; pesquero/a (2, 6, 8)
fit el ajuste (12)
fit, to quedar; encajar (**8**)
fitting room el probador (**8**)
fix, to arreglar (12)
flag la bandera (1)
flamenco flamenco/a (2)
flank, to flanquear (15)
flat plano/a (10)
flavor el sabor (1)
flight el vuelo (4, **9**)
flight attendant el/la asistente de vuelo (**9**)
flood, to inundar (4)
floor el piso (5, **8**)
flower la flor (2, **9**)
flower bed el cantero de jardín (14)
flower shop la florería (**8**)
flu la gripe (**10**)
flute la flauta (1, **14**)
flute, Andean la quena (8)
fly, to volar (ue) (8)
fog la niebla (9)
folkloric folklórico/a (3)
following siguiente; a continuación (4, 6)
foods los alimentos (**10**)
foot el pie; la pata (*animal*) (8, **10**)
football el fútbol americano (**2**)
footwear el calzado (8)
force la fuerza (15)
forecast el pronóstico (4)
foreign extranjero/a (13)
foreign expression el extranjerismo (12)
foreigner el/la extranjero/a (7)
foreman el capataz (15)
forest el bosque (5, **9, 12**)
form la forma; el formulario (4, **11**)
form, to formar (8)
formulate, to formular (8)
fortify, to fortalecer (**15**)
fortune teller el/la adivino/a (12)
forum el foro (14)
found, to fundar (14)
foundation la fundación (15)
founded fundado/a (9)
founding la fundación (13)
fountain la fuente (6)
fourth cuarto/a (**8**)
fox zorro (8)
fragment el fragmento (13)
free libre (6)
free of charge gratis (7)
freezer el congelador (**6**)
French el francés (**2**)
frequent frecuente (11)
frequently con frecuencia; frecuentemente (8)
fresh fresco/a (6)
Friday el viernes (**1**)
fried snack la fritura (7)
friend el/la amigo/a (1, **2**)
friendship la amistad (5)
frighten, to asustar (11)
frightened asustado/a (13)
frog la rana (5)
from desde (2)
from then on a partir de (10)
from time to time de vez en cuando (2)
front of, in delante de (2, **3**)
front page la primera plana (**13**)
front, in enfrente (12)
frontier la frontera (3)
frustrated frustrado/a (4)
fry, to freír (i,i) (**6**)
frying pan la sartén (**6**)
fulfill, to (*a promise*) cumplir (con) (**15**)
full lleno/a (8)
fun divertido/a (9)
function la función (7)
function, to funcionar (10, **12**)
functional funcional (10)
funds los fondos (14)
fur la piel (**14**)
furnish, to armar (15)
furnished amueblado/a (5)
furniture los muebles (**5**)
furor el furor (11)
fusion la fusión (14)
future el porvenir (12)

G

gabardine (*lightweight wool*) la gabardina (**14**)
gain weight, to subir de peso (**10**)
game, (to go to a) (ir a un) partido (2, **4, 7**)
game show el concurso (**13**)
garage el garaje (**5**)
garbage can el basurero (**5**)
garden el jardín (5)
garlic el ajo (6)
garment la prenda (**14**)
gastronomy la gastronomía (2)
gather, to agregar (15)
genealogical genealógico/a (4)
general general (9)
generate, to generar (15)
generation la generación (10)
generosity la generosidad (15)
generous generoso/a (10)
genetic genético/a (10)
genius, of genial (7)
Genoese genovés/-esa (7)
genre el género (8)
gentleman el caballero (2)
geography la geografía (**3**)
geology la geología (**3**)
German el alemán (**2**)
gesture el gesto; el ademán (8, 11)

get, to conseguir (i,i); sacar (*a grade*) (5, 9)
get along, to llevarse bien (4)
get down (from), to bajarse (de) (**9**)
get in shape, to ponerse en forma (**10**)
get off (of), to bajarse (de) (**9**)
get up, to levantarse (**5**)
get up early, to madrugar (13)
get well, to mejorarse (**10**)
giant el gigante (6)
gigantic gigantesco/a (15)
girl la muchacha; la chica (**2, 3**)
girlfriend la novia (3, **4**)
glance la mirada (13)
glass el vidrio (7)
glasses las gafas (15)
glyph el glifo (15)
GNP el PIB (9)
go, to ir (**3**)
go around, to recorrer (**9**)
go away, to alejarse; marcharse; irse (9, 11)
go out, to salir; dar un paseo (**4, 7**)
go to a game, to ir a un partido (**7**)
go to bed, to acostarse (ue) (2, **5**)
go up, to subir (6)
go well with, to hacer juego (con) (**8**)
goal la meta (6, **11**)
god el dios (9)
gold ring el anillo de oro (**8**)
golf el golf (2, **7**)
good bueno/a (**1**)
Good afternoon. Buenas tardes. (**1**)
Good evening. Buenas noches. (**1**)
Good morning. Buenos días. (**1**)
Good-bye. Adiós. (**1**)
good-looking guapo/a (**2**)
goods los bienes (5)
gosh caramba (7)
gossipy chismoso/a (5)
government el gobierno (2)
governmental gubernamental (12)
governor el/la gobernador/a (**15**)
grab, to agarrar (11)
grade la nota (3)
graduate, to graduarse (12)
grandfather/grandmother el/la abuelo/a (**4**)
grandma la abuelita (*diminutive*) (4)
grandson/granddaughter la el/la nieto/a (**4**)
grapefruit la toronja (**6**)
grapes las uvas (**6**)
grass el pasto (7, 12)
grave el sepulcro (14)
Great Depression la Gran Depresión (3)
great fabuloso; qué padre (*Mexico*); magnífico/a (**7**)
green verde (**1**)
Green Peace la Paz Verde (12)
greeting/s el/los saludo/s (**1**)
grey gris (**1**)
grey-haired, to be tener canas (13)
griddle la comal (15)
grill la parrilla (6)
groceries los comestibles (6)
groom el novio (**4**)
ground el suelo (13)
group el conjunto (4)
grow up, to criarse (4)
grow, to crecer (8)
Guarani language el guaraní (10)
guard el/la guardia (9)
guava la guayaba (1)
guess, to adivinar (5)
guide book la guía (**9**)
guide, to guiar (12)
guitar la guitarra (1, **14**)
guitar-like instrument el charango (4)
gymnasium el gimnasio (2, **3**)
gymnastics la gimnasia (**7**)

H

haggle over, to regatear (**8**)
hair el pelo (**5**)
hair dryer el secador (**5**)
hair salon la peluquería (13)
hairstylist el/la peluquero/a (**11**)
half medio/a (12)
hallucinogenic alucinógeno/a (5)
hallway el pasillo (12)
ham el jamón (**6**)
hamburger la hamburguesa (**6**)
hand la mano (**5, 10**)
handicapped discapacitado/a (3)
handicraft la artesanía (3)
hang, to colgar (ue) (13)
hanging guindando (7)
happiness la felicidad; la alegría (2, 6)
happy contento/a (**5**)
hard duro/a (10)
hard drive el disco duro (**12**)
hard-working trabajador/a (**1**)
harm el daño (15)
harmful nocivo/a; dañino/a (10)
harp el arpa (*fem.*) (7, **14**)
hatchet el hacha (7)
have a good/bad/wonderful time, to pasarlo bien/mal/de maravilla (**9**)
have a point, to tener razón (**3**)
have, I tengo (**2**)
have, to tener (ie) (1, **2**)
hay el heno (11)
he él (**1**)
head la cabeza (**10**)
headache el dolor de cabeza (10)
headline el titular (**13**)
health la salud (4, **10**)
health insurance el seguro médico (**11**)
healthy saludable (10)
hear, to oír (8)
heart el corazón (2, **10**)
heartrending desgarrador/a (11)
heat, high/medium/low fuego alto/mediano/bajo (**6**)
heat, to calentar (ie) (**6**)
heaven el cielo (2)
hectare la hectárea (15)
helicopter el helicóptero (13)
hell el infierno (4)
hello hola (**1**)
helmet el casco (12)
help, to ayudar (**2**)
helper el/la asistente (3)
hen la gallina (15)
her su/s (**3**)
herb la hierba (10)
here aquí (**1**)
heritage la herencia (7)
hers suya/as (7, **13**)
hi hola (**1**)
hide, to esconder (7)
hieroglyphic el jeroglífico (15)
highway la autopista (9); la carretera (14)
hill la loma (15)
hire, to contratar (**11**)
his su/s; suyo/os (**3, 7, 13**)
Hispanic hispano/a; hispánico/a (1)
history la historia (**3**)
hockey el hockey (**7**)
hold that, to sostener (ie) (13)
hole el hoyo (15)
holy santo/a (14)
Holy Week la Semana Santa (1)
home el hogar (4)
home, at en casa (2)
homeland la patria (10)
homework la tarea (2)
honest honrado/a; honesto/a (**11**)
honesty la honradez; la honestidad (**15**)
honored honrado/a (14)
hope la esperanza (12)
hopeful esperanzado/a (10)
horoscope el horóscopo (4, **13**)
horrified horrorizado/a (14)
horseback riding, to go montar a caballo (**9**)
hospital el hospital (3)
host/hostess, show el anfitrión/la anfitriona (7, **13**)
hot caliente; cálido/a (**6, 9**)
hot, it is hace calor (**7**)
hot, to be tener calor (**3**)
hotel, (luxury) el hotel (de lujo) (**9**)
house la casa (**5**)
house, in the en casa (2)
house, to albergar (3)
house specialty la especialidad de la casa (**6**)
housewife la casera; el ama (*fem.*) de casa (7, 12)
housing la vivienda (15)
How are you? ¿Cómo está usted? (*for.*); ¿Cómo estás? (*inf.*) (**1**)
how much/many cuanto/a/os/as (**1**)
how cómo (**1, 2**)
howling aullador/a (5)
hug el abrazo (4)
human rights los derechos humanos (4)
humanistic humanista (8)
humanity la humanidad (11)
hummingbird el colibrí (9)
humoristic humorístico/a (4)
hundreds los centenares (4)
hungry, to be tener hambre (**3**)
hunt, to cazar (8)
hurricane el huracán (4)
hurried apurado/a (14)
hurry, in a volado/a (12)
hurry, to be in a tener (ie) prisa (**3**)
hurt oneself, to lastimarse (**10**)
hurt, to doler (ue) (9, **10**)
husband el esposo (3, **4**)
hut, little la chocita (15)
hydromassage el hidromasaje (10)
hydrotherapy la hidroterapia (10)
hyperlink el hipervínculo; el enlace (**12**)
hypermarket el hipermercado (6)
hypothesis la hipótesis (15)
hysterical histérico/a (13)

I

I yo (**1**)
I am soy; estoy (**1**)
I know sé (4)
I would love to. Me encantaría. (**4**)
I'll come by for you. Paso por ti. (**4**)
ice el hielo (**7**)
ice cream el helado (**6**)
ice cream shop la heladería (**8**)
ideal ideal (1)
identical idéntico/a (10)
ignorant of, to be ignorar (11)
illness la enfermedad (5, **10**)
illumination la iluminación (15)
illusion la ilusión (6)
illustrious ilustre (10)
image la imagen (8)
immediate inmediato/a (9)
immediately de inmediato (15)
immense inmenso/a (8)
immigrant el/la inmigrante (13)
immigration la inmigración; la migra (*slang*) (15)
immunology la inmunología (1)
impact el impacto (15)
impassion, to apasionar (11)
impatient impaciente (**5**)
impress, to impresionar (9)
impressive impresionante (2)
improve, to mejorar (6, **15**)
improvise, to improvisar (**14**)
improvised improvisado/a (15)
in demand en demanda (14)
in need of, to be faltar (**6**)
inaugurated inaugurado/a (3)
inauguration la inauguración (6)
Inca inca (15)
incentive el incentivo (11)
incite, to incitar (13)
include, to incluir (2)
including inclusive (5)
incorporate, to incorporar (6)
increase, to aumentar (13, **15**)
incredibly increíblemente (15)
indefinite indefinido/a (7)
indicate, to indicar (8)
indifferent indiferente (8)
indigenous indígena (4)
indiscrete indiscreto/a (13)
industry la industria (4)
inequality la desigualdad (5)

inexpensive barato/a (**1**)
infection la infección (**10**)
inferno el infierno (4)
infidelity la infidelidad (13)
inflation la inflación (**15**)
influenced influido/a (12)
influential influyente (13)
informal informal (3)
information el dato (1)
infrastructure la infraestructura (5)
ingredient el ingrediente (6)
inhabit, to habitar (6)
inhabitant el/la habitante (8)
inherit, to heredar (5)
initiated iniciado/a (9)
injured herido/a (9)
inn el hostal (**9**)
innate innato/a (14)
innovative innovador/a (14)
insect el insecto (5)
insert, to insertar (8)
inside adentro (6)
inside of dentro de (**5**)
inspect, to inspeccionar (14)
install, to instalar (**12**)
instant el instante (8)
instrument el instrumento (2)
insurrectionist el/la insurrecto/a (13)
intelligent inteligente (1)
interesting interesante (1)
interesting, to be interesar (**6**)
international internacional (2)
Internet la Red informática (**12**)
interpreter el/la intérprete (4, **11**)
interrupt, to interrumpir (15)
intervention la intervención (15)
interview la entrevista (2, **11**)
intestine el intestino (6)
intimate íntimo/a (10)
intonation la entonación (14)
invasion la invasión (7)
invent, to inventar (15)
investigation la investigación (14)
invite, to invitar (3)
involve, to involucrar (4)
Irish el/la irlandés/esa (9)
iron el hierro; la plancha (**5**, 6)
iron, to planchar (**5**)
ironic irónico/a (14)
irrigated land el regadío (8)
irrigation la irrigación (15)
island la isla (2, **9**)
It's all the same to me. Me da igual. (**7**)
Italian el italiano (**2**)
itinerary el itinerario (4)

J

jacket la chaqueta (**8**)
jade el jade (15)
jaguar el jaguar (9)
jail la cárcel (15)
January enero (**1**)
Japanese el japonés (**2**)
jealous celoso/a (11)
jealousy los celos (11)
jeans los vaqueros (**8**)
Jesuit el jesuita (10)
jewel la joya (7)
jewelry store la joyería (**8**)
jewels las alhajas (13)
Jewish judío/a (14)
job application la solicitud de empleo (**11**)
job candidate el/la aspirante (**11**)
jog, to hacer jogging/footing (**10**)
joke la broma; el chiste (11, 15)
journalist el/la periodista (4, **11**, **13**)
journalistic periodístico/a (15)
judge el/la juez/a (8, **15**)
juice el jugo (**6**)
July julio (**1**)
June junio (**1**)
jungle la selva; selvático/a (4, 5)
jury el jurado (14)
just justo/a (**11**)
just, to have (*done something*) acabar de (hacer algo) (**11**)
justify, to justificar (14)

K

keep, to guardar (10)
key la llave (12)
keyboard el teclado (**12**)
kick, to patear (**7**)
kill, to matar (11)
kilogram (= *2.2 pounds*) el kilo (**6**)
kindness la bondad (15)
king el rey (2, **15**)
kingdom el reino (8)
kiss el beso (4)
kiss, to besar (10)
kitchen la cocina (**5**, **6**)
knee la rodilla (**10**)
kneel down, to arrodillarse (15)
knife el cuchillo (8)
knotted anudado/a (15)
knotted string el quipu (*Inca*) (15)
know, to saber; conocer (*someone*) (**4**)
knowledge el conocimiento (15)
known conocido/a (6)
Korean el coreano (**2**)

L

label la etiqueta (10)
laboratory, (language) el laboratorio (de lenguas/de idiomas) (2, **3**)
laboriously afanosamente (5)
lace el encaje (10)
lack la falta (12)
lack, to carecer de (6)
lacking, to be faltar (6)
lake el lago (**9**)
lame cojo/a (13)
lamp la lámpara (**5**)
land el terreno; la tierra (4, 6, 8)
land, to aterrizar (**9**)
landlord/lady el/la casero/a (12)
landscape el paisaje (8)
language el idioma (**2**)
languish, to languidecer (11)
laptop computer la computadora portátil (**12**)
last último/a; pasado/a (2, 6)
last night anoche (**6**)
last, to durar; perdurar (8, 14)
lasting duradero/a (15)
late tarde (**2**)
late, to be tardar (13)
lately últimamente (15)
laugh, to reírse (i, i) (**5**)
laughter la risa (13)
laundry la lavandería (12)
law la ley; el derecho (**3**, 6, **15**)
lazy perezoso/a (2)
leader el caudillo; el/la líder (15)
leadership el liderazgo (9)
leading lady la primera actriz (**13**)
leading man el galán (**13**)
leaf la hoja (15)
leap, to saltar (8)
learn, to aprender (**2**)
leather el cuero; la piel (**8**, **14**)
leave, to salir; dejar (**4**)
lecture la conferencia (3)
left (of), to/on the a la izquierda (de) (**3**)
left, to be quedar (**6**)
leftist de izquierdas (8)
leftovers los restos (10)
leg la pierna (**10**)
legendary legendario/a (6)
lemon el limón (6)
lemon pie la tarta de limón (**6**)
lemonade la limonada (4, **6**)
lend, to prestar (12)
Lent la Cuaresma (9)
less... than menos... que (**5**)
lessen, to disminuir (15)
lesser inferior (3)
lesson la lección (**1**)
let go, to soltar (ue) (2)
let's go vamos (**4**)
letter (of recommendation) la carta (de recomendación) (1, **11**)
lettuce la lechuga (**6**)
level el nivel (10)
lexicon el léxico (15)
liberate, to liberar (9)
liberty la libertad (5)
librarian el/la bibliotecario/a (11)
library la biblioteca (**3**)
license plate la placa (12)
life la vida (2)
light ligero/a (13)
light up, to alumbrarse (15)
like, to gustar (**6**)
likewise igualmente (**1**)
limit el límite (6)
limit, to limitar (10)
limousine la limosina (14)
linguistic lingüístico/a (13)
lip el labio (8)
lipstick el lápiz labial (**5**)
liquid el líquido (5)
Listen. Oye. (*command*) (**7**)
listen, to escuchar (**2**)
listener, radio el/la radioyente (**13**)
liter el litro (**6**)
literature la literatura (**3**)
live (*on television*) en directo; en vivo; en vivo y en directo (13)
live, to habitar; vivir (**2**, 6)
living room la sala (3, **5**)
loan el préstamo (11)
lobster la langosta (**6**)
located ubicado/a (8)
location la ubicación (5)
lodging el hospedaje (**9**)
long-awaited ansiado/a (15)
long-sleeved de manga larga (**8**)
look la mirada; fíjese (*for. command*) (9, 15)
look at, to mirar (**2**)
look for, to buscar (**2**)
lose, to perder (ie) (**4**)
lose weight, to adelgazar; bajar de peso (**10**)
lotion, (shaving) la loción (de afeitar) (**5**)
loud sonoro/a (14)
love el amor (2)
love, to querer (ie) (**4**)
lover el/la amante (7)
lower bajo (12)
lower, to bajar (6)
lozenge la pastilla (**10**)
luck la suerte (**7**)
lukewarm tibio/a (7)
lunch el almuerzo (2, **6**)
lunch, to have almorzar (ue) (**4**, **6**)
lungs los pulmones (**10**)
luxurious lujoso/a (3)
luxury el lujo (5)
lyrics la letra (3)

M

macaw el guacamayo (5)
magic la magia (14)
mail el correo (2)
mail carrier el/la cartero/a (**11**)
mailbox el buzón (2)
majority la mayoría (8)
make haz (*command*) (9)
make, to hacer (**3**)
make good, to (*on a promise*) cumplir (con) (**15**)
make up, to confeccionar (15)
makeup el maquillaje (**5**, **8**)
mall el centro comercial (**8**)
man el hombre (**1**)
manage, to manejar (12)
manager el gerente (9, **11**)
mandatory obligatorio/a (**12**)
manifest, to manifestar (ie) (6)
manner (of dressing) el modo (de vestir) (11, **14**)
mansion la mansión (5)
mantilla la mantilla (10)
manufacture la fabricación (2)
manufacture, to fabricar (12)
map el mapa (**1**, **9**)
maracas las maracas (**14**)
Marathon in Madrid Mapoma (1)
March marzo (**1**)
Mardi Gras el carnaval (9)
mariachi musician el mariachi (*Mexico*) (3)
marine marino/a (6)
maritime marítimo/a (5)
market el mercado (4)
married, to casado/a (**4**)
marry, to casarse (4)
martial marcial (13)
marvelous maravilloso/a (4)
Mass la misa (15)
massacre el masacre (4)
masses, the el pueblo (**15**)
masterpiece la obra maestra (9)
match, to emparejar (*pair up*); hacer juego (con) (*to go together with*) (6, **8**)

material el material (5)
mathematics las matemáticas (2, **3**)
matriarchy el matriarcado (5)
mattress el colchón (13)
maximum máximo/a (9)
May mayo (**1**)
mayor el/la alcalde/alcaldesa (12, **15**)
meal la comida (2, **6**)
means los medios (14)
measure la medida (**12**)
measure, to medir (i, i) (6)
measurement la medida (**6**)
mechanic el/la mecánico/a (**11**)
medicine la medicina (**3**)
melancholic melancólico/a (7)
melody la melodía (14)
member el miembro (4)
memory el recuerdo (4)
memory card la tarjeta de memoria (**9**)
mention, to mencionar (4)
mentioned mencionado/a (15)
menu el menú (**6**)
merit el mérito (11)
message el mensaje (8)
metal sheet la plancha (8)
meteorological meteorológico/a (4)
meter el metro (8)
Mexican mexicano/a (**2**)
Mexican chicken dish el mole poblano (10)
Mexican-American chicano/a (12)
mezzanine el entresuelo (7)
microphone el micrófono (15)
microscope el microscopio (1)
microwave el microondas (**6**)
migrant migratorio/a (15)
mile la milla (15)
military militar (4)
milk la leche (**6**)
milk, to ordeñar (15)
milky lácteo/a (10)
millennium el milenio (3)
million/s el/los millón/millones (2)
mine la mina (*noun*); mío/a/os/as (6, **13**)
miner el/la minero/a (10)
mineralogy la mineralogía (6)
minimum mínimo/a (9)
mining la minería (4)
minister el/la ministro/a (4, **15**)
minority la minoría (13)
mirror el espejo (**5**)
miscellaneous misceláneo/a (3)
misery la miseria (8)
Miss señorita (Srta.) (**1**)
miss, to echar de menos; extrañar (*someone*) (2, 3)
mission la misión (5)
mist la bruma (11)
mistaken equivocado/a (15)
mix, to mezclar (8)
model el/la modelo (**14**)
moderate moderado/a (15)
moderator el/la presentador/a (12, **13**)
modern moderno/a (3)
monarch el/la monarca (13)
monarchy la monarquía (**15**)
Monday el lunes (**1**)
money el dinero(4)
monkey el mono (5)
monotonous monótono/a (11)
monster el monstruo (5)
month el mes (**1**)
monument el monumento (**9**)
moon la luna (8)
Moor (*Arab*) el/la moro/a (13)
moral la lección; la moraleja (8)
more… than más… que (**5**)
Moslem musulmán/ana (14)
mother la madre (**4**)
mother-in-law la suegra (**4**)
motive el motivo (10)
motto el lema (**15**)
mountain la montaña (2, **9**)
mountainous montañoso/a (4)
mouse el ratón (**12**)
mouth la boca (7, **10**)
move la mudanza (12)
move away, to alejar (13)
move up, to ascender (ie) (**11**)
move, to mudarse (5)
movement el movimiento (8)
movie la película (**4, 7, 13**)
movie theatre el cine (2, **4**)
Mr. señor (Sr.) (**1**)
Mrs. señora (Sra.) (**1**)
mulatto mulato/a (7)
multinational multinacional (15)
mural el mural (12)
muralist el/la muralista (3)
muscle el músculo (10)
muscular musculoso/a (13)
museum museo (2, **3**)
music la música (**3**)
musical comedy la comedia musical (**14**)
musical rhythm el son (14)
musician el/la músico/a (8, **14**)
mutton el carnero (6)
my mi/mis (**1, 3**)
My name is… Me llamo…; Mi nombre es… (**1**)
mysterious misterioso/a (11)
mystery el misterio (4)

N

nailed enclavado/a (15)
name el nombre (**1**)
name, to denominar; nombrar (4, 6)
named mentado/a (15)
narrate, to narrar (4)
narrative narrativo/a (*adj.*) (14)
narrator el/la narrador/a (11, 14)
nationality la nacionalidad (2)
natural resource el recurso natural (**12**)
nature la naturaleza (5, **12**)
navigable navegable (5)
navigate, to navegar (12)
navigator el/la navegante (7)
nearby cerca (de); cercano/a (**3**, 8)
necklace, (pearl) el collar (de perlas) (7, **8**)
need, in necesitado/a (9)
need, to necesitar (1, **2**)
negative negativo/a (7)
neighbor el/la vecino/a (5)
neighborhood el barrio; la vecindad (3, 5)
neither… nor ni… ni (**7**)
nephew el sobrino (**4**)
nervous nervioso/a (3, **5**)
nest el nido (11)
never nunca (2, **7**)
nevertheless sin embargo (3)
new nuevo/a (**2**)
New Year's Eve la Nochevieja (9)
New Yorker neoyorquino/a (12)
news las noticias (**13**)
newscast el noticiero (**13**)
newscaster el/la comentarista (**13**)
newspaper el periódico (**7, 13**)
next próximo/a (6)
next to al lado (de); junto a (**3**, 8)
nice simpático/a (**1**)
nickname el apodo (2)
niece la sobrina (**4**)
night la noche (**2**)
nightclub, to go to a ir a una discoteca (**7**)
nightstand la mesa de noche (**5**)
ninth noveno (**8**)
no one ninguno/a; nadie (**7**)
no way ni modo (3)
nobility la nobleza (15)
noble noble (15)
noise el ruido (11)
nominated nominado/a (12)
nomination la nominación (13)
none ningún/ninguna (**7**)
nose la nariz (**5, 10**)
nostalgic nostálgico/a (7)
not even ni siquiera (15)
note el apunte (5)
notebook el cuaderno (**1**)
nothing nada (**7**)
notify, to notificar (14)
novel la novela (2, **7**)
novelist el/la novelista (2)
November noviembre (**1**)
now ahora (**2**)
nowadays hoy en día (3)
nuclear plant la planta nuclear (**12**)
nucleus el núcleo (4)
nude desnudo/a (15)
nun la monja (12)
nun, little la monjita (14)
nurse el/la enfermero/a (**11**)
nutrition la alimentación (6)
nylon el nilón; el nylon (**14**)

O

obesity el sobrepeso (**10**)
obituary la esquela funeraria (**13**)
object el objeto (9)
obligation el compromiso; la obligación (11, 15)
observatory el observatorio (**3**)
observe, to observar (8)
obstruction la obstrucción (10)
obtain, to obtener (ie) (11)
occupy, to ocupar (2)
occur, to ocurrir (3)
ocean el mar (**7**)
October octubre (**1**)
odor el olor (8)
of course claro; por supuesto (**4**, 14)
offer la oferta (1)
offer, to ofrecer (9)
office la oficina; el despacho (2, **11**)
official oficial (13)
often a menudo (2)
oil el petróleo (9, **12**)
okay de acuerdo (**4**)
old viejo/a; antiguo/a (**2**)
old person el/la anciano/a (12)
older mayor (**4**)
olive la aceituna (2)
olive oil el aceite de oliva (2)
Olympic Games los Juegos Olímpicos (3)
omelet la tortilla (*Spain*) (6)
on sobre (**5**)
on demand en demanda (14)
on the back a cuestas (14)
on the dot en punto (2)
on time a tiempo (3)
on top encima (13)
on your own por su cuenta (11)
one must ha de; hay que (8)
one un/o/a (**1**)
only solamente; sólo; nomás (*slang*) (**3**, 15)
open abierto/a (2)
open, to abrir (**2**)
opera la ópera (1, **14**)
operate, to operar (**10**)
opinion, to express an opinar (5)
opponent el/la contrincante (12, **15**)
oppressed oprimido/a (15)
or o (**1**)
orange anaranjado/a (*color*); la naranja (*fruit*) (**1, 6**)
orchestra, (symphony) la orquesta (sinfónica) (**4, 14**)
orchid la orquídea (5)
order el orden (4)
order, to pedir (i, i); ordenar (**6**, 15)
ordinary ordinario/a (12)
origin el origen (3)
originality la originalidad (13)
originate, to originar (8)
originating proveniente (14)
ornament el ornamento (8)
orphan el/la huérfano/a (9)
our/s nuestro/a/os/as (**3, 13**)
out of place fuera de lugar (12)
out of work, to be estar en el paro; estar sin trabajo (**11**)
outfit el conjunto (**14**)
outgoing extrovertido/a (1)
outing la gira (11)
outing, to go on an ir de excursión (**9**)
outrage la barbaridad (5)
outside fuera (de) (4)
oven el horno (**6**)
overcome, to superar (12)
overpopulation la sobrepoblación (13)
owing to debido a (5)
own propio/a (13)
owner el /la dueño/a; el/la propietario/a (5, 8)
oxygen el oxígeno (10)

P

pacifist el/la pacifista (**15**)
pack the suitcase(s), to hacer la(s) maletas(s) (**9**)
pack, to empacar (10)
packaged empaquetado/a (10)

pageant el concurso (**13**)
pain el dolor (**10**)
painful doloroso/a (10)
painted pintado/a (3)
painter el/la pintor/a (2)
painting la pintura; el cuadro (2, **5**)
palace el palacio (3)
Panama monetary unit el balboa (5)
Panamanian panameño/a (**2**)
Panamanian embroidery la mola (5)
panpipe la zampoña (8)
pants los pantalones (**8**)
paper el papel (**1**)
parade el desfile (9)
paradise el paraíso (6)
paragraph el párrafo (5)
parents los padres (**2**)
park el parque (1, **4**)
park, to estacionar (11)
part la parte (3)
participant el participante (1)
participate, to participar (3)
particularly particularmente (2)
parting la partida (9)
partner la pareja (4)
party la fiesta (1)
pass (by), to aprobar (ue) (*a test*); pasar (por) (4, 13)
passion la pasión (13)
passionate apasionado/a (9)
past el pasado (15)
pastime el pasatiempo (**7**)
path el sendero (5)
patient el/la paciente (**10**)
patio el patio (**5**)
patio, small el patiecito (12)
patriarch el patriarca (14)
patriarchy el patriarcado (5)
paw la pata (7)
pay (cash), to pagar (en efectivo) (**8**)
peace la paz (4)
peaceful pacífico/a (15)
peach el durazno (14)
peak el pico; el auge (8, 15)
pearls las perlas (**8**)
pedicure la pedicura (10)
peel (*fruit*) la cáscara (7)
peel, to pelar (**6**)
peeling descarapelado/a (12)
pelican el pelícano (6)
pen el bolígrafo (**1**)
penalties los penales (*Latin America*); los penaltis (Spain) (7)
pencil el lápiz (1)
penguin el pingüino (6)
people la gente; el pueblo (8, **15**)
pepper el pimiento (**6**)
percussionist el/la percusionista (7)
perennial perenne (11)
perfect perfecto/a (2)
perform, to representar (**14**)
perfume el olor; el perfume (6, **8**)
perfume shop la perfumería (**8**)
perhaps quizás (4)
period período (2)
permanent permanente (3)
permission el permiso (15)
perpetuate, to perpetuarse (15)
perseverance la perseverancia (13)
person la persona (**1**)
personality personalidad (7)
personify, to personificar (6)
personnel el personal (11)
pertinent pertinente (11)
Peruvian peruano/a (**2**)
pesticides los pesticidas (**12**)
pet la mascota (6)
petrified petrificado/a (7)
pharmacy la farmacia (**8**)
phenomenal fenomenal (6)
phenomenon el fenómeno (10)
philharmonic filarmónico/a (14)
photocopier la fotocopiadora (**12**)
photocopy la fotocopia (12)
photocopy, to fotocopiar (**12**)
photographer el fotógrafo/a (1)
physical físico/a (5)
physical education la educación física (**3**)
physics la física (**3**)
piano el piano (1, **14**)
pick, to pizcar (*Mexico*) (15)
pick up, to recoger (9)
pickup truck la camioneta (1)
picnic, to have a hacer un pícnic (**7**)
picture el cuadro (2)
pie el pastel (**6**)
piece el pedazo (**6**)
piece, (musical) la pieza (musical) (3, **14**)
pile el montón (12)
pile, to apilar (15)
pill la pastilla (**10**)
pilot el/la piloto (**9**)
pinch la pizca (**6**)
pink rosado/a (**1**)
pipe el tubo (12)
pirate el pirata (7)
pirate, to piratear (11)
pity la pena (2)
place el puesto; el sitio (5, 10)
plaid de cuadros (**8**)
plain el llano (10)
plains of Argentina las pampas (11)
plan, to planear (14)
plane el avión (**9**)
plant, to plantar (12)
plastic el plástico (3)
plastic arts las artes plásticas (14)
plate el plato (15)
plateau, high el altiplano (10)
platform el andén; la plataforma (13, 15)
play (*theatre*) la obra (**13**)
play, to practicar (*a sport*); jugar (ue) (*a sport*); tocar (*an instrument*) (**2, 4**)
player el/la jugador/a (2)
please, to complacer (11)
Pleased to meet you. Mucho gusto.; Encantado/a. (**1**)
pleasure el placer (7)
plumber el/la plomero/a (**11**)
poem el cantar; el poema (15)
poet el/la poeta (2)
poetry la poesía (6)
point (of view) el punto (de vista) (1, 13)
point out, to señalar (12)
political político/a (15)
political post el cargo politico (**15**)
political science las ciencias políticas (**3**)
politician el político (15)
politics la política (15)
pollute, to contaminar (**12**)
pollution, there is hay contaminación (**7**)
polyester el poliéster (**14**)
poor pobre (**2**)
population la población (2)
pork el cerdo (10)
port el puerto (2)
portrait el retrato (14)
Portuguese el portugués (**2**)
pose, to posar (modelo); plantear (14, 15)
posed posado/a (14)
position el cargo; el puesto (**11**)
possible posible (3)
possibly posiblemente (2)
potatoes las papas (**6**)
pound, to golpear (12)
poverty la pobreza (5, **15**)
power el poder (15)
practice, to practicar (**2**)
praise la alabanza (12)
pray, to rezar (15)
precious precioso/a (6)
pre-Colombian precolombino/a (5)
precursor el/la precursor/a (10)
predict predecir (i) (15)
predominate, to predominar (8)
prefer, to preferir (ie, i) (**4**)
preference la preferencia (5)
preferred preferido/a (9)
prehispanic prehispánico/a (3)
prehistoric prehistórico/a (3)
preoccupation la preocupación (10)
prepare, to preparar (**2**)
prescribe, to recetar (**10**)
present oneself, to acudir (11)
presentation la representación (14)
preservative el conservante (10)
preserve, to preservar; conservar (5, 8, **12**)
preside, to presidir (15)
presidency la presidencia (15)
president el/la presidente/a; el/la rector/a (*of a university*) (8, **15**)
president's office la rectoría (**3**)
press la prensa (4)
press conference la conferencia de prensa (6)
prestige el prestigio (14)
prestigious prestigioso/a (2)
pretend, to fingir (11)
pretty bonito/a; lindo/a (**2**, 8)
price el precio (5, **8**)
prince el príncipe (2)
print, to imprimir (**12**)
printed impreso/a (12)
printer la impresora (**12**)
priority la prioridad (15)
prisoner el/ la prisionero/a (15)
privacy la privacidad (5)
prize el premio (8)
process el proceso (15)
process, to procesar (12)
procession la procesión (1)
procreate, to procrear (10)
produce, to producir (8)
producer el/la productor/a (**13**)
product el producto (2)
professor el/la profesor/a (**1**)
profile el perfil (11)
profound profundo/a (5)
profoundly profundamente (10)
program, to programar (**12**)
programmer programador/a (12)
progress el progreso (15)
prohibit, to prohibir (15)
prohibited prohibido/a (6)
project el proyecto (5, 15)
prolific prolífico/a (2)
promise la promesa (6)
promise, to prometer (6)
promote, to ascender (ie); promover (ue) (*an idea*) (**11, 15**)
property la propiedad (10)
proportion, to proporcionar (10)
propose, to proponer (15)
prosperity la prosperidad (10)
prosperous próspero/a (6)
protagonist el/la protagonista (**13**)
protect, to proteger (8, **12**)
protected protegido/a (6)
proteins las proteínas (**10**)
prove, to comprobar (ue) (15)
provide, to proporcionar (1)
provisions los comestibles, las provisiones (15)
psychological psicológico/a (14)
psychologist el/la psicólogo/a (3, **11**)
psychology la psicología (**3**)
public el público (13)
publicity la publicidad; publicitario/a (*adj.*) (13)
publish, to publicar (6)
Puerto Rican puertorriqueño/a (**2**)
purple morado/a (**1**)
purse el bolso (**8**)
put, to poner; meter (**4, 6**)
put out (fires), to apagar (fuegos/incendios) (**11**)
pyramid la pirámide (3)

Q

qualifications las calificaciones (**11**)
quality la calidad (4, **8**)
quantity la cantidad (6)
quarter el trimestre (3)
quartet el cuarteto (**14**)
queen la reina (7, **15**)
question la pregunta (**1**)
questionnaire el cuestionario (10)
quit (smoking cigarettes), to dejar (de fumar) (**10, 11**)
quite a few bastantes (13)
quite bastante (**3**)

R

raccoon el mapache (8)
race la raza (5)
radio station la emisora (*business entity*); la estación de radio (*on the dial*) (**13**)

radioactivity la radioactividad (**12**)
raging furibundo/a (14)
rail el riel (15)
railroad el ferrocarril (6)
rain la lluvia (4)
rain, heavy el chubasco (7)
rain, to llover (ue) (**7**)
raise el aumento (**11**)
raise, to subir (6)
raising la cría (10)
ranch la estancia (11)
ranch, small el ranchito (15)
rape, to violar (**15**)
rapid rápido/a (2)
rarely raramente (4)
rascal el cabrón (13)
rate (of unemployment) la tasa (de desempleo) (6, **15**)
raw fish with lemon el ceviche (6)
rayon el rayón (**14**)
razor blade la navaja de afeitar (**5**)
reach, to alcanzar (2)
react, to reaccionar (10)
read, to leer (**2**)
reader el/la lector/a (12, **13**)
ready dispuesto/a (**12**)
real menudo (*slang*) (2)
real estate los bienes raíces (5)
realistic realista (4)
really de verdad (**1**)
reason la razón (2)
receipt el recibo (**8**)
receive, to recibir (**2**)
receiver el receptor (12)
recently recientemente (6)
rechargeable recargable (12)
recipe la receta (**6**)
recognition el reconocimiento (12)
recommend, to recomendar (ie) (9)
reconquest la reconquista (13)
reconstruct, to reconstruir (15)
record, to grabar (**12, 13**)
recorded grabado/a (13)
recording la grabación (12)
recovery la recuperación (9)
recreational recreativo/a (7)
recuperate, to recuperar (10)
recycle, to reciclar (**12**)
recycling el reciclaje (**12**)
red rojo/a (**1**)
reduce, to reducir (15)
referee el árbitro (**7**)
reflect, to reflejar (8)
reforestation la reforestación (**12**)
reform, to reformar (12)
refreshing refrescante (9)
refreshment el refresco (3)
refrigerator el refrigerador (**5**)
rehearse, to ensayar (11, **14**)
reign, to reinar (10)
reinforce, to reforzar (ue) (15)
relate, to relatar (7)
relation la relación (4)
relative relativo/a; pariente (*family*) (4, 15)
relax, to relajarse (10)
religious religioso/a (15)
remain, to quedarse; permanecer (**9,** 14)
remaining, to be quedar (6)
remains los restos (10)
remedy el remedio (**10**)
remedy, to remediar (13)
remember, to recordar (ue) (**4**)
remove, to remover (14)
renewable renovable (11)
renown el renombre (14)
rent la renta (*Mexico*) (12)
rent, for de alquiler (14)
rent, to alquilar (11)
repair, to reparar (**11**)
repeat, to repetir (i, i) (**4**)
repertoire el repertorio (**14**)
report, to informar; reportar (13)
reporter, (television) el/la reportero/a (4, **13**)
represent, to representar (2, **13, 14**)
representative el/la representante (**15**)
representative representativo/a (3)
republic la república (15)
request, to pedir (i, i) (**4**)
require, to requerir (ie) (11)
requirement el requisito (5)
research la investigación (3)
researcher el investigador/a (1)
reservation la reservación; la reserva (6, **9**)
residence la residencia (2)
resin la resina (7)
resolve, to resolver (ue) (12)
resource el recurso (5)
respect, to respetar (15)
respectable respetable (14)
respective respectivo/a (7)
respiratory respiratorio/a (10)
response la respuesta (5)
responsibilities las responsabilidades (**11**)
responsibility, to take responsabilizar (1)
responsible responsable (3)
rest, to descansar (12)
restaurant el restaurante; el restaurán (**6,** 13)
restore, to restaurar (5)
result el resultado (6)
résumé el currículum vitae (**11**)
retire, to jubilarse; retirarse (7, **11**)
retirement plan el plan de retiro (**11**)
return, to devolver (ue) (*something*); regresar; volver (ue) (**2, 4, 8**)
return, on de regreso (11)
reveal, to revelar (15)
review el repaso; la reseña (*article*) (6, 13)
revolutionized revolucionado/a (12)
revolver el revólver (11)
reward, to premiar (11)
rhythm el ritmo; la cadencia (1, 15)
rice el arroz (**6**)
rich rico/a (**2**)
richness la riqueza (5)
ride, to montar (11)
right el derecho; verdad (8, **15**)
right away enseguida (**6**)
right, to/on the a la derecha (**3**)
right, to be tener razón (**3**)
rise up, to surgir (10)
risk el riesgo (10)
ritual el ritual (3)
rival el rival (8)
river el río; fluvial (*adj.*) (2, 9)
river bank la orilla (14)
road el camino (8)
rob, to robar (6)
role el papel (12)
romantic romántico/a (4)
room el cuarto; el salón (**5,** 9)
room, little el cuartito (5)
round redondo/a (15)
roundtrip ida y vuelta (**9**)
route la ruta (10)
routine la rutina (5)
row la fila (7)
royal real (14)
rub, to frotar (15)
ruin la ruina (4)
ruling el reglamento (10)
rumor el rumor (13)
run, to correr (2, **7**)
Russian el ruso (**2**)

S

sacred sagrado/a (13)
sacrificed sacrificado/a (15)
sad triste (**5**)
safe and sound sano/a y salvo/a (11)
sail, to navegar (14)
sailor el/la marinero/a (3)
salad la ensalada (**6**)
salary el salario; el sueldo (3, **11**)
sale la rebaja (**8**)
sale, on en rebaja (**8**)
salsa performer el/la salsero/a (12)
salt la sal (**6**)
salutation/s el/los saludo/s (11)
Salvadorian salvadoreño/a (**2**)
same mismo/a (8)
same as, the al igual (15)
same, to be the dar igual (7)
sample la muestra (15)
sandals las sandalias (**8**)
sandwich el bocadillo; el sándwich (3, **6**)
Sanfermín festival los sanfermines (2)
sanitation la sanidad (15)
SARS el SRAS (10)
satellite dish la antena parabólica (**12**)
satellite TV la televisión por satélite (**13**)
satisfactory satisfactorio/a (6)
satisfied satisfecho/a (8)
satisfy, to satisfacer (9)
saturated saturado/a (10)
Saturday el sábado (**1**)
sauce popular in Argentina la chimichurri (6)
saucepan la cazuela (**6**)
sausage, (blood) la morcilla (6)
save, to guardar; archivar (*a file*); salvar (**6, 12**)
saxophone el saxofón (**14**)
say, to decir (i) (**6**)
scam el doble juego (4)
scandalized escandalizado/a (5)
scanner el escáner (**12**)
scar la cicatriz (13)
scarce escaso/a (15)
scarlet escarlata (5)
schedule, (class) el horario (de clases) (**3,** 8)
schedule, work el horario de trabajo (**11**)
scholarship la beca (10)
scholastic escolar (12)
school la escuela (5)
School of Art la Facultad de Arte (**3**)
School of Engineering la Facultad de Ingeniería (**3**)
School of Humanities la Facultad de Filosofía y Letras (**3**)
School of Law la Facultad de Derecho (**3**)
School of Mathematics la Facultad de Matemáticas (**3**)
School of Medicine la Facultad de Medicina (**3**)
School of Science la Facultad de Ciencias (**3**)
science fiction la ciencia ficción (7)
scientist el/la científico/a (1)
score la partitura (14)
scorpion el escorpión (7)
screen la pantalla (**12**)
script el guión (10, **13**)
script writer el/la guionista (13)
scuba dive, to bucear (**9**)
sculptor el/la escultor/a (8)
sea el mar (2, **9**)
sea bass la corvina (6)
sea lion el lobo marino (6)
seafood los mariscos (**6**)
search la búsqueda (**11**)
search engine el buscador (12)
seasick, to become marearse (13)
season la estación; la temporada (**1, 7**)
seat, (aisle/window) el asiento (de pasillo/ventanilla) (6, **9**)
seat of government la sede (8)
second segundo/a (**8**)
secrecy la clandestinidad (13)
secretary el/la secretario/a (1, **11**)
secrete, to segregar (5)
security seguridad (9)
see you later hasta luego (**1**)
see you soon hasta pronto (**1**)
see you tomorrow hasta mañana (**1**)
see, to ver (**2**)
seem, to parecer (**6**)
select, to seleccionar (15)
selection la selección (7)
self-defense la defensa propia (14)
sell, to vender (**2**)
semester el semestre (**3**)
senator el/la senador/a (**15**)
sensationalist sensacionalista (13)
sensuous sensual (7)
sentence la oración (7)
sentimental sentimental (4)
separate, to apartar (15)
separated separado/a (13)
September septiembre (**1**)
sequins las lentejuelas (**14**)
serenade la serenata (3)
serious (sickness) grave; serio/a (5, 7)
servant sirviente/a (4)
serve, to servir (i, i) (**4**)
service servicio (2)

set the table, to poner la mesa (**5**)
seventh séptimo/a (**8**)
several varios/as (9)
severe severo/a (8)
sewer la alcantarilla (13)
sex el sexo (13)
sextet el sexteto (**14**)
shake, to sacudir (15)
shameless (person) el/la sinvergüenza (13)
shampoo el champú (**5**)
shape, in en forma (10)
share, to compartir (4)
sharp puntiagudo/a (9)
shave, to afeitarse (**5**)
she ella (**1**)
sheep la oveja (8)
shell la cáscara (7)
shell, to desgranar (15)
shine, to brillar; lucir (8, 14)
shirt la camisa (4, **10**)
shock el sobresalto (13)
shoe store la zapatería (**8**)
shoes los zapatos (7, **8**)
shoot, to disparar (11)
shopping center el centro comercial (**8**)
short bajo/a (*in stature*); corto/a (**2**, 6)
shortage la escasez (**12**)
short-sleeved de manga corta (**8**)
shot la inyección (**10**)
should we go vamos a (**4**)
shout el grito (11)
shout, to gritar (**7**)
show la función; la exposición (4, 8)
show a movie, to poner una película (**4**)
show, to mostrar (ue) (8)
shower el chubasco (7)
showy vistoso/a (9)
shrimp los camarones (**6**)
shrink, to encogerse (15)
shy tímido/a (**1**)
side el lado (11)
sidewalk la banqueta (12)
sign el letrero (9)
sign, to (*a letter, a treaty, etc.*) firmar (7, **15**)
signature la firma (11)
significant significativo/a; significante (7, 13)
silk la seda (**8**)
silverware la platería (3)
similar parecido/a; semejante (12, 14)
simplicity la sencillez (**14**)
since desde (2)
sincerely yours atentamente (**11**)
sing, to cantar (8)
singer el/la cantante (1)
single soltero/a (**4**)
sister la hermana (**4**)
sister-in-law la cuñada (3, **4**)
sit, to sentarse (ie) (**5**)
situated situado/a (3)
situation la situación (5)
sixth sexto/a (**8**)
size el tamaño (14)
size, clothing la talla (8)
skate, to patinar (**7**)
skater el/la patinador/a (12)
skating el patinaje (**7**)
ski, to esquiar (**7**)
skiing, (water) el esquí (acuático) (**7**)
skill la destreza (15)
skillet la sartén (**6**)
skin la piel (5)
skinny flaco/a (**2**)
skirt la falda (**8**)
skull la calavera (15)
sky el cielo (8)
slave el/la esclavo/a (9)
sleep, to dormir (ue, u) (4)
sleepy, to be tener sueño (**3**)
sleeveless sin manga (**8**)
slogan el lema (publicitario) (13)
slope la falda (8)
sloth el perezoso (5)
slow lento/a (9)
slowly despacio (5)
small pequeño/a (1, **2**)
small, very chiquito/a (5, 15)
smell el olor (6)
smile la sonrisa (2)
smile, to sonreír (i, i) (10)
smog, there is hay contaminación (**7**)
smoke el humo (**12**)
smoke, to fumar (8)
snack la merienda (**6**)
snake la culebra (7)
snorkel, to bucear (9)
snow, to nevar (ie) (**7**)
so, so más o menos (**1**)
soap el jabón (**5**)
soap opera la telenovela (**13**)
soccer el fútbol (**2**)
social page la crónica social (**13**)
social science las ciencias sociales (**3**)
social security el seguro social (6)
social welfare programs los programas sociales (**15**)
socialist el/la socialista (8)
society la sociedad (5)
sociology la sociología (**3**)
sodium nitrate el nitrato de sodio (6)
sofa el sofá (**5**)
soft suave (8)
soft drink el refresco (**6**)
softly dulcemente (5)
solar solar (15)
solid sólido/a (6)
solitary solitario/a (11)
soloist el/la solista (**14**)
solution la solución (2)
solve, to resolver (ue); solucionar (**15**)
some alguno/a/os/as (**7**)
someone alguien (**7**)
something algo (3, **6**)
son el hijo (**4**)
son, my mi'jo (*slang*) (15)
song la canción (3)
son-in-law el yerno (**4**)
soon pronto (10)
sophisticated sofisticado/a (14)
sophistication la sofisticación (14)
sorbet el sorbete (6)
sorrow la pena (10)
soul el alma (2)
sound el sonido (*fem.*) (14)
soup la sopa (**6**)
soup, a bit of la sopita (10)
souvenir el recuerdo (**9**)
sow, to sembrar (ie) (8)
spa el balneario (9)
Spanish español/a; el español (**2**)
speak, to hablar (**2**)
specialty shop la tienda especializada (6)
species la especie (5)
spectacle el espectáculo (8)
spectacular espectacular (2, 5)
spectator el/la espectador/a (**13**)
speculate, to especular (13)
speech el discurso (**15**)
speed la velocidad (12)
spend, to gastar; pasar (*time*) (**4**, **8**)
spicy picante (**6**)
spider la araña (8)
spider, little la arañita (10)
spider web la tela de la araña (10)
sponsor el/la patrocinador/a (12, **13**)
sponsor, to patrocinar (**13**)
sport el deporte (1, **7**)
sporting deportivo/a (7)
sports section la sección deportiva (**13**)
sportscaster el/la comentarista deportivo/a (**13**)
spreadsheet la hoja electrónica (**12**)
spring la primavera (**1**)
spy, to espiar (11)
square cuadrado/a (5)
squash la calabaza (11)
squeak, to rechinar (15)
squid el calamar (6)
squirrel la ardilla (8)
stadium el estadio (**3**)
stage la etapa (*phase*); el escenario (*theatre*) (3, 13, **14**)
stair step la escalonada (8)
stairs las escaleras (12)
stall el puesto (6)
stamp el sello (2)
stamped estampado/a (14)
stand in line, to hacer cola (**9**)
stand out, to destacar (12)
stand up, to levantarse; pararse (8, **15**)
standing parado/a (15)
stanza la estrofa (11)
star el/la protagonista (**13**)
state el estado (7)
statement la afirmación (12)
station la estación (**13**)
stationery shop la papelería (**8**)
statistics las estadísticas (**3**)
statuary la imaginería (4)
statue la estatua (**9**)
stay la estadía (**9**)
stay, to (*somewhere*) quedarse (**9**)
stay in bed, to guardar cama (**10**)
stay in shape, to mantenerse (ie) en forma (**10**)
stay trim, to guardar la línea (**10**)
steak el bistec (**6**)
steal, to robar (6)
steam el vapor (9)
step el paso (4)
step on, to pisar (11)
stepbrother/stepsister el/la hermanastro/a (**4**)
stepfather el padrastro (**4**)
stepmother la madrastra (**4**)
stereotype el estereotipo (12)
stew el estofado (6)
stew, Chilean el curanto (6)
stewpot la cazuela (**6**)
stick el palo; la vara (7)
still todavía; aun (3, 4)
still life la naturaleza muerta (6)
stimulate, to estimularse (9)
stimulus el estímulo (11)
Stockholm Estocolmo (4)
stomach el estómago (**10**)
stone la piedra (4)
stop la parada (15)
store la tienda (**8**)
storm la tempestad (8)
story el relato; narrativo/a (12, 14)
storyteller el/la cuentista (11)
stove la estufa (**6**)
stove, little la estufita (15)
straight ahead todo recto (3)
strange extraño/a (11)
strange, to seem extrañar (12)
straw la paja (**14**)
strawberry la fresa (15)
stream el chorro (15)
street la calle (2)
strengthen, to fortalecer (**15**)
stress el estrés (**10**)
string, to ensartar (15)
striped de rayas (**8**)
stroll el paseo (1)
struggle la lucha (15)
student el/la estudiante; estudiantil (*adj.*) (**1**, 6)
student union el centro estudiantil (**3**)
studies los estudios (2)
studio el estudio (**13**)
study el estudio (3)
study, to estudiar (**2**)
stunning impactante (5)
stupid tonto/a (13)
style el estilo (2, **14**)
style, in de moda (**8**)
subject, academic la materia (**3**)
substance la sustancia (15)
success el éxito (11)
such as tal/es como (4)
suckling pig el cochinillo (8)
suffer (from), to sufrir (de); padecer (de) (3, 10)
sufficient suficiente (11)
sufficiently suficientemente (4)
sugar la azúcar (**6**)
suggest, to sugerir (ie, i) (9)
suggestion la sugerencia (8)
suit el traje (**8**)
suitcase la maleta (4)
summarize, to resumir (7)
summary el sumario; el resumen (2, 5)
summer el verano (**1**)
Sunday el domingo (1)
sunglasses las gafas de sol (7, **9**)
sunny, it is hace sol (**7**)
superficial superficial (11)
supermarket el supermercado (6)
supervisor el/la supervisor/a (**11**)
support el apoyo (4)

support, to apoyar; mantener (ie) (*a family, etc.*) (8, **15**)
supposed supuesto/a (9)
sure seguro/a (4)
surely seguramente (3)
surf, to surfear (7)
surname el apellido (2)
surprise la sorpresa (6)
surprised maravillado/a (4)
surprising sorprendente (11)
surrealist surrealista (13)
surrounded rodeado/a (12)
surroundings el ambiente (3)
survey la encuesta (10)
susceptible susceptible (4)
suspicion la sospecha (11)
sweater el suéter (4, **8**)
sweep, to barrer (**5**)
sweets los dulces (15)
swell, to hinchar (12)
swim (in the ocean/in a pool), to nadar (en el mar/en una piscina) (**2, 7**)
swimming natación (**2**)
swimming pool la piscina (5, 7, **9**)
swimsuit el traje de baño (**7**)
symbolize simbolizar (6)
symphonic la sinfónica (14)
symphony la sinfonía (**14**)
symptom el síntoma (**10**)
synthesis la síntesis (9)
synthetic sintético/a (14)
system el sistema (4)

T

table la mesa (**1, 5**)
tablespoon la cucharada (**6**)
tail la cola (7)
take, to tomar (**2**)
take advantage of, to aprovechar (7)
take care (of oneself), to cuidar(se) (6, **10**)
take off, to despegar (*on an airplane*); quitarse (**5, 9**)
take on, to encargar (14)
take one's blood pressure, to tomarse la presión (**10**)
take out (the garbage), to sacar (la basura) (**5**, 9)
take pictures, to sacar fotos (9)
take turns, to turnarse (5)
talcum powder el talco (**8**)
talent el talento (9)
talented talentoso/a (**14**)
tall alto/a (**2**)
tank el tanque (10)
task la tarea (2)
taste el gusto (5)
tasty sabroso/a (4)
tattoo el tatuaje (13)
taxes los impuestos (11, **15**)
taxi driver el/la taxista (4)
tea el té; la yerba mate (*Argentina, Paraguay, Uruguay*) (3, **6**, 11)
teach, to enseñar (**2**)
teaching la pedagogía; la enseñanza (**3**, 12)
team el equipo (**7**)
tear la lágrima (8)
tear down, to derribar (13)
teaspoon la cucharadita (**6**)
technique la técnica (14)
technological tecnológico/a (**12**)
teeth los dientes (**5, 10**)
telephone telefónico/a (*adj.*) (3)
television la televisión (**7**)
tell, to contar (*a story*) (10)
temperate templado/a (6)
temperature la temperatura (6, **10**)
temple el templo (8)
temporary temporal; temporario/a (3, 12)
temptation la tentación (6)
tend to, to soler (ue); atender (ie) (4, 7)
tendency la tendencia (14)
tenderness la ternura (14)
tennis el tenis (**2**)
tennis court la cancha de tenis (**3**)
tens las decenas (5)
tense tenso/a (14)
tension la tensión (13)
tent la carpa (15)
tenth décimo (**8**)
terms los términos (11)
terrace la terraza (**5**)
terrain el terreno (4)
terrestrial terrestre (8)
terrific estupendo/a (**7**)
territory el territorio (13)
Thank you. Gracias. (**1**)
thankful agradecido/a (13)
that (one) eso (*neuter*); ese/a; ése/a (*that one*); aquello (*neuter*); aquel/la; aquél/la (*that one over there*) (**4**)
that which (lo) que (5)
the el/la/los/las (**1**)
theatre el teatro (**3, 4**)
theft el robo (11)
their su/s; suyo/a/os/as (**3**, 7, **13**)
theirs suyo/a/os/as (7, **13**)
theme el tema (7)
theory la teoría (8)
therapy la terapia (3)
there allá; allí (9)
there is/are hay (**1**)
therefore por eso (2)
thermal termal (10)
these (ones) estos/as; éstos/as (*these ones*) (**4**)
they ellos/as (**1**)
thick espeso/a (15)
thin delgado/a (**2**)
thing la cosa (**1**)
think, to pensar (ie) (3, **4**)
third tercer/o/a (**8**)
thirsty sediento/a (12)
thirsty, to be tener (ie) sed (**3**)
this (one) este/a; esto (*neuter*); éste/a (this one) (**4**)
thorax el tórax (13)
those (ones) esos/as; ésos (*those*); aquellos/as; aquéllos/as (*those over there*) (**4**)
thought el pensamiento (3)
throat la garganta (**10**)
throw in, to echar (**6**)
throw out, to arrojar (12)
throw, to tirar (15)
Thursday el jueves (**1**)
ticket, (roundtrip) el boleto; el pasaje (de ida y vuelta) (4, **9**)
tie la corbata (**8**)
tie, to atar; empatar (*the score*) (**7**, 8)
tight estrecho/a (*clothing*); apretado/a (**8**, 12)
time el tiempo; el rato (*length of*) (1, 13)
timid tímido/a (**1**)
tin el estaño (10)
tip punta; la propina (*monetary*) (4, **6**)
tire, to cansar; aburrir (*bore*) (**6**, 7)
tired cansado/a (4)
title el título (2)
toad el sapo (8)
toast, to tostar (ue) (**6**)
toaster la tostadora (**6**)
together juntos/as (4)
tolerance la tolerancia (15)
tomato el tomate (**6**)
tomb la tumba (15)
tomb stone la lápida (14)
tomorrow la mañana (**2**)
tongue la lengua (7, **10**)
too much demasiado (9)
toothbrush el cepillo de dientes (**5**)
toothpaste la pasta de dientes (**8**)
toothpick el palillo (14)
topic, current el tema actual (**15**)
tortoise el galápago (8)
toucan el tucán (11)
touch el toque; el tacto (6, 13)
tour la gira (**14**)
tour, to ir de excursión (**9**)
tour guide el/la guía (**9**)
tourism el turismo (5)
tourist el/la turista (2)
touristy turístico/a (9)
tournament el torneo (2)
tow truck la grúa (4)
towel la toalla (**7**)
town el pueblo; la villa (8, 15)
town crier el pregonero (7)
town, small el pueblecito (10)
trace la huella (12)
track and field el atletismo (**7**)
trade el oficio (**11**)
tradition la tradición (3)
traffic el tráfico (15)
traffic, to traficar (13)
traffic jam el atasco (14)
tragedy la tragedia (7)
tragic trágico/a (4)
train el tren (6, **9**)
trainer el/la entrenador/a (**7**)
training el entrenamiento (**11**)
tranquilizer el calmante (**10**)
transaction la transacción (15)
transform, to transformar (10)
transition la transición (12)
translate, to traducir (15)
translator el/la traductor/a (15)
transmit, to transmitir (10, **13**)
trap, to atrapar (11)
trapped atrapado/a (7)
travel, to viajar (**2, 9**)
travel agency la agencia de viajes (**9**)
travel agent el/la agente de viajes (**9**)
travel through/across, to recorrer (**9**)
traveler el/la viajero/a (**9**)
traveling salesperson el/la viajante (**11**)
treasure el tesoro (8)
treatment el tratamiento (10)
tree el árbol (4)
tremor el temblor (14)
tresses (*of hair*) las trenzas (8)
trilogy la trilogía (13)
trimester el trimestre (3)
trip, to tropezar (12)
trip, (to take a) (hacer un) viaje (**9**)
trombone el trombón (2, **14**)
truck el camión (*Mexico*) (15)
true cierto/a (2)
trumpet la trompeta (1, **14**)
trumpeter el/la trompetista (5)
trunk la cajuela (15)
truth la verdad (8)
try, to probar (ue) (6)
try on, to probarse (ue) (4, **8**)
Tuesday el martes (**1**)
tulle (*silk or nylon net*) el tul (**14**)
turkey el pavo (**6**)
Turkish turco/a (10)
turn off, to apagar (**12**)
turn on, to encender (ie) (**12**)
turnover la empanada (empanadilla) (6)
tuxedo el esmoquin (**14**)
twist around, to enredar (7)
twist, to torcer (ue) (**10**)
typical típico/a (8)

U

ugly feo/a (**2**)
umbrella la sombrilla (**7**)
UN la ONU (12)
uncle el tío (**4**)
uncomfortable incómodo/a (9)
under debajo (de) (**5**)
underscore, to subrayar (5)
understand, to comprender; entender (ie) (**2, 4**)
uneasiness la inquietud (13)
unemployment el desempleo (6, **11**)
unfaithful infiel (13)
unfinished inacabado/a (13)
unforgettable inolvidable (8)
unfortunately desgraciadamente (10)
uniform el uniforme (7)
union el sindicato (12)
unique único/a (8)
unite, to unir (15)
university la universidad (**1**)
unknown desconocido/a (15)
unmarried soltero/a (**4**)
unraveled deshecho/a (10)
use, to usar; utilizar (11, 14)
useful valioso/a; útil (12, 15)
useless inútil (15)
utensil el utensilio (6)
utility la utilidad (10)

V

vacancy la vacante (**11**)
vacation las vacaciones (8)
vacuum cleaner la aspiradora (**5**)
vacuum, to pasar la aspiradora (**5**)
value el valor (1)
variety la variedad (5)
various varios/as (9)
vary, to variar (6)

VCR la videograbadora (**12**)
vegetarian el/la vegetariano/a (**6**)
vegetation la vegetación (13)
velvet el terciopelo (**14**)
vendor, street el/la vendedor/a ambulante (8)
venerated reverenciado/a (15)
Venezuelan venezolano/a (**2**)
venomous venenoso/a (5)
version la versión (10)
very muy; sumamente (**1,** 10)
very truly yours lo(s)/la(s) saluda atentamente (**11**)
veteran veterano/a (12)
veterinarian el/la veterinario/a (**11**)
veterinary science la veterinaria (**3**)
vibrate, to vibrar (15)
viceroyalty el virreinato (11)
victim la víctima (7)
video camera la cámara de video (**9**)
video pirate el/la videopirata (13)
view la vista (5, **9**)
viewer el/la televidente (**13**)
viola la viola (**14**)
violate, to violar (**15**)
violence la violencia (13)
violent violento/a (14)
violin el violín (1, **14**)
vision la visión (3)
visitor el visitante (9)
vitamin la vitamina (10)
vivid vívido/a (10)
voice la voz (8)
voicemail la mensajería (12)
volcano el volcán (5, **9**)
volleyball el vólibol (**7**)
voluntary voluntario/a (5)
volunteer el/la voluntario/a (2)
voluptuous voluptuoso/a (9)
voluptuousness la voluptuosidad (14)
vote el voto (13)
vote (for), to votar (por) (**15**)
voter el/la votante (13)
vulture el buitre (14)

W

wages el sueldo (3, **11**)
waiter el camarero (**6**)
waiting area la sala de espera (**9**)
waitress la camarera (**6**)
wake up, to despertarse (ie) (**5**)
walk, to caminar; andar (**2,** 6)
walk, to take a pasear; dar un paseo (**4, 7**)
wallet la cartera (15)
want, to querer (ie) (**4**)
war la guerra (5)
wardrobe el armario (5)
war-like bélico/a (13)
warm cálido/a, caluroso/a (8, **9**)
warn, to advertir (ie, i) (14)
warrior el guerrero (3)
wash, to lavarse (**5**)
wash clothes, to lavar la ropa (**5**)
wash dishes, to lavar los platos (**5**)
washing machine la lavadora (**5**)
waste los desechos (**12**)
watch el reloj (**1**)
watch (television/a movie), to ver (la televisión/una película); vigilar (**7,** 15)
watch one's figure, to guardar la línea (**10**)
water, (mineral) el agua (mineral) (*fem.*) (3)
water skiing el esquí acuático (**7**)
waterfall el salto (**9**)
wave la ola (5)
way (of dressing) el modo (de vestir); la vía; la manera (5, 6, 11, **14**)
we nosotros/as (**1**)
wealth la riqueza (9)
weapon el arma (*fem.*) (**15**)
wear a shoe size, to calzar (**8**)
wear, to llevar (**8**)
weather el tiempo (**7**)
weatherman/woman el/la meteorólogo/a (**13**)
weave, to tejer (10)
weaving el tejido (4)
web site el sitio Web (**12**)
web page la página Web (**12**)
wedding la boda (3)
Wednesday el miércoles (**1**)
week la semana (**1**)
weight el peso (**10**)
weightlifting levantar pesas (**7**)
welcome la bienvenida (8)
well bien (*fine*); pues; el pozo (*of water*) (**1, 3,** 15)
well made bien hecho/a (**14**)
well-being el bienestar (**10**)
wet húmedo/a (13)
wet, to mojar (14)
what qué; cómo (**1, 2**)
What's happening? ¿Qué pasa? (**1**)
What's up? ¿Qué tal?; ¿Qué pasa? (**1**)
What's your name? ¿Cómo se llama usted? (*for.*); ¿Cómo te llamas? (*inf.*) (**1**)
whatever you hear oyeres (13)
whatever you see vieres (13)
when cuando (**2**)
where donde (**2**)
which (one/s) cual/es (**2**)
while mientras (4)
while, a little el ratito (15)
whistle el silbato (15)
white blanco/a (**1**)
who quien (**2**)
whose cuyo/a/os/as (5)
why por qué (**2**)
wide ancho/a; amplio/a (5, 8)
widow/er viudo/a (4)
wife la esposa (3, **4**)
wild montuno/a (14)
will la voluntad (15)
willing dispuesto/a (**12**)
win, to ganar (2, **7**)
wind el viento (6)
window la ventanilla (**9**)
windy, it is hace viento (**7**)
wine el vino (**6**)
winner el/la ganador/a (15)
winter invierno (**1**)
wintertime invernal (*adj.*) (6)
wire la alambrada (15)
with con (**1**)
withdraw, to retirarse (15)
within dentro de (**5**)
woman la mujer (**1**)
wonderful magnífico/a (**7**)
wood la madera (3)
wool la lana (**8**)
work la labor; la obra (*art*) (2, 10)
work, to trabajar; funcionar (*mechanical*) (**2, 12**)
work on commission, to trabajar a comisión (**11**)
worker el/la trabajador/a (1)
world el mundo; mundial (1, 15)
world heritage el patrimonio mundial (10)
World Series la serie mundial (4)
worn out gastado/a (10)
worry, to preocuparse (8)
worth, to be valer (2, **8**)
would you like te gustaría (**4**)
wound, to herir (ie, i) (4)
wounded herido/a (10)
wristwatch el reloj de pulsera (**8**)
write, to escribir (**2**)
writer el/la escritor/a (6)
wrong, to be no tener razón (**3**)

X

X-ray la radiografía (**10**)

Y

yard el patio (**5**)
year el año (**1**)
years old, to be... tener...años (**3**)
yellow amarillo/a (**1**)
yesterday ayer (**6**)
yogurt el yogur (**6**)
you tú; usted/es (*for.*); vosotros/as (*inf. pl.*) (Spain) (**1**)
you were, if si fueres (9)
you're welcome de nada (**1**)
young joven (**2**)
younger menor (**4**)
your tu/s (*inf.*); su/s (*for.*); vuestro/a/os/as (*inf. pl.*) (**1, 3**)
yours tuyo/a/os/as (*inf.*); suyo/a/os/as (*for.*); vuestro/a/os/as (*inf. pl.*) (**3, 13**)
youth la juventud (12)

Z

zinc el cinc (10)
zone la zona (8)

CREDITS

Text Credits

p. 33 "Salsa a Nueva York." Courtesy of TTH Records, Inc.; **p. 69** "Cuentáme alegrías" (Salvador Puerta) by Tachú © and (p) Pasarela SL; **p. 107** "La bamba" Interpretada por El Mariachi Vargas de Tecatitlán aparece por autorización de Sony BMG Music Entertainment (México) S.A. DE C.V.; **p. 147** "Marimba con punta" by César Castillo ©MC Productions, Inc. **p. 183** Music courtesy of SONIDO Inc.; Lyrics © 1981 Ruben Blades Publishing, all rights administerd by Sony/ATV Discos Music Publishing LLC (ASCAP); **p. 217** "Tren al sur" by writer/composer Jorge González Rios, SCD, Chile; **p. 251** "El pregonero," courtesy of TTH Records, Inc.; **p. 253** "Sensemayá" by Nicolás Guillén. Used by permission of Juan Pablos Editor; **p. 285** "Junto a ti," by Yawar ©Producciones Iempsa, S.A.C.; **p. 287** "Los rivales y el juez," Ciro Alegría. Used by permission of Los Morochucos; **p. 323** "Tu ausencia," ©Discos Fuentes S.A.; **p. 354** "Sol de primavera" by Gonzalo Vargas ©Celestial Harmonies; **p. 356** "El ñandutí," Aitor Bikandi-Mejías; **p. 388** "Todo cambia." Music courtesy of Universal Music Latino; Lyrics: Letra y Música: Julio Numhauser ©1984 Editorial Musical Korn Intersong/Warner/Chappell Music Argentina; **p. 396** "No hay que complicar la felicidad" by Marco Denevi ©Denevi, Marco, *Falsificaciones,* Buenos Aires, Corregidor, 1984, pp. 159–160. Used by permission; **p. 401** Reprinted with permission from Toshiba; **p. 415** Reprinted with permission from Nokia; **p. 430** "Caminando." Music courtesy of Warner Music Latina, Inc.; Lyrics: Words and music by Millo Torres; **p. 433** From "La Casa en Mango Street." Copyright ©1984 by Sandra Cisneros. Published by Vintage Español, a division of Random House Inc. Translation copyright ©1994 by Elena Poniatowska. Reprinted by permission of Susan Bergholz Literary Services, New York. All rights reserved; **p. 469** "Se vende," (Benjamín A. Estacio, Octavio Cruz) by A.D.N. © and (p) Teddysound SL; **p. 471** "Solos en la noche by Paloma Pedrero." Reprinted with permission; **p. 498** "Que viva el son montuno." Courtesy of TTH Records, Inc.; **p. 500** ©Anderson Imbert, Erique, "El crimen perfecto," en *El gato de Chesire Cuentos 2, Obras Completas,* Buenos Aires, Corregidor, 1999, pp. 101–102; **p. 533** "Tu música popular." Courtesy of TTH Records, Inc.; **p. 535** "Bajo la alambrada" from *Cajas de Carton* by Francisco Jiménez. Spanish translation copyright ©2000 by Francisco Jiménez. Reprinted by permission of Houghton Mifflin Company. All rights reserved

Photo Credits

Photos in the Observaciones sections are stills from *¡Pura vida!* video to accompany *¡Arriba!, Comunicación y cultura,* 5th edition, ©2008

Cover Getty Images, Inc. Laura Ronchi Collection; **p. 3 (top)** Salvador Dali (1904–1989), "The Discovery of America by Christopher Columbus, 1958–1959, oil on canvas, 410.2 x 310 cm. Salvador Dali Museum, St. Petersburg, Florida, USA. The Bridgeman Art Library International Ltd. ©2004 Salvador Dali, Gala-Sal; **(bottom right)** Diego Rivera, "Mexico from the Conquest to 1930." Mural. (Detail) Location: National Palace, Mexico City, Mexico. Photo: Leslye Borden/Photoedit. ©Banco de Mexico Diego Rivera & Frida Kahlo Museums Trust. Av. Cinco de Mayo No. 2, Col. Centro, Del. Cuau; **p. 7** Jupiter Images–FoodPix–Creatas–Brand X–Banana Stock–PictureQuest; **p. 11** PhotoEdit Inc.; **p. 15** Aurora & Quanta Productions Inc.; **p. 17** ©Jimmy Dorantes / Latin Focus.com; **p. 27 (left)** Corbis/Bettmann; **(right)** Corbis/Bettmann; **p. 29 (top)** AGE Fotostock America, Inc.; **p. 31 (top left)** SuperStock, Inc.; **(top right)** Stock Boston; **(middle left)** Getty Images Inc.–Stone Allstock; **(middle right)** Getty Images Inc.–Image Bank; **(bottom)** Corbis/Bettmann; **p. 33** Mauricio Smith; **p. 34** The Granger Collection; **p. 35** Getty Images Inc.–Image Bank; **p. 36** Getty Images Inc.–PhotoDisc; **p. 39** Art Resource, N.Y; **p. 39** Getty Images, Inc.–Allsport Photography; **p. 46** ©Robert Frerck/Odyssey/Chicago; **p. 43 (top left)** Agence France Presse/Getty Images; **(top right)** Getty Images, Inc.; **(bottom left)** Getty Images, Inc–Liaison; **(bottom right)** Getty Images Inc.–Hulton Archive Photos; **p. 50** ©Oliver Benn/Stone/Getty Images; **p. 51** Daniel BerehulakAllsport Concepts/Getty Images; **p. 62 (top left)** PhotoDisc/Getty Images; **(top right)** The Image Works; **(bottom right)** PhotoEdit Inc.; **p. 65** Ian Aitken ©Rough Guides; **p. 67 (top left)** J. Pavlovsky/Corbis/Sygma; **(top right)** Mercury Press; **(middle left)** Index Stock Imagery, Inc.; **(middle right)** ©Daniel Aubry/Odyssey/Chicago; **(bottom left)** ©Reuters NewMedia Inc./CORBIS; **(bottom right)** Getty Images Inc.–Stone Allstock; **p. 69** TEDDYSOUND, S.L.; **p. 72** Reuters Limited; **p. 75 (top left)** Art Resource, N.Y.; **(bottom right)** ©Reuters NewMedia Inc./CORBIS; **p. 83** Images.com; **p. 87** Getty Images, Inc.; **p. 88** Agence France Presse/Getty Images; **p. 89** Photodisc/Getty Images; **p. 98 (top)** ©Tony Perrottet/Omni-Photo Communications, Inc.; **(bottom)** Frida (Frieda) Kahlo, "Frieda and Diego Rivera," 1931, oil on canvas, 39 3/8 in. X 31 in. (100.01 cm x 78.74 cm). Ben Blackwell/San Francisco Museum of Art. ©2003 Banco de Mexico Diego Rivera & Frida Kahlo Museums Trust. Estate of Frida Kahlo.; **p. 101** Omni-Photo Communications, Inc.; **p. 103** "Courtesy of Marcie A. Bahn and Elizabethtown College;" **p. 104** Getty Images Inc.–Stone Allstock; **p. 105 (top left)** ©Robert Frerck/Odyssey/Chicago; **(top right)** Getty Images Inc.–Image Bank; **(middle left)** D. Donne Bryant Stock Photography; **(bottom left)** Susan M. Bacon; **(bottom right)** Corbis/Bettmann; **p. 107** Mariachi Nuevo Tecalitlan; **p. 109 (left)** David R. Frazier Photolibrary, Inc.; **(middle)** Ceremonial procession—detail of musicians. From Mayan fresco series found at Bonampak. (East wall, room 1). Museo Nacional de Antropologia, Mexico City, D.F., Mexico. ©SEF/Art Resource, NY; **(right)** ©Erich Lessing/Art Resource, NY; **p. 115 (top left)** AP/Wide World Photos; **(bottom right)** AGE Fotostock America, Inc.; **p. 118** Pearson Education/PH College; **p. 122** AP Wide World Photos; **p. 126** Werner Forman/Art Resource, NY; **p. 127** Rob Crandall; **p. 131** Photo Researchers, Inc.; **p. 135** Corbis/Outline; **p. 143** PhotoEdit Inc.; **p. 145 (top left)** ©Robert Frerck/Odyssey/Chicago; **(top right)** Index Stock Imagery, Inc.; **(middle left)** D. Donne Bryant Stock Photography; **(middle right)** U of Cincinnati International Programs; **(bottom left)** Neil Lukas ©Dorling Kindersley; **(bottom right)** Viesti Associates; **p. 147 (left)** Rafael Larios; **(right)** Index Stock Imagery, Inc.; **p. 149** Latina Media Ventures; **p. 151** Getty Images Inc.–Stone Allstock; **p. 155 (top left)** Getty Images, Inc.; **(bottom right)** PhotoDisc/Getty Images; **p. 161** AP Wide World Photos; **p. 162** Photo Researchers, Inc.; **p. 165 (left)** Agence France Presse/Getty Images; **(right)** Stephane Cardinale/Corbis/Sygma; **p. 167 (top)** Susan M. Bacon; **(bottom)** Susan M. Bacon; **p. 174** Getty Images, Inc.–Taxi; **p. 175** Getty Images Inc.–Hulton Archive Photos; **p. 179** Peter Wilson ©Dorling Kindersley; **p. 180** D. Donne Bryant Stock Photography; **p. 181 (top left)** Getty Images, Inc.–Liaison; **(middle left)** ©kevinschafer.com; **(middle right)** Cindy Karp/Time Life Pictures/Getty Images; **(bottom left)** Susan M. Bacon; **(bottom right)** Susan M. Bacon; **p. 183** Instituto Panameno de Turismo–IPAT; **p. 185 (top left)** Corbis/Bettmann; **(bottom left)** Susan M. Bacon; **(top right)** PhotoDisc/Getty Images; **p. 189 (top left)** Claudio Bravo, "Ajos y Col," 1984, oil on canvas, 52.1 x 65.2 cm. ©Claudio Bravo, courtesy, Marlborough Galley, New York; **(bottom right)** AFP/Getty Images, Inc.; **p. 194** Chilean National Tourist Board; **p. 196** AP Wide World Photos; **p. 198** Susan M. Bacon; **p. 200** Susan M. Bacon; **p. 201** Susan M. Bacon; **p. 202** Grant LeDuc; **p. 205** Getty Images, Inc–Liaison; **p. 208** ©Fernando Pastene/Latin Focus.com; **p. 211** PhotoEdit Inc.; **p. 213** StockFood America; **p. 215 (top left)** Viesti Associates; **(top right)** Omni-Photo Communications, Inc.; **(middle left)** Getty Images Inc.–Stone Allstock; **(bottom left)** D. Donne Bryant Stock Photography; **(bottom right)** Panos Pictures; **p. 217** Loreto

Otero; **p. 218** Getty Images, Inc.–PhotoDisc; **p. 219** ©Jack Parsons/Omni-Photo Communications, Inc.; **p. 223 (top left)** Getty Images, Inc.–Agence France Presse; **(bottom right)** Jaime Colson, Merengue, 1937. Courtesy of Museo Bellapart, Dominican Republic.; **p. 228** Getty Images, Inc.– Liaison; **p. 230** Ricky Davila/International Cover; **p. 232** Getty Images, Inc.; **p. 235** NAOS Photo; **p. 238** AP Wide World Photos; **p. 242** AP Wide World Photos; **p. 245** David R. Frazier Photolibrary, Inc.; **p. 247** John MacDougall/Agence France Presse/Getty Images; **p. 249 (top left)** Agence France Presse/Getty Images; **(top middle)** eStock Photography LLC; **(top right)** Getty Images Inc.–Stone Allstock; **(middle left)** Neg./Transparency no. 578(3). Photo by Jackie Beckett. Courtesy Dept. of Library Services, American Museum of Natural History.; **(middle right)** Photo © www.danheller.com/Dan Heller Photography; **(bottom left)** Photo © www.danheller.com/Dan Heller Photography; **(bottom right)** Woodfin Camp & Associates; **p. 251** Tito Nieves Productions, Inc.; **p. 252 (top)** Getty Images, Inc.; **(bottom)** Europa Press Reportajes, S.A.; **p. 254** PhotoDisc/Getty Images; **p. 257 (top right)** Fundacion Guayasamin; **(bottom right)** Getty Images Inc.–Stone Allstock; **p. 262** Getty Images Inc.–Stone Allstock; **p. 264** Stock Boston; **p. 265** ©Robert Frerck/Odyssey/Chicago; **p. 269** Susan M. Bacon; **p. 272** Susan M. Bacon; **p. 273** Susan M. Bacon; **p. 274** ©Jimmy Dorantes/Latin Focus.com; **p. 276** Corbis/Bettmann; **p. 278** Dave King ©Dorling Kindersley; **p. 279** Lebrecht Music & Arts Photo Library; **p. 281** PhotoEdit Inc.; **p. 283 (top left)** ©Jack S. Grove/Mira.com; **(top right)** Rob Reichenfeld ©Dorling Kindersley; **(middle left)** Photography: Angel Hurtado, Art Museum of the Americas, OAS; **(middle right)** The Image Works; **(bottom left)** Affordable Photo Stock; **(bottom right)** Getty Images Inc.–Stone Allstock; **p. 285 (top)** Getty Images, Inc.–Taxi; **(bottom)** PhotoEdit Inc.; **p. 293 (top left)** Corbis/Bettmann; **(bottom right)** AP Wide World Photos; **p. 300** Les Stone/Corbis/Sygma; **p. 301** Getty Images Inc.–Image Bank; **p. 302 (top)** Getty Images Inc.–Hulton Archive Photos; **(bottom)** Museo del Oro, Banco de la República; **p. 305** Getty Images Inc.–Stone Allstock; **p. 306 (top)** Getty Images Inc.–Stone Allstock; **p. 308** Getty Images Inc.–Stone Allstock; **p. 310** Getty Images Inc.–Stone Allstock; **p. 313** Fernando Botero. "Nauturaleza muerta con sopa verde" (Still Life with Green Soup). 1972. ©Fernando Botero, courtesy, Marlborough Gallery, New York.; **p. 316** AP Wide World Photos; **p. 317** PhotoEdit Inc.; **p. 319** Nature Picture Library; **p. 321 (top left)** Jeffrey A. Scovil Photography; **(top right)** ©Marcelo Salinas/Latin Focus.com; **(middle)** ©Jan Butchofsy-Houser/CORBIS; **(bottom left)** PhotoEdit Inc.; **(bottom right)** ©2004 Peter Menzel/menzelphoto.com; **p. 323 (top)** Fernando Jaramillo; **(bottom)** David Ashby ©Dorling Kindersley; **p. 324 (top left)** Getty Images Inc.–Stone Allstock; **(top right)** Photo Researchers, Inc.; **(bottom left)** The Stock Connection; **(bottom right)** Peter Arnold, Inc.; **p. 325** Prentice Hall School Division; **p. 329 (top left)** Nancy Humbach; **(bottom right)** ©Robert Frerck/Odyssey/Chicago; **p. 333 (top)** Getty Images, Inc.–Taxi; **(bottom)** ©Wolfgang Kaehler 2004 www.wkaehlerphoto.com; **p. 335 (top)** Photofest; **(bottom)** PhotoEdit Inc.; **p. 337** Corbis/Bettmann; **p. 339** The Image Works; **p. 340** ©Hubert Stadler/CORBIS; **p. 345** Corbis Digital Stock; **p. 348** SAMUEL GOLDWYN/STARZ! ENCORE ENT / THE KOBAL COLLECTION; **p. 350** Sri Maiava Rusden / PacificStock.com; **p. 351** Photo Researchers, Inc.; **p. 353 (top left)** Itaipu Binacional; **(top right)** ©Ken Laffal; **(middle left)** D. Donne Bryant Stock Photography; **(middle right)** Woodfin Camp & Associates; **(bottom left)** Andrew W. Miracle; **(bottom right)** PhotoEdit Inc.; **p. 354** Celestial Harmonies; **p. 356** Visuals Unlimited; **p. 357** Victor Englebert; **p. 360** Getty Images, Inc - Artville LLC; **p. 363 (top left)** Nature Picture Library; **(bottom right)** ©Sophie Bassouls/CORBIS Sygma; **p. 369** AP Wide World Photos; **p. 371** PhotoEdit Inc.; **p. 375** PhotoEdit Inc.; **p. 378 (top)** Susan M. Bacon; **(bottom)** Susan M. Bacon; **p. 382** Aurora & Quanta Productions Inc.; **p. 383** PhotoEdit Inc.; **p. 385** Getty Images, Inc.–PhotoDisc; **p. 387 (top left)** Corbis/Bettmann; **(top right)** ©Carlos Goldin/Focus/DDB Stock Photo. All Rights Reserved; **(middle left)** Getty Images, Inc.–Liaison; **(middle right)** SuperStock, Inc.; **(bottom left)** Corbis/Bettmann; **(bottom right)** ©Max and Bea Hunn/DDB Stock Photo. All Rights Reserved. MBH35-15087; **p. 388** Omar Torres/Agence France Presse/Getty Images; **p. 389** Editorial Atlantida S.A.; **p. 394** Photo Researchers, Inc.; **p. 397 (top left)** "Humanscape 65", Mel Casas, Acrylic, 72" x 96", Collection of Jim & Ann Harithas, New York, New York; **(bottom right)** Getty Images, Inc.–Agence France Presse; **p. 401** Yoshikazu Tsuno/Agence France Presse/Getty Images; **p. 402** Photo Researchers, Inc.; **p. 405** ©Tillman Paul McQuien and Kim G. Hochmeister; **p. 406** NASA/Johnson Space Center; **p. 407** PhotoEdit Inc.; **p. 412** PhotoEdit Inc.; **p. 415** Nokia; **p. 422** AP Wide World Photos; **p. 423** AP Wide World Photos; **p. 426** Jim McIsaac/Allsport Concepts/Getty Images; **p. 427** Getty Images Inc.–Stone Allstock; **p. 429 (top left)** Juanishi Orosco V. and Esteban Villa, "Idaho Migrant Council Murals," 1978, one shot enamel paints on concrete wall. Dimension: stairway 20'x 14'. Idaho Migrant Council, Burley, Idaho Art Center. Courtesy of the California Ethnic and Multicultural Arch; **(top right)** Getty Images, Inc.; **(middle left)** Jamie Squire/Getty Images, Inc.; **(middle)** ©Michael Grecco/Stock Boston; **(middle right)** Prentice Hall School Division; **(bottom left)** Frank Cantor/Cantomedia; **(bottom right)** Stock Boston; **p. 430** Eric Laguna; **p. 432** AP Wide World Photos; **p. 439 (top left)** Getty Images Inc.–Image Bank; **(bottom right)** Robert Harding World Imagery; **p. 444** Robert Fried/robertfried-photography.com; **p. 445 (top)** Corbis/Bettmann; **p. 447** Getty Images, Inc.; **p. 448** AP Wide World Photos; **p. 451** Getty Images, Inc.; **p. 453** Robert Fried/robertfriedphotography.com; **p. 454** Getty Images, Inc.; **p. 465** AP Wide World Photos; **p. 467 (top left)** ©Robert Frerck/Odyssey/Chicago; **(top right)** ©Robert Frerck/Odyssey/Chicago; **(middle)** Aurora & Quanta Productions Inc; **(middle left)** Getty Images Inc.–Stone Allstock; **(middle right)** ©Robert Frerck/Odyssey/Chicago; **(bottom)** Linda Whitwam ©Dorling Kindersley; **p. 468 (top left)** ©Quike H. Novoa /MercuryPress.com; **(bottom left)** ©Dorling Kindersley; **(bottom right)** David Murray and Jules Selmes ©Dorling Kindersley; **p. 469** TEDDYSOUND, S.L.; **p. 477 (top left)** Art Resource, N.Y.; **(bottom right)** Art Resource, N.Y.; **p. 478** Marv Sloben; **p. 480** Guitar Society; **p. 482** AP Wide World Photos; **p. 485** Corbis/Reuters America LLC; **p. 487** AP Wide World Photos; **p. 488** AP Wide World Photos; **p. 491** AP Wide World Photos; **p. 492 (top)** Getty Images, Inc.–Taxi; **(bottom)** PhotoEdit Inc.; **p. 495** Getty Images Inc.–Stone Allstock; **p. 497 (top left)** ©Robert Frerck/Stone/Getty Images; **(top right)** Esto Photographics, Inc.; **(middle left)** Oswaldo Guayasamin, "La Madre el Nino." 1989. Photo Nicolas Osorio Ruiz. Museo Fundacion Guayasamin, Quito–Ecuador; **(middle)** Art Resource, N.Y.; **(middle right)** Joan Miro, Spanish, 1893–1983. The Owl. Photograph ©SuperStock, Inc. ©2004 Successio Miro/Artists Rights Society ARS, NY; **(bottom left)** Self Portrait #8 (desnudo frente al espejo), 1988, 420 cm x 165 cm, mixed media and oils on canvas. Co. Museo de Arte Contemporaneo de Puerto Rico. Painter: Maria de Mater O'Neill.; **(bottom right)** Getty Images Inc.–Stone Allstock; **p. 498 (top)** ©Goldberg Diego/CORBIS SYGMA; **(bottom)** Photo Courtesy: Tipica Novel and Mauricio Smith, Jr.; **p. 499** Eduardo Comesana Agencia de Prensa; **p. 502** PhotoDisc/Getty Images; **p. 505 (top left)** Viesti Associates; **(bottom right)** AP Wide World Photos; **p. 506** PH College Archives category PS Portraits; **p. 508** CONGRESSWOMAN ILEANA ROS-LEHTINEN; **p. 510** Demetrio Carrasco ©CONACULTA-INAH-MEX. Authorized reproduction by the Instituto Nacional de Antropologia e Historia; **p. 512** Andy Crawford ©Dorling Kindersley, Courtesy of the Royal Museum of Scotland, Edinburgh; **p. 514** Sebastian Szyd/The World Bank; **p. 515 (top)** AP Wide World Photos; **(middle)** ©Horst Wagner / EFE / CORBIS All Rights Reserved; **(bottom)** Getty Images, Inc.; **p. 521** Getty Images–Stockbyte.; **p. 525** Juan Mabromata/Agence France Presse/Getty Images; **p. 526** Getty Images, Inc.–Taxi; **p. 527** Felipe Guaman Poma de Ayala: Neuva coronica y buen gobierno (1615), page 337 of the autograph manuscript GKS 2232 4to. Courtesy of The Royal Library, Copenhagen. Complete digital facsimile: www.kb.dk/elib/mss/poma/; **p. 529** Getty Images, Inc.–Liaison; **p. 531 (top left)** Corbis/Bettmann; **(top right)** D. Donne Bryant Stock Photography; **middle left)** Photo Researchers, Inc.; **(middle right)** ©The British Museum **(bottom left)** CORBIS- NY; **(bottom right)** D. Donne Bryant Stock Photography; **p. 532** Landov LLC; **p. 534** Charles Barry, Santa Clara University; **p. 539 (top)** Bob Fitch/Take Stock; **(bottom)** Stephen Oliver ©Dorling Kindersley; **p. A6** TM and ©Twentieth Century Fox Film Corp./Photofest

INDEX

Mar Caribe
OCÉANO
ATLÁNTICO
Barranquilla
Cartagena
Maracaibo
Caracas
Barquisimeto
Río Orinoco
VENEZUELA
Medellín
Manizales
Bogotá
Cali
COLOMBIA
CORDILLERA DE LOS ANDES
Georgetown
GUYANA
Paramaribo
SURINAM
Cayenne
GUAYANA
FRANCESA
(Francia)
Salto Ángel
Quito
ECUADOR
Guayaquil
Cuenca
Islas
Galápagos
(Ec.)
Ecuador
Río Amazonas
Belém
Manaus
Iquitos
Fortal
Río Madeira
Cajamarca
Trujillo
PERÚ
Río Branco
B R A S I L
Rec
Machu
Picchu
Lima
Ayacucho
Cuzco
BOLIVIA
Lago
Titicaca
Salvad
Arequipa
La Paz
Brasília
Cochabamba
Santa Cruz
Arica
Sucre
Potosí
Iquique
Desierto de Atacama
Belo
Horizonte
PARAGUAY
São Paulo
Río de Janeiro
Santos
Trópico de Capricor
Antofagasta
Salta
Asunción
Salto
Iguazú
CHILE
San Miguel
de Tucumán
ARGENTINA
Coquimbo
Río Paraná
Río Uruguay
Pôrto Alegre
Córdoba
Rivera
Rosario
URUGUAY
Valparaíso
Mendoza
Santiago
Buenos Aires
Montevideo
La Plata
Río de la Plata
OCÉANO
ATLÁNTICO
Concepción
Bahía Blanca
Puerto Montt
CORDILLERA DE LOS ANDES
OCÉANO
PACÍFICO
Estrecho de
Magallanes
Islas
Malvinas
(Br.)
Punta Arenas
TIERRA DEL FUEGO
Cabo de Hornos
OCÉANO
PACÍFICO
I. Pinta
I. Fernandina
I. Marchena
I. San Salvador
Santa Cruz
I. Isabela
I. Santa Cruz
Puerto
Ayora
Puerto
Villamil
I. San
Cristóbal
Puerto
Baquerizo
Moreno
ISLAS GALÁPAGOS
(ECUADOR)
OCÉANO
PACÍFICO
Cabo Norte
Volcán
Katiki
Hanga Roa
Cabo
Cumming
Mataveri
ISLA de PASCUA
(CHILE)
América del Sur